Liquid
Assets

Liquid Assets

EXPANDED EDITION

A History of New York City's Water System

DIANE GALUSHA

PURPLE MOUNTAIN PRESS
Fleischmanns, New York

COLORPAGE
Kingston, New York

Liquid Assets: A History of New York City's Water System
Expanded Edition 2016

First Edition 1999

Published by Purple Mountain Press, Ltd.
1060 Main Street
P.O. Box 309
Fleischmanns, New York 12430-0309
845-254-4062
845-254-4476 (fax)
catskill.ne/purple
www.catskill.net/purple

Library of Congress Cataloging-in-Publication Data

5 4 3 2 1

Manufactured in the United States of America

Table of Contents

LIQUID ASSETS: THE STORY CONTINUES

Introduction xi   Water System Infrastructure Projects xii   Watershed Protection Programs xviii
Below the dams xxii   Climate change, invasives and hydropower xxiii   Conserving a finite resource xxiv
Floods and their legacy xxv   Education and Recreation xxviii   Farm and Forest xxxi
Land Acquisition xxxv   Preserving history xxxvii   Other programs xl
Watershed Protection and Partnership Council (WPPC) xlii   The Coalition of Watershed Towns xliii
Sources and Acknowledgements xliv

Introduction	7
1. The Thirsty Settlement	11
Water, water everywhere. . .	12
2. Claiming the Croton	19
John B. Jervis: An engineer's engineer	20
3. Of "Life and Stir": The City Grows	33
A visit below	36
An unquenchable demon	40
4. Lake Effects	43
Island tapping	46
5. Liquid Links	51
Disaster in Pennsylvania	54
6. A New Aqueduct	63
Jerome Park's "Hay Days"	69
7. The New Croton Reservoir	73
"On the move!"	76
8. Finishing the Croton System: Cross River and Croton Falls	83
The terror of typhoid	85
9. To the Catskills	89
10. The Catskill Aqueduct	99
Tunneling under the Hudson	104
11. Beneath City Streets	113
Crossing the Narrows to Staten Island	121
12. Building the Ashokan	125
On patrol	136
13. Kensico and Hill View Reservoirs	141
To filter, or not to filter. . .	150
14. Fire and Flood: The Schoharie Project	155
An ancient forest	159
15. Fighting for the Delaware	167
New sources, new conduits	176
16. The Delaware Aqueduct	179
Sam Rosoff: Rags to riches	184
17. Waiting for "The Water"	187
Courts and compacts	194
18. Pepacton	201
Building reputations, too	214
19. Cannonsville	217
When the rains didn't come	227
20. Assessing the Damage	231
Tax disputes	242
21. Tunnel Vision	245
22. To the Future. . .	255
Conclusion: Pride and Sorrow	263
Appendix	265
The System	265
Collecting Reservoirs	266
Storage/Balancing Reservoirs	271
Distributing Reservoirs	271
Aqueducts and Tunnels	272
Chapter Notes	275
Bibliography	286
Acknowledgments	289
Index	291

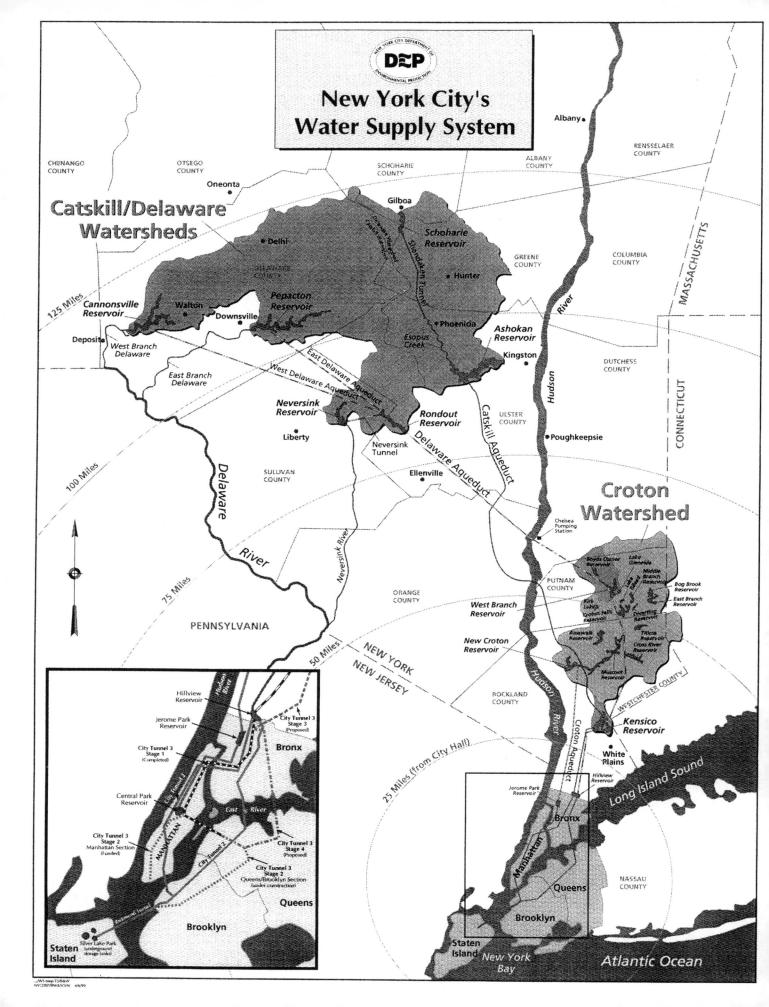

Highlights: 1997-2015

The Filtration Avoidance Determination, signed in November 2002, kept most of the original Memorandum of Agreement environmental protection programs in place and added others. The ceremony took place on the chilly shores of the Ashokan Reservoir, where New York City Mayor Michael Bloomberg shook hands with Environmental Protection Agency Region II Administrator Jane Kenny. New York City's Department of Environmental Protection Commissioner Christopher Ward looked on. *CWC photo*

The $3.6 billion Croton Filtration Plant took eight years to build in Van Cortlandt Park in the Bronx. Mosholu Golf Course was reconstructed atop the facility. *NYC DEP photos*

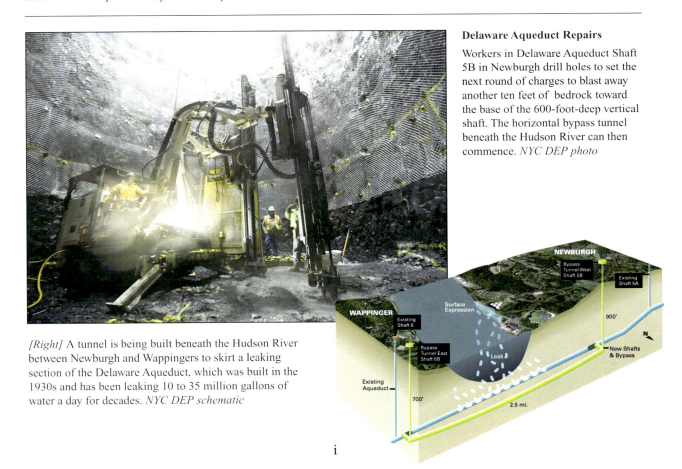

Delaware Aqueduct Repairs

Workers in Delaware Aqueduct Shaft 5B in Newburgh drill holes to set the next round of charges to blast away another ten feet of bedrock toward the base of the 600-foot-deep vertical shaft. The horizontal bypass tunnel beneath the Hudson River can then commence. *NYC DEP photo*

[Right] A tunnel is being built beneath the Hudson River between Newburgh and Wappingers to skirt a leaking section of the Delaware Aqueduct, which was built in the 1930s and has been leaking 10 to 35 million gallons of water a day for decades. *NYC DEP schematic*

Gilboa Dam Reconstruction

Reconstruction of the Gilboa Dam included remodeling the stepped spillway and repaving the spillway basin. *NYC DEP photo*

Proud workers with the Barnard-D.A. Collins Joint Venture posed for a celebratory portrait following a ceremony marking the completion of the reconstruction of the Gilboa Dam. *CWC Photo*

A walk-through inspection gallery was added to the rebuilt Gilboa Dam. The gallery entrance is shown here. *NYC DEP photo*

Bald eagle nests were monitored and protected during reconstruction of the Gilboa Dam visible in the background. This photo was taken by the NYS DEC in May 2014.

Catskill Watershed Corp. Programs

The 10th anniversary of the MOA was celebrated with a special dinner in April 2007, when (left to right) Alan Rosa, executive director of the CWC; Marilyn Gelber, former commissioner of the NYC DEP; and Perry Shelton, former chairman of the Coalition of Watershed Towns and long-time president of the CWC Board of Directors, reflected on how far the Watershed partnership had come. *All CWC photos*

The "Payment for Ecosystem Services" model in which upstream landowners are remunerated for keeping the water clean for downstream consumers has drawn observers and researchers from around the globe to the NYC Watershed. This group of South Korean visitors met with a CWC staff engineer to discuss water protection programs.

An historic boarding house in Mount Tremper was renovated with help from a CWC low interest loan, one of more than 300 loans awarded since 1998. Rechristened the Foxfire Mountain Inn, it opened in 2015.

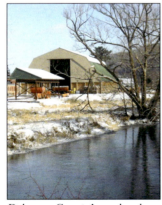

Delaware County's sand and salt storage facility near the West Branch of the Delaware River was among 39 built in the Catskill-Delaware Watershed.

The Catskill Watershed Corp. Board of Directors, shown here with long-time head Perry Shelton presiding over his final meeting in 2008, manages a host of water and community protection programs.

Conserving A Finite Resource

Hydrants refitted with sprinkler heads reduce illegal opening of hydrants in the heat of summer. Young people on the Hydrant Education Action Team (HEAT), a program created by DEP in 2007, convey the conservation message citywide. *All NYC DEP Photos*

[Top Right] DEP staff spreading the word about conserving water.

A DEP employee collects a water sample from the delivery system to be tested for quality.

Invasives and Hydropower

Thousands of ash trees have been removed from city lands at the Ashokan Reservoir because of the march of the Emerald Ash Borer, whose destructive tracks can be seen beneath the bark.

Water chestnuts, one of many alien invaders, clogging the waters of the Muscoot Reservoir.

The DEP obtained a federal license to harness the power of the Cannonsville Dam's releases to the West Branch of the Delaware River, but in late 2015 was reevaluating the project.

Floods and Their Legacy

[Top left] The Walton Reporter Office was a jumble of muddy filing cabinets and computer stations following the Flood of 2006 which brought heavy damage to western Delaware County. *Walton Reporter photo*

[Top Right] The Greene County community of Prattsville sustained unparalleled damage from Irene in 2011. The image of this precariously tipped Victorian house was seen around the world.

[Below] This is Prattsville's dream of a community reborn. *Drawing by Ian Law/PLACE Alliance*

Ten days after Tropical Storm Irene caused such havoc in the Catskills, the Ashokan Reservoir was still spilling into the lower Esopus Creek. *Aaron Bennett photo*

Hikers on the Shavertown Trail examine a weather station that feeds information to the NYC DEP. The agency's sophisticated Operations Support Tool relies on data collected from many such stations to help predict supply and meet its downstream flow obligations. *Author photo*

Watershed Education and Recreation

[Clockwise from top left] How streams behave—and misbehave—was the focus of this exercise by Tri-Valley Central School students on a tributary of the Rondout Creek. *CWC photo*

Students from PS 84 discovered an unknown world of macroinvertebrates in a pond study class at Ward Pound Ridge Reservation in Westchester County. *CWC photo*

Students from Sidney in Delaware County and the New York Harbor School in Manhattan became partners in a three-week journey on foot and afloat from the Catskills to Central Park. The Mountaintop to Tap Trek was organized by Stroud Water Research Center and assisted by DEP, CWC and other organizations. *John Schwartz/NYC DEP photo*

Forester Brent Feldweg explains timber grading and selection to educators at a Watershed Forestry Institute for Teachers, who learn the connections between healthy forests and healthy water. *WAC photo*

Franklin students raised trout from eggs to explore the connection between clean water and healthy living systems. *CWC photo*

Walton students share their history with New York City peers, with the help of new technology. *CWC photo*

Recreational, non-mechanized boating was piloted at the Cannons-ville Reservoir and extended to three other reservoirs in 2012. *Bob Moses photo*

Many miles of foot trails on city lands beckon to hikers, like this one overlooking the Pepacton Reservoir. *Author photo*

A Canadian visitor stopped to read about the making of the New York City water system at one of six kiosks erected by the CWC in 2002. *CWC photo*

The world famous Gilboa tree fern fossils are prominently displayed at the Gilboa Museum. *Author photo*

Kids can learn how to dig a tunnel at Time and The Valleys Museum in Grahamsville, where the focus is on water. *Time and the Valleys Museum photo*

Like miniature Spidermen, workers in this 2013 photo inspect the face of the Kensico Dam, which was cleaned and repaired as part of a $42 million upgrade project. *NYC DEP photo*

A technician at work in the DEP's Kingston water quality testing lab. *NYC DEP photo*

A solar-powered robotic buoy for collecting water quality data being installed on the Rondout Reservoir. *NYC DEP photo*

DEP police are alert to security threats, but also train for emergencies like cold water rescues. *NYC DEP photo*

Liquid Assets: The Story Continues

Liquid Assets: The Story Continues

hey passed out cigars and breathed a collective sigh of relief on January 17, 1997, the day the hard-fought New York City Watershed Memorandum of Agreement was signed at the state capitol. There were smiles and handshakes on that cold winter day in Albany, but none among the 86 signers was under any illusion that implementing the historic pact would be easy.

They were in uncharted waters, as it were, creating a brand new model of water quality protection based on collaboration instead of coercion, dialogue rather than demands. The city that needed the water and the upstate communities surrounding its reservoirs would be partners in protecting the resource so crucial to everyone's survival.

A tall order, to be sure. After a century and a half of running its far-flung water system by fiat, the city was now required to pay for programs, many to be run by outside organizations, to keep the water clean at its source and avoid building an expensive filtration plant. "Payment for Ecosystem Services (PES)" would become the label for this system of procuring the cooperation of Watershed municipalities, businesses, farmers and residents. City money, lots of it, would pay for septic systems, salt sheds, stream repairs, community wastewater treatment systems, stormwater controls and much more. A separate agreement paid farmers to undertake water protection measures. Still more money would buy land to keep it from ever being developed (See Chapter 22).

In fact, to keep water flowing to the faucets of millions well into the future, the NYC Department of Environmental Protection (DEP) has committed an estimated $1.4 billion for Watershed protection, including the expense of major infrastructure. Additional or revised protection programs to address new or emerging concerns have been incorporated in each of three Filtration Avoidance Determinations (FADs) issued by the US Environmental Protection Agency (EPA) since 1997, and in the Water Supply Permits issued by the NYS Department of Environmental Conservation (DEC).

Too, the DEP itself has been forced to adapt to changing circumstances and to address issues that were barely on the radar in 1997:

- Climate change. More frequent and intense storms and rising sea levels are affecting water and wastewater operations. The DEP has been forced to manage and retrofit its reservoirs for flood control and to take into consideration downstream interests affected by weather-related reservoir releases. City-funded flood hazard mitigation programs have been devised in concert with partner agencies to reduce future flood damage.

- Terrorism threats. After the attacks of September 11, 2001, the city implemented a number of security measures in consultation with the FBI and US Army Corps of Engineers. It also bolstered its DEP police force with 145 new officers.

- New technology. High-tech water meters and high-efficiency toilets and fixtures installed throughout the city have significantly cut consumption. Water testing, snow pack monitoring, mapping of city lands, modeling systems, public communication and other DEP functions have also advanced with the march of technology.

- Invasive species. Threats from non-native aquatic and terrestrial organisms, animals and plants have prompted the DEP and partner agencies to establish monitoring and eradication efforts.

- Pharmaceutical contamination and hydrofracturing for natural gas are other water quality issues that have demanded DEP attention. The latter was banned in New York in 2015; the former remains an area of study.

Here, then, are highlights among watershed protection programs and New York City Water Supply projects from the past two decades.

Water System Infrastructure Projects

Croton Water Filtration Plant

This $3.6 billion facility, constructed deep beneath the Bronx, was activated in the spring of 2015. Unlike the more remote Catskill-Delaware System, filtration of the older Croton System was mandated by the US EPA because of the potential for contamination of the reservoirs in this heavily populated area of Putnam and Westchester Counties.

Controversy over siting, jobs, cost overruns and local environmental impacts beset the plant for years. The project required permission from the NYS Legislature to "alienate" public parkland, as it would be built beneath Mosholu Golf Course of VanCortlandt Park. In exchange, the City agreed to spend $40 million on improvements to the park, and $200 million to restore and build parks in other areas of the Bronx.

Site work and excavation of a million cubic yards of rock and soil began in 2004, and construction of the 400,000-square-foot facility began in 2007. At the height of the project, 1,300 laborers were on site. The DEP reported in 2009 that the project required enough concrete to build a sidewalk from New York to Miami, and enough pipe to reach the top of the Empire State Building 140 times over.

Ten million feet of electrical wire was also required in the plant, which was constructed 100 feet below the surface and subjects water to aeration, sand filtration and ultra-violet treatment.

Meanwhile, the 1890 New Croton Aqueduct was rehabilitated. The 33-mile-long, 13-foot diameter brick lined tunnel connects the New Croton and Jerome Park Reservoirs and runs at one point beneath the Harlem River. Ground penetrating radar, a remotely operated vehicle and other means of inspection had found the tunnel in remarkably good shape. After draining, the aqueduct was re-grouted, shaft sites were updated, and pumps and valves repaired.

A 58-foot long, 12-foot wide concrete plug was built inside the aqueduct beneath Jerome Park Reservoir to divert water to the filtration plant. In addition, three tunnels totaling more than a mile in length were constructed to carry the water from aqueduct to plant and back to the distribution network. A subsurface distribution facility for the treated Croton water was built between 2009 and 2013 and features a grade-level vegetated roof.

The Croton plant can supply up to 290 million gallons of water – 30% of the city's supply -- every day, and is considered key to satisfying demand when the Delaware Aqueduct is taken off line in 2022 as part of the multi-faceted "Water for the Future" program.

In a scene straight out of history, workers are shown re-grouting the 1890-brick lining of the Croton Aqueduct. *NYC DEP photo*

Delaware Aqueduct Repairs

The Delaware Aqueduct is leaking. Cracks in the concrete lining in two sections of the tunnel are allowing 10 to 35 million gallons of water a day — that last is enough to supply the City of Rochester every day -- to migrate upwards through limestone, some 600 feet to the surface. The misplaced water is coming up beneath Wawarsing in Ulster County, where it has flooded septic systems, basements and back yards, and beneath Roseton near the Hudson River in Orange County, where ponding has occurred on the surface.

Tests done in 1991 indicated that dye injected into the tunnel surfaced in about an hour at a Newburgh sinkhole. The City was criticized for failing to divulge this information publicly until 2000, for the slow pace of the repair plan, and for dragging its feet on reparations to affected homeowners. Sump pumps, bottled water and disinfection units were initially provided to residents while the DEP, Ulster County Health Dept. and the US Geological Survey monitored and mapped conditions there. Unhappy residents crowded public meetings and wrote letters to local newspapers. As of August 2015, 37 Wawarsing area parcels had been bought out with $15 million in NYC and NYS funds; five more were pending. Thirty-two properties were declared ineligible or were withdrawn from buy-out consideration.

To explore the interior of the Rondout-West Branch section of the Aqueduct where the leaks were occurring, the DEP turned to Woods Hole Oceanographic Institute. Engineers there designed a self-propelled, nine-foot long torpedo-shaped vehicle equipped with five digital cameras to take 360-degree photographs every eight feet of the 45-mile aqueduct section. In 2003 the Autonomous Underwater Vehicle collected 160,000 photos, as well as sonar, velocity and pressure data to pinpoint and quantify the leaks. Two more trips by the AUV gathered additional data.

After examining the voluminous information provided by the AUV, the DEP devised a plan that is perhaps the most expensive ($1 billion) and complex repair project in its history. It will build a 2.5-mile long bypass tunnel around the most significant leak between Newburgh on the west side of the Hudson River and Wappinger on the east. Excavation of a pair of vertical construction shafts, 600 feet deep on the Newburgh side, 400 feet on the Wappinger side of the river, began in 2014 (ten dwellings and a tavern on some 75 acres of land were acquired for this purpose). Blasting every three or four days, each blast loosens about eight to ten feet of rock, which is then hoisted out of the shaft in seven-ton bucket loads. The 14-foot diameter shafts will be lined in steel and concrete.

When the shafts are finished in 2016, boring of the horizontal bypass tunnel will begin. A Tunnel Boring Machine (TBM) will be lowered to tunnel

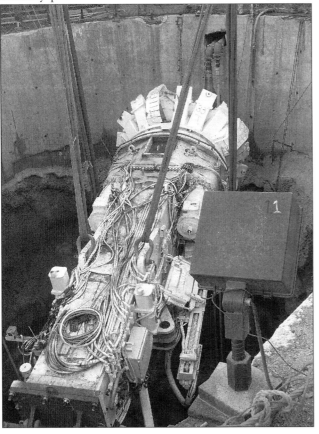

The remarkable Tunnel Boring Machine was lowered down a shaft to excavate a tunnel connecting the Croton Aqueduct with the new Croton Filtration Plant. The TBM is also being used to dig City Tunnel #3 and will be employed on the Delaware Aqueduct Bypass tunnel. *NYC DEP photo*

level on the Newburgh side and assembled before it is set on course to drill the 22-foot diameter bypass tunnel, which will be about 150 feet away from the existing tunnel. Advancing 50 feet a day, the TBM is expected to complete its work in 2022.

Then, the Delaware Aqueduct, which carries half of the City's water, will be shut down and drained so that the bypass can be connected to the existing tunnel, and the leaky section can be plugged and abandoned. Workers will also enter the Wawarsing section to seal with grout the cracks along 500 feet of the tunnel.

The tunnel could not be drained at all were it not for six intrepid deep sea divers who spent a month in 2008 in a pressurized tank above Aqueduct Shaft 6 in Dutchess County. They took turns descending in a diving bell to the bottom of the water-filled shaft to chip away at concrete encasing a broken valve and then fixing it so that pumps will work when it's time to empty the tunnel for the first time since it was last inspected in 1958.

This will be accomplished by three massive vertical turbine pumps and six centrifugal pumps that were lowered into the aqueduct in 2013 replacing 1930s-era pumps.

The eight- to 12-month shut-down period is what keeps DEP planners awake at night. They've developed a plan, dubbed "Water for the Future" that couples the Aqueduct bypass project with a series of actions designed to ensure that nine million people, including 25,000 customers in Newburgh and Marlborough who will be impacted by the shut-down of the Delaware Aqueduct, are not left without water when the tunnel is drained.

Reactivating the Croton Aqueduct has already been accomplished, making this supply available again to water customers who have been solely dependent on the Delaware and Catskill Aqueducts for several years. The DEP also plans to get inside the Catskill Aqueduct before the Delaware is turned off to clean the harmless 'biofilm' layer from the tunnel walls and coat the interior surface with an epoxy sealant to improve the speed of water flow and thus increase its capacity. For the same reason, new air vents will be added and some old ones replaced on the Catskill Aqueduct between the Ashokan and Kensico Reservoirs.

Water conservation initiatives, such as retrofitting city-owned buildings, schools and residences with low flow toilets and other fixtures (see *Conserving a Finite Resource*) will add another 25 million gallons daily.

Additional key pieces of infrastructure that have been upgraded in advance of the aqueduct repair project include flow control stations at Shafts 9, 10 and 17 in Putnam and Westchester Counties and the Cross River and Croton Falls pumping stations. The Catskill and Delaware Aqueducts have been connected at Gardner to allow greater capacity and flexibility of use.

With the four Delaware System Reservoirs off line for as much as a year, a system of voiding excess water from those reservoirs is being developed.

Gilboa Dam and release works

A $400 million project prompted a decade ago by fears that the Gilboa Dam of the Schoharie Reservoir did not meet New York State standards for safety is expected to be completed in 2020.

The project began with the full-scale rehabilitation of the dam, work that was finished in November 2014. Eight months later, construction began on a project to build release works that will provide the capability of releasing water from the reservoir into the north-flowing creek to facilitate dam maintenance, respond to potential emergencies, mitigate flood risk for downstream communities, and enhance downstream habitat for fish and wildlife.

DEP began a thorough investigation of the integrity of Gilboa Dam after the flood of 1996, which overtopped the spillway by 6.7 feet (a record eclipsed by Tropical Storm Irene in 2011). An initial investigation, completed in 2003, found that Gilboa Dam would require a comprehensive rehabilitation and upgrade because it likely did not meet modern standards for dam safety. Additional engineering work in 2005 found that Gilboa Dam had a marginal factor of safety for flood conditions similar to 1996, and that the dam could potentially fail under the pressure of a larger flood.

Following that report, DEP moved immediate-

City Tunnel #3 Work continues on City Tunnel #3, a concreted portion shown in this 2008 photo, which was taken three decades after the project was begun. *NYC DEP photo*

ly to make emergency repairs to the dam. In 2006, a 220-foot-long by five-foot-deep notch was cut from the top of the westernmost portion of the dam to control water spilling from the reservoir and to allow for the installation of 80 anchoring cables into the top and outer face of the dam to the bedrock below. Giant siphons were also installed to remove water from the reservoir over the dam's spillway and into the creek below.

The full-scale rehabilitation of the nearly century-old dam included addition of an inspection gallery inside the dam that runs its entire length. The gallery, which also includes instruments to constantly measure stress on the dam, allows engineers to visually inspect the inside and outside of the dam on a regular basis.

The dam face was designed with three-, six- and 12-foot steps that dissipate the energy of water as it spills from the reservoir. Some 234 million pounds of concrete was molded and dyed to resemble the original bluestone face of the dam. The east and west abutment walls were also strengthened through the installation of 40 post-tensioned anchors.

The rehabilitation was completed two years ahead of schedule despite a nine-month setback in the wake of Hurricane Irene.

The project also adapted to limitations on some construction work after a pair of bald eagles built two nests near the dam's west support wall. DEP was required to curtail some construction work during the eagles' breeding season, along with monitoring the eagles and their hatchlings, which are protected by federal law.

The reconstruction of the Gilboa Dam earned the DEP the 2015 National Dam Rehabilitation Project of the year award from the Association of State Dam Safety Officials.

The release works under construction in 2015 include an intake structure, a valve chamber, and two sections of tunnel that will run as deep as 185 feet below the surface. The nine-foot-diameter tunnel will be drilled by a micro-tunnel boring machine. The first leg of the tunnel will stretch 1,188 feet from a future gate shaft on the east side of Route 990V in Gilboa to a valve chamber on the eastern bank of Schoharie Creek. The valve chamber will be located about 1,000 feet downstream of the dam.

A second leg of the tunnel, stretching 930 feet, will run from the gate shaft to an intake structure at the bottom of Schoharie Reservoir, several hundred feet south of the dam. Once workers bore into the bottom of the reservoir, a specialized dive team will remove the micro-tunnel boring machine from the 135-foot-deep water and install the intake structure. Roughly 10,000 cubic yards of sediment will also be dredged from around the intake.

The valve chamber, which acts as the portal that releases water into the creek below the dam, will include two valves capable of releasing 65 million to 1,550 million gallons of water each day. A third, smaller valve will be capable of smaller releases up to 65 million gallons per day.

Upgrades to the Shandaken Tunnel Intake Chamber where Schoharie water begins its journey under the mountains to the Esopus Creek and thence to the Ashokan reservoir are also planned.

The members of Laborers Local 147 Tunnel Workers, the sandhogs who have been building the City's third water delivery tunnel since 1970, are slowly, methodically working themselves out of a job.

Stage 1 of City Tunnel #3 (CT3), 12.5 miles of tunnel between Hillview Reservoir and Astoria, Queens, including three massive underground valve chambers, was finished in 1998, providing water to parts of the Bronx, northern Manhattan and Astoria (*see Chapter 21*). In October of 2013, the 8.5-mile Manhattan leg of Stage 2 was activated, allowing delivery of 350 million gallons of water that is consumed in Manhattan daily. The ten-mile Brooklyn-Queens leg of Stage 2, begun in 1993 has

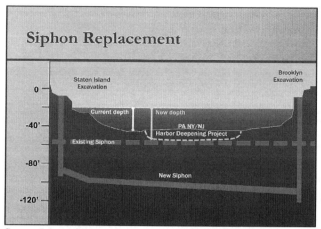

Siphon Replacement

Staten Island
Excavation

Brooklyn
Excavation

0

Current depth   New depth

-40'   PA NY/NJ
                  Harbor Deepening Project

Existing Siphon

-80'   New Siphon

-120'

Staten Island Siphon Cutaway of the deeper siphon connecting Manhattan to Staten Island to enable dredging of New York Harbor.

been bored and lined, and five distribution shafts constructed. As of 2015, two additional shafts, installation of instrumentation and controls and some mechanical work remained to be completed. A proposed Stage 3 of the 55-mile delivery tunnel, to link Kensico Reservoir in Mt. Pleasant with the CT3 valve chamber beneath VanCortlandt Park in the Bronx, has been deemed unnecessary.

The tunnel sections range from 10 to 24 feet in diameter and burrow 400 to 800 feet below the busy streets of New York. Digging them involves incredible logistical planning, meticulous coordination with many agencies, communication with residents and businesses and a lot of patience. Imagine: The amount of rock excavated during the first two stages of the project could fill both the Empire State Building and Yankee Stadium. A staggering amount of concrete – 30 million cubic feet – was used to line the tunnel sections. In the Manhattan section alone, ten shafts, spaced 20 blocks apart, were excavated to bring the water up from the tunnel to large trunk mains. More than six miles of the latter, and 11 miles of smaller distribution mains, were installed in the service area of the Manhattan leg, designed and managed by the City's Design and Construction Commission.

Draining and inspecting City Tunnels 1 and 2 will be possible once CT3 is in operation, now anticipated to be in in the early 2020s, more than half a century after it began. It is the largest public

works project in the City's history, with a price tag to match: $1 billion in the last decade alone.

Staten Island Siphon

A new deep siphon has been bored beneath New York Harbor between Brooklyn and Staten Island.

This tunnel, completed in late 2014, will replace two shallower pipes which first brought Catskill System water to the residents of Staten Island in 1917 and 1925. They were replaced in 1970 by the Richmond Tunnel constructed deep in bedrock (*See Chapter 11*). The original pipes have served as backup delivery mechanisms since that time; the 72-inch siphon completed in 2015 will serve as the new backup.

The removal of the two older mains is to enable the harbor channel to be dredged to a depth of 50 feet to accommodate larger ocean going ships. The current Anchorage Channel is 45 feet deep. The Port Authority of New York and New Jersey and the NYC Economic Development Commission partnered on the $250 million siphon project, which was halted for a year and a half after the storm surge caused by Hurricane Sandy on October 28, 2012. The surge flooded the construction shafts in Brooklyn and Staten Island and severely damaged the Tunnel Boring Machine (TBM), which had been lowered into the tunnel of July of that year and had progressed 1600 feet before the devastating storm hit.

After dewatering the tunnel and shafts, the TBM was repaired and tested, and was finally put back into service April 14, 2014. The TBM simultaneously excavated and installed four-foot wide concrete pre-cast segment rings to line the tunnel wall. The new tunnel was expected to be put in service by the end of 2015.

Ultraviolet Disinfection Plant

Adding chlorine to water supplies is pretty good at killing bacteria, but it's not effective against cryptosporidium, a microorganism that can sicken and even kill those with compromised immune systems. But when exposed to ultraviolet (UV) light, those pathogens are rendered sterile, and thus cannot colonize and infect people.

The US EPA recognizes UV as an effective

Ultraviolet Treatment facility Although it is not filtered, all water from the Catskill and Delaware systems is directed through chambers holding ultraviolet lamps to render pathogens sterile. The UV treatment facility is located at Eastview in Westchester County. *NYC DEP photo*

treatment method, and in fact requires two forms of disinfection for surface water supplies nationwide. So, while the DEP is not required to filter its Catskill-Delaware Supply, it meets the two-treatment rule by the addition of chlorine, and UV disinfection at a facility in Westchester County.

Located at Eastview, where the former NYC Board of Water Supply had intended to build a filtration plant back in 1910 (*see Chapter 13*), the gigantic UV facility, largest in the world, was begun in 2006 and was completed in 2012. It is connected to both the Catskill and the Delaware Aqueducts, so all water that comes from the West of Hudson Watershed is treated here. The plant can handle up to two billion gallons of water a day, more than the total UV capacity in the rest of the US.

The custom designed system sends water through 56 chambers, each containing 210 ten-foot long lamps, rather like florescent lights, but these low pressure/high output lamps emit a more powerful dose of ultraviolet rays that disrupt the DNA of cryptosporidium.

The plant measures 410x200 feet. Its first floor is underground. (Some of the dirt excavated for the plant was used to bury the concrete former aerators at the Kensico Dam in Valhalla.) Construction included the installation of more than a mile of cement-lined 12-foot diameter pipe, 10,000

linear feet of steel pipe, 1,200 tons of structural steel, 20,000 square feet of aluminum grating, and 121,000 cubic yards of concrete.

Work also included improvements to the existing Delaware Aqueduct, approximately 500 feet below ground, which required months of nightly shutdowns of the aqueduct. The facility cost $1.2 billion to construct, and the electric bill is somewhere around $20 million annually, with another $2 million for staff and other operational expenses.

The use of the more benign UV process may allow the DEP to reduce the amount of chlorine it adds to the water, but the two-treatment rule means it will likely never discontinue chlorination.

East-of-Hudson Dam Upgrades

A million here, a million there, pretty soon you're talking about real money.

While the big ticket items ($1.5 billion UV facility; $1 billion Delaware Aqueduct repair, and the mega-billion City Tunnel #3) tend to capture the headlines and the imagination, a host of smaller projects are always underway somewhere in the NYC water system. Dams, dikes and other facilities at all but one (New Croton) of the 13 reservoirs in the East of Hudson Watershed have been upgraded at a cost of $263 million, through August 2015. Some examples:

• Repairs and upgrades to Amawalk, Titicus and Middle Branch Dams, built between 1894 and 1897, were conducted to bring them into compliance with state dam safety standards. Flow control equipment replaced, spillways and dam faces rehabilitated, roads and boat ramps rebuilt. Completed in 2010. $51 million.

• Improvements to Hillview Reservoir, including modernization of four chamber buildings, installation of advanced security systems, roadway and landscaping alterations, elevation of the 2,750-foot-long basin dividing wall by ten feet, and installation of a bird deterrent system on the 90-acre reservoir, the last stop for Catskill and Delaware water before it enters the distribution system. Completed in 2013. $41 million.

• Rehabilitation of Kensico Dam. Cleaning of spillway, waste weir, façade and colonnades; replacement of the gate house and valve chamber, repair of pavilions, terrace and fountains, installation of new electrical equipment, landscaping and new fencing. The 1,843-foot long dam was closed to vehicular traffic after the terrorist attacks of 2001, but was later reopened for recreational use, only to be shut down for six years during the rehabilitation work. Completed in 2011, reopened to walkers, joggers and skaters in the spring of 2012. $42 million.

Watershed Protection Programs

The geographic, cultural, and political landscapes of the West of Hudson (WOH) and East of Hudson (EOH) New York City Watersheds are poles apart. So while the goal of maintaining water quality in the city's reservoirs is the same, the methods used to develop and deliver water quality assurance programs under the 1997 NYC Watershed Memorandum of Agreement (MOA) have been different depending on which side of the river you're on.

WEST OF HUDSON (WOH)

The original list of MOA programs to be managed by the 15-person Catskill Watershed Corporation (CWC) was short, but it towered over the first CWC Board of Directors back in '97. To be sure, most of the locally-elected directors had been in the trenches as members of the Coalition of Watershed Towns; they'd been dreaming and talking about this moment for years. But when the ink dried on the MOA, it was time to put words into action and deliver the programs they'd pledged to their Catskill region constituents: septic remediation, sand and salt storage, stormwater controls, education programs, and economic development loans and grants. Those programs, along with $126 million from the City, would come with a lot of responsibility for a group that had no office, no staff, not even a bank account.

But within a year after its first Annual Meet-

One of eighteen absorption beds being installed for the hamlet of Lexington's community septic system.

This installation in Willow, Ulster County, is one of thousands of septic systems replaced or repaired since 1997.

Tourism promotion is a key element of economic development initiatives in the West-of-Hudson Watershed, where the Delaware & Ulster Rail Road excursion train received support from the Catskill Fund for the Future.

ing in April of 1997, the CWC was ensconced in a rented (later purchased) former newspaper plant in Margaretville. It had an executive director and a staff of 13. And it was putting money on the streets. In addition to 12 local officials representing the five WOH watershed counties, the CWC board includes two people appointed by the NYS Governor – one to represent the State's interests, the other to represent the environmental signatories to the MOA – and one appointed by the Mayor of NYC. With a host of partner agencies and advisory committees, the Board sets policy and rules for its programs. Here's a summary of the CWC's accomplishments through late 2015:

Septic Repair and Replacement: The first dollars out the door in 1997-98 – more than $1 million in fact -- reimbursed 289 WOH homeowners who had replaced their septic systems after Nov. 2, 1995. Since then more than 4,800 on-site residential septic systems have been replaced, the cost of each ranging from $5,000 to well over $40,000, depending on terrain, size of the lot and soil characteristics. Permanent residents are reimbursed 100 percent of eligible costs, non-permanent residents 60 percent. A handful of commercial systems have been replaced for small businesses, with CWC paying 75% of the cost, up to $40,000.

Sand and Salt Storage: Thirty-nine facilities were constructed between 1998 and 2003 for the storage of municipal road de-icing supplies. Total cost was over $9.6 million. A small facility for a Watershed hospital was also constructed under a lesser used program for institutions.

Stormwater controls: A Margaretville bank and a pharmaceuticals firm in Hobart were the first applicants to the Future Stormwater Program in 1998. The program reimburses the cost of DEP-required Stormwater Pollution Prevention Plans for new construction. A Stormwater Retrofit Program, launched in 1999, provides grants to municipalities, businesses and institutions for correcting runoff problems that degrade water quality. The program has assisted dozens of projects, large and small, across the watershed.

Education: A program to provide grants to schools and non-profit organizations in New York City and the WOH Watershed was developed in early 1998 and by July the first $100,000 was awarded to 13 recipients. Since that time nearly 500 grants totaling more than $2.5 million have supported projects designed to enhance understanding and appreciation of the NYC water system and the region that is the source of 90 percent of the water for half of the State's population. The MOA also earmarked funds for a regional watershed museum *(See Education and Recreation)*.

Economic Development: Initially capitalized with $59.7 million in City money, now wholly owned and managed by the CWC, the Catskill Fund for the Future (CFF) was established as a revolving low-interest loan fund to help businesses located in Watershed Towns. A team of consultants was first hired to produce an Economic Development Study to guide the use of the CFF. But even before the study report was adopted in July of 1999, and before permanent program rules were approved the following summer, the CWC board voted to establish a $2.5 million interim loan program, assisting 10 businesses as well as providing another $250,000 for tourism promotion.

Since then, 326 loans valued at $61 million have been given to businesses of all sorts, leveraging another $80 million and creating and saving hundreds of jobs. But even with CFF assistance, not all of these businesses have been successful. More than a few failed to weather periodic financial downturns. And despite emergency assistance provided to hundreds of damaged businesses after floods in 2006 and 2011, several did not recover from those disasters.

From 2001 to 2004, a grant program using CFF investment interest deployed funds to 122 non-profit organizations before falling interest rates called a halt to the initiative.

The CFF has been employed for many special projects: Assistance to hospitals and health care facilities; installation of renewable energy systems at community institutions; erection of six outdoor exhibits commemorating communities lost to the city's reservoirs; and support for tourism efforts, including the Reservoir Recreational Boating Program established in 2009 and the Catskill Interpretive Center which opened in 2014.

In its first five years, the CWC had expended $32 million on environmental protection, economic development and education programs. When the Filtration Avoidance Determination (FAD) was renewed in 2002, allowing the DEP to avoid filtering Catskill-Delaware water for another five years, the **Community Wastewater Management Program (CWMP)** was added to the CWC to-do list.

The CWMP was established as part of an effort to address the wastewater needs of 22 hamlets identified in the MOA. The top seven on the priority list were handled under the New Infrastructure Program managed directly by the DEP. The CWC would be responsible for dealing with the other 15 under the CWMP program, funded by the City.

Bovina's community septic system had gotten a kick-start as a pilot project using a federal Water Resources Development Agency grant, so it was the first CWMP project completed. Similar systems in Bloomville and Hamden, a wastewater treatment plant in Boiceville and a septic maintenance district in Delancey followed. Funding for the program was continued under the ten-year 2007 FAD, and community systems were subsequently completed in Ashland, Trout Creek, Lexington and South Kortright. In late 2015, the last five communities on the priority list were under study or design.

Hundreds of vulnerable on-site individual septic systems are being decommissioned through this program. The municipalities own the community systems when they are complete and receive operation and maintenance funds as part of the block grant that covers construction. Annual fees on district homeowners are capped at $100 per year, adjusted for inflation. Businesses pay according to water usage.

The CWC has also provided towns and villages with planning grants, assistance with the review of City land acquisition proposals, and funds to hire attorneys and consultants to meet City challenges to local tax assessments on their properties.

EAST OF HUDSON (EOH)

Most of the reservoirs in Westchester and Putnam Counties were developed as part of the Croton System to capture water that is now filtered at the new Croton Filtration Plant. But the West Branch Reservoir in Putnam and the Kensico Reservoir in Westchester receive waters from the Catskill-Delaware System, and, because the reservoirs in that WOH system are not filtered, source water protection in these EOH basins is vitally important.

The MOA required the City to allocate $68 million to be used for a "Water Quality Investment Program" to fund a variety of water protection purposes in Westchester and Putnam Counties.

Putnam County

In Putnam, the county holds the money ($30 million) and the Board of Legislators decides which projects proposed by the towns are to be funded. These have included repair of approximately 160 residential septic systems, stormwater best management practices and regulatory compliance, sand and salt storage facilities, stream channel improvements and other water quality enhancement efforts. Those funds have been expended.

A new program, funded directly by the City and run by the NYS Environmental Facilities Corp. (EFC), has been set up to partially reimburse homeowners for septic system repairs in the Boyds Corners and West Branch Reservoirs, which are part of the Delaware Water Supply System.

Putnam County municipalities include the Towns of Carmel, Kent, Patterson, Putnam Valley and Southeast, and the Village of Brewster.

Westchester County

In Westchester, the county is the custodian of the funds ($38 million) but the Northern Westchester Watershed Committee, made up of representatives of 12 towns and villages, recommends projects to receive those funds. Local sewer district improvements and stormwater controls have been accomplished with this money, and $500,000 was spent to create a county-wide Septic Database Management program.

All Westchester septic haulers were already licensed. The database program created a reporting system in which results of residential pumpouts and inspections are sent to the County to track pumpouts in Watershed towns.

In addition, each Westchester municipality received a grant of $312,500 in 2006 to do a potpourri of locally chosen projects relevant to water quality. The municipalities are the Towns of Bedford, New Castle, North Castle, Yorktown, North Salem, Lewisboro, Pound Ridge, Somers, Cortlandt, Mt. Pleasant and Harrison, and the Village of Mt. Kisco.

Though millions have been spent, the original Westchester allocation has grown through investment earnings to almost $45 million. The most significant current project on the drawing board is a residential septic repair program in the Town of Bedford, which would help homeowners pay for repairs, or to connect their septic systems to an existing sewage collection system. This program may be used as a model for other Watershed towns.

In the four Westchester towns within the Kensico Reservoir basin (Harrison, Mt. Pleasant, North Castle and Newcastle), the DEP reimburses homeowners half the cost of repairs to their failed septic systems. The NYS EFC administers this program, which is funded directly by the City as a requirement of the 2007 Filtration Avoidance Determination (FAD) issued by the EPA and NYS DEC as distinct from the county initiatives funded under the MOA.

Stormwater

In this highly developed watershed, with impervious surfaces such as rooftops, paved streets and parking lots creating significant runoff and pollutant potential, stormwater controls are needed. More than that, they are required by the NYS DEC. Acting under federal authority, the DEC designated EOH communities as MS4s (Municipal Separate Storm Sewer Systems), which require the development of stormwater management programs and permit systems.

These of course cost money, and under terms of the 2010 Water Supply Permit issued by the DEC, New York City agreed to allocate $15 million for MS4 compliance activity. Matched by Westchester and Putnam, as well as Dutchess County, which has a small amount of land in the EOH Watershed, the funds ($30 million total) are overseen and distributed by the East of Hudson Watershed Corporation, formed exclusively for this purpose. Modeled after the Catskill Watershed Corporation, the non-profit organization is made up of elected EOH municipal officials.

An initial five-year roster of dozens of stormwater projects was completed in 2015.

No-action items

The 1997 MOA allocated $1 million for each county to be used for planning to identify significant sources of pollution to the Croton Watershed, recommend measures to prevent it, and to protect "the character and special needs of Croton Watershed communities." That money, however, was left on the table, perhaps because the regulatory atmosphere was already saturated. "No one wanted to do it," according to William C. Harding, Executive Director of the Watershed Protection and Partnership Council.

Also left undone was the proposed diversion of wastewater from dozens of treatment plants to a plant or plants outside the NYC East of Hudson Watershed. Feasibility studies funded by the City were done, and Westchester County-operated plants in Peekskill and Ossining on the Hudson River were identified as possible recipients of combined waste-water. However, many technical and political issues, together with the unpopular notion of transporting "effluent from the affluent" to someone else's backyard left the idea dead in the water.

Below the dams

New York City's upstate reservoirs were built for one reason – to supply people, institutions and industry in the city and its suburbs with clean, abundant water. Downstream water releases have also been required to maintain river flow levels and stream ecology.

Increasingly, however, those downstream interests have received more attention as citizen activists and sportsmen's groups argue on behalf of dam safety, flood control, fishery health and recreational activity.

Dam Concerned Citizens (DCC) was established in 2005 in response to information that the Gilboa Dam was being examined for possible structural vulnerabilities. The safety of thousands of people living along 55 miles of the Schoharie Creek from the dam to the stream's confluence with the Mohawk River was suddenly an issue, and the organization was formed to make sure their voices were heard during dam repairs and subsequent reconstruction. DCC and Schoharie County officials secured DEP-funded emergency notification systems downstream, and participated in countless meetings and site tours to stay abreast of the work.

DCC launched a website to provide information on weather events, reservoir and stream levels and project information. They have lobbied for additional stream gauges downstream, and for improved water releases from the reservoir, whose original lower level outlet release works have long been silted in and inoperative, rendering the Schoharie Creek occasionally bone dry below the dam. In March of 2015 the DEP announced that it would begin minimum releases of 10 to 15 million gallons a day to the creek, and would implement a storage protocol that would allow it to release water whenever actual storage exceeded the objective. Some aspects of the plan may have to wait until the lower level outlet works are completed at the reservoir in 2020.

Meanwhile, anglers in the Esopus Creek, where Schoharie Reservoir waters are diverted via the Shandaken Tunnel, have demanded cleaner releases to protect trout and their habitat. A world renowned fishery, the Esopus has been called Yoo-Hoo Creek by some, a reference to the chocolate drink the stream occasionally resembles downstream of the tunnel's portal due to sediment load from the Schoharie basin.

Litigation brought by environmental groups resulted in a finding that the City violated the federal Clean Water Act with these turbid releases, and in 2006 the New York State Dept. of Environmental Conservation issued a State Pollutant Discharge Elimination System (SPDES) permit requiring the City to limit highly turbid discharges, maintain targeted flows, continuously monitor water parameters and develop a cold water release plan. Those activities are reviewed twice a year at meetings attended by vigilant interest groups.

Another constituency affected by the operations of the Schoharie Reservoir are people, parks and businesses many miles away, below the Ashokan Reservoir in Ulster County, destination for Schoharie waters. The Lower Esopus Watershed Partnership, a coalition of community and government organizations in the Esopus drainage area between the reservoir and the Hudson River, has insisted that the City manage its dual-reservoir Catskill Water Supply with their interests in mind. Uncontrolled Ashokan spillage during high water events, and deliberate releases to provide seasonal voids in the reservoir, have caused stream degradation, farmland flooding, beach erosion and some structural damage in the Lower Esopus watershed.

Similar complaints have been raised far to the west, below the Cannonsville and Pepacton Reservoir dams. The Friends of the Upper Delaware River (FUDR) is another coalition of groups and individuals that serves as a watchdog over the activities of the Delaware River Basin Commission and argues for "a more equitable plan that will provide cold water to protect both habitat and our fishery while considering the vital issue of flood mitigation, and adding missing elements like a thermal release component to protect the ecosystem during times of stress."

Complaints about DEP's water management have persisted through periodic reviews and revisions of the Flexible Flow Management Program (FFMP) that sets procedures for water releases from the Pepacton, Cannonsville and Neversink Reservoirs, and despite development of the Operations Support Tool (OST), a monitoring and modeling system designed to more accurately predict water storage levels in all of the city's reservoirs and better manage the movement of water throughout the system.

The FFMP is an agreement between the Delaware River Basin states of New York, Pennsylvania, New Jersey and Delaware, and the City of New York (members of the Delaware River Basin Commission established in 1954 – *Chapter 17*). It attempts to balance water supply demands, fish habitat requirements, flood mitigation and the need to repel salt water encroachment in the Delaware Bay estuary. The FFMP relies on the City's Operations Support Tool (OST) to help juggle those often conflicting needs.

Costing more than $5 million to create in 2010, the OST was designed to respond more effectively to changing weather, climate, and emergency events. It links DEP's water quality and quantity models; assimilates near-real-time data on reservoir levels, stream flow, snow pack and water quality; and ingests National Weather Service forecasts. At the same time, it takes into account the rules and laws that govern water supply operations, including Delaware River Basin Commission's flow agreements.

Climate change, invasives and hydropower

The Climate Change Coordinator at the DEP's Bureau of Environmental Planning and Assessment has the unenviable and maybe impossible task of preparing the agency for rising sea levels and more frequent and potent storms.

A few major issues include how to retrofit or armor wastewater treatment plants; prepare for floods that may damage infrastructure, contaminate the water supply and overtop dams to inundate downstream communities; and predict the impact of warmer, wetter winters on the amount and timing of mountain snowpack which in large measure determines how the water system is managed.

Alien invaders

Climate change is also aiding and abetting the spread of invasive species which threaten water and woodland. Agencies across the Watershed are meeting the challenge with studies, biological control experiments, monitoring and recruitment of citizen scientists to keep an eye out for tree killers like Asian longhorn beetle, hemlock wooly adelgid and emerald ash borer; water borne pests like didymo, zebra mussel and water chestnut; and streamside nuisances like Japanese knotweed and marsh thistle, Aggressive stranglers like mile-a-minute vine, and dangerous plants like giant hogweed whose sap can burn and blind a person, are menacing and worrisome to land managers.

These insects and plants have the power to upset native ecological balance, kill trees that shade water and shelter fish, colonize water pipes, and suffocate macroinvertebrates and other aquatic creatures.

The advance of the emerald ash borer into the Catskills prompted the DEP in 2014 to begin removing vast swaths of this species from the Ashokan Reservoir basin. An estimated 4,000 ash trees were harvested ahead of the insect's advance, sold to a Dutchess County furniture maker with its own mill. Many more trees that have already been infested and are considered a hazard were scheduled for removed in 2016. Ash makes up an estimated seven percent of the Catskill forest.

Hydropower

The adverse impact of fossil fuel use on our changing climate has prompted calls on many fronts for increasing development of renewable energy sources. Hydropower seems a natural in the water-rich Catskills.

Four electric generating stations have long been positioned at the Rondout and Ashokan Reservoirs to take advantage of the energy of falling water. The DEP itself operates power plants with a combined capacity of 43 megawatts at the Rondout Reservoir outlets of the East Delaware and the Neversink Tunnels. Brookfield Renewable Energy operates a third Rondout Reservoir hydro facility at the outlet of the West Delaware Tunnel. A fourth station, operated by the New York Power Authority, generates power from water as it moves from Ashokan Reservoir into the Catskill Aqueduct. The City garners millions in electricity sales and lease revenue from these plants annually.

A hydropower facility had been located on the Catskill Aqueduct at the Kensico Reservoir but was discontinued when the aqueduct was taken off line during construction of the ultraviolet treatment facility at Eastview. The future of that hydro plant is undetermined.

The DEP is also reevaluating its plan to construct a 14-megawatt hydroelectric facility at the Cannonsville Dam after workers taking preparatory earth borings in July 2015 unexpectedly released ground water under natural (artesian) pressure. Turbid water emerged from a rock face below the dam, prompting the DEP to draw down the reservoir in case the earthen dam had somehow been compromised by internal erosion.

Worried communities as far downstream as Trenton, NJ were apprised of the situation as the DEP monitored conditions 24/7, called in experts and hired consultants to drill relief wells and cap the bore holes. The crisis was shortlived – by August 2 normal operations had resumed -- but DEP officials were pledging to take another look at whether a marginally profitable hydroelectric facility that it had planned to operate, and for which it had obtained a license from the Federal Energy Regulatory Commission, would justify the cost of these repairs and future construction estimated at $72 million.

Conserving a finite resource

Back in 1984, per capita water use in New York City's five boroughs was 207 gallons a day. Thirty years later, in 2014, a variety of conservation initiatives had brought that figure down to 118 gallons per day.

Despite increasing population, in-city consumption has decreased by 30 percent since the early 1990s, when the average daily distribution was above 1.4 billion gallons per day. In 2014, average daily distribution was recorded at 996 million gallons per day (mgd), and since 2009, water usage has been well below the 1.045 billion gallons consumed daily during the record 1966 drought when severe water use restrictions were in place.

In 2012, the DEP launched a Water Demand Management Program to reduce citywide use by an additional five percent (50 mgd). With the shutdown of the Delaware Aqueduct looming in 2021 or 2022, and the city's population expected to rise to 9.1 million by 2030, water efficiency will be crucial to assure ample supply as well as to create additional storage and treatment capacity in the city's 14 wastewater treatment plants.

The DEP is pursuing six key strategies for managing water demand:

- Retrofit plumbing fixtures in public buildings and parks, including a $50 million project that in 2015 had replaced 10,000 inefficient toilets in 129 schools with low-flow fixtures, resulting in a 70% reduction in water use at each building. The goal is to replace 40,000 toilets in 500 schools by 2019, saving four million gallons of water each day. Activation buttons are being installed on spray showers at 400 playgrounds to save an estimated 1.5 mgd.

- Encourage homeowners to replace inefficient toilets with low-flow (1.3 gallon/flush) models by providing $125 vouchers towards the purchase of new ones. It is hoped that 800,000 toilets will be replaced through this program, which is similar to a rebate program in the mid-1990s in which 1.3 million toilets were replaced and water consumption was reduced by 90 mgd. The old toilets (typically using as much as five gallons per flush) are being recycled as tile, bathroom fixtures, road beds and drainage material.

• Engage non-residential properties to save water. Eleven of the City's premier hotels agreed in 2013 to cut water consumption by five percent, saving a total of 13 million gallons per year.

• Automated Meter Reading (AMR). This system began in 2008 and now serves 836,000 customer accounts, providing detailed water use information that can be monitored by each customer as well as by DEP's Water Leak Notification Program, which can detect spikes in usage.

• Expansion of leak detection efforts to include not just water mains (7,000 miles of them, including 394 miles of pipe that date from 1870 or earlier) to parcels with multiple buildings, such as housing projects and educational institutions.

• Improve pressure management to prevent drastic fluctuations in pressure zones that can cause water main breaks, which have been reduced by 40 percent in recent years.

Other efforts to reduce consumption have included assisting upstate wholesale water customers to develop conservation plans; offering lower water rates to building owners who recycle waste water for use in toilets, irrigation and cooling towers; installing sprinkler caps on fire hydrants during the summer; distributing conservation kits to retrofit faucets in homes and apartments, and expanding educational messaging to schools and the public.

Floods and their legacy

Irene. Lee. Sandy.

They are names that make hearts drop in the nation's largest city and in its Watershed. But they are only the latest storms to claim lives and bring monumental damage to communities and infrastructure.

Watershed residents well remember the unnamed Flood of 1996, when up to four feet of snow, melting in a surge of 60 degree warmth on January 19, was augmented by four inches of rain,

sending torrents of water through homes, businesses, schools. Roads became rivers, bridges were twisted from foundations, buildings collapsed. The National Guard was called in, the NYC DEP deployed workers and heavy equipment to assist local highway crews, the Red Cross moved in to help shell-shocked residents.

The trauma, and response, was repeated in 2006, when up to 12 inches of rain fell on western Delaware County on June 27. Several feet of water

The Village of Margaretville was under water after Tropical Storm Irene swept through in August of 2011.

coursed down Walton's Delaware Street. More than 70 businesses reported damage estimated at $20 million. The Village Hall, the library, the police department, the theater were all flooded. Dozens of farms in the West Branch Watershed were hit hard, and the Watershed Agricultural Council ultimately spent more than $327,000 repairing barnyards, watering systems, access roads and other farm infrastructure.

The DEP deployed police officers, scuba divers, boats, dozens of vehicles and a helicopter to assist with rescues and evacuations. It supplied dump trucks, graders and other equipment to help clear roads, sent huge pumps and leak detection crews to locate water main breaks, and in an ironic twist, sent a 1000-gallon tanker truck with fresh drinking water – from New York City -- to the Town of Walton.

Clean-up took weeks. Recovery took much longer. But this time, in addition to the usual emergency funding sources, there was financial assistance from the Catskill Watershed Corp., which established a $5 million fund to provide no-interest loans to stricken businesses in the Village of Walton.

Just five years later, Tropical Storm Irene laid waste to a wider swath of the Watershed. Again, more than a foot of rain fell on the Catskills on August 28. Death and destruction returned with a vengeance. The hamlet of Prattsville on the Schoharie Creek was very nearly wiped off the map, with well over 100 buildings destroyed or heavily damaged. Margaretville, Fleischmanns, Windham and many other communities were stunned by the devastation. More rain fell when Tropical Storm Lee arrived on September 9.

The DEP once more provided crews and equipment to help with the recovery, and to repair and clean up its own facilities that had been damaged, including wastewater treatment plants in Tanners-ville and Margaretville, where staff members were stranded by high water and washed out roads, and the Downsville operations center and police precinct, located just downstream from the Pepacton Reservoir dam and spillway.

More worrisome was the impact on the Gilboa Dam, where contractors had been working to reconstruct the facility for several years. Irene sent eight feet of water – more than ever recorded -- over the dam's spillway that harrowing day in 2011. Although electronic monitoring sensors failed, prompting the DEP to trigger downstream emergency notifications and evacuations, the dam held firm. However, much of the construction staging area, access roads and work platforms were destroyed. The dam has since been updated with modern telemetry and the structure of the dam itself upgraded, including new discharge conduit and operating areas. (*See Water System Infrastructure Projects*)

Highly turbid water in the Ashokan Reservoir persisted for months after Irene, and the DEP obtained State Health Department approval to add significant amounts of aluminum sulfate to the water to help settle out the particulates before sending it to consumers.

Emergency funding was again generated by the CWC, which met in special session to approve a $5 million fund that would ultimately provide 150 grants of up to $30,000 each to help damaged businesses get back on their feet. The City added $1 million to the business recovery fund. More money was spent over the next several months in a CWC program to clear trees and debris from streams and floodways.

A new forest was planted in 2014 at the Kensico Reservoir after a tornado uprooted a wide swath of trees. In 2012, Superstorm Sandy felled thousands of trees there, mostly giant Norway spruce that were planted when the reservoir was built. *NYC DEP photo*

The city funded evacuation route signs and warning sirens in the Schoharie Valley below the Gilboa Dam when questions about the dam's integrity made downstream residents uneasy neighbors.

Extending the flood plain of the Stony Clove stream is intended to reduce downstream damage in future floods. *Ashokan Watershed Stream Management Program photo*

The Watershed Agricultural Council, too came to the aid of farmers, where fields had been gouged and strewn with debris and piles of gravel, fences were flattened, and acres of crops destroyed at the peak of the harvest season. More than $423,000 from the Agricultural and Community Recovery Fund was distributed by WAC to 20 farm families in Delaware and Greene Counties. A separate Farmer Relief Fund channeled public donations to assist with repairs and lost income.

And then came Sandy, a year later, on Oct. 29, 2012. The Superstorm, eclipsed only by Katrina as the costliest in American history, was felt most powerfully in New York City and the Croton Watershed. The record storm surge that accompanied Sandy submerged many of the City's sea-level wastewater treatment plants. Ten plants and more than 40 sanitary sewer pumping stations were temporarily disabled by Hurricane Sandy. In a reversal of earlier patterns, upstate workers were sent downstate to help with the recovery, using industrial pumps to, among other tasks, drain Manhattan's Battery Underpass of floodwater.

Hurricane Sandy resulted in more than 16,000 downed trees in the City, and caused massive damage to the forest surrounding the Kensico Reservoir in Westchester County. In some areas, 90 percent of the trees were toppled or damaged. Many were 100 feet tall, most of them century-old Norway spruce planted when the reservoir was built. The DEP contracted for the trees to be removed the following year. Logs were shipped to a mill in Quebec where they yielded hundreds of thousands of board feet of lumber.

These disasters brought many changes to the watershed. Dozens of homes were purchased through the Federal Emergency Management Agency buy-out program, with partial funding supplied by New York City. The lots have been cleared, and the City is now a major property owner in several communities. (*See Land Acquisition*)

In the years since Irene, several sections of torn up streams have been repaired with more than $13 million in funding from the federal Natural Resources Conservation Service Emergency Watershed Program, and the DEP's Stream Management Program. Channel relocation, streambank armoring, slope re-vegetation and floodplain widening were among the projects on the West Kill, Stony Clove, Vly, Dry Brook and other Catskill streams. In some cases, stream rehabilitation projects that had been accomplished years earlier had been undone by the wild waters. Principal partner agencies in these efforts are County Soil & Water Conservation Districts.

Perhaps the most notable "Irene effect" was the flurry of flood mitigation efforts launched at every level of government. The State made money and consultants available to the most heavily damaged communities through a "New York Rising" program to determine how to minimize future flood hazards and bolster local economies. The City allocated more than $1 million to pay for Local Flood Analyses in a number of inundation areas to see how flood impacts might be reduced. Another $10 million from the DEP's Stream Management Implementation Program was earmarked for projects recommended in Flood Hazard Mitigation Plans developed through the above two programs. And the CWC is administering a new Flood Hazard Mitigation Implementation program, also funded by the City to the tune of $17 million. This will be tapped to help municipalities and property owners enact flood protection measures, including relocation out of the floodplain.

Education and recreation

Education

Since the Watershed agreements were enacted in the mid-1990s, a generation of students have grown to maturity, many thousands of them carrying into adulthood new understanding of what it means to be water consumers, and water stewards.

Lessons about water quality, conservation, watershed history and more have been provided by many agencies, organizations and educators. They have been conveyed through stream and water studies, authentic research, theatrical presentations, music and art projects, field trips to reservoirs, environmental education centers and City water sites, and through direct communication between urban and rural peers.

Funds provided by the NYC DEP, the US Forest Service and other agencies support these far reaching programs.

The Watershed Agricultural Council (WAC) has coordinated more than 200 bus tours to introduce New York City school groups and adults to the Watershed. More than 10,000 people have visited the place where their water begins in order to appreciate the complexities of the water supply system, the roles of the forest and Watershed residents in maintaining water quality, and the sacrifices that were made by former communities on their behalf.

WAC also runs an intensive professional development program, Watershed Forestry Institute for Teachers, that reached more than 270 educators between 1999 and 2015. Many of those teachers have formed partnerships through a program called Green Connections in which Watershed and NYC classes share water lessons and meet each other in upstate and downstate visits. More than 4,500 students have benefitted from this exchange program.

Thousands of young people have been directly affected by the Catskill Watershed Corporation's (CWC) Education Grant Program. Since 1998, when the first annual funding round was conducted, the CWC, in partnership with the NYC DEP, awarded 488 grants to schools and organizations in New York City and in the West-of-Hudson Watershed. In 18 rounds, more than $2.5 million was distributed for projects and programs that directly touched more than 120,000 people.

Grants have been used to study macroinvertebrates; create anthologies of student writing about water; build nature trails; purchase microscopes and digital cameras, waders and snowshoes; raise trout; compose songs; create water-themed computer games; study flood impacts and climate change;

Roxbury Central School students stir up some macroinvertebrates from the East Branch Delaware River to study later. *CWC photo*

explore environmental careers and, of course, enjoy personal encounters with the great outdoors. Teacher conferences and training sessions have been held, and many programs have been offered for the general public by libraries, arts organizations and Watershed agencies.

The NYC DEP has an Education Office with a full time staff that provides background and instructional materials, visits classrooms in the City, participates in teacher training, assists with educational exhibits, gives tours and public presentations and coordinates with other agencies and organizations supplying water-related curricula and programs on water, wastewater and other environmental issues. They run the annual Water Resources Art and Poetry Contest which in 2015 attracted entries from 1,350 students from 75 schools in New York City and Watershed communities. Their artwork and poetry reflected an appreciation for New York's water resources and wastewater treatment systems and the importance of water conservation.

The DEP, at its Queens offices, hosts the regional coordinator of Trout Unlimited's Trout in the Classroom (TIC) Program. In 1997, this national initiative was started in New York through the efforts of the late Joan Stoliar, volunteers from Trout Unlimited (TU) and the Theodore Gordon Flyfishers. With early support from a 1998 CWC education grant, the program has grown from four participating classrooms to more than 200 schools in the City and in the East- and West-of-Hudson Watersheds. Through TIC, a bit of the wild world is brought indoors, where students help raise brown and brook trout from eggs to fingerlings and learn how clean water is crucial to the habitat, food source and survival of this critical species.

Recreation

Learning also takes place today in an informal way through outdoor recreation on City lands and reservoirs. But when the MOA was signed in 1997, only fishing was allowed on the reservoirs; if you weren't carrying an access permit, a fishing license and a pole, you faced arrest for trespassing. In the MOA, the DEP agreed to consider eventually permitting other uses for its existing lands and waters,

and to listen to Sporting Advisory Committees and local communities about what activities should be allowed on the Watershed lands it would acquire in the future. These might include hiking, birdwatching, cross country skiing, nature study and hunting (in certain areas, under certain conditions). But, warned the DEP, it was not likely to allow boating, camping, or mountain biking.

Years of discussion between landowners, outdoor enthusiasts, public officials and the other major landowner in the region – New York State – helped soften that position and led to a recognition that more eyes on the Watershed would mean better security, increased public stewardship and better resource management.

In 2007, the NYC DEP agreed that a City permit was not needed to hike, fish, hunt and trap on the 11,000 acres of city lands that adjoined State Forest Preserve lands. The NYS DEC agreed to patrol adjoining city property and assist in its management. Since then, the number of acres open for recreation without a permit has grown to 63,612.

Permits are still needed for many places, and they can now be obtained for free and almost instantly online. Today 118,000 people hold permits. So, while the DEP continues to stock the reservoirs with trout, bass and other fish, they're not just welcoming anglers these days: More than 125,000 acres of lands and reservoirs are open for hiking, hunting, boating and other forms of low-impact recreation.

In 2009, the DEP opened the Cannonsville Reservoir to non-mechanized boating (no fishing pole required!). Following a three-year pilot to determine whether there were any adverse effects on water quality (there were none), the program was extended to the Pepacton, Schoharie and Neversink Reservoirs. With funding from the CWC, a network of boat cleaning vendors was established to prevent the spread of aquatic invasive plants and organisms. A dozen launch sites were developed by DEP, boat rental outlets sprouted up and brochures were created to publicize this new recreation and tourism resource. More than 800 canoeists, kayakers and sailors took advantage of the recreational boating program on four reservoirs in 2015. (Fishing remains the only activity allowed on the Ashokan and

Rondout Reservoirs, where the Catskill and Delaware Aqueducts begin.)

Ten hiking trails have been constructed on City lands by non-profit groups who manage and monitor them. These include the Catskill Mountain Club, New York-New Jersey Trail Conference, Putnam County Land Trust, Teatown Lake Reservation, the Finger Lakes Trail Conference and the Windham Area Recreation Foundation. The DEP claims such trails are good for public health and the recreation and tourism economy.

In 2013, the DEP waded into a local controversy when it committed $2.5 million towards developing an 11.5-mile trail along an easement owned by Ulster County on the north side of the Ashokan Reservoir. The County's plan is to reclaim the former Ulster & Delaware Railroad railbed from the Catskill Mountain Railroad (CMR) which had intended to restore the rails to extend its tourist excursion train from its station in Phoenicia to Kingston. Despite valiant volunteer efforts over nearly 30 years, the CMR was not able to accomplish its aim, and the county saw the idle right of way as an ideal hiking and biking path which could link to other recreational paths to the east and south. Entreaties, and threats of litigation, from CMR to maintain the rails so that they might one day be reutilized by trains again fell on deaf ears, and as of late 2015, the plan was to tear up the rails and develop a foot and bike trail. And after decades of restricting access to its premier Catskills reservoir, the DEP will help fund the rail trail and maintain a number of access points along the trail.

And in other turnabouts, the DEP began allowing licensed guides to offer outdoor trips on City lands and waters in 2013. (Some 29 guides signed up to do so). Even mountain bikers and snowmobilers have found places to play on city lands. Just don't expect to pitch your tent anytime soon.

Meanwhile, far from its forested Watershed, the NYC DEP in early 2015 committed $4 million towards a $12 million pedestrian bridge to span the Major Deegan Expressway and connect the Croton Woods and Allen Shandler Recreation Area of Van-Cortlandt Park in the Bronx. The park, where the City built the nation's first municipally owned golf course in 1925, was fragmented by highways built from the 1930s to the 1950s.

The bridge will allow people safer access to these disjointed areas in the City's third largest park. The project is part of mitigation efforts associated with the construction of the Croton Water Filtration Plant beneath the park's nine-hole Mosholu Golf Course. New York State and the City Parks Department will also provide funds for the bridge, expected to be completed by 2019.

Farm and forest

When the NYC DEP allocated $4 million in 1993 to fund an experimental, voluntary program to install pollution controls on ten farms in its Catskill-Delaware Watershed, it had no way of knowing that it was making a down payment on a radical idea that would soon gain traction around the world – paying upstream land owners to preserve water quality for downstream consumers.

This "payment for ecosystem services" (PES) model, instituted by the fledgling Watershed Agricultural Council (WAC) long before the term had been coined, has become one that many nations and urban centers would like to implement: It benefits both landowners who are remunerated for managing their lands with water quality in mind, as well as the folks at the other end of the pipe, who depend on clean water and, more often than not have no idea where it comes from.

The catch – and it's a big one – is that PES requires money. Lots of money. Between 1993 and 2015, the DEP committed $235 million to WAC contracts funding not only its farm program that has grown to 332 active farms throughout its watersheds, but also its forestry and conservation easement programs that were barely on the radar screen at the beginning. So while resource managers and policy wonks visit the Watershed every year from places like Brazil, India and South Korea to learn more about PES, few have the deep pockets to replicate it. And so the New York City Watershed protection model remains unique on the planet.

Agriculture

Still, much has changed in the nearly quarter century since farmers warily shook hands with the city on a deal that promised exemption from Watershed regulations if they would install Best Management Practices (BMPs) on their dairy operations (*see Chapter 22*). Of the ten original pilot farms, only three continued to maintain dairy herds in 2015. A few had horses or small livestock; three were raising beef cattle, a less labor intensive occupation that is on the rise – Delaware County is now the third largest beef producer in New York State, according to WAC.

The economics of milk production has in fact contributed to the cessation of many dairy farm operations in the West of Hudson Watershed. But there remain 190 large farms ($10,000 in gross annual sales) and 100 small farms ($1,000 in sales annually) with Whole Farm Plans governing 159,230 acres. In the Croton Watershed east of the Hudson River, 77 farms, mostly horse boarding operations, have Whole Farm Plans.

A 17-member Council (12 of them current or former farmers) oversees the activities of this now sprawling organization with 50 staffers in three offices. Its attentions are focused on owners of farms, because open space is a preferred use of Watershed lands, and also because a lot can happen on a farm to foul the water: pesticides applied to fields, phosphorus from feed excreted by livestock, inadvertent fuel spills, parasite infestations, sediment loading and more.

This temporary bridge, loaned by the Watershed Agricultural Council, helps prevent stream damage and erosion caused by logging equipment. *WAC photo*

Concreting barnyards allows easier manure removal and storage, preventing uncontrolled runoff. It also keeps the animals healthier and presumably happier. *WAC photo*

Best Management Practices

Basically, teams of WAC staff members and personnel from federal, state and county partner agencies work with farmers to determine what can be done to prevent pollution from barnyards and fields while at the same time improving work efficiency and cutting farm operating costs. Examples of Best Management Practices include concreting barnyards where animals congregate, making these areas easier to clean and healthier for livestock; development of springs and other water sources away from streams to keep animals out of running water; housing calves, whose manure has high concentrations of pathogens, separate from the larger herd; employing rotational grazing to reduce erosion and improve livestock health; building manure storage facilities to allow this natural fertilizer to be spread at dry times of the year, and constructing safe farm fueling stations.

WAC keeps tabs on participating farms to make sure they are still active and that the BMPs are being used and maintained properly (there's funding for that, too.). What happens when a farm stops operating? Trucks, tillers, manure spreaders and other rolling stock is either taken back to be used by other farmers, or is sold to the owner at a pro-rated cost. Barnyards and fencing systems usually stay on the land, hopefully to be used by a new operator. In

one case, a giant 886,500-gallon manure storage tank was dismantled and relocated to a functioning WAC farm.

Many Whole Farm Plans allow farmers to benefit from the Nutrient Management Credit Program, which gives cash credits as a reward for following prescribed manure spreading schedules on fields distant from watercourses. The credit is affirmed through soil testing and can be utilize to pay for increased transport costs and equipment expense. The idea is to reduce the amount of nitrogen and phosphorus that gets into water bound for New York City reservoirs. The practice is credited in part with getting the Cannonsville Reservoir removed from the Federal phosphorus restricted list in 2002, a designation that prevented addition or expansion of wastewater treatment plants in the basin.

Precision Feed Management, a system promoted by Cornell Cooperative Extension in Delaware County, encourages farmers to use more home-grown feed and forage, minimize overfeeding and optimize outside feed purchases to reduce nutrient accumulation. PFM has become a requirement of the NYC Filtration Avoidance Determination, and the City has contracted with WAC to begin implementation in late 2015.

Another incentive for farmers is the federal Conservation Reserve Program which pays farmers to vegetate streamside buffers and keep them undisturbed. In the NYC Watershed, the DEP pays what would be the farmer's half of the cost of BMPs needed to complete their water quality program. The DEP also allows WAC farmers and others to lease farmlands that the City has purchased. There were 100 such leases in 2015, most for hay production, others for row crops, livestock grazing and maple sap collection.

Over the years, WAC has facilitated and participated in research to evaluate methods for reducing on-farm phosphorus loss and pathogen risks. With funding from the DEP and other agencies, a wide range of county, state and federal researchers have studied the value of cover crops, solar calf housing, manure management and other activities, research that in some cases has led to enhancements or modifications of WAC programming.

Conservation easements

Through its city-funded conservation easement (CE) program, WAC has become the largest working lands conservation easement program in New York State. As of late 2015, WAC had purchased 160 agricultural CEs encompassing nearly 25,000 acres from 135 property owners. CEs limit property development but allow for continued commercial activity like agriculture, timber harvests and blue stone quarrying so long as those activities have a conservation plan approved by WAC.

The program is a component of DEP's Land Acquisition Program which is keen to secure or protect relatively large, contiguous land holdings with significant water resources. Its importance to the City is indicated by the growth in funding for the CE program, from $20 million in 1997 to more than $70 million in 2015.

Economic Development

A recognition that unprofitable farms are not good for water quality has been key to WAC's programs from the start. Its stated mission places the promotion of "the economic viability of agriculture and forestry," ahead of "the protection of water quality, and the conservation of working landscapes." The establishment of a regional brand – "Pure Catskills" – and a comprehensive directory of producers puts the mission into practice.

Pure Catskills in 2015 counted among its members 280 farm- and forest-based businesses, restaurants, artisanal producers and organizations. Members are listed in the widely distributed directory and in a searchable online website. They are featured at outreach events and have access to promotional materials, scholarships and grant opportunities. The Pure Catskills Marketplace, an online collection of high-quality farm, food and forest products grown, raised and made in the Catskills, is another marketing outlet.

A four-year Agricultural Development Grant Program ran from 2008 to 2011 and distributed 73 grants totaling more than $244,000 to help farmers develop new products and improve their marketing tools.

WAC also supports area farmers with educational programs, conferences, and producer discussion groups. In addition, a number of organizations intent on encouraging, assisting and promoting new and sustainable farm operations have sprouted with WAC support. They include Farm Catskills, which seeks to develop and support new farmers and diverse agricultural practices; Catskills CRAFT (Collaborative Regional Alliance for Farm Training); and Catskills FarmLink, which helps link aspiring farmers to land and equipment and offers information on funding and educational opportunities.

There remain 18 or 20 large farms in the Watershed that have refused to participate in WAC programs, whether because they remain foes of the City's presence here, or are philosophically opposed to government's involvement in agriculture or private life. But WAC's goal remains 90 percent participation among active large farms. WAC is also required to develop 50 new Whole Farm Plans – East and West of Hudson, large and small farms – by 2017. In late 2015, they had 16 to go.

Forestry

Here's a stunning factoid: 76 percent of the 2,000-square-mile (1.26 million acre) New York City Watershed is forested. The State owns a good chunk of it, the City, too. But much of that forest land is privately owned. And since most farms also contain forest, it was given to the Watershed Agricultural Council to figure out what to do with $500,000 in City funds allocated in the 1997 MOA towards a new Forestry Management Program.

WAC's Whole Farm Plan program seemed to be bearing fruit, so, to encourage forest owners to think about preserving and managing their forested land rather than dividing, clear cutting or developing it, WAC instituted a Forest Management Plan program.

Trained foresters (there are 48 consulting foresters on WAC's approved list) helped landowners consider their aims for their property: improve it for eventual timber harvest? enhance wildlife habitat? control invasive plants and insects? The plans were labor intensive and covered a lot of ground. They cost $1.2 million. A Management Assistance Program (MAP) which provides funds for implementing actions recommended in the plans paid for 487 projects, ranging from riparian improvements to fruit tree planting. That cost another half a million dollars.

Then WAC and its partners took a hard look at the Forestry Management Program. This critical appraisal revealed that many of the plans were sitting on the shelf, either because the owner had to sell land to pay taxes, or had died and left it to offspring who had no interest, or because other, personal priorities eclipsed the need to protect water and trees.

A more cost-effective solution was adopted, encouraging woodland owners to enroll in New York Forest Tax Law 480-a, a property tax reduction program for those owning at least 50 wooded acres. Eligible landowners receive an enrollment incentive check from WAC of $450, plus $5.50 per acre of land within the NYC Watershed. WAC then pays for the State-mandated timber management plan, and landowners receive up to an 80 percent reduction in taxes by committing to 10 or more years of limited subdivision or development.

Those who own less than 50 acres of forested land can now write their own management plan for free by using "My Woodlot," a new, US Forest-Service and NYC DEP-funded website administered by WAC. Plans created by their owners reflect specific preferences and because they are invested in this customized process, those landowners can be expected to follow through to apply for MAP funds, which are still available for specific projects.

Forest land owners will soon have another option: Forest Conservation Easements. WAC will launch a pilot program in 2016, funded with $6 million in City money, to determine whether anyone is interest in selling the rights to develop, parcelize or build impervious surfaces in their woods.

Logging BMPs

WAC works with more than 20 loggers, providing money, materials and technical support to employ Best Management Practices on more than 50 timber harvest jobs a year. These include erosion control measures (water bars, hay bales, silt fences and culverts) on forest roads; the loan of temporary bridges for use by skidders and other equipment in crossing streams; and a program that provides log-

gers with free samples of things like geotextile fabric, grass seed and organic bar oil to encourage their use.

Between 2001 when the program started, and 2015, WAC paid out $1.5 million for BMPs on 606 projects. An estimated 500 miles of logging trail was stabilized.

Model Forests

Four demonstration forests in and near the Watershed provide outdoor laboratories and classrooms for the study of various timber management techniques and strategies. Hundreds of professional foresters and loggers, researchers, students and the general public have toured the Frost Valley Model Forest (240 acres, Ulster County), Lennox Memorial Model Forest (18 acres, Delaware County), Siuslaw Model Forest (140 acres, Greene County) and Clearpool Model Forest (264 acres, Putnam County). Visitors can see the relative merits of clear cutting and selective harvesting, how to plant and manage tree lots for birds and wildlife and how water protective mechanisms are employed in a working forest.

The Model Forests are overseen by WAC, funded by DEP with research coordinated by State University of New York College of Environmental Science and Forestry.

Economic Development

Wood means money, to property owners, loggers and builders. To crafts people, too. Between 2000 and 2008, 85 Forestry Economic Development Grants were awarded by WAC to furniture makers, artists and log home companies with $2.4 million in US Department of Agriculture funds. Projects included renovating woodshops and showrooms, upgrading production equipment, installing kilns and safety devices, and developing promotion materials and marketing strategies.

Several demonstration projects were initiated to determine the feasibility and cost effectiveness of the use of wood biofuel to heat schools and other buildings. Frost Valley YMCA, Cairo-Durham Central School and Catskill Craftsmen wood products plant in Stamford were among sites where nine wood-fired boilers were installed to heat water and structures.

Land acquisition

In 1997, when New York City was granted a permit by the NYS Department of Environmental Conservation to buy land from willing sellers in the NYC Watershed, it owned 44,600 acres of land surrounding its reservoirs in six counties – three percent of the Watershed.

Over the next 18 years, the City purchased outright another 87,992 acres, and acquired standard and farm conservation easements on nearly 50,000 acres more. Added to the buffer lands it already owned, that's a lot of real estate.

The bulk of the land buys occurred in the Catskill-Delaware Watershed, where 78,608 acres had been purchased, and 48,109 acres acquired in easement, as of August 2015. Sixteen percent of the five-county Catskills is owned by NYC. Another 12 percent is owned by the State. That makes some municipal officials, planners, real estate brokers and businesses uneasy.

They are worried that continued City land purchases have reduced the potential for economic development and increased the value of remaining properties, putting them out of reach of many local residents and expediting the departure of the region's young people.

And while the City pays millions of dollars in taxes on its reservoir infrastructure and the vacant lands it owns ($159 million in fiscal year 2015), it also frequently challenges tax assessments levied on those properties. A fund created by the MOA to help municipalities pay experts and lawyers to meet those challenges was drained and a template system was negotiated in 2010 to try to avoid these annual conflicts. Thus far settlements based upon these templates are holding firm.

The land acquisition program has its supporters too. They laud the preservation of open space and the willingness of the City to open much of its land to fishing, hiking and hunting, even trapping in some areas.

Following major floods in 1996 and 2011, the City agreed to partner with several Counties at their request to match federal and state dollars to purchase heavily damaged homes in Federal Emergency Management Agency (FEMA) flood buy out programs.

Under the 1996 partnership with Delaware County, 28 properties totaling 14 acres were acquired and the City became the owner of record. Under the 2011 partnerships, 60 properties totaling 84 acres were or are expected to be acquired in three counties; 37 of these will be paid for by NYC but owned by a local municipality.

All structures are cleared from these parcels, and the land is to remain vacant forever, although some can be utilized for non-intensive purposes (playgrounds, walking paths, etc) under permit from the DEP. Many of these properties are in hamlets that had been declared off limits to City land acquisition, until Mother Nature changed the rules.

High Bridge, a monument to 19th-century engineering and construction, has been restored. The Harlem River span that once carried Croton water into Manhattan, is now a linear park enjoyed by walkers, bikers, and joggers. *Tom Tarnowksy/ Friends of Croton Aqueduct photo*

Preserving history

The history of the New York City water system has everything – brilliant minds and eccentric personalities, mind boggling accomplishments and political intrigue, tragedy and triumph, joy and sorrow.

It would make a great movie.

In fact, the documentary "Deep Water, Building the Catskill Water System" tells the story of the development of at least part of the system, primarily the Ashokan Reservoir known as "the last of the handmade dams." The film, by Willow Mixed Media, was created in 2002 with a Watershed Education grant from the Catskill Watershed Corp. in partnership with NYC DEP.

"City That Drinks the Mountain Sky," a staged interpretation of the same story by Arm of the Sea Theater, uses giant masks, puppet figures and original music to tell this larger than life tale. It was created in 1999 with support from the CWC and the DEP.

Indeed, between 1998 and 2015, the sad yet stunning history of this incredible system has been embraced, celebrated and reverently preserved in many different formats by agencies, community groups, municipalities and dedicated individuals. Books, plays, art and music, exhibits and historic restoration projects have been the result.

Here are some of the highlights:

Gilboa Fossils and Museum

Our understanding of the world famous Gilboa Fossils (*Chapter 14*) was greatly expanded in 2004 when NYS Museum paleontologists Linda Van Aller Hernick and Frank Mannolini discovered the tree fern's crown. Van Aller Hernick, whose 2003 book on the fossils documented the incredible finds of the late 19th and early 20th centuries, wrote of the new discovery in a 2007 issue of the journal *Nature*. It was declared one of the "100 Top Science Stories of 2007" by *Discover* magazine.

The following year, contractors building an access road for the reconstruction of the Gilboa Dam uncovered additional 380-million-year-old specimens in the same quarry where they caused such a stir when they were unearthed in 1920. The DEP donated the latest finds to the NYS Museum, which now holds the largest collection of fossils from what is believed to be the world's oldest forest.

The Gilboa Historical Society, established in 1997, features the fossils in a museum established in 2005. The museum, located in a relocated schoolhouse/town hall, also highlights the history of Old Gilboa and the drowned Schoharie Reservoir valley. The Society, working with the DEP, moved an outdoor fossil exhibit originally installed by the NYC Board of Water Supply a mile from the dam to the grounds of the Gilboa Town Hall where an interpretive panel was erected to explain their significance.

An expansion project to double the size of the museum was launched in 2015.

Croton Aqueduct, High Bridge and the Central Park Fountain

Some of the oldest elements of the early Croton Water Supply system have been the focus of renewed attention in recent years.

Friends of the Old Croton Aqueduct began restoration of an 1857 **Keeper's House** in 2014. This Italianate house in Dobbs Ferry was occupied for many decades by the superintendent of the aqueduct, a 26-mile portion of which is now a walking and biking trail maintained by the New York State Office of Parks, Recreation and Historic Preservation (OPRHP). The house has not been occupied since 1962. For more than a decade, "Friends" raised the necessary funds to accomplish the restoration which has proceeded under the direction of OPRHP staff. The Keeper's House was expected to open to the public, with programs and exhibitions, in 2016.

High Bridge, the engineering masterpiece of the Croton Aqueduct, was restored and reopened to pedestrian traffic in 2015. The oldest bridge in New York City, the 1848 span originally carried Croton water in cast iron pipes across the Harlem River (*Chapter 2*). The 15-arch granite bridge linking the Highbridge section of the Bronx and the Washington Heights section of Manhattan, had been a popular destination for urbanites for decades after its construction. But access to the bridge was ended in 1970.

Its restoration was 20 years in the making and was led by the New York City Department of Parks and Recreation. The High Bridge Coalition, a consortium of interested organizations and agencies, including the NYC DEP, NYC Parks, National Park Service Rivers and Trails, and many others, was established in 2001 to get the job done. The ancient stone was scrubbed, the pipe chamber below the walkway was restored, brickwork was re-laid and –mortared and safety fencing installed. Bronze medallions noting key historic elements of the bridge and aqueduct were set into the walkway. The 1928 steel span, which replaced five of the original arches to accommodate river traffic, was painted and the entire bridge illuminated. At the completion of the three-year, $62 million project, a huge celebration atop the now sparkling High Bridge was held June 9, 2015 when grateful residents of both sides of the river praised the return of this once-crucial link between the boroughs.

The **fountain** that announced the arrival of Catskill water to Manhattan in 1917 was reactivated in 2003 to help commemorate the 150th anniversary of the completion of New York's Central Park. The fountain, submerged 38 feet beneath the surface of the Central Park Reservoir, had been located, retrofitted and turned on in 1998 to celebrate completion of the first leg of City Tunnel #3 (*Chapter 21*). Five years later, it dazzled once again as New Yorkers hailed their magnificent park, and the 1862 reservoir (originally called Lake Manahatta) that once distributed Croton water to millions. Renamed the Jacqueline Kennedy Onassis Reservoir, it is now a favored place for birdwatchers, joggers and educational and historical tours.

Watershed Model and the Queens Museum

From Watersheds to Faucets: The Marvel of the NYC Water Supply System, is a permanent exhibit at the Queens Museum in Flushing Meadows Park. The focal piece is a 540-square-foot relief model of the New York City water system as it existed in 1938, on extended loan from the NYC Department of Environmental Protection (DEP). It was built by cartographers employed by the Works Progress Administration (WPA) for the 1939 World's Fair to demonstrate the enormity and intricacy of the system. It was intended to be shown in this building, originally the fair's New York City Pavilion. By some monumental error in planning or execution, the model turned out to be too big for the space, so it was warehoused, and only shown once a decade later before it was put back in storage. In 2005, the 28-piece model was re-discovered by the NYC DEP which sent it to a conservation lab in Ohio to be restored. It was subsequently reassembled and in 2013 was installed in a new gallery at its original intended home, now the renovated and expanded Queens Museum. The Watershed Model is located steps away from another inspiring model, the Panorama of the City of New York, built to be housed in this same structure at the 1964 World's Fair. The model serves as an introduction for exploration of how the understanding of our water system intersects with contemporary art, conservation, and climate issues.

Watershed Commemorative Project

Six outdoor exhibits explaining the NYC Water System and recognizing the communities sacrificed to make way for the water were installed in 2002 at each reservoir in the West-of-Hudson Watershed. A project of the Catskill Watershed Corp. (CWC), the commemorative effort involved committees from each reservoir basin who helped map the former towns, provided historic images and articulated key points about their communities. The kiosks also show how the water system fits together, and explain the ongoing measures to protect water quality in the Catskill-Delaware Watershed. The kiosks were renovated in 2010. Signs denoting the approximate locations of the communities lost to the reservoirs were installed by the CWC on watershed roadways in 2004.

Time and the Valleys Museum

Water is the overarching theme of Time and The Valleys Museum in Grahamsville, located mid-way between the Rondout and Neversink Reservoirs. The museum, developed and operated by a non-profit group who raised more than a million dollars to make it happen, opened in June, 2011 as a three-level wing of the expanded Daniel Pierce Library. Its permanent exhibits include "Water in the Valleys" showing how water shaped the landscape and provided sustenance and energy for settlers; and "Tunnels, Toil and Trouble" on the development of the reservoirs and the history of the towns that were uprooted.

Meticulous dioramas show the locations of every structure in the two reservoir basins, and recorded interviews allow displaced residents to tell their personal stories. Construction images, artifacts and oral histories of engineers and workers explain just how the dams and tunnels were built. Hands-on activities help children grasp the engineering concepts behind tunnel boring and dam building.

A Watershed Museum was originally envisioned in the 1997 Memorandum of Agreement, and $1 million for exhibits was earmarked within the Catskill Watershed Corp.'s education program. A site in the Town of Shandaken was identified, but later rejected in favor of a larger parcel in the Town of Middletown where the non-profit group charged with developing the museum announced a proposal to build the "Water Discovery Center." The group drew up initial plans and attempted to attract the estimated $25 million needed to build the facility, but it had not been constructed as of 2015.

Electronic history

"Behind the Scenes: The Story of the Watershed Agreement" is a collection of 12 audio interviews conducted in the years after the NYC Watershed Memorandum of Agreement (MOA) was signed in 1997. Producer Nancy Burnett talked with City, State, Watershed and environmental representatives who shared their positions and reflections on the process and the outcome. Interview transcripts and photos of the participants were placed on the website of the CWC, which funded the project. A separate website includes guidelines and activities for teachers.

Some of those interviewees were revisited in 2012 by filmmaker Drew Harty of Galene Studios who was engaged by Time & The Valleys Museum to create an interactive component for its "Tunnels, Toil & Trouble" exhibit. "The Price of Water" illuminates the process by which farmers came to terms with the City over payment for water protection services, as well as how the MOA was achieved covering non-farm activities three years after the agricultural deal was reached. Those interviews can be seen at the museum, and are also accessible from its website.

Prehistoric artifacts

Archaeological excavations prior to construction of the Catskill/Delaware Ultraviolet Treatment Facility in Eastview, Westchester County, yielded a treasure trove of prehistoric artifacts. Some 400 artifacts included stone tools, cache blades and quartz projectile points from the terminal Archaic Era and early Woodland Period. Many were found near Mine Brook and suggest that the site was periodically utilized by hunting groups as much as 5,000 years ago. The NYC DEP donated the finds to the Historical Society of Tarrytown and Sleepy Hollow in 2012. DEP dedicated a plaque at the UV Facility to commemorate the discovery and created a web page with information about the artifacts.

Wooden water mains preserved

Two hollowed out yellow pine logs that once carried water beneath the streets of lower Manhattan were unearthed in 2006 and subsequently donated by the NYC DEP to the New-York Historical Society. Believed to be part of the original municipal water system installed by the Manhattan Company in the 1820s, the interlocking wooden mains carried water from a series of groundwater wells in the vicinity of City Hall. Remarkably preserved, the pipes, 12 and 14 feet long and two and a half feet around, were revealed during routine utility upgrades on Beekman Street by the city's Department of Design and Construction. They will be used to educate museum visitors about the critical role water played in the development of the city.

Belden House

The Belden House in Carmel, Putnam County, acquired by the city in 1896 during construction of the West Branch Reservoir, was used as a residence for a custodian and later for city offices. Originally built in 1760, the house was renovated in grand style by George M. Belden more than 100 years later. Over the years, DEP undertook maintenance of the house, while looking for a partner who would raise funds to restore and take over the house. Despite local interest, no viable partner has emerged and the future of the house is uncertain.

Other programs

Here are a few more programs that have changed the physical and economic landscape in the years since the MOA was signed in 1997:

Stream Management

The DEP's Stream Management Program has established offices in the Ashokan, Schoharie, Pepacton/Cannonsville and Rondout/Neversink basins. DEP staff, along with county Soil & Water Conservation District and Cornell Cooperative Extension personnel, work with landowners and other agencies to repair streambanks, restore historic stream function and educate property owners about living streamside.

Some projects are as complicated as reconstructing entire reaches of streams devastated by flooding. Others are as simple as planting native shrubs and trees to prevent future erosion.

A total of 287 stream construction and Catskill Stream Buffer Initiative (CSBI) projects were completed through the end of 2014 at a cost of $15.6 million (federal cost-sharing brought the overall project costs to $31.2 million). This represents a total of 31.8 miles of riparian treatment.

Sewer Extensions

The service areas of wastewater treatment plants built and operated by New York City in conjunction with WOH Reservoirs have been extended to connect another 342 properties in six communities – Haines Falls and Showers Road in the Town of Hunter, Neversink in the Town of Neversink, Grand Gorge in the Town of Roxbury, Pine Hill in the Town of Shandaken and Margaretville in the Town of Middletown.

More than 61,500 linear feet of sewer line will have been installed when all extensions are completed in late 2016.

WWTP Upgrades

Treatment processes and equipment have been improved in nearly all municipal, commercial and privately held wastewater treatment plants in East and West of Hudson Watersheds. The City expended nearly $354 million on the upgrades including the addition of micro-filtration and ultraviolet treatment to replace chlorination of effluent which in most cases is discharged to nearby waterways. A few plants were consolidated, so that 95 non-city owned WWTPs now operate in the Watersheds. Five facilities east of the Hudson serving small establishments or subdivisions remained to be upgraded as of 2015.

New laboratories

The DEP operates four water quality testing laboratories that have all been upgraded to utilize state of the art technologies and methodologies. The newest facility, at Hawthorne, Westchester County, was completed in October, 2015, replacing a lab that had been built alongside the Kensico Reservoir in 1955. The other labs are located at Grahamsville, Kingston and Queens. 195 chemists, microbiologists and limnologists work at those labs conducting multiple tests on 48,000 water samples taken each year from reservoirs, streams, wastewater treatment plants and various points within the distribution system. A network of robotic sampling devices stationed on the reservoirs analyzes the drinking water an additional 320,000 times annually.

A rootwad revetment being built on the West Branch Neversink River. The vegetated buffer directs water to the center of the channel and away from the roadway. *Photo by Vickers & Beechler*

Bonus cash

"Good Neighbor Payments" provided counties, towns and villages in both Watersheds an added inducement or reward (some cynics called them 'bribes') to sign the MOA. More than $13 million was distributed to 75 municipalities according to the amount of land area in each town and county that lay within the Watersheds. (The East-of-Hudson Watershed encompasses 234,527 acres of land. The West-of-Hudson Watershed stretches across 1,002,028 acres of private and public lands.)

This money has been used for new fire halls, community centers, structural improvements and other capital purposes (funds could not be used to reduce the tax levy.)

Examples of expenditures include swimming pools in Andes and Olive, ambulances in Tompkins and Hobart; computers in Franklin and Halcott, police cars in Fleischmanns, and Roxbury, sidewalks in Walton, a soccer field in Prattsville and heavy equipment and town halls nearly everywhere. 18 years after Good Neighbor monies were distributed, several towns are still hanging on to some of it, watching it grow with investment, ready for a rainy day.

Post-911 security

In the weeks and months after September 11, 2001, when terrorists crashed four passenger planes into the Twin Towers of the World Trade Center in New York City, the Pentagon in Washington, DC and into a field in Pennsylvania, the NYC DEP was on high alert for suspicious activity on and around its dams, reservoirs and water supply facilities.

Fishing, hiking and hunting on city lands were forbidden. Roads over Ashokan and Kensico Dams were closed to vehicles, requiring long detours. NYS Conservation Officers were brought in to bolster DEP's 75 environmental police officers in patrolling the Watershed. The Army Corps of Engineers was enlisted to assess security measures at the city's many rural and urban facilities, and the DEP implemented its recommendations, without revealing what they were.

They did make some noise about beefing up their police force, though, adding 145 officers between 2002 and 2003 (the force is up to 245 in 2015) and opening five new precincts in the Watershed. A new Environmental Police Academy was established in November 2002 to provide training specific to water supply protection, as well as counter-terrorism tactics, and traffic, penal law and environmental law enforcement.

In 2015, the DEP dedicated a new training facility at a former Army Reserve Center in Kingston. The 16,000-square-foot facility on four acres is named for Robert H. Dietz, a World War II Medal of Honor winner. Recruits undergo 1,275 hours of training over seven months and eventually patrol the Watershed on foot, bicycle, ATV, boat, car and helicopter. They are stationed at seven precincts: Ashokan, Beerston, Downsville, Eastview, Gilboa, Grahamsville and Yonkers.

Watershed Protection and Partnership Council (WPPC)

The 27-member WPPC was established to exchange ideas and concerns and serve as a forum among the disparate parties to the Memorandum of Agreement. The Council operates under the New York State Department of State and is run by a staff of three, including its first and to date only Executive Director, William C. Harding. The City and New York State provided initial funding of $1.5 million for salaries, office expenses and other costs of running the council. Initial finding has been exhausted and the State now provides funding for the Council and its activities.

Eleven of the members serve as the WPPC's Executive Committee to review watershed protection efforts and resolve disputes. Only three disputes have actually reached that level: the wording of Watershed 'welcome' signs erected by the City; the maximum allowable slope for on-site septic systems, and whether the Town of Harrison could use East of Hudson (EOH) watershed improvement funds on a sewer project located outside Watershed boundaries.

An EOH Advisory Committee was named to provide an avenue for intermunicipal dialogue and program planning among the Croton Watershed officials (West of Hudson municipalities had the Catskill Watershed Corp. for that purpose); and an East of Hudson Sporting Advisory Committee was established to review New York City land purchases in Westchester and Putnam Counties and to recommend recreational uses for them.

A Technical Advisory Committee was established to examine scientific and technological advancements in the realm of water quality. In 2000, the Council organized the first Watershed Science and Technical Conference to share experience and research papers stemming from the groundbreaking studies, projects and programs that had been launched in the New York City Watershed. The conference has been held annually, expanding to encompass research and developments in other watersheds around the country and the world, and addressing issues like climate change, flooding and emerging contaminants.

The WPPC's role over the past decade or so has become more programmatic than policy oriented, according to Director Harding, but it is still tuned in to its mission. "We have the same issues and concerns as we did back on Day 1 of the MOA, but through time we have created a fabric of partnership and to a certain extent trust.

"Many of us there at the beginning are still here. That long term relationship is priceless. But our job now is to have a plan for transition to the next generation, to train, educate and impart, beyond the mechanical, the whys and wherefores of watershed partnership, before we go."

The Watershed Protection and Partnership Council coordinates an annual conference to share scientific research and technical advancements in the field of water quality. *WPPC photo*

The Coalition of Watershed Towns

For several months after the signing of the Memorandum of Agreement that ushered in the future for Watershed communities, the Coalition of Watershed Towns stepped back, took a long breath and, yes, rested on its laurels. For seven years the band of West-of-Hudson municipal leaders had played David against the City's Goliath to help shape the historic agreement. Many of them afterwards stepped up to become the first Board of Directors of the Catskill Watershed Corporation to implement the programs the CWT had envisioned in those hard-fought negotiations. For a time, then, the CWT became dormant, their work, they thought, finished.

But in early 1998, a tempest in the Village of Tannersville over City stormwater requirements for a proposed bike path raised the hackles of local officials, including the new Town of Hunter Supervisor, Dennis Lucas and Windham Supervisor Pat Meehan, who was on the CWC Board. They urged that the CWT be reconstituted to continue as a watchdog over the City, and the MOA. Meehan resigned from the CWC to become chairman of the CWT. Dennis became the Vice Chair. The CWT was back in business, taking on the role of MOA watchdog while the CWC worked directly with the DEP to find solutions on the ground.

The CWT later participated in the review of MOA deliverables and the new programmatic requirements of the 2002 Filtration Avoidance Determination. Then, with the 2007 FAD on the table, with the New York State Department of Health assuming primacy over the agreement from the federal EPA, Governor George Pataki, credited with facilitating the MOA, left office. The new administration of Manhattanite Eliot Spitzer was seen by the Coalition as deaf to the interests of Watershed communities. The CWT felt the City had the ear of the new Governor, and "blindsided" the upstaters with a ten-year, rather than a five-year FAD renewal that included ambitious new land acquisition targets.

"'The Troubles' began all over again," according to Lucas, who took over as CWT chairman when Meehan resigned in disgust.

The CWT thus became involved in protracted negotiations to secure important concessions in the State-issued 2010 Water Supply Permit. Key successes, Lucas says: The City's permit to acquire land was linked to continuation of CWC programs, and agreement was reached to develop a template for valuing City properties to avoid "bankrupting" municipalities facing assessment challenges from the City.

In 2015, with the FAD nearing renewal again, the CWT was preparing to examine what's been done, and what is needed in the Catskill-Delaware Watershed. The FAD's renewal will come in the 20th anniversary year of the original Watershed Agreement. The CWT, which had such a crucial role in birthing that document, still has a vital role to play in keeping it alive, according to Lucas.

"Our role was from the outset and continues to be one of oversight and review of how the partnership is being implemented," he says. "The historic MOA is like no other agreement known to governance. This is a living Watershed, and it takes everyone involved to bring their best intentions to the table to move it forward."

Sources and Acknowledgments

Information for the 2016 addendum to Liquid Assets was gathered from a variety of printed and electronic sources, interviews and correspondence:

Publications: Annual reports, newsletters, press releases, program reports and presentations developed by the NYC Department of Environmental Protection (DEP), the Watershed Agricultural Council (WAC), the Catskill Watershed Corp. (CWC) and the East of Hudson Watershed Corp. (EHWC)

Websites: DEP, WAC, CWC, EHWC, Dam Concerned Citizens, Lower Esopus Partnership, Friends of the Upper Delaware River

Interviews and Correspondence: NYC DEP: David Warne, Adam Bosch, John Schwartz, Kim Estes-Fradis; Watershed Agricultural Council: Brian LaTourette, Rob Birdsall, Larry Hulle, Tom Pavlesich, Ryan Natz, Kristen Morley, Heather Magnan; Catskill Watershed Corp.: Alan Rosa, Timothy Cox. Coalition of Watershed Towns: Dennis Lucas; Watershed Protection & Partnership Council: William Harding; East of Hudson Watershed Corp.: Kevin McCarthy

Introduction

EPTEMBER 8, 1996. Fog, damp and heavy, envelops a crowd of people clustered in a small parking lot along Route 55, a few miles east of Liberty in Sullivan County, New York.

They are a mostly older group. Grey heads prevail. Pulling coat collars tightly against the chill, they greet each other warmly with hugs and handshakes, inquiring after family members and mutual friends. A few, unsteady on their feet, are helped to metal folding chairs set up in rows in front of a little three-sided kiosk, its pitched, shingled roof sheltering the historical marker they have come to see dedicated:

Neversink Reservoir
Completed in 1955 to provide water for New York City. The Neversink River flowing through the valley was an attraction for trout fishermen and fly-tiers. This valley was settled over 200 years ago. The villages of Neversink and Bittersweet lie beneath these waters. There were farms, a sawmill, a casino, a bowling alley, general stores, boarding houses, churches, schools and more here.

As the plaque is read and short speeches are recited by historians, local officials and New York City representatives, many of the listeners gaze off into the fog. There is indeed a reservoir out there, somewhere, still and deep beneath the swirling mist. The waters, in turn, hide history, and the poetic hush that falls over the assembly allows each one to envision this valley as it used to be:

There is Pluma Cross, sorting the mail at the Neversink post office; William Lawrence selling ice cream and souvenirs at Bill's Casino, with its pool hall and bowling alley; Morris and Dora Begun catering to the whims of well-heeled patrons of their Neversink Inn.

The trees in F. D. Vanderlyn's orchards are heavy with apples. Charlie Freer is busy at his grist mill, while all hands in the Misner family help bring in the hay on their Hollow Road farm. Voices are raised in song at choir practice in the Methodist Church as sunshine streams in through the stained glass windows. Kids romp in the Bittersweet schoolyard and splash in the swimming hole at a bend in the river.

It was the river that brought life and a simple, country version of prosperity here. And, in one of history's small ironies, it was the Neversink, so called because the rapid current carried its cargo swiftly along without sinking, that ultimately submerged the valley.

Now, barely 200 feet from where these former residents stand looking into the past, the impounded waters of the Neversink gush noisily through a 10-foot tunnel 126 feet beneath the surface, bound for the Rondout Reservoir five miles away. There, blended with water from the Pepac-

The Kellogg children enjoyed an afternoon of fishing on the Cross River in Katonah, Westchester County, in the 1880s. New York City later laid claim to much of the area as it developed its water supply, a process that extended over several lifetimes and was neither free nor easy. Katharine Kelly.

ton and Cannonsville Reservoirs from far-off Delaware County, it is sent in a head-long rush southward, through rocky mountains, beneath rivers wide, to flow into other reservoirs and then into a 6,000-mile network of water mains and pipes throughout New York City.

It might almost be called a miracle, this system that funnels fresh water from clear mountain streams to a metropolis of nine million souls 120 miles away. Even those who bemoan the loss of entire communities to New York City's need for life-sustaining water acknowledge the foresight and fortitude that brought about this marvel of planning, engineering and construction.

The city's water system was largely built over a period of 130 years. It encompasses 18 collecting reservoirs and three controlled lakes spread out over a 1,969-square-mile watershed in nine counties both east and west of the Hudson River. The reservoirs store 550 billion gallons of water and supply, by gravity alone, 1.2 billion gallons daily to the faucets and hydrants of thirsty New York and its northern suburbs.

Almost continuously, from the day in 1842 when a joyful Manhattan celebrated the long-awaited arrival of water from the first Croton Reservoir 45 miles to the north, until 1967, when the Cannonsville Reservoir was completed in distant Delaware County, the city has been planning, building or improving its water system. Indeed, it is not done yet. For the past 25 years, it has been burrowing beneath the streets of the Bronx, Manhattan and Queens, digging a third major delivery tunnel which is not expected to be finished until the year 2020.

The building of the New York water system has been called one of the wonders of the modern world and has been compared to the Panama Canal as among humankind's most impressive achievements. Untold worker-hours, countless millions of dollars, hundreds of lives have been expended in the city's quest for water. But this is most of all a story of individual accomplishment and sacrifice, a story that mere recitation of dimensions and dollar signs can't begin to convey.

Triumph and tragedy, skill and scandal, recklessness and resolve have shared the stage on which this long-lasting drama has been played. Careers have been built and destroyed, fortunes won and lost. Social reverberations of these massive construction projects were as profound as their imprints on the landscape, as scores of immigrant laborers were recruited to cut stone or dig tunnels, then stayed to leave their cultural mark on nearby communities. Politicians rode the waves of the water system's successes, or paid dearly when drought or deception resulted in water famines.

While some communities were completely obliterated, homes, barns and businesses bulldozed and burned, others were relocated, lock, stock and blacksmith shop, using horses, stout ropes and strong backs to move them out of the water's way. Lives were altered slowly, as small towns worried for decades about rumored New York City takeovers. Or they were changed in an instant, by a fall from scaffolding atop a 100-foot dam, or in a premature dynamite explosion in a tunnel 1,000 feet beneath the surface.

The hostility and resentment engendered by the city's upstate incursions has been as predictable as the ebb and flow of the waters on its reservoirs'

shores. The bitterness in the hearts of people whose homes and livelihoods were claimed by powers they could not fight or understand has merely lessened with time. But while New York City condemned vast tracts of land, it was also required to compensate its owners, some would say rather generously. In addition, it built and continues to operate, at its own expense, many wastewater treatment plants for communities in its watershed, and is among the largest of taxpayers in dozens of municipalities.

Inextricably and forever linked by a substance that is taken for granted more often than not, the upstate-downstate relationship is a complicated one, made more so in 1997 with the signing of the New York City Watershed Memorandum of Agreement. The 1,000-page document is a pact between the city and the towns that provide its inhabitants with water. In it, the city is allowed by the federal government to avoid filtering the bulk of its reservoir supplies as long as it ensures the quality of the water by enforcing tough new land use regulations on watershed residents and businesses. The city may also buy----from willing sellers----thousands of acres of land near those reservoirs and their feeder streams with the intent of keeping them from development. In exchange, the city must fund road and bridge improvements, build more treatment plants, repair individual septic systems, and fund economic development efforts as well as educational and environmental improvement programs.

It was an agreement worked out over six long years, upstaters and downstaters overcoming mistrust and animosity to feel out a tentative new partnership. As it happened, while the lost communities beneath the Neversink were being remembered that foggy morning in September of 1996, a telephone conference among local leaders was being held to decide whether they concurred on the final draft of the agreement that would take them into the future.

They did. The pact was signed. The future has begun. It is important, then, to see how far we have come.

Remains of a well of the old Manhattan Company, c. 1800, were unearthed in 1926 during excavation for a building foundation near the corner of Reade and Centre Streets. NYC DEP.

1. The Thirsty Settlement

WHEN a British naval force led by Col. Richard Nicolls sailed into the harbor of the Dutch settlement of New Amsterdam in September of 1664, spelling the beginning of the end of Dutch rule in America, it may have been water, rather than weaponry, that played a deciding role in the conflict.

Historians say it was the despotic 20-year reign of Peter Stuyvesant, director general of the province of New Netherlands, that led to the Dutch downfall. The inflexibility of the one-legged governor, his refusal to allow citizens a voice in their government and his strict pronouncements regarding religion and other matters, prompted New Amsterdam's residents to welcome, or at least fail to resist, the British invaders. So the stone fort on the island was handed up with nary a shot from its 20 cannons.[1]

Stuyvesant, however, is said to have claimed it was the lack of water within the fort----limited to 20 or 24 barrels brought in from ships in the harbor----that prompted him to surrender the stronghold.[2]

Assuming that story is correct, Stuyvesant might have avoided capture had he pursued earlier proposals to drill a well within Fort Amsterdam. But digging wells had, up to that point, been a largely private pursuit, with individual settlers providing their own water from the sandy soils.

There were an estimated 1,000 people living in New Amsterdam on the southern end of Manhattan Island in 1650. A year earlier Adriaen van der Donck, in a report to officials in the motherland, declared that the waterfalls, streams and brooks in New Netherland provided good drinking water and were "all very clear and pure. . ."[3]

By 1667, though, the English occupants of the fort had finally sunk wells both within and just outside the enclosure at the foot of Bowling Green.[4] In 1677, the common council of the renamed New York ordered "Several weells bee made in the places hereafter menconed (for the publique good of the Cytie) by the inhabitants of Each Street where the said wells shall bee made. . ."[5]

In 1686, the council specified that nine more wells be dug, the expense shared between the users and the city. Each well was surmounted by a long pole with a weight at one end and a chain with a bucket on the other. An order issued in 1696 placed responsibility for the public wells on an alderman and councilman in each ward. They were to "Supervise the Public Wells of this Citty and take care that they be kept Sweet Usefull and in Good repair. . ."[6]

But with the growth of the settlement's population the shallow wells became polluted with seepage from cesspools, privies and street run-off. Many were brackish, infiltrated by salt water, so that even animals shunned them. Swedish visitor Peter

Water, water everywhere . . .

New York's need for a clean, copious water supply has led to suggestions that it build canals, harness the tides, tap rivers in other states, even go as far as the Great Lakes or the Adirondacks to fulfill ever-growing demands. Here are some proposals that never got off the drawing board:

1798. Dr. Joseph Browne suggests building a small dam across the Bronx River below Williamsbridge to turn the river through a canal to the Morrisania Creek and then into the Harlem River where part of the water would be used to turn a water wheel to fill a reservoir on Manhattan.

1819. Robert Macomb proposes bringing water from Rye Pond to a reservoir on the Harlem River before distributing it to the city.

1830. Francis B. Phelps suggests taking water from the Passaic River above the falls in Paterson, N.J., and conducting it in iron pipes across the Hudson River to New York. Also in 1830, John L. Sullivan proposes building a navigable canal from the Passaic River for both water and commerce between eastern Pennsylvania and New York.

1834. Bradford Seymour proposes building a dam across the Hudson River from the foot of Christopher Street in New York to the New Jersey shore. Seymour says the dam would prevent salt water encroachment, and locks would allow navigation on the river, while river water would be pumped to a reservoir for city consumption.

1876. Harvey G. Eastman suggests augmenting supplies in the Croton Reservoir and associated lakes by building a pumping plant to transmit Hudson River water from a site north of Poughkeepsie to a reservoir on Flagler Hill, then through 15 miles of pipes to tributaries of the Croton River in northern Dutchess County.

1901. The Merchants Association of New York City suggests damming the Wallkill River at Philipsburgh to create a 50-square-mile lake from which water would be sent to the city in a gravity-fed aqueduct.

1905. Charles Armstrong, a former state engineer in Wisconsin, Illinois and South Dakota, proposes tapping the Great Lakes and running a pipeline along the route of the old Erie Canal. The water, he claims, would supply local communities, as well as New York,

where it could turn waterwheels to generate power for municipal lighting.

1926. The Board of Water Supply (BWS) proposes laying an aqueduct diverting water from tributaries of Wappingers, Sprout, Jackson and Fishkill Creeks in Dutchess, Columbia, and Rensselaer Counties to the Kensico Reservoir. The BWS plan also includes a new reservoir on the East Branch of the Croton River in Putnam County.

1927. As part of the plan to develop tributaries of the Delaware River, the BWS proposes damming the Beaver Kill near Beaver Kill, and the Willowemoc Creek near Parkston. That portion of the three-phase Delaware project was never implemented, but the Rondout, Neversink and Pepacton Reservoirs were constructed.

1950. Lawrence T. Beck offers an alternative to the city's plan to dam the West Branch of the Delaware River at Cannonsville, proposing a plan to dam the Hudson River at Haverstraw, 15 miles below Poughkeepsie, sending salt-free water to the city through an aqueduct, allowing river traffic to pass through locks, and New York State Thruway traffic to drive atop the dam. Additional proposals to dam the Hudson and East Rivers at Manhattan, and the Hudson at Hyde Park, are brought forward by others several years later.

1966. Some planners suggest damming Long Island Sound and developing a freshwater lake by treating and pumping salt water from the impoundment back into the sea. Dikes would be built at both ends of the sound, the eastern dike measuring more than seven miles long and perhaps doubling as a causeway for traffic between Connecticut and Long Island. Navigation locks and pumping stations would have to be constructed.

1969. In a report on alternative regional water supply plans conducted for the Army Corps of Engineers, additional potential dam sites are listed on the Delaware River, and other dam and diversion projects proposed for the Susquehanna River system in New York and the Housatonic River, which drains eastern New York and parts of New England.

1974. A report on potential additional water sources for the city suggests damming the Hoosic River in Rensselaer County, the Schoharie Creek in Montgomery County, and the Black River in Oneida County.

Principal sources: Charles H. Weidner's *Water for A City* (1974); Edward H. Hall's *Water for New York City* (1917); a chapter by Robert Boyle in *The Water Hustlers* (1971); a 1974 report to the Board of Water Supply on "An Additional Water Supply for the City of New York," submitted by Metcalf and Eddy.

Kalm, visiting in 1748, said the "want of good water lies heavily upon the horses of the strangers that come to this place; for they do not like to drink the water from the wells of the town."[7]

For decades, however, one source of water remained untainted and highly sought. This was the fresh-water pond known as The Collect (the Dutch had called it Kalch-Hook), a 48-acre pond fed by springs and bordered by a marsh. The Collect, located just north of the city where the prison called the Tombs now stands, was near what was known as the Tea Water Spring. The water from this spring, pure enough for the making of tea and for other kitchen uses, was peddled around town by vendors who carried the water in casks, selling it for one cent a gallon.[8] These "teawater men" eventually became so numerous that the common council had to pass a law in 1757 to license them and regulate the trade.[9]

The Tea Water Spring, fitted with a pump whose handle extended over Chatham Street, was the focal point of a beautifully ornamented public park frequented by "rich and fastidious" persons who apparently considered it something of a rural resort. Near the spring, the Kissing Bridge crossed a small stream and was part of a tradition outlined by a Rev. Mr. Burnaby, who traveled to America in the mid-1750s:

The amusements are balls and sleighing parties in the winter, and in the summer going in parties upon the water and fishing, or making excursions into the country. There are several houses pleasantly situated up the East River, near New York, where it is common to have turtle feasts. Those happen once or twice a week. Thirty or forty gentlemen and ladies meet and dine together, drink tea in the afternoon, fish and amuse themselves till evening

A view of 1667 New Amsterdam "a small city on Manhattan Island, New Holland, North America," depicted in a wood engraving by G. Hayward. Cornelia Cotton Gallery.

and then return home in Italian chaises. . . Just before you enter the town there is a little bridge, commonly called the 'Kissing Bridge,' where it is customary, before passing beyond, to salute the lady who is your companion.[10]

Some used the Collect for dumping rather than courting, though. In 1778, Major General Valentine Jones, commandant of New York, issued a public notice declaring it illegal "to wash cloathing of any kind in the Fresh Water Pond, or heave filthe, carbage or dirt in or near the same."[11]

Some years earlier, in 1774, engineer Christopher Colles received the common council's backing for development of a municipally-owned water supply using wells dug near the Collect. Colles, an Irish immigrant, was an inventive man who proposed to erect a reservoir on Broadway, between Pearl and White Streets, to be filled with water pumped by a steam engine from a well or wells. The city bought land from Augustus and Frederick VanCortlandt and there built a reservoir, along with a pump house. A well 50 feet deep and 40 feet in diameter was also dug. In November of 1774, the council contracted with Isaac Mann and his son of Stillwater, far upstate, to furnish 60,000 linear feet

of pitch or yellow pine logs to be delivered the following year.[12]

Colles worked diligently on the enterprise and was named superintendent of the works when it was placed into partial operation in 1776. On March 4 of that year, he demonstrated his steam-powered pump, which was capable of lifting 17,400 gallons of water an hour into the reservoir.[13]

The public marveled, but history intervened as the outbreak of the Revolutionary War interrupted the project. The common council paid Colles in May 1776 for supervising the works for one month, then adjourned for the duration of the war.[14] The water works was abandoned, never to be revived. As it happened, 1776 was the year a great fire swept through the city, 400 buildings reduced to ashes without adequate water to fight the flames.[15]

For the next quarter century, the Tea Water Pump was heavily utilized as a drinking water source, though the spring and the nearby Collect were becoming seriously degraded. One newspaper writer in the 1780s called the pond "a common sewer," used by nearby residents for washing themselves and their clothes, and emptying "all their

The inventive Christopher Colles

The engineer who set in motion New York's first attempt at a municipal water supply had been in America less than a decade when he got the common council's approval to replace the haphazard hodge-podge of wells and springs with a reservoir and a network of wooden distribution pipes.

Born in Ireland in 1738, Christopher Colles emigrated to this country in 1765. The years that followed were inventive ones, despite the failure of his water system plans, which were thwarted by the city's financial difficulties and the onset of the Revolutionary War.

During the war, Colles was an artillery instructor for the Continental Army. He was among the first to design a steam engine, publish-

ed many scientific essays and pamphlets, did astronomical calculations and, during the War of 1812, designed and built a semaphore—a visual telegraphic device.

Solving transportation problems intrigued Colles, who was reportedly the first to propose linking the Great Lakes with the Hudson River by means of natural and artificial waterways. In 1808, he proposed construction of a wooden, above-ground canal to operate between New York and Philadelphia.

Colles also went into business in New York in the late 1790s, manufacturing a variety of items, from mouse traps to fireworks, and selling furs and Indian goods.

Christopher Colles died in 1816.

Source: *Dictionary of American Biography*, 1946

suds and filth"—not to mention dead livestock—into the Collect. [16]

After many more years of use and abuse, the pond was filled in by 1803 and the surrounding hills later leveled.[17]

The clamor for clean water became louder and more desperate as New York City's population grew to 33,000 in 1790, and tripled to 96,000 by 1810. At that time, some 250 public wells dotted the streets traversed by hundreds of horses and countless unpenned hogs. Doctors pleaded in vain for better cleaning of the filthy thoroughfares, but the wells could not meet the demand for flushing, or for firefighting.[18]

In 1798, a yellow fever epidemic killed 2,000 people in the city, and other diseases like cholera and typhoid fever attributable to poor sanitation and unclean water regularly visited the growing city.[19]

Ultimately, disease and fire were the twin terrors that pushed the city to explore development of a municipal water system, but for the better part of two decades, officials and citizens debated whether it should be publicly or privately operated. Numerous proposals were brought forward and tabled, including one from Dr. Joseph Browne, who was the first to suggest moving beyond Manhattan to secure a wholesome water supply.

"The health of a city depends more on its water than all the rest of the eatables and drinkables put together," declared Dr. Browne. He proposed that the Bronx River be dammed below Williamsbridge, the water turned into a canal leading to Morisania Creek and thence into the Harlem River. Water was to be pumped through a cast iron pipe to a reservoir on Manhattan Island. Dr. Browne felt a private company should build the system, an opinion not shared by the common council.[20]

The council did, however, appoint a committee, and British engineer and canal builder William Weston, to further explore the Bronx River idea. They issued favorable reports, and the common council submitted a bill to the state legislature seeking the authority to build its own waterworks. On March 30, 1799, state lawmakers passed "An Act for supplying the City of New York with pure and wholesome water." The law conferred a charter on the Manhattan Company, which was given the exclusive right to convey water to the city.

However laudable its purpose, the act also made possible the back-door establishment of a bank, and may have contributed to the famous duel between Aaron Burr and Alexander Hamilton in 1804. Hamilton and the Federalists controlled The Bank of New York, the only chartered institution in the city. Since Hamilton founded the bank in 1784, he and his political compatriots had successfully prevented the establishment of any rivals to their monetary monopoly. But leading members of the Republican (now Democratic) party engaged Aaron Burr, a United States Senator, to add to the bill of incorporation for the water company a measure allowing it to use surplus capital in any transactions consistent with state law. The company thus formed developed a modest water system, sinking a well near the Collect, building a 550,000-gallon reservoir on Chambers Street and laying six miles of wooden mains to supply 400 families, all in its first year.[21]

But it also wasted no time in getting into the banking business, establishing a "house of discount and deposit" at 40 Wall Street Sept. 1, 1799.[22] It soon became apparent that company officials, including Burr and a dozen other directors, found banking far more profitable than water sales, which likely displeased Hamilton and colleagues. Of course Burr and Hamilton were political opponents with no lack of contentious issues between them. Burr had defeated Hamilton's father-in-law for the Senate in 1791, and in 1800, Hamilton backed Thomas Jefferson for president, rather than Burr, who became vice president. The powerful Hamilton, who'd been named the nation's first secretary of the treasury by George Washington and who had signed the Constitution for New York State, later used his influence to defeat Burr's bid for governor in 1804.[23] Burr demanded that Hamilton retract what he considered slanderous statements made against him during the campaign, and the two men squared off in a duel on July 11, 1804 in Weehawken, N.J. Hamilton, whose own son had died in a duel in 1801, was killed when struck by a ball from Burr's pistol.[24]

Meanwhile, the Manhattan Water Company, which had expanded its water system to include 25 miles of main and 2,000 customers, was the target of complaints from people who claimed the water it was providing was unfit for consumption and often just plain unavailable, its wooden mains clogged by roots or taken out of service for weeks at a time.[25] But as it fumbled with management of the ambitious city project, the company invested in other engineering marvels, including, in 1801, the mile-and-a-half-long Cayuga Bridge, a wooden span which crossed the northern end of Cayuga Lake and the Montezuma Swamp in west central New York. The $150,000 project was financed by a loan from the Manhattan Company, which today does business as Chase Manhattan Bank.[26]

In 1804, continuing dissatisfaction with the water system in New York City prompted Mayor DeWitt Clinton to appoint a committee to confer with the Manhattan Company about ceding its works and water supply privilege. Nothing came of the effort, however, and the company continued as a waterworks for another 35 years as the city fathers entertained many suggestions for tapping new sources of supply.[27]

The combination of the Manhattan Company's small reservoir and the public and private wells that had proliferated in the polluted city continued to serve the growing metropolis in a haphazard and inadequate manner until a disastrous fire in 1828 destroyed about $600,000 in property. The following spring the common council, which had already ordered the erection of 40 cisterns to collect water for fighting fires, voted to build a reservoir for fire-fighting purposes at Broadway and 13th Street in the Bowery.[28]

An account in an 1838 issue of *Family Magazine* reprinted in *Catskill Water System News*, Nov. 20, 1911, described its construction :

After breaking ground to obtain water, and penetrating through the earth to the distance of 11 feet, the workmen employed in digging the well of the reservoir came to the bed of rock forming the base of the city. Through this rock

they bored a well 113 feet in depth by 17 feet in diameter, with two shafts extending in opposite directions, east and west, 75 feet each way, another branch from the westerly shaft northerly 22 feet.

The well furnished 21,000 gallons of water a day, which was raised by a steam-powered pump into a cast iron tank enclosed by a stone building 27 feet high. "It forms a very picturesque object to boats passing through both the East and North Rivers," the article enthused. Pipes carried the water to hydrants. Each could supply two hand-pump fire engines with water "the force of which is so great that, in case of emergency, it can be thrown to any necessary height by attaching the apparatus of the hydrants to the engine leaders."

This humble precursor of the city-owned and operated water system cost $42,233 to build.[29]

It did not solve the overriding need for clean drinking water, though. Scientists in 1830 estimated that 100 tons of human excrement were being put into Manhattan soil every day. There was no city-wide sewer system to serve the 202,000 residents, and open pits held dead animals and offal. Travelers declared they could smell the city two or three miles away.[30]

Then, in 1832, came the menace of Asiatic cholera. This dread disease brought acute diarrhea, spasmodic vomiting, dehydration, and, often, death to its victims, who could be identified by their bluish skin tone and puckered, darkened extremities.

Cholera's arrival in North America was described by ex-New York City Mayor Philip Hone, who kept a diary from 1828 to 1851 and wrote on June 15, 1832:

The Albany steamboat which came down this afternoon brought the alarming news that the cholera, which has of late been the scourge of the eastern continent, has crossed the Atlantic and made its appearance first in Quebec and from there has travelled with its direful velocity to Montreal. It was brought to the former city in a vessel called the "Carricks" with a cargo of Irish immigrants of whom many died on the way. . . There can be little reasonable ground to hope for our exemption in New York from this dreadful scourge. The city is in a more filthy state than Quebec and Montreal, and I do not know a European city which is worse. . .''

In *Leslie's History of the Greater New York* (1898), a writer recalled the epidemic:

> It is still remembered where it [the disease] made its first appearance, a house on Cherry Street, near James, and the fateful date was June 25. The next week the alarm had become universal, and the exodus toward the open portions of the island began. . .Four or five hospitals were improvised where the patients could be treated with greater convenience and better effect than in their own homes.

Its spread hastened by infected immigrants, unwashed foods, garbage-strewn streets and sewage-contaminated water, the epidemic raced through the city. At its peak in July, cholera claimed 104 New Yorkers in a single day. In August, 100,000 people fled the city, the roads leading out of town thronged with coaches and wagons bearing panic-stricken people. City streets, by contrast, were empty and "deathly silent." By late October, 3,500 men, women and children had died.[31]

With an urgency spurred by tragedy, the Fire and Water Committee of the common council hired Col. DeWitt Clinton, Jr. to investigate the many water supply sources that had been suggested, from the Passaic to the Bronx Rivers. Six weeks later, Col. Clinton recommended the Croton River, which had first been proposed in 1830 by Francis B. Phelps.

Clinton recommended bringing water from the Croton River in an open aqueduct crossing valleys and streams and drawn by gravity for about 30 miles to the city. He envisioned a 1,000-foot-long aqueduct bridge to carry the water across the Harlem River.[32]

In January of 1833, the common council applied to the state legislature to have Gov. William

Marcy appoint five commissioners to further examine the plans, make surveys, test the water and estimate the expense of developing a water supply. The legislature complied and on February 26 the governor named a five-member water commission, which in turn hired Major David B. Douglass, former professor of engineering at the U.S. Military Academy at West Point, to survey all proposed sources of water supply.

Major Douglass' report, submitted on Nov. 1, 1833, recommended a plan similar to Col. Clinton's except that the open aqueduct would be a closed masonry conduit, and four reservoirs for receiving, equalizing pressure and distributing the water in Manhattan would be constructed.

The commission recommended the Croton River as the only adequate supply available, and the common council subsequently asked the legislature to pass an act allowing the city to construct its own waterworks. It did so on May 2, 1834, and the water commission was reappointed to conduct yet another detailed study with an eye toward putting a specified project before the voters. Nine months later the commission, after reviewing investigations done by three engineers, recommended damming the mouth of the Croton River to form a 700-acre reservoir, and taking the water across the Harlem River in a siphon beneath the waterway rather than on a bridge above it.

After all of the proposals, delays and studies, the electorate got its chance to speak on Apr. 14, 1835. The question of whether or not the Croton water project should be built was endorsed, 17,330 to 5,963. The common council on May 7 ordered the water commissioners to proceed with construction of what has become known as the Old Croton Reservoir and Aqueduct. A loan of $2.5 million was authorized, and Major Douglass was appointed chief engineer.[33]

The city was on its way to providing its inhabitants with a sure, pure source of water. But it would not be ready in time to save New York from the greatest disaster in its history.

Ruins after the 1835 fire that consumed 700 buildings in a 17-square-block area of New York City.
Detail of an aquatint by W. J. Bennett after a painting by N. Calyo.
Eno Collection. Miriam and Ira D. Wallach Division of Arts, Prints and Photographs.
The New York Public Library. Astor, Lenox & Tilden Foundation.

2. Claiming the Croton

SEVEN months after New York City's leaders had given the go-ahead for the development of a municipal water system, and while engineer David Douglass was preparing surveys of the 42-mile aqueduct, a devastating fire provided proof that time was of the essence when it came to tapping the Croton.

The Great Fire of 1835 began about 9 P.M. on a frigid December 16, when gale winds blew off New York Harbor and the temperature dipped to below zero. Smoke and flames were first seen issuing from a five-story building at 28 Merchant Street, between Wall Street and Hanover Square. The fierce wind carried the flames from street to street, destroying homes, stores and warehouses in a 17-block area occupied largely by shipping and wholesale merchants. An estimated 700 buildings were consumed in the inferno, which stymied the city's volunteer firemen who took water from the river only to have it freeze solid in the pipes of their hand-pump carts.[1]

Although a train of flatcars carrying fire engines was rushed from New Jersey, little could be done to stop the wall of fire. Many of the stores were new, and featured iron shutters and copper roofs. Their burning, said one account, "gave the appearance of an immense iron furnace in full blast. The heat at times melted the copper roofing and the liquid ran off in great drops."[2]

At one time the East River was ablaze when barrels of turpentine burst and spread across the water.[3]

"The flames were unmanageable and the crowd, including the firemen, appeared to look on with the apathy of despair," wrote Philip Hone in his diary December 17. Hone's son, son-in-law and nephew were among merchants who lost their businesses in the blaze, despite frantic efforts to save stock by dumping it in the middle of the street. Most of their inventories burned anyway.

It took a brave band of sailors from the Brooklyn Navy Yard to finally quell the blaze 16 hours after it began, carrying kegs of gunpowder through showers of sparks to blow up several buildings in the fire's path.[4] One eyewitness described the aftermath:

> The morning of the 17th of December opened upon New York with a scene of devastation sufficient to dismay the stoutest heart. The fine range of buildings and splendid stores in Exchange Place, Merchant Street and all the adjoining streets down to the river lay, literally levelled to the earth, with their contents consumed, the Merchants Exchange and Post Office entirely destroyed, the whole one heap of smoking ruins.[5]

The Merchants Exchange, a three-story marble building just seven years old, was gutted in the fire, its 60-foot cupola crashing into the vaulted rotunda

John B. Jervis: An engineer's engineer

John Bloomfield Jervis, the "practical" engineer who implemented the Croton project started by the more academic David B. Douglass, most definitely got a hands-on education.

Born on Long Island on December 14, 1795, to Timothy Jervis, a carpenter, and his wife, Phebe Bloomfield Jervis, the future engineer grew up in the wilds of Rome, New York, where his father kept a farm and ran a sawmill. Though insatiably curious and a voracious reader, young John went to school only to age 15. He worked with his family until, in 1817, he was hired as an axeman, cutting trees for a crew surveying the line of the Erie Canal.

Jervis absorbed all he could on the job, seeking out the post of rodman the following year. "I had only a common school education, with no view to the science of engineering," he wrote in his memoirs toward the end of his life. "The thing appeared a mystery... [but] I had faith to believe that what others had learned, I could learn."

And learn he did, spending eight years on the Erie, where he eventually became supervising engineer for a 50-mile stretch of the canal. In 1825, Benjamin Wright, the dean of American civil engineering and the man who had hired Jervis to hack a path for the surveyors seven years earlier, brought him on as principal assistant engineer for the Delaware & Hudson Canal. Jervis succeeded his mentor as chief engineer on the D&H in 1827, and three years later took the job of chief engineer of the Mohawk & Hudson Railway. A three-year stint as chief engineer on the Chenango Canal preceded his appointment to the Croton post.

In more than a half-century as a civil engineer, Jervis established a reputation as an inventor and an innovator. He constructed the first railroad in North America designed for steam locomotives, developed an air convoy system for braking loaded railroad cars on downgrades, and applied the moveable forward truck to steam locomotives, allowing trains to negotiate curved tracks. Jervis used his own invention of a rainfall and runoff gauge to calculate development of a controversial system of artificial reservoirs to feed the Chenango Canal. And his employment of a reverse curve on the spillway of the Croton Reservoir dam was much copied by later dam builders.

Fresh from his success on the Croton, Jervis became a consultant on development of the Boston public water supply, completed in 1848. He was chief engineer for the Hudson River Railway from 1845 to 1850, and subsequently became involved in the operations of several Midwestern railroads, serving as president of the Chicago and Rock Island during its construction. A banking and real estate investor, he also helped organize the Rome Merchant Iron Works.

Jervis died on January 12, 1885, in Rome.

Sources: Neal FitzSimons' *The Reminscences of John B. Jervis*; Larry D. Lankton's *The "Practicable" Engineer: John B. Jervis and the Old Croton Aqueduct*; F. Daniel Larkin's *John B. Jervis: An American Engineering Pioneer* and Larkin's *The Mohawk & Hudson and The Saratoga and Schenectady*; and Michelle McFee's *Limestone Locks and Overgrowth, The Rise and Descent of the Chenango Canal*. Illustration: Jervis as he appeared about the time of the Croton project. Jervis Public Library.

and taking with it a statue of Alexander Hamilton that had been erected eight months earlier.

"Goods and property of every description are found under the ruins in enormous quantities," wrote diarist Hone. Silks and laces, recently arrived cargoes of coffee and tea, "costly indigo and rich drugs add to the mass of mud which obstructs the streets."

Losses were estimated at $18 to $20 million. Scores of businessmen were ruined, and every insurance company in the city went bankrupt.

The disaster made city residents more anxious than ever to see a reliable source of water brought to their doorsteps, but that didn't happen as quickly as they might have hoped. It took a full year after his appointment for chief engineer David Douglass to provide water commissioners with their first map of the aqueduct line, and to conduct appraisals of land to be acquired. More months went by as Douglass took additional surveying parties into Westchester County to further refine the route. When the chief engineer requested more time and staff to develop specifications, the commissioners lost patience and fired him in October of 1836.[6]

Supporters said Douglass was unfairly dismissed by commissioners who failed to define his perogatives, interfered with his disciplining of subordinates, and "treated this vast undertaking as little more than an extended job of plain masonry, which might be carried out with trifling expense."[7]

Douglass, an 1813 graduate of Yale and a decorated officer of the War of 1812, claimed his firing was politically motivated because he was a Whig, and four of the five water commissioners were Democrats, as was the man named to replace him, John B. Jervis.[8]

But Stephen Allen, a former New York City mayor and chairman of the commissioners, insisted Douglass was removed because, while he was a learned man and a professor at West Point and New York University, the Croton project was a job for a man with practical experience, not theoretical knowledge.[9]

Unlike Douglass, John Jervis had been schooled only to age 15, and had no formal engineering training. But by the time he took over the Croton project, Jervis had hungrily learned all he could in the field, working his way from a teenage axeman clearing timber for the Erie Canal, to chief engineer on the Delaware & Hudson and the Chenango Canals, as well as on the Mohawk and Hudson Railway.

Jervis wasted no time putting his 20 years of experience to work implementing the Croton water project that Douglass had laid out. He was charged with building a dam on the Croton River to hold back a 400-acre reservoir six miles from the Hudson; a 38-acre receiving reservoir between 6th and 7th Avenues; and a distributing reservoir on Murray Hill at 5th Avenue and 42nd Street in Manhattan. A closed aqueduct, laid just beneath ground level and covered with earth, would be 41.5 miles long and 166 feet above mean tide. It would connect the reservoirs, feeding water to the city by gravity. Its most challenging features? An 80-foot stone arch bridge across the Sing-Sing Kill in what is now Ossining; the crossing of the Harlem River into Manhattan, and no fewer than 16 tunnels beneath hills and ridges, totalling 7,000 feet in length.

A dispute over whether to send the water over or under the Harlem River held up construction on that part of the project, so that, while water was introduced into the city in 1842 and most of the system was on line by 1844, the 1,450-foot, pipe-carrying arched bridge that was ultimately built was not completed until 1848.

After organizing a squad of assistant engineers to collect rock and soil samples and prepare profiles of the aqueduct route, Jervis gathered information on labor and materials costs and design precedents. Bids for the dam and the northernmost part of the aqueduct were opened on Apr. 26, 1837, and work began the following month.

The aqueduct was divided into four 10-mile divisions, with a resident engineer responsible for each division. These units were then divided into sections of about a half-mile long on which contractors bid. By October of 1838, all sections of the aqueduct, and the city reservoirs, were under contract.[10]

The Croton Aqueduct at Yonkers. Ossining Historical Society.

The project was built on lands acquired from owners who, not surprisingly, sometimes balked at the city's authority to condemn their property. According to Croton Aqueduct Commission reports from the period, 534 acres were taken from 36 property owners who were paid $85,785 for land needed for the reservoir. Another 292 acres were purchased along the aqueduct line from owners who got a total of $165,000, an average of $571 per acre.

In an 1837 report the water commissioners cited "opposition we had to encounter from some of the land owners in Westchester, who insisted upon remuneration for their property far above the damage they were to sustain by its occupation, and others who attempted to prejudice the people against the proceedings of the commissioners, and otherwise to embarrass them."

The same report noted that a group of 20 residents petitioned the state legislature, claiming the act of 1834 allowing the city to go forward with the project was unconstitutional. Others took their pleas to court, or threatened to. Pierre VanCortlandt in 1837 warned a contractor to discontinue working on his land or face trespass charges despite the fact that he had been paid $2,350 for his property, more than $100 an acre, "much of which is steep side-hill and entirely unfit for cultivation," according to the commissioner.

In 1838, however, the commissioners' report acknowledged that a good portion of seized land was "valuable meadow, which may account for the very high price awarded for it by the appraisers, equal to $229 an acre."

Not everyone was opposed to the city's presence, or its purchase offers. In November 1835, while still chief engineer, Major Douglass reported to Commissioner Allen that he was welcomed by several landowners who were personally approached for their property. "I am happy to say that our location generally in the vicinity above this appears to give very general satisfaction. . . J. Wells of this place [Yonkers] whom I met today expresses the greatest cordiality and good feeling," wrote Douglass.[11]

Although possession of some of the lands required for the project was delayed, work on the acquired property nonetheless went forward, with as many as 4,000 laborers on the job at one time. Most were Irish immigrants who worked for as little as 68 cents for a 10-hour day early in the project. In 1838, workers struck for higher pay, as described in the water commissioners report of that year:

> It commenced on section 15, under contract to Timothy N. Ferrell. The per diem pay, during the winter months, was 68½ to 75 cents, and the contractor posted a notice that the pay for the month of April would be from 75 to 81¼ cents. The demands of the men, however, was 87½ to 100 cents per day, and the contractor refusing to comply with these terms, the laborers on that section (it did not extend to the mechanics) quit the work in a body and proceeded along the line of aqueduct in a tumultuous manner, from the Croton dam to Sing Sing; compelling those who were willing to work to join them until they amounted to several hundred persons. The prompt interference of the magistrates of the town of Mount Pleasant, however, prevented the mob from proceeding further. . .

Most of the strikers subsequently went back to work when the contractor met their demand for 87½ cents a day, but the leaders of the walk-out, and "the most riotous" of the workers, were denied employment, the commission report said.

Sometimes it was the contractor who literally walked out. On Aug. 2, 1838, John McGregory, who had the contract to build two sections of the aqueduct, was paid $2,880 for work and materials for the month of July, then "absconded with the whole of the money, leaving his mechanics and labourers unpaid, with several debts . . . contracted with other persons."[12]

Some disturbances had nothing to do with money, and everything to do with liquor, at least according to the commissioners, who required contractors to promise not to provide spirits to their workmen or to allow anyone else to bring it to the aqueduct line. It was liquor, the commissioners reported in 1837, that had caused a "riot" spurred by sectional differences fostered in Ireland. "The fight was most desperate, resulting in broken heads, and maimed bodies and limbs, and eventually in the death of one of their countrymen, named Baxter." Indictments were brought, but no one was convicted in the killing.[13]

The workers, many of whom were recruited for the aqueduct job as soon as they arrived in New York from their home country, lived in camps along the line and, like many another immigrant group, became the butt of bigotry and stereotypical jokes. Writer Washington Irving, whose home, Sunnyside, was near the aqueduct line in Tarrytown, made fun of the Irishmen's supposed penchant for whiskey and fear of goblins in a letter to a friend in 1840. Describing a "colony of Patlanders" encamped in the woods near the stone arch bridge carrying the aqueduct over the Pocantico [Mill] River, Irving, creator of the legendary Headless Horseman, said the workers had been "most grievously harassed by all kinds of apparitions" including "mishapen monsters . . . invariably without heads, which show that they must be lineal descendants of the old goblin of the Hollow."

Irving wrote that the workers so feared going out at night that a local whiskey shop was forced to close for lack of customers, which, he quipped, could prompt the laborers to "abandon the goblin region of Sleepy Hollow" and "seriously retard" completion of the Croton waterworks.[14]

But another prominent author, Charles Dickens, expressed his admiration for the Irish and other immigrants following an 1842 visit to the United States. "It would be hard to keep your model republics going without [them]. For who else would dig, and delve, and drudge and do domestic work and make canals and roads and execute great lines of Internal Improvement?" asked the British visitor in *American Notes*, his account of five months of travel here during the year the Croton water system was inaugurated.

Many of the Irish, when the water system was finished, found jobs on later public works projects and settled nearby, prompting the establishment of the first Catholic churches in the region and leaving a distinctive cultural mark that endures today.

The aqueduct these men were building was an arched tube of brick and stone, buried 15 to 30 feet beneath the surface of the earth on a line roughly parallel to the Hudson River. Carrying the aqueduct across small streams along the route were 114 stone culverts up to 25 feet across; 33 circular stone ventilators 14 feet high were constructed at one-mile intervals to circulate air through the tunnel. Six waste weirs, surrounded by stone buildings with brick arched roofs, allowed excess water to escape from the aqueduct.[15]

The bottom of the aqueduct was an inverted arch, the side walls vertical. The greatest interior width was seven feet, five inches, the greatest height eight feet, five inches. The masonry was held together by cement made with hydraulic (waterproof) lime. Masonry inspectors were installed every two miles along the line to examine all cement work and inspect and test all loads of hydraulic cement. Explained Jervis, "It was deemed important to guard against a very common fault in hydraulic masonry, namely, the want of full bedding of the stone and brick in mortar."[16]

Jervis knew his reputation was on the line should any portion of the massive undertaking fail. "In a canal or a railway, any failure would only suspend traffic until repairs could be made; no comparison to the suspension of the supply of water to a large city," he related later in his life. But though he felt a heavy weight of responsibility, and was subjected to scrutiny and criticism by other builders, engineers and city officials who predicted the aqueduct would not withstand the pressure, or that the Croton would not supply as much water as anticipated, Jervis remained confident that the project could be successfully completed.[17]

He was assisted in this daunting task by a staff of some 20 able engineers, including Peter Hastie and Edward Tracy, who had worked with him on the Chenango Canal; Horatio Allen, who had worked with him on the Delaware & Hudson Canal; James Renwick, who later became a prominent architect; and Jervis' younger brother William.

Second assistant engineers earned $50 a month; first assistants made $75 to $100. The four resident engineers were paid $1,500 a year. Allen, as principal assistant to Jervis, made $3,500, while the chief engineer himself earned $5,000 annually.[18]

One of the young engineers employed on the aqueduct was Fayette Tower of Oneida County, who wrote to his mother in Waterville of his experiences in the fall of 1837:

> I truly believe I could not find a place so aside from the world----yet so near the great emporium of the United States. Tho I am within two hours ride of the city of New York I am in a country where there is less communication by any thoroughfare and where there is less intelligence and enterprise among the inhabitants than in the remotest corner of Brookfield. Yet my sojourn among these people is not without some instruction to me. I learn to compare the different people I am thrown among with each other and to notice the causes which produce those differences.[19]

Tower, writing from Sing Sing in "the wild region of the Croton," drew an illustration of a building used as an office and living quarters for engineering staff members. A woman, presumably, the landlady, "does all her cooking in one vessel, that is what she calls a 'spider'. . .with that she can roast a piece of beef, broil a steak, bake a loaf or perform anything in the cooking line."[20]

In Sing Sing, the aqueduct was carried across the 63-foot deep gulf of the Sing Sing Kill on a massive stone conduit, 88 feet across, built by Young & Scott of Philadelphia.[21] A second arch was later constructed beneath the viaduct to carry a local road across the stream. The double arch remains an attraction in Ossining more than a century and a half after its construction. In fact, the entire Old Croton Aqueduct was designated a Civil

Engineering Landmark by the American Society of Civil Engineers in 1975.

Indeed, stonework was a hallmark all along the aqueduct, and the identities of some communities were closely linked with it. Archville, a hamlet a mile north of Tarrytown, took its name from an arched bridge that carried the water line over Broadway, which was reduced to 18 feet wide beneath it. Stories abound of trucks and large vehicles being damaged or stuck in the narrow arch, and many accidents occurred there until the city, taken to court by the town of Mount Pleasant for encroaching on the highway, demolished the arch and put a siphon beneath the road in 1924.[22]

Twenty-five streams crossed the line of the aqueduct, which passed through valleys with musical names like Indian Brook, Mill River and Jewell's Brook. But the controversy that surrounded the traverse of the Harlem River was anything but melodic.

While David Douglass had suggested that a high masonry bridge should carry the water over the river at about the line of the aqueduct, Jervis recommended a low structure, 50 feet above the river, using a single arch to span most of the waterway. Four 36-inch cast iron pipes would carry up to 50 million gallons of water a day across the bridge and into Manhattan. "The object was economy as compared to a bridge on the grade of the aqueduct," Jervis wrote in his memoirs. Noting that eminent engineers Canvas White and John Martineau had suggested similar plans years earlier, Jervis also pointed out that "there was no navigation on this part of the river" so a low bridge would not interfere with ship traffic.[23]

The water commissioners supported Jervis'

The Croton Aqueduct was carried over this arched bridge at Sing Sing (now known as Ossining). A second arched pedestrian bridge was later added below the first. Ossining Historical Society.

recommendation, claiming it was the plan approved by voters in 1835, was the easiest, safest and
cheapest to build and would take less time to complete.[24]

But some members of the city council held out
for a high bridge, and a group of adjoining property
owners also agitated for the loftier structure. On
the day a call for bids on the low bridge was
advertised in metropolitan papers in October 1838,
another ad appeared warning contractors and the
public that "we will use every means the law will
justify to prevent any and all persons obstructing
the water at the natural channel of said river, so as
to prevent a free and uninterrupted passage
through said channel by vessels with masts and
spars of the usual and proper height and dimensions of vessels of the draft of water said channel
will now allow to pass."[25]

Jervis claimed the high bridge proponents were
more interested in enhancing the value of their
property by "giving an ornament to the district"
than in improving navigation. But they took their

case to the state legislature, which passed an act in
May of 1839 compelling the city to construct either
a bridge 100 feet above the water, or a tunnel
beneath the river. The commissioners then vacated
the contract which had been awarded to six partners from Pennsylvania, and directed Jervis to draw
up plans and estimates for the two methods of
crossing the Harlem outlined by the legislature.

One month later he did so, recommending a
high bridge, though it would cost $200,000 more
than a tunnel, which he claimed would be too
dangerous to build. The project went out to bid
June 15, 1839, and the contract was let August 13.[26]

Jervis' bridge was 1,450 feet long and was supported by 15 granite arches, eight of them with
spans of 80 feet, seven with 50-foot spans. Originally, two lines of 36-inch cast iron pipe were laid
atop the bridge and then covered with earth, 12 feet
below grade level of the aqueduct, to handle 36
million gallons of water a day.[27]

The bridge, which cost $963,427, took nearly
a decade to build. While it was under construction

by laborers engaged by contractors George Law, Samuel Roberts and Arnold Mason, water was directed through pipes laid in the river alongside the bridge. Water first passed over High Bridge in May of 1848. Between 1860 and '63, the top was raised by six feet and a third pipe, 90-inches in diameter, was laid.

The bridge did indeed become "an ornament to the district," attracting tourists and visitors from the city eight miles away. James Miller's *Stranger's Guide for the City of New York*, published in 1861, noted that pedestrians were invited to stroll atop the covered viaduct. Carriage fare, and a two- or three-hour stay at the bridge, was $5. Hourly trains on the Harlem Railroad also carried passengers to the bridge. Fare: 12½ cents. Among its admirers was Edgar Allen Poe, who lived and wrote (the poems "Annabel Lee" and "Ulalume") in nearby Fordham, the Bronx, from 1846 to 1849, according to *The WPA Guide to New York*, written in 1939.

The aqueduct itself----at least 26 miles of it----remains a modest attraction 150 years after its construction, serving as a hiking trail that is a National Historic Landmark. The Old Croton Trailway State Park is headquartered at Dobb's Ferry, where the sole surviving overseer's house along the aqueduct is currently (1999) under restoration.

The Reservoirs

Work on the 50-foot-high Croton Dam was begun in 1837. It was to create a 400-acre lake five miles long to store up to 600 million gallons of water. The river was closed off by a 100-foot stone dam, and a 250-foot earthen embankment, 55 feet wide at the top.[28] A 180-foot tunnel was cut through solid rock on the south side of the river to channel the water to the head of the aqueduct.[29]

The dam was nearing completion in the winter of 1841 when disaster struck. Warm temperatures,

Above: High Bridge was built to carry the Croton Aqueduct over the Harlem River. Ossining Historical Society.

Croton Aqueduct Engineer F. B. Tower produced this 1843 illustration of the
first Croton Reservoir Dam, completed in 1842. Ossining Historical Society.

and rain that began falling the night of January 5, combined to melt 18 inches of snow on the ground and fill the lake to overflowing. Water behind the dam was rising 14 inches an hour by January 8, until the waste weir could not handle the volume. In the early morning hours, the earthen embankment gave way two or three feet from the top.[30] An estimated 200 feet of the dam washed out, sending a wall of water down the valley. Albert Brayton, son of one of the dam contractors, tried to alert sleeping residents downstream by blowing a horn, but many people were caught unawares.[31]

"Fifty or sixty people were thrown into the flood and their possessions swept away," relates one Westchester County history, naming several people who were rescued by rafts as they clung to trees. "William Evans, sometimes called 'Uncle John,' and Robert Smith sought refuge in a tree which was swept away and were drowned. Mr. Bailey waded waist deep in water carrying his

father and a bag of gold and fortunately reached a place of safety."[32]

Three bridges, several houses, three mills and other structures were destroyed in the flood. "It appears that three lives were lost, one at the dam, and two at Bailey's wire factory," reported Engineer Jervis to the water commissioners the day after the flood.[33] Later, in his memoirs, Jervis recalled his first look at the devastated valley, which he called "indeed sad . . .the aspect severe in the extreme." Wrote Jervis, "No one without such experience could imagine the severity with which this scene, with its attending circumstances, affected me."[34]

Damage claims against the city by those who had lost property in the flood went on for years, but Jervis got right to work rebuilding the dam, whose masonry portions survived the onslaught. He started by acknowledging he'd made a mistake. "It was manifest I had been in error in regard to the extent of waterway necessary for so great a flood," he wrote in his memoirs. "For three years, I had seen no flood that gave me suspicion of one of this magnitude."[35]

But enlarging the weir presented a problem, as the extension would have to be based on gravel, and the overflow from a height of 40 or 50 feet would likely undermine the foundation. So Jervis designed a reversed curve masonry dam, to gradually turn the water from a vertical to a horizontal position, and then built a nine-foot high secondary wooden dam 300 feet below the main structure to form a pool that would absorb the force of the water as it spilled.[36]

Contractors McCulloch, Back, McManus and Hepborne "evinced a high degree of energy" in reconstructing the dam over the next two years, when two more floods stalled progress. "This was a season of intense anxiety to me," related Jervis. "I watched the indications of rain very closely and devoted as much personal attention to this as I could possibly spare from other work."[37]

Meanwhile, work was progressing on the receiving reservoir (the Yorkville Reservoir), which extended from 79th to 86th Streets between 6th and 7th Avenues. The impoundment consisted of earth embankments up to 38 feet high. The reservoir was 1,826 feet long and more than 800 feet wide, covering 35 acres. Its capacity was 180 million gallons of water.[38]

Most of the land taken up by the reservoir was city property, but 10 acres were acquired from private owners, to whom the city paid $22,000. In 1853, the area became part of Central Park.[39] Use of the reservoir was discontinued in 1890.

From the Yorkville Reservoir, a double line of three-foot iron pipes was laid to 5th Avenue and the Murray Hill distributing reservoir. This grand, Egyptian-style masonry structure occupied the west side of the avenue between 40th and 42nd

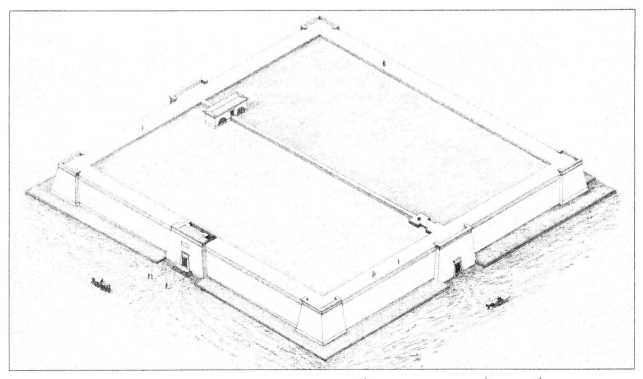

The Egyptian-style Distributing Reservoir at Murray Hill, on 5th Avenue between 40th and 42nd Streets, held 24 million gallons of water, carried in a brick-lined aqueduct from the Croton Reservoir 42 miles to the north.
Ossining Historical Society.

Streets, now the site of the main branch of the New York Public Library.[40]

Rising 45 feet above street level, the reservoir covered four acres in what was then a rather wild section three miles north of city hall. It was built with hollow granite walls connected by cross walls and, at the top, by brick arches. "An opening was left in the cross walls so that a man may go around the whole and discover any leak there may be in the masonry," said Jervis in his memoirs.

A stone staircase led to a railed promenade atop the reservoir, which was 420 feet square. From the walkway, sightseers could look across 24 million gallons of Croton water, sail toy boats on its surface, or enjoy the view of the growing metropolis to the south.

On June 8 and 9, 1842 five water commissioners and chief engineer Jervis, along with several of his assistants, made a final inspection of the aqueduct and reservoirs. They walked the 33-mile water line from Croton Dam to the Harlem River. Two weeks later, when a small amount of water was released into the aqueduct, four of them rode a boat, christened the *Croton Maid*, inside the same passageway. On June 27, the first Croton water flowed into Yorkville Reservoir to the applause of Governor William Seward, Mayor Robert Morris and other dignitaries.[41]

In the wee hours of Independence Day, the water was allowed to flow into the distributing reservoir on 5th Avenue. Later in the day, Croton water coursed its way through Manhattan's new mains.[42]

Former Mayor Philip Hone and his wife visited the Yorkville and Murray Hill Reservoirs on July 12, 1842. In his diary, Hone described the former:

The outer walls are of a handsome wrought stone, the basins lined with a dry slope wall, one 20, the other 30 feet in depth. They are, at present, about one-half full, and the clear, sweet, soft water (clear it is, and sweet and soft, for to be in the fashion I drank a tumbler of it and found it all of these) is flowing in copiously. There were a great number of visitors at this place----pedestrians, horsemen, railroad travellers and those who, like myself, came in

their own carriages. . . for it has become a fashionable place of resort. . .

Some were not as impressed with the accomplishment, however. George Templeton Strong, lawyer and literary critic, wrote in his diary on July 5, 1842, "There's nothing new in town, except the Croton Water, which is all full of tadpoles and animalculae, and which moreover flows through an aqueduct which I hear was used as a necessary by all the Hibernian vagabonds who worked upon it. I shall drink no Croton for some time to come. Post drank some of it and is in dreadful apprehensions of breeding bullfrogs inwardly."[43]

Such concerns notwithstanding, the new water system was inaugurated with pomp, ceremony and a parade to end all parades on October 14, 1842. The day began with the firing of cannons and the ringing of church bells, followed by a five-mile-long procession consisting of military units, politicians and nearly every civic and trade organization in the city and environs, including 4,000 firemen belonging to 52 fire companies. Temperance societies, touting clean water over spirits (no liquor, only Croton water, was served at the day's events), joined butchers on horseback, scientists and clergymen who were watched by thousands of spectators.[44]

John B. Jervis, whose engineers and contractors reportedly threatened to stay out of the parade if he was made to walk, as initially planned, in the end accompanied Gov. Seward in his horse-drawn barouche.

There were fireworks, balloon ascensions and receptions all over the city. The Astor Hotel lit 700 lamps in its windows. And at city hall, where the parade ended, the New York Sacred Music Society sang George Pope Morris' Croton Ode: "Water leaps as if delighted while her conquered foes retire! Pale contagion flies affrighted with the baffled demon fire! . . ."[45]

Indeed, Samuel Stevens, president of the Board of Water Commissioners, recalled the Great Fire of 1835, when businesses, warehouses and merchandise sustained millions of dollars in damage. "If it had been dwelling houses, it would have turned 100,000 of our citizens into the streets," Stevens claimed. Noting that the Croton water works cost $12 million to construct ($7 million to contractors, $408,000 for land, $1.8 million for pipes and $436,000 for "incidentals," including commissioners' salaries), Stevens asserted, "Security against such awful calamities cannot be too dearly bought."[46]

J. L. Lawrence, president of the Croton Aqueduct Board, was another of the day's orators hailing the achievement of Jervis and company. "The hill has been levelled or pierced, the stream and the valley have been overleaped, the rock has been smitten!," Lawrence said. "Nature, yielding to human industry, perseverance and skill, no longer holds the boon she had before denied us."[47]

But ex-mayor Hone wondered in his diary about the long-term expense of the project: "It is astonishing. . . how cheerfully (citizens) acquiesce in the enormous expense which will burden them and their posterity with taxes to the last generation. Water! Water! is the universal note which is sounded into the masses. . ."

A five-mile-long parade celebrated the introduction of Croton water to thirsty Manhattan in 1842.
Cornelia Cotton Gallery.

3. Of "Life And Stir": The City Grows

EW YORK CITY in 1842 was a metropolis of more than 300,000 people, a busy, bewildering place described in profuse detail by British author Charles Dickens, who arrived in the harbor on board the steam packet *New York* early in that year:

> There lay stretched out before us, to the right, confused heaps of buildings, with here and there a spire or steeple, looking down on the herd below; and here and there, again, a cloud of lazy smoke; and in the foreground a forest of ships' masts, cheery with flapping sails and waving flags. Crossing from among them to the opposite shore were steam ferry-boats laden with people, coaches, horses, waggons, baskets, boxes, crossed and recrossed by other ferry-boats: all travelling to and fro, and never idle... Beyond were shining heights, and islands in the glancing river. The city's hum and buzz, the clinking of capstans, the ringing of bells, the barking of dogs, the clattering of wheels, tingled in the listening ear. All of which life and stir, coming across the water. . .hemmed the vessel round. . ."[1]

Facing page: High Bridge and tower, shown in this 1880 illustration from *Harper's Weekly*, was a fashionable destination for New Yorkers, who traveled eight miles from the city by train or carriage to stroll atop the waterway. Collection of Robert J. Kornfeld, Jr., A.I.A.

During the 1840s, 20,000 new people were joining the city's throngs each year, pushing the population of Manhattan to 515,547 by 1850.[2] The demands of so many people and their businesses, coupled with the now-ready availability of Croton water, put great pressure on the new supply. Pipes were soon laid to Randall's, Ward's and Blackwell's Islands to serve burgeoning communities there, and it wasn't long before "water closets," first patented in the U.S. in the 1830s, were being installed in growing numbers. Plumbing businesses sprang up to install these indoor bathrooms, and the seemingly inexhaustible supply of water even prompted the opening, in 1844, of a water cure hospital where the hydropathic school of medicine was practiced.[3]

Between May 1844 and June 1845, the number of permits issued to water takers rose by 2,255, to 9,582, according to the annual report of the Croton Aqueduct Board. These included 7,171 private dwellings and 2,411 businesses and institutions, among them 177 manufactories, 420 stores and offices, 265 barrooms, 63 slaughter houses and 83 steamboats. The city took in more than $131,000 in user fees but the aqueduct board complained that too many people were taking water for free from hydrants, or were just plain wasting it. In the board's report to the common council in December of 1849, it noted,

Street hydrants are opened and kept running

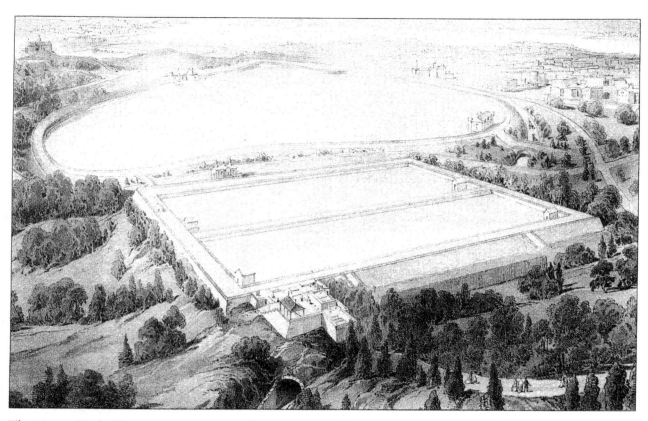

The 38-acre Yorkville Receiving Reservoir (foreground) and Lake Manahatta, built in 1862 to add storage capacity for the growing city. The latter reservoir still exists but is no longer used. The Yorkville Reservoir is now the Great Lawn in Central Park. Cornelia Cotton Gallery.

for months together; street washers are converted into jets for the amusement of children and domestics; sweepers, instead of collecting into heaps and carting away the accumulations of the gutters, find it more convenient, with a full head of water from a street hydrant, to wash the whole into a receiving basin and thence to the public sewers, to be removed at four-fold greater cost, while in many of the stores in the lower wards, no care is taken to close the various openings supplying water closets and wash-basins, and the water may be heard during the still hours of the night, rushing through numerous lateral drains into the street sewers.

The board noted that liveries cleaning their horses in the streets added to congestion and filth, and steamboat owners were careless about shutting off hydrants at the wharves to fill their boilers. The

board called for more rigid policing and stricter rules to curb the abuse, which had led to the average daily per capita consumption of 60 gallons of water during the summer of 1849, "a supply three times greater than any legitimate use of it would demand."

Increased water rates were instituted in May 1850. Buildings were charged by frontage and height. Other users, like bakeries, schools, warehouses and stables, were assessed special rates. Liveries, for example, were charged $2 a year for each horse, public bathing tubs $5 each per year, builders ten cents per thousand bricks laid.[4] The state was charged three-quarters of a cent per hundred gallons for water consumed at the prison at Sing Sing.

When appeals to curb water use did not stem the flow, the Croton Aqueduct Department began, about 1852, installing water meters at commercial establishments. This was not always effective in cutting waste, however. In the department's annual report to the common council in 1858, "the enormous and extraordinary consumption of water by the St. Nicholas Hotel" was cited. Meters indicated the hotel, a massive structure built in 1854, was taking 36,172,774 gallons a year, water its owners would not or could not pay for. "Suppose there were ten or twenty such enormous establishments on the island—as well they may be, if the anticipations of the increase in its population and business are realized—how is the water to be preserved?" asked the aqueduct board.

Meter installation was not vigorously pursued until after 1878, when 529 meters were in place. The following year, the number of meters had risen to 1,398, and by 1880, more than 4,000 meters were registering commercial water flow (residences were still charged by street frontage). That year, the commissioner of public works reported that one hotel had decreased its use from 80,000 to 24,000 gallons per day after meters were installed.[5] Still, water consumption soared, from 12 million gallons a day in 1842 to 40 million gallons in 1850.[6]

And so, just nine years after the Croton Reservoir and Aqueduct had appeared to solve the city's water crisis, the common council directed the Croton Aqueduct Board to look for a site to build a second storage reservoir where a 60-day water supply could be accommodated. In February 1852 the board voted to appropriate land in what was to become Central Park, and in June 1853, an act of the state legislature allowed the purchase of 106 acres for a reservoir to be called Lake Manahatta.[7]

Work on the project did not begin until after Central Park was created by the city in 1856. In 1857, while clearing, grading and landscaping was being done on the rocky tract, dotted with a few farms and squatters' shanties, the aqueduct board was stymied in its efforts to develop the reservoir by a suit brought by Dinsmore, Wood & Co., whose low bid had been rejected as incomplete. The dispute reached the Supreme Court before the city was allowed to formally award the job to Fairchild & Co.[8]

Ground was broken Apr. 17, 1858, and the reservoir was built over the next four years under the guidance of Chief Engineer Alfred Craven. Upwards of 2,000 men worked on the project as city finances allowed during that period of financial depression. It occasionally took its toll on laborers, many of them immigrants, and on ordinary citizens. The June 11, 1861, edition of *The New York Times* reported that 10-year-old William Mealy drowned while bathing in a water-filled trench dug for aqueduct piping.

The Civil War also interfered with the project during the last year of construction. The engineer in charge of the daily work, George Greene, was called into Army service and led a brigade into battle at Cedar Mountain, Va. Aug. 9, 1862, just 10 days before Lake Manahatta was formally opened with great fanfare.

The New York Times of August 20 called it the largest artificial lake in the world, its water covering 96 acres. The reservoir, 30 feet deep, was divided into two basins and could hold one billion gallons. The inside of the 15-foot embankment around the reservoir was lined with hydraulic cement. Two gatehouses, at north and south, were imposing stone features of the reservoir. The Croton Aqueduct was extended to connect Lake Manahatta with the older Yorkville Reservoir nearby and pipes were laid to allow distribution to the city from either or both facilities. The project cost about $2 million, including $500,000 for the land.

Thousands of people lined the reservoir's banks to watch the first gush of water cover its bottom Aug. 19, 1862, accompanied by booming cannon, music and speeches. The *Times* reported that hundreds of curious spectators wandered inside the two basins until engineer Craven gave the word for the 10 influent gates to be opened. The awestruck crowd applauded, the newspaper said, then watched for an hour as the water made scant progress over the bottom of the vast reservoir. It took a week for the bed to be covered, six months to fill the two basins.

Luther Marsh, speaking for the contractors, noted that many of the laborers had been called off to war, "but still the toil of peace went steadily on.

A visit below

Whatever its insufficiencies by the 1870s, the Croton system was still considered a marvel, its dams, underground aqueduct and distribution network almost a miracle. Two lengthy, illustrated articles—in *Harper's Magazine*, July 6, 1872, and in *Scribner's Monthly*, June 1877—described the system, which was as much admired for its form as its function.

Scribner's visited Croton Dam keeper Henry Munyers, "for nearly a quarter of a century a devoted servant of the department. Henry is not a very presentable object personally. His face is blue with a gunpowder wound received in an unfortunate blasting operation, and his eyesight is almost gone. But he loves his work and does it faithfully. . .Politicians may come and politicians may go, but Henry is a life incumbent; indeed, they say it would break his heart to remove him."

Munyers showed the reporter a small building covering an opening to the aqueduct just west of the dam where "with gauge and lantern in hand, old Munyers is placed on watch during stormy nights, and when the water rises above the proper level, the gates are lowered and the supply reduced."

The reporter then followed the line of the aqueduct, which employed keepers at station houses at Sing Sing, Mill River, Dobb's Ferry, Yonkers and Tibbits Brook. Thirty years earlier, in a report to the Croton Aqueduct Commissioners, Chief Engineer John B. Jervis had complained to the aqueduct board that the line was being encroached upon by nearby property owners who "plough and cultivate the lands, and go so far as to sell the crops of grass that grow upon the aqueduct to strangers." That manicure was favored by the *Scribner's* visitor in 1877 however:

There is an admirable neatness in the manner with which all the appurtenances are kept. In all the gatehouses and wasteweirs, every bit of brass and steel work is as bright as a new pin; every bit of sod on the line of the aqueduct is trimmed like an English gentleman's lawn, and the water, take up a glass of it where you will, is nearly as clear as when it came out of the spring.

The south gate-house in Central Park is an exemplification of this. From the roof to the foundation; from the walls to the floor; from the benches provided for inquisitive visitors who want to rest their legs and their curiosity; to the policeman in charge, the most exacting housekeeper might search in vain for a particle of dust. And the scrupulous cleanliness to be seen on the groundfloor of the gatehouse is repeated in the tunnels far below. . .

We descend a spiral stair-way placed in a circular well with moist, dripping walls, to a whitewashed chamber lighted for our particular benefit by several gas jets. Our attendant is a one-legged pensioner of the late war, a son of Erin, with the inevitable name of Pat. . .Pat, carrying a brilliant torch, now leads us into a wide tunnel, stalking over the pipes on his wooden leg with greater security than we do. The tunnel curves toward the Eighty-fifth Street entrance to the Park, and the six mains running along its bottom gradually sink into the ground until they are buried completely. One pipe extends to First Avenue,

"Shutting off the Croton at the Central Park Reservoir." *Harper's Weekly*, Nov. 12, 1881.
Cornelia Cotton Gallery

another to Third, another to Madison, and so on, into nearly every building in the city.

But once a year, when the aqueduct was inspected from end to end, the task was more challenging. Related *Scribners*:

Many strange and exciting adventures befall the men detailed for this service. Though but one life has ever been lost, large parties have sometimes been in imminent danger. . .The laborers under charge of Mr. (Benjamin) Church, dressed in rough suits, enter the aqueduct at the dam, and travel downward either afoot or in an ingenious car propelled by a crank like the hand-cars used on a railway. . .Some of the men carry torches, whose smoke and wavering blaze curl and flash in the darkness and throw fantastic shadows and reflections on the moist walls. The voices reverberate like peals of thunder and seem to awake responsive vibrations in the massive stone and brick work itself. In some conditions of the atmosphere, labor-

Above: Laying Croton water mains on 10th Ave. *Below:* The pipe vault below the Central Park gatehouse. Cornelia Cotton Gallery.

ers repairing the masonry five miles below can be distinctly heard by those at the entrance. . .

Thousands of tons of water are pressing against the gates at the entrance, and should a bar give way or an order be misunderstood, the flood would rush down upon the unfortunates and engulf them with irresistible force. . .

In some cases, it is not necessary to empty the aqueduct when a local inspection is to be made, and five feet of water is allowed to remain, enough to float the small metallic life-boat to convey the laborers from point to point. . .The explorations sometimes occupy 24 successive hours, and Mr. Church was once on duty over 72 hours without sleep. . . The whole length of the aqueduct is carefully inspected twice in every twenty-four hours and any negligence or delay on the part of the keepers in reporting a leak might cause a disaster of unprecedented horror.

High Bridge over the Harlem River was raised six feet in the early 1860s, and a 90-inch water main was added atop the two smaller original pipes to accommodate increased demand. Cornelia Cotton Gallery.

When we contemplate this benign achievement which muscle has reared and money pays for, how does the wickedness of the rebellion seem aggravated——a rebellion which has laid so many stalwart forms in the dust and squandered so many millions of treasure. How many benevolent enterprises might not those lives and that treasure have accomplished for the benefit of man."

Two years later, the war threatened to exact a toll on the water system itself. When Union authorities got wind of a Confederate plot to burn several buildings in New York City, Major General Benjamin F. Butler, commanding 3,500 troops on special detail, stationed a gunboat in the Harlem River to protect High Bridge and its aqueduct from possible sabotage.[9]

Among the conspirators was Col. Robert Martin, who had reportedly discussed with fellow Kentuckian Dr. Luke Blackburn poisoning the city's water supply before concluding that the amount of poison needed to do an adequate job could not be obtained without prompting suspicions.[10]

In the end, an Election Day attack by a gang of expatriot Canadian southerners resulted in fires being set at a number of New York hotels, including the St. Nicholas, the extravagant 600-room landmark so criticized for its gluttonous water use, which sustained $10,000 in damage.[11]

That year, 1864, was one of drought——no water flowed over the Croton Dam for 52 days straight. The following year, the dry spell stretched for 42 days.[12] The aqueduct board had anticipated the need for additional sources of water back in 1857, when, even as it prepared to build Lake Manahatta, it ordered a team of surveyors north, into Putnam County, to find more reservoir sites.

The surveyors, under the direction of engineer James Morley, spent from July to December 1857 in the field, and the aqueduct board, in its annual report for that year, anticipated the examination would show the entire Croton watershed "as being very favorable for the construction of dams, and the preservation, in proper condition, of large bodies of water. When the daily consumption of the city shall exceed the quantity afforded by the river, in seasons of drought, these storage reservoirs will be required to make up the deficit. It is the part of prudent foresight to acquire the sites for these contemplated reservoirs at an early day, even though the actual construction of them should be delayed until called for by necessity."

That day arrived in July 1866, when work began on Boyd's Corners Reservoir on the West Branch of the Croton River in the Town of Kent. A year earlier, state legislators had empowered the aqueduct board to acquire land in Westchester, Dutchess and Putnam Counties for water supply purposes. The Boyd's Corners project would be the city's first foray into Putnam, where, over the next 44 years, 8,300 acres would be condemned in the Towns of Kent, Carmel, Patterson and Southeast for city water supply and protection.[13]

The dam at Boyd's Corners formed a 300-acre lake that inundated a farming valley named for one of its first settlers, Ebenezer Boyd, a Revolutionary War veteran and tavern keeper. The *Putnam County Courier* of October 6, 1866, reported that 11 families, a school and a church would be forced to vacate the area. A cemetery, including the grave of Ebenezer Boyd, deceased since 1792, was also relocated.

The farm and sawmill of Laban Barrett on the site of the dam was the first property sold to the city. The church was rebuilt in 1869 on higher ground donated by Platt Parker, who himself lost property to the reservoir.[14] While the *Courier*'s initial article on the project chided "avaricious" landowners for demanding more from the city than their land was worth, it later expressed doubt that the Commissioners of Appraisals appointed to hear those claims would treat residents fairly. Noting that the three commissioners lived in Dutchess and Westchester Counties, the newspaper said, "Gentlemen residing along the Hudson River are

The Boyd's Corners Dam and Reservoir was completed in the Town of Kent, Putnam County, in 1873.
Cornelia Cotton Gallery.

not apt to place a very high estimate upon the value of lands in the interior." Nonetheless, the paper reported the following spring that the commission had awarded Platt Parker $12,400 for his land.[15]

The reservoir was built under the direction of George S. Greene, the major general who had worked on the Lake Manahatta project, and High Bridge before that, then served in the Civil War, where he was wounded before returning to engineering. The contract for the job was won by Edward Roach and Joshua and Simon Jenkins, who bid $201,000.[16] The dam, 670 feet long, 57 feet tall, was begun under the auspices of the Croton Aqueduct Department, but in 1870 the state legislature passed an act to reorganize city government. The Department of Public Works was thus created, superseding the aqueduct board. Mayor A. Oakley Hall appointed William Marcy Tweed to head the new department, placing in his hands most city development projects.[17]

"Boss" Tweed and his associates, the so-called Tweed Ring within the Democratic Tammany Society, ruled city politics for years, receiving kickbacks and commissions from contractors who padded bills and skimped on their work with no fear of penalty. The "Boss," who speculated extensively in real estate, held many offices while he was superintendent of public works, including county supervisor and state senator. Exposed by newspaper articles and vilified in editorial cartoons, Tweed, a U. S. Congressman from 1853 to 1855,

An unquenchable demon

Fire—the terror that helped motivate New York to develop a reliable water source—did not release its frightening grasp on the city just because there was now water in the pipes.

A blaze that nearly rivaled the Great Fire of 1835 in intensity and destruction swept through the business section below Wall Street on July 19, 1845, leveling 345 buildings. Starting in a box factory—some said a sperm oil establishment—the fire set off explosions and made diarist George Templeton Strong think "the days of '35 had returned. . . Everything in New Street as I looked down from Wall seemed withering away and melting down in absolute white heat . . . Then I came into Broadway just in time to see the iron shutters on the stores three or four doors south of Exchange Place beginning to grow hot, and the Waverley House beginning to disgorge occupants, furniture, and smoke from every convenient outlet. . . One of St. John's people told me awful stories of the Croton giving out and the fire having it all its own way. . ."

But the Croton had not given out, and the fire was eventually quelled. Thirteen years later, however, a gigantic blaze turned the famed Crystal Palace in Bryant Park into a heap of melted glass and iron. Despite its location next door to the Murray Hill distributing reservoir at Fifth Avenue and 42nd Street, the famed "fairy palace" was consumed in just 30 minutes on Oct. 5, 1858.

Built in 1853 to house the Exhibition of the Industry of All Nations, the Crystal Palace was a wonderland of art and implements, from English armor to Sevres china, tapestries, jewelry and statuary. All was lost in the fire, including, ironi-

The Crystal Palace was destroyed by fire in 1858.
Cornelia Cotton Gallery.

cally, fire apparatus that had been on display. Miraculously, none of the 2,000 people in the building when the fire broke out at the hands of an arsonist were killed.

Another spectacular fire claimed Latting Observatory, just north of the Crystal Palace. The 350-foot wooden tower went up in flames on Aug. 30, 1856.

The introduction of Croton water in 1842 spurred the development of improved fire fighting equipment. The first steam fire engine in this country was built in New York in 1840-41. But in at least one instance, fire fighters went directly to the source to battle a blaze in Sing Sing. When a fire broke out at Olive Hall during a dance one winter night in 1874, the Croton Aqueduct, which runs through the village, was tapped. Nonetheless, the fire ultimately devastated two acres in the heart of the village.

Still, insurance companies apparently felt more confident about the safety of their clients' buildings with Croton water so near. The 1845 Annual Report of the Croton Aqueduct Board touted the monetary savings the system had procured for city residents: "The tax to defray the interest of the Croton Water debt is 20 cents on the 100 dollars," the report stated, "and the average reduction on the rates of insurance is at least 40 cents on the 100 dollars. Every person who pays tax on real or personal estate actually pays less money now than he did previous to the introduction of the water."

Sources: Kenneth Holcomb Dunshee's *As You Pass By;* William Thompson Bonner's *New York, The World's Metropolis, 1623-1923.*

was convicted of embezzlement in 1874 and died in prison four years later. Estimates of the amount of money stolen from the city by Tweed and his associates over the better part of a scandalous decade ranged from $40 million to $100 million.[18]

During his tenure as public works commissioner, the Boyd's Corners Dam was beset with delays and graft. Its upstream face was banked with earth that was not rolled or rammed, a condition that may have led years later to the dam's ultimate reconstruction.[19]

The reservoir was designed as a hedge against drought. It would serve as a feeder for the original Croton Reservoir, whose supply would be augmented during the summer by upstream releases from Boyd's Corners into the Croton River. "If the demand for water should increase to such an extent that this reservoir would be insufficient, others similar can be built," said a prophetic *Putnam County Courier* on Oct. 6, 1866. "In the Croton Valley, there are fourteen other available sites capable of storing sixty billions of gallons, or enough to supply New York at the present rate of consumption for one thousand days."

The reservoir was finished in 1873. On Apr. 12, the *Brewster Standard* reported that the four-billion-gallon reservoir was overflowing.

Four years later, with New York in the grip of a prolonged drought, the Boyd's Corners Reservoir was nearly bone dry, exposing former pasture walls, stone foundations and traces of old cross roads. "Save in the very lowest points, where the water has stood fifty-four feet deep, all is brown, bare and black," related the *Putnam County Standard* on Nov. 10, 1876. "Below the dam is seen the four huge fountain pipes, from which, when the dam is full, the water rushes up 100 feet in the air, making a spectacle which draws many sight-seers."

Activity in the area that autumn, though, was focused on construction of yet another reservoir on the Middle Branch of the Croton River near Brewster, and on feverish attempts to capture the water from several Putnam County lakes to divert their flow into the city's two existing storage reservoirs.

"Everywhere the old outlets are being sunk lower," said the *Standard* of the work being conducted by 300 men on seven lakes and ponds. The task involved cutting down lake outlets by several feet, blasting new outlets and hand-digging six-foot-deep canals through quicksand and swamps of man-sized water lily roots to make pathways from one dwindling water source to another.

The battle between stubborn nature and shovel-wielding workmen mirrored the one between the city and the people who lived along those lake shores. It was a fight that continued for decades.

N. L. Thompson's Hotel, Lake Mahopac. To prevent contamination of the Croton Watershed, New York City in the 1890s ordered removal or relocation of properties lining the lakes of Putnam County. Seventy-five buildings on Lake Mahopac alone, including several hotels and boarding houses, were forced to move. Cornelia Cotton Gallery.

4. Lake Effects

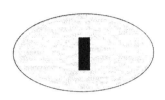

I N the summer of 1870, an unfamiliar man with deep pockets and an apparent lust for water made his appearance in the Putnam County lakes district.

First he approached Joseph Smith, owner of Rock Mill and 60 acres of land at the lower end of Lake Gilead. Mr. Smith, who had paid $4,000 for the property a few years earlier, was paid $25,000 for his holdings.

Isaac Hill, who owned 52 acres south of Kirk Lake, was paid $5,200 for the land which he had acquired for half that amount. Tillott Cole, who owned the outlet to Lake Gleneida, declined the purchase offer of Edward H. Tracey.

The local press, of course, was abuzz with speculation. "All kinds of rumors are in circulation concerning the object of these purchases," reported the *Putnam County Courier* of Carmel on Aug. 20, 1870, "but the most reasonable is that Mr. T. is connected with a heavy sewing machine company, which, foreseeing a brilliant future for this section of country, induced in part by the certainty of railroad communication therewith, desires to own and control all valuable water privileges, where sufficient power can be had to drive machinery. Soon after the completion of our railroad, we expect to see large factories erected at all the points named, and at many others also. The future for this section of country is full of promise."

In reality, the wheeling and dealing done by E. H. Tracey, an engineer for the Croton Water Department, had more to do with the Big City than with Big Business. For it was his task to buy up the water rights to natural lakes that could supplement the Croton Reservoir supply while the Boyd's Corners Reservoir was being built. A serious drought had occurred in 1869, and the city, whose 942,000 people were demanding 77 million gallons of water a day in 1870, was trying to stave off another water famine.[1]

And, with Boss Tweed and cohorts firmly in control of the city and its public works, money was apparently no object. Even Tillott Cole had his price, eventually leasing his property, including the water rights to Lake Gilead, to the Croton Water Department for $10,000, with the city having first option to buy the property for $30,000 at the end of five years.[2]

It didn't take long for the press and the public to realize what was happening. On Sept. 10, 1870, the *Putnam County Courier* reported that E. H. Tracey, the man who had supervised the building of High Bridge under John B. Jervis, had come to Carmel the previous week "armed with weapons more effective than the chassepot or needlegun"— $25,000 in cash, handed to Joseph Smith for his Rock Mill property. The deed, the paper reported, was given to William M. Tweed, not the corporation of the city of New York. "One thing is certain," the *Courier* said, "that he who furnished

the $25,000 and received therefore the considera-
tion named, paid a good round price for the whistle
and is fully entitled to all the music that can be
drawn from that instrument."

The following week the paper reported that the
dam at 179-acre Lake Gilead had been partially
removed to allow the water to drop three inches
per day into the Croton. The city, the *Courier* said,
planned to lower the lake by several feet. "It is a
great mistake for New York people to suppose that
they can come into the rural districts and do about
as they please, without reference to the rights or
interests of residents," warned the *Courier* on Sept.
17, 1870.

By October, a petition was submitted to the
city's water commissioners bearing the signatures
of Putnam County residents protesting the draining of the lakes and ruining the natural beauty of
the area, as well as endangering the public health
by baring lake bottoms. A public meeting was held
at Smalley's Hotel in the county seat of Carmel on
Lake Gleneida, where angry property owners contributed money for a court action seeking an injunction against the city's further drawing down
the lake.[3] A Kirk Lake resident, Solomon Hill, also
sought to stop the city's excavating the outlet of
that lake, and sued for $10,000 in damages. His
brother, Isaac Hill, reputed several years earlier to
have sold to New York City 52 acres of his farm
on the opposite side of the lake, testified in Supreme Court in 1878 that the city's draining of the
lake left four or five acres of his land bare. This, he
said, made it difficult for his cattle and horses to get
to water and caused every member of his family
and several neighbors to come down with "fever
and ague."[4] Another property owner, J. G. Miller,
took Tillott Cole to court for damages he said
resulted when Cole dammed Lake Gleneida on
behalf of the city and raised the water level above
the normal high water mark, flooding his lands.[5]

A bill proposed by Tweed to give him the
authority to buy or condemn land for New York
City water supply purposes, or to draw down
watershed lakes by four feet—more if he deemed
it an emergency—was debated during the fall of
1871 by the state legislature. But few doubted the

outcome, given Tweed's reputed propensity to co-
erce, cajole and buy off opponents. "No despot in
Europe has such limitless power over the exche-
quer of his country as this bill confers upon Mr.
Tweed," complained the *Courier* on Feb. 18, 1871,
when it reported the bill's passage. "If Mr. Tweed
should introduce a bill in the legislature ceding
Putnam County to him and his heirs forever, we
have no doubt of his ability to pass it. To such ends
have we come at last."

Some, however, responded to the act with wry
humor. "It is reported that a spring of pure Holland gin has been discovered at Croton Falls,"
wrote the *Brewster Standard* on Dec. 16, 1871. "We
learn that every effort is being made by the inhabitants of Westchester County to keep it out of the
river. The city of New York is therefore fully
guaranteed against getting any."

In 1872 came a bill to repeal the 1871 act. The
city was quick to object, claiming the additional
water had led to more and larger buildings in the
city, which would be unprotected against fire if the
water rights were withdrawn. Tweed's successor,
new Public Works Commissioner Van Nort,
pleaded to the legislature that the increased water
supply had also led to "a general substitution of
water closets in place of noxious and unwholesome
privies," and requested that the 1871 bill be allowed
to run out in 1875. By then the city would have
two new reservoirs in place on the West Branch of
the Croton River and would no longer need the
lakes.[6]

But Lakes Gleneida, Kirk and Gilead remained
under the city's control, as do they still. However,
in 1877 came state legislation that, while allowing
the city to collect and retain Westchester and Putnam waters, prevented it from claiming water from
resort-lined Lakes Mahopac and Gleneida between
March and September. And it required damage and
riparian rights claims to be heard in the county of
origin, a right that several wealthy landowners
along Lake Mahopac took advantage of. Property
owners claimed there were aesthetic drawbacks and
health risks to lowered lake levels (although Engineer E. H. Tracey, suffering from heart disease,
chose Smalley's Hotel on the shores of Gleneida to

spend his final days in September of 1875). Others pointed to efforts by residents to benefit from extended shorelines.

"Some owners are taking advantage of the low water to dig the shore deeper and build walls father out, as land is valuable here, especially on deep water fronts," the *Putnam County Standard* reported. The battle continued on many other fronts, including Peach, Haines and Waccabuc Lakes, and White, Barrett and Mud Ponds. In fact, Water Department Engineer Thomas Eddis Emmet, whose task was to divert as much water as possible from Putnam lakes, declared in the *Putnam County Standard* of Nov. 10, 1876, that the city should buy up the east half of the county, dam all the lakes, turn the region into a public park and sell the timber to pay for the work.

While, in 1877, published accounts spoke of the "crystal clear" lakes in the Croton watershed, their shores "luxuriously wooded," their environs "romantic,"[7] others found them undependable, vulnerable to drought conditions and too often stagnant. "The whole Croton system is a sham and a delusion," declared H. G. Eastman in a proposal to New York Mayor William Wickham on Nov. 24, 1876. Water, said Eastman, a professor from Poughkeepsie, "hasn't reached the second story in the higher districts since 1868. For the hundredth time, we are now told again by officials not to be alarmed, that there is an abundance of water lying around loose up in Putnam and Dutchess Counties and it only needs plenty of new ponds to give us a bountiful supply. We don't believe it."[8]

Eastman had a plan to pump water from the Hudson and pipe it into the Croton system. The city didn't buy into that idea, but some years later agreed with his contention that much of the city's water supply was foul and a likely source of contagion.

Even as Manhattan and environs were growing (by an average of 22,000 people a year during the 1870s, 27,000 annually in the 1880s),[9] so were the northern "rural districts," which would ultimately be called the "suburbs." In 1888, when the State Board of Health surveyed the region, an estimated 20,000 people resided in the Croton Reservoir watershed. Horses, cows and other livestock numbered more than 12,000.[10] Animals and their human masters were accompanied, of course, by barns and manure-filled barnyards, privies and cesspools, tanneries, mills and slaughter houses. With so much effort and money having gone into its reservoirs and lakes, the city was not anxious to have all that hard-won water debased.

Enter Michael T. Daly, commissioner of Public Works for the city, who, acting under the orders of the Webster Act passed by the state legislature in March 1893, launched what became known as Daly's Raids in the Croton watershed. Armed with a law to "provide for the sanitary protection" of New York's water, and a directive from the Common Council to provide a 300-foot margin around reservoirs and along streams that fed them, Daley and his men fanned out across the countryside, ordering homes evacuated, barns and pigsties removed, privies burned.[11] Time was of the essence, they claimed, for cholera was once again threatening the city.

Those who failed to obey verbal warnings to get out found condemnation posters nailed to trees and outbuildings:

> *The property occupied by you in the Town of Bedford, Westchester County, has been condemned by the Commissioner of Public Works of the City of New York under provisions of Chapter 189 of the Laws of 1893. You have been notified to vacate, and no steps have as yet been taken. If you desire to avoid a summary removal, you will vacate the premises within 8 days from the service of this notice. Yours &c, H. T. Dykman, Counsel in Charge.*[12]

The *Illustrated American* of Apr. 22, 1893 likened Daly's forays into Putnam, Westchester and Dutchess Counties to "Sherman's march to the sea, or the Vandals' descent upon Rome. Mansion and hut, factory and shop, cottage and pig-sty, farm and barnyard, stable, hen-coop, pigeon roost, an infinity of what the law construes to be nuisances, were laid waste without pity or sentiment, or the remotest consideration for the feelings or fate of their owners."

Island tapping

In their compulsion to tap every available water source for the growing metropolis, the City of Brooklyn and a host of private water companies laid pipes and installed pumps all over Long Island.

Ponds, wells and subsurface infiltration chambers captured surface and groundwater, which was relayed to Brooklyn, located on the western end of the 115-mile-long island, through miles of underground brick-lined conduits.

Long Island was eyed for its water potential as far back as the 1850s, when a steady stream of experts proposed tapping subterranean rivers, exploiting springs or building an open canal. A plan proposed by Brooklyn's Common Council to convey the waters of Baisley's Pond through a nine-mile conduit to a reservoir on Mt. Prospect near Prospect Park was defeated in a public referendum in 1853, but that didn't stop the city from buying land and water rights. In 1856, the council subscribed $1.3 million to the stock of the private Nassau Water Company on the condition that it build a water system capable of supplying 20 million gallons a day, and that the City of Brooklyn have the right to buy the whole plant at cost.

In July 1856, ground was broken by the Nassau Water Company for the Ridgewood Reservoir in Cypress Hills, the highest point in Brooklyn. The following year, the city did indeed buy out the company, completing the project by the end of 1858. In April 1859, the public hailed the accomplishment, which signaled a departure from the exclusive use of wells and cisterns on the island.

By 1896, just before its consolidation with Greater New York, the City of Brooklyn had expanded the Ridgewood system to encompass 2,700 acres of land drawing from a watershed that embraced almost all of Nassau County. The system, which included 16 supply ponds connected by a network of conduits and pumping stations, had cost Brooklyn $22 million to develop.

When the New York City Board of Water Supply was established in 1905, it set up a Long Island Department. Engineer Walter Spear supervised division offices at Freeport and Babylon, and a team of more than 70 people proceeded to conduct surveys and install test wells, rain gauges and observation stations with an eye toward improving the existing system and further developing groundwater sources in Suffolk County adjoining the Ridgewood system.

In 1908, a plan to develop a groundwater supply of 250 million gallons per day from Suffolk County was submitted to the State Water Supply Commission for approval. The BWS proposed to sink a continuous line of wells along the south shore, from Amityville to Quogue, and in the Peconic Valley. The water would be transmitted by gravity in a 40-mile-long masonry aqueduct from Great River to the Ridgewood pumping station in the now-Borough of Brooklyn. The three-stage project would carry an estimated price tag of $47 million.

Meanwhile, construction of the Catskill System had begun and the BWS held off on its Long Island plans. In 1912, the Board of Estimate and Apportionment recommended that the petition to the re-named State Conservation Commission for permission to begin Suffolk County development be withdrawn. Citing "satisfactory progress in the Esopus watershed, on the Catskill aqueduct, [and] the pressure tunnel and pipelines in the city," the BWS, in its 1912 Annual Report, explained that "It seemed better business policy to develop the Catskill supply to the full capacity of the present aqueduct, 500 million gallons daily, before incurring the great expense to which the city would be subjected in the development of further supplies of water from Long Island."

However, the city continued to draw on and improve the Ridgewood System, which in 1916 supplied 73 million gallons a day from wells, and 20 million gallons daily from surface supplies, including Hempstead Reservoir. Two infiltration galleries—tiled, open-jointed sewer pipe totaling six miles in length and laid 10 to 15 feet below groundwater—collected another 34 million gallons a day. It cost an estimated $1 million to pump Ridgewood water to the highest points of the system in 1916, the year before the introduction of Catskill water eliminated that expense.

A number of private water systems also supplied water to Long Islanders. They included the Flatbush Water Works, the Citizens Water Supply Company and the Woodhaven Water Company. Over the years, the city acquired these systems, and subsequently closed them as their supplies fell victim to pollution or overpumping, followed by salt water intrusion. The state water authorities, citing the overdevelopment of the subsurface sources, rejected a 1932 BWS application to drill more wells in Kings, Queens and Nassau Counties that the city said would have provided up to 94 million gallons per day in times of drought.

The ponds and wells used for the Ridgewood system were ultimately abandoned.

Still, underground aquifers currently contribute approximately two percent of the city's daily water supply. Ever mindful of the need for more water, the city purchased the last remaining private water system, the Queens portion of the Jamaica Water Supply Company, in 1996. The

acquisition represented the first new water supply source for the city since the addition of the Cannonsville Reservoir in Delaware County in 1965.

The system purchased by the city included 69 wells, 12 storage tanks, 700 miles of water mains, 7,500 fire hydrants and 90,000 accounts. The city currently operates 45 of the wells, which yield 33 million gallons per day. This water from the Southeast Queens System is mixed with surface water from the Catskill-Delaware System to supply 500,000 residents of Richmond Hill, Kew Gardens, Jamaica, Ozone Park, Briarwood and other communities.

Sources: Edward H. Hall's *Water for New York City* (1917); *Water Supply System of the City of New York* (BWS, 1952); *The Water Supply of the City of New York* (Dept. of Water Supply, Gas and Electricity, 1937); BWS Annual Reports (1906, 1907, 1908, 1912); *New York City Municipal Water Finance Authority Bond Prospectus* (1998); *Thirsty City, A Plan of Action for New York City Water Supply* (1986)

The magazine noted, however, that the action was necessary to preserve the water for the 1.8 million people who now lived in the city. It included photographs showing a sewer pipe draining into the outlet of Tonetta Brook and pig pens lined up on the shore of Lake Gleneida in Carmel. The article also pointed out that "Those who have suffered by it will receive liberal compensation for their pecuniary damage."

The damage, was, in fact, fairly substantial. From the time the raids began on Apr. 12, 1893, through late May of that year, the number of "principal nuisances abated" was 529. More than 150 buildings, including seven mills, one tannery and one slaughter house, were sold and removed, and 33 additional estates situated close to reservoirs had been condemned.[13]

Property owners were paid for the land and buildings the city took, and then were allowed to

buy the structures back at auction if they wished, and dismantle or move them back behind the buffer zone. The *Brewster Standard* of Sept. 15, 1893 reported that 203 structures sold for $4,443 under the gavel of auctioneer Frank Townsend, who strode through village and fields trailed by 200 bidders and twice as many spectators. E. E. Birch bought back his steam mill with its cider press and saws, for $42. Mrs. J. H. Holmes claimed her barn and storehouse for $19.50 and planned to move them a few feet to just outside the city boundary. F. R. Hall, the paper related, "took the tallest house in town, the Chase place erected 20 years ago by George F. Bailey. He paid $230 for it and will move it to the rear of his Main Street lot."

Twenty-five structures in the hamlet of Thomasville were sold and the area cleared. The hamlet of Towners was nearly eliminated—a hotel, two feed stores, a shop and several homes, leaving the Harlem Railroad depot the only building standing. Parts of the villages of Patterson and Mt. Kisco were taken, and old communities like Southeast Center, Mill Town, Farmers Mills and Red Mills were claimed. Along the Muscoot and the Middle Branch, Branch Creek and Tonetta Brook, inspectors and demolition crews examined every parcel.

"A slaughter house near Lake Mahopac was one of the worst nuisances," related the *Brewster Standard* on Apr. 12, 1895. "Along the lake about 75 houses were condemned and the proprietors of seven or eight summer hotels upon the lake shore, which accommodate about 1,200 persons in the summer, were ordered to remove their outbuildings outside the danger line."

Even the dead were not safe from Daly's reach. Hearing that a destitute man who'd been strangled in Carmel had been interred in Potter's Field on the Putnam County Farm within 75 feet of a stream, the city's health commissioner urged Daly to issue an order requiring metal caskets and special permission from the city to be buried within 1,000 feet of a watercourse. The order applied to a dozen cemeteries in just the immediate vicinity. The pauper whose untimely exit had caused such a stir was exhumed from Potter's Field, and reinterred in a new cemetery on the County Farm, an acceptable distance from the stream.[14]

Condemnations and subsequent auctions went on through the end of that year and much of 1894. Frank Townsend, the *Brewster Standard* said on Dec. 8, 1893, "made quick work of the sale at Carmel yesterday, knocking down over 100 structures in less than seven hours." They included a schoolhouse and two privies ($25), a blacksmith shop, a feed store, and the New York Milk and Cream Co. factory ($83). The factory's ice house sold for $36.

David Lockwood's hotel in Carmel was another establishment doomed in Daly's Raid, but he appeared to profit from the action. Lockwood bought the hotel back from the city for $7 at auction, and a year later, after a damage commissioner had heard his claim for remuneration, he was awarded $24,858 for the property. While some of the buildings were the subject of spirited bidding, most were allowed to go to their former owners if such was their desire. One newspaper account described the scene outside Ellen Morgan's house in Brewster when it came time to see her home auctioned. "The old lady covered her face with her apron, and with many sobs and sighs moved her tottering form down to the gate. She cried out, 'Five dollars!' 'Let her have it,' said a chorus of voices on the piazza. It was as good as a play. . ." reported the paper. "No one could go up against such an exhibition as that." Mrs. Morgan got her house for $5, and all the outbuildings for 50 cents.[15]

It is not hard to imagine the activity that must have consumed those villages over several months as families looked for new homes or land on which to move their old ones. "Housemovers and contractors have been busy negotiating with purchasers for the removal of buildings, the work in many instances has been commenced and scarcely an idle man can be found," said the *Brewster Standard*, ON Sept. 22, 1893. Buildings were moved over rolling logs, using horses, ropes and capstans.

In the spring of 1894, the *Putnam County Republican* in Carmel reported on an industrious scene:

> The Hazen store building is well along toward its new foundation in the park. The brick house has been advanced as far as the triangle. The south half of the Gleneida Hotel is being prepared for removal by C. Vorndran's men. Work was commenced Tuesday by a gang of Italians on the foundation for the Palmer Block on the new site purchased by Mrs. B. D. Crane.

The newspaper was actually printed in the Palmer Block as it was being moved. "Business is being carried on as usual in all the stores and offices in the building," reported the *Republican* on June 9, 1894. "It is expected that the building will reach its new site by Saturday night." (The Palmer Block was destroyed by fire on its new site four years later.)

In Brewster, Lincoln Frank was a house mover of renown. "Since September 23, he has moved 16 dwellings and without a mishap worth speaking of," said the *Standard* of Nov. 17, 1893. "So sure and steady is the transit that families, if they choose, occupy the house from the time it leaves the old foundation until is set down on the new site."

But the same reporter decried the chaotic appearance of Marvin Avenue, where all the buildings on one side of the street had to be moved to the other. "Every property owner has located his building irrespective of every other building, no two buildings are on the same line, and every other house faces in a different direction."

Work of a different sort was going on all across the region as contractors hired by the city cleaned and filled in outhouse pits and cesspools. The *Brewster Standard* reported on Sept. 29, 1893 that the New York Fertilizer Company had arrived in town and expected to hire 25 to 50 men and several teams of horses to do the work. "In each vault and cesspool, the sewage will be treated with a powerful absorbant made of marl, copperas and chloride of lime. The sewage will thus be converted into an odorless and harmless powder, no more obnoxious than Pillsbury's flour, and as easily handled. This material will be put up in barrels and sold as a fertilizer of high grade."

There was, of course, opposition to the city's heavy-handed intrusion in these communities. In Mount Kisco, local authorities, in an act of protest, arrested two city contractors for breaking the Sabbath as they filled in a "filthy hole" in the rear of Henry Boehmer's beer bottling establishment on a Sunday.[16]

And William Tilford, a farmer from Lake Mahopac, sued the city for $5,000 after health officers quarantined his house when one of his sons was stricken with typhoid fever. None of the family was allowed to leave the residence for a month, and for two weeks several men were engaged digging a deep ditch around the house. Tilford wanted recompense for false imprisonment and for prolonging his son's illness because of noise of the ditch diggers. Another son, unable to return to the house from his farm job, took to drinking, his father said, claiming another $1,000 in damages.[17]

The purification effort included an experimental "electrozone" sewage-treatment plant set up in Brewster. The brainchild of Col. Albert E. Wolf, the system mixed common table salt with water and ran electric current through the resulting sodium chloride creating a "hypochloride" disinfectant. This chlorine solution was passed into a tank where it was mixed with raw sewage piped from Brewster's business district and ultimately discharged to a subsurface tile field. City records show that the electozone plant was relocated years later and burned down in 1911. It was replaced with a sewage-treatment plant that used chlorine bleach as a disinfectant.[18]

Back in 1894, however, New York City still had to take drastic action to curb pollutants. Mayor Gilroy, in an address reported in the Jan. 12, 1894, *Brewster Standard*, explained the actions taken to "permanently remedy the evils." Up to that point, the city, he said, had removed 356 privies, 120 barnyards, five factories, and 1,000 "miscellaneous" nuisances.

It was imperative, after all, that the city protect its investment in Putnam and Westchester Counties, an investment that by 1894 included several lakes, seven completed reservoirs, and four reservoirs under construction.

5. Liquid Links

HILE workers toiled to finish the Boyd's Corners Dam and drought pushed the city to siphon rural lakes, a desperate Croton Water Department forged ahead with plans for its third major reservoir project.

In November 1871, two years before completion of Boyd's Corners, surveyors found a site for a new dam on the Middle Branch of the Croton River, a mile west of Brewster Station and just north of Drewville in the Town of Southeast, Putnam County. The 500-acre Middle Branch Reservoir would cover the Isaac Kelly flats, and, reported a local newspaper on Nov. 25, 1871, Mr. Kelly's recently constructed mansion was expected to make a "comfortable and commodious boarding house" while the work was going on.

It was another two years, though, before contractors Belden & Denison began work in earnest. The project was a big one---build a stone and cement core wall for an earthen dam 500 feet long,

94 feet high and 660 feet wide across its base; dig a 700-foot masonry tunnel 15 feet wide and 12 feet high to divert the water during construction; construct five miles of macadamized road around the new lake, and nine miles of stone fence to mark its boundaries, "all to be finished in two years," related the *Putnam County Standard* of Dec. 18, 1873.

But the Middle Branch actually took twice that long to build. Known locally as the Tilly Foster Reservoir after a magnetic iron ore mine located nearby, the project employed hundreds of men, many of them Swedish immigrants. Shovel-bearing laborers were paid $1.12 a day during 1877. Tunnel workers got $1.50 for 10-hour days spent drilling and blasting. Masons who cut and placed the stones on the face of the dam and on the abutment of a 75-foot-long highway bridge received $3 a day.[1]

A steam shovel on a moveable track scooped up rock and dirt blasted off the hillsides and loaded railroad cars pulled by a small locomotive named "The Pioneer." The cars hauled the material to a dump site, where men filled horse carts with dirt. Sixty to 80 teams made 35 trips a day to the dam site. It took the average worker a minute and a half to load a cart. "There is a great difference in shovelers," declared a reporter writing for the *Putnam County Standard* of June 8, 1877. "We noticed some of them would pick up but 12 shovel-fulls a minute, while others would handle 15 or 18 in the same time."

Facing page, top: The Middle Branch Reservoir, known locally as the Tilly Foster Reservoir for an iron mine nearby, was built near Brewster between 1873 and 1878. Photo by Robert Kornfeld, Jr., AIA.

Bottom: The Amawalk Reservoir Dam, built in the 1890s and repaired a century later, impounds the Muscoot River, Town of Somers. Robert Kornfeld, Jr., AIA.

The old Kensico Reservoir, shown in this 1908 photograph, was created in 1881 by damming
the Bronx River and claiming much of Kensico village in Westchester County. NYC DEP.

A Waring steam drill, an "ingenious, labor saving invention," was used to drill blasting holes in the tunnel heading. "Only eight to ten men can work comfortably in the heading since all their work is done with sledge hammers and drills, therefore it is not a very comfortable place for human hands and heads," reported the *Standard* on July 30, 1875.

Six or eight blacksmiths were employed sharpening drills and replacing horseshoes, and many youngsters were hired to sprinkle water on the dirt dam and bring drinking water to the workers. Other laborers cleared trees, shrubs, stone walls and rail fences from the 500-acre reservoir after an assortment of buildings, including several homes and barns, a schoolhouse, and a saw and feed mill, were purchased by the city, auctioned and either moved or razed.[2]

It was appetite-inducing work. "The laborers get good substantial board, and in two days will put away 300 pounds of meat, an average of 2 and 1/2 pounds a day. Mr. Mackey keeps 60 boarders, Mr. Fay has about 20 boarders, Cap Manville about the

same number. There are several other places where from three to ten men find bed and board, and from the number of meat and grocery wagons which daily go the rounds, it is probable they all get enough to eat."[3]

Tuesdays were paydays when $3,000 was disbursed by the paymaster. The boarding house keepers got a big proportion of that—about $1 a week per man. Some workers lived in shanties on the hillsides. They found danger, and sometimes pleasure, on the project. The *Brewster Standard* of June 4, 1875, reported that a 22-year-old Swede named Martin Bangston died when he was hit in the head by a rock near a blasting site. The following March, another Swedish worker was killed when his drill struck blasting powder that had not fired on a previous round.

But at least one dam laborer met his bride on the project. John Conklin married Mary Mackey, daughter of the boardinghouse keeper, in May 1876.[4]

Overseeing the job were the Syracuse contractors Belden & Denison. While building the Middle

Branch Reservoir, the firm was enlarging a canal in St. Catherine's, Ontario, and constructing another canal in western New York. The firm was accused of manipulating state canal contracts, and in 1875 H. D. Denison was arrested for contempt for refusing to hand over company books to a commission investigating the matter.[5]

Despite the controversy, the Middle Branch project was completed, its impounded water stored and sent downriver to the Croton Reservoir as needed. The city was growing—in 1874, another 13,000 acres in part of Westchester County had been annexed and 50,000 people added to the population. The demand for water ballooned, so at about the time the Middle Branch was sewn up, Commissioner of Public Works Allan Campbell directed that a survey be made of the Bronx and Byram Rivers to see if it was feasible to tap into those sources.[6]

In 1879, Campbell proposed a multi-faceted system that involved building four dams: a small one to convert the twin Rye Ponds into a 280-acre reservoir; a larger dam across the Bronx River near Kensico Station to create a 250-acre reservoir; another on the Byram River near the Connecticut state line, and a receiving reservoir at Williamsbridge. The plan also entailed laying 15 miles of 48-inch pipeline, the Bronx Conduit, from Kensico Reservoir to the Williamsbridge facility.[7]

By 1881, in the midst of another water shortage, the city was putting this latest plan in motion with the construction of the first Kensico Reservoir to serve the newly annexed Westchester towns of Morrisania, Kingsbridge and West Farms.[8]

The 45-foot-high masonry dam on the Bronx River created a reservoir one and a half miles long and less than a half-mile wide. The 230-acre lake had a storage capacity of 1,797,000 gallons.[9]

A few hundred people lived in old Kensico village, where, from the hilltops to the east, one could see Long Island Sound 24 miles away. This was largely a farming region, dotted with water-powered industries and mills. Its residents included the Raven family, who had immigrated from Germany, purchased a farm along the Bronx River and turned it into a hotel to service travelers. John and Caroline Raven, undeterred by the coming of the reservoir, engaged teams of horses and oxen and many men to pull their little hotel on logs up the hill, where it served as a boarding house for dam workers.

Later, visitors who had come to admire the lake and fish its waters spent time at what had been named the Lake View Hotel. In the winter, people skated on the lake and the hotel cut ice from its surface to serve as refrigeration the rest of the year.[10] But the Ravens, who had raised 11 children along Lake Kensico, were dislocated once more less than a quarter century later when their establishment, part of an extended community that had grown up around the reservoir's shores, was obliterated to make way for a larger dam.

That facility, the so-called new Kensico Dam, was built just 300 feet upstream from the old dam on the Bronx River, creating a many-tentacled lake that swallowed the original reservoir and much of the surrounding countryside. The Raven family finally abandoned their hotel and farm at the intersection of Old Orchard St. and old Route 22, and moved to a new farm near Armonk.

Meanwhile, the population of Manhattan was ballooning, from 1.1 million in 1880 to 1.4 million a decade later.[11] Water consumption rose from 92 million gallons per day in 1880 to 100 million gallons daily in 1885, and 145 million gallons in 1890.[12]

The strain on the old Croton Aqueduct had become evident in the 1870s, and surveys for a new aqueduct had been undertaken as early as 1873. Engineers from the Department of Public Works had begun a survey for a new and larger dam on the East Branch of the Croton River in 1877.[13] But it was not until 1881, with a severe drought in progress, that Isaac Newton, chief engineer of the Croton Aqueduct, presented a special report to Public Works Commissioner Hubert Thompson outlining the problem and recommending a new, larger Croton Reservoir and Aqueduct.

Detailed plans for the new dam, and the aqueduct which would deliver 250 million gallons of water daily to the city, were delivered to Mayor William R. Grace. On Jan. 9, 1883, the state senate

Disaster in Pennsylvania

The East Branch and Bog Brook Reservoirs (Double Reservoir I) were under construction in Putnam County during the spring of 1889 as a catastrophe unfolded in western Pennsylvania downstream from another earthen dam.

There, after a night of heavy rain, the South Fork Dam 12 miles from Johnstown gave way on May 31, sending a 37-foot wall of water crashing down the Conemaugh Valley. Within minutes, 20 million tons of water laid waste to several villages and four square miles of the city of Johnstown, killing at least 2,209 people and destroying 1,600 homes and 280 businesses.

For weeks afterwards, readers of newspapers in the U.S. and abroad were swept up in daily accounts of the tragedy—85-ton locomotives swept nearly a mile; huge steel mills obliterated; 99 entire families wiped out; bodies found as far away as Cincinnati; $12 million in property lost; mass burials, misery and disease. All this because a 72-foot high dam impounding a recreational lake had burst.

Croton Aqueduct Chief Engineer Alphonse Fteley was dispatched to Johnstown to both report back to the commission on the cause of the disaster and participate in a professional examination of the dam break. Fteley, along with engineers James Frances, F. E. Worthen and M. J. Becker, formed a committee which issued a report on the failure of the South Fork Dam for the American Society of Civil Engineers in June 1891. In general they blamed the South Fork Fishing and Hunting Club, whose members included wealthy businessmen and industrialists such as Andrew Carnegie, Andrew Mellon and Henry Clay Phipps, for failure to maintain the dam, clear the spillway, and properly repair an earlier break.

It may be that the Pennsylvania tragedy made the Aqueduct Commission particularly cautious as it built the New Croton Dam from 1892 to 1906. At one point, cracks in the unfinished masonry of the earthen dam's core wall—the dam was to be more than twice as tall as the South Fork Dam—led to trepidations that it would not be watertight, so the commission ordered it torn down and rebuilt (Chapter 7).

Nearly a century later, another dam failure, this time in Idaho, had similar repercussions in the Croton system. The collapse of the Teton River Dam as it was being filled for the first time June 5, 1976 flooded 300 square miles, killed 14 people and caused damage estimated at $1 billion. It resulted in passage of the federal Dam Safety Act and inspection of all dams across the country.

The Boyd's Corners Dam, the oldest in the Croton system, was red-flagged because inspectors claimed there was no adherence between the concrete core wall and its rock foundation. Although city officials disagreed, the reservoir was drained in 1978 and remained a 273-acre mud flat until reconstruction was begun in 1988. Boyd's Corners was placed back in service in 1993.

Sources: Johnstown Flood Museum; Anwei Skinsnes Law's *The Great Flood, Johnstown, Pennsylvania, 1889* (1997); Charles H. Weidner's *Water for a City* (1974); Gordon Carruth's *Encyclopedia of American Facts and Dates* (1987); Carl Picha, District Engineer, NYC Water Supply, 1998.

passed a resolution authorizing the mayor to appoint a commission to investigate the situation and report on its feasibility. A five-man committee named on Mar. 7, 1883, reported back to the senate, recommending a new aqueduct and storage reservoirs be developed under the eye of a special commission. Three months later, the legislature passed "An Act to provide new reservoirs, dams and a new aqueduct. . . for the purpose of supplying the City of New York with an increased supply of pure and wholesome water." [14]

The act placed authority for developing the project in the hands of a Board of Aqueduct Commissioners, and designated the Department of Public Works as the agency for making surveys and designing and drafting the plans. The first Croton Aqueduct Commission consisted of Mayor Franklin Edson, Comptroller and former Public Works

Commissioner Allan Campbell, current DPW Commissioner Hubert Thompson and three citizens: James C. Spencer, George W. Lane and William Dowd.[15]

The commission directed the Public Works Department to come up with plans for a new aqueduct and sufficient supply reservoirs "to secure all the water that can be obtained from the Croton Lake and River," and to build immediately a reservoir or reservoirs to store the waters of the East Branch of the Croton and its tributaries.[16]

This quest for water for New York was the start of a spate of dam-building that over the course of the next generation brought wealth to dozens of contractors, work to thousands of mostly immigrant laborers, and woe to many landowners in Putnam and Westchester Counties.

As surveys were made and construction begun for the new Croton Aqueduct and dam (Chapters 6 and 7), the East Branch Reservoir and four others like it also took form between 1888 and 1897, under the auspices of Alphonse Fteley, the commission's chief engineer.

The East Branch Reservoir near the village of Brewster was formed by the Sodom Dam across the East Branch of the Croton. It was connected by a 1,773-foot tunnel to the Bog Brook Reservoir, which was built at approximately the same time. Thus the projects were designated Double Reservoir I.

Sullivan, Rider & Dougherty were the successful bidders for the Sodom Dam and resulting 553-acre reservoir. They built a masonry dam 500 feet long across the river, and a 600-foot-long, 75-foot-high earthen dam with a masonry core wall on a ridge perpendicular with the 78-foot-high masonry dam. That dam was 53 feet thick at its base and 12 feet thick at is crest. [17]

Construction was begun in February 1888, an inauspicious time, since the famed Blizzard of '88 paralyzed the region a month later. The river was diverted by a temporary cribwork dam while a trench for the permanent dam's foundation was excavated. "In the center, near the bottom, large iron pipes with gates are built into the foundation, the pipes being eventually the escape or outlet for

The East Branch Reservoir, Putnam County, during construction in the 1880s.
Reports on the New Croton Aqueduct Reservoirs and Dams, 1895-1907.

the water, and while the dam is being built, they serve as a waste weir or outlet for the river," related *Harper's New Monthly Magazine* in 1889.

The first stone, quarried from a nearby hillside, was laid on the dam in August 1888. A 637-foot steel cable was stretched across the valley between two towers anchored into bedrock. The cableway, perhaps the first instance of its use in dam construction, allowed materials and equipment to be transported to any spot on the dam, eliminating the need for derricks and increasing efficiency and safety.[18]

The East Branch reservoir was placed into service July 4, 1892, and was finished October 31. From a gatehouse built on the upstream face of the dam, water was allowed to flow from any of three elevations through two 48-inch outlet pipes to a circular fountain basin 80 feet in diameter. There the water was aerated before it was discharged into the river channel to flow to the new Croton Reservoir, completed some years later.[19]

Harper's noted that the taking of 1,472 acres for the East Branch Reservoir required the removal of several homes. "The million people in the city need a reserve of drinking water, and twenty-one families must move out of their quiet rural homes and see their hearths sink deep under water," the magazine said. Three saw and grist mills, a sash and blind factory and a carriage factory were among the buildings on 111 parcels taken for the project.[20]

Exactly a year after the contract was let for the Sodom Dam, the contract for the Bog Brook Reservoir was awarded to David R. Paige and Company. The project consisted of two earthen dams with masonry core walls. Dam #1, 1,340 feet long, 60 feet high and 25 feet wide at the top, impounded tiny Bog Brook. Dam #2, 1,956 feet long, 24 feet high and 12 feet wide at the crest, traversed a depression between the brook and another small stream. A gatehouse and aeration jets were provided at Dam #1, which was started in February 1889. Dam #2 was begun in April of the following year, and both were completed by Aug. 15, 1893.[21]

The East Branch Reservoir was served by a 73-square-mile watershed and had a storage capacity of 5.2 billion gallons. The Bog Brook Reservoir could store 4.4 billion gallons, taken from a much smaller watershed of just 3.5 square miles. To equalize the supply, the reservoirs were connected by a tunnel 10 feet in diameter, excavated through rock and lined with brick, backed by rubble masonry. The flow between the two reservoirs was regulated at a gatehouse at the north portal of the tunnel, near the Bog Brook Reservoir.[22]

The city acquired 1,962 acres of land for Double Reservoir I, including additional surrounding parcels taken in 1896 and 1897 to "abate nuisances and prevent the erection of objectionable buildings near the reservoirs."[23] One area resident, A. F. Avery of Katonah, writing in the *Putnam County Courier* of Oct. 23, 1891, declared that the "nuisances" contaminating the water supply originated not along the shorelines of its reservoirs, but on what had been allowed to remain within the flow line.

"Yesterday I took occasion to visit some of the reservoirs in Putnam County, especially the one at Sodam [sic]," Avery wrote. "Upon examination, I found that no attention had been paid to the natural filth that necessarily exists in a new basin, the old tanyard of Chester Crosby, barnyards, privies, etc. have been allowed to remain and to be submerged, and at the present moment, the people of New York City are using water reeking with these impurities. Under such circumstances, why should anyone expect the water free from bad tastes and smells."

Despite such complaints, and objections raised by people forced to relinquish their properties, the commission took control of additional acreage and tallied the cost for all of the land acquired for the double reservoir at $473 per acre. According to the aqueduct commission's reports, the total cost for the two projects, including land, construction, engineering and legal expenses, came to almost two million dollars.

The cost to area communities was great as well. Most of Southeast Center, the original center of the Town of Southeast, was taken for the East Branch Reservoir, and parts of the New York and New England Railroad had to be relocated. More than 200 buildings were auctioned and torn down or moved to make way for the reservoirs (four reser-

The Village of Brewster in the Town of Southeast saw four New York City reservoirs built in its environs.
Cornelia Cotton Gallery.

voirs were built in the township).[24] Because prime farmland and many industrial sites were removed, the area saw a precipitous decline in population. The 1892 census showed 14,165 people in Putnam County, a decline of 684 since the 1890 counting of 14,849 residents. That number was down significantly from the 1880 census of 15,181 and the 1875 record of 15,799.[25]

The impact of reservoir construction sometimes took years to be fully felt. The Borden Condensary in Southeast, where evaporated milk was made from milk provided by as many as 200 farms, saw its fortunes dwindle as those farms were displaced. It finally closed in 1915. The Tilly Foster Mine, once an important source of iron ore for the eastern U.S., not to mention substantial regional employment, was spared from destruction by the Middle Branch Reservoir in the 1870s, but its owners blamed the reservoir for the mine's underground flooding in 1897. The courts ordered the reservoir drained, but the flooding continued. An errant spring was ultimately found to be the culprit. The mine, beset by accidents as well, subsequently closed.[26]

Such clashes did not deter the city from continuing development of the Croton Water System, however. On Mar. 12, 1890, ground was broken for the 734-acre Titicus Reservoir near the hamlet of Purdys in northern Westchester County. Washburn, Shaler & Washburn got the contract to build what was known as Reservoir M, and spent nearly five years on the project.[27]

The Borden Condensary in Brewster closed in 1915 because so many farms that had supplied it with milk were taken for reservoirs. Southeast Museum, gift of Louse Townsend.

The following description of the dam and its construction is excerpted from Edward Wegmann's *Water Supply of the City of New York 1658-1895*:

The 534-foot central part of the dam and its spillway were constructed of masonry on bedrock foundation. Two earthen wings, of 732 and 253 feet respectively, extended from the central portion, which rose 109 feet from the surface. The upstream face of the dam was lined with stones of up to 30 cubic feet in size, with cement mortar filling the spaces between. Cement was brought to the dam over a spur of the New York and Harlem Railway. The sand with which the cement was mixed was delivered by teams of horses to a large cement house. During freezing weather, the sand was first heated, the mortar mixed with brine, and the stones steamed before being laid. Some 36 masons, using six derricks, laid an average of 3,240 cubic yards of masonry per month. One month they laid 5,700 cubic yards, enough to pave 46th St. in Manhattan six inches deep from the Hudson River to the United Nations Building.

Granite for the spillway, the cornice of the dam and the gatehouse was obtained from a quarry a mile-and-a-half from the dam. A railway was constructed which utilized gravity to pull empty cars from the far end of the quarry to the stone yard or the crusher, where they would be loaded, then run to the head of an incline, attached to a cable, and sent downhill. There, a locomotive would take the loaded train to the dam site, switching it to the proper place for unloading. As the dam got higher, the track for the locomotive was raised on the hillside, and a trestle was built 50 feet over the stream in front of the dam wall. From there, stones were placed in the wall with boom derricks. The loaded train, usually four eight-ton cars, would, in descending from the quarry, pull a train of empty cars to the top of the incline and the process would begin again.

The earthen wings of the dam were built atop 124-foot masonry core walls. Dirt, excavated by steam shovels from three pits on nearby hillsides, was delivered to the dam in gravity-fed rail cars. Earth was laid on the dam in six-inch layers and thoroughly rolled. But before the dam could be built, a 24-foot high,

1,000-foot long crib dam had to be built to divert the Titicus River into a 1,000-foot canal and timber flume around the dam site. Two big freshets during the winter of 1890-91 proved too much for the diversion system, and the contractor sustained significant damage to the works.

A total of 1,045 acres of land and numerous buildings in the communities of North Salem and Salem Center were taken by the city for the Titicus Reservoir, which was completed in 1896. New roads were built around the reservoir, and in 1901 the Town of North Salem took the Aqueduct Commission to Supreme Court to force it to build an additional road along the south side of the lake. The court ordered it done, and, after two unsuccessful appeals by the city, the new highway was built by John Twiname. It was completed in 1905. The total cost of the project, including land purchases, was $1,797,000.[28]

The valley submerged by the Titicus was dotted with large country retreats, some of which were converted to boarding houses for dam laborers, according to the *Brewster Standard* of May 4, 1894. One estate that escaped being taken was "Merryweather," the home of Ulysses S. Grant Jr. and family. The palatial estate in North Salem had been given to the Grants in 1881 as a wedding present by Mrs. Grant's father, Senator Jerome Chaffee.

The Titicus Dam in Westchester County, shortly after its completion in 1893. Reports on the New Croton Aqueduct Reservoirs and Dams, 1895-1907.

There the couple reared four of five children, frequently hosting the owner's father, former president Ulysses S. Grant, who kept a stable of prized Arabian horses there. The Grants sold the property at the turn of the century, and it went through a succession of owners until in 1998 the house, containing eight bedrooms, Tiffany windows, marble baths and a grand portico, was placed on the market. Asking price: $3.8 million.

Not all of those within the path of the reservoirs were so well-heeled, of course, nor were some of them well-pleased at the amount they received for their condemned properties. Darius Lobdell, incensed at the power of the city to take his land, did not stand idly by when Italian workers began to erect a stone boundary fence across a hayfield that remained in his possession. "My father told me that when Darius came around and saw what they were doing, he had a big corn knife that was like a machete, so he gave a hoot and a holler and brandished this knife and started chasing [the workers]," related Thomas L. Purdy in 1970. "They got scared to death and disappeared up over the hill and never came back to build that wall. To this day, I understand, that wall has never been built along that particular section because Darius Lobdell chased the workmen out with a corn knife."[29] Lobdell and a hired man were, however, arrested for trespass when they stood firm against a deputy sheriff and Division Engineer Alfred Craven who had come to investigate the matter.[30]

Sometimes it was hard for the city to please anybody. In the fall of 1895, citizens above the dam became upset that the city was drawing off 40 million gallons a day from the reservoir, leaving behind foul-smelling, decaying vegetable matter. The North Salem Board of Health urged the city to do something about the problem, so the outlet gates were shut tight, leaving downstream a dry river bottom, dead fish, and residents complaining about the lack of normal river flow. The American Condensed Milk Co. at Purdys was forced to shut down, lay off its employees and send farmers elsewhere with their milk. The city's need for water won out, and releases downstream to the Croton Reservoir were resumed.

As the Titicus was being built, a new reservoir was being constructed just a few miles away in the Town of Somers. Constructed not by the Aqueduct Commission but by the Department of Public Works, the Amawalk Reservoir was built on the Muscoot River between 1889 and 1897.

The 1,280-foot-long main dam is 80 feet high. It was built by contractor John McQuaid and consisted of earth banked against a masonry core that extends 85 feet down to bedrock. A 50-foot-wide spillway is also of masonry. The dam was finished with faced stones, as was an accompanying fountain aerator. An auxiliary dike that closes a depression in the ground just west of the main dam completed the 600-acre reservoir, which is three miles long and holds seven billion gallons of water.[31]

As with other reservoir projects in this farming area, the city auctioned off the forage crops on lands it acquired. Reported the *Putnam County Courier* of July 10, 1891: "To show the quality of grass that grows on lands that are to be taken for reservoir purposes near Amawalk, some heads of timothy taken from a meadow on the Parent place last week measured 9 inches in length."

As the Amawalk was being built, workers under the direction of contractor M. S. Coleman were erecting yet another dam, or rather two of them, to form the West Branch Reservoir. Built between 1890 and 1898, the main dam impounded the West Branch of the Croton River near the village of Carmel, and the auxiliary dam crossed a small tributary valley near the hamlet of Crafts.

Ground for both was broken in November 1890 for the oddly-shaped, three-sided masonry and earth dam across the West Branch, and the 720-foot-long auxiliary dam made of earth with a masonry core. The main dam, designed by Alphonse Fteley, included a 250-foot spillway 65 feet high. A gatehouse on one side of the spillway regulated the flow of water through two 48-inch pipes into a stone-lined channel in the river bed to flow 15 miles to the Croton Reservoir, where a new, larger dam was being built almost simultaneously with this one. Contractor Coleman, who won the contract for the new Croton dam in 1892, a year later took as partners Frank S. and Elmer Washburn, contractors on the Titicus Dam, to help complete the West Branch project.[32]

Hundreds of men converged on the area to find work. But that work required horse-power, too. "Contractor Coleman has a lot of fine horses in the stables at the new dam," reported the *Putnam County Courier* on Feb. 27, 1991. "They are all Norman horses ranging in weight from 1400 to 1800 pounds and they are as choice a lot of working horses as one seldom sees at a public work."

The newspaper was not so flattering in its description of the human toilers, though. "Last Saturday was pay day at the dams here," read the *Courier* on Apr. 24, 1891. "Out of every 100 men, 75 went on a drunk and did not report for work on Monday. This is probably a fair sample of the men we will have to deal with for the next four years."

It was, admittedly, a rough job, frought with danger. A violent explosion in January 1891 rocked the auxiliary dam site near Crafts. "Flashed Into Eternity" was the *Courier's* headline over the story telling of the death of foreman "Con" Connolly, a 28-year-old Irishman "blown to atoms" when a powder box containing 12 cases of dynamite somehow erupted. The blast showered dirt 2,000 feet away, tore window sashes out of a workers' boarding house, and jarred plaster from ceilings in Croton Falls, Purdys and Somers.

Laborers were killed and injured regularly in falls, cave-ins and explosions. The *Courier* told on July 24, 1891, of a Swede who broke his arm in a fall onto some rocks. It hailed Contractor Coleman

The West Branch Reservoir being built in the early 1890s.
Reports on the New Croton Aqueduct Reservoirs and Dams, 1895-1907.

for not only having the man's arm set by a local doctor, but taking him to St. Francis Hospital in New York under the care of paymaster McGrath. But the laborers weren't always in Coleman's corner. In 1893, a group of them rebelled against the contractor's order that they board on the dam property. There was only one boarding house there, kept by Angelo Paladino and Henry Episcobo, and several workers, claiming they were charged "exhorbitant rates" refused to board there. They were fired from their jobs. Eleven of them, the *Putnam County Republican* said on Oct. 28, 1893, took clubs to the boarding house, beat Episcobo over the head, and threw him down an embankment.

Meanwhile, area residents waged their own battle for what they considered fair prices for their condemned property. Some 1,690 acres were taken, and those who refused the city's initial offer for their property put their faith in three-man Commissioners of Appraisal, who would balance valuations claimed by owners and the city's appraisers, and issue compromise awards.

The system seemed to meet with grudging local approval, at least after the first set of awards was announced by Appraisal Commissioners Hamilton Fish Jr., Henry Mabie and John F. Dawson in July of 1891. Gideon Lee was awarded $21,000 for the property he'd claimed was worth $34,000; S. F. Best was awarded $25,600 for a 73-acre parcel he'd wanted $27,000 for, and Benjamin Secor was awarded $4,160 for his 32 acres. "While the awards are large, they are none too large, when we take into consideration that so much productive property is laid waste at our very doorstep and we derive no benefit from it whatsoever," opined the *Putnam County Courier*.

The West Branch absorbs the overflow from Lake Gleneida where such a hue and cry was raised 20 years earlier when the city claimed its waters. Building the later reservoir involved not just constructing two dams and clearing the basins of buildings and vegetation. It also meant relocating highways and laying stone boundary walls, erecting a highway bridge at Cole's Mills, and an 1,800-foot causeway, now Route 301, which runs above the reservoir.[33]

Indeed, the 1890s were lush times for contractors involved in the city's water projects. Up to 1895, 37 contracts had been let for the construction of the East Branch Reservoir, seven for the Titicus, and eight for the West Branch.[34]

By far the greatest number——165——had been awarded for construction of the New Croton Aqueduct that would tie the system together.

Placing iron lining in Shaft 25 on the Manhattan side of the Harlem River.
Reports on the New Croton Aqueduct Reservoirs and Dams, 1895-1907.

6. A New Aqueduct

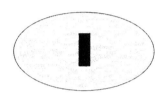 N EARLY 1884, Croton Aqueduct Commission engineers were busy surveying and boring to determine the best route for the new subsurface water line, which would have three times the carrying capacity of the existing 42-year-old aqueduct. By the end of the year, the first 10 contracts for construction of the aqueduct from the existing Croton Dam to the Harlem River were awarded, and work began in January 1885.[1]

The new aqueduct, which totals 33 miles in length, was made up of three distinct sections.

For 24 miles, from the Croton Dam to just north of the Jerome Park Reservoir (built between 1895 and 1906 to service The Bronx), the aqueduct is almost entirely a horseshoe-shaped masonry and brick-lined tunnel whose average depth beneath the surface is 125 feet. The tunnel, 13 feet high and wide except for a wider section beneath Gould's Swamp at Ardsley near Tarrytown, runs south along the Pocantico and Sawmill Rivers and Tibbets Brook at a grade of 0.7 feet per mile.

The next section of the aqueduct is a masonry conduit from Mosholu Avenue to the gatehouse at 135th St. in Manhattan. This is a circular inverted siphon whose diameter is 12 feet, three inches, except for a 1,300-foot section that runs 300 feet beneath the Harlem River at High Bridge. This section was reduced to 10.5 feet to increase the velocity of the water and prevent the deposition of silt.

From the 135th St. gatehouse, several water mains----48 and 60 inches in diameter----conveyed water to the Central Park Reservoir and thence to the city's distribution system.[2]

Benjamin Silliman Church, who had been a division engineer on the old aqueduct for 26 years, was chief engineer of the Aqueduct Commission at the start of the new undertaking, and was responsible for its design and planning. In his 1883-87 reports to the commission, he described the exacting surveying process: "Field parties were at once organized and equipped with accurate instruments . . .to insure great accuracy of lines and grades which could be afterwards transferred from such surface lines and levels, down the shafts, into the tunnels, to guide the work when in progress. . . Alignment bolts of copper were ordered to be placed in solid ledge rock where possible or in the center of stone monuments, whose foundations were to be built below the influence of frost. After the bolts and monuments were placed, the lines were again run and marked with a fine centre-punch and hair line. Much of this had to be accomplished at night by sighting to plummet lamps to prevent errors from radiation of reflected heat rays of the sun during hot weather."

Surveyors ran the line between the Croton Dam and the Central Park Reservoir and back again, "testing within a few thousandths of a foot."

The New Croton Aqueduct as constructed beneath the Harlem River at High Bridge, which had carried the Old Croton Aqueduct high above the river. *Scientific American*, collection of Robert Kornfeld, Jr., AIA.

Beginning in January 1884, the aqueduct was excavated from 40 vertical shafts ranging from 21 to 391 feet deep. Concerns about security helped prompt planners to design the aqueduct as a deep tunnel rather than to parallel the old aqueduct on or near the surface. A tunnel, it was reasoned, would be protected from shelling by "hostile ships that might force their way into the Hudson, or by guns placed on the New Jersey shore," explained *Harper's New Monthly Magazine* in 1889. A surface aqueduct, the magazine continued, "could easily be destroyed by a mob."

It took many weeks to dig each of the shafts to tunnel grade. The actual work of driving the tunnel began in March 1885 at Shaft 11A, where during the first week workers burrowed 40 feet to the north and 24 feet to the south. The city purchased land on which to dump the rock that was dug from shafts and the tunnel. The New York City and Northern Railroad, a short, single-line carrier, hauled brick and cement for the tunnel lining from barges and canal boats docked at the Harlem River near High Bridge. Within the city, tunnel materials were delivered by teams and wagons shuttling from supply points on the Hudson River.[3]

According to Chief Engineer Alphonse Fteley's report on the New Croton Aqueduct (1895-1907), the most difficult section to excavate was a 110-foot stretch south of Shaft 13. The tunnel was driven through this water-logged, 160-foot deep pocket of mud, using a special system of supports. It took 92 weeks to complete the aqueduct through that 110-foot section.

At the south heading of Shaft 17, laborers encountered a pocket in the rock filled with wet sand and gravel. Again, supports were used to get through the 135-foot stretch, and a heavy bulkhead was built at the end of the excavation to keep the sand from flowing into the tunnel. But on Sept. 9, 1887, the bulkhead collapsed, killing three work-

The 135th St. Gatehouse, where the old and new Croton Aqueducts connected, was completed in 1890. The elaborate design concealed what was essentially a mechanical shed. The tower had no real function. Reports on the New Aqueduct, Reservoirs and Dams, 1895-1907.

Below: Excavating Shaft 26. Reports on the New Aqueduct, Reservoirs and Dams, 1895-1907.

A trench at the Sawmill River Crossing of the new aqueduct.
Reports on the New Croton Aqueduct, Reservoirs and Dams, 1895-1907.

ers. A stronger bulkhead was built, and the job completed.[4]

The tunnel beneath the Harlem River was originally planned for 150 feet beneath the surface of the river, where test holes had indicated a 30-foot roof of solid rock. But 300 feet into the tunnel (excavated from Shaft 25 on the Manhattan side of the river), workers reached a pocket of sand from which water flowed freely into the tunnel. Reported the chief engineer, "Borings showed it extended 75 feet below the tunnel and 26 feet ahead of it. To avoid a possible loss of life in excavating through such treacherous material with a river overhead, the commission abandoned that heading and drilled Shaft 25 150 feet deeper to locate the tunnel 300 feet below the surface of the river." The tunnel was then successfully driven through solid limestone.

In another area, south of Shaft 30 near 149th St. in Manhattan, a tunnel collapse prompted the lining of the aqueduct with cast iron rings for 234 feet. The rings were backed with 18 inches of brick and rubble masonry grouted with cement.[5]

In the first two years of the project, 166 accidents were recorded, and 59 lives were claimed, according to a Jan. 1, 1887, report to the Aqueduct Commissioner. Before the job ended, 92 men had been killed, including Commissioner Walter Howe, who drowned in August 1890, and Robert E. Morris, a young, newly-married assistant engineer, who died in an accident at Shaft Zero (the Croton Dam) Sept. 25, 1885.[6]

Most of the laborers were Italian, but the *Brewster Standard* of May 28, 1886, reported that contractors were "importing" more and more black workers from Virginia. "We are informed that a society furnishes them at $2 a head," the newspaper said.

At the peak of construction, as many as 10,000 workers, hundreds of mules and horses and a great number of steam engines, were reportedly employed on the aqueduct project.[7] More than 1,000 laborers at five shafts along the line went on strike in April 1886, demanding a pay raise of 25 cents a day. At that time, the foreman was paid $3 a day, drill runners $2.50, muckers who dug and moved blasted rock and dirt $1.50.[8] The work environment was dark, dank and dangerous. Early on in the project, the only light was furnished by lanterns and torches. Electricity was instituted along the line in 1887. To lay stone and mortar fills, workmen often had to crawl into cramped cavities. Broken bones and other injuries were common.[9]

Nor was that the only threat to life and limb. In 1889, unidentified arsonists attempted to burn down a building in South Yonkers used as an aqueduct office and living quarters for employees. "The incendiaries scattered oil on the blinds and placed oil soaked rags on the inside of the window sill," reported the *Putnam County Courier* on Sept. 4, 1889. The rags failed to burn, however, and the perpetrators got away, their motive unknown.

The Aqueduct Commission engaged some 222 inspectors to examine the tunnel work as it progressed, but many contractors cut corners, leaving empty spaces behind the brick lining and false partitions to hide holes between the lining and the excavation. When, in 1888, one contractor objected to the fact that his pay had been withheld because of defective work, an investigation was instituted along the entire line from the Croton Dam to the Harlem River. Three separate committees examined the work. They included State Engineer John Bogart; F. Collingwood, who later became secretary of the American Society of Civil Engineers; five masons and builders; and engineers of the Aqueduct Commission. They discovered defects from one end of the tunnel to the other, and as a result more than half a million dollars in contractors' fees were ordered withheld. Many large portions of the brick lining had to be torn out and rebuilt, and nearly 400,000 barrels of cement were used to fill in cavities and holes.[10]

Charles Bernard, in *Century Illustrated Magazine* of December 1889 described one such empty space:

> As we walk on, there are sounds in the air—echoes from unseen workmen. Soon, through the murky air are seen starlike spots of light. There is a flash from an electric light. We meet

Laying the brick lining. Reports on the New Croton Aqueduct, Reservoirs and Dams, 1895-1907.

piles of brick, stone and cement. We come to a wooden staging, climb a short ladder and stand close to a roof among a group of workmen.

There is a square cut in the arched ceiling and much crumbling. We crawl through and sit directly on the top of the tunnel lining. The space between the lining and the rock is not high enough for one to stand, yet it makes a comfortable seat. Candles light up the wet ragged rocks overhead. You can see some heavy timbers in the distance and the clean red bricks of the arch.

This space over the tunnel lining is only one of a great number found at different points along the aqueduct at the top or sides or over the lining. . . But masonry wasn't supplied here, for three or four courses of solid brick laid in cement. In the upper course in the cave, the spaces are not laid in cement but laid loosely in place and left there.[11]

Benjamin Silliman Church, designer of the New Croton Aqueduct.
Ossining Historical Society.

Repairs continued for 30 months. In July 1890, the Aqueduct Commission decided to suspend repairs and place the line in service because of yet another water shortage. Ironically, many fissures in the rock contributed four million gallons of infiltrating groundwater per day to the normal flow of Croton water. The new Croton Aqueduct, the longest and largest water conduit in the world at that time, was finally completed and turned over to the Department of Public Works June 24, 1891.[12]

The project was first directed by Chief Engineer B. S. Church. A resident of Ossining, he occasionally took his young daughter, Angelica Schuyler Church, to work with him. She later studied mechanical engineering, an unusual field for a woman of that time, although she became more noted for her sculpture.[13]

Alphonse Fteley took over from Church in November 1888 and, ill with tuberculosis, retired

in 1900, to be succeeded by William Hill. Engineer of Construction H. S. Craven was the immediate supervisor of the work. It cost $19.6 million, about $700,000 more than estimated. More than 312,000 cubic yards of bricks were used to line the tunnel, enough to construct thirty 14-story buildings.[14]

Over the next several years, dozens more contracts were let for ancillary projects along the aqueduct line. In 1901, John J. Hart & Co. got the bid to build a brick conduit connecting the old and new Croton Aqueducts at Dunwoodie so both could be used while the upper portion of the old tunnel was being rebuilt during construction of the New Croton Reservoir. A rock slide in 1897 sent 2,000 cubic yards of earth down the face of a cliff near Shaft 25 in Manhattan so that two large retaining walls—along with a winding stairway, ornamental iron railings and lamp posts for the benefit of pedestrians in the area—were added. In 1902, a new system for dewatering the aqueduct under the Harlem River was introduced to replace one that was capable of emptying the siphon in 73 hours through a second shaft on the east side of the river. Over this pump shaft, a hoisting plant had originally been installed consisting of two iron bailing buckets, 14 feet deep and four feet wide, with a capacity of 1,390 gallons each. The buckets were lowered and raised by a high-pressure engine and the water discharged into the river. An improved system, installed in 1902 by Pneumatic Engineering Co. of New York, used a direct air pressure pump, run by a compressor and a steam engine, designed by Prof. Elmo Harris of the University of Missouri School of Mines. The new system speeded the dewatering process to just 12 hours.[15]

Of the 300 million gallons of water a day the aqueduct carried, about 50 million eventually went

Jerome Park's "Hay Days"

When a three-member "Commission of Estimate and Assessment" was appointed in February 1895, allowing the city to begin condemning land to build the Jerome Park Reservoir, it laid claim to a storied race track and social center dating back to Civil War days.

Among the properties in the 300-acre taking area was Jerome Park, established in 1866 by the American Jockey Club, whose members included such wealthy horsemen as William R. Travers, August Belmont, John F. Purdy, William Butler Duncan and P. S. Forbes. The track, the first formal, commercial racetrack in New York City, was the original home of the Belmont Stakes. The park was named for Jockey Club president Leonard W. Jerome, a Wall Street speculator whose daughter, Jennie Jerome Churchill, later became the mother of Winston Churchill.

The inaugural meeting at the park was held Sept. 25, 1866, when 25,000 people attended races and an auction of fine horses presided over by Mr. Belmont, the financier who was the jockey club's first president. "Many of the leading turfmen of New Orleans, Mobile, St. Louis, Cincinnati, Cleveland and other western cities had come East purposely to witness the race between Asteroid and Kentucky," reported *The New York Times* the following day. Many others had simply come to see and be seen, and to participate in what by all accounts was the social event of the season.

"The City, from Fourteenth Street up, was alive with preparations for the meeting. By eleven o'clock, long lines and processions of pilgrims to the new Mecca were wending their rapid pace. Every style of conveyance, from the old fashioned Concord coach and the modern caleche with four spanking horses, to the hired livery buggy and the dandy tandem team, spun along the common way," the *Times* reported. Club members and guests occupied the Club Stand to the left of the track; thousands of others sat on wooden benches in the Grand Stand to the right of the track, while myriad *hoi polloi* stood outside the picket fence to take in the sights without paying the price.

A highlight of the event was the arrival of Gen. Ulysses S. Grant, who stepped into the Grand Stand to the cheers of an adoring crowd and the strains of "See! The Conquering Hero Comes," played by Dodworth's Band.

"Jolly little picnics" were enjoyed on the grounds, where club members and visitors partook of chicken, tongue, apple pie, cheese, biscuits, cognac, champagne and, of course, cigars. The presence of about 1,000 women, the *Times* reporter wrote, did much to enhance the order and decorum of the races, which, heretofore, had been male-only affairs.

From the time it opened until the American Jockey Club held its last race in 1889, Jerome Park was the scene of two two-week racing meets per year, as well as amateur races by "gentlemen jockeys"—young members of the club. "Of all days at Jerome Park, Decoration Day was the one that deserved the red letter," explained John Brewster Dane in a 1901 article for *Cosmopolitan Magazine*. "From 10 to 20 thousand people would betake themselves thither for the sport. . .Every coach had stored away in its capacious interior an elaborate lunch. Their owners had butlers and footmen on the grounds and in the cool of the afternoon the cloths were spread on top of the coaches or on the shady turf."

The narrow valley occupied by the track ultimately proved irresistible to a thirsty city looking for ways to store more water, however, and Jerome Park was claimed for the greater good of the metropolis.

Sources: *The New York Times*, Sept. 26, 1866; *Cosmopolitan Magazine*, vol. 30, p. 246, 1901; Jerome Park Conservancy Preservation Report, by Robert Kornfeld, Jr., August, 1998

The west basin wall of the Jerome Park Reservoir
under construction in 1902.
Collection of Robert Kornfeld., Jr., AIA.

The Jerome Park Reservoir Keeper's House
and storage-room extension.
Reports on the New Aqueduct, Reservoirs and Dams, 1895-1907.

to the Jerome Park Reservoir to meet the demands of the annexed district, the 25th Ward. This project had been the subject of debate from the time it was first proposed in 1884 until the contract for its construction was awarded in 1895 to John B. McDonald. The Aqueduct Commission only voted to proceed in the face of increased consumption of water that followed completion of the new Croton Aqueduct, and the threat of speculators purchasing property and constructing buildings only to sell at inflated prices when the city finally decided to develop the reservoir. Also, warned Commission President James Duane in an appeal to the rest of the commission, "Until this reservoir shall be constructed, if any serious accident should happen to the New Aqueduct above the city line, or if any disaster should fall upon the Croton dam, requiring any considerable number of days to repair, we should find the city reduced to a condition, so far as its water supply is concerned, which would be extremely embarrassing, and which might prove absolutely dangerous."[16]

It was another year before a public hearing was held on the proposed reservoir, and several more months before final plans for a two-basin, 228-acre, 1.9-billion-gallon facility were adopted.

The mile-long, half-mile-wide reservoir was sited in a natural depression, but required the excavation of about seven million cubic yards of dirt and rock to dig a basin with a uniform depth of 26 feet. Some of the material was hauled to fill in nearby swampy areas. But most was carried on specially constructed railroad dump cars to the headwaters of Westchester Creek four miles away. Trains of ten to 15 flat cars loaded by steam diggers or derricks, were run from the excavation area to the so-called "Meadows," where a plow-bearing car was attached to the rear, the plow winched forward to clear the material off the sides of the cars. The arrangement reportedly dispensed with the labors of 150 men.[17]

The project became a focus of controversy in 1903 when the city's Merchant's Association claimed Jerome Park contractors were making "extravagant and useless" changes to the undertaking, including applying six inches rather than three inches of concrete to the base of the reservoir, a change that added a quarter million dollars to the cost. The association urged Mayor Seth Low to oust the Aqueduct Commission for misfeasance and neglect of duty.[18] A subsequent inquiry resulted in testimony that contractor John B. McDonald, who was also constructing parts of the new subway in the city, had made unnecessary changes and delays in the Jerome Park work, had abandoned a construction trestle which was then embedded in the retaining wall, and had had a $77,000 house built for an assistant engineer who was a son of a commission member. Engineer William Hill was accused by inspectors and others of allowing the contractor to violate specifications. Hill, claiming he was distressed by the investigation, resigned as chief engineer on July 8, 1903, and later, when called to testify at the inquiry conducted by the District Attorney, he reportedly went to Atlantic City, N.J., outside the DA's jurisdiction. No charges were ever filed against Aqueduct Commission members William TenEyck, John Ryan and John Windolph.[19]

The Jerome Park Reservoir was designed to receive and distribute water from both old and new aqueducts. It was ultimately reduced to a single basin, 94-acre, 773-million-gallon reservoir. Work on the second basin was suspended in December of 1905 when, in light of the pollution threats uncovered during the previous decade in the Croton watershed, a special commission recommended constructing a water filtration plant at the Jerome Park site.[20] Work on the east basin of the reservoir was halted because, if it were to be used to store filtered water, it would have to be covered and otherwise altered.[21]

Although the filtration project was finally put out to bid in 1913, the facility was never built. With the arrival of chlorine and other chemicals as effective purifiers, talk of a filter plant subsided.

Almost a century later, however, Jerome Park became one of several sites eyed for a filtration plant as the city came under federal orders to filter its increasingly stressed Croton supply. Area residents protested, citing the historic and park-like nature of the 125-acre reservoir zone, which includes the sites of two Revolutionary War-era forts. Opponents said a filter plant would add to the industrialization and congestion of the neighborhood, home to 50,000 people. The city, in 1998, selected an alternative site (Chapter 13).[22]

The New Croton dam under construction in 1905. Reports on the New Aqueduct, Reservoirs and Dams, 1895-1907.

7. The New Croton Reservoir

THE NEW CROTON Aqueduct had been in service less than a year when city officials reported that water consumption had jumped from 110 to 165 million gallons per day. Four years later, in 1895, 183 million gallons per day were being sent down the pipeline to New York.[1] By then, the city had launched its largest storage project to date, the New Croton Reservoir, consuming thousands of acres of Westchester County and taking 14 years to complete.

The New Croton Dam had been discussed and debated since the early 1880s, when Isaac Newton, chief engineer of the Croton Aqueduct, had presented plans for the new aqueduct along with a high masonry dam designed by B. S. Church to be located some four miles below the Old Croton Dam near Quaker Bridge. These plans had the backing of John B. Jervis, designer and builder of the first Croton Reservoir; George S. Greene, who had overseen the Central Park and Boyd's Corners Reservoirs and Robert Martin, constructor of the Baltimore waterworks.

But the opinions of various engineers differed on the site, profile and height of the dam, and numerous reports were contracted and engaged before, in 1890, Paris-born Chief Engineer Alphonse Fteley, who had engineered the Sudbury, Mass., water system before coming to New York, recommended a smaller dam at a different location,

claiming it could be built faster and cheaper than a high dam. Ultimately, the commissioners decided on Jan. 22, 1891, to construct the impoundment three miles downriver from the old dam, on lands belonging to A. P. Cornell and others. Plans were approved in May 1892, and after the first set of bids were rejected, the project was re-advertised, with James S. Coleman awarded the job at his bid of $4.1 million.[2]

The following description of the project was taken from the "Reports on the New Croton Aqueduct, Reservoirs and Dams, 1895-1907":

> Construction started in October of 1892. As originally planned, the dam was to be half masonry (stone and cement), half earth. It would consist of a 600-foot masonry portion 260 feet high, 216 feet thick at the bottom and 18 feet wide at the top. A 600-foot earthen section, 120 feet above the ground, with an 18-foot-thick masonry core wall was to extend from the central masonry dam to the south side of the valley. A masonry spillway, 1,000 feet long, was to run at right angles from the main masonry dam on its north side. A 20-foot-wide roadway was to run along the top of the dam, and two gatehouses would draw water from the reservoir and control the flow through the aqueduct.

A railroad, dubbed the Oscawana and Cornell, was built to take supplies and equipment from the Oscawana station on the New York Central and

Above: Steam shovel and crew on the job at the New Croton Reservoir, 1898.

Top left: Cyclopean masonry was cleaned and hauled to the dam site on railroad cars, 1898.

Top right: Pointing up masonry on upstream face of the dam, 1898.

All Croton-on-Hudson Historical Society.

Hudson River Railroad to Mamaroneck, "chosen as the terminus because of its excellent harbor advantages," related the *Sing Sing Republican* in April 1893.

It took four years to excavate a diversion channel for the Croton River and to dig the foundation before the first masonry was laid May 26, 1896. Over the next six years, the Aqueduct Commissioners would order various aspects of the project changed—the masonry portion of the dam was extended 110 feet; the height of the dam was raised six feet, the waste weir raised four feet. Then, in 1901, when cracks were discovered in the unfinished masonry core wall of the earthen dam, William Hill, who had succeeded Alphonse Fteley as chief engineer in 1900, expressed doubts about its stability. He recommended that a committee of outside engineers have a look. The committee, made up of J. J. R. Croes, Edwin Smith and Elnathen Sweet, recommended that a significant portion of the earth dam be replaced with masonry to guard against "disaster" and to satisfy "the general feeling of security in the public mind."

The commission voted Apr. 16, 1902, to extend the central masonry dam 290 feet. The core wall that had already been built was torn out and its foundation widened and deepened.

Before work on the dam itself could begin, a new channel, 1,600 feet long and 125 feet wide, had to be dug for the river. A 600-foot-long masonry wall, 23 to 25 feet high and 13 feet wide at its base, helped keep the river in the temporary channel, which was excavated from solid rock. The channel kept the river at bay while workmen excavated the dam foundation 100 feet below the stream bed.

Explained engineer Edward Wegmann, as cited in Charles Weidner's *Water for a City*, "The excavation below the river-bed was made at first with a large dredge having a 2½-cubic yard dipper on an 80-foot boom. This dredge, which excavated about 800 cubic yards in 10 hours, had to be kept floating in the foundation-trench and was replaced by a steam shovel of the same capacity when bed-rock was reached. At one time, three steam shovels were used in making the excavation. . ." Excavated material was shoveled into skips, which were hoisted

and transported by three cableways that stretched across the trench. As the excavation became bigger, the cableways were supplemented by railway inclines operated by stationary engines and cables. From the inclines the rock and dirt was hauled by locomotives on a 36-inch track to spoil banks.

"The contractors are meeting with grave difficulties in excavating the bottom for the new Croton dam," reported the *Brewster Gazette* on Feb. 22, 1895. "The best they can do is take out 30 carloads of muck per day, and this does not pay expenses. The steam shovel has proved a failure so far, as it comes in contact with boulders, some of them weighing as much as ten tons. It requires the constant use of two large pumps, working day and night, to keep the water from submerging the steam shovel. The contractors are under the constant surveillance of inspectors from New York, and the slightest imperfection is not allowed to escape their notice."

The work was under the immediate eye of Division Engineer Charles Sewall Gowan from 1892 until his resignation in 1905. "Now let us be severely logical" was a favorite expression of the engineer, who had superintended part of the Boston water project before joining the Croton Aqueduct Commission to work on the new water line. "The building of the protective work for the main excavation of the new Croton Dam received his close personal attention," related an account in the Oct. 23, 1909, Ossining *Democratic Register* at the time of the engineer's death. "The comparative immunity from excessive infiltration to a pit that was at one point nearly 130 feet below the Croton River seemed to justify the care which he bestowed on this important preliminary."

Some 1.2 million cubic yards of earth and rock, enough to cover Central Park six inches deep, were removed for the dam foundation. The surface of the bedrock was then washed by high-pressure streams of water, seams were grouted and the surface painted with grout cement. Eight derricks were mounted on platforms while masonry was raised on the foundation. At the height of work, the contractors' plant consisted of more than 500 pieces of heavy machinery. Some 745,000 barrels

"On the move!"

In addition to the heavy construction taking place at dam and reservoir sites throughout Putnam and Westchester Counties in the 1890s and early 1900s, much activity centered around communities being displaced by the projects. Like Brewster and other towns where homes and businesses had been moved back from streams and lakes the city had claimed, villages like Katonah, Whitlockville and Purdy's Station were in large part physically relocated behind the high water lines of the New Croton and Muscoot Reservoirs.

In Katonah, more than 50 houses, stores, offices and barns were dragged as much as a mile to a new village site when civic leaders and area residents decided they wanted the bustling community to remain intact. A syndicate whose members included Clarence Whitman, Joseph Barrett and William Henry Robertson acquired a tract of land on the farm of William Ashbee a mile south of the original Katonah railroad station, and sold lots to those interested in moving their structures there.

Noted landscape architects B. S. and G. S. Olmstead were engaged to design the new community, and it became one of the first planned hamlets in the country. It featured wide streets, a main boulevard ("The Parkway") with a central landscaped promenade and businesses located on side and parallel avenues. Strict covenants on deeds to the parcels prohibited such things as slaughter houses, ink manufactories, vicious dogs, chickens and even liquor sales.

Buildings acquired by the city were put up for auction, usually before their owners had been paid for them. The owners often bought them back at bargain prices at those auctions, and either tore them down to rebuild them elsewhere, or engaged contractors who moved them, using horses, ropes and plenty of muscle, to higher ground. Frances R. Duncombe, in her 1961 book *Katonah, The History of A Village and Its People*, described the moving process:

First, each house had to be lifted from its foundations by jacks and two heavy carrying-timbers made

fast crosswise under its house beams. A tow rope was then attached to both ends of the front timber and secured to the main towing rope which extended somewhat beyond a capstan (like a turnstile) placed out ahead of the house and to which the house was to be drawn.

The house was pulled along over a track made of two long timbers, sturdy and smooth, (cut from Georgia pines) starting under the raised house and extending toward the capstan. To keep these timber tracks nearly level, their elevation had to be controlled by cribbing under them. The track timbers were lubricated with ordinary yellow laundry soap. As soon as one set of timber rails had been passed over, they were picked up and moved ahead to make another section of track.

A horse hitched to the far end of a long pole attached to the top of the capstan circled round and round, drawing the house forward. After about three turns had been laid around the capstan, the forward end of the rope was pulled out ahead towards what would be the next position of the capstan, capstan and horse were moved ahead another lap, and the process began over again.

Temporary bridges spanned the Cross River, and some of the buildings had to cross the waterway more than once. The first buildings were erected in and moved to the new village in 1895, and the exodus from Old Katonah continued through 1898 and beyond. "James Clark has arrived in Katonah with H. W. Kellogg's house and barn," reported the *Katonah Times* June 10, 1898. "They are now sliding down Bedford Road and in another week will be near their foundation next to the residence of E. B. Newman."

A similar sight was seen in the hamlet of Purdy's Station at the confluence of the East and West Branches of the Croton, midway between the Titicus and Muscoot impoundments.

Thomas Purdy, 88, explained in a 1998 interview that some folks moved to Somers, Ridgefield, Conn., or North Salem, but several homes, along with the post office, were moved to hillside land owned by his uncle, Isaac Purdy, to begin a new community.

The Methodist Church and other buildings condemned as part of the buffer zone along the river were also moved. "Speaking of building movers," reported the *Katonah Times* July 14, 1899, "Messrs. Edward Hunt and George Johnson of Henry Parent's force moved the Corson house at Purdys (36x63, first story brick-lined), nearly 100 feet in less than two days. Only these two men, mind you, no other help, blocking, slides, jacking, team, work——all done by these two in the time mentioned. That shows ability."

Life continued uninterrupted during the moves, with business conducted and families carrying on life as usual. There were reports of dentists seeing patients, weddings being conducted and retail trade going forth in buildings as they were pulled to new locations. Edith Martin Voris, recalling her family's move in a 1970 interview, said workers "moved the house across the railroad tracks after the 1 o'clock train went up. That was the last train at night. So they moved across the track that night and my mother slept all through it. She went to bed just as though she was going

to bed anytime, and next morning she was on the other side of the tracks."

McKeel's Store, Reynold's Hotel, the Purdy family's cider mill and the home of Nathaniel Voris, real estate appraiser and auctioneer who sold many a city-acquired building throughout the region, were among the buildings to be moved in this way. Immovable amenities that were destroyed to become city property included a popular bicycle race track ("I used to ride my pony around it," Mr. Purdy recounted) and a ballpark.

Purdy Station resident John Rowe, ruefully acknowledging "the sin of force and greed" that took his neighbors' properties, nonetheless expressed optimism——and some tongue-in-cheek humor—— in a poem titled "On the Move," published in the *Katonah Times* May 19, 1899. "Of many places, some may say, they're not at a standstill, dead! But if you come by Purdys way, you'll see we're going ahead. You'll say with an emphatic, yes, that Purdys is alive! Having survived the past, I guess, in future, it will thrive."

Moving day coincided with wash day for the family of Dr. James Chapman, whose home was dragged away from the encroaching waters of the New Croton Reservoir to the new Village of Katonah. Katharine Kelly.

Sources not named above: North Salem Historical Society Bulletins; *Westchester Life*, January, 1953; "A History of the Voris Family," by Hester A. Voris Teed (1984); author interview of Merwin Voris, Purdys, Mar. 1, 1998.

of cement were used, and 100,000 tons of coal consumed in operating machinery. At one point, 1,500 men were on the payroll.[3]

Seventeen gangs of masons were on the job when a reporter from the *Katonah Times* paid a visit to the construction site in 1899. On April 21, the paper related:

> Upon the stone work there are between 30 and 40 large derricks and their accompanying engines. These are handling the immense blocks of stone that are being put into place by hundreds of workmen. From the three great cables stone, cement and sand are constantly being lowered down, while the structure is surrounded with narrow gauge railroad tracks upon which run platform cars drawn by small locomotives that bring the stone in from the quarries a couple of miles east of the dam.
>
> By close observation, men looking as small as ants on an anthill, and quite as busy, may be seen. . . A little engine comes puffing into sight drawing six or seven platform cars upon which are great blocks of stone. The train stops at the north end of the mason work. Presently, from one of the great cables above, a chain descends. It reaches one of the cars, the chain is fastened to an immense block of stone. In a minute, the block is being rapidly raised toward the cable. At the proper time it stops in its upward movement and begins to travel across the ravine suspended from the cable. Again it stops and is rapidly lowered down upon the stone work to become part and parcel of the great structure, there to remain for all time.
>
> On the south bank, high up over the scenes of operations, are the shanties of the boilers and engines that operate the great cables. The engineers obey signals by electric bells, just as engineers do on ship-board.

Masonry work proceeded year-round. Salt was added to the cement and sand was heated in steam-coiled boxes during very cold weather. The quarry where the dark granite, called gabbro rock, was hewn was near Hunter's Brook. The rock weighed 185 pounds per cubic foot. Granite blocks were layered in mortar, with spaces between filled with mortar and small stones. In early 1903, Chief Engineer William Hill reported to the Aqueduct Commission that the foundation upon which had rested the section of core wall that had earlier been removed was limestone, much of it disintegrated. Steps were taken to widen and deepen the foundation, and place cyclopean (extremely large) blocks of granite as the heart of the dam.[4]

William Hill, successor to Alphonse Fteley who retired in 1900 and died of tuberculosis in June 1903, was himself replaced as chief engineer in October 1903 following a controversy involving the Jerome Park Reservoir (Chapter 6). J. Waldo Smith took over, but resigned in 1905, just prior to the New Croton Reservoir's completion, to become chief engineer of the newly created Board of Water Supply to establish New York City's Catskill water supply system (Chapter 9).[5]

The gates of the New Croton were closed Apr. 1, 1905, and the last stone laid on the dam Jan. 17, 1906. In March of that year, the *Katonah Times* reported, "Soon, the once narrow Croton River will be a great lake, 2,400 feet across at the dam breast, filling the valley behind it for nearly 20 miles and spreading at Hunter's Brook to an extreme width of two miles. When the waters have risen to the top of the new dam, the top of the old dam will be 33 feet below the surface."

The Old Croton Aqueduct between the Old and New Croton Dams was also submerged by the expanded reservoir, and 15,400 feet of it had to be repaired and the brickwork reinforced with concrete. Some sections, totalling 1,600 feet, were relocated.[6]

To replace roads that were submerged by the reservoir, 32 miles of new highway and 21 new bridges were built. Seventy-three miles of stone boundary walls were also constructed. Several miles of track operated by three different railroads had to be moved. The New York Central & Hudson River Railroad Company, which leased the track to the three rail lines, settled with the city for $478,341 in compensation for the taking and damaging of its real estate. AT&T Co. was paid $3,965 for expenses and damages involved with relocating its utility rights of way within the reservoir lines.[7]

So, too, were farmers, homeowners, businesspeople and institutions ousted from the valley of the Croton to make way for the reservoir. In addition to the removal of churches, schools, stores, homes and an estimated 2,000 residents, 1,600 bodies in six cemeteries were reinterred in higher ground.[8] The *New York Herald* of July 8, 1903 reported that 58 eviction notices were given to "squatters" on city lands----church trustees, farmers, hotel proprietors and others----for occupying their properties after the city had taken them, and failing to pay rent for them.

Several towns were affected, including Katonah, Golden's Bridge, Purdy's Station and Croton Falls, parts of which were in the way of the Muscoot Reservoir. The Muscoot was built at the foot of Muscoot Mountain on the Croton River upstream from the Croton Reservoir to retain water over that area when the big reservoir was drawn down. "Fears were entertained that if the water in the reservoir were lowered below the level of these flats, the neighborhood would be rendered unhealthy by malaria," it was explained in the Reports of the Croton Aqueduct, 1895-1907. The bid for the Muscoot Reservoir, built in the towns of Somers and Bedford, Westchester County, was awarded to Williams & Gerstle for $209,000. Work was begun in 1901, but the contractor later abandoned the project, and in 1904, William Flanagan won the award to complete the 1,130-foot masonry dam, which was finished Jan. 1, 1906.[9]

Both the Cornell and the Muscoot Dams were built largely by immigrant laborers, many of them Italian. They lived in "The Bowery" or the shanty town dubbed "Little Italy," near the Cornell Dam, or in abandoned buildings in the hamlets. "The old optical factory building and other old houses nearby are the scene of much life and activity," said the *Katonah Times* in a report on the Muscoot Dam June 6, 1901. "Many Italians swarming about campfires can be seen every evening."

Single workers lived in boardinghouses for the most part, while those with families occupied small houses, where they raised gardens, fruit trees and children, who grew to maturity during the life of the projects. Mary Josephine D'Alvia of Croton-on-Hudson estimated that 50 members of her extended family, the Pettinatos and the Guzzis, lived

at or near the New Croton Dam works. Her mother, Lena Pettinato Rucci, was the first child born there. Lena's father was a stonemason who had first found work on a New York City water project in Putnam County, then migrated to the New Croton job, where he acquired a house near the dam and built eight more in an area called Larkintown to rent to other workers. Mrs. D'Alvia's uncles and great-uncles worked on the dam. One of them, the story goes, was occasionally lowered by rope off the face of the dam to retrieve fallen hammers and other tools. An aunt bicycled around the dam delivering fresh-baked buns; a grandmother sold tomatoes for 50 cents a basket.

Another of Mrs. D'Alvia's uncles kept one of many saloons at the Bowery, an area so rowdy with bars and bawdy houses that children and young women were not allowed to go there. But there was also an Italian school and St. Michael's Chapel, where the Italian and Irish Catholics worshiped. A commissary fed the workers, and a local bakeshop supplied 2,000 loaves of bread a day.[10]

Lena Pettinato Rucci, reminiscing in 1974 about her life as a youngster in a construction zone, recalled her father taking her to see the masons, small and dark against the sun-drenched granite, working diligently against the towering dam. "Everything was done with precision," she wrote. "They didn't raise an eye." [11]

She explained that a boardinghouse was run by Mrs. Jack O'Neill and her two daughters, Nora and Alice. "[It] had a long table that could seat 60 people with long benches on each side and each end. In another room in the sleeping quarters, there were cots all around. Most of the boarders were Irish and Swedish. The best of food was served there to people of the dam, and people who visited the dam. At Christmas one of the boarders would dress up like Santa Claus. A fiddler played while guests danced and sang Christmas carols."[12]

Even John B. Goldsborough, the six-foot, six-inch superintendent on the project, lived at a boardinghouse, owned by the Riekert family, before he married the daughter of the man responsible for materials transportation at the dam.[13]

Workers celebrated Italian feast days with ethnic music and food. Saturday nights were for drinking home-made wine and playing bocci; Sunday was for church. The reporter who visited the dam site for the *Katonah Times* in April 1899 stopped by on wash day. "All the colors under the sun filtered from the many clotheslines of the vicinity. The women, having finished their laundrying, were gossiping before their front doors, settling accounts with refactory children or driving hard bargains with the numerous peddlers that frequent the place. The sidehill gardens generally showed where the winter's freshets had about swept off all of last season's top soil, but cold frames and some attempt at beginning this season's gardening were in evidence."

There was danger, of course. The *Katonah Times* reported two accidents May 8, 1903, when a driller lost three fingers to a blasting cap explosion, and a laborer suffered a fatal blow to the head when struck by a rock as he worked in the "hole" of the coffer dam at the Muscoot project.

Italian workers were also the targets of the so-called Black Hand Society, countrymen who preyed on the immigrants by threatening them or their families if they did not hand over money. There were so many public works projects employing immigrants in Westchester and surrounding areas that the Black Hand's activities were widely dispersed. In July 1905, local papers reported that Sheriff James S. Merritt planned to swear in all the area contractors employing Italians and arm them with revolvers so they could drive away the bandits. "The sheriff will also import a staff of Italian detectives from New York and Philadelphia to go disguised as laborers and mingle among the Italians at Croton Dam, Cross River Dam and other projects to find the hiding places of the brigands and break it up."[14]

Italians got short shrift in wages, too. A document itemizing wages for various types of workers on the Croton project showed not only that "intelligent labor" was paid $1.50 to $1.60 per day (20 to 30 cents more than "common labor"), but that "common labor" was further differentiated by

Resembling a scene from the Civil War, a steady stream of National Guardsmen marched to the New Croton Dam to keep order during a labor strike in the spring of 1900. Croton-on-Hudson Historical Society.

whether the worker was white ($1.30-$1.60 per day), colored ($1.25-$1.40) or Italian ($1.15 to $1.25 per day).[15]

In the spring of 1900, 700 to 1,000 Italian laborers at the Croton dam went on strike, demanding their pay be increased to $1.50 per day. They reportedly threatened to blow up the dam, and stationed armed pickets on the hillsides above the dam to watch sheriff's deputies and National Guardsmen from New York, Mount Vernon, Yonkers and Brooklyn march into the valley. Tensions mounted when Sgt. Robert Douglas of Company B, First Regiment, New York National Guard, was shot dead while on guard duty. Twenty-seven strikers were arrested. Contractor James Coleman said there would be no pay raises; strike leader Angelo Rotella was adamant that his men would not work; cavalrymen stood watch to make sure nothing amiss happened at the dynamite cave at Muscoot Dam. Meanwhile, Governor Teddy Roosevelt made an appearance on horseback and Italian Consul General Giovanni Branchi acted as an intermediary to try to settle the strike.[16]

Eventually, perhaps softened by Easter Mass at which strikers and soldiers worshiped side by side at St. Michael's Chapel, hostilities were defused and the men went back to work three weeks later. A baby girl, born to a striker and his wife, was christened Anita Douglas Rotello for the soldier who had been gunned down. It was not the last stoppage, however. Three thousand stonecutters, bricklayers and plasterers seeking higher wages went on strike throughout the county in May 1900, and in 1902, Muscoot workers struck, demanding an eight-hour day (they worked 10-hour days despite an 1897 state law that provided for shorter days). The following year, about 100 workers walked off the Muscoot job in sympathy for a discharged foreman. The sheriff guarded the camp bakeshop out of fear the bread would be poisoned.[17]

The original Croton gatehouse, center left, was ultimately submerged beneath the waters of the enlarged reservoir. The new gatehouse, at right in this photo was itself replaced by a new facility in 1993. Reports on the New Aqueduct, Reservoirs and Dams, 1895-1907.

This was a time of big projects across the country and around the world. While club-toting deputies patrolled the works at Croton, the Duchess of Connaught was placing the last stone in the mile-long dam across the Nile at Assouan, Egypt.[18] And while local newspapers decried the endless changes and delays in the construction at the New Croton Reservoir, they wondered whether the immense Wachusett Reservoir, which was to claim four towns, 5,000 acres, six mills, 360 homes and six miles of railroad line north of Boston, would beat New York City to completion.[19]

Some, though, saw silver linings in the local shadows. Citing the near-completion of the New Croton and the Muscoot reservoirs, the *Katonah Times* sounded an optimistic note May 25, 1906: "We are all anticipating the beautiful sights when both lakes are filled and, in a few years more, another lake, covering the valley of Cross River, with the hills of old Bedford and Lewisboro on its shores, will perhaps surpass in beauty all of the dozen or more artificial lakes made by the city."

The Clock Barn, a training barn for carriage horses at Forest View Farm, was among the buildings claimed for the Cross River Reservoir. *Below:* The Cross River Dam, Westchester County, under construction in 1907.
Both Katharine Kelly.

8. Finishing the Croton System: Cross River and Croton Falls

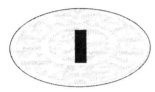N the decade following the 1898 consolidation of New York City to include Brooklyn, Staten Island and other areas, about as many people moved into the five boroughs as would later populate Boston and San Francisco.[1] Thus, with every drop of water a precious commodity, the city's Board of Estimate and Apportionment in 1901 authorized the issuance of $4 million in bonds to enhance water systems in Brooklyn, drill wells in Queens and build a dam to create the Cross River Reservoir.[2]

Surveyors had already been in the field the previous spring looking for a Cross River dam site, but actual construction would not begin for another five years, as controversy swirled about whether Westchester should play host to yet another New York City project.

Following the lead of Dutchess County officials, who rose up to successfully protest city proposals to develop water sources there (Chapter 9), Westchester Assemblyman James Apgar introduced a bill in January 1905 that would have prohibited the city from taking additional lands in Westchester. But the Aqueduct Commission moved swiftly to approve Cross River plans in time to thwart the legislative effort to stop them. "The commission believes that it is a race between the city and the legislature to control the water supply,

and acted quickly to get the advantage," reported the *Katonah Times* on Feb. 10, 1905. About 20 Westchester County representatives attended a hearing on plans to construct the three-mile-long reservoir, but the only one who spoke was Col. William Jay, owner of 157 acres earmarked to be taken for the project. "He said he had no objection to the plans, but he hoped the Aqueduct Commission would spare his trees," reported the *Times*. "They promised to do what they could in that regard."

By April, the Supreme Court had appointed appraisal commissioners to hear damage claims from residents to be displaced, and the lands thereupon officially became city property. On June 20, the contract to build the dam was awarded to McArthur Bros. Company and Winston and Company, and work began almost immediately. Their bid of $1.2 million had not been the lowest received, however; Dunn, Naughton & Co., jointly with the Ryan-Parker Company, had submitted a bid that was $116,000 lower, but political considerations, and the fact that the second-lowest bidder had just completed a big dam at Clinton, Mass., for the city of Boston, were reportedly involved in tossing the job to McArthur *et al.*[3] Frederick Walters, in the interest of Bart Dunn, brother of a former sheriff who was one of the unsuccessful bidders, brought an injunction to halt the project, and work was stopped from September until November 1905, when the case was dismissed and construction resumed.[4]

The Cross River Dam, and the Croton Falls Dam to follow, were intended to feed the New Croton Dam downstream, and to retain more of Croton water that might be wasted over it in periods of high water. Plans for the former called for a dam 840 feet long and 170 feet high to impound the Cross River less than a mile east of the new village of Katonah. The Aqueduct Commission's reports of 1895-1907 described the pending Cross River project: "At the southerly end, the dam will terminate with an abutment from which a masonry core wall will be built for 100 feet into the hillside. A circular structure called the bastion will be built at the northerly end of the dam. From the bastion a waste-weir about 240 feet long will be constructed along the hillside. A waste channel, cut in rock, is to extend from the waste-weir around the main dam to the river channel below the dam."

An earthen diverting dam was built 300 feet upstream of the main dam to send the river down a 16-foot-wide wooden flume around the construction zone, then back into the channel about 500 feet below the dam's foundation, which was excavated in time to lay the first stone on May 25, 1906.

The plans called for 47,000 feet of wooden fence and guard railings along reservoir roadways, and 90,000 feet of stone walls to designate the boundaries of city lands around the reservoir. They also required five miles of new highways to replace those submerged. A Supreme Court decision also forced the city to change its plans and build a roadway across the top of the dam, requiring it to be widened from 17 to 23 feet, adding 5,000 cubic yards of masonry to the edifice.[5]

A narrow-gauge railway known locally as the Boutonville Express, named for a hamlet nearby, brought supplies to the construction site. It was infamous for its tip-overs and derailments.[6]

A large crushing operation was erected to produce stone for the cast-concrete blocks used as facing on both upstream and downstream sides of the dam. Blocks were two to three feet wide and two to three feet thick.[7] Stone for crushing came from nearby quarries. Accidents, of course, were

fairly common. The *Katonah Times* of Aug. 17, 1906, reported that two foremen and several workers were injured when a laborer using a pick struck an unexploded stick of dynamite. In October, foreman Fred Gardner was killed when a gravel box he was standing on was accidentally connected to a derrick chain and flipped over. Two months later, an 18-year-old Italian worker died when he fell into the main shaft of the crusher plant and was horribly mangled.

A ferryboat strike delaying shipments of cement for concrete work threatened to hold up the project during the autumn of 1906. The contractors, the *Times* reported on August 17, "use at the rate of two carloads of cement a day and the supply has been exhausted for over a week."

The community of Cross River was cut in two by the project, the local correspondent for the *Katonah Times* providing weekly reports of who had moved, and where. "Those already gone from this place are George W. Ruscoe, Abram Knapp, Hiram Reynolds, John S. Hunt, A. C. Pullen, and Harry Hobby," related the paper on July 13, 1906. "Those who have moved from city property but still remain in the place are Joseph Ferguson, William S. Reynolds and Miss Jennie Ferris. Will Van-Tassell hasn't yet moved from the McTavy house but soon will. He will not have far to go as he owns a house just across the street, not taken by the city."

Hillbourne Farms, "better known as Sharp's Sanitorium," was among the businesses taken, according to the local paper of July 7, 1905. A blacksmith shop, the post office and several other buildings were moved beyond the taking lines, and some displaced residents found temporary housing at the so-called Brick House on the Old Post Road, not far from the Methodist Church, where services had to be suspended because so many people had left the area.[8]

An historic grist mill, said to have been erected around 1800 by Governor John Jay and through much of the 1800s operated by the Hoyt family, was claimed for the reservoir. "The people near Hoyt's Mill seem to be anxious to have the city purchase the property, but the owner of the old mill appears to think more of the place than of the

The terror of typhoid

The wholesale cleansing of the Croton countryside that took place during the 1890s when city agents targeted for demolition privies, pigpens and other "nuisances" did not eliminate all threats to the public health. In the early 1900s, typhoid fever reared its ugly head. This time, the labor camps of the city's own reservoir projects were suspected as the source of the contagion.

An infectious disease caused by the bacillus *Salmonella typhi*, typhoid fever is transmitted by milk, water or solid food contaminated by feces of typhoid victims or symptom-free carriers of the disease. It causes chills, high fever, headaches, cough, intestinal distress, vomiting and diarrhea. Before the advent of antibiotic treatment, many sufferers died as the disease progressed to pneumonia or intestinal hemorrhage.

The *New York Herald* reported Dec. 7, 1902, that Dr. A. Seibert, a New York Polyclinic professor and an expert in cholera and typhoid, estimated one in every 8,000 New York City residents was a victim of typhoid fever. He urged construction of a water filtration plant, a concept endorsed by Dr. Ernst Lederle, president of the New York City Health Department. But Lederle also suspected that decomposing leaves falling into reservoirs and the streams that fed them added to the health threat. So in January 1903 the city began cutting down trees lining the streams and rivers in the Croton watershed, a move decried by botanists, engineers and others who suggested catch basins instead.

The *Katonah Times'* Mount Kisco correspondent pointed a finger in another direction on Jan. 30, 1903: "While they are protecting the water by clearing away all the trees, they are overlooking about a dozen houses that are occupied by twice as many families, all of whom have hogs and chickens and are located less than 20 feet from one of the largest and most important branches of Croton Lake, three of which houses are so close

to the brook that one can stand on the back stoop and throw wash water and worse stuff right into the water."

The State Health Commissioner, Dr. Eugene Porter, later instructed local health authorities to get rid of deleterious conditions, by force, if need be. But when several cases of typhoid were diagnosed in the new village of Katonah in spring 1907, the labor camp at the Cross River Reservoir construction site was fingered as the probable source.

New York Health Department inspectors examined the entire village, testing springs near the schoolhouse, milk from the local dairy, and Katonah's own water supply. They also examined the Italian camp at the dam site, which contractors claimed was maintained in an hygienic manner, although four people were found to be infected. They never pinpointed the actual source, but theorized that the culprit was a temporary outhouse utilized by a band of 20 to 30 laborers who had spent part of 1906 working near a pumping station that supplied the village of Katonah.

Two people died during the 1907 outbreak, which sparked plans for municipal sewering at Mt. Kisco and other locations in the watershed. Edward Hatch Jr., chairman of the New York Merchants Association Pollution Committee, went a step further, taking the case for sewage control straight to President Theodore Roosevelt.

Requesting the President to use his influence to stop "water poisoning," Hatch wondered why the federal government imposed safety regulations on steamboats and railroads, but "does nothing to save the 25,000 lives which are annually sacrificed to typhoid fever—a preventable disease-because of the habit of the American people of drinking diluted sewage."

Sources: *New York Herald,* Dec. 7, 1902; *New York Tribune,* Jan. 2, 1903; *Katonah Times,* Jan. 30, 1903, April-August 1907; *New York Times,* April 10, 1908.

money it might bring," the *New York Tribune* reported on Aug. 5, 1900, long before dam construction was begun. Five years later, mill owner Seth Hoyt conceded defeat in a notice in the *Katonah Times*, July 7, 1905: "New York City having condemned our mill property two miles east of Katonah, I wish to notify the public that there will be no more grinding done at that place."

Perhaps the most celebrated place taken for the Cross River project was Forest View Farm, a 90-acre estate formerly owned by New York City hotel and livery owner George S. Green, who raised hackney ponies there. The facility, "on the limpid Cross River in one of the most picturesque sections of Westchester County," was acquired in 1901 by the Fiss, Doerr & Carroll Horse Company, which supplied "95 percent of the horses used by the dry goods houses of the metropolis," according to a brochure for the company.[9]

During construction of the Cross River reservoir, mules and their black drivers were housed at the farm, and contractor James Winston and his family occupied one of its houses. The Winstons' third child was born at the farm, where Mr. Winston also kept a bevy of fighting cocks.[10]

Despite the ill feelings that must have been engendered by the city's incursions into the area, there remained an element of civility between the locals and those engaged in claiming part of the community. The July 20, 1906, *Katonah Times* described a "very successful and largely attended" lawn party at the Cross River home of Mr. and Mrs. Wilbur Hunt, noting, "The superintendents and foremen of the Cross River dam turned out in full force."

By August 1907, the work was largely completed, and in October, John F. Cowan, president of the Aqueduct Commissioners, placed the final stone in the dam with a specially-made silver trowel. Speakers delivered congratulatory messages from atop an oil drum in the middle of the dam roadway, then "repaired to the camp dining room, where a bountiful luncheon was served," the *Times* reported November 1, 1907.

By that time, work on the two-part Croton Falls Reservoir up in Putnam County was well under way. It consisted of a main dam impounding the West Branch of the Croton River in the Town of Carmel just north of the hamlet of Croton Falls, and a diverting dam across the East Branch of the Croton at Dean's Corners in the Town of Southeast, two miles southeast of Brewster and downstream from the East Branch and Bog Brook Reservoirs.[11] The two dams are connected by a 3,500-foot-long paved channel.

The main dam, dubbed the Hemlock Dam, is 1,100 feet long and 173 feet high. It is notable in that this may have been the first time masonry was reinforced with steel in dam construction; an estimated 575 tons of steel bars were used to reinforce both the cyclopean concrete of the main section and the top 42 feet of the facing blocks of the dam.[12]

As had become common practice, a special construction railroad was built from the Harlem Division of the New York Central Railroad at Brewster to transport an amazing assemblage of machinery and equipment two-and-a-half miles to the dam site. Altogether, 20 miles of rail line were laid about the quarry and construction sites for both dams. Thick woods in the area supplied material for railroad ties. A power plant consisting of five boilers and two 125-foot-high smokestacks operated a 300-horsepower engine that ran the stone crushers. A massive system of steam-driven compressors operated machinery at the quarry and main dam, where steam shovels excavated the foundation. Much of the machinery was housed in a wooden building 200 feet long, 50 feet wide and 40 feet high. A mixing plant delivered finished concrete to two 1,400-foot-long cableways, allowing an average of 800 cubic yards of concrete to be placed in an eight-hour shift. A temporary dam to divert water from the foundation was built 600 feet above the main dam, with an 800-foot-long wooden flume carrying the river around the site until the three 48-inch pipes making up the outlet for the reservoir were able to carry it.[13]

The diverting dam at Dean's Corners is made of earth with a concrete core. It has a 1,000-foot stepped concrete spillway. In times of high water, if the East Branch, Bog Brook, Diverting and Croton Falls Reservoirs are full, the spillways of the latter two allow the excess to flow into the river and ultimately into the New Croton Reservoir.

The contract for building the Croton Falls project was awarded Aug. 21, 1906, to James Malloy & Co. at their bid of $3,028,000. As was the case at Cross River, Malloy was the second lowest bidder, after Ashbel G. Vermilyea, who claimed he could do the job for $200,000 less. But the city claimed Vermilyea didn't have sufficient plant to carry out the project.[14]

The *Katonah Times* of Jan. 1, 1907, described the camp where many of the laborers lived: "On a hill near Daisy Lane a small village has been built for the housing of the laborers. Twenty dwellings have already been erected together with a bakery, blacksmith shop, and general store. The houses are at present one-room affairs about 25 by 40 feet. Plans have been made for a jail and a hospital. A spring has been found nearby and pipes have been laid, giving the settlement a good supply of water. The bakery turns out about 500 loaves of bread a day. Over 200 Italians are already there, and many more are expected in the spring."

So many Italians had taken up residency in Putnam and Westchester Counties as laborers on public works projects that in March 1907 several prominent Italians put up $20,000 to form Minerva Publishing Co. and start an Italian-language daily newspaper called *L'Avenire* ("The Venture"), based in Mount Vernon.[15]

Irish workers, too, were employed on the project. "The cornerstone of the new Hemlock Dam was laid on Wednesday afternoon," related the *Katonah Times* Apr. 17, 1908. "The flag of Erin appeared to be in the ascendant at that time. . ." Cement blocks were again used in building the Hemlock Dam, the first laid in the facing in July 1908. Large cableways stretched across the valley to deposit them on the dam.

Railroad and blasting accidents killed and injured many workers, and the Black Hand Society of Italian "bandits" claimed some as well. One Italian worker was killed and two seriously injured in August 1906 when two other Italians entered a saloon and demanded money. They got a fight

instead, and afterward fled by train to Brooklyn, where the Croton Falls constable, accompanied by the local barber and two Brooklyn cops, found the perpetrators and jailed them.[16] Two months later, a peddler was held up and shot, and Sheriff James Merritt established a squad to patrol the dam vicinity on horses supplied by Winston & Company. There were soon eight suspects in jail, but that didn't satisfy area residents, who petitioned the sheriff to provide a uniformed officer to protect the community against the "bold and reckless lawless element."[17] The request bore fruit, for the following month two officers were escorting grateful women to and from the train station after dark.[18]

C. Elmore Smith was assistant city engineer directly in charge of the work on the Hemlock Dam, with William Hauck supervising the Diverting Dam work. In October 1908, about 350 people----city engineers, their families and other guests---were entertained by the contractors, who attached seats to railroad flat cars and gave them a tour of the works before treating them to lunch.[19]

This "great celebration" was not shared by people displaced by the projects. "Money cannot pay for the heartaches and sorrow caused by being forced to take up a new life among strangers," Albert Chamberlin, a resident of Croton Falls, wrote in a letter to the *Katonah Times* on June 27, 1905. "Is the average award given by the city a fair compensation? In most cases, it is not. For instance, a physician, the only one in the place, having a lucrative practice and a delightful home---- where is he going? A new practice is to be built up and a new home to establish. Again, here is one who is a tradesman and doing a good business. His home is taken, his store is closed, his customers scattered. Where is he going to locate?"

It was not until 1911 that the Croton Falls reservoirs were finished. A year earlier, the Aqueduct Commission had been abolished and its projects transferred to the Department of Water Supply, Gas and Electricity for operation. All eyes were now on the Catskill System, where the grasp of the world's second-largest city had extended into the mountains across the Hudson River.[21]

By the time New York City surveyors arrived looking for dam sites, the Catskills had long been famed for pure water. The Crystal Spring Water Company of Pine Hill, shown here on the side of Belleayre Mountain where it operated from the 1880s to the 1930s, was one of several companies that shipped bottled water to urbanites. Shandaken Historical Museum. *Below:* Board of Water Supply President J. Edward Simmons addressed the crowd at the Catskill Aqueduct groundbreaking ceremony near Garrison, Putnam County, June 20, 1907. NYC DEP.

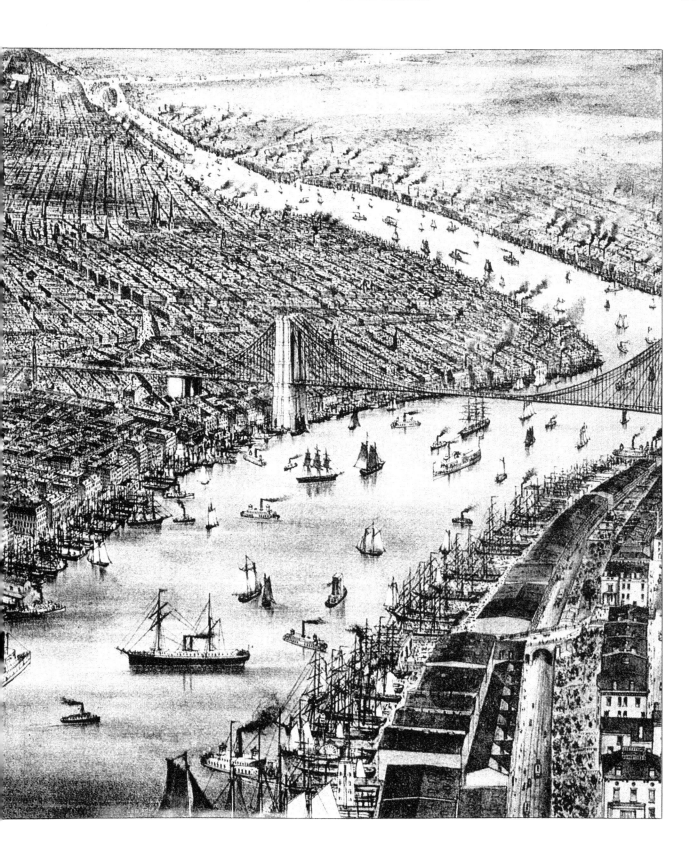

who cited the need for additional protection for the higher buildings that were sprouting up all over Manhattan Island.

"People here are enthusiastic over the project," claimed Ulster County's *Kingston Freeman* on Apr. 6, 1899. "The formation of a large number of lakes in this section of the mountains will make the Catskills more of a summer paradise than ever." The article noted, however, that Davis Winne and Henry Hudler, owners of hundreds of acres of wild lands near Mount Pleasant, had thus far refused to sell options to the Ramapo Company, which also wanted to tap the mountain streams to supply electrical power throughout greater New York. The *Kingston Weekly Leader*, on the other hand, in an Apr. 29, 1899, article, worried about the potential that a large dam at, say, Big Indian might break and threaten property as far east as Kingston.

The proposed Ramapo contract was brought unexpectedly to a vote at a Board of Public Improvements meeting Aug. 16, 1899, pushed by Water Commissioner William Dalton and the board president. City Comptroller Bird S. Coler, saying the contract had been put together without his knowledge, opposed taking action on the measure, and succeeded in getting it put off for two weeks. He used the time to campaign for its defeat. Newspapers condemned the proposal, a public outcry ensued, taxpayers filed suit and an injunction was issued, precluding further action by the improvements board.[4]

The Ramapo Water Company was eventually forced to dissolve and in 1901 the state legislature repealed its charter. Thus was the way cleared for the city to develop its own Catskill supply.[5]

Acting under the authority of Comptroller Coler, prominent engineer John Ripley Freeman launched an investigation into the city's water supply and its potential for expansion. Freeman, an 1876 graduate of Massachusetts Institute of Technology and a consultant on the Grand Canal in China, the Panama Canal, and the water supplies of such cities as Mexico City, San Francisco and Baltimore, spent seven months reconnoitering the territory east and west of the Hudson. His report to Coler in March 1900 recommended tapping the

Ten Mile River watershed in Dutchess County and the Upper Housatonic watershed in Massachusetts and Connecticut, both of which could be connected to the existing Croton system with relative ease and less expense than other sources. He felt constitutional authority could be found for this interstate water shift, and suggested that a boundary change be made to place a proposed Housatonic Reservoir entirely within New York State.[6]

Freeman also looked into the Ramapo, Hudson and Wallkill Rivers, and the Esopus Creek watershed, as well as ways to curb water waste in the city, where he estimated half to two-thirds of the water delivered to Manhattan was lost to leaks and wastage. Freeman recommended that the city construct a high-level reservoir at Yonkers, install meters on all city taps, consider filtering Hudson River water, abandon plans for any Ramapo or Wallkill developments, investigate the Schoharie Creek as an additional source of water, and make test borings at Bishop's Falls on the Esopus to determine the feasibility of building a high dam there.[7]

Although the city's Department of Water Supply, Gas and Electricity thereupon conducted surveys of the Esopus watershed, no formal city action was taken on Freeman's report. But in 1902, Mayor Seth Low, former Mayor of Brooklyn and a past president of Columbia University, appointed an independent committee to once again study the city's water situation.

John R. Freeman was one of three men delegated for this task. The others were William Hubert Burr (chairman), professor of civil engineering at Columbia University and Rudolph Hering, a German-born sanitary engineer. The Burr-Freeman-Hering Commission was charged with reporting on the best methods for reducing water waste, estimating future water consumption, recommending permanent sources to meet those future needs and determining whether temporary supplies should be developed while the permanent sources were established.[8]

To accomplish this far-ranging mandate, the commissioners divided the work into departments covering aqueducts and reservoirs, filtration and pumping, Long Island sources and other subjects. The departments were headed by engineers from throughout the Northeast, and employed a total of 200 people—engineers, draftsmen, chemists, biologists, secretaries and laborers.[9]

The Report of the Commission on Additional Water Supply for the City of New York, filed Nov. 30, 1903, was a weighty 980 pages, not including maps, diagrams and tables. It included the following findings and recommendations:

- Long Island wells be further developed to supply Brooklyn and Queens.
- More stringent plumbing regulations and inspections be made, and universal metering be instituted, to eliminate the estimated 40 million gallons of water lost per day—enough to meet the needs of 380,000 people.
- The Hudson River be utilized as a source, employing filtration of a sort used by the City of Poughkeepsie.
- Five watersheds be explored for the development of reservoirs: Fishkill and Wappinger Creeks in Dutchess County, the Roeliff Jansen Kill in Dutchess and Columbia Counties, and the Esopus and Rondout Creeks in Ulster County west of the Hudson. Fishkill was considered the top choice, with dams proposed for Stormville and Billings. Dams could be built in the Wappingers watershed at Hibernia, Clinton Hollow and Rochdale; and on the Roeliff Jansen Kill at Silvernails. Proposed dam sites in the Esopus watershed included Olive Bridge, and/or lesser facilities at Wittenberg, Willow, Cold Brook Station, Shandaken Station and Big Indian. Rondout reservoir sites included Napanoch, Lackawack and Eureka.
- The Catskill Creek watershed (featuring potential dam sites at Franklinton in Schoharie County, Preston Hollow in Albany County and Oak Hill and East Durham in Greene County) be investigated, along with the Schoharie Creek watershed, but not until after the development of the Ulster County supplies.
- Some 325 acres be acquired to build a concrete reservoir at Hill View.

Alarmed at the commission's suggestions, Dutchess County residents and officials sought legislative protection from the acquisition of land and water rights by New York City. The Smith Dutchess County Act of 1904 thus barred the city from reaching northward into that county.[10] City attorneys fearful of legal challenges had similarly advised against the Ten Mile and Housatonic River proposals made earlier by John Freeman. And the general disdain toward the idea of drinking polluted Hudson River water meant that suggestion was not given serious consideration, either.

Thus the Esopus and Rondout studies took precedence. With the support of city Mayor George B. McClellan, the development of the Catskill system began, facilitated by three major legislative acts, which in essence recognized that the growth and well-being of the state was tied to the growth and well-being of its largest city. In November 1904, state voters ratified an amendment to the constitution exempting water bonds from the city's debt limit. Seven months later, the legislature passed, and Gov. Frank Higgins signed, Chapters 723 and 724 of the Laws of 1905. The first established a five-person state water supply commission with the authority to approve or reject any New York City water plan. The second, known as the McClellan Act, provided "for an additional supply of pure and wholesome water for the city of New York; and for the acquisition of lands or interests therein, and for the construction of the necessary reservoirs, dams, aqueducts, filters and other appurtenances for that purpose; and for the appointment of a commission with the powers and the duties necessary and proper to attain these objects."[11]

The lengthy McClellan Act allowed cities and villages in Westchester County to take water from any of the city's reservoirs or aqueducts. And while it guaranteed protection from the courts for property owners and owners of riparian rights seeking compensation for direct and indirect damages from city takings, it allowed the city to take possession of land and/or dwellings just 10 days after an appraisal commission was appointed and upon payment to the owner of one-half the assessed valuation of the property.

The act also required the appointment of a board to oversee the process of water system development. Less than a week after the passage of Chapters 723 and 724, the mayor named the first Board of Water Supply, selecting one nominee from each of three lists supplied by the city's Chamber of Commerce, the Manufacturers' Association of Brooklyn and the Board of Fire Underwriters. Named to the board, and paid $12,000 per

board appointed John R. Freeman, William Burr and Frederick Stearns as consultants, and J. Waldo Smith as chief engineer, with Alfred D. Flinn as his deputy.[14]

Like his contemporary, John Freeman, Smith was a New England native and a graduate of MIT. Seemingly born with an intuitive grasp of water

Chief Engineer J. Waldo Smith, second from left, posed with consulting engineers (l. to r.) John R. Freeman, Frederic Stearns and William Burr for this 1907 photo. NYC DEP.

year, were J. Edward Simmons, a banker who was president of the chamber; Charles N. Chadwick, who had headed a special water investigation committee named by the Manufacturers' Association in 1896 and Charles A. Shaw, president of the Hanover Fire Insurance Co.[12]

The board immediately set about the task of establishing the foundation for the huge mission ahead, dividing the work between the Administrative and Engineering Bureaus and securing offices for the headquarters of both on the ninth and tenth floors of the newly completed Barclay Building at 299 Broadway and Duane Street in the city.[13] Bringing in some of the best minds of the day, the

works design and construction, Smith, at the tender age of 17, served as chief engineer of the water system in his hometown of Lincoln, Mass., a system he once described as "a one-lung pump and two miles of pipe."[15] After college and an impressive early career developing water systems in several New Jersey cities, as well as what was then the largest mechanical filtration plant in the world in Little Falls, N.J., he accepted an offer to become chief engineer for the Croton Aqueduct Commission in 1903.

Smith supervised the completion of the New Croton and Muscoot Reservoirs, untangled problems at Jerome Park and designed the Cross River

Reservoir before leaving the commission to take the BWS job at an annual salary of $15,000. He surrounded himself with noted engineers, including Thadeus Merriman, Walter Spear and Charles Clark, who would, in their own time, succeed him as chief engineer of the BWS.[16]

Chief Engineer Smith reported for duty at the BWS on Aug. 1, 1905. On Aug. 9, the board directed him to come up with plans, maps and profiles aimed at capturing Catskill Mountain water. It also ordered the engineering staff to give special attention to the pressing situation in Brooklyn, Richmond and Queens, and passed a resolution that steps should be taken to secure Long Island waters to make up the deficit.[17]

Survey crews were quickly placed in the field to take soil samples and borings at Olive Bridge and Tongore, prospective sites for a high dam to hold back Esopus Creek. As they worked, the State Water Supply Commissioners, who would rule on the water plan to come, were given an August railroad tour of the Esopus Valley as far as Highmount, where they spent several days in conference at the elegant Grand Hotel on the Ulster-Delaware County border. Commissioners Henry Persons of Erie County, Milo Acker of Steuben County, Charles Davis of Ulster County, and Dr. Ernst Lederle and John A. Sleicher of New York City, were escorted on the trip by Edward Coykendall, general manager of the Ulster & Delaware Railroad, who perhaps wished to convince them of the folly of a project that would destroy many communities and submerge miles of his rail line. Coykendall, in comments made later that fall, urged the city to go to the Adirondacks for water and called the McClellan Act "one of the most outrageous acts of confiscation ever passed by a legislature in a civilized country."[18]

Coykendall's sentiments were expressed at one of seven public hearings held between November of 1905 and February of 1906 after the BWS submitted its plans for the development of the Esopus, Rondout, Schoharie and Catskill Creek watersheds to the city's Board of Estimate and Apportionment. On Oct. 27, 1905, that body approved the expenditure of $161.8 million to obtain 500 million gallons of water per day from the proposed system.[19]

Mayor McClellan petitioned the State Water Supply Commission to okay the plans, and the commission in turn slated the public hearings, which drew 126 objections and a parade of lawyers representing towns, businesses, organizations and individuals from half a dozen counties opposed to the plans. Chief among them was powerful Kingston attorney A. T. Clearwater, a former district attorney and county judge, who had as his clients the Ulster & Delaware Railroad and its owner, Samuel Coykendall; the Board of Trade and the Chamber of Commerce of the City of Kingston; the Cornell Steamboat Company; the First National Bank of Kingston and others.[20]

Clearwater, in front of an audience of 500 spectators at the first hearing November 27, 1905, in the Ulster County Courthouse in Kingston, argued that Chapter 724 of the Laws of 1905 was itself unconstitutional in part because it deprives people of property without due process of law, and takes private property for public use without just compensation. Exhibiting the turn of phrase that made him a sought-after public speaker, Judge Clearwater told the commission, "The powers asked by New York are too great. They ask power that the Almighty would not delegate to an archangel, let alone, if I may use such an irreverent comparison, a Tammany contractor."[21]

Representing the city were Corporation Counsel John Delaney, his assistant George Sterling, and engineers Smith, Burr, Freeman and Stearns. Sterling, speaking before the commission on December 11, argued that the city had done everything legally and under constitutional restraints; that the proposed plan was the product of objective studies done by professional engineers over the course of three city administrations and that those studies had determined the city had nowhere to go for water but the Catskills.

"Some of the objections assumed that the city would immediately, on the approval of its plan, proceed to devastate the whole Catskill mountain region, that it would seize buildings, tear them down on ten days notice to the owners and turn them out without a roof to shelter them," Sterling said. "A moment's consideration will convince anyone that this cannot be the case... No lands can be flooded until a dam has been constructed, no water can be diverted until an aqueduct has been built." But, he pointed out, the city justifiably retained power to summarily seize and destroy buildings in "extraordinary" cases to prevent unreasonable delay of the monumental project "by one or two individuals who are the owners of buildings worth but a few dollars."[22]

Sterling went on to say that those relocated would receive the market value of their property, and would likely be "better housed than they were before." Water in the brooks above the dams, he observed, would be just as copious, and just as free, to people living in the vicinity as it always was. He added, "If some of them are compelled to live in a little more cleanly manner than they have been accustomed to, and not to pollute the streams unnecessarily, they will have been taught a useful lesson in decency, cleanliness and healthfulness."[23]

The city's arguments won the day, and the State Water Supply Commission approved its plans May 14, 1906. "It is admitted that this undertaking will destroy several small hamlets and a vast amount of valuable property, and that the State cannot afford to permit the City of New York to enter an interior county nearly 100 miles distant and condemn property there, unless the conditions demand it," read the commission's decision. "But if the circumstances warrant it, the State cannot afford, by refusing to permit such entrance, to retard the growth of the great metropolitan city or to jeopardize the interest of its inhabitants... The commission is therefore of the opinion that the plans proposed are justified by public necessity."[24]

The commission did, however, sponsor amendments to the McClellan Act to provide better protection for property and business owners. Thus the legislature adopted Chapter 314 of the Laws of 1906, further defining the city's responsibility in respect to acquiring property; requiring the city to pay indirect damages to businesses whose value has been lowered by the projects and to employees who lose their jobs at firms acquired

by the city; providing police protection for communities near BWS projects; allowing municipalites within the Rondout and Esopus watersheds to connect to any BWS reservoir or aqueduct; and requiring the city to reconstruct some of the City of Kingston's sewers. The city was also prohibited from taking any water from Mink Hollow Stream above the City of Kingston's water source at Cooper Lake near Woodstock.[25]

By the time the city received the commission's conditional but anticipated blessing, the Board of Water Supply had more than 400 employees drawing plans or making surveys. By the end of 1906, according to the BWS Annual Report for that year, it had appointed 882 Civil Servants, housed in 31 leased properties used for engineering staffs, laboratories, store yards and drafting rooms. Auditors, bookkeepers and clerks were at work creating an accounting system to vouch for the estimated $162 million in expenditures. The Engineering Bureau was organized into six departments: Headquarters, Reservoir, Northern and Southern Aqueduct, Long Island and Filtration. They were divided into divisions and in turn into sections.

To Headquarters Department fell the daunting task of producing designs, specifications and contracts; hiring employees; purchasing supplies and equipment; testing materials, and planning the 18-mile-long City Tunnel #1 and the distribution conduits from Hill View Reservoir to the five city boroughs. This included the cast-iron pipeline laid beneath the Narrows to Staten Island, where Silver Lake Reservoir was developed.

The Reservoir Department had its headquarters in Brown's Station, Ulster County, and was assigned to do topographic surveys (18,000 acres the first year) and land surveys of 674 properties to be taken, along with investigation of impoundment sites. During 1906 this involved the taking of 21,400 linear feet of core borings to find a secure foundation for the Ashokan Dam, and 1,000 soil samples to determine whether to strip the surface earth from the reservoir floor. (A portent of the ill will the city's presence would instigate could be found in newspaper articles like one published Aug. 16, 1906, in which the attack on surveyors in the Beaverkill Swamp by swarms of hornets was used as something of a metaphor: "[The hornets] resent the invasion of their ancient solitary domain by even college graduates from the great City of New York. So far the hornets have escaped few casualties, but the invading engineers are a sight to see.")[26]

The Northern Aqueduct Department was housed at Poughkeepsie and was responsible for plotting the 62-mile section of the underground Catskill Aqueduct stretching from the Ashokan Reservoir to the Croton system, including planning the difficult Hudson River crossing. The Southern Aqueduct Department, headquartered in White Plains, was in charge of the remaining 17 miles of aqueduct, plus planning the Kensico and Hill View Reservoirs.[27]

The Long Island Department was charged with surveying and mapping potential ground water and estuary impoundment sites, along with a possible pumping station and distributing reservoir on the south side of the island.

Investigations were also conducted for a proposed filtration plant near Eastview, and surveys were run for the anticipated reservoir on Schoharie Creek, the next phase of the Catskill system. The Rondout Creek watershed would not be developed for another 30 years; Catskill Creek and its tributaries would never be tapped.

The Board of Water Supply had already accomplished much in office, field and lab when it paused June 20, 1907, for an official groundbreaking ceremony marking the start of the first contract on the line of the Catskill Aqueduct, an 11-mile section to be excavated by Thomas McNally Company of Pittsburg for $4.1 million. The 1907 BWS Annual Report noted that the Hudson River Dayliner *Albany* carried Mayor George McClellan and 350 invited dignitaries to Cold Spring, Putnam County. From there they were conveyed by automobiles and carriages to the Newell property near Garrison, where the city had acquired two acres for an aqueduct shaft.

About 1,000 people were waiting. They joined in as the BWS Glee Club sang "The Star Spangled Banner," heard a welcome address by Board President J. Edward Simmons and saw Commissioner Charles Chadwick present to the mayor a souvenir spade, specially made by Tiffany and Company with inlaid silver blade and a mahogany handle fashioned to represent a cross-section of the aqueduct.

Mayor McClellan, son of the famous Civil War general, who had opposed Abraham Lincoln for President, was a journalist, an attorney, a Congressman by the age of 27 and by age 30 president of the New York City Board of Aldermen. His two terms in office were marked by a fondness for great public works, including the city's first subway, which opened in October 1904, when the Mayor drove the first train from City Hall Station to 145th Street.

His speech at the start of the Catskill works hailed not only the commissioners and the engineers, but "the men with the picks and shovels, the men who carry the hods. The course of human events is not permanently altered by the great deeds of history, nor by the great men," McClellan said, "but by the small daily doings of the little men."[28]

More than 17,000 such "little men" would toil over the next decade, felling trees and buildings, constructing dams and dikes, shoveling muck, blasting through solid rock hundreds of feet beneath the earth, to bring soft, pure Catskill water to the metropolis 120 miles distant. It would be among the greatest engineering accomplishments of that or any age, rivaling the Panama Canal, which was even then being driven through the swamps of Central America.

Workers being lowered into Shaft 5 of the Rondout Pressure Tunnel. NYC DEP.

10. The Catskill Aqueduct

WAMPS were not the biggest problem facing the builders of the Catskill Aqueduct, but they were indeed among many natural obstacles waiting to be overcome, both above and below ground. Glaciers, earthquakes and floods had, over eons, created a patchwork of geologic conditions that would ultimately take the aqueduct through what geologists know as the Catskill Plateau, the Great Appalachian Valley, the mountainous Hudson Highlands, the Piedmont Region of Westchester County and the Coastal Plain represented by Long Island. Plotting an aqueduct through such varying terrain would be no mean feat.

Toward this end, the Board of Water Supply appointed eminent geologists W. O. Crosby, a professor at the Massachusetts Institute of Technology, and J. F. Kemp, on the faculty of Columbia University, to work with city engineers to find the most efficient, cost-effective and safest aqueduct route and conduit types.[1]

Field studies and test borings were conducted all along the route to determine such things as drainage, location of fold and fault zones, contours of underground bedrock, probable depth of buried gorges and the nature of underground water circulation. These investigations led to two major changes in the aqueduct route as initially proposed: The out-take of the Ashokan Reservoir was shifted from West Hurley to a point nearer the dam site at Olive Bridge to take advantage of more favorable topographical conditions; and the Hudson River crossing, first proposed for New Hamburg, was changed to Storm King farther south to avoid several faults, penetration of problematic limestone, and the necessity of building a nine-mile-long pressure tunnel from Marlboro to Fishkill.[2]

Gravity would do most of the work in getting the water to the city (from the Ashokan Reservoir at 587 feet above sea level to Hill View Reservoir at 295 feet above sea level), but engineers had to design the aqueduct to maintain a gentle grade to take advantage of the descending elevation.

As finally developed, the aqueduct included four distinct kinds of water conveyance systems for the 92 miles of water line between the Ashokan Reservoir and the city:

- *Cut-and-cover.* 55 miles. The least costly alternative, used where topography and elevation allowed, this involved digging a trench 28 feet wide within which was laid a horseshoe-shaped concrete conduit 17 to 18 feet in height and width, covered by earth. The cut-and-cover gradient is one foot to the mile.
- *Grade tunnel.* 24 sections totaling 14 miles. Where hills or mountains were encountered and circumventing them was impractical or too expensive, horseshoe-shaped concrete tunnels were driven through them. As in cut-and-cover stretches, water flows through grade

Above: Catskill Aqueduct surveyors traversed rough terrain, as shown in this 1907 photograph from the side of Storm King Mountain. *Below:* Excavation of a shaft of the Rondout Pressure Tunnel. Both NYC DEP.

tunnels as it would in open channels, but the tunnels are narrower (13 feet wide) and their sides steeper. The gradient (slope of descent) of these tunnels is two feet to the mile.

- *Pressure tunnel.* Seven tunnels, totaling 17 miles. Used to traverse large valleys and deep rivers, circular concrete pressure tunnels were placed below the hydraulic gradient, deep enough below the valley bed so that the weight of the rock overburden would exceed the internal pressure of the water. Varying in diameter from 14 to 16 feet, these tunnels were connected at either end to the aqueduct by vertical circular shafts, also lined with concrete, and ranging from 300 to 700 feet deep (except in the case of the Hudson River tunnel, where the shafts were 1,100 feet deep).
- *Steel-pipe siphon.* Six miles. Riveted steel pipe was encased in concrete, lined with cement, and laid on concrete cradles in earth-covered trenches. Siphons crossed smaller valleys, or were used where the rock was not suitable for a pressure tunnel. Parallel lines of pipe were added to existing siphons once the Schoharie system was operational, doubling the aqueduct's carrying capacity to 500 million gallons per day. [3]

Concrete for *cut-and-cover* sections was mixed at stationary plants using aggregate from sand and gravel banks or stone-crushing plants. (Some contractors used old stone boundary walls as material for crushing.) Concrete was generally carried in bottom-dump buckets on flat cars to be deposited in bottom invert forms. The top arch was fashioned by collapsible steel forms, concrete deposited on them by locomotive cranes. The largest area of fill on the aqueduct was on a cut-and-cover section at the lower end of the Newburgh Division, where "Monell's Fill"—a 975-foot-long, 23-foot deep trench (90 feet wide at the top, 188 feet wide at the bottom) required 68,000 cubic yards of material to fill in after the conduit was laid, according to BWS Division Engineer Lazarus White. Another special feature of the aqueduct involved a cut-and-cover section at St. Elmo Brook, where, to avoid a high

embankment, the aqueduct was carried on a viaduct with arches supporting the invert, then covered with earth fill, the final appearance being the same as the usual mounded cut-and-cover.

In *grade tunnels*, drilling and blasting through hillsides was conducted from portals at the surface, with muck removed in wagons pulled by mules, although electric locomotives were used in some cases. Some tunnels were reinforced by timbers or steel forms, and all were subsequently lined with up to 22 inches of concrete. A portion of the mile-long East View Tunnel, south of Kensico Reservoir, was reinforced with an interlining of vitrified brick when it was discovered that groundwater percolating through rock containing an acid-forming mineral was eating away at the concrete lining. [4]

Pressure tunnels started with vertical shafts excavated by men who, once surface material was dug away, used drills mounted on tripods to drill circles of holes in the rock surface. The holes were loaded with dynamite, blasted, and the resulting debris hoisted out. Men were lowered back into the hole via an open cage or lift, to drill, blast and muck out repeatedly, timbering the shaft as necessary, until the desired depth was achieved. Then the bottom area was "belled out" to a height and diameter that would accommodate track, rolling cars and other equipment, which was also lowered down the shaft mechanically. The tunnel was then excavated horizontally by much the same drilling and blasting procedure used in the shafts, as workers headed toward their counterparts who were making progress in the opposite direction from other shafts. The muck was shoveled into cars, which were rolled to the belled out area, then hauled out to the surface.

Steel-pipe siphons, ranged in length from 600 feet to 6,700 feet. Each section of pipe was 9½ feet long, and weighed five tons. They were delivered to siphon sites by rail. Laid on concrete cradles in excavated trenches, the pipe was riveted together, lined with two-inches of mortar, enclosed in con-

Tunnelers pierced uneven shale in driving through
the Shawangunk Mountains. NYC DEP.

crete six to eight inches thick and covered with
earth.[5]

The administration of the project was divided
into the Northern and Southern Aqueduct Departments, with each department organized into divisions, as outlined in BWS annual reports.

The Northern Department, under Robert
Ridgway, department engineer, consisted of 60
miles of aqueduct, 44 miles west of the Hudson
River and 16 miles east. It stretched between the
upper end of the Esopus Creek siphon and the
north side of Hunter's Brook, extending from the
headworks near the Ashokan Reservoir to the
north edge of the Croton watershed, crossing five
counties: Ulster, Orange, Dutchess, Putnam and
Westchester.

The Northern Department was divided into
five geographic divisions: The Esopus (13 miles),
Wallkill (12 miles), Newburg (14 miles), Hudson
River (eight miles) and Peekskill (13 miles). There
was also an Executive Division, with offices at
Poughkeepsie.

The Southern Aqueduct Department was
headed by Department Engineer Merritt H. Smith.
It consisted of 31 miles of the aqueduct between
Hunter's Brook and Hillview Reservoir, along
with the Kensico and Hillview Reservoirs and a
filter plant which was planned for the vicinity of
Eastview.

Five divisions operated within the department:
The Croton (10 miles), Kensico (five miles), White
Plains (12 miles) and Hill View (four miles). The
Executive Division was headquartered at White
Plains.

The first aqueduct construction contract let by
the BWS was to Thomas McNally Co., the lowest
of eight bidders seeking to build a little over 10
miles of aqueduct from Hunter's Brook near Peekskill to Cold Spring in the towns of Cortlandt and
Yorktown, Westchester County, and Phillipstown
in Putnam County.[6] The section included eight
miles of cut-and-cover and 2.8 miles of grade tunnels at Cat Hill, Garrison and McKeel. The 11,430-
foot Garrison tunnel traversed the "roughest and
most difficult country between the Catskills and
New York," related White in his 1913 book, *The
Catskill Water Supply of New York City, History,
Location and Sub-surface Investigations and Construction.* The shaft for the tunnel was sunk in 1907,
but the tunnel took five years to complete, partly
because the contractor had cash flow problems
stemming perhaps from a financial "panic" that
occurred in 1907. "Physical obstacles are more
readily overcome than financial," opined White in
his overview of the Catskill system to that point.
But the engineer recounted physical obstacles
aplenty.

Contract 11 for $2.3 million went to Stewart-
Kerbaugh-Shanley Co., for construction of the
Esopus Cut-and-Cover (6.5 miles) and the Peak
Grade Tunnel (3,470 feet). The section ran from a
mile south of Brown's Station to 2.5 miles north of
High Falls. White considered it "wild and inaccessible country, remote from railroads and reached
only by very rough country roads with numerous
steep grades. . .a very puzzling country in which to
place the aqueduct." At the little town of Atwood,
a rock cut 900 feet long and 25 feet deep was carved

into a hill overlooking the Esopus to place the aqueduct "well back from the cliff face in sound rock."

A quarry and a stone crushing plant at the foot of Bonticou Crag, a steep cliff at the outlet of the 6,800-foot Bonticou Grade Tunnel, supplied crushed stone for concrete work but could only be reached by an inclined cable-operated railway. Though it was "picturesquely located," White said, "Large boulders at the foot of the crag (loosened by blasting) had a tendency to roll into the workings of the quarry and cramp men and the plant," often burying the track as well. The cut-and-cover section of aqueduct that began at this eastern edge of the Shawangunks was subsequently relocated to avoid damage from recurring shale slides, the largest of which amounted to 2,000 cubic yards.

When bad ground was encountered in the 6,150-foot Hunter's Brook Grade Tunnel, north of Croton Lake, workers laid up timber lagging dry-packed with mortar to keep the tunnel from caving in. In December 1910, when the timbering was 1,470 feet from the head of the tunnel, a serious fall occurred, bringing down five sets of timbers. A few days later, White related, another fall wrecked 19 sets of timbers. The next three months were spent replacing and concreting them. A similar cave-in occurred in the 3,650-foot-long Reynold's Hill Tunnel, between the Sawmill River and the Bronx. It took four months to reclaim 60 feet of tunnel there.

The four-mile-long Rondout Pressure Tunnel west of the Hudson crossing was exceptionally difficult. Constructed from eight shafts and stretching 23,608 feet beneath the Rondout Creek and valley, it was the longest of the pressure tunnels on the aqueduct: Others pass beneath the valleys of the Wallkill River (23,391 feet), Moodna Creek (25,200 feet) and the Hudson River (3,785 feet); Croton Reservoir (2,900 feet); and Yonkers (11,000 feet). The variety of rock conditions in the Rondout Tunnel (workers encountered 12 different kinds of rock) resulted in great differences in rates of excavation progress from one section to the next. In shales, workers advanced 350 feet per month. Where the rock was more dense, progress was

reduced to 160 feet per month. A total of 250,000 cubic yards of solid rock were excavated from the Rondout Tunnel, which cost $248 per linear foot to construct, compared to $146 per linear foot in the less problematic Wallkill Tunnel.[7]

The sinking of 498-foot Shaft 4 on the Rondout Tunnel, begun July 20, 1908, was delayed for a year because of water infiltration. At 200 feet, workers struck sulphur water; at 260 feet, the flow was 900 gallons per minute. At the foot of the shaft, pumps worked furiously to remove 2,000 gallons per minute. "The sulphur content made it very difficult to get men to do the work," acknowledged contractor T. A. Gillespie Company in a 1911 company booklet. Indeed, the BWS Annual Report of 1909 indicated workers were on duty for just three hours at a time because of the irritating effects of hydrogen sulfide gas.

Simply inhaling the dust that clouded the shafts was unpleasant enough. To remedy that, workers in some shafts wore the "Automatic Respirator and Smoke Protector," a mask that covered the nose and housed a wet sponge to collect inhaled dirt and dust. The sponge had to be removed and rinsed out every three hours, according to the *Catskill Water System News*.

Many of the workers were immigrants or southern blacks. Lazarus White described the organization at Shaft 1 (the Rondout Tunnel), where an American superintendent and foreman supervised a largely Slavic workforce excavating the vertical shaft down to tunnel level. "These men had all had previous experience in Pennsylvania or West Virginia (mine) shafts, the workmen being particularly steady and hard working. During March 1909, an average of 5'9" was made per advance, which corresponds to 57 yards of rock shoveled into buckets in about 14 hours, each man filling five buckets of muck in his shift."[8]

The men were encouraged to do their best work by being paid bonuses based on a monthly progress of 90 feet. During the record month, workers received 40 percent of their wages in bonus payments, and "the contractor (was) more than compensated by the decreased cost per foot of the shaft excavation."

Tunneling under the Hudson

The subterranean crossing of the Hudson River between Storm King Mountain on the west and Breakneck Mountain on the east was just one of several options considered by engineers puzzling over this immense challenge. They discussed building a bridge to carry steel pipes across the waterway; laying steel or iron pipes in trenches dredged in the river bottom; or going 100 feet or so below the river's surface to drive one or more "shield tunnels," either steel lined or containing one or more pipes.

Instead, they decided to drill a tunnel through bedrock, considering it the cheapest and most durable method. But finding that bedrock took years of boring and test drilling—so long, in fact, that at one point, "people began to believe the river bottomless," according to Division Engineer Lazarus White writing in 1913.

Scows, held in position on the river by 10 anchors weighing two to three tons apiece, carried men and equipment to bore through bottom muck, gravel and rock. For four years they did battle with rough water, tides and passing traffic to recover core samples that would yield assurance of at least 150 feet of solid granite above the prospective tunnel. One scow found bedrock at 600 feet, but results of other borings were incon-

clusive. Under the supervision of geologist Charles Berkey, a second method of determining the extent of bedrock was utilized. Test shafts were sunk on both riverbanks, and, at a depth of 300 feet, diamond-bit drills worked toward each other at 43 degree-angles. They met 1,500 feet below the surface, their cores showing continuous, sound granite from shore to shore. Another set of inclined borings was made, meeting at 950 feet, convincing engineers it would be safe to drill the tunnel somewhere between those depths. They settled on 1,114 feet beneath the surface of the river.

The test shafts were enlarged for use as construction shafts; the east was 1,132 feet deep, the west 1,159 feet deep. As many as 300 workers per shift tunneled toward each other to span the 3,030-foot gap between the shafts with a 17-foot-diameter circular tunnel. At first, the Board of Water Supply conducted the work with its own forces, but in mid-1911, with both shafts completed and all but 450 feet of tunnel driven, the job was contracted out to the T. A. Gillespie Co.

Working conditions were dangerous. At one point, crews driving west struck a seam of water and the tunnel was flooded, "causing the report to spread that the Hudson River had been broken

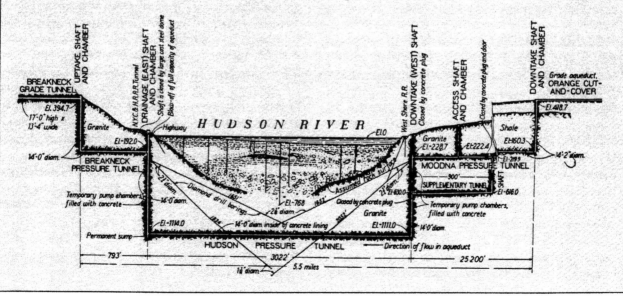

into and the tunnel was lost," White related. But the water was pumped out, the fissure concreted, and a concrete bulkhead with a steel door was built 200 feet from the east shaft to guard against a recurrence. A pumping plant was installed between the bulkhead and the shaft. An exploratory drill hole driven into the face of the heading found no indication that more groundwater was ahead.

"Popping rock," sheets of rock that peeled off with a loud report, injured several workers, prompting 646 feet of steel roof support to be erected in 13 locations. But even those protective supports proved hazardous to a group of workmen placing rivets in the material on Christmas morning, 1911. The *Newburg Daily News* reported that eight men were nearly killed when a large sheet of steel fell into the tunnel, cutting the air line and the electricity, and trapping them in a small space between the heading and the obstruction. They spent several hours waiting for rescue, as water seeping into the dark tunnel rose to their hips.

In early 1912, opposing drill crews finally reached each other. On January 30, in a ceremonial "holing through," New York City Mayor William Gaynor pulled the switch, setting off a blast that breached the last nine feet of granite blocking the tunnel. The two sides were less than an inch from being perfectly aligned. The mayor, wearing boots and a yellow slicker, was greeted by cheering workmen who scrambled through the opening and heard him call their achievement "one of the greatest engineering feats in history."

There remained the matter of lining the shafts and tunnel with concrete. A plant was built at the west shaft, where barges of sand and crushed stone were unloaded at a special dock on the river, mixed and lowered down the shaft and hauled by electric trolley cars to be dumped into forms inside the tunnel, creating a 17-inch barrier between Catskill water and the granite that would contain it.

Late in 1912, a 50-foot concrete plug sealed off the construction shaft on the west side of the crossing, while the uptake shaft on the east side, designed as the drainage and access shaft for the entire Breakneck-Hudson-Moodna pressure tunnel system, was topped with a 46-ton cast steel cap manufactured in Nicetown, Penn. Transported by rail to Jersey City, and by boat up the Hudson, the dome was hoisted by two 60-ton cranes at the river landing, where it was upended for placement of reinforced mortar lining. The cap's installation required 34 nickel-steel bolts, each 55 feet long, to resist the internal pressure of the city-bound water.

In 1914, when the aqueduct was first filled with water, leaks were detected at the Breakneck shaft, and a supplemental shaft was built the following year to circumvent the weak area.

Sources: Board of Water Supply Annual Reports, *Transactions of the American Society of Civil Engineers, Catskill Water System News, Newburg Daily News, Catskill Mountain News, Cornwall Local*, Lazarus White's *Catskill Water Supply of New York City*, Edward Hall's *Water for New York City*.

Facing page: Cross-section of the Hudson River crossing of the Catskill Aqueduct between Breakneck Mountain on the east and Storm King Mountain on the west. *Above:* Headworks of the east shaft of the Hudson River crossing can be seen at right, while the portal to the Breakneck Mountain grade tunnel is at top of inclined rail line. A horizontal tunnel was drilled from the east shaft through the mountain to connect with a vertical shaft driven down from the portal. NYC DEP.

Once shafts were sunk, horizontal tunnel excavation began. A good description of tunnel muck removal is provided in the 1910 BWS Annual Report, in which is detailed the work of the Dravo Contracting Co., which built 1,184 feet of the Yonkers Pressure Tunnel, a 143-foot-deep uptake shaft leading to Hillview Reservoir, and a 300-foot-deep downtake shaft connecting the reservoir with City Tunnel #1 and the distribution system:

> After the shafts were concreted, structural head frames 60 feet high were erected above the shafts. In them were operated two balanced Connellsville self-dumping shaft cages, worked by a Vulcan mine hoist. . . A special low steel muck car sat very low on the frame and was equipped with a front door, the arrangement such that when the cage reached the top of the head frame its floor was tilted by wheels entering a curved trackway, the floor of the cage being mounted on shafts. The car was held fast while the front door was automatically opened and the muck deposited in a high timber bin, from which it was run into a crusher and through a screen, the screen feeding onto a long belt conveyor, supported on high trestles so as to dump the crushed rock into a high conical storage pile.
>
> All the rock of the tunnel was directly crushed up in this manner to stone grading up to about two inches in size. The fine screening or stone dust made excellent sand which was used in the concrete as a substitute for natural sand, which in this neighborhood is very scarce. The stone crushing arrangement was most excellent, as it economically disposed of the tunnel muck by converting 100 percent of it into materials used in the concrete.

Contractors were required to supply living quarters for the workers in their employ. BWS regulations stipulated that "each inmate should have an individual bed, bunk or cot, and not less than 400 cubic feet of air space." The contractor constructing five miles of cut-and-cover near Newburgh housed its workers in two camps, one for American workers, another for Italian laborers. There were 50 houses, with eight men living in each. Cooking stoves were provided in small lean-tos attached to the Italian barracks, but not for the Americans, who ate in a common dining room because, the contractors said, Americans didn't cook.[9]

"Camp Bradley," on private land 140 feet above Croton Lake near a section of the aqueduct built by the Bradley Contracting Co., consisted of several buildings housing 345 men. With sanitation a major consideration, the camp was sewered, and all rain and washwater, along with run-off from spoils piles, was filtered.[10]

The Board of Water Supply required contractors to provide their workers with individual cots and "not less than 400 cubic feet of air space." This cabin, photographed in 1910, was decorated with magazine illustrations and pictures of loved ones. NYC DEP.

The George W. Jackson Co., which in 1910 won the contract to build 2.1 miles of Yonkers Pressure Tunnel, provided a house, rather than a camp, as sleeping and dining quarters for 100 white workers. About 30 black employees lived in another house, on Bennett Place, and a hospital was built on Seminary Avenue, according to the BWS Annual Report for 1910.

The *Cornwall Local*, in regular updates on progress of the Hudson River crossing nearby, also related the impact of so many strangers in their midst. Apr. 7, 1909: "73 Italians direct from the city passed through the village Friday, bound for Shafts 4 and 5 to be employed by the Mason & Hanger Co." Feb. 16, 1911: "About 1,500 people is the largest number that has been employed on the aqueduct in the town at one time. Of these, [by] far the greatest number are Negroes. Hungarians outnumber any of the white race. However, a majority of the countries of Europe, as well as the states of the union, have been represented." March 23, 1911: "A gang of about 20 Russians has moved into one of the shacks at Shaft 5. One of them is a muck boss who has a wife and one child and the others are his help."

During the life of the Hudson crossing project (from test boring that started in 1907, to completion of the tunnel in 1913) the *Cornwall Local* reported on baseball games between workers from east- and west-side shafts; on improvements to the town landing to enable the BWS boat *Ashokan* to dock there; on the chase of a dozen mules that had made a break for it in 1909 after arriving by train from Kentucky to work for Mason & Hanger; on the wedding in October 1910 of BWS engineer Charles Gavin to eccentric "Free Thinker" Antoinette Gazzam of Cornwall-on-Hudson. In July 1910, the newspaper reported that Baptist preacher Albert Watson was holding Sunday afternoon meetings for the workers, and was about to form a Bible class among the most "riotous" of them.

The newspaper also reported that six "Spaniards" were arrested in August 1910 after trying to kill a foreman. Fined $10 each and sentenced to jail time, they got a local lawyer to appeal the conviction on the grounds that they didn't understand English or the American legal system.

A more serious outbreak occurred in May 1913, when 300 laborers in the White Plains area attempted to drive from their work 400 men employed by the Pittsburgh Construction Co. on the aqueduct line at Elmsford. "The construction company herded the men together and put up a stubborn fight," reported *The New York Times* on May 22. Confronted with mounted and armed BWS policemen, stone-throwing strikers "were forced to retreat after many heads had been cracked." Several arrests were made, the offenders fined $3 each. A subsequent meeting of area contractors and state mediation officials resulted in an agreement by the employers to grant the workers' demand for a pay raise, to $2 a day.

Civil Service wages for BWS forces during this period were $60 a month for axemen; $80 for rodmen; $100 for transitmen or levelers; $120 to $130 for inspectors, and $1,350 to $3,000 per year for assistant engineers. Still, some BWS employees found it more lucrative to go to work for contractors along the aqueduct line. The Aug. 20, 1911 issue of *Catskill Water System News* published weekly by the BWS reported that "M. M. Hale, senior section engineer in the Manhattan Division, resigned from the BWS to go with Holbrook, Cabot & Rollins Corp. of Contract 67," and "P. W. O'Grady, formerly an assistant engineer on Section 5, Croton, has started work on a sub-contract for the cut-and-cover concrete south of Reynold's Hill."

Jesse Denniston, a Cornwall boy who'd gone to Cornell to study engineering, spent one of his summer vacations earning $2 a day helping with the aqueduct survey, and in 1909, fresh out of college, took the civil service exam for masonry inspector. He got a pay raise, to $5 per day. Working out of the engineer's office at Vail's Gate, Denniston lived at Canterbury and usually walked to work. Since the project proceeded 24 hours a day, he often found himself on foot at night. "Once in a snowstorm, I got lost," he recalled in a 1970 interview on tape at the Cornwall Public Library. "The only way I could tell where I was, I listened to the hoist running at the shaft at Vail's Gate."

In 1915, when the aqueduct was undergoing hydrostatic tests, a rupture occurred where the Moodna Tunnel joined the Hudson's west shaft, and, on the east side of the river, where the Breakneck Tunnel was connected to the east Hudson shaft. Denniston, assigned to help with the repairs at Breakneck, "commuted" from his home on one side of the Hudson, to his work on the other, via canoe. Recalled an aging Denniston, "Someone expressed concern about my going across the river, alone, ice sometimes, dark sometimes, and a blacksmith who worked over there said, 'Oh, he's just as safe as in the Lord's vest pocket.' "

Moodna Pressure Tunnel power house at Cornwall-on-Hudson. Huge, coal-fired boilers supplied power to run hoists, forges, and compressors. NYC DEP.

Many of those employed on the line were not so fortunate. "Since the first pick was struck on the work, more than 200 men have been killed in the course of their daily work," reported the *Pine Hill Sentinel* of January 18, 1913. "Approximately ten out of every 100 (workers) are killed or injured every year. More than 3,800 accidents, serious and otherwise, to workers on the great aqueduct have been recorded. . . The men doing the rough work are virtually all foreigners or negroes. Owing to the laborers being so inconspicuous, the death by accident of one or more of them attracts no public attention."

Some, though, sought recompense for their losses. Rose Colligan, sister of a man who died when struck in the head by a falling rock in Shaft 4, was awarded $11,000 in damages from the city in 1912. And four laborers, injured in various ways during the early part of 1910 while working for the Dravo Company, sued the contractor for $10,000 to $15,000 each.[11]

A freak lightning strike injured two men in July 1911, when a bolt struck the power house at Shaft 6, followed the cable down the shaft to the rail cars below and along the rails in both directions. At the west end of the tunnel, Thomas Brown, one foot on the rail, had just dropped a stick of dynamite in a hole when the lightning travelled through his body and the wire he still held, igniting the dynamite to cause an explosion that severely injured Brown and companion David Emery.[12]

Neither were the contractors nor BWS employees immune from the dangers of the job. Joseph Hanger of Kentucky, nephew of H. B. Hanger of Mason & Hanger, lost a leg, and ultimately his life, when he stepped on an unexploded blasting cap with hob-nailed boots.[13] And a BWS photographer named Bresnan suffered serious facial burns when flash powder exploded prematurely as he was taking pictures in the Garrison tunnel: "With eyes blinded so that he was unable

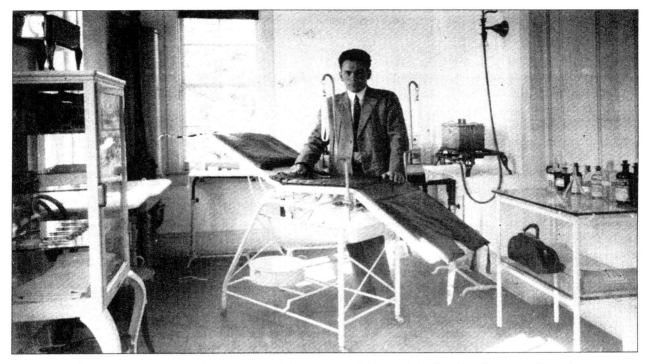

The operating room at the contractor's hospital on the line of the Yonkers Pressure Tunnel. Nearly 12,000 surgical cases were recorded by the BWS in 1911 alone. NYC DEP.

to see anything, and face burning with pain, sitting on the edge of the raft, supporting himself with one hand, with feet trailing in four feet of water, he held the torch aloft with the other hand so that his only companion could see to pole the raft through the tunnel a half-mile to the shaft," read an account in the BWS periodical *Catskill Water System News* of Nov. 10, 1911.

Fridays were thought to be unlucky, a superstition that led workers tunneling beneath the Croton Reservoir to "hole through" on Thursday night Sept. 7, 1911, in order to avoid doing so the following day. The milestone occurred without incident, but Friday retained its unlucky reputation when two laborers, working for the same contractor on another portion of the contract, were killed as the boom of a derrick carrying a concrete bucket fell on them.[14]

Hospitals and quarantine facilities were constructed at contractors' camps, and by all accounts the resident doctors and nurses were busy people.

In 1911, contractors' forces reached a high of 17,243 men, and the BWS Annual Report of that year summarized hospital activities in the camps: 11,973 surgical cases, 12,849 medical cases, 1,400 communicable diseases reported, and 98 deaths. That year, malaria was a particular problem in camps near the Hudson River between Storm King and Peekskill, with 633 cases registered. A swamp in and around Constitution Island off West Point was considered the prime breeding site for malarial mosquitos, but it was not found feasible to drain the swamp, or even treat it.

Contractors also made significant investments in machinery and equipment to handle their sections of the aqueduct. The Elmore & Hamilton Contracting Co., engaged to build three miles of cut-and-cover aqueduct between the Wallkill Pressure Tunnel and the northern end of the Newburgh Division, started work in September 1908. In 1909, they won the contract for another stretch of siphon in the White Plains Division, where they had on site a specially-designed steam shovel, two locomotive cranes, two concrete mixers, concrete forms, eight boilers, two derricks, one hoisting engine, two steam pumps, 35 scrapers (pulled by draft animals), 10 drills, and an assortment of cars, track and wagons.[15]

The Pittsburgh Contracting Company, building the mile-long Eastview Tunnel and the Elmsford Tunnel, utilized a mucking machine designed by the company's superintendent. It consisted of a rail-riding carriage with a 28-foot boom equipped with a special mechanism for picking up boxes loaded with muck at the heading and placing them on flat cars to be taken back to the shaft. The aim was to eliminate rolling wheelbarrows up an incline and into box cars for the trip out of the tunnel. But the device still required brawn to fill those boxes with rocks and dirt.[16]

The Glyndon Company, building a small section of cut-and-cover and 1.2 miles of grade tunnel within the Croton Lake drainage area, had an extensive compressor plant to power its operations as well as its worker camps. To provide water, the contractors built a concrete dam across the brook near the power house and developed a pumping system. To get sand for concrete, they acquired rights to a 12-acre parcel near the Hunters Brook

tunnel and built a cableway supported by 15 towers from 10 to 85 feet high, to convey sand to the site.[17]

Mason and Hanger, at Shaft 6 of the aqueduct, had four 60-horsepower boilers which furnished power for two air compressors, steam for a hoisting engine and a motor for blowing the forge in a blacksmith shop. Those boilers consumed 20 tons of soft coal daily, coal that was shipped from the company's own mines near Pittsburgh.[18]

The Dravo Company laid an incline cable road from the New York Central Railroad 1,000 feet up the side of Breakneck Mountain to get men and materials to the shaft site on the east side of the Hudson. Construction of that shaft set a U.S. record for speed----588 feet excavated in 93 days, or 6.3 feet per day. In the tunnel, a special hammer drill was tested which used hollow steel through which a combined stream of air and water was blown in to clear the bottom of the hole of chippings. Though plagued with breakdowns, use of the drill was to be encouraged, said Engineer Lazarus White, "because it eliminates the dust of drilling, the breathing of which undoubtedly shortens the lives of tunnel workers."[19]

A 2,000-foot section of cut-and-cover bisected the farm of Oscar and Abbie Washburn near Chappaqua, Westchester County. Their daughter Al-

berta (known as "Jack"), was a child of six when the work was being done in 1912. She and her four sisters watched the activity of men and mules with fascination, and 86 years later recalled how rocks from blasting operations 500 feet away rained through the barn roof one day. Barracks for the workers, mostly southern blacks, were built on nearby property, which is now a Girl Scout center. "Sometimes workers would come and steal chickens, so my father kept a pistol by the bed," Miss Washburn remembered. She recalled that her father's sister, her Aunt Antoinette, lived with the family and fought "tooth and nail" the city's incursion onto their property. It made no difference, though, and the grassy hump snaked its way through the farm. The family had a right of way over the aqueduct, paying $10 rent per year to the city in order to graze their cows atop the waterway.[20]

Upon formally filing maps, naming appraisal commissions and thus claiming lands for the aqueduct, dams and reservoirs, the city posted notices of area takings in conspicious public places. It paid owners half their properties' assessed valuations. If they did not accept the purchase offer made directly by the city, owners could rely on the appraisal commissioners to come up with a better price. If still dissatisfied, they could take the matter to Supreme Court. Sometimes the direct sale method worked. The 1907 BWS Annual Report noted that a 24-acre farm near Kensico in Westchester County was purchased from the owner for $21,000, or $883 per acre. Sometimes, property owners tried to get more for their holdings than they were worth. The same BWS report crowed that Commissioners of Appraisal awarded a Phillipstown man just $550 for a 10-acre parcel he said was valued at $45,000 because it contained a trolley line. The city convinced commissioners that the rails had only recently been placed on the

ground to bolster the man's claim. Most often, though, the commissioners weighed the claims of both city and landowner, and arrived at a compromise.

Some 70 buildings were built along the aqueduct line, and at the reservoir sites. They included granite siphon chambers at each end of every steel-pipe siphon to connect them with adjoining cut-and-cover sections and to house water control gates. The superstructure built atop the drainage shaft on the east side of the Hudson River crossing was given special consideration. "With Breakneck Mountain for a background, it was recognized that a masterful, simple, dignified architectural treatment alone would be satisfactory," related the 1911 BWS Annual Report. Local granite was selected for the building and its approaches because it "best harmonizes in color and texture with the rugged mountainside."

So proud was the city of its accomplishment that it paraded a reproduction of a concrete section of the Catskill Aqueduct through the streets of New York during the Silver Jubilee celebration May 26, 1923, accompanied by BWS employees and patrolmen on horseback.

Facing page: Concreting the arch of the Peekskill cut and cover section of the aqueduct, June 27, 1911.

Right: Twelve horses were needed to haul 11-foot-diameter sections of steel pipe for the Bryn Mawr siphon.

Both NYC DEP.

A section of the Queens conduit on Willoughby Avenue, near Kent Avenue, looking east, Sept. 1914.
NYC DEP.

11. Beneath City Streets

DESIGNED to deliver Catskill Mountain water to millions of waiting customers in New York City, City Tunnel #1 was, at the time of its construction (1911-15), the longest pressure tunnel in the world.

Although significantly shorter than the Catskill Aqueduct proper, the 18-mile-long tunnel involved a daunting set of challenges distinct to urban construction: It crossed two rivers and New York Harbor; required the use of thousands of pounds of high explosives in a heavily populated area; posed problems in the disposal of millions of tons of rock and debris; and demanded care and caution in avoiding underground sewer and subway lines.

The tunnel was drilled through solid rock and ranged from 15 to 11 feet in diameter. It crossed beneath three boroughs (subsurface pipelines were laid in two more) and burrowed beneath the Harlem and East Rivers. It was constructed from 24 shafts ranging from 250 to 750 feet deep and included a 10,000-foot line of cast-iron piping laid in a trench on the floor of the Narrows of New York Harbor. On the other side of the Narrows, at Staten Island, the water reached the Catskill System's terminus in Silver Lake Reservoir.[1]

To avoid excessive interference with streets, buildings and utilities, construction shafts were largely located in parks and other public spaces. Situated about 4,000 feet apart, the shaft sites generally included wooden hoist frames over the vertical openings, bins for transferring muck, and temporary offices and shops.[2]

At 22 of the shafts, water was delivered to street mains through vertical riveted steel pipes, called risers, embedded in concrete in the upper part of each shaft. Shafts and risers were lined with concrete to prevent corrosion. Provisions were made at Shaft 11 in Morningside Park and at Shaft 21 on the Manhattan shore of the East River at Clinton and South Streets for de-watering the tunnel for inspection or repairs.[3] At Shaft 3, a connection was made to the Croton Aqueduct system through an eight-foot tunnel to the gatehouse at the north end of the Jerome Park Reservoir.[4]

The work went on for six years, largely unnoticed by the general populace because the shaft sites were the only visible indication that a tunnel was being built. From two terminal shafts in Brooklyn, however, the aqueduct took the form of large steel and cast-iron pipes laid in surface trenches to Queens and Richmond on Staten Island, the total length of the delivery system being 34 miles.[5]

The original plan for the Catskill water system, as outlined in 1905 and approved in 1906, provided only for the delivery of 120 million gallons per day to the Boroughs of Brooklyn and Richmond, deferring consideration of distribution to Manhattan, Queens and the Bronx to a later date. Studies and debate on what that distribution system would entail proceeded over the next few years, as experts

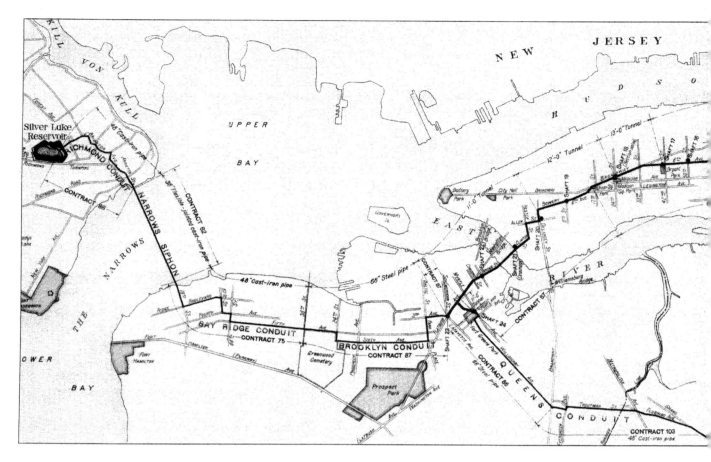

The route of City Tunnel #1 from Hillview Reservoir in Yonkers through Manhattan, under the East River, through Brooklyn and under the Narrows of New York Bay to Silver Lake Reservoir on Staten Island.

considered whether to use the conventional system of laying metal pipes through city streets, or to bore a deep rock tunnel far beneath the surface.

To carry 500 million gallons of water per day to the city under the same head as a single 15- to 11-foot diameter tunnel would require thirty-two 48-inch pipes or sixteen 66-inch pipes. That would cost an estimated $47 million.[6] Board of Water Supply (BWS) engineers favored the tunnel approach because it would cost less, be less disruptive and involve fewer repairs over the long run, while reducing pumping costs and increasing the height to which the water could be elevated. A tunnel would also allow delivery of larger amounts of water, at greater pressure, at any point along the line in case of fire, reducing insurance rates.[7]

In November of 1909, the BWS submitted to the city's Board of Estimate and Apportionment a plan for a pressure tunnel from Hill View Reservoir, beneath the Bronx and Manhattan to Brooklyn, with lines of metal pipes to Queens and Richmond. Two consulting engineers and a geologist, reviewing the plans for a committee of city officials, studied data already collected in 125 rock borings conducted by the BWS. They reviewed records from the seven-mile tunnel from Jerome Park to 135th Street along the city's own Croton Aqueduct, the first pressure tunnel ever built, in 1885-91. They also looked at pressure tunnels constructed for the Pennsylvania Railroad, the East River gas tunnel, the Webster Avenue sewer and the Bronx Valley storm sewer. Much information had also been collected during the building of the

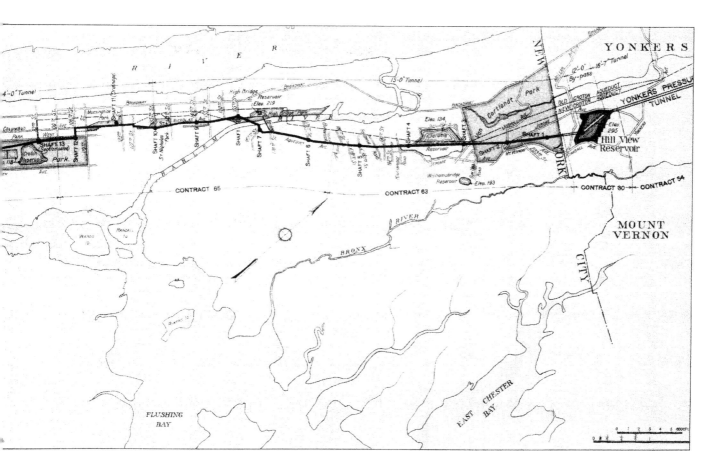

Rondout, Wallkill and Moodna pressure tunnels on the Catskill Aqueduct then under construction. After considering all this material, the consultants backed the tunnel concept, and the Board of Estimate's committee, made up of the president of the Board of Aldermen, the Comptroller and the president of the Borough of Manhattan, recommended that the city go forward with the plan and appropriate $25 million to the undertaking.[8]

The Board of Estimate concurred, and petitioned the State Water Supply Commission for permission to build the project. The petition was granted on Oct. 20, 1910, and the following spring, four contracts for construction of City Tunnel #1 were awarded, totalling $19 million.[9]

Of these four contracts, two went to firms that were already engaged on portions of the Catskill Aqueduct (Mason & Hanger and the Pittsburgh Contracting Co.) The other city tunnel contracts

were awarded to Grant Smith & Co. and Locher (later known as Smith, Hauser & Locher); and to Holbrook, Cabot & Rollins Corp., George B. Fry and T. B. Bryson.

The work was conducted under the auspices of the City Aqueduct Department, headed by Department Engineer Walter Spear. The department was divided into the Bronx Division, the Manhattan Division and the Conduit and Reservoir Division, the latter being responsible for the pipelines in Brooklyn, Queens and Staten Island, and for the Silver Lake Reservoir.

Much of the following construction description was provided by Lazarus White, Manhattan Divison Engineer, who wrote *The Catskill Water Supply of New York City* in 1913.

The tunnel section extending four miles south from Hillview Reservoir was constructed from five circular concreted shafts, a departure from the Catskill Aqueduct practice of timbering rectangular shafts. The Dravo Company was once again subcontracted to sink the shafts. Engineer White provides a description of the initial excavation, and then the drilling of holes for blasting Shaft 4 at Jerome Park Reservoir, 196th St. and Jerome Ave.:

> The upper portion of the shaft was sunk by the aid of a stiff-legged derrick which was later replaced by temporary head frames. After excavating and timbering 14 feet of earth overlaying the rock at Shaft 4, very good progress was made for the next 150 feet, the maximum weekly progress being 32 feet. The diameter of this shaft is 17 feet 6 inches and was excavated by three circular rows of holes on 4½-foot, 7-foot and 8-foot radii. The first row of holes 8 feet deep was drilled to an inward slope of 1 to 4, the second row 8 feet deep was drilled to an inward slope of 1 to 2, the third row of holes six feet long was drilled vertically. The two outer rows contained 17 holes and the inner nine. All the holes were drilled in one shift by six drill runners and helpers. The next two shifts were engaged in shooting and mucking, eight men working in each shift. This rotation was maintained so that an advance of about 6 feet per day was made. The best monthly progress was 99 feet on Shaft 4.

At one point in sinking Shaft 4 water was struck by drillers, prompting concern that it came from Jerome Park Reservoir through seams which had been opened in the rock by heavy blasting during reservoir construction. Testing of the shaft water showed that it differed from Croton water, however. Drill holes were grouted, and the flow cut off.

After the shafts were sunk, headings were excavated at the base of each, from which the tunnel itself was driven. Three shifts of seven drillers and helpers and three shifts of about 20 muckers were employed per day. It took from eight to 11 hours to drill a heading, and about a week to make 12 advances of from six to seven feet each.

The Pittsburgh Contracting Co. built five miles of the tunnel from 179th St. in the Bronx to W. 99th St. in Central Park. Considered among the more progressive companies in the field, the firm electrified most of its operations. Transformers which stepped the current down from 7200 to 220 volts, and switchboards were installed at each of seven shafts.

At Shaft 7, 167th St. and Sedgwick Ave. near the Harlem River, several problems were encountered. A 48-inch brick sewer had to be rebuilt, and an open concrete caisson had to be used to drive

Workers drill the belled-out area at the bottom of a shaft prior to beginning the horizontal tunnel in this 1913 photo. NYC DEP.

Forms for concreting the arch are in place in this 1914 photograph. NYC DEP.

the shaft past an area of wet sand and clay. A metal "shoe" was set atop the sandy section, and a 13-foot concrete cylinder built on it. The weight of the concrete drove the cutting shoe through 47 feet of bad ground. Additional concrete was added and the lining reinforced with horizontal bars as the caisson was sunk to sound rock. Drilling and blasting were used from then on to reach the 350-foot shaft depth prior to drilling the tunnel beneath the Harlem River.

At some other shafts, like Shaft 18 at 24th and Broadway, Madison Square, steel sheet piling driven by steam hammers was used to reach rock through water-bearing gravel. When bad ground was encountered in the tunnel itself, the roof was supported by 12-foot-long, 9-inch steel I-beams bolted together longitudinally, held up by temporary timber caps and legs known as "horseheads." Wooden lagging was then placed transversely between two or three lines of these steel "crown bars," which were left in place when the tunnel was concreted.

The contract under which Shaft 18 was built involved 4.8 miles of the tunnel between 100th St. at Central Park and 4th Ave. at 14th St. Although all six shafts in this section were located in the heart of Manhattan, only one site, Shaft 16, had to be acquired by eminent domain, the other five being located in Central, Bryant and Worth Monument Parks.

City regulations prohibited blasting between the hours of 11 p.m. and 7 a.m. until horizontal tunnels had been excavated 250 feet in from the shaft bottoms. Most shafts initially received licenses to store 100 pounds of gelatin dynamite on site, but later, 200- to 400-pound licenses were issued as explosives were stored in fortified surface magazines, supplied with heating systems to prevent freezing, covered with sheet iron to make them bullet-proof and tended by licensed personnel.

The Dupont Company usually made two deliveries of dynamite daily to the magazines. When tunnel driving commenced and larger quantities of explosives were needed, approval was granted to store up to 1,000 pounds of dynamite in 19 underground chambers at tunnel grade. Entrance was through side tunnels having several right-angle turns and heavy, automatically-closing doors to seal off gases in case of explosion. During the first three years of construction, 10,000 pounds of dynamite were used daily----2.5 million pounds by the end of 1912, a year in which 14 men had been killed in blasting accidents.[10]

What might have been a major disaster occurred in August 1913, when fire broke out in the blacksmith's shop and spread to the headframe over Shaft 9. All but one of the contractor's buildings at the site, located at 150th St. and St. Nicholas Ave., were destroyed, and several apartment houses and homes on St. Nicholas Ave. were heavily damaged. "The fire demonstrated the great value of having the magazine underground, where 968 pounds of dynamite were stored at the time," the 1913 BWS Annual Report ventured. Sixty men were in the tunnel when the blaze broke out. After the fire was doused, they had to climb out using ladders. A group of drillers waiting to descend the shaft jumped to the street; five were hospitalized, according to the *Catskill Water System News* of Aug. 20, 1913.

The fourth contract on the City Tunnel stretched from Union Square to the Bowery, Delancey and Clinton Sts. and under the East River to Brooklyn, where the two terminal shafts were located. The six shafts in this section varied from 310 to 757 feet deep, and all required compressed air caissons to reach rock through ground water.

Caissons served both as a safe place for workers to excavate the shafts, and as permanent shaft lining. They ranged from 15 to 18 feet in inside diameter and were from two to three feet thick. A caisson began with a two-foot high steel cutting ring or shoe placed at the bottom of the chamber that had been excavated from the surface. Atop the cutting ring, a hollow cylinder of very dense concrete was laid higher and higher as the caisson slowly descended. Sand and muck were hoisted out of the cylinder by teams of four to six men filling a bucket with shovelfuls of material as the caisson descended with the help of gravity. The caisson was gradually heightened by the use of steel forms and

A 123-foot high caisson was used to drive Shaft 23 through groundwater to solid bedrock. The caisson towered 73 feet above the ground and weighed 2,300 tons. At right is a post-construction view of the same Brooklyn street corner (where Lafayette, Third and Flatbush Avenues meet Schermerhorn Street), 1915. NYC DEP.

made heavier as needed by the placement of pig iron on a platform at its top. The tallest caisson erected for the city tunnel was at Shaft 23, where it rose 123 feet from the cutting edge, towering 76 feet above ground level and weighing 2,300 tons before it finally reached solid rock 100 feet below groundwater.

Once the heavy caisson reached groundwater, a thick, reinforced concrete deck was constructed about six feet above the cutting edge to form the roof of a working chamber into which air was pumped under pressure to keep out water and seeping sand. The concrete deck was pierced by two wells into which men and materials could be lowered.

In those chambers the "sand hogs" labored, drilling and digging sand, shale and rock under air pressures that ranged up to 45 pounds per square inch. They were lowered to their jobs in buckets operating in a special steel shaft equipped with air locks that raised the pressure to that of the working chamber when the men descended, and lowered it gradually as they returned to the surface. Lowering the pressure too quickly could result in the release of nitrogen into the blood and tissues, forming

bubbles. There were several cases of "Caisson disease," also known as "the bends," among sand hogs who worked on the city tunnel, and at least one fatality resulted.

Sand hogs were members of the Compressed Air and Foundation Workers' Union, and were paid higher wages because of the dangers of their job. Those working in air pressure up to 22 pounds per square inch could work a total of eight hours per shift and were paid $4 for that shift, about twice that of regular laborers. Those who toiled in higher pressures were allowed to work fewer hours per shift, time on interspersed with time off. Workers operating under pressures of 40 to 45 pounds per square inch, for example, could work only two hours per shift—one hour on, five hours off, another hour on, and for those two hours of labor, they were paid $5.

The average crew when the Shaft 20 caisson was being sunk in late 1911 consisted of six sand hogs, a foreman and a lock tender. Dozens of laborers, mechanics, compressor engineers, hoist runners and other workers toiled at the surface during each shift. Excavation of the rock on Shaft 23 was made under 45-pound pressure, each man working two hours a day. To keep the work going continuously, 12 seven-man gangs were employed. "Although the men worked with a will, it took 351 hours to excavate 161 yards of rock," related Lazarus White.

Once the caisson was bedded on sound rock, it was sealed to the rock with concrete so that compressed air could be safely taken off without water leakage occurring. The tunnel was then excavated horizontally from a belled-out chamber in the rock. Men then went to work drilling precise patterns in the tunnel headings in both directions, ramming gelatin dynamite and blasting caps into the holes and setting off the charges that would loose another six or seven feet of bedrock from its ancient footings. Ventilation hoses were dragged to the heading to clear smoke and dust, and soon, workers were back in the hole to set up electric lights and haul muck six feet or so back from the new heading so drillers could prepare for the next round of explosives. An hour after shooting, a gang of 17 to 22 muckers descended into the tunnel, to extend the narrow rails for battery-operated train cars so that dinky engines could be loaded with debris and hauled back out of the tunnel.

"Three-car trains are hauled by General Electric storage battery cars at a speed of 400 to 500 feet per minute [six to eight miles per hour]," White explained in his 1913 book. "A mucking shift will load 52 to 60 cars in eight hours." On Shaft 19, he reported, 179 men were employed on a typical three-shift day. This sort of progress did not prevent complaints from contractors about the high turnover in these back-bending jobs and the "increasing wage [$2 for eight hours] demanded by the muckers." There were frequent efforts to find a reliably designed and constructed mucking machine to do away with the need for so many men, but none had proven successful by 1913.

Spoil from the shafts and tunnels was used to fill low areas in the Bronx, and along the bulkhead at Riverside Park. Much of the rest was hauled to scows and dumped at sea. "Stone which in the country would be crushed and used for concrete is wasted in the city because of the small shaft areas

and the nuisance from the operation of crushers," the engineer said.

The contractors erected concrete mixing plants at locations convenient to the shafts. At Shafts 10 and 12, gravel and sand from storage bins on the Hudson River were delivered in skips on trucks, hoisted in these skips to 150-yard steel bins, and conveyed to hoppers and mixers to be combined with cement, which was elevated to the mixing platforms by bag hoists. The mixed concrete was hauled to the shaft head by hoisting engines and lowered in cages to the bottom of the shafts before being drawn to moveable concreting forms in trains of five to seven cars pulled by electric engines.[11]

Although urban construction had its drawbacks, including higher labor costs, the city environment paid off in another respect, Division Engineer Lazarus pointed out: "New York and its vicinity has been the scene of extensive tunnel operations since the beginning of work on the New Croton Aqueduct in 1890. The 30 miles of tunnel on that aqueduct was the means of training many men; this was followed later by tunnel and rock excavation on subways, and a little later by the Pennsylvania [Railroad tunnels under the Hudson], and finally by the aqueduct tunnels."

Hundreds of men worked not in the tunnels, however, but in the trenches dug to lay distributing pipes through parts of Brooklyn and Queens. Trenching machines and men with picks and shovels dug up pavement and excavated pipeline trenches at the rate of 500 to 900 feet per week in 1912 and 1913. Surface rail systems cooperated with the contractors during construction. On 5th Avenue, for example, the work was carried on in 300-foot sections, while the Brooklyn Rapid Transit Company put in temporary cross-overs and abandoned its westerly track for the length of each section until the pipe was laid and the trench refilled. The company also assisted by removing carloads of excavated material from 5th Avenue. The Long Island Railroad excavated and underpinned its tracks at four points where they crossed the pipeline. The Queens County Railway Company also had tracks affected by the project.

A 66-inch bronze section valve about to be lowered down Shaft 13 in 1913.
NYC DEP

Although many were inconvenienced by the building of the city tunnel and conduits, some experienced unexpected benefits. The New Netherland Bank at 41 W. 34th St. had, since its construction in 1904, employed an automatic pump in the cellar to get rid of water from a never-failing spring that had been struck when the building was erected. When the city tunnel passed beneath 10 years later, the spring was cut off and the bank was finally able to dispense with the cellar pump.[12]

Bronze riser valves to regulate the flow of water from the tunnel to the distribution mains were installed in shafts and were located 100 feet below the top of sound rock. Their placement was a feat to rival tunnel construction: 72-inch riser valves weighed 21 tons; 48-inch valves were a hefty nine tons. Designed to close automatically in case of a break in the valve chamber or in the street mains, they were carefully lowered in pieces from street level.

Two 66-inch section valves----20 tons each----crossed the main pressure tunnel at Shafts 13 and 18 to permit the tunnel to be divided and drained without putting the entire tunnel out of commission. Thirty-one bronze shaft caps were also installed, and weighed five to 11 tons each.[13]

On January 12, 1914, New York City Mayor Purroy Mitchel pressed an electric switch 400 feet beneath 150th Street, detonating a charge to blow out the last section of rock in the entire Catskill Aqueduct-City Tunnel network. Accompanied by oilskin-clad members of his cabinet and the three-member Board of Water Supply, the mayor ceremoniously discharged 200 pounds of dynamite to open the passageway. "As the three-foot ledge was penetrated, the laborers set up a wild cheer in which the city officials and distinguished visitors joined," related the *Catskill Mountain News*.

Though located in upstate Margaretville, more than 100 miles to the northwest, the newspaper's readers had more than a passing interest in the aqueduct project, designed as it was to carry water captured in the nearby Esopus valley, a valley even now disappearing before their very eyes.

Crossing the Narrows to Staten Island

Rather than conduct laborious boring and sampling to determine the depth of bedrock beneath New York Harbor, the Board of Water Supply chose a novel approach for reaching city residents across the Narrows on Staten Island: They would lay flexible-jointed, cast-iron pipe in a trench on the bottom of the harbor, thus connecting the City Tunnel in Brooklyn with the Catskill System's terminal reservoir at Silver Lake.

The contract to do the work was awarded in February 1914 to Merritt & Chapman Derrick and Wrecking Co. for $996,862. They were to lay 10,570 feet of submarine pipe from 79th St. and Shore Rd., Brooklyn, to the junction of Arrietta St. and Stuyvesant Place on Staten Island.

The operation included a 120-foot-long dredge with a six-yard shell bucket, seven bottom-dumping scows with 1,000-cubic-yard capacity each, two tugs to haul the scows out to sea to dump the dredged material, a 70-ton derrick scow with a steel skidway for laying pipe, two other derrick scows and a 35-ton derrick tug.

Excavation to remove part of the Brooklyn seawall and dig an area to contain a derrick scow commenced in April 1914, and dredging operations began in August in the Bay Ridge, Brooklyn channel. The 13-ton dredge bucket dug the trench, which was 30 feet wide and varied in depth from 10 to 35 feet. After a section of trench was dug, an A-shaped drag of I-beams weighing 20 tons was hauled along the bottom of the trench by three tugs to smooth the bottom prior to laying pipe.

A 168-foot-long structural steel cradle or skidway was suspended over the front end of the scow, which carried a 70-ton derrick. A second derrick scow was positioned alongside to lift 12-foot lengths of pipe into position onto the cradle, where sections of pipe were connected by pouring a joint of 300 pounds of hot lead. Lead pellets were then forced into each screw hole, and grease was forced into all holes to lubricate the joint and make it flexible.

Cables holding the pipe fast to the skidway were then removed, the scow was allowed to move forward slowly, and the pipeline was gently slid down the skidway into the trench. About 25 men working on the pipe scow could lay an average of 2½ lengths of pipe in an eight-hour shift.

The trench was refilled to a depth of eight feet using mostly subway and foundation excavation material, since trench dredging was practically completed before back-filling commenced.

About 1,400 feet of pipe was laid the first season. The work continued during 1915, when the Staten Island approach trench was dredged and lined with 575 tons of steel sheeting. In June 1916, the submarine pipe was finally connected to the land conduit, two Venturi meters to register and record water flow were installed on both sides of the Narrows, and the entire line was ready for testing by July 10.

A 48-inch cast-iron pipeline—the Richmond Conduit—carried the water from the shore gatehouse at the foot of Arrietta St., beneath Victory Blvd. to Silver Lake, where, since 1913, workers had been transforming a former resort area to a storage reservoir.

From the late 1800s through the early years of the 20th century, Silver Lake Park had been a popular recreation spot originally called Fresh Pond. In the 1880s, guests of the Silver Lake Hotel enjoyed swimming, boating, walks along a shoreline promenade and moonlit dancing in a large pavilion. Stages and trolleys ran from Tompkinsville to the hotel, which was later known as Raisch's Casino Hotel. Ice was harvested from the tree-lined lake in the winter, when skaters also flocked to the site.

Staten Island residents had gotten their water from an assortment of private companies, which were acquired by New York City in 1909. Estimated capacity was about 12 million gallons, most of it from driven wells. Bids were let in the summer of 1913 for construction of a 56-acre reservoir

Clockwise from the top: Building the earthen dike in Silver Lake Reservoir in 1914. The derrick scow used by contractors Merritt & Chapman to lay more than 10,500 feet of submarine pipeline in a trench along the bottom of the Narrows of New York Bay between Brooklyn and Staten Island. Laborers worked in close quarters to dig the Richmond Conduit tunnel between the Narrows siphon and Silver Lake. Silver Lake as it looked in 1896 when it was a recreation area for Staten Islanders. Staten Island Historical Society, all others NYC DEP.

to encompass the old Silver Lake, and the Beaver Engineering and Contracting Co. was awarded the contract for $821,000.

The lake was drained, the top soil and all organic material removed, and a two-basin, earthen-banked reservoir constructed to impound 435 million gallons of water. About 165 acres of land (10 parcels) were taken by the Board of Water Supply for the project. The reservoir, about four times the size of the original lake, was surrounded by about 100 acres under BWS control.

The reservoir, located about two miles from St. George, was 35 feet deep, 2,400 feet long and 1,500 feet wide, with a 1.5-mile shoreline. By Feb. 20, 1917, it was filled with its first water from the Catskill Mountains 120 miles away. The reservoir also became a selling point for developers seeking to market nearby homesites with a view of the lake, the Statue of Liberty and the Orange Mountains in New Jersey.

A second submarine pipeline was laid to Staten Island between 1923 and 1925 (Chapter 15).

Four decades later, in 1962, a new, five-mile-long pressure tunnel was begun beneath Upper New York Bay to connect Staten Island and City Tunnel #2 in Brooklyn. The 10-foot-diameter Richmond Tunnel runs for 25,000 feet beneath the bay. Built from 950-foot-deep shafts located in the Red Hook section of Brooklyn and the Tompkinsville section of Staten Island, the tunnel dispensed with the Narrows pipeline while increasing the delivery capacity from 100 million to 300 million gallons of water a day to burgeoning Staten Island.

The Perini Corp. and the Morrison-Knudsen Co. teamed up on the $16 million tunnel project. A special feature of the Brooklyn shaft-sinking job was the freezing of the earth above bedrock to prevent water infiltration. Brine was circulated through pipes sunk around the perimeter of a circle, prompting the ground to freeze in ever enlarging cylinders so that excavation and subsequent concreting could take place without the problem of water seepage. This alleviated the necessity of pumping the water out, which could have lowered the surrounding groundwater levels, destabilizing area buildings.

A tunnel-boring machine, the Alkirk Hardrock Tunneler, was utilized for a time to drill through bedrock beneath the Narrows, but it proved inefficient because of extensive breakdowns and modifications, so conventional methods were employed in round-the-clock excavation of the tunnel, which was finished in 1968.

A 96-inch conduit connects meter and distribution chambers, and a mile of 86-inch concrete pipe carries water from the distribution chamber to the largest underground storage tanks in the world. Holding 100 million gallons, the reinforced concrete storage structure is 1,720 feet long, 226 feet wide and 38 feet high. It is divided into two units so that half may be removed from service for cleaning or repair. The system was installed on a hillside, the added elevation above the old lake improving water pressure to Staten Island customers.

The start of tank construction in 1967 was delayed for four months when a citizens' group took the city to court to prevent the use of park land for the project. The court sided with the city and the Walsh Company got right to work on the $15 million project. The north basin of the Silver Lake Reservoir had to be drained to allow for construction, so a booster pumping system was installed in one of the existing Narrows siphons to maintain the level of the reservoir's south basin for the duration of the project.

The new system went on line in 1970. Silver Lake itself was discontinued as a water source and has reverted to its former use as a recreational area.

Sources: *Staten Island and Its People* (Vol. 1, 1930); *Catskill Water System News* (Oct. 30, 1913); Staten Island Historical Society; E. H. Hall's *Water for New York City* (1993 reprint); Weidner's *Water for A City* (1974); NYC Board of Water Supply Annual Reports, 1914-1917; NYC Municipal Water Finance Authority Bond Prospectus for Fiscal 1998; *Delaware Water Supply News*, April and July 1965; Board of Water Supply Annual Reports, 1962, 1965, 1968.

East face of the upper gate chamber, shown in November of 1912. Shandaken Historical Museum.

12. Building the Ashokan

ORK on the Catskill Aqueduct had been under way for two months before bids were opened in August of 1907 for Contract #3, construction of the reservoir dam at the head of the pipeline. The job of building the Ashokan Reservoir would not begin for several more months, however, as opponents of the project prompted a state investigation of the bid-letting process and nearly brought to trial the three-member Board of Water Supply.

Five bids were received from firms anxious to take on the monumental task of building the huge dam and its auxiliary dikes, structures consisting of 5.5 miles of masonry and earth that would hold back 128 billion gallons of water. The lowest bid, for $10.3 million, was submitted by John Pierce Co. of New York City; the highest was for $14.7 million. Chief Engineer J. Waldo Smith, backed by consulting engineers, believed the Pierce bid was too low and the company was not in a position to complete the task. Pierce agreed to step aside, and the city engineers recommended awarding the job to the second-highest bidder, MacArthur Brothers Co. and Winston & Co. of New York City and Katonah, whose bid was $2 million higher, at $12.6 million. The BWS accepted the MacArthur/Winston proposal August 31.[1]

This launched a storm of controversy. Publisher Joseph Pulitzer, whose *New York World* had questioned the expense of the project, branded it the "Esopus Folly" and demanded an investigation. Mayor George McClellan named a three-person committee, including Col. Thomas Symons, former military aide to President Theodore Roosevelt, to look into the matter. In November, the committee reported back that the MacArthur Bros. bid was "excessive" and that Pierce should have gotten the job, whereupon the Commissioners of Accounts recommended putting BWS members Simmons, Chadwick and Shaw on trial for malfeasance.[2]

McClellan's counsel reassured the mayor that the BWS had acted in good faith and on sound information, and no action was taken against the board, although Simmons tendered his resignation in early 1908. The bid award was confirmed, and so, ultimately, was the board's judgment, as John Pierce's company, which had earlier built the new Customs House in New York and the Chicago Post Office, went into the hands of receivers soon after.[3]

Given the green light, MacArthur and Winston wasted no time in transforming the placid Esopus Valley into a bustling conglomeration of men and machines. They hauled cableways, derricks, pumps, compressors and other equipment from Westchester County, where Winston & Co. had just finished the Cross River Dam. They laid a railroad from Ulster & Delaware tracks at Brown's Station to the dam site at Olive Bridge, opened a

Bishop's Falls on the Esopus Creek was about a quarter-mile above the Olive Bridge Dam site
and was ultimately submerged beneath the Ashokan Reservoir.

bluestone quarry and built another rail line, including an 89-foot-high, 390-foot-long steel trestle over the Esopus, to get to it. They erected a machine shop for the repair of locomotives, steam shovels, traction engines and steamrollers; established labor camps; and put up cement storage buildings, stone crushing operations, power houses and other buildings.[4]

Contract #3, which began in earnest in 1908, required the building of a 4,650-foot-long dam across the Esopus Gorge at Olive Bridge to re-create, in a sense, a lake geologists said had been there in pre-glacial days. The dam's 1,000-foot main section, made of concrete and large blocks of bluestone, would be built just downstream from Bishop's Falls, where John I. Boice owned the oldest gristmill on the Esopus. Two wings of the dam would be primarily earth, with concrete cores. The contract also involved construction of the Beaver Kill Dikes (three earth impoundments with concrete core walls, totaling 2.3 miles); a 1,000-foot

masonry waste weir over which surplus water would pass to the spillway channel; a 2,200-foot-long dividing weir to separate the 128 billion-gallon reservoir into East and West Basins; a gate chamber within the dividing weir; and a double underground conduit, as much as 80 feet beneath the surface. The two conduits, one above the other in the same rock trench, would total 8,700 feet in length and would permit water to be carried from either basin to the "headworks"—a second gate chamber, aeration plant and the connection to the Catskill aqueduct—which would be built under separate contract.[5]

Also under separate contract would be accomplished the task of clearing all trace of humanity and vegetation from the 12-square-mile reservoir. There, nearly 2,000 people lived in eight villages and outlying farms. The city would claim 504 dwellings, perhaps 1,500 barns and outbuildings, 10 churches, 10 schools, seven sawmills, nine blacksmith shops, and several stores, mills and other

The first concrete block was laid on the downstream face of the Olive Bridge Dam in October 1908. NYC DEP. *Top left:* J. Waldo Smith surrounded by ducklings. Smith was the first chief engineer of the Board of Water Supply, credited with developing the Catskill Water Supply. A granite tower, built as a surveying tower at the start of the reservoir project, was dedicated in his honor in 1935. Olive Free Library. *Top right:* Pupils at the Ashokan Reservoir school for workers' children posed with their teacher Oct. 30, 1908. NYC DEP.

An unidentified water boy brings a pail and dipper to workers on the dam.
Boys worked ten hours a day for ten cents an hour. Lonnie Gale.

establishments. More than 2,600 bodies in 40 cemeteries had to be exhumed and reinterred elsewhere. The coming of the reservoir also required the relocation of 13 miles of Ulster & Delaware Railroad tracks serving six stations in the valley.[6] Miles of telephone and electric lines were also moved.

While four communities (Olive City, Brown's Station, Broadhead's Bridge and Ashton) were forever eliminated, and four more (West Hurley, Shokan, West Shokan and Boiceville) were relocated, an entirely new, temporary village was built to house, feed, educate and tend to the medical needs of up to 4,000 laborers. This camp, near Brown's Station, contained dormitory-style barracks, equipped with lights and running water, where single workers lived; 200 cottages for married men and their families; a sewage disposal plant and paved and lighted streets. There were a hospital with quarantine and surgical areas, three churches, police and fire stations, a bank, several stores, a post office, a bakery turning out 5,000 loaves of bread a day and schools where immigrant laborers learned English and many of their children studied the three Rs. Smaller camps were operated at other locations around the reservoir site.[7]

Many of the workers were newly arrived European immigrants. About half were Italian, but many hailed from Austria, Poland, Russia, Sweden, Finland, and Germany. A great number were southern Blacks who handled the mule teams shipped up from Virginia. Labor camps were largely segregated according to race and nationality, the locals referring to the Italian camp as "Little Italy."

Unskilled workers received $1.20 to $1.60 per day. Pipe fitters, pumpmen and plumbers earned

More than 13 miles of track belonging to the Ulster & Delaware Railroad had to be relocated. A U&D train is shown here at the Brown's Station depot, which was itself moved to Shokan on the relocated track. Lonnie Gale.

$2, stonemasons made $3 a day, and powdermen $10.16 a week. Out of their earnings, workers had to pay $20 to $22.50 per month for room and board in the company camp. They bought provisions at the company store for substantially more than stores outside the camp charged.[8]

About 100 workers went on strike for one day in 1908, seeking a five-cent daily pay hike. The strike and complaints about living conditions brought an organizer from the International Workers of the World to Ashokan in an attempt to organize the work force. A subsequent investigation by the Federal Bureau of Factory Inspection turned up some recommendations for change, but there was no pay hike, and no unionization.[9]

Water boys earned $1 a day. One of those water boys was Claude Barringer. He was a local boy who was just nine in 1909 when he got a job hauling two 12-quart pails a half-mile from Winchells Corners to the dam site and back, several times a day, providing laborers with drinking water. "I worked 10 hours a day for 10 cents an hour," Barringer related to a reporter in 1985. "I got six dollars a week. My mother took it."[10]

Indeed, pay days usually found the foreign workers lined up at the camp post office to send money to their own families back in the Old Country, while area merchants spread their wares on the ground nearby.

Genevieve McLean was also a child of nine when the reservoir was begun, but her memories were different ones. The daughter of a general store owner whose property was taken for the project, she recalled the novelty of the arrival of big men and bigger machines. "My brother and I roamed around everywhere, riding on the equipment and building things," she said many years later.[11]

During 1908, the foundation for the Olive Bridge dam was excavated and masonry laid to a height of 15 feet. The gorge was effectively closed, and the Esopus Creek diverted through an opening in the dam. Masonry continued to be placed throughout the following year, supplied by stone crushing and concrete mixing plants at several locations. Nine steam shovels and 13 steam rollers excavated and compacted the earth; nine locomotives, 58 dump cars and 75 flat cars carried supplies over 13 miles of standard gauge track, and another six locomotives hauled 62 dump cars on three miles of narrow-gauge track. The average workforce between May and November 1909 was 1,900 men and 300 animals. The maximum force was 2,218 men and 331 animals in August.[12]

The Board of Water Supply itself was a big employer during this period, with a maximum of 1,710 people drawing city paychecks in 1910. The following year, BWS expenditures totalled $25.9 million. Both were records during the board's first 30 years in existence.[13]

By the end of 1909, the city had condemned or directly purchased all 15,222 acres required for the reservoir, except for the Ulster & Delaware property.[14] Homes and buildings not directly in the way of construction were used by BWS or contractors' forces, or rented to workers or engineers. In 1910, the city realized monthly rental income of $1,235 for 239 houses it owned in the Reservoir Department.[15]

The city also harvested the hay crop within the reservoir basin, gathering, in 1911, 300 tons of hay which was fed to the horses of the Board of Water Supply Police force. Nor did the apple crop go to waste; they were sold on the trees to the highest bidders, yielding $457, according to the 1911 BWS Annual Report.

In May of that year, a compensation agreement was reached between the city and Samuel Coykendall, owner of the U&D Railroad, whose tracks bisected the valley. Coykendall and his attorney, A. T. Clearwater, claimed physical damages amounting to $2.9 million and in addition de-

manded that the city pay for the relocation of 13.5 miles of rails, which they estimated would cost $1.6 million. After months of negotiations, a court battle, and a face-to-face meeting between Coykendall and New York City Mayor Gaynor in Kingston, the railroad settled for a total of $2.8 million.[16]

Winston & Co. was awarded the job of moving the railroad to higher ground, and work was started in June 1911. Within six months, there were 800 men, 200 teams of horses and mules, eight steam shovels, a half-dozen dinky engines and more than 100 dump cars at work on the project.[17] Two new depots were built to replace those that had to be abandoned, and the Brown's Station depot was moved to Shokan on the relocated track.

The new rail line took property whose owners had thought they were safe from reservoir condemnation. "The farms of the Elmendorfs and Greens were gone; 80 acres of the VanSteenbergh farm, and a newly set-out apple orchard were left on the inaccessible side of the track and eventually grew into wilderness," recalled Vera VanSteenbergh Sickler. "I can remember the steam shovel, half-submerged in the cut in front of our house. I was nine years old at the time. I heard the tap, tap of the hammers as they laid down the ties and rails. I saw the loads and loads of dirt that raised the high bank that closed off the old Ashokan Road, a road that had been there before there was a Town of Olive!"[18]

The U&D switched to its new track on the north side of the reservoir June 8, 1913. The very next day, trying to make up some time by running on the as-yet-undisturbed old line, the Rip Van Winkle Flyer smashed into a car operated by Curtis Peters, 54, chief mechanical engineer for Winston & Co. He had reportedly just dropped his boss, James O. Winston, at Brown's Station, and was crossing the old track when the train shot through a tunnel and struck him just west of the station. All work on the dam project was stopped as, two days later, 1,000 men attended services for Peters, whose body was taken by train for burial in his native Massachusetts.[19]

The Ashokan project claimed many lives and injured scores of workers. One man was badly

The "dinky" railroad used in building the Ashokan Reservoir. Chet Lyons.

scalded by steam when his locomotive collided with another; several workers perished in the collapse of a scaffold; another was killed, his partner losing both legs, when the two were pulled into a stone crusher.[20]

Twenty-three-year-old Elwyn Davis, writing in his diary on Mar. 22, 1913, recorded the death of Charles Eckert, killed when he was struck in the head by a piece of scaffold being removed from beneath the newly completed Traver Hollow Bridge. Davis, a mechanically-inclined man, picked up some work fixing drills, traction engines and rollers for the contractors, and himself suffered a mangled hand when he caught it in the gear of a Monarch steamroller. [21]

Among the unpleasant tasks to be accomplished before water could flood the land was the disinterment of 2,637 bodies from burial grounds large and small. The city allowed families $15 to engage "an undertaker or other person" to remove the remains and reinter them elsewhere, and another $3 to replace head and footstones. "This practice developed a new industry in the towns of Olive and Hurley," said the *Catskill Water System News* of May 20, 1912, "farmers, stone cutters, liverymen, boardinghouse keepers and undertakers engaging in the work of removing these bodies from the reservoir site."

Unclaimed graves were exhumed, many of them relocated to a special section of the Burgher Cemetery at the end of Watson Hollow. Mathias and Alonzo Burgher and Joseph Hill were awarded this contract in July of 1911, and by November 24 had completed the job, moving 368 graves well above the taking line.[22]

That year the C. P. Bower Company had finished grading 22 miles of new highways (40 miles of roadway would ultimately replace those flooded by the reservoir); and Harrison & Burton had begun construction of six reinforced concrete bridges: Traver Hollow, Esopus, Boiceville, Olive and two Bushkill spans.[23]

Rice & Ganey subcontracted from J. F. Cogan Co. the work of clearing and grubbing 9,500 acres of reservoir lands. The work, which started on Mar. 19, 1912, involved burning or tearing down all buildings, felling trees and large bushes to within six or 12 inches from the ground depending on their size, cutting brush and pulling stumps. Hand tools and gas-powered "endless-chain" saws mounted on horse-drawn carts were utilized. Stubborn trees and stumps were removed with explosives or pulled out by gas-driven caterpillar-type traction engines or horses and ropes.[24]

The city had considered stripping the soil from the bottom and sides of the basin to avoid the potential of decomposing vegetable matter affecting water quality, but decided instead to install aerating fountains, and perhaps filtration, to alleviate taste and odor problems.[25]

In 1910, nature removed a landmark so that man would not have to: the Bishop's Falls covered bridge, washed off its piers in a freshet, was swept against the partially-constructed dam just downstream.

Area residents were allowed to buy their own or others' homes from the contractor, and dismantle or move them. Elwyn Davis recorded in his 1913 diary that "Uncle Watson and I started to remove the house, fence and outbuildings from the Case Winnie property he purchased from Mr. Rice, the contractor." The work of tearing off interior lath and taking down the porch, siding and roof of the buildings, went on for weeks, until Davis recorded that his father, helping his uncle, was struck in the back by a nail-studded board. That injury, in the days before antibiotics were used to treat infections, kept the elder Davis bedridden for several weeks.

In late 1911, the masonry portion of the Olive Bridge dam was finished; in 1912, the Beaver Kill dikes were finished, rolled and seeded, the upper gate chamber was nearly completed, and the waste weir and concrete spillway were practically done.

The young Elwyn Davis, whose youth bridged the era between horses and airplanes, appeared torn between the image of progress as epitomized by the massive construction project, and the loss of the familiar. On Sunday, May 11, 1913 he wrote in his diary that he and 13 friends went to High Point Mountain, where "a great view can be had of the reservoir from the peak, and the look-off rocks." A closer encounter yielded a different image on May 26, when he drove through Ashokan: "It certainly looks desolate through the village, the houses most gone. . ."

Not surprisingly, resentment ran high among those who were being displaced. Most had spent their whole lives in the vicinity, many on homesteads that had been in their families for generations. The oldest among them remembered the days when the old plank road through the valley was a thoroughfare for hides, butter, bluestone and four-horse Concord coaches. Later, summer tourists flocked to the region by train, filling local farmhouses and boarding establishments. Mills of

every description took advantage of falling waters along the Beaverkill and Esopus Creeks. Residents had grown up in these communities, raised their own families and cared for aged parents there. They had toiled through planting season, harvested ice from mill ponds, listened to fiddles at local dance halls, buried loved ones in churchyards and farmstead cemeteries.

Told they must leave their homes, uproot their dead and see their lands inundated, they cried, they howled in protest, and then many hired lawyers to argue for the best deal they could get from the city. Those lawyers included A. T. Clearwater, of course, along with Harrison Slossen, John G. VanEtten, Arthur Brown, Edward Alexander and William Brinnier. They appeared for their clients at numerous hearings held in Kingston by the three-man commissions appointed to hear damage claims and make awards.

These commissions took testimony from residents, their lawyers and witnesses, and from city attorneys and their appraisers. There were usually wide differences between what a long-time farmer thought his property or business or water rights were worth, and the value placed upon them by the city. The BWS Annual Report of 1913 shows that 184 claims seeking $626,000 had been brought before commissions through December 31 of that year. Awards in 1913 totalled just $123,000 (about a third of that appealed to the Supreme Court).

Mary Weeks, for example, wanted $10,000 for the 25 acres that had been handed down from a great-great-grandfather who had served in the French and Indian War. The city said the Olive property was worth $4,000. She was awarded $4,900.[26]

On the other end of the spectrum, former state Assemblyman Charles Weidner claimed $40,000 for his 21-bedroom home with its 100-foot veranda, cider and sawmills, smokehouse, barn, orchard and vineyard near the Bushkill. The house had been a popular summer retreat for "distinguished Americans, foreigners and St. Louis bankers" for some 20 years, according to the *Kingston Freeman* reporting on commission testimony on June 15, 1909. The city claimed the Weidner estate was worth $20,000.

The Winchell brothers, Azarius and Elwyn, wanted $25,000 for their store, which not only housed the post office, the Western Union Telegraph and Citizen's Standard Telephone offices, but served 18 area boardinghouses as well.[27]

West Shokan farmer Silas Terwilliger wanted remuneration for injury done to his dairy business, since he could no longer sell 800 quarts of milk a week to summer guests at Mrs. James' boardinghouse, among others. Dressmaker Ermie Elmendorf put in a business damage claim for the general store, boardinghouse and dressmaking shop she and her husband Ira operated a block from the railroad station in Broadhead's Bridge. The city had paid them $8,000 for the property in 1907; they were the next to last to leave town in 1913, when they became caretakers at the Kenosha Lake Clubhouse. But Mrs. Elmendorf wanted to be compensated for $600 per year she lost in summer boarders, the $350 lost in dressmaking fees, the $1,000 to $1,500 annual profit from the store, the income from rent paid by the Oddfellows who used the building and from the livery stable Ira operated.[28]

Some of the cases both perplexed and amused the public, which followed the proceedings in the region's newspapers. Trustees of the Glenford Methodist-Episcopal Church, for example, were arrested for trespass and sued when they moved the church to a new site without paying the city for it. They claimed the church was at least half on land owned by the Ulster & Delaware, whose owner, Mr. Coykendall, said they could take it. The city considered it stolen property. A judge ultimately agreed, and the congregation had to pay $45 for the building.

Another widely publicized case was that of Stella Flood, who claimed $20,000 because the diversion of the Esopus Creek left her 3,200-foot river frontage below the dam spillway filled with "stagnant, dead water." She wanted another $7,665 for damage done to her Tongore property in 1905 by drillers and surveyors looking for a site for the dam. Her itemized account included loss of a Jersey cow which escaped through a fence destroyed by surveyors ($50), loss of milk from that Jersey cow ($144.28), occupancy of her wood lot for a season

West Shokan's Main Street before the village was razed for the reservoir. Town of Olive Archives.

The Traver Hollow Bridge, one of six reinforced concrete bridges built in the reservoir vicinity, was under construction in this 1913 photograph. NYC DEP.

($100) and damage to 1,165 feet of stone wall ($1,715) and to 388 feet of "corduroy road" by heavy wagons and machinery ($503).

Not only that, claimed Mrs. Flood in testimony before Commissioners William Murray, Patrick Walsh and Joseph McGrath, "They put a saloon at each side of us while they were there and there were drunken men wandering around. . . Before that it was a nice quiet place."[29] She was awarded just $1,750.[30]

In general, the city claimed not only that residents were inflating property values, but that the coming of the reservoir was actually improving the area. It noted that 484 new buildings had been constructed outside the taking line between 1907 and 1913, resulting in "remunerative occupation" to carpenters, masons and other tradesmen. And far from scattering to the four winds, reservoir residents had for the most part stayed in the area. Of 1,907 people identified as living in Olive, Hurley and Marbletown in 1907, 712 (37 percent) had relocated near the reservoir, 472 (24 percent) had settled in the Kingston area, and about 230 had gone north of Woodstock or south of Port Ewen; 162 had died.[31]

Frank L. DuMond, recalling in 1988 that period of movement and change, said many buildings in his town of West Hurley were reincarnated elsewhere. Temperance Hall was rebuilt as a general store, a two-story schoolhouse re-emerged as a one-story school, and the Dutch Reformed Church was rebuilt on a smaller scale at Zena. Even "St. Patrick's Cathedral," the Catholic church constructed for reservoir workers, was moved to Phoenicia for use as a parish hall for St. Francis de Sales Church, according to another area historian.

Six of the new buildings counted by the BWS in 1913 were churches, and at least one local newspaper saw that as a good sign. Noting that the area's Protestant congregations had lost three-quarters of their members because of re-aligning territories, the *Catskill Mountain News* projected on Dec. 20, 1912, that the "nucleus of enterprising young men who are building new villages" could be counted on to "build in the future a spiritual ediface more lasting than the Ashokan Dam."

By that time the dam was almost finished. Grubbing concluded the following year. The 500-foot Traver Hollow Bridge, with its 200-foot concrete arch, was opened to traffic Aug. 7, 1913 as design progressed for the Ashokan Bridge atop the reservoir's dividing weir. This would be a bridge of 15 arches, each span 67 feet wide and 11 feet high. It would be supported on 14 piers extending through the weir, the bridge having a total length of 1,110 feet. Under the floor of the bridge conduits for electric and telephone cables would be embedded in reinforced concrete.[32]

Indeed, work continued on the earthen dikes, and on the roadways around the reservoir, which residents of the new communities hoped would at least provide stellar views of their watery valley. The Brown's Station labor camp remained a lively place, as Mrs. C. S. Bergner, a child whose father worked for Winston & Co., recalled years later:

> The camp. . .was galvanized into action each workday by the company whistle which could be heard for miles around. At exactly ten minutes of five o'clock, somewhere out on a core wall, a weary mule, endowed with ESP, would suddenly begin to bray. Quickly joined by others, it seemed all 365 mules were braying in unison. That chorus reverberated against the hills and alerted all wives that it was time to put the kettle on, and children that they must get off the roads, because the Chariot Race was coming through. On each of the roads leading to the big mule barns they came, the three-mule teams with their colored drivers, standing up, cracking the long whips above the mules' backs, just for effect.[33]

Those mules were heard braying in terror the night of Feb. 24, 1915, when a big barn where 105 of them had just been fed caught fire and burned to the ground, killing 87 animals and injuring many of the rest. "Many mules, their sides smoking from burning hair and frantic with pain, ran wildly through the streets. Many were found dead in yards and gardens next day," recalled Mrs. Bergner. A newly rebuilt locomotive in the attached roundhouse was also lost in the fire. The contractor

Ashokan Reservoir workers, c. 1910. Southern blacks, many of them expert mule handlers, were brought north for the project. Olive Free Library.

replaced the mules with others kept on his stock farm near Saugerties.[34]

Throughout 1913, valley residents who had remained in their old homes until the final eviction order was issued finally left them. It was a year in which the village of Ashokan had to worry as well about a typhoid outbreak that had infected 14 dam workers. A health department inspector found the source to be a local dairy where the men had gotten their milk. He quarantined the dairy, hospitalized the workers, and declared there was no danger of transmission of the disease to villagers, according to the *Catskill Mountain News* of September 26.

The West Shokan correspondent for the *Kingston Freeman* kept up a litany of departing neighbors: "Dr. DuMond has purchased land of A. D. Winne and will erect a new residence and office at Olive; Mrs. Jerome Gulnack contemplates build-

ing and conducting a new up-to-date hotel in the new village; The St. Patrick's Day ball to be given in the Pythian Hall on Monday next will be the last one to be enjoyed by the young people of Shokan, as the building is to be torn down the first of April; George Siemon still runs his blacksmith and wagon making shop but will soon have to close up and move out; D. N. Mathews is about to close his store business of 42 years standing. . . The A. D. Winne house, Van Etten's ice house, and Herman Bell's house are being torn down. . . People who knew every foot of this section find themselves lost when they go to Brown's Station and Olive City, with all the land cleared and the houses gone, they have to inquire their way around. . ."

And finally, Aug. 16, 1913, "Very few buildings are left now to be burned. The trees are all cut down and the village is fading as a dream. . ."[35]

On patrol

As thousands of workers took up residence along the line of the new Catskill Aqueduct and the Ashokan Reservoir, they brought with them to upstate communities and rural areas all the social and criminal problems common to small cities, from drunkeness to burglary, assault and even murder.

Residents East of the Hudson River had long complained that local police organizations were not providing adequate protection from "lawless and troublesome" elements at dam construction sites. Still, the 1905 law establishing the Board of Water Supply did not include provisions for a city-run police force on the new Catskill system, and it was not until 1906 that an act amending the original law corrected that omission, requiring creation of the Board of Water Supply Police Bureau.

Debate over whether applicants should be taken from the Civil Service ranks delayed the formal organization of the force until 1908. The initial stations were established at Peekskill, Garrison and Brown's Station, and a fourth was soon added at High Falls. They were manned by temporary patrolmen until July 9, when the first 49 appointments were made from among 830 people who had passed the Civil Service exam for aqueduct patrolman. Rhinelander Waldo was named Chief of Patrolmen at an annual salary of $3,600. He resigned in late 1908, succeeded by his deputy, Douglas McKay, a 1905 graduate of West Point who supervised operations from Kingston headquarters for three years.

Thirteen men and a commanding officer staffed each of the four squads. Patrolmen were paid $75 a month, and had to provide their own food, board and uniforms, which consisted of olive drab shirts, pants, leather leggings, shoes, buckskin gauntlets, slicker and overcoat. The city furnished their equipment, which included a Colt .38 revolver, a night stick and a whistle. Patrolmen were housed in buildings taken by the city for reservoir and aqueduct purposes.

The first year's activities included 164 arrests. As construction increased, the police force grew, until, by the end of 1910, 280 patrolmen, supervised by 61 sergeants, made 1,519 arrests. Most were misdemeanors, but 138 were felonies. New precincts were added at New Hurley, Mohonk, Gardiner, Pleasantville, Kensico, Valhalla, Elmsford and Yonkers. Additional, smaller detachments of from one to three men were formed at Shokan, Olive Bridge, New Paltz, Wallkill, Yorktown Heights, Pleasantville, Hawthorne and Ardsley.

Many of the original BWS patrolmen and officers had been in the military, and had seen service in the Spanish American War. They were often compared to Teddy Roosevelt's Rough Riders.

Their jobs were by all accounts difficult: investigating armed robberies, raiding taverns and brothels, protecting BWS personnel, contractors' forces and the general public, breaking up fights between laborers who often could not speak English. They also helped trace pollution threats and searched for missing children, but their most publicized activities had to do with murder and mayhem. BWS police were credited, for example, with catching the killer of Gardiner aqueduct inspector Gilbert Sanborn, who was nearly decapitated in September 1910 by a knife-wielding worker who had been reprimanded by Sanborn. A week later two patrolmen saved a Gillespie Co. foreman who was being beaten by two irate laborers at the bottom of Shaft 7 on the Rondout tunnel at High Falls.

The most spectacular case involved the stabbing murder of Mary Hall, wife of a BWS engineer, who was killed in 1911 in her Yorktown Heights home by a gang of Italian workers allegedly seeking $3,000 rumored to be stashed in the house. Six perpetrators were later apprehended in New York City by BWS police. They were convicted of first degree murder and were electrocuted at Sing Sing Prison in July of 1912. The case was recalled in the memoirs of Edward Ocker Sr., who wrote that a New York City undertaker who claimed the bodies placed them on exhibit at his funeral parlor and charged admission to see them until authorities compelled him to bury the corpses.

A 23-year member of the BWS Police, Ocker was born in 1876 in Pennsylvania. He saw the last of the Indian wars while serving at Fort Riley, Kansas, in 1898, and later went to Puerto Rico during the Spanish American War. He joined the BWS force in 1910, and for much of his early service rode a horse named Bud.

Many patrolmen did their jobs on horseback; by 1912, when George Shrady commanded the force, 151 animals were stabled in buildings constructed of lumber salvaged from homes and barns in the Ashokan basin.

The most skilled equestrians among the police force formed a precision and trick riding unit that appeared at fairs, exhibitions and parades in the early teens. Among the celebrated riders was Sgt. Fred E. Walker, a former U. S. Cavalry officer and daring stuntman noted for his ability to

A special exhibition equestrian team of BWS patrolmen. NYC DEP.

vault over a trio of galloping horses. The squad's drill team practiced in 1913 on what would soon become the floor of the Kensico Reservoir, and in May of that year they impressed the crowds as they passed in regimented review in a New York City parade of municipal employees. A total of 130 BWS mounted and foot patrolmen and officers marched in the parade, accompanied by their mascot, "Sam," an aged white bulldog reputed to have "licked all other dogs between Yonkers and West Hurley."

Gradually, horses gave way to motorcycles and patrol cars, reducing the number of patrolmen needed to cover the 240-square-mile aqueduct zone. The completion of work on the aqueduct, and on the Ashokan, Kensico and Hillview Reservoir projects, also reduced the force, until, in 1917, the BWS police consisted of just 34 patrolmen, 16 sergeants, 42 horses, seven motorcycles and one car.

With the threat of war and the severing of diplomatic relations with Germany in 1917, the National Guard began patrolling the line of the aqueduct, especially the cut-and-cover portions on the surface. They were quartered during the winter in village homes and farmhouses. Alberta Washburn recalled that about a dozen of them, "big strapping guys, most of them Indian," camped for two years to patrol a section of aqueduct near her family's Chappaqua farm. Guards used the Washburn barn to get out of the weather, and used their telephone to call families in the city. The water line, she says, "was very vulnerable, anyone could have put a bomb there and blown it to bits." Particularly vulnerable was the Ashokan Reservoir headworks, where special detachments of BWS police stood guard.

The commencement of construction of the Schoharie Reservoir and Shandaken Tunnel prompted the establishment of BWS precincts at Allaben, West Kill, Prattsville and Gilboa, with a detachment at Grand Gorge. Additional detachments were formed in 1921 when second pipes were added at siphon locations on the Catskill Aqueduct to accommodate Schoharie water.

In 1924, BWS police, with State Troopers from Cooperstown and Stamford, raided and shut down a so-called "disorderly house back in the mountains from Gilboa," where the proprietor and 31 patrons were arrested for gambling and vagrancy and were fined $10 each. Frequented by many dam laborers, the gambling house "had come to be a stench to the people of that section," one newspaper account read.

Local residents sometimes criticized BWS police inaction, though. Ulster County citizens petitioned New York City Mayor William Gaynor to investigate conditions along the Catskill Aqueduct line, claiming "a horde of divekeepers, gamblers and women have camped near the workmen, who as a result spend all their earnings in debauchery." This situation, they said, went unchecked by the BWS police.

A local newspaper also pointed out that robbers made off with $150 from the Brown's Station depot while agent Harry Ennist was at dinner, despite the fact that 50 BWS police were stationed nearby.

The BWS police force reached a low point in the 1930s as unneeded patrolmen and officers left the ranks, many taking jobs with the city police and corrections departments. The four remaining BWS horses were sold in 1933; the following year there were just eight patrolmen, three sergeants and one clerk working out of a single precinct, Yonkers.

But in 1937, the Police Bureau was reorganized in anticipation of the construction of the new Delaware Aqueduct and the Rondout Reservoir. Precincts were opened at Elmsford, Kerhonkson, Modena and Cold Spring, and patrolmen's duties included filing construction accident reports and accompanying paymasters as they made their rounds on contractors' pay days.

In 1938, a precinct was established at the Lackawack Dam of the Rondout Reservoir; 86 patrolmen were assigned to the BWS, getting around in squad cars marked with "BWS Police, N.Y." in green, white and black. Tensions rose when a home-made bomb—a 10-inch long winged cylinder stuffed with two sticks of dynamite—was found at the base of the Traver Hollow Bridge near the Ashokan. Believed tossed from the bridge, it had not exploded. With the outbreak of war in Europe in 1939, vacations and leaves were cancelled and 24-hour patrols were instituted at vulnerable points on the system.

The discovery of a bomb in the British pavilion at the New York World's Fair in the summer of 1940 prompted heightened scrutiny of movement around the city's reservoirs. That fall, Mayor LaGuardia revoked 22,000 reservoir fishing permits to keep people off the water. Between 1941 and '45, the BWS police force was beefed up to provide security against potential foreign attack. A total of 184 patrolmen and 250 guards worked out of nine precincts. Appointees (more than 14,000 were screened from Civil Service lists) were investigated and their patriotism ascertained. Those hired went through three weeks of training at the Neversink precinct, where they received instruction in the use of automatic weapons and tear gas; first aid for victims of gas attacks; the handling of bombs, dynamite and explosives and the use of pistols (target practice was held at Napanoch Prison). Despite these grim forebodings, there were only 34 misdemeanor arrests during the period. About the biggest problem faced by the police bureau was keeping its employees, who were lured away by higher-paying defense plants or drafted into the military.

In 1952, the precincts at Neversink and Lackawack were discontinued, and a new one established at Grahamsville. Of the 97 arrests that year, 29 were for disorderly conduct, and 37 for motor vehicle violations.

The tone became more serious with the deepening of the Cold War throughout the 1950s. *The New York Times* reported the placement of 15 armed guards and 24 radio-equipped jeeps in round-the-clock patrols of the watersheds east and west of the Hudson River. Mobile laboratories were equipped to "make quick water analysis in the event of an atomic bomb attack." By 1960, a total of 1,762 water samples had been collected, radioactivity levels proving to be within acceptable thresholds.

Security concerns re-emerged as an issue in the wake of numerous terrorist attacks during the 1980s and '90s. Critics of the city's administration of the system claimed parts of the network of reservoirs and aqueducts remain vulnerable to such attacks, with just 50 Department of Environmental Protection police officers on duty to patrol the vast watershed. In 1999, as the city considered beefing up the force, DEP officers worked from four precincts: Downsville, Neversink, Olive and Yorktown.

Sources: Board of Water Supply Annual Reports 1907-1960; "The Catskill Reign of Terror, 1907-1917," an unpublished booklet by Sgts. Carmody and Ocker; 1997 interviews with Edward Ocker, Jr. and Alberta Washburn; *Pine Hill Sentinel, North Westchester Times, Cornwall Local, Catskill Mountain News, New York Herald, New York Times, New York World, Ellenville Journal*; correspondence with NYC DEP (1999).

On Sept. 9, 1913 the gates of the dam were closed and water began to fill the completed west basin. The following day, Mayor William Gaynor, who had succeeded George McClellan as New York City mayor in 1909, died suddenly from the lingering effects of a gunshot wound suffered in 1910 when a disgruntled city employee shot him in the throat. The planned celebration of the start of storage of Catskill water was thus delayed for about a month. On October 11, Acting Mayor Ardolph Kline presided over a special luncheon attended by 500 engineers, officials and invited guests who also toured the dam site and reservoir,[36] a reservoir whose name may be derived from the Indian word "sokan," meaning "to cross the creek."[37]

Still, there was much to do. During 1914, the wings of the dam were paved with three- to four-ton bluestone blocks from the Yale quarry delivered in rail cars, hoisted by derricks and navigated into place by gangs of workers. Fires continued to burn day and night as debris from the east basin was burned; 780 men and 244 mules and horses worked to place macadam surfacing on most of the 40 miles of new roads. And a 250-kilowatt hydro-electric generating plant was installed in the lower gate chamber to power gate and screen chambers, a machine shop, and the superintendent's dwelling, as well as to light dike roads and grounds.[38]

The crowning glory of the magnificent new dam was the aeration basin, a small reservoir, 500 by 250 feet, whose bottom was lined with water pipes four to five feet apart and capable of ejecting stored water 40 to 60 feet in the air. This process oxidized vegetable organisms and removed taste and odors, while providing a visually stunning sight against the evergreen forest lining the new lake.[39]

Finally, on June 24, 1914, said the *Pine Hill Sentinel*, all of the steam whistles throughout the reservoir work zone "screamed with joy" for an hour signifying the completion of all construction work on the dam and dikes.

However, limited rainfall, and releases of millions of gallons of water per day to test the Catskill Aqueduct, slowed the filling of the west basin. The

Above: More than 376 million gallons of water went through the Ashokan aerators daily. NYC DEP

Sentinel cited unnamed BWS sources that placed the blame of the lack of storage on a porous reservoir bottom, which would be remedied, the paper said, by draining it and applying a patented preparation made of asphalt, creosote and another material "known only to the inventor." The job, which the June 27, 1914, report said was to cost $2.5 million, was never undertaken.

The *Poughkeepsie Evening Star*, asserting that the Croton system was still adequate for the city's needs, wondered whether the Catskill project had been a mistake. Describing the Ashokan outlet as "dry as a cuttlefish, and as still as the Sahara," the newspaper asked, "Was it worth a hundred millions of taxpayers' money to work a cyclopean miracle in those mountains. . . ?"

But during 1915, the east and west basins slowly rose with rains that pounded the mountains during several heavy storms. Soon, more than 100 feet of water covered the area where once Bishop's Falls had powered mills and delighted travelers. And on November 22, water was released into the now-operational Catskill Aqueduct, on its way, at long last, to New York City.

Traveling stiff-legged derricks handled materials as the Kensico Dam progressed in 1914. NYC DEP.

13. Kensico and Hill View Reservoirs

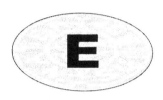 VEN before the city awarded the contracts for the Catskill System's storage and balancing reservoirs at Valhalla in Westchester County and Hill View in Yonkers, some New York City businesses and politicians were complaining that the city was wasting time and money tapping and transporting Catskill Mountain water.

In commentary dated Apr. 25, 1909, the Republican Club of the City of New York estimated that the city had spent to that point $358 million on waterworks, "enough to build three barge canals and have $50 millions to spare [enough] to complete both the Nicaragua and the Panama Canals. . . The sum is over one-half the total amount of gold in circulation in the United States." Recalling engineer John Freeman's initial 1900 report on water supply alternatives, in which he estimated vast losses due to waste and leakage, the Republican Club urged metering of all domestic consumers to save water. It advised postponing further construction and criticized "guesswork engineering" and questionable bid awards for portions of the work thus far accomplished. It also suggested that the city build a third Croton aqueduct to guard against breakage, "rather than build miles of unneeded aqueduct in Ulster County that will be useless for years until the whole Catskill line is finished."[1]

Such criticism notwithstanding, the Board of Water Supply proceeded with development of the Catskill System. In fact, 1909 was the highwater mark for construction contracts, the BWS that year awarding 39 contracts totaling $38.2 million for various aspects of the work. Two of those contracts were for the construction of the Kensico Reservoir, where a 50-day supply of Catskill water would be stored, and Hill View Reservoir, whose purpose would be to equalize hourly differences between city water consumption and the steady flow in the aqueduct, particularly in times of fire.[2]

The job of building the 1,800-foot-long, 300-foot-high Kensico dam went to John and James Rodgers and John Haggerty, whose bid of $7.9 million included not only the massive dam but substitute roads and bridges and a temporary water supply system to replace the old Kensico Reservoir just downstream of the larger new impoundment. The work was later assigned to H. S. Kerbaugh Inc.[3]

The big new reservoir, which would hold 30 billion gallons, would dwarf the original Kensico Reservoir, built in 1885. Four miles long and from one to three miles wide, it required an additional 3,200 acres of land to expand the 1,300-acre reservoir and buffer zone the city already owned. The impounded waters of the Bronx River would rise to a maximum depth of 155 feet, lapping 110 feet above the surface of the old reservoir.[4]

Top: The Rye Outlet Bridge under construction in 1911. NYC DEP. *Above left:* H. S. Kerbaugh, Inc., builders of the Kensico Dam, built their principal work camp about one-half mile south of Valhalla Station to house hundreds of workers and their families. The camp, divided into Italian and American sections, included a school, social hall, hospital, police and fire stations, even a library stocked with foreign language newspapers. Wilfred Hurley. *Above right:* Placing granite on the downstream face of the Kensico Dam in 1915. NYC DEP.

Before the new dam could be built, provisions had to be made to replace the so-called Williamsbridge service, water supplied by the existing reservoir to the 1889 Williamsbridge Reservoir in the Bronx through a pipeline known as the Bronx Conduit. Initial plans called for the bigger dam to be placed downstream from the old, to avoid interruption of service, but tests conducted in 1908 showed a better location about 300 feet upstream from the old earthen dam, which was ultimately dismantled. So for the first two years of the Kensico project, workers were largely involved in building

two rolled-earth dikes with timber core walls, one across the Bronx valley, the other across the valley of the outlet from Rye Pond, which had served as an auxiliary to the original reservoir. The ponds were connected by a small tunnel and water was first aerated and chlorinated before passing into the Bronx conduit through a 36-inch riveted steel pipe.[5]

Some 186 acres of swampland were cleared and re-covered to form the floor of the temporary reservoirs created by the dikes. All standing timber and stumps were cut to within six inches of the ground, and all brush, grass and tussocks sheared to the surface. A 12-inch covering of non-organic material was spread atop the surface. "All during last season, two 70-ton steam shovels were kept busy, together with six 18-ton narrow gauge locomotives, running about 10-car trains," related *The Catskill Water System News* July 5, 1911. Each shovel loaded an average of 500 cars per day. "At first the material was spread by hand, but later a scraper, hung on a truck (railroad wheels with frame) and attached to the rear of the train, was used. In some places considerable difficulty was encountered in holding up the tracks and plant in the wet portions of the swamp.'"

To further increase the supply, the Byram River was tapped and water led to the Rye Reservoir through a tunnel and an open ditch called the "Bear Gutter." Before the old Kensico Reservoir was drained, hundreds of fish were captured in 500-foot seines and, under the direction of county and state game officials, transferred to Rye Reservoir, which would ultimately lie 54 feet beneath the surface of the new lake.[6] Water was furnished to the Bronx from the temporary supply in 1911, when the the old lake was drained and excavation for the new dam was begun.

By 1910, an impressive collection of men, machines and animals had been assembled at the reservoir site, three miles north of White Plains. George Angell was superintendent and B. C. Collier resident engineer for Kerbaugh, which established a labor camp on city land about a half-mile south of Valhalla Station. A railroad spur was built from the Harlem Division of the New York Central and Hudson River Railroad to a storage yard where coal, cement and ice houses, a machine shop, two blacksmith shops, stables for 68 animals, and a granary were located. Thousands of feet of standard- and narrow-gauge railroad track (there would be 15 miles of track and three long trestles in use by the end of 1912) were laid to connect highway excavations, the substitute reservoir works, and a quarry about a mile away. There, rock was blasted from the earth and either crushed as concrete material or chiseled by expert stonecutters to serve as the facing for the dam. A power plant and cement

mixing facilities were erected near the site where the Rye Outlet Bridge, a 625-foot-long, 110-foot high span, would cross the reservoir about two miles north of the dam.[7]

Excavation for the foundation of the dam began in 1911 with steam shovels digging as much as 130 feet beneath the surface to sound rock. Two cableways spanning 1,860 feet were installed at the dam, supported by four timber towers 125 feet high. The cableways first removed most of the excavated material, and were later utilized to lay the concrete core (one million cubic yards of it) and cyclopean (very large) stone facing. The facilities which supplied these materials were themselves immense.[8]

The contractors purchased a 50-acre quarry at nearby Cranberry Lake, where a crushing plant was erected capable of handling 500 cubic yards of rock per hour. Drills and dynamite dislodged granite from a 3,000-foot ridge, and four steam shovels loaded the rock into train cars. Strings of 15 to 20 cars, hauled by four 40-ton locomotives, were taken to the crushing plant, where cars dumped their loads into an initial crusher. This device featured a huge 13x7-foot jaw weighing 74,000 pounds, which reduced 10-ton boulders to rocks of nine inches and smaller. Rocks of about four inches passed through a grate, with the bigger pieces run through a second crusher, and then between two heavy rollers. All material was used to make concrete: Crusher dust one-quarter inch and finer was added to sand excavated from a pit at the north end of Rye Lake, and stone between one-quarter and two-and-a-half inches in diameter was utilized as aggregate.[9]

The quarry also supplied the stone for a full-sized model of the upper 25 feet of the downstream face of the dam so that engineers could study the architectural details of the edifice.[10]

The largest charge of dynamite ever set off to that point occurred Mar. 21, 1914, when a single blast of 32.5 tons of dynamite blew uncounted tons of rock as high as 50 feet in the air. It took 60 days to load the 142 dynamite holes ranging from 32 to 45 feet deep. The blast provided 120,000 yards of

The stone yard at the Kensico Reservoir, where about 80 stone cutters, most of them Italian immigrants, worked to shape one- to 16-ton blocks for the dam face. NYC DEP.

cyclopean stone, 9,000 cubic yards of dimension stone and 70,000 cubic yards of crusher dust.[11]

By the end of 1914, more than a third of the masonry had been laid on the dam. Between July 25 and Aug. 24, 84,450 cubic yards were placed, breaking all records for placing masonry in dam construction. (The best progress made on the Olive Bridge dam at the Ashokan Reservoir was 35,300 cubic yards.) The process was watched carefully not only by the engineers and contractors, but by the public and the press, which was at times skeptical of the durability of this "new material." Several reinforced concrete buildings had collapsed in the early years of the century, and the BWS took great pains to be sure it was using good quality material. In 1908, BWS inspectors tested samples from every 300 barrels of portland cement intended for use in tunnel and reservoir concreting.

Of 162,000 barrels sampled, 32 percent were rejected.

The upstream face of the dam was built of precast concrete blocks, mixed at a block yard south of the dam and seasoned for three months before placement. The concealed portion of the downstream face below ground level was concrete molded against wooden forms. The remainder of the downstream face was cut stone blocks ranging from one to 16 tons each.[12]

The stone-cutting yard was equipped with a 25-ton electric crane, nine surfacing machines and 50 drilling machines. About 80 stonecutters were employed there.[13] They were largely Italian immigrants, men like Saverio Conforte, who came to the United States from the Province of Salerno with his brother, a bootmaker. Saverio's granddaughter, Josephine Conforte Pofill, recalled that he was an imposing man, with dark hair and a red beard, who rode his bicycle to the quarry every day from his home near the city. "Once he fell asleep as he cut stone on a table, and fell forward, cutting his face," Mrs. Pofill recalled in a 1998 interview. "It left a scar that ran from under his eye to his chin."

He was one of many to be hurt on the works. A great number did not survive their injuries. In just two months, May and June 1913, the *White Plains Daily Argus* reported five accidents, the worst of which resulted in the deaths of five men, when a dynamite charge in the quarry went off prematurely. During a single 48-hour period, two men died in separate accidents, and the wife of an Italian worker was killed when she was struck by a train on a trestle as she walked back to the labor camp. The worst accident on the project occurred Apr. 27, 1915. Eight Italians, aged 21 to 40, died when their supervisor, who was subsequently arrested, mistakenly discharged 18 sticks of dynamite in a cut-off trench 55 feet beneath the surface.[14] The descendants of Jack Paolo, who came to this country from Italy with his two sons, have long accepted the family story that their immigrant ancestor died when he fell into unfinished concrete and was entombed forever in the great dam. It is an unconfirmed story common to most of the city's big public works projects.[15]

More than 1,500 workers toiled on the Kensico project. About half of them, and their families, lived in the principal work camp near Valhalla. The camp, maintained by the contractor, consisted of 24 houses that accommodated 24 single men each, along with 20 two-family houses. Other laborers boarded at homes taken over by the BWS, or in private homes in the vicinity.

The camp, a few hundred feet downstream from the dam, was divided into Italian and American sections. Sewage, electric and water systems were supplied, and there was a police station, fire protection and a school, run by the North American Civic League for Immigrants. The school, opened in 1910, was located in a two-story, eight-room building, where more than 40 children were taught the three Rs to prepare them for regular public school. At night, foreign-speaking laborers took classes in English and American government, and their wives learned sewing, cooking and hygiene.

A hospital provided medical care for injured workers and attempted to keep at bay infectious diseases like poliomyelitis, which made a frightening appearance in the area in July of 1916, but failed to infect any of the 100 children living in the camp.

A one-story building constructed by the contractor served as a social hall and a gymnasium, with a stage. There was a small library, where workers and their families could read books or Russian, Polish or Italian language newspapers. Saturdays were given over to dances or movies; Sundays offered story hours for youngsters.[16]

Many men were also employed by another contractor, Rinehart & Dennis Co., charged with construction of the tunnels from the temporary reservoirs, the influent and effluent chambers and the aeration works, a concrete basin into which were set 1,750 bronze nozzles to send water skyward in jets that were at once purifying and beautiful. The inflow and outflow gatehouses are separated by a little over two miles, and are connected outside the reservoir by a concrete conduit which allows the bypassing of the reservoir if necessary.

To house and care for the workers and the contractor's organization, Camp Columbus, a temporary village of 60 buildings, was constructed. Rinehart & Dennis maintained their own power plant, stone crushers, cement mixing plant and other operations at locations strategic to the work, which included .8 miles of grade tunnel and 2.7 miles of pressure tunnel.[17]

The entire project, overseen by BWS Chief Engineer J. Waldo Smith, and more directly by Department Engineer Merritt Haviland Smith, attracted a cadre of ambitious engineers who wanted to be part of it. One of them was Harold Traband, who went to night school at Cooper Union to study surveying and engineering while working on the railroad. His daughter, Virginia Fish, in a 1998 interview, remembered him studying for the Civil Service exam before landing a job at Kensico and later with the city's finance department. Like many

Posing atop a pile of precast concrete blocks used to build the upstream face of the dam were (l. to r.) Alice Jones, Pearl Pietschker and Orphelia Swenson. Cranberry Lake Preserve.

of his contemporaries, Mrs. Fish said, "They called him a self-made man."

The Kensico project also captured the attention of engineers and architects the world over: 500 members of the American Society of Civil Engineers toured the works in 1913; 100 members of the American Water Works Association drove to Valhalla from their Hotel Astor convention in New York City in 1916. A 1915 visitor was the celebrated Army officer George Washington Goethals, who as chief engineer of the Panama Canal had supervised 50,000 workers in the construction of the 1.5-mile-long Gatun Dam and the 40-mile-long canal, completed only the year before his Kensico tour.[18]

The Kensico Dam was indeed a sight to see, designed to be the focal point of the Bronx River Parkway, which had its terminus at the reservoir, "a suitable approach and setting for the most monumental structure of the Catskill system."[19] The profile of the downstream face shows 21 panels of squared stone separated by 15-foot-wide expansion joints made of rusticated stone projecting from the surface. Diamond patterns of dimension stone are spaced throughout the panels. The length of the dam is crowned by a richly ornamented stone band. A highway traverses the top of the dam, and a sweeping, brick-paved plaza featuring rectangular pools and landscaped in 1919 with 1,176 evergreen trees and bushes is spread out at its base. At both ends of the top of the structure are circular granite "rotundas" in which are inscribed the names of BWS commissioners and engineers and New York City mayors. An historical account of the building of the Catskill System is carved in the curved walls, as is this: "He causeth the wind to blow and the waters to flow; He maketh the grass to grow upon the mountains. . ."

A resident displaced by the great reservoir also turned to Biblical terms to try to describe his feelings about being forced to give up property for the project. "What is it the Bible tells us about building our house on a sure foundation, so that when the winds and the rains come they won't wash it away?" questioned the unidentified property owner in an article of the day. "I guess back in those times, they didn't have any New York water system to deal with."[20]

Kensico area residents had been pushed out once, back in the 1880s, when the city dammed the Bronx River the first time. Now, some of the same folks were being asked to move again. "Richard C. Keeler, who lives over in the Rye Pond section, has as good cause to grumble as anybody. When the city acquired the pond a few years ago, Mr. Keeler had to move back 300 feet from the water's edge. Four years ago, the city pushed him back half a mile, and now he's got to go away back. He is 75. He has the original grant given to his ancestors, and he will show it to you and tell you he thinks it is a ding-dang shame that he can't even fish in the pond now without getting a permit from Commissioner O'Brien."[21]

About 500 residents were displaced by the project, but, unlike in the Ashokan basin, just a few cemetery plots had to be unearthed and reinterred.[22] A portion of the community of Valhalla was taken, including a hotel and a few stores. About 25 more buildings in "New Kensico" at the north end of the reservoir were condemned, as were several outlying farms.[23]

Gone were Ravens Farm and Hotel, Wyckoff's and Pfister's General Stores, Lane's Saloon, a file factory, a textile mill, Woodman's farm and Whimpenny's rag carpet mill, District #6 one-room schoolhouse, and homes owned by Mr. Butts (a violin bowmaker), Ed Riley (the poormaster), Willis Husted (a cider mill operator) and the Pietschker family.[24]

Del Pietschker, in recollections published more than 70 years later, recalled Kensico as "a small, quiet community, a secure little hamlet nestled in the valley below the North Castle hills." He was eight years old when his family's property was claimed by the city, and recalled that most displaced families settled in what remained of Valhalla, Armonk or North White Plains. There his father, a painting contractor, started over with his family, alongside many dam laborers, in a community that grew exponentially in the coming decades.[25]

Indeed, said an account of the second flooding of Kensico, the community made little effort to stop the city's plans. "People whose homes were taken objected to it of course, but there was no organized opposition," related Edmund Ward. "They figured New York had to have the water and it was no use kicking against the prickles, as it were."[26]

The city compensated property owners for homes and land seized for both the reservoir and for nine miles of new substitute roadways. Fourteen miles of old highways were discontinued; the Town of Mount Pleasant settled with the city for $60,000 for the cost of losing them, and laying out new highways.[27] The Methodist Church, which had spruced up its building, installed a new furnace and put on a new roof, received $21,000 for the property, inspiring others to improve their holdings in hopes of getting big settlements from the three-member damage commissions.[28]

When, in late 1916 and early 1917, the end came for Valhalla businesses at the base of the reservoir, their owners attempted to put as bright a face on it as possible, purchasing the most desir-

able land on the north side of Davis Brook and adopting a uniform design for their new buildings—wood exteriors and Swiss-style red roofs.[29]

Fifteen miles to the south, there were fewer condemnations of private property as the Hill View Reservoir was built. "It was a most fortunate circumstance to find a hill so near the city line, largely unoccupied and at a price comparatively small," explained Lazarus White in his 1913 book *The Catskill Water Supply*. The Millard Construction Co., later named the Keystone State Construction Co., was awarded the $3.2 million contract to construct the 90-acre reservoir, 3,000 feet of underground aqueduct to its north and south, and the uptake and downtake shafts connecting the impoundment to the tunnels.[30]

Hewn from the top of a large glacial hill, the highest point in Yonkers, the reservoir was excavated to a depth of 20 to 45 feet. The wooded site (133 acres just south of the Empire Racetrack, now Yonkers Raceway) was stripped of its trees, brush and topsoil. Trees were cut into railroad ties and lumber at the contractor's sawmill. Topsoil, preserved to line the reservoir's future embankments, was loosened from stumps and boulders with mattocks, excavated with hand shovels and transported to storage piles on wagons or rail cars, which were delivered to the spoils piles by gravity and returned to the top of the hill by horses.[31]

Drilling, blasting and steam shovels did much of the heavy work excavating the twin basins of the 900-million-gallon reservoir. The inside of the embankments was formed of finely graded material spread in five-inch horizontal layers rolled to a four-inch thickness. A double line of three-foot gauge track was laid on the east and west embankments. After a full train of cars dumped its load the length of the track, a spreader car pushed by a locomotive was run along the track to smooth the material. The track was then moved back 13 feet by horses, and the next section was lined. Sixteen locomotives, 19,000 feet of narrow-gauge track, 90 dump cars, five road scrapers, three 10-ton steam rollers, 112 dump wagons and six sprinkler wagons were among the contractor's equipment inventory.[32]

Top left: Lining the embankment slopes at Hillview with concrete in 1915. *Above:* The chamber through which water from the 143-foot-deep Catskill Aqueduct uptake shaft would pour into the east basin of Hillview Reservoir. *Left:* The mess hall at Camp Hillview, Oct. 1910. All NYC DEP.

The 69-acre bottom of the reservoir was lined with six inches of concrete. The embankment's slopes 21 feet above the bottom were covered with eight inches of concrete to protect against erosion, not to provide water tightness. Rubble stone paving lines the upper portions of the slopes, which were ringed with an 8,600-foot walking path.[33]

The 2,740-foot-long dividing wall between the east and west basins contains the 12-foot circular by-pass aqueduct, which connects the 143-foot-deep uptake shaft of the Yonkers pressure tunnel, and the 200-foot-deep downtake shaft of City Tunnel #1. Either one or both basins may be used or by-passed whenever required.[34]

Shaft and tunnel excavation and lining were conducted in much the same manner as elsewhere on the aqueduct, except that electric dynamite firing was replaced with fuse firing. Instead of connecting the exploders in the cartridges with electric wires, they were crimped to waterproof fuses loaded with gunpowder so as to burn 24 inches a minute, allowing men sufficient time to leave the tunnel before the blasts occurred. "Before the next shift entered the tunnel, the air would be clear," Lazarus White explains in his examination of the Catskill System. The Yonkers tunnel to the north of the reservoir was 16 feet, seven inches in diameter, the Van Cortlandt siphon to the south 15 feet.

A labor camp accommodating up to 450 workers was named Camp Hill View.[35]

On Nov. 22, 1915, the first Ashokan water entered the Kensico basin. It had taken 22½ hours to make the 75-mile trip from the Catskills. "When the water rushed out of the opening, it made a wild dash and soon formed a channel, but it was several days before it began to pond back against the new dam. . . In two weeks, the water has risen two feet above the high water mark of the old dam," reported the *North Castle Sun* on Dec. 3, 1915.

The newly concreted Hill View Reservoir was next filled, and then, finally, water reached the Borough of the Bronx Dec. 27, 1915. Manhattan was supplied with Catskill water for the first time one year later, Nov. 29, 1916; Brooklyn and Queens received theirs Jan. 22, 1917.[36] A week later, water arrived across the narrows at Silver Lake, and the reservoir there was full by Feb. 20.[37]

Back upstate at Ashokan, the finishing touches had been put on the dividing weir bridge, the Olive Bridge Dam and the highways around the reservoir. The Brown's Station work camp was demolished, and MacArthur Brothers and Winston packed up their equipment and left town. Downstate, Kerbaugh Co. closed the books on the Kensico project, where BWS policemen on brand new bicycles patrolled the roads and footpaths to keep an eye on throngs of visitors who came to view the newly changed landscape. Aside from the Kerbaugh commissary, which burned in October 1916, most of the other camp buildings had been torn down. Elsewhere on the barren fringes of the new reservoirs and the aqueduct, new growth was taking hold, as hundreds of thousands of conifer seedlings, grown in BWS nurseries, began to replace evidence of human habitation. Bookkeepers and auditors tallied the cost of the first phase of the Catskill project at $184,707,540, including the acquisition of 21,330 acres of land and prepared for the initial disbursements for the next phase, development of the Schoharie supply.[38]

It was not until October 1917 that the city celebrated its new and abundant water source. A three-day spate of concerts, parades and ceremonies, reminiscent of the festivities that marked the opening of the Croton sluice gates 75 years earlier, was staged October 12-14. It was no coincidence that the event was planned for Columbus Day weekend, a holiday that Italians especially take to their hearts, and so thousands of members of various Italian societies marched in a parade to commemorate the accomplishment in which their countrymen had played so large a role.

The parade passed Columbus Circle where Mayor Purroy Mitchel viewed the procession following a ceremony at City Hall in which he formally accepted the completed system, praised the engineers who designed it and introduced his predecessor, George McClellan. The ex-mayor, who had pushed the enterprise when others scoffed, quipped, "The amount of mud that was thrown at me, had it come in another shape, would have furnished almost enough material to build the great Ashokan Dam."[39]

Then it was on to Central Park, where Catskill water was turned into a donated fountain in the old reservoir. Onlookers cheered the sight, until a sudden downpour scattered them, ironically cancelling a pageant called "The Good Gift of Water," written by Edward Hagaman Hall and involving 15,000 waiting schoolchildren.[40]

The storm clouds of war were also building that autumn weekend in 1917. Ex-mayor McClellan, who had left politics to join the service, would ultimately attain the rank of lieutenant colonel. Mayor Mitchel, defeated for re-election, signed up the following year, only to die in a flying accident at a Louisiana training field in July 1918. Members of the Tenth Regiment of the New York National Guard patrolled the perimeter of the new Kensico Dam, on the lookout for "fanatical foreigners" armed with bombs.

But for a few golden days in October, there was real joy, real pride in the achievement that had laid such priceless bounty on the tables of almost every New York City resident. Just a week before the speeches and songs in Central Park, an unusual find from the still waters of the Kensico reflected that gift. A man named Howard Quinby, preparing the perch he'd caught during a morning of fishing, discovered an unexpected favor hidden within— two small pearls—thus adding to the lore of treasures lost, and treasures found, in the building of the New York City water system.

To filter, or not to filter . . .

The Board of Water Supply embarked on the Catskill Water System with the intention of building a filtration plant to remove any impurities. It had also talked for years of doing the same in the Croton system, but chose instead, for reasons of economy, to attack contaminants at the source, requiring the destruction of entire communities if they threatened nearby water sources. Armonk was an example of one of those. About half of the Westchester County village of 500 people was condemned in 1903 to preserve the quality of the Wampus River, which was diverted into the old Kensico Reservoir via Byram Lake and the Bear Gutter Tunnel, part of the Williamsbridge project of the 1890s.

In the sparsely settled Catskill region, water quality was not nearly as threatened as in the more congested areas north of New York City. Still, said the BWS Annual Report for 1909, "The Board realized that no matter how pure Catskill water may be, with the increasing population of the watersheds, filtration will eventually become imperative." The city thus purchased a 315-acre site in the Town of Mt. Pleasant near the Catskill Aqueduct for the future Eastview filtration plant. It hired filtration consultants, prepared 68 drawings of preliminary plant designs, came up with cost estimates, visited filter plants in Washington, Baltimore and Philadelphia, even tested various

Placing one-ton drums of liquid chlorine on a truck in Valhalla in the 1920s. Source protection and chlorine treatment has long been favored over expensive filtration for the city's water. NYC DEP.

types of sand found in the Hudson Valley, Long Island and New Jersey.

But with construction of the actual water supply system the most pressing consideration, the BWS put expensive filtration plans on the shelf, and concentrated instead on cleaning up the immediate localities of its new reservoirs. In 1912, for example, it successfully prevented the Westchester County Board of Supervisors from establishing a tuberculosis hospital near Yorktown Heights in the Croton watershed. The city argued that the health of city residents would be endangered if hospital discharges polluted Croton water, which could, at times, be mixed with Catskill water.

And it pressed for legislation that would give the city the same authority to enforce sanitation regulations in its Catskill watershed as it had on the east side of the Hudson River. It noted that the 5,300 year-round population of the Catskill region swelled to 11,000 in the summertime, thus increasing probability of contamination, and it wanted the authority to construct sewage treatment plants and require buildings to tap into them. Those proposals riled area residents, who saw in them a threat that the city would take over the entire region, or would force property owners to pay for a service they did not want or even think was necessary. One local editor even accused powerful New York City Democrats of nominating for State Assembly a bookkeeper for one of the Ashokan Reservoir contractors, claiming the candidate was registering ineligible workers to vote and do the city's bidding.

State legislators, perhaps reacting to constituent concerns, defeated city-sponsored sanitation bills in 1913 and 1914. But in 1915, Chapter 665 of the laws of that year was adopted, allowing the BWS to promulgate and enforce standards subject to approval of the state Department of Health. The city thereupon developed "Rules and Regulations for Protection Against Pollution of the Waters of Ashokan Reservoir and Tributary Watercourses."

Those rules prohibited the location of privies, compost heaps, stables, slaughter houses, cemeteries or other potentially contaminating uses near watercourses or reservoirs; outlawed the disposal of garbage, manure, dead animals, factory wastes or other "putrescible matter" into watercourses; and forbid the washing of animals or laundry in watercourses or reservoirs controlled by the city. Swimming was not allowed, either. The city also required that the toilets of all cars on the Ulster & Delaware Railroad be locked between West Hurley and Cold Brook along the Ashokan Reservoir.

Sanitary inspectors sought out polluters in its newly-won watersheds. This outhouse near the Esopus was one of hundreds built by the BWS to replace substandard privies that emptied directly into streams.

Town of Olive Archives.

The BWS then began drawing up plans to build sewage treatment plants in Pine Hill, Chichester and Phoenicia. Board President Charles Strauss met with property owners and wrote to the local press insisting that the city had no intention of buying any more homes or lands, but simply wanted to keep sewage out of its water. It would pay all expenses of hooking up homes and businesses so as to "get results quickly, on a basis of friendliness, if possible." But, replied a mistrustful *Pine Hill Sentinel*, "The City has never done anything it agreed to do."

Strauss persisted, adding that if cooperation of residents was not forthcoming, they would "be compelled by due process of law to cease polluting the watercourses." Meanwhile, the BWS organized a team of sanitary inspectors to seek out polluters along Esopus Creek and its tributaries. By 1916, 583 privies were improved, 122 new outhouses were installed, 46 new cesspools built, and one farm building moved. "As these men were natives, they encountered little, if any, opposition," said the BWS Annual Report for 1916.

Ten years earlier, the law that had allowed the city to go to the Catskills for water had also required it to reconstruct part of the sewer system in the City of Kingston. Before the city could divert water from the Esopus Creek, which had been the receptacle for Kingston's sewage, it had to build an intercepting sewer leading to the Rondout Creek and the Hudson River. King, Rice & Ganey performed that job, which entailed building 6,200 feet of tunnel through rock and earth, and 1,300 feet of pipe laid in open cut.

It was not until the 1920s that the city built its own sewer plants. Acting on Chapter 630 of the Laws of 1923 the BWS entered into agreements with the Village of Tannersville and the Town of Roxbury to build sewage treatment plants in Tannersville and Grand Gorge for the protection of Esopus and Schoharie waters. A plant was also built in Pine Hill, and a community septic system installed in the hamlet of Chichester. Although 1937 newspaper accounts estimated it would be cheaper for the city to buy and raze all homes and businesses in Margaretville and Arkville rather than build a sewage treatment facility upstream from the proposed Pepacton Reservoir, the city, in the mid-1950s, built a treatment plant in Margaretville and another in Grahamsville, between the Rondout and Neversink Reservoirs.

As water quality appeared assured—the city had installed a chlorination system at Kensico, and a sediment-removing coagulation plant just north of that reservoir's intake on the Catskill Aqueduct at Pleasantville—the need to build the Eastview filtration plant abated, and the city sold off much, but not all, of its Eastview property. In 1919, the BWS pushed its plans onto the back burner, "until some later time, when the need for filtration should become pressing."

A decade later, as the BWS embarked on development of the Delaware River supply, the state's Water Power and Control Commission addressed the issue, noting its approval of the city's plans to protect the new source using "rigid restrictions" and "multiple chlorination" rather than filtration. But, in okaying the city's plans May 25, 1929, the commission acknowledged, "It is our opinion that the time is close at hand when the use of surface waters collected from inhabited watersheds should not be permitted without adequate filtration. We reserve the right to require filtration, additional purification or the taking of additional precautions at any time we may find it necessary."

By the 1950s, the city was exploring the use of covers to keep its urban distributing reservoirs clean. But the cost and problems associated with placing concrete or aluminum and steel roofs atop reservoirs ranging in surface area from 38 to 96 acres discouraged that idea.

In 1986 the U. S. Environmental Protection Agency (EPA) finally forced the filtration issue by posting directives requiring all surface water supplies in the nation to be filtered. New York City, was ordered to build such a plant to clean its Croton water. Years of controversy ensued over a location for the plant, until in December 1998 the city announced it had chosen Mosholu Golf Course in Van Cortlandt Park, the Bronx, as the preferred site. It proposes to build a 10-acre treatment facility, including a 20-million-gallon reservoir, beneath the city-owned golf course. Completion of the $660 million facility is anticipated in 2006.

Catskill water was treated at this coagulating plant near Pleasantville before entering the Kensico Reservoir. This 1917 photo shows guards who were among a contingent that patrolled the Catskill Aqueduct and other vulnerable water system facilities during World War I. NYC DEP.

The city's water system is among just 100 surface supplies from 10,000 in the nation that remain unfiltered. But the federal government, recognizing the expense involved in filtering 1.2 billion gallons of water a day, has allowed the city time to prove it can, through regulations, land acquisition—and the construction of more wastewater treatment plants—retain the purity of its Catskill and Delaware supplies and thus avoid filtration there (Chapter 21).

Still, it is required, under terms of the 1997 New York City Watershed Memorandum of Agreement, to go forward with designs for a filtration plant should one ultimately be needed. The city is eyeing the old Eastview site in the Towns of Mount Pleasant and Greenburgh as a preferred location, after examining 600 potential sites along the Catskill and Delaware Aqueduct routes. Public information meetings on initial

plans for the plant were held in February 1999. The city must prepare preliminary designs and a Draft Environmental Impact Statement by December 2000.

But unlike the early years of this century, when the BWS considered filtration a foregone conclusion, the city is attempting, through watershed protection measures, to avoid that very expensive prospect for its West-of-Hudson supply.

Sources: BWS Annual Reports, 1909-1929; *Pine Hill Sentinel*; *The New York Times*; *Katonah Times*; *Catskill Mountain News*; 1958 BWS Annual Report; Dec. 1, 1998, announcement on filter plant site by NYC Department of Environmental Protection; published comments by EPA Administrator Jeanne Fox, Jan. 1999; Information Sheet, Catskill/Delaware Water Supply, February 1999.

A mucking machine and its operators at Shaft 5 of the Shandaken Tunnel. The Ulen Corp., which took over tunnel driving when the original contractor failed, reported that its workers removed 584,000 cubic yards of rock to create the longest continuous tunnel in the world. Empire State Railway Museum.

14. Fire and Flood: The Schoharie Project

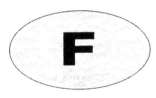LORENCE HINMAN was just a child, but she knew something was amiss in Gilboa when she looked out the windows of the one-room schoolhouse to see strange men walking about outside, wielding transit poles and chains. They were surveyors, studying the lay of the land, making maps and charts that would determine the outlines of the city's 14th dam and reservoir.

Those marks on paper would also translate into the destruction of Gilboa and its environs; some 500 people would be displaced, homes, barns and businesses in a six-mile-long valley razed to build the Schoharie Reservoir. When they saw those men in the schoolyard, Florence and her curious classmates had only the vaguest notion of what was to come. "I don't think even the older people realized what was going to happen," Florence Hinman Brandow related nearly 80 years later.[1]

How could they have envisioned the scope and impact of a project that would redirect the waters of a north-flowing river and send it southward; build the longest underground tunnel in the world; and uncover a fossilized forest, the oldest and most extensive ever found? How could they have foreseen the army of workers that would invade their valley, or the conflagration that would claim their town before the city could tear it down?

It was but an accident of geography that placed Gilboa in the path of the steam shovels. As originally planned, the Schoharie Creek was to have been dammed at Prattsville, Greene County, six miles upstream from the Schoharie County town of Gilboa. The State Conservation Commission in October 1914 approved the city's plans to build a reservoir in Prattsville that would capture the run-off from 228 square miles and send it through a 10-mile tunnel to the Esopus Creek and thence to the Ashokan Reservoir. An estimated 200 million gallons per day could be provided to the New York City supply, they said.[2]

Others, though, were convinced it would never happen. New York was short of money. The Ashokan provided plenty of water. And, suggested the *Catskill Mountain News* in March 1915, the city's water-drinking population was shrinking since "thousands of citizens and aliens who reside in New York have returned to their parent countries, called to the colors by the European war."

Still, a confident Board of Water Supply collected soil and rock samples in the vicinity of Prattsville to find a good spot for the dam, and it appeared for a time that the Platner Farm would be the chosen location. With all the activity of drilling rigs and operators, homeowners renovating buildings to accommodate the anticipated demand for offices and apartments, and a parade of men looking for jobs, "boom conditions" began to develop in Prattsville. Residents prepared for the

Above: The Gilboa Dam begins its march across the Schoharie Valley. Construction of the dam commenced in 1919. Zadock Pratt Museum.

Left: The dam rose to dwarf, and later drown, the community of Gilboa, home to 350 people. Beatrice Mattice.

onslaught of hundreds of construction workers who were expected to begin the eight-year project in the summer of 1915.[3]

But during that year, crews also fanned out to six other sites to take exploratory borings (203 of them, totalling 22,000 feet in earth and rock). They examined an area near Devasego Falls, just north of Prattsville; the nearby Ditmar site; the Caswell site farther north near the Schoharie-Delaware County border; the Manor Kill site near the junction of the Schoharie and Manor Kill Creeks at West Conesville on the Manor Kill; and in the hamlet of Gilboa, just below Gilboa Falls. The latter site would tap into a 314-square-mile watershed and provide 250 to 300 million gallons of water each day, enough, when added to the Ashokan supply, to operate the Catskill Aqueduct at full capacity. An 18-mile tunnel would be required to carry the water under the mountains to enter the Esopus Creek at Allaben.[4]

The BWS sought state approval to modify its plans to allow it to build at the more productive Gilboa site, and the Conservation Commission conducted four public hearings on the new outline in early 1916. Not surprisingly, residents of Gilboa, where 2,500 acres would be condemned, as well as property owners and businesses north of the reservoir, argued against the plan. Because the Schoharie Creek is a tributary of the Mohawk River, utility companies dependent on that water source worried that the new dam would restrict flows farther north.

As it was responding to these concerns, the BWS was fighting for its life. Some New York City interests argued that the board's work was done, and the Ashokan supply, delivered by the magnificent Catskill Aqueduct, was sufficient to meet the city's needs for some time to come. In early 1916, a bill which would have abolished the BWS was introduced by State Senator William Bennett with the support of the Real Estate Board of New York City. The BWS' Schoharie plans, Bennett said, "merely shows that there is no limit to the disposition of the board to spend the city's money."[5] The argument was also brought before the city's Board of Estimate and Apportionment in February 1916, when opponents pointed out the municipality's "perilous" financial situation and declared that the project had no support outside of the contractors who would benefit from it.[6]

Despite these objections, the city's finance board okayed the expenditure of $22 million for the Schoharie project, and the State Conservation Commission followed suit June 6, 1916. BWS engineers and contractors set to work taking more borings to determine the exact location for the dam foundation and for the Shandaken Tunnel. Topographical and real estate surveys were run, and hundreds of deeds copied to prepare condemnation maps.[7]

Plans called for the creation of a five-mile-long reservoir impounded by a masonry dam 1,324 feet long and 160 feet high. An earth embankment section, with a concrete core wall, would extend another 700 feet. The masonry section would be of concrete into which stones of varying sizes would be embedded. The overfall of the dam would be stepped on the downstream side to reduce the force of the water tumbling into the rock-paved spillway channel below. The contract for construction of this dam was awarded June 20, 1919, to Hugh Nawn Contracting Co. of Roxbury, Mass. The company's bid of $6,819,000 included the dam, two stream diversion facilities, three miles of substitute highways and a temporary bridge. Nawn started the job July 10, 1919.[8]

By that time, the Degnon Contracting Co. of Long Island City had already had its forces at work on the Shandaken Tunnel for a year and a half. Degnon's $12,138,000 bid was the lowest of three received in November 1917. The project included the construction of intake and outlet chambers, and a horseshoe-shaped, concrete-lined tunnel, 11 feet six inches high by 10 feet three inches wide.[9]

Driven almost entirely through solid rock, the 18-mile tunnel was to be constructed from seven shafts ranging in depth from 320 to 630 feet. The tunnel, designed to carry up to 600 million gallons of water daily, would slope an average of 4.4 feet per mile. At its deepest point, it would be 2,215 feet beneath the crown of a 3,200-foot mountaintop just east of Deep Notch near Westkill, in the Town of Lexington.[10]

For most of its length, the tunnel burrows beneath Greene County. Water enters the 174-foot-deep intake shaft about four miles from the dam (elevation 1,130 feet). It exits 18 miles to the south through a portal and a stone-lined channel that leads to the Esopus Creek, seven miles west of the Ashokan Reservoir (elevation 610 feet). From there, gravity continues to pull the water to Kensico (elevation 355); Hillview (elevation 295); and finally, to Silver Lake (elevation 228).

During the first full year of work on the tunnel, Degnon's forces managed to excavate 716 feet of the 3,238 feet of vertical shaft that would be required before horizontal tunneling could begin. Several feet of earth was first removed from the top of each 14-foot-diameter shaft before jackhammers were used to drill six- to eight-foot-deep blasting cavities in circular patterns of sump, relief and trim holes. An average of one to two pounds of blasting powder were used to loosen each cubic yard of

rock, which was hoisted out of the shafts by derrick and dumped in spoils banks.[11] Grout was injected when water seams were breached, and shafts were then lined with concrete in stretches of 100 to 300 feet.

Because of the remoteness of the shaft sites, work camps were established at each location. These camps featured 22- and 8-man houses, equipped with kitchens and dining rooms. Two men slept in each room. Buildings were lighted by lamps, heated by stoves and served by chemical toilets and water piped from nearby springs and brooks.[12]

In 1919, Degnon bought 18 acres of land just north of the Ulster & Delaware Railroad's Shandaken station along the Esopus Creek, where a switch yard, machine shop and storage building were erected to serve the south end of the tunnel. Another six acres were leased on the U&D just south of the Grand Gorge station where supplies would be unloaded for the northerly portion of the tunnel. A reinforced building for the storage of 20

Entertainment for tunnel workers included this wrestling match between a Russian and a Swede. Many nationalities were represented among the work force, which at one point averaged 1,200 men. Empire State Railway Museum.

An ancient forest

Workers hewing face stones at the Riverside Quarry for the Gilboa Dam uncovered more than they expected when, in 1921, they revealed fossilized tree stumps that proved to be among the most important paleontological finds ever. The discovery of hundreds of roots, stems, even spore cases from 350-million-year-old tree ferns prompted a special investigation of the quarry, and two other nearby sites, by a team of experts from the New York State Museum.

They had known for more than half a century that these fossils existed in the Gilboa area. Reformed Church minister and naturalist Samuel Lockwood had discovered the cast of a fossilized fern stump on the banks of the Schoharie Creek in the 1850s.

Fossil tree fern stumps. Empire State Railway Museum.

Decades later, blasting at the Riverside Quarry revealed more of the fossils, bases resting on shale beds, the sizes of their stumps varying from 12 inches to more than three feet in diameter. One particularly large stump was 11 feet around. Altogether, several hundred tree fern sections were found at three distinct elevations in these three sites that ranged over an area of 1.6 miles.

Museum officials trucked 40 fossils to Albany, where paleobotanist Dr. Winifred Goldring named the plant *Eospermatopteris*. In 1923, she helped Jules Henri Marchand, maker of natural history models and exhibits for museums, design a prominent diorama for the New York State Museum. Re-creating the "First Forest," the exhibit used 15 of the fossils to depict tree ferns 25 to 40 feet tall, with fronds six to nine feet long and roots that extended nine feet or more. The diorama included running water depicting the Schoharie Creek and its tributaries, and showed the now-famous ferns living along the swampy shores of what was then the Devonian Sea, evidenced by small marine fossils found near the fern fossils.

The exhibit officially opened Feb. 12, 1925. The affair was attended by geologists and museum directors from around the country, state regents and legislators, and engineers of the Gilboa Dam who had cooperated in the fossils' preservation. For 50 years a centerpiece of the museum's main exhibit hall, the First Forest was dismantled and placed in storage when the museum moved from the State Education Building to new quarters in Empire State Plaza in 1979.

The Board of Water Supply placed several of the ferns on display in a grove of trees about a mile from the Gilboa Dam. Some went to other institutions, including museums in Ireland, Sweden and England. Many of the heavy stumps were shipped directly from the Gilboa quarries to recipients around the world at the expense of Gilboa dam contractor Hugh Nawn, who took great interest and pride in the timeless discovery.

At least one fossilized stump found its way to a New York City high school where Frances Ogbin, a former student who later moved to Gilboa, said earth science students occasionally used it as an extra seat. "We never heard anything about the destruction of the town, nor the geologic significance of the fossil," said Frances in 1988.

Sources: "The Oldest Forest" (undated, NYS Museum and Science Service); "Stories of Old Gilboa" (1988-89, Gilboa Central School); "Gilboa Fossil Group Finished" (unidentified newspaper clipping); Linda VanAller Hernick's *The Gilboa Fossils* (1996) tons of gelatin dynamite was built at a secluded spot along the Bearkill, from which smaller magazines at the shafts were supplied.[13]

Work on the intake chamber and the portal proceeded during 1919, when a maximum of 500 men worked along the line. Once the desired shaft depths were reached, drilling, blasting and mucking were conducted in both directions, so that tunneling was progressing simultaneously from 12 headings. Compressors furnished air for the drills, and a full-time inspector went from shaft to shaft to repair drills and keep them running efficiently.[14]

In 1920, four $10,000 mucking machines were purchased. This device, 25 feet long and weighing nine tons, consisted of a 34-inch shovel with a 10-foot reach. Rolled forward on track laid in the center of the tunnel, it tossed muck onto an endless belt, which carried it to the rear and dumped it in muck cars for the trip to the surface. The machines were supposed to load a ton of muck a minute, but they were plagued with breakdowns.[15]

These and other problems associated with war-related shortages of material and money apparently caused Degnon to withdraw from the tunnel contract, which was assigned Nov. 11, 1920, to the Shandaken Tunnel Corp., formed and financed by two banks, engineers Stone & Webster, Inc., and the Ulen Contracting Corp.

Ulen, based in New York City, had built water and sewer projects in 90 cities in the U. S. and 25 more in South America. When it took on the Shandaken Tunnel, the company was also building a 128-mile, $10 million railway connection between the Bolivian and Argentine rail systems. The company employed 25 superintendents, managers and engineers on the Shandaken Tunnel project, headed by Thomas S. Sheppard.[16]

Once engaged, Ulen immediately picked up the pace of the Shandaken project, which by then was a year behind schedule. The workforce was increased from 200 men on November 11 to 650 by year's end.[17] Equipment was repaired, adequate supplies acquired. In 1921, bonuses were paid to crews making the highest average "pull" per shot for the week, and tunnel driving progress sped up appreciably. Ulen's forces averaged 1,070 men that

year, with a maximum of 1,440 and a minimum of 720 men on the job.[18]

The push was on to bore the remaining 83,731 feet of tunnel in three eight-hour shifts, around the clock. All but one heading was holed through in 1922. A 1923 booklet prepared by the company about the project cites several noteworthy statistics: 584,000 cubic yards of rock—650,000 carloads—were removed from the tunnel; holes totalling three million feet in length were drilled for placement of explosives; 2.5 million pounds of dynamite were detonated to carve the tunnel, enough to stretch 525 miles if the sticks were laid end to end. During the week of Feb. 1, 1922, the tunnel was advanced a record 1,431 feet. Water was not a problem, but about half the tunnel was timbered where softer shales were encountered.[19]

For every 1,000 cubic yards of rock removed from the tunnel, 380 cubic yards of concrete was placed as lining averaging from 10 to 12 inches thick; 425,000 barrels of cement were used, enough to fill the cars of a freight train 25 miles long.[20]

Roads had to be built and kept passable year-round to get materials to the shafts. In 1922 alone, 609 carloads of cement and 387 carloads of other freight were hauled by truck from the Allaben rail yard.[21]

Theodore "Ike" Carmen and his brother John were local truckers who got the contract to transport three million bags of cement from the Grand Gorge siding to the shafts. As many as eight trucks were used, but only 100 to 125 bags could be loaded per truck because of weight limits on some of the area bridges. "If a shaft needed 1,000 bags, that meant 10 trips to Grand Gorge, no eight-hour day," recalled Mr. Carmen. Strong backs were the order of the day. The trucker remembered the time two tunnel workers held a contest to see who could push the most cement. A brawny Polish fellow won, loading and pushing a wheelbarrow with 13 bags weighing 1,222 pounds.[22]

Concrete was mixed at the mouth of each shaft, where stone crushers reduced some of the rubble that came from deep within the earth into sand and aggregate. Mixed concrete was sent down the shaft through an eight-inch pipe to a hopper at the bottom of the shaft, from which it was drawn off into a train of side-dump cars. Concrete was first poured onto the invert (base of the tunnel), then cars, running on tracks centered over the invert, were hoisted up a 60-foot incline to a deck from which concrete was poured behind collapsible steel sidewall forms. To place concrete in the arch (top) of the tunnel, it was pumped behind forms using a pneumatic gun fitted with a pipe.[23]

Over each shaft was a 50-foot head frame with two balanced steel platform cages for lowering men and material. In 1922, as workers were removing concrete forms at the mouth of the intake shaft, scaffolding inexplicably gave way, hurling two brothers to their deaths at the bottom of the shaft. Lawrence Van Dyke, 27, and his brother Nelson, 21, had grown up in nearby Broome and had survived front-line service in World War I, only to meet their end not far from the farmhouse they shared with their parents.[24]

The tunnel contract included construction of an inlet chamber and gatehouse containing valves that regulated the discharge of water into the tunnel. The Coffin Valve Co. supplied the big gate valves, hydraulic cylinders, bronze castings and other equipment for the facility, which also included living quarters for a "keeper" and his family. The first person to serve as resident "keeper" was Keith Proper, a diminutive man with extraordinary strength, who took depth and turbidity readings and operated the eight bronze gates that controlled the water flow. "Whenever they called for water, he opened the gates; if they didn't want so much, he closed them," explained his son, Churchill Proper, in a 1996 interview. Water would rush through the gates far below the apartment with a roar loud enough to make the windows rattle, recalled Churchill Proper. His brother, Edward, took over the keeper's job from their father and maintained that position for another 20 years. The resident caretaker post was discontinued in the mid-1970s.

The tunnel project employed many other local men, like Leonard Ford of Shandaken, a hoist operator at one of the tunnel shafts, who had the peculiar habit of always wearing a tie to work; and

Floyd Kirk of Spruceton, a blacksmith's helper in 1917, who had a knack for making tools and drill bits "because growing up on a farm, we learned everything."[25]

But many laborers came from farther afield. Striking miners from Pennsylvania found work on the project, as did others brought in by bus. Ulen was among the first to use buses rather than trains to transport workers in groups of 30 or 40 from as far as Philadelphia and Buffalo. Most nationalities were represented, and there were numbers of Blacks and Native Americans. But turnover was substantial----Ulen had to hire a total of 10,000 men to maintain a force that averaged 1,200 between April 1921 and February 1923. More than a million meals were served at Ulen's commissaries. Married executives and their families were housed in a "cottage colony" near the company's Allaben headquarters; single men lived in a staff house adjacent to the office.[26]

While supervisors and laborers worked toward completing the tunnel, the Hugh Nawn Co. orchestrated the dam project and another firm, Rice & Ganey, built the diversion works which in February of 1924 allowed delivery of the first Schoharie Creek water through the tunnel to the Esopus. The event was marked with a celebration that included a subterranean concert by the Hen-

A temporary dining room was set up in the Shandaken Tunnel to celebrate the hole through between Shafts 5 and 6. The tunnel was completed in 1924. Empire State Railway Museum.

sonville Band.[27] The Ulen Corp.'s tunnel work was completed Nov. 6, 1924, two months ahead of deadline. The company had succeeded in building the longest continuous tunnel in the world. At 95,740 feet in length, it eclipsed the second longest tunnel---New York's own City Water Tunnel #1, completed in 1915---by just under 2,000 feet. The third longest, Hetch-Hetchy, delivering water from Yosemite National Park to San Francisco, was 73,334 feet in length.

It would be another three years, though, before the reservoir itself would be ready.

In 1919, preparations were made to begin the massive job. A special electric transmission line was stretched 50 miles from Kingston. Hugh Nawn's work camp was situated on Broome Center Road north of the hamlet of Gilboa where 20 eight-man bunkhouses, a commissary, carpenter shop, infirmary, blacksmith shop, storehouses and wash houses with chemical toilets were initially erected.

(Workers on other contracts would later occupy the Devasego Inn and the Gilboa Hotel.) The dam and dike areas were partially cleared and the Steen Kill diversion culvert where that stream crossed the dike site was nearly completed.[28]

The following year, excavation for the dam and spillway began, coffer dams were constructed to keep the Schoharie out of the building zone, and two quarries---Riverside and Stevens Mountain---were developed. While BWS engineers tested small scale models of the dam and spillway to determine the most effective size and shape to carry maximum flood flows, the contractor was literally struggling to keep his head above water: Rainfall totals in 1920 exceeded any on record, six times flooding the coffer dam work area.[29]

Workers started laying masonry and large stone blocks on the dam in 1921. Concrete operations were complex, involving three separate materials sites and as many overhead tramways. The

Building the stepped spillway. Engineers built scale models of the dam to determine what size and shape of spillway would handle maximum floods. Empire State Railway Museum.

following description is taken from the 1921 Board of Water Supply Annual Report:

Sand from the so-called Patchin sand pit was delivered to a washer on a narrow gauge railroad, dumped into a hopper and fed onto a conveyor which elevated it to a revolving screen washer. The clean sand was automatically transferred to another hopper, thence to buckets on an overhead tramway, 585 feet long. Buckets traveling 500 feet per minute carried the sand to a huge bin over the distant concrete mixer.

At the Stevens Mountain quarry, stone was dumped by railroad cars into a Traylor "Bulldog" crusher, screened, collected in bins and discharged onto a 90-foot conveyor transporting it to a storage pile. The storage pile was located over a 180-foot-long wooden tunnel in which cars were drawn by a hoist engine to receive the stone, and then discharge it into one-yard buckets on another tramway, 3,670 feet long. Supported by 10 towers averaging 22 feet high, the tramway took the stone to bins over the mixer.

Cement, stored in a storehouse on Conro's flats along what is now State Route 30, was delivered to the mixer at a rate of six bags every 48 seconds by yet a third tramway, 3,300 feet long. Storage for 2,000 bags was provided at the mixer, where water was supplied by a four-inch gravity line from the Manor Kill. The two-cubic yard mixer accepted sand, stone, cement and water, and dumped the mix into elevator buckets operated by electric hoists which raised the concrete to the top of a 135-foot distributing tower. From there, the material was dumped into a hopper feeding steel chutes suspended from a 430-foot cable swung between two towers and delivered directly to the dam for placement.

Gray sandstone facing blocks five to six feet thick were mined and shaped at the Riverside Quarry, and delivered to the dam first by truck, and later, railroad cars.

Emerson Meade of Conesville, interviewed in 1988, remembered going with two cousins one day up to Steven's Mountain where his uncle worked at the giant stone crusher. The boys marveled at the complicated arrangement that funneled stone from one mountain, cement from across the valley, and sand from the direction of Prattsville. "Altogether, they had materials coming from three directions."[30]

Other contractors employed on the works included the Schunnemunk Co., which built more than seven miles of substitute roadway; Lupfer & Remick, builders of two bridges over the Schoharie and the Mine Kill Creeks, and Rice & Ganey, which cleared and grubbed 1,300 acres of trees and brush as they did in the Ashokan basin.[31]

Coordinating the work of the contractors were BWS officials headquartered in Grand Gorge, where Department Engineer George Honess held sway. Division offices were located at Prattsville, Allaben and Gilboa, headed respectively by Division Engineers William Hunter, Charles Clark and James Guttridge. (Clark and Guttridge later went on to supervisory posts in the construction of City Tunnel #2.) Midway through the Schoharie project, in May 1922, J. Waldo Smith, the first chief engineer of the BWS, retired after 17 years of spearheading development of the Catskill Supply. He was succeeded by Thaddeus Merriman.[31]

Regular contact with the public directly affected by the changes in their midst was the job of BWS "foot soldiers" like Sidney Clapp, an assistant engineer in charge of watershed sanitation. It was his job to see that privies and pig pens were not polluting the Schoharie and its tributaries. He was, therefore, well known in the vicinity. Wrote *New York Times* reporter Alvin Meland in September 1925, " Some residents hate him cordially."

But mostly they hated the process by which their property (nearly 2,500 acres) was summarily taken. Some people took what the city offered for their holdings; others held out for more, taking their claims to damage commissions. Both sides prepared early for those commission hearings. In 1917, the board had taken a census of all mills, creameries and other businesses in the region, and had taken photographs of all buildings to serve as evidence. Said the 1917 Annual Report, "In several instances, claimants were pictured in the act of making extensive repairs and painting structures that had stood for years unpainted."

But, opined V. D. Mattice in a poem, "The Passing of Old Gilboa," what's fair is fair:

"Many damage claims are pending, some are large and some are small;
There should be this stipulation, "A square deal for one and all."
It's a case of sheer compulsion, taking what another owns;
Surely, it's no trifling matter, forcing people from their homes."

Gilboa residents' attitude toward the city was colored, too, by the upheaval all around them, upheaval that extended to their graveyards. A total of 1,330 bodies had been located in two large cemeteries and five smaller burial grounds. Relatives had been given the opportunity to have the bodies exhumed and reburied elsewhere. Bodies with no living descendants were moved, along with head and foot markers, to the New Gilboa Cemetery during the summer of 1921. Charles Mead & Co. of New York landed the grisly job of unearthing and relocating unclaimed bodies. Graves were opened, remains placed in individual yellow pine boxes and taken in trucks to the new cemetery.[32]

Henry Young of West Conesville helped with that task, according to his daughter, Evelyn Young Haskin. "Back then, he was glad to do anything," she said of her father, who was a farmer, blacksmith and later a town highway worker. "He used to tell us that when they opened the graves, the only thing that wasn't deteriorated was the silk ties." Other family members also earned money at the Schoharie project. Henry's wife, Sarah, did laundry for workers and their families in a copper boiler on a woodstove on their back porch. The couple's two daughters, Evelyn and Emma, picked strawberries and blackberries and sold them to the occupants of Gilboa's two hotels before the community was razed.[33]

Contemporaries of Evelyn Haskin were Winfield Maben of North Lexington and Harry Keator of Olive. Mr. Keator was the oldest of nine children. His father was a stone mason who worked a quarry on his own farm. Together they went to Shandaken looking for work. They landed jobs at the tunnel outlet, where bluestone imported from Shinhopple in western Delaware County, and some mined in a nearby quarry, was being laid in the channel. "I had no business being there, I was

The Devasego Inn, a handsome vacation destination that could accommodate 150 guests, was claimed by the city and housed contractors' forces before it was torn down to make way for the reservoir. Zadock Pratt Museum.

only 16," Mr. Keator says. But the $4 he earned each day helped support his family.[34]

Winfield Maben was a water boy on the dam, supplying laborers with drinking water and keeping the new concrete wet for 36 cents an hour. He and his family lived in the old Devasego Inn, a landmark with ties to trucker Ike Carmen. Mr. Carmen's uncle and aunt, Starr and Lottie Mase, had once hosted as many as 150 guests at a time there. Ike earned 50 cents a day setting pins in the bowling alley, slaughtering and dressing dozens of chickens each week and washing dishes until 9 at night. The Mases were evicted when the city came to Gilboa. They joined people like Sidney and Della Rivenberg, owners of the Gilboa Telephone Company; Dr. Ernest Billings; dressmaker Hazel Hoagland Baker and her mail carrier husband Asa; Fred Seabal the barber; and storekeeper Van Palmer. The Methodist Church was in the way of the new dam, which cut through the center of town.

the Masonic Hall and the silent movie
And so was the home of Mary Brooks,
story goes, refused to vacate her home,
instead burned out by authorities when
to visit a neighbor.

roved the ultimate demise of the rest of
unity in October 1925. A blaze ravaged
gs which by then had been acquired by
d were being rented to their occupants prior to issuance of the final eviction notice. The structures included several homes, two stores, Becker's Hotel and the Methodist Church. Some said the blaze was deliberately set to keep the city from selling the rights to a movie company that wanted to film a last conflagration. The official explanation held that a rubbish fire left smoldering behind H. S. Slover's Department Store consumed the community.[35] By the end of the year BWS forces had burned the remaining buildings in town.

Flames took a further toll just after Christmas in 1926, when a tar-papered boardinghouse occupied by laborers employed by Hugh Nawn burned down, killing two men and injuring two others.[36]

And after the fires, there was flood. The sluice gates at the dam were closed July 24, 1926. Following a dry spell, a great storm arrived November 16,

delivering 11 billion gallons in rainfall and runoff into the new reservoir. A billion gallons more spilled into the basin for each of the next six days. On November 24, a record 660 million gallons of water was sent down the Shandaken Tunnel.[37]

Florence Brandow, grown to young adulthood since she first saw those surveyors out the schoolhouse windows, remembers cheering as the water first rolled over the lip of the spillway. "A group of us went down that night. They had a big searchlight they fixed with car batteries so we could see when it first went over. There was loud hollering: 'There is goes! It did it!'" Despite the heartache of the past seven years, excitement prevailed that dark night. Said Mrs. Brandow, "I think once it was finished, and looked good, people sort of settled back and didn't think any more about it."

Some, like garage owner, car dealer and entrepreneur Imer Wyckoff, looked forward to new ventures. Mr. Wyckoff tried to launch a new town around a small retail settlement known as "Imerville" a couple of miles from the reservoir. But his little development——a Socony Garage, the general store of Leland Lewis, the East Side Lunchroom which also housed the post office——failed to attract his fellow townfolk, who had scattered to other locales.

It did, however, provide a home for Hayward and Ettie Mercer Regular and their three children, who rented an apartment at the new Wyckoff block. Hayward, a native of Newfoundland where he had learned the fine art of rigging aboard fishing vessels, had brought his family down from Montreal to take a job rigging and tending cranes on the dam project. They had lived in the old village until its demise, the kids had gone to school there, and had enjoyed leading the tired work horses from the dam up to a hillside farm for equine R&R. Mr. Regular longed to become a U. S. citizen. And so they stayed to become part of a reborn community.[38]

But the family lost all their possessions——including Hayward Regular's naturalization papers—— when, in 1928, another fire, caused by an exploding oil lamp, destroyed Imerville, thus putting an end to the dream of New Gilboa.[39]

Delaware River Basin

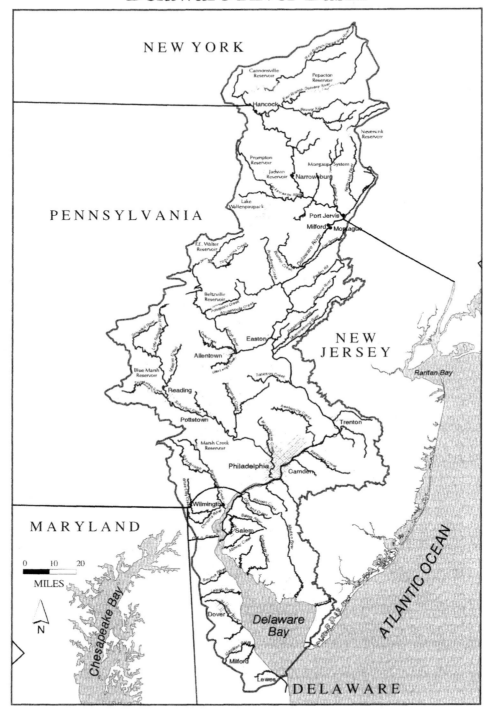

The Delaware River drains parts of four states: New York, Pennsylvania, New Jersey and Delaware. Delaware River Basin Commission.

15. Fighting for the Delaware

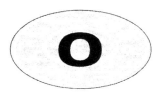

O VERCOMING the physical obstacles and community opposition to development of the Catskill System was tough. But the Board of Water Supply was to face an even longer and costlier battle, one that raged all the way to the U. S. Supreme Court, as it tangled with three other states for control of the Delaware River System.

Heeding a 1920 warning from BWS Chief Engineer J. Waldo Smith that galloping water consumption in the ever-growing city threatened to eclipse the new Catskill Supply by 1932, the BWS in the early 1920s launched a search for new water sources.[1]

It must have seemed like old times for the city's consultants----engineers John Freeman and William Burr, who had authored the 1903 report that led to the development of the Esopus, and geologist Charles Berkey, who had helped the city locate its Hudson River crossing for the Catskill Aqueduct.[2] Once again they were called upon to help compile an updated survey of water sources, and they explored many of those scrutinized nearly two decades earlier. They looked close to home, revising the original report on Long Island well sources, and farther afield, reconnoitering potential dam sites within 200 miles of New York City. In 1921 the BWS sent a six-person team upstate to make topographical surveys of eight dam sites: three on Cat-

skill Creek near Oak Hill and Preston Hollow; one on Schoharie Creek at Burtonsville; one on the East Branch of the Delaware River in Margaretville and three on the Basher Kill at Phillipsport, West Brookville and Godeffroy.[3]

During 1922 and '23, the board examined possible new aqueduct lines and additional conduits to expand the delivery system in Brooklyn, Queens and Staten Island, and routes for a second city water tunnel. Throughout the period, the BWS issued specific reports and recommendations to the Board of Estimate: In 1924 it urged the construction of a 20-mile-long, deep-rock tunnel to take water from Hill View Reservoir through The Bronx, beneath the East River to Queens and Brooklyn. The project, which would provide back-up for City Tunnel #1 and allow the delivery of more water, would cost an estimated $67 million and would take six to seven years to build.[4]

As it explored these and other proposals, the city, which had long eyed the deep valleys of the Delaware River, was participating in a venture it hoped would allow it to tap into that source. In March 1923, the state legislature passed an act establishing a commission to work with representatives from New Jersey, Pennsylvania and the federal government to formulate a treaty outlining the conservation, use and development of the Delaware River drainage basin. New Yorkers appointed by Gov. Alfred E. Smith to the Delaware River Treaty Commission included Chairman George

Engineers of the Board of Water Supply in 1912. Front (l. to r.): Merritt Smith, J. Waldo Smith, Robert Ridgway; rear: Walter Spear, Thaddeus Merriman, Alfred Flinn, Carleton Davis, Frank Winsor. NYC DEP.

MacDonald, Rudolph Reiner and Jefferson De-
Mont Thompson.[5]

The BWS provided data and materials it had
collected as eight commissioners settled in to negotiate the use of the waterway, whose East and West
Branches originate in Delaware County, N.Y., and
meander southward 74 and 68 miles, respectively,
to converge at Hancock, N.Y. From there, the
main trunk of the Delaware River flows 330 miles
south, forming the boundaries of New York, Pennsylvania, New Jersey and Delaware. The river
passes through Trenton, Philadelphia and Wil-
mington before emptying into Delaware Bay. In
January 1925, the tri-state commission came up
with a 24-article "treaty" which included plans to
develop dams to supply not only New York City
but also Philadelphia and Northern New Jersey.

Impoundments were proposed for the East Branch
in the Margaretville area and the West Branch near
Cannonsville, both in Delaware County, and the
main stem at Port Jervis, where the three states
adjoin. Dams were also proposed for Sullivan
County, N.Y., where a correspondent for the *Sullivan County Review* had, five years earlier, on Jan.
29, 1920, expressed the hope that rumors of dam
construction and jobs would prove true "as we are
all wishing for something to start in this old for-
saken place that would make it boom, for it has
been dead long enough."

The commission estimated $500 million would
be required to provide Pennsylvania, which com-
mands half the Delaware watershed, with three
billion gallons a day, New York and New Jersey
1.5 billion gallons each. The treaty also addressed

A mountain stream feeding the Rondout Creek was just the pure-water source
the city needed as demand began to outstrip supply in the 1920s. NYC DEP.

sanitation needs, industrial uses and navigation issues.[6]

The agreement was subject to ratification by all three state legislatures, and was a subject of considerable debate. It failed to be adopted by lawmakers in Pennsylvania and New Jersey not once, but twice, and was never ratified. But as the treaty discussion went on, so, too, did the city's water planners.

In November 1926, anxious to begin work on supplementing its water supply, the BWS reported on potential development of East-of-Hudson sources. "Continuing delays in adjusting questions of importance to other sovereignties do not justify neglect of the needs of the City of New York," the board said. It thereupon proposed going to Dutchess, Columbia and Rensselaer Counties to

tap streams including the Kinderhook, Stony Kill, Claverack, Taghkanic, Roeliff Jansen Kill and tributaries of the Wappingers, Sprout, Jackson and Fishkill Creeks. These creeks, diverted into the Kensico Reservoir, could provide 422 million gallons a day. Additionally, yet another new reservoir on the East Branch of the Croton River could yield 133 million gallons more. Developed over 15 years, these projects would cost about $348 million. Engineer Smith recommended the city begin working on them immediately so that more water would be available by 1935, when he now anticipated demand and supply would merge.[7]

Throughout 1926, drought conditions prevailed in the city's Catskill watershed, and officials urged restricted water use as it battled the perception, fueled by press reports, that the Ashokan

Reservoir was leaking and "millions of gallons of water are running away in underground channels." The *New York Herald Tribune* described the Ashokan basin as one of "unutterable desolation. Here lie visible mile on mile of stone fences, the twin walls of the old wagon road that once wound through the valley, tree stumps, acres of them, where once stood forests, (and) mounds of stone rubble, relics of the dam's construction. Of water there is little, scarcely more than a broad and sluggish stream. Of the 130 billion gallons the reservoir is designed to hold, less than 16 billion remain." [8]

Mayor Jimmy Walker appointed former Chief Engineer Smith, now a consultant, to look into the matter, but the issue faded away as heavy autumn rains filled the parched basin. Then, tales of destruction from November floods filled local newspapers, which speculated about the liability of the city for some of the damage. Phoenicia residents, in particular, wondered whether the extra water now being funneled from the Schoharie watershed down the Shandaken Tunnel into the Esopus had added to the mass of water that surged through town, collapsing buildings and bridges.[9]

In 1927, abandoning its earlier plan to expand on its East-of-Hudson supply, the BWS recommended to the city's Board of Estimate that New York State tributaries of the Delaware be dammed to provide 600 million gallons of water a day. The plan would first tap the Rondout Creek (actually a tributary of the Hudson) between Eureka and Lackawack, then would impound the Neversink River at Curry, the East Branch of the Delaware a mile east of Downsville, and, later, the Little Delaware a mile below the Village of Delhi, the Beaverkill seven miles above Roscoe and the Willowemoc one mile above Livingston Manor. The city contended that 70 percent of the water flowing past Tri-State Rock, 115 miles from the river's source, originated in New York State, and so New York alone had the right to determine how to use it. The water thus obtained would be sufficient through 1950, and would require the fewest reservoirs, shortest aqueducts and the least disturbance to communities than other alternatives. Those al-

ternatives included East-of-Hudson proposals (15 reservoirs on 11 streams), the Housatonic River (which lies in Connecticut), groundwater sources on Long Island (which would require continuous pumping) and the Adirondacks (too far away and too costly to develop).[10]

Nor did the city pursue its idea, approved by the state as part of the Esopus-Schoharie plan back in 1906, to dam Catskill Creek and its tributaries in Greene County. While the city had reserved the right to do so, the state, in September 1927, modified the earlier approval to exclude that area from potential development by New York City after the City of Albany filed for permission to build a dam there, on Basic Creek.[11]

Hearings were held on whether the city should expend $272 million on the proposed Delaware plan, and the Board of Estimate gave its approval in January 1928. Then it was the public's turn to comment on the specifics of the proposal. At a two-day hearing in March held by the State Water Power and Control Commission, attorneys spoke for several municipalities and large companies. Among the opponents was A. T. Clearwater, who had stood up at a similar hearing on the Ashokan project 23 years earlier. Then, he had berated the city for usurping much of the best land in that area, predicting, "The streams of Ulster County can meet the needs of New York City only temporarily."[12] Now, he warned the people of the Delaware basin to beware the damage commissioners, chosen more for their political connections than for their aptitude in the field of appraisals. For the city's part, Acting Corporation Counsel Arthur Hilley said the city was prepared to allow municipalities along the line of the new aqueduct to take water from it and anticipated building sewage treatment plants for a number of villages in the region.[13]

That was small comfort to the 1,500 people who would be displaced from communities like Arena, Pepacton and Shavertown; Montela and Neversink; Bovina Center and Lew Beach. They had been hearing rumors of city dams, fueled by periodic appearances throughout the region of surveyors and boring crews, since 1912. The Sullivan County towns of Wurtsboro, Cuddebackville and

Westbrookville would be annihilated in a reservoir with dams at Summitville and Valley Junction; the Mamakating Valley, also in Sullivan County, would be drowned by a big dam at Phillipsport; Margaretville in Delaware County would be split by a dam that would result in a reservoir with branches as far north as Roxbury and as far east as Fleischmanns.[14]

Now that the city had applied preliminary plans to paper, communities like Margaretville, Delhi, Downsville and Parkston, which were near projected dam sites, weren't sure whether to be nervous about potential inundation or optimistic about the economic benefits to be derived from being situated near a huge construction site. The *Livingston Manor Times*, in a Jan. 30, 1930 editorial just two months after the 1929 stock market crash, projected that the Delaware projects "will provide work for thousands of men and help in a large way the solution of the unemployment problem in New York State." Job needs notwithstanding, few of those most likely to be affected by the reservoirs were happy about the state commission's May 25, 1928, decision to approve the plans. But many were cheered when the State of New Jersey subsequently brought an action to stop the massive undertaking.[15]

New Jersey, seeking a permanent injunction, contended the city was wasting its water and refusing to install meters to curb the waste. It said there was no public necessity for the project because the city could use the Hudson River or go elsewhere in its upstate watershed for additional water instead of tapping an interstate supply. The withholding of Delaware River water would mean the encroachment of salt water at the river's tidal Delaware Bay outlet, a condition that would harm the state's oyster industry, New Jersey said. The city countered that placing five dams on the river and its tributaries would actually improve the river downstream by minimizing future floods, and by augmenting, with periodic water releases from those dams, stream flows during dry periods of the year. The projects would enhance electric generating potential and improve sanitary conditions, fishing

and recreation along the river, according to the city.[16]

The U. S. Supreme Court appointed Charles Burch of Memphis, Tenn., as Special Master to investigate the matter. Judge Burch held hearings in Trenton, New York City, Philadelphia and Memphis in late 1930. Meanwhile, confident that it would emerge victorious, the BWS went forward with preliminary work on the project, surveying and taking borings at dam sites and along the line of the proposed 70-mile Delaware Aqueduct, before the court reached its verdict.[17]

That verdict came May 25, 1931, when the Supreme Court denied New Jersey's suit and accepted Special Master Burch's recommendation that the city be permitted to withdraw 440 million gallons of water a day from the Delaware, not the 600 million for which it had sought approval. But, adding the 100 million gallons it anticipated drawing from the Rondout Reservoir (a Hudson River tributary and thus not affected by the Supreme Court decision), the city would still be able to deliver 540 million gallons of water a day to its residents. The city was also required to release water from its dams to maintain a specified flow at Port Jervis, where it was also required to build a sewage treatment plant.[18]

Supreme Court Justice Oliver Wendell Holmes, in delivering the court's decision, made a classic contribution to the literature of the law:

> A river is more than an amenity, it is a treasure. It offers a necessity of life that must be rationed among those who have power over it. New York has the physical power to cut off all the water within its jurisdiction. But clearly the exercise of such a power to the destruction of the interest of lower states could not be tolerated. And on the other hand, equally little could New Jersey be permitted to require New York to give up its power altogether in order that the river might come down to it undiminished. Both sides have real and substantial interests in the River that must be reconciled as best they may be. The different traditions and practices in different parts of the country may lead to varying results but the effort always is

to secure an equitable apportionment without quibbling over formulas.[19]

That landmark decision would not be the final word on the division of the Delaware; the issue would return to the Supreme Court's doorstep in 1954 (Chapter 18).

But for now, Thaddeus Merriman, Chief Engineer of the BWS since the retirement of J. Waldo Smith in 1922, wasted no time in proceeding with work on the new Delaware Aqueduct. There was, he said, no time to lose. Each year, water consumption was rising an average of 35 million gallons per day, and it would take 10 years to bring the Delaware System on line.[20]

In fact, the Great Depression and World War II would delay for more than a generation the introduction of the first Delaware water into New York City. Neither Chief Engineer Smith nor his successor Merriman would live to see it happen.

The city had, however, gotten a start on expanding its delivery capabilities with the construction of City Tunnel #2. Proposed in 1924, it was not until 1927 that the project was authorized by the Board of Estimate and Apportionment and the State Water Power and Control Commission. In May 1927, the City Aqueduct Department was formed, with engineer Charles Clark at its head. The department was divided into the Executive, Yonkers, Brooklyn and Queens Divisions, headed respectively by engineers Roger Armstrong, James Guttridge, Royal Gilkey and John M. Fitzgerald.[21]

The tunnel was built from 19 vertical shafts ranging from 361 to 766 feet beneath the surface. Fifteen of those concrete-lined shafts, spaced 7,000 feet apart, served, upon the tunnel's completion, as conduits to the surface delivery pipes. Designed to carry up to 700 million gallons of water a day, the tunnel is circular with a 17-foot interior diameter for most of its 20-mile length. For about 1.3 miles it is 15 feet in diameter. Sixteen miles of the tunnel are located under streets, parks and other city property; .8 miles under river and harbor waters and 3.2 miles under private lands. Unseen, it passes deep beneath Calvary Cemetery in Queens, the Walla-

bout Canal, Fort Greene Park and Brooklyn Hospital. While the route of the tunnel had been determined from test borings conducted in 1923 and '24, tunnel grades and shaft locations were determined by further borings made in 1927 by the Osborne Drilling Company of New York City. Geologic studies, design of shafts, underground explosives magazines, valve chambers and connections to Hillview Reservoir and to City Tunnel #1 were worked out in 1927 and '28. Commissioners of Appraisal were also appointed to hear damage claims from owners of 409 parcels affected by the project.[22]

Bids were let in 1928 for the tunnel's construction in four distinct sections. Patrick McGovern, Inc. was awarded the entire job for $42.6 million. By the end of 1930, all shafts had been sunk and "McGovern's Tunnel," as it was known by the "sandhogs," was half excavated. Electrically-operated mine hoists mounted over the shaft openings carried men and materials below ground in cages nine feet high, nine feet long by six feet wide. Shaft 2A, the deepest shaft, was the last to be completed because water infiltration that threatened to flood the shaft required numerous work stoppages to inject grout into the rock to cut off the flow. Once shafts reached the required depth, and work space was hewn at the bottom, drilling and blasting of the horizontal tunnel proceeded from two directions at once. Typically, three advances were made from each shaft per day, two in one heading and one in the other, resulting in weekly progress of from 75 to 100 feet per heading. It took about six hours to drill the 62 blast holes for one advance, and about two hours for loading and firing the explosives. The succeeding shift would muck out the tunnel using short-boomed steam shovels that maneuvered on railroad tracks within the tunnel, dumping rock into rail cars to be hoisted to the surface for disposal. Much of the muck was carted by truck and dumped into the East River to form a bulkhead. Muck from Brooklyn excavations was disposed of at sea.[23]

Other work required by the contractor included the construction of uptake and downtake chambers to regulate flow from Hillview Reser-

Top left: Rock and soil samples, cement and many other materials were tested in BWS labs like this one in the basement of 147 Varick Street, New York City. *Top right:* Surveying inside City Tunnel #2. *Above left:* Mucking machines couldn't eliminate all of the post-blast clean-up work inside City Tunnel #2; men, using shovels and air hoses, loaded the remainder of the debris into muck cars for hoisting out of the shaft. *Above right:* Excavating Shaft 7A at Bryant Ave. and E. 167th St. in 1929. All NYC DEP.

voir; 14 subsurface valve chambers to control flow to the city's delivery system and a drainage chamber on the Queens side of the East River. The tunnel at this point was divided into two sections by a pair of 66-inch hydraulically operated bronze gate valves to allow the unwatering of either section while the other remained in service. By the end of 1931, all but a few feet of the tunnel had been excavated, and 80 percent of the concrete lining, or 85,000 linear feet, had been poured. Batching plants for the concrete were located at the Bronx and East Rivers, Eastchester and Flushing Creeks and the Gowanus Canal so that materials could be delivered by scow.[24]

The tunnel was very nearly completed when the city's declining fiscal condition brought construction to a grinding halt. In September 1933, the city applied to the federal government under provisions of the National Industrial Recovery Act for $1 million in grants and loans. The money was awarded in December, allowing the BWS to let contracts for valves, sluice gates, overhead cranes, pipes, pumps and other equipment to permit the operation of the conduit.[25]

City Tunnel #2, all 105,265 feet of it, was completed and tested by 1935, and was finally placed in service in 1936. It eclipsed the Shandaken Tunnel as the longest continuous tunnel in the world, just as the Shandaken conduit had surpassed City Tunnel #1. Within a decade, the new Delaware Aqueduct would claim the title of the world's longest tunnel, a distinction it continues to hold more than half a century later.[26]

The year 1933 marked the death of former Chief Engineer Jonas Waldo Smith, followed a year later by the passing of Prof. William Burr, chairman of the Burr-Hering-Freeman Commission that had laid the foundation for the BWS in 1904 and for 30 years a consultant to the city on development of its water supply.[27]

J. W. Smith's successor, Thaddeus Merriman, retired in 1933. Mr. Merriman, whose early career had included surveying and designing the Nicaragua Canal and Jersey City's Boonton Dam, had spent 28 years with the BWS. Turning the reins over to Walter Spear, the former Chief Engineer would continue as a consultant for the board, and also on water supply projects in Southern California and Boston, and flood control projects in Los Angeles and Tennessee, before his death in 1939 at the age of 57.[28]

The old guard was passing, ushering in a new era of New York City's water development.

Above: Water inflow, which at one point reached 500 gallons per minute, shown at Shaft 2A, City Tunnel #2, in August 1931. Grouting was required to cut off the flow. *Facing page:* City Tunnel #2 curved at this point, Shaft 2A south. Both NYC DEP.

New sources, new conduits

With the addition of the Schoharie supply and the anticipation of Delaware water came the need to add delivery capacity along the Catskill Aqueduct and in the city.

When the Catskill Aqueduct was completed in 1915, it featured a single steel siphon at each of the 14 valleys it traversed. That was sufficient to carry the 250 million gallons per day yielded by the Ashokan Reservoir, but when the Schoharie Reservoir doubled the supply, more siphon pipes had to be installed to carry the flow. In 1921, anticipating this demand, work was begun to add two additional lines of conduit at each siphon. Rice & Ganey, Frederick Snare and Thomas Crimmins were awarded sections of the total project. Their bids came to approximately $6.2 million. Fourteen years after the first siphon pipes were laid, contractors were back excavating earth and rock (601,000 cubic feet); riveting together 66,000 linear feet of steel pipe; and encasing it in 100,000 cubic yards of concrete.

The work was completed at all but one of the siphon locations by the end of 1924, the same year the Shandaken Tunnel was finished.

Meanwhile, contractors Angelo Paino, T. A. Gillespie and P. F. Connolly were installing 11 miles of new delivery pipes in Brooklyn and on Staten Island. The Mt. Prospect, Park Slope and Fort Hamilton conduits were 66- and 72-inch pipelines designed to improve water pressure and availability. Those contracts amounted to $3.2 million and involved up to 500 laborers.

Air hammers first broke up the pavement, followed by steam-powered excavators which removed about three feet of broken pavement and earth into waiting trucks for disposal. Gasoline- and steam-operated caterpillar-traction trenching machines then came in to excavate a trench nine to 10 feet deep and seven to eight feet wide. Where street railways or other obstructions prevented use of the big trenching machines, picks and shovels, aided by cranes, did the job. Pipes were laid by cranes onto temporary wooden blocking in the trenches, where they were riveted, caulked and, if necessary, enclosed in concrete, before the trenches were backfilled.

This work was carried on for two years beginning in early 1923. At the same time, Narrows Siphon #2 was being laid in the bottom of New York Harbor. To avoid reliance on other, "inferior" local water sources on Staten Island, the BWS chose to expand the delivery system from the city by adding a second submarine pipeline, and three more miles of conduit, labeled the Clove Conduit, from the shore at Clifton to Silver Lake.

Merritt-Chapman & Scott Corp. was awarded this job in March 1923 for $1.5 million. It involved the laying of 8,800 linear feet of 42-inch flexible-jointed, cast-iron submarine pipeline from the Fort Hamilton conduit at 86th St. and Shore Rd., Bay Ridge, Brooklyn, across the Narrows to Vanderbilt Ave. and Bay St. at Clifton, in the Borough of Richmond, Staten Island. The new line, added to the existing 36-inch line, would deliver about 32 million gallons of water a day into Silver Lake Reservoir, according to engineers, who worried that water use was outpacing availability. In 1921, Staten Island residents consumed 18 million gallons per day, a 5.5 million gallon increase since Catskill water had been introduced just three years earlier.

A clam-shell dredge with a 10-ton, seven-cubic-yard bucket excavated the submarine trench. The dredge was attended by six bottom-dumping scows which deposited the removed material at sea. Work went on 24 hours a day digging a cut that ranged from 12 to 30 feet deep in the bottom of the harbor. A timber-and-steel drag towed from a scow smoothed the trench before pipe was laid between September and December 1924. Pipe was delivered by derrick from the scow *Collegian* to a sister vessel, *Colossus*, where workers joined pipe sections with lead, greased the joints and slid the sections off a curved launchway into the water.

The Staten Island improvements were completed in 1925.

The previous year, the Board of Estimate and Apportionment approved the expenditure of $2.7 million to construct the Williamsburg Conduit, nearly six miles of six-foot steel pipeline to connect Shaft 24 of City Tunnel #1 in Fort Greene Park, Brooklyn, with Long Island City, Queens. This was intended to add to the water supply of the Borough of Queens and improve distribution in the Williamsburg and Greenpoint sections of Brooklyn.

Beaver Engineering and P. F. Connolly were the contractors on the new conduit, which was laid in two sections. The first ran along Myrtle, North Portland, Park, Franklin and Wythe Avenues and Hooper, South First, Maujer and Leonard Streets. The second section extended from Leonard Street along Calyer and Oakland Streets; under Newtown Creek to East Avenue in Queens; then along East, Jackson and Ely Avenues to Nott Avenue.

Pipes were laid in trenches excavated just under street level, except where the conduit encountered subways or other obstacles. At the Newtown Creek crossing, a 426-foot-long tunnel was dug through rock between two shafts, one on the Brooklyn side of the creek, 136 feet deep, the other, on the Queens side, 131 feet deep. Work was conducted around the clock. Excavation of the shafts was begun in April 1925, and the tunnel was "holed through" August 20. Pipes were laid, encased in concrete and tested by December 7. A similar tunnel, though not as deep, was dug beneath the Long Island Railroad crossing of Jackson Avenue.

The Williamsburg Conduit was placed in operation Jan. 22, 1927.

Sources: Board of Water Supply Annual Reports, 1922-1927; Charles Weidner's *Water for a City* (1974).

Above: At Shaft 2 of the Delaware Aqueduct, a 20-foot-long safety bulkhead provided a barricade against possible heavy inflows of water while workers tunneled beneath the Rondout Valley at Wawarsing. Ventilation pipes are shown above. *Top:* Steel interlining of the Delaware Aqueduct being placed prior to concreting, 1942. Both NYC DEP.

16. The Delaware Aqueduct

O GET the water from the newly-claimed Delaware River basin, the city had to once again outdo itself in the arena of tunnel building. Its efforts produced what was then, and remains, the longest continuous tunnel in the world.

The Delaware Aqueduct, a circular, concrete-lined tunnel 13.5 to 19.5 feet in diameter, stretches 83.8 miles connecting the Rondout and Hillview Reservoirs. Built from 31 vertical shafts, the aqueduct is actually three distinct pressure tunnels driven through bedrock at depths ranging from 300 to 1,550 feet below the surface. The tunnel was built on an approximate two percent grade, except for a half-mile stretch of inclined tunnel between the Rondout effluent chamber and Shaft 1, where the grade is about 10 percent.

The six-mile Neversink Tunnel, the 25-mile East Delaware Tunnel and the 44-mile West Delaware Tunnel funneled water to the Rondout and thus the Delaware Aqueduct, from the Neversink, Pepacton and Cannonsville Reservoirs as they were constructed.

The Board of Water Supply had hoped to get under way with the big project by 1932, when most of the test borings and topographic and real estate surveys along the proposed route had been completed. But in April of that year, the city's precarious fiscal status in the midst of the Great Depression prompted the withdrawal of a $50 million appropriation for the launch of the undertaking, and for the next four years work on the aqueduct was restricted to the drawing board as BWS employees prepared plans for the tunnel, surface structures, valve chambers and other aspects of the project.[1]

It was not until 1936 that the city's Board of Estimate and Apportionment approved more than $17 million to commence construction. A re-organized BWS, under command of Chief Engineer Walter Spear, established field offices, added 176 staffers and got to work preparing bid and contract specifications.[2] That year, too, Appraisal Commissions were appointed to determine awards to be made to property owners in six real estate sections along the aqueduct route. A total of 139 parcels were purchased outright, and 1,242 permanent easements were acquired, according to the 1936 BWS Annual Report.

The aqueduct's three sections include:

- *The Rondout-West Branch Tunnel.* This 48-mile section runs from a mile below the Rondout Reservoir near the hamlet of Lackawack to the West Branch Reservoir in the Croton watershed. It tunnels southeast across the Hudson River Valley through the towns of Wawarsing, Rochester, Gardiner, Plattekill and Marlboro in Ulster County; the Town of Newburgh in Orange County; the Towns of Wappinger, Fishkill and East Fishkill in Dutchess County, and the Towns of Kent, Putnam Valley and Carmel in Putnam County.

- *The West Branch-Kensico Tunnel.* A 23-mile section connecting the West Branch Reservoir in Putnam and the Kensico Reservoir in Westchester, this portion of the aqueduct runs through the Town of Carmel, and the Westchester County Towns of Somers, North Salem, Lewisboro, Bedford and North Castle. A 2.4-mile by-pass tunnel was constructed beneath the West Branch Reservoir, and a 2.3-mile by-pass tunnel, 650 feet below sea level, was dug beneath the Kensico to allow Delaware water to be joined with, or skirt, Croton and Catskill waters, respectively.

- *The Kensico-Hill View Tunnel.* This carries water 13 miles from Kensico to the start of the city's delivery system at the outlet of Hill View Reservoir, where City Tunnel #2 commences. This section of the aqueduct traverses the Towns of Mount Pleasant and Greenburgh, and the City of Yonkers.[3]

The project was divided into 11 contract sections ranging from five to 14 miles in length, not including the first mile of tunnel in Ulster County, which was part of the contract for construction of the Rondout Reservoir dam. Ten companies won those 11 contracts at bids totalling $140,109,000.[4]

But before the tunnel could be driven, vertical construction shafts had to be built down to tunnel grade. Contracts totalling more than $9 million for sinking the 31 shafts were awarded in 1937 to the Dravo Corp. of Pittsburgh, Frazier-Davis Corp. of St. Louis and W. E. Callahan and J. P. Shirley of Dallas.[5]

The deepest of the shafts was Shaft 2A, 1,551 feet beneath the Shawangunks, three miles south of Kerhonksen. Another notable aspect of shaft construction included, at Shaft 4, two miles south of Gardiner, the installation of riser pipes to connect the Delaware Aqueduct with the Catskill Aqueduct. Provisions were also made to allow connection of the Croton Falls Reservoir to the Delaware Aqueduct at Shaft 11. A coagulating plant to reduce suspended solids in the water was erected at Shaft 17. And at Shaft 19, the aqueduct was designed to connect with a potential Eastview Filter Plant.[6]

The ceremonial beginning of the project took place March 24, 1937, when New York City Mayor Fiorello LaGuardia set off a blast at Shaft 3, two miles south of Lake Minnewaska in Ulster County. An estimated 1,200 people attended the event, which sent showers of splintered rocks onto some of the spectators. The Right Rev. Michael J. Lavelle of the Catholic Archdiocese of New York was called upon to deliver the invocation, as he had 30 years earlier at the start of the Ashokan project.[7]

Actual work on the aqueduct had, in fact, begun February 10 at Shaft 17 at the Kensico Reservoir. This was part of a contract held by Dravo that called for the sinking of 10 shafts in Westchester County and Yonkers. Those shafts were finished in June 1938, but the completion of other shafts along the line took until spring 1939.[8] That year, construction rolled into high gear both in the tunnel and at the Rondout reservoir site, so that by the end of 1939, 6,000 men were employed by the various contractors.[9] Their wages ranged from 75 cents an hour for unskilled surface laborers, to $2.12 an hour paid to operating engineers. Stonemasons were paid $1.50, concrete mixer operators $1.65, crane engineers $1.87.[10] Many of the workers were furnished by unions including Hod Carriers, Operating Engineers, Teamsters, the Brotherhood of Electrical Workers, the Carpenters and Joiners, and the Bridge and Structural Iron Workers.

In contrast to earlier aqueduct and reservoir projects, contractors did not maintain work camps for laborers, who were now able to drive to work and so lived or boarded independently in neighboring communities. There were, however, change houses with lockers and showers near the job sites.[11]

Another difference between the Delaware Aqueduct and earlier projects was its speed. By the end of 1939, 35 of the 84 miles of tunnel had been driven at an average weekly rate per heading of 134 feet for the 13.5-foot diameter tunnel, and 105 feet for the 19.5-foot tunnel. By comparison, City Tunnel #2 recorded an average weekly progress of 75 feet per heading; the Catskill Aqueduct 55 to 70 feet; the 1890s Croton Aqueduct project 25 to 40 feet per week.[12]

In the 1930s, rail-mounted drilling carriages called jumbos, and track-riding mucking machines speeded the task of tunnel driving. Jumbos carried six to nine pneumatically powered drills, mounted on adjustable columns on top and side decks where drill operators stood to create in the wall of rock the meticulous patterns of 40 to 55 holes into which gelatin dynamite was placed. After each blast, fumes and dust were drawn out through ventilation pipes, and clean air blown in. Lights were replaced, and the mucking machine brought up by a battery-operated locomotive running on temporary tracks. The machine's shovel collected debris from the blast and deposited it on conveyors which dumped it into a muck car coupled to the machine. Filled cars were uncoupled and attached to the front end of the train, while empty cars were brought forward. Loaded trains were rolled back to the shaft to be hoisted out on elevator cars for dumping. Portable electric transformers provided power to run trains and lights, and to set off the dynamite blasts that advanced the tunnel an average of nine feet per shot.[13]

Drills needed sharp bits, of course. At a sharpening plant maintained by the Walsh Construction Co. at Shaft 5 near Plattekill, two men operated three furnaces turning out 2,250 pieces of sharpened steel every 24 hours.[14]

Mayor LaGuardia got a first-hand look at the operation when, accompanied by Comptroller Joseph McGoldrick and another city official, he visited Shaft 11 in the Town of Somers and set off a charge 330 feet beneath the surface that tore out 180 tons of rock from the tunnel heading 2,500 feet away. "[It] all but lifted the three highest elected officials of New York City out of their boots," reported the *Downsville News* on Nov. 2, 1939. "The concussion was so great the visitors were blown against each other."

Such explosions could sometimes be felt on the surface. Thomas L. Purdy Jr., in recollections published in 1985, remembered visiting friends on Mustato Rd. in Katonah, Westchester County, soon after war had been declared in Europe. "Suddenly we heard and felt an ominous boom and the house shook." Mr. Purdy related. "Our friends reassured us and said it was only a blast for the construction of the Delaware Aqueduct several hundred feet beneath their house."[15]

"Tunneling is being carried out with the scheduled precision equal to high-class railroad operations; every minute counts, and timing of the blasts on some sections doesn't vary more than five minutes from day to day," reported the *Engineering News Record* in August 1940. That month, workers who'd been blasting toward each other from shafts in Newburgh on the west side of the Hudson River, and Wappingers on the east, "holed through" the tunnel 600 feet beneath the river.[16]

Most of the aqueduct was driven, and much of it concreted, by 1941. But progress on the Rondout Reservoir, and completion of the aqueduct, slowed considerably with the approach of U. S. participation in European hostilities. Early in 1941, the federal government set up a system of controls to assure that materials would remain available for shipment to its lend-lease partners and for stockpiling for its own potential defense. Users of essential construction materials were given preference ratings according to their relative importance to defense, public safety and the country's welfare. BWS officials appealed personally on behalf of the city's numerous applications for higher ratings to acquire equipment and materials to finish the dam and associated aqueduct. But with the nation's full involvement in the war effort, supplies were hard to get, and high preference ratings even harder. The BWS therefore suspended much of its bidding and construction activity for the duration of the war.[17]

However, in April 1944 the aqueduct was placed into emergency service by diverting the Rondout Creek near Lackawack down an 800-foot tunnel into Shaft 1 to provide water for the growing city until the Rondout and Neversink reservoirs could be finished. The water flowed 45 miles through the aqueduct to the West Branch Reservoir of the Croton System, where combined waters were sent to the Kensico Reservoir of the Catskill

System. The West Branch-Kensico tunnel had been placed into operation Mar. 3, 1943. The emergency use of the Rondout Creek constituted the first siphon from the long-sought Delaware Supply.[18] It yielded 37 million gallons of water a day (MGD) in 1944; 150 MGD in 1945, and 72 MGD in 1946, the year construction resumed on the Delaware reservoirs. At the same time, water demand grew from 1,031 MGD in 1944 to 1,141 MGD in 1946.[19]

The war also claimed workers, both from contractors forces and the BWS itself, which saw 277 employees enter the service. Eight of them were killed.[20]

By 1941, when most of the aqueduct was finished, some 58 men had lost their lives on the project. Some died in accidents involving tunnel trains or falling rock. Methane gas was encountered at some locations. Eight men were injured in Aug. 1938 when a lit match touched off a gas explosion 1,550 feet underground at Shaft 2A in Kerhonkson. The Dravo Corp. crew suffered burns, bruises and broken bones when they were hurled against the tunnel wall by the massive blast, which roared upward through the shaft at 4:50 a.m. August 23.[21]

There were many near misses, too. More than 500 pounds of dynamite that had already been set with blasting caps plunged to the bottom of Shaft 2A in April 1940 when the shaft's lowering mechanism malfunctioned. Miraculously, the dynamite did not explode, reported the *Ellenville Journal*. On another occasion, workers placing steel guides at the headframe of a shaft somehow dropped a 20-foot-long, 600-pound rail down the shaft, where a crew was excavating muck from the base of the shaft, 900 feet below. The shaft penetrated 10 feet of muck and stood vertically, "quivering like a tuning fork in the midst of the mucking crew, none of whom was injured," reported the BWS' *Delaware Water Supply News* in a Sept. 1, 1949, article about tunnel safety.

The *News* went on to note that while 25 million pounds of dynamite was used in shaft and tunnel work prior to 1943, only one fatality was due to explosion. More careful attention to safety and inspections reduced the number of lost-time accidents per mile of tunnel by 60 percent, and the number of fatalities by 75 percent, compared with BWS tunnel projects prior to commencement of the Delaware Aqueduct. The *News* cited statistics showing that there were more accidental deaths in the average 15 days in New York City homes in 1948 (82) than there were on the Delaware project in 10 years (79). Traffic deaths in the city claimed 576 lives in 1948, compared with 507 fatalities on BWS work in the previous 42 years.

However, lung conditions resulting from inhaling dust and fumes in the confined spaces of the tunnel in time took their toll on workers' health. In 1937, just as the Delaware Aqueduct was getting under way, the state labor department enacted new codes governing rock drilling and dust control, including ventilation specifications, and requirements on the use of water during drilling and mucking operations. At about the same time, an amendment to the Workmen's Compensation Law recognized the special hazard of silicosis, a scarring of the lung tissue common among tunnel workers and miners that predisposes its victims to pulmonary tuberculosis. The new act allowed affected individuals to be compensated for that disease.[22]

Tunnelers pierced a variety of rock types and formations. Geologists identified Binnewater sandstone, High Falls shale and Shawangunk grit; Inwood limestone, Manhattan schist, Fordham gneiss and Yonkers granite. Decayed rock resulted in tunnel cave-ins; fault zones yielded infiltrations of sand, water and clay. At Shaft 19, the site of the proposed Eastview filter plant, a zone of decayed rock required special excavation and shoring methods which took seven months to go 117 feet; 23,750 barrels of cement were used to grout weak areas in that stretch. Permanent structural steel roof support had to be erected in about half the entire aqueduct, 227,758 feet. In about 40 percent of the aqueduct, where steel support was not utilized, the tunnel roof was coated with cement mortar sprayed over the rock surfaces by compressed air.[23]

One of the toughest sections to build was the 12-mile stretch in Ulster County from about a mile south of Shaft 1 to Gardiner. A zone of seriously decayed rock was encountered south of Shaft 2 at Vernooy Creek and resulted in a 10-month delay in completing the contract. Virtually all of the 74,000 feet of this part of the aqueduct had to be shored with steel. Methane gas was also a problem, and prompted the State Department of Labor and the U. S. Bureau of Mines to provide information, oversight and training, including a course on gas detection and mine rescue for the BWS and contractor Samuel Rosoff, Ltd. of Kerhonkson.[24] The "hole through" between Shafts 1 and 2, the last on the Delaware Aqueduct, was accomplished May 7, 1942.[25]

Like other contractors, Rosoff erected a sand-and-gravel processing plant to provide aggregate for the concrete to line the tunnel. He acquired a 158-acre parcel near Wawarsing, where the plant produced 800 cubic yards of crushed stone a day. Portland cement was delivered by rail from a mill at Alsen to Wallkill Valley Railroad sidings at Gardiner and Kerhonkson, where it was stored in steel silos before being trucked to batching plants adjacent to Shafts 2A and 3. From the mixers, concrete was dropped down the shafts through 12-inch pipes to receiving hoppers at the bottom. There it was loaded into agitator cars for transporting through the tunnel and placement behind collapsible forms that were moved down the tunnel as concreting progressed.[26]

BWS engineers and contactors' personnel inspected the tunnel upon completion. Unlike earlier jobs, when inspections were conducted on foot, motorcycle or, in one unsuccessful instance, rubber-tired tricycles, the Kensico-Hillview portion of the aqueduct was viewed from an eight-passenger wagon towed by a Ford car modified to traverse up to 30 inches of water.[27]

A number of underground valve chambers and above-ground structures were built along the aqueduct route. Pleasantville Constructors erected a drainage chamber at Shaft 6 on the east side of the Hudson River to allow the unwatering and inspection of 44 miles of the Rondout-West Branch Tunnel. Frazier-Davis Construction Co. built influent and effluent chambers at Shafts 9 and 10 at the West Branch Reservoir. The effluent chamber, designed to control the flow of water from either the reservoir or the by-pass tunnel into the West Branch-Kensico Tunnel, was built to handle 1.1 billion gallons per day, twice the capacity of the Catskill Aqueduct. Chlorinating facilities were also positioned at the effluent chamber, which could not be built until a coffer dam consisting of five million pounds of steel sheet piling was constructed to provide a dry, enclosed area.[28]

Associated Contractors of Valhalla were required to build an influent chamber at Shaft 17 at Kensico Reservoir, where a four-story coagulating plant was also built. Here, alum, delivered by trucks from Cooney Hill Rd., could be added to the water to reduce suspended solids. A 1,900-foot dike, made of spoils from tunnel construction, was built from the shore west of the spillway to Snake Island, to form a channel allowing a longer course for the chemically-treated water to run before it enters the reservoir proper.[29]

An aeration basin was also built at Kensico. Up to 1.2 million gallons of Delaware water a day could be directed through 3,492 nozzles in a basin 386 feet long. This was in addition to the aeration facilities for Catskill water.[30]

Difficult, dangerous work requires toughness in the people who do it. Tunnel workers, also known as sandhogs, were noted for their thick skin, their camaraderie, and their work-hard-play-hard philosophy. Tunnel workers in the Newburgh area reportedly hung out at Ray Shea's Corner Bar and Grill and Eddie Wong's, an area known as Hard Rock Corners. Workers partied together and supported one another when they got into trouble. When one of their number, Red Hammer, was arrested for some infraction by Newburgh Police, a fellow sandhog, dressed nattily as an "attorney," appeared with him in court, accompanied by imposing comrades with names like Jughead Mitchell, Slim "Six Fingers" Merrick and Hay Bag Grant. Red Hammer was allowed to go free.[31]

BWS and contractors' forces let off steam and had some fun at sporting events, picnics and dances

Sam Rosoff: Rags to riches

If ever there was a man to epitomize the big and boisterous complexity of New York City in the early days of the twentieth century, it was Samuel Rufus Rosoff.

Known in later years as "Subway Sam" for the $50 million in subway contracts he'd won from the city, Rosoff might have been the model for his own Horatio Alger story. Born in Minsk, Russia in 1883, he worked on a cattle boat plying the Black Sea before, as a fatherless 12-year-old, he emigrated to the U.S. with his mother in 1895. When others in the family moved to the Midwest, Sam stayed in New York City, hawking newspapers on street corners. Rosoff sometimes slept on street grates, but also found lodging in the Newsboys' Home on East 42nd St., where, for eight cents he recalled years later, he got a bed, a clean nightshirt, and breakfast of coffee, oatmeal and a roll.

As a teenager he became a "candy butcher," selling candy on the West Shore Railroad, where he made the acquaintance of A. A. Low, brother of New York City Mayor Seth Low, and thereupon made some connections that enabled him to branch out and enter the business world on his own. Early ventures included a company he formed to raise the steamship, *Bavaria* which had sunk in the Gulf of St. Lawrence; a disastrous potato purchasing enterprise; a stone brokerage to supply materials for the Cape Cod Canal; a real estate development firm in Queens; and an excavation company that won several contracts on the New York State Barge Canal.

He managed road building contracts in Delaware County, N.Y., during World War I, organized the East Side Omnibus Corp. with a franchise to run buses along three of New York's avenues and, with his own sand and gravel mining operation near Marlboro, was able to secure numerous New York City jobs and subway contracts, which ultimately made him a millionaire. He returned to his homeland in 1929 to discuss a proposal from officials of the Russian government that he build a subway in Moscow, but those talks fell through.

Rosoff, with his expansive girth, dandy suits and ever-present cigar, cut a colorful figure in New York, where he was often in the public eye. "Sam Rosoff is as much a phenomenon of contemporary New York as the Empire State Building," spouted *The New York Times Magazine* in 1934. "He is a character, an eyeful and a local wonder." Called a "Paul Bunyan of industry," "a living dynamo" and a "loveable roughneck," Rosoff lived in an expensive apartment high above Central Park, where he occasionally went trail riding when he wasn't personally supervising his far-flung financial empire.

That empire stretched to Margaretville, Delaware County, where, in 1928, he purchased for $70,000 the failing Delaware & Northern Railroad. He was described as an "angel" by locals thankful for the passenger and freight service along the 38-mile line which had been operating since 1906 but had fallen into receivership. Others, though, suspected his motives. Rosoff claimed he wanted to revitalize the line, extend it to the Pennsylvania border and make some money off the coal trade. Skeptics claimed he'd only purchased the property to sell it at an inflated price to the city when the East Branch Valley was condemned for the Pepacton Reservoir, which would be Phase 2 of the Delaware water supply development. About half of the rail line would have to be submerged or be relocated, as was the Ulster & Delaware in the Ashokan basin. The latter was a costly undertaking the BWS preferred to avoid, and after a long, contentious battle, Rosoff and the city settled for $200,000 in 1939, ending the rail line's short life.

That was the year he won Delaware Aqueduct Contract 331, to build 75,157 feet of pressure tunnel beneath the Shawangunk Ridge for $18,916,650. An estimated 800 workers were employed on Rosoff's section of the tunnel, but he had not endeared himself to laborers, many of whom suspected he was involved in the murder of sandhog union leader R. Norman Redwood.

Metropolitan newspapers were filled with sensational accounts of the assassination of Redwood in the driveway of his Teaneck, N.J., home Feb. 19, 1937. Redwood was the 54-year-old business agent for Local 102 of the Compressed Air, Tunnel and Subway Workers, which had gone on strike against two of Rosoff's contracts—the Sixth Avenue subway and a sewer line under the East River. A day after Rosoff obtained an injunction against the union, Redwood was murdered, and the wealthy contractor, who had reportedly been overheard to say he would kill Redwood "stone dead," was arrested as a material witness.

Rosoff vehemently denied that he knew anything of the killing, and many suggested that inter-union rivalry had spawned the deed. Four days after Redwood's death, the steamship *Benjamin Odell*, one of the vessels on the Hudson River Nightline which Rosoff owned, burned at its winter berth at the contractor's sand and gravel company dock in Marlboro. The fire was thought to be arson, but, like the Redwood murder, was never solved.

After the scandal, Rosoff went on to amass the fortune that allowed his two sons to attend Yale University. This from a man who boasted he had not gone to school a day in his life. "I haven't got any education. What I got is what it takes to get guys with an education to do the job I want done," he once explained.

Sam Rosoff was in the midst of building a water tunnel for the City of Baltimore when he fell ill and died after surgery for an intestinal ailment Apr. 9, 1951 at Johns Hopkins Hospital, Baltimore.

Sources: *New York Times, Life Magazine* (Mar. 8, 1937); *Board of Water Supply Annual Report 1939; Catskill Mountain News*; Gerald Best's *The Ulster & Delaware Railroad Through the Catskills* (1972).

detailed regularly in the *Delaware Water Supply News*. The Mar. 1, 1939, edition, for example, carried stories about bowling matches between the Utah Construction Co. and BWS engineers from Shafts 11 and 12 "in the Northern Westchester wilderness." There were baseball games and ping pong tournaments, clambakes and dinner dances. A highlight of the year for the BWS in the watershed and in New York City was the annual picnic pilgrimage to the J. Waldo Smith monument, erected in 1936 at the Ashokan Reservoir to honor their first chief engineer.

Sam Sigman, who started his long career with the city as a junior engineer in 1938, came early to admire the fortitude of tunnel workers. His first assignment as a surveyor on the aqueduct line took him to Shaft 5A on the west bank of the Hudson River. The tunnel was being driven beneath the river, and, because of unstable geology, it was supported with steel lining. Mr. Sigman made his first ride down the 1,020-foot shaft alone in an elevator cage, to which was attached a section of that 15-foot-diameter steel lining. The cage was stopped near the bottom as workers maneuvered the circular section in place aboard a rail car to deliver it to its tunnel destination. Meanwhile, Sigman waited in the darkened, jerking cage. "What have I gotten myself into," he remembered wondering. "That was a long, tortuous introduction to the tunnel."[32]

The Delaware Aqueduct was completed in 1945 but would wait another nine years to carry the impounded waters of the Neversink River and the Rondout Creek. These were waters so pure the *Delaware Water Supply News* reported that vacationing Assistant BWS Engineers Louis Lockwood and Edward Craig "rendered a service to the nation" when they emptied a gallon of Neversink River water into Isa Pond in Yellowstone National Park. Located on the Continental Divide, the pond's outlets emptied toward the Pacific and the Gulf of Mexico, the Neversink waters helping to "purify" both.[33]

Drillers prepare holes in the rock for dynamiting an eight-foot "slot" for the
concrete cut-off wall of the Neversink Dam, Aug. 22, 1947. NYC DEP.

17. Waiting for "The Water"

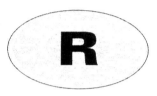

RESIDENTS of the Rondout Valley had lived with the specter of the city's coming for decades. As early as 1907, Board of Water Supply surveyors had combed the Rondout and Vernooy Creek watersheds, making topographic maps of 4,900 acres in anticipation of later reservoir development.[1] Those plans were solidified in 1927 and debated in public hearings and in court through the early 1930s, when the Supreme Court approved a modified city proposal.

But it wasn't until 1936 that the prospect of the valley's inundation became real to people, recalled Margaret Dolan. "Then the headlines came out in our local paper: 'Mammoth Water Project in Rondout Valley to Begin This Fall.' And then they began putting up eminent domain posters on the buildings they were taking over. And my dad came home and said, 'You know, after all these years of hearing this, they're really going to do it.' "

After that, said Mrs. Dolan, whose family had lived in the area for four generations, people began referring to the coming reservoir as "The Water," as in, "When The Water takes our house."[2]

Homes, farms and businesses were indeed taken almost immediately for the Rondout Reservoir, but "The Water" did not come for another 15 years, the project put on hold during much of World War II. In the late 1930s, however, it must have seemed imminent, as contractors set up shop to excavate a trench for the dam in the hamlet of Lackawack and to build a coffer dam and diversion tunnel to redirect the Rondout Creek during construction.

"Shock troops of the Perini Construction Company have taken the village of Lackawack by storm and this week are proceeding to wipe it from the face of the earth," declared the *Downsville News* on June 16, 1938. "Giant cranes, huge steam shovels, blasting gangs and fleets of thundering trucks are at work moving aside and flattening out the doomed hamlet, preparatory to actual work on the construction of the diversion tunnel. . . Hundreds of jobless are reported pouring into the area, most of them fruitlessly, but enough are striking jobs to keep the spark of hope alive in the breasts of those still straggling in."

A month earlier, Perini, a Framingham, Mass., firm, had won the $2.8 million contract to build the stream control works. These included a 1,500-foot-long, 55-foot-high earthen coffer dam, which directed the Rondout Creek away from the main dam site, 400 feet downstream. Water was sent into a 600-foot-long channel and thence into a concrete-lined diversion tunnel 2,400 feet long and 30 feet in diameter. The diversion tunnel later became part of the main dam's spillway channel.[3]

In June of 1937, the Triest Construction Co. of New York City won the job of excavating a cut-off trench and dropping two exploratory caissons for the main Lackawack Dam in the Town of

Above: The cut-off wall at the center line of the Merriman Dam as sheepsfoot rollers at the base of the wall work over the first layer of earth fill, Aug. 13, 1946. *Top left:* Workers building and stripping forms and laying concrete for the intake works at the start of the Neversink Tunnel appear tiny against the massive excavation. Gene Fuller. *Top right:* While fill was being graded and rolled on the Merriman Dam of the Rondout Reservoir, BWS Section Engineer Irving Guttridge, Foreman Jack Killeen of contractor S. A. Healy Co. and BWS Division Engineer Charles Hoerner posed for a photo on July 31, 1947. NYC DEP.

Wawarsing, Ulster County. The firm was to install pumping plants to lower the groundwater level in those caissons.[4]

The dam would have a concrete core wall which, because of heavy concentrations of ground water, was built as a series of connected caissons. These caissons (20 of them sunk at the Lackawack dam, 21 at the Neversink Dam a few miles away, started four years later) consisted of heavily reinforced concrete. They were 45 to 38 feet long and 10 to 12 feet wide, with four-foot-high structural steel cutting edges on the bottom. Several 14- to 15-foot sections of concrete, called "lifts," were poured, and tons of cast-iron weights added to push the caissons through 53 to 137 feet of overburden to sound rock. An enclosed working chamber occupied the area within the cutting shoes at the bottom of each caisson, where half a dozen men and machines dug out the dirt and rock as the caisson dropped and sent it to the surface in muck elevators.[5]

Compressed air was pumped into the working chambers to keep the groundwater out. Working in the caissons was dangerous, and caisson disease—"the bends," a constriction of the abdominal muscles which could cause strangulation—was always a possibility if workers were not properly reacclimated to the surface air pressure in special chambers before they emerged from the caisson. Men worked one three-hour shift per day, and wore badges that read "COMPRESSED AIR WORKER. If this man is stricken on the street, do not send him to the hospital, send him at once to the medical lock at Lackawack, Ulster County."[6]

Three men died in the caissons, including a civil engineer who drowned while conducting an inspection, and a 52-year-old Newburgh worker who fell 76 feet to the bottom of the caisson when a board on which he was walking atop the shaft broke.[7]

Aside from the experimental caissons, built in 1937 and '38, work on the Lackawack caissons was conducted around the clock from Jan. 2, 1940 to Jan. 23, 1941. The average total rate of descent of all the caissons was 1.76 feet per shift.[8]

The 2,400-foot earthen dam at Lackawack was renamed Merriman Dam in November 1939, two months after the death of former BWS Chief Engineer Thaddeus Merriman. Mr. Merriman had been with the BWS since its start in 1905 and succeeded J. Waldo Smith as chief engineer in 1922. Overseeing construction of the Schoharie Reservoir, the Shandaken Tunnel and City Tunnel #2, he had also fought vigorously for the city's right to develop the Delaware River basin. Mr. Merriman retired as chief engineer in 1933, but remained a BWS consultant whose cement and concrete specifications were used on the board's tunnels and underground structures for many years. (*The Delaware Water Supply News*, in a Dec. 1, 1944, article, reported on the launch of the *SS Thaddeus Merriman*, a 365-foot ship built of reinforced concrete. The vessel was commissioned for the U.S. Maritime Commission and named in recognition of Mr. Merriman's contributions to the science and manufacture of portland cement.)

Mr. Merriman had turned over the task of actual Delaware System development to his successor, Walter Spear. Spear supervised initial contracts amounting to $172 million, but was stricken at his desk Mar. 26, 1940, and died three days later. He was succeeded by his deputy chief engineer, Charles M. Clark, a man who had risen from a laborer with the Croton Aqueduct Commission in 1893 to supervise portions of the Catskill Aqueduct and later construction of City Tunnel #2. When Clark took over the Delaware work, he became one of a handful of engineers who had been involved in all three of the city's water systems. But he would not live to see the completion of the Delaware work; he died soon after his retirement in 1945. Two more chief engineers—Roger Armstrong (1945-48) and John Fitzgerald (1948-52)—would make their marks on the Delaware development before the Rondout Reservoir would go on line.[9]

The Merriman Dam was begun Aug. 28, 1939, by Mason and Hanger Co. of New York City. Their bid of $15.4 million included the reservoir's effluent valve chamber, a 3,100-foot inclined tunnel from that chamber to Shaft 1 of the Delaware Aqueduct the shaft itself, and nearly a mile of deep pressure tunnel at the northern end of the aqueduct. Mason and Hanger built the caisson cut-off wall for the dam, which would rise 220 feet above the original stream bed, its upstream face covered with heavy stone, the downstream face seeded, and a road running across its top.[10]

Progress on the dam and other parts of the contract was steady until the middle of 1941, when federal restrictions on procurement of equipment and materials for non-defense uses forced a significant slowdown both at the Rondout Reservoir and at the Neversink, where work had commenced in 1940. In April 1944, when an emergency connection diverted the waters of the Rondout directly into the completed Delaware Aqueduct (Chapter 16), both projects shut down almost entirely. In August 1944, the Mason & Hanger contract was terminated. The city paid the firm nearly $8 mil-

lion for work already done and acquired the contractor's physical plant for use after the war.[11]

It was not until 1946 that the twin projects were reactivated. In March of that year, S. A. Healy Co. of Chicago was low bidder to complete the Merriman Dam at Rondout Reservoir for $14.3 million.[12] And in July, the same company won the $4 million contract to excavate the cut-off trench and build 19 caissons to form the core wall of the Neversink Dam.[13] Two years later, it was awarded the $24 million job of building the rest of the dam and appurtenant structures.

Construction of the Merriman dam required 6.9 million cubic yards of earth embankment and one million cubic yards of rock fill. Working the night shift on board a big Euclid dump truck (commonly called a "Euc") was Horace Sheeley of Grahamsville. His father, Earl D. Sheeley, had run

Above: The "grizzly" (earth processing) plant at the Merriman Dam site allowed bottom-dumping trucks to empty loads of excavated material from the platform behind the control house at center. Below the control house are two revolving rock screens that emptied fill for the dam embankment into waiting trucks, and courser rocks into suspended hoppers. NYC DEP.

a trucking business for years, and Horace had always been enamored of big, powerful machinery. So when he got out of the service in 1948, Horace signed on with the Teamsters and got a job carting gravel and dirt on the Merriman Dam.

"I made $1.50 an hour. I worked a lot of overtime, so in a good week, I might take home $100," recalled Mr. Sheeley. "That was real good money around here." But one wet night he wondered briefly if it was worth it. The Euc ahead of him slipped down the greasy clay road going downhill toward the grizzly, the stone crushing and sorting plant. "He dumped his load, and I straddled that load, jackknifed, dumped my own load and got stuck. They called off work that night—too dangerous."[14]

By that time, work on the Neversink Reservoir was also going full bore. It had begun in 1940, with a contract awarded for the construction of 4.5 miles of substitute highways and a three-span bridge over the Neversink River. In 1941, George M. Brewster & Son of Bogota, N.J. got the contract to build a 1,400-foot coffer dam and a diversion tunnel to steer the Neversink River away from the main dam construction site, as well as two exploratory caissons for the new dam in the Town of Neversink, Sullivan County, just a few miles from the Rondout Reservoir. The contract also included removal of 259 buildings, a task largely completed by the end of 1942.[15] In November of that year, the *Liberty Register* reported on a surprise inspection of the project by New York Mayor Fiorello LaGuardia.

The location of the dam was changed in 1939 from a site near Curry to the hamlet of Neversink to increase the watershed area from 70 square miles to 93 square miles. [16] Construction of the dam was done in much the same way as at the Rondout. Fill on both coffer and main dams was laid by bottom-dumping Eucs (90 of them at the height of activity) that picked up graded materials at the grizzlies and dumped them on the dams' embankments. The fill was then leveled by 12 bulldozers and rolled to precise specifications by 15 tractor-drawn sheepsfoot rollers (so named because of the hoof-like tamping plates attached to the rollers).[17]

Ensuring that the rolled fill was compacted properly was Sam Sigman's job. An assistant engineer with the BWS, Mr. Sigman had worked at the Lackawack project before spending the war years helping to put in dry docks for the construction of landing craft at the Brooklyn Navy Yard. After the war, he returned to the BWS' Neversink project. Mr. Sigman and his wife made their home in an apartment over the Rubenzahl Brothers' chicken hatchery. The incubators kept the apartment nice and toasty, and the young engineer was pressed into service delivering eggs to his co-workers until the Sigmans and their two children moved to Liberty.

Mr. Sigman said he was sympathetic to the plight of displaced local residents, who didn't seem to show much resentment toward the BWS personnel doing the city's bidding. Mr. Sigman recalled one old man who steadfastly refused to yield his home until the bitter end, but still showed the engineer some hospitality by sharing some homemade applejack.[18] On Halloween night, 1940, related the *Downsville News*, about 65 BWS employees and guests enjoyed a harvest social, square-dancing to the music of Slaver's Orchestra at Max Begun's Neversink Inn. Begun donated the hall for the event. The inn later became a reservoir casualty.

Nor did Ben Musso feel any antagonism from local residents. The son of Division Engineer Frank Musso, Ben Musso was an 18-year-old college engineering student when his dad became the man in charge of the Neversink Dam and Tunnel. The younger Musso helped survey the line for the tunnel, the underground conduit that connected the Rondout and Neversink Reservoirs. He also measured material removed from the tunnel (the contractor was paid by the cubic yard) and inspected concrete used in the tunnel lining. "The Board of Water Supply was so fussy, we had our own inspectors in the cement plants on the Hudson River making our own specifications," Ben Musso related. Rather than take a BWS job in the city when the Neversink job was finished, he stayed on as section engineer in charge of maintaining the facili-

ties at the Rondout and Neversink Reservoirs. He retired after 25 years in that position.[19]

The hamlets of Lackawack, Montela and Eureka were claimed for the Rondout Reservoir; the community of Neversink, and smaller ones named Aden and Bittersweet, were taken for the Neversink project. In between was Grahamsville, population 300, which narrowly escaped inundation and so became a beehive of activity. "Grahamsville was like a boom town, between the two reservoirs and the tunnel projects," recalled Horace Sheeley, who remembers a busy 24-hour diner, several stores and a number of homes that boarded reservoir workers. The community, where Routes 44 and 55 intersect, was also the location of the Neversink Tunnel's outlet portal and the tunnel contractor's offices and shops, along with concrete mixing and batching plants.

"Most local people worked on the projects," said Ben Musso. "Every young guy, soon as he got out of school, went to work on the dams or in the tunnel." Brothers Milton, Sherman and Albert Kortright were among them. Milton made 65 cents an hour when he started for S. A. Healy, operating a "turnapple," a loader with a rubber-tipped blade to clean out beneath the grizzly at the Neversink project. Earlier, his two brothers were working together on the night shift as a section of the dam's core wall was being built in November 1947, stationed atop steel-reinforced forms into which concrete was being poured. The forms collapsed. Milton said Sherman managed to grab a concrete bucket and hang on until he was lowered to the ground. Albert, 22, who had just gotten out of the Navy after seeing service in World War II, died in the 50-foot fall. Also killed, buried beneath tons of concrete, were two co-workers, Werner Gilles, 30,

of Grahamsville, and Lee Bridges, 53, a Rosendale father of five.[20]

By 1946, the Delaware projects, including the aqueduct and both reservoirs, had resulted in 5,500 accidents, 74 of them involving fatalities.[21] Gene Fuller, a local man who also drove a Euc on the Neversink dam, said none of those deaths occurred in the Neversink Tunnel. "They figured they'd lose a man a mile (on the five-mile tunnel), but they didn't lose any," he said.

Placing granite on the east wall of the weir channel of the Neversink Dam, 1952. NYC DEP

There were injuries, though. One man, he recalled, was run through by a welding rod dropped by a worker above him. When he recuperated and returned to work, the same man was struck in the head by a falling rock. "But we didn't worry," said Mr. Fuller, who twice barely escaped electrocution, was nearly buried in two cave-ins and came close to being struck by a piece of falling ice at the portal to the Neversink Tunnel. "You can't be superstitious. You gotta say, if it's your time to go, there's no way of getting around it." Mr. Fuller was another who turned a post-war job into a lifetime occupation, becoming an electrician who maintained pumps, lights and compressors and wired the intake chamber at the Neversink Tunnel, then stayed on with the Board of Water Supply, Gas & Electricity for 30 years to maintain the facilities.[22]

Labor troubles punctuated the work at both ends of the decade. In early 1940, a dispute between the Newburgh Iron and Steel Workers Local 417

Facing page, top left: Falling ice was an occupational hazard at the Neversink Tunnel portal, shown here in December of 1947. Walter Deyo. *Top right:* Drillers worked atop "Jumbos" like this rig in the Neversink Tunnel, 1950. Walter Deyo. *Bottom:* Aerial view of the Neversink Dam in 1952, showing the future reservoir in the vacated basin in top of photo, with the outlet channel of the diversion tunnel at lower right. NYC DEP.

Courts and compacts

The U.S. Supreme Court's 1931 limitation of New York City's Delaware River water withdrawal to 440 million gallons per day did not end the squabbling between New York, New Jersey and Pennsylvania over rights to the Delaware supply, nor did it stop the city from continuing to search for more dam sites in the basin.

In 1936, the states, joined by Delaware, came together to form the Interstate Commission on the Delaware River Basin (Incodel). As the city proceeded to develop the Rondout and Neversink Reservoirs, the new commission, rejecting the federally-sponsored Tennessee Valley Authority model, worked toward a states-run organization based on interstate cooperation.

Incodel first provided a forum for discussion on the clean-up of the lower Delaware River, which had become a floating sewer, the recipient of an estimated 500 million gallons of sewage a day and untold quantities of industrial pollutants. Millions of tons of coal dust from Pennsylvania mines also found their way into the river, used, along with the Schuylkill River, by the City of Philadelphia as a drinking water supply. Incodel backed state officials in getting that city and Camden, N.J., to initiate wastewater treatment.

In 1947, as the Board of Water Supply endeavored to complete the Rondout and Neversink and launched work on the Pepacton Reservoir, it was prompted by burgeoning water consumption to find a temporary emergency supply. It also petitioned the Supreme Court to allow development of the third phase of the Delaware supply and began searching for new permanent sources. It sent its engineers into the field to gather soil samples and test borings in the Beaverkill and Little Delaware Valleys, along with the East Branch between Hancock and Fish's Eddy, and the West Branch between Cannonsville and Deposit. In late 1949, the BWS' New Sources Division recommended diverting the West Branch at Cannonsville as the third stage of the system, and it recommended pumping 100 million gallons of water a day from the Hudson River at Shaft 6 of

the Delaware Aqueduct at Chelsea should the need arise. That plant was constructed in 1950 but was not used until 1965 after being removed and reconstructed. (Chapter 18).

At the same time, Incodel, authorized by its respective state legislatures, had employed the engineering firms of Malcolm Pirnie of New York and Albright and Friedl of Philadelphia to develop a master plan for the multi-state use of the 330-mile Delaware River. Their report, issued in 1950, incorporated the Cannonsville project, along with a pair of reservoirs 75 miles to the southeast, on the Delaware River at Barryville, straddling the New York-Pennsylvania line, and on the Neversink River between Godeffroy and Summitville. A huge tunnel would carry the mingled waters from Godeffroy to reservoirs in Brooklyn and New Jersey. Further development, the study suggested, could include dams at Wallpack Bend between New Jersey and Pennsylvania; on Flat Brook in New Jersey; and at Fish's Eddy in Delaware County, N.Y. A proposed compact to create the Delaware River Basin Water Commission to finance, build and administer the projects was brought before all four state legislatures but fell through in 1953 because Pennsylvania declined to join in the agreement.

Meanwhile, the city, though declaring its support for Incodel's plans, said it could not wait for the states to move, and in 1950 sought, and received, approval from the city's Board of Estimate and Apportionment and the State Water Power and Control Commission to proceed with the Cannonsville project, subject to modification of the 1931 Supreme Court decision.

It was not until April 1952 that the city filed the petition with the Supreme Court, which appointed Special Master Kurt F. Pantzer to take testimony and explore the matter. Pantzer recommended that the city be allowed to withdraw up to 800 million gallons a day from the Delaware and its tributaries once the Cannonsville project was completed. The court, in an amended decree issued June 7, 1954, adopted the recommendation of the Special Master, and required the city to release water from its impoundments in order to maintain the flow of the main river at 1,750 cubic feet per second at Montague, N.J., The decree also provided for the appointment of a River Master to administer the agreement.

It was also in 1954 that the Neversink and Pepacton Reservoirs were completed (the Rondout was finished the previous year). Ground was broken for the Cannonsville Reservoir in 1955.

Efforts to establish a cooperative commission to control and develop Delaware water resources resurfaced in July 1955, when the Delaware River Basin Advisory Committee was formed. In 1961 the committee proposed establishment of a five-member Delaware River Basin Commission (DRBC), which would include the governors of the four states and the federal government as a full participant.

Following ratification of the Delaware River Basin Commission compact by the state legislatures, President John F. Kennedy signed the measure into law Sept. 27, 1961. It was the first time in the nation's history the federal government and a group of states had joined as equal operating partners in a river basin planning, development and regulatory agency.

The expectation was that the commission would follow a plan developed over the preceding three years by the Army Corps of Engineers in response to clamors for flood control measures in the wake of deadly Hurricane Diane in August 1955. The 50-year, $591-million plan, designed to increase water supply and recreational usage, limit flood damage and provide hydroelectric power, included the proposed construction of 58 storage facilities in a populous region extending from the Catskills to Delaware Bay.

Included in the hefty 11-volume document was a proposal to build several major reservoirs along the Delaware and its main tributaries, the largest of which would be at Tocks Island, seven miles north of the Delaware Water Gap in Pennsylvania. The 3,200-foot-long, 160-foot high dam would impound a reservoir extending 37 miles up the Delaware to Port Jervis, and would create a national park proponents estimated would draw 10 million visitors a year. The project was authorized by Congress in 1962 but criticisms about cost and environmental impacts caused Congress to rescind its authorization in 1975.

The parties to the 1954 decree spent the next few years re-thinking their water supply policies and goals. A 1982 "Good Faith Agreement," proposed 14 recommendations, only one of which involved construction of a new reservoir. That was Merrill Creek Reservoir in Warren County, N.J., a 650-acre impoundment completed in 1987 by a consortium of seven electric utilities to restore to the Delaware River during low-flow periods water depleted by electric generating plants.

The remaining recommendations, which were formally adopted by the DRBC, involved adding water supply to existing storage reservoirs (including a proposal, never carried out, to enlarge New York City's Cannonsville Dam capacity by 13 billion gallons); developing drought management initiatives (the basin has experienced eight droughts since the early 1980s) and decreasing consumption through regulations, metering and education. In 1987, the DRBC required some 304 water purveyors in the four states to install service meters within 10 years. New York City, the largest user of Delaware Basin water, anticipated spending $290 million to implement universal metering, and had virtually completed the task by the end of 1998 (Chapter 19).

The DRBC's thrust toward conservation has included requirements for source metering or measuring as well as leak detection by water suppliers. It also set performance standards for toilets, faucets and showerheads, reinforced by federal guidelines that went into effect in 1992. The aim is to reduce unaccounted-for water by 15 percent by the year 2020, thus minimizing the need for further reservoir development.

Sources: BWS Annual Reports for 1950, 1952, 1954; U.S. Supreme Court decisions May 4, 1931 and June 7, 1954; *Catskill Mountain News*, *Liberty Register*, *The New York Times* (Feb. 2, 1961); *Saturday Evening Post* reprint ("Look What They're Doing to the Delaware!," 1950); Delaware River Basin Commission Annual Reports 1985, 1987, 1996; Journal AWWA "Conservation in the Delaware River Basin"), January, 1996.

and Newburgh Local 17 of the Laborers and Hod Carriers Union briefly came to blows as the two groups battled for jurisdiction over who should do the iron handling. Neversink Tunnel workers went on a five-week strike in the fall of 1949, demanding a ten-cent-per-hour pay raise. That year, an average of 665 men were employed by the contractor at the Neversink Dam.[23]

The year 1948 saw contracts awarded for the bulk of the Neversink Dam (S. A. Healy, $24.8 million) and for the Neversink Tunnel and associated control works to the Delaware Aqueduct (Frazier-Davis Construction Co. of St. Louis, $15.6 million). The tunnel would carry water from the Neversink Reservoir to the Rondout and from there into the aqueduct to the city. It was a 5.2-mile concrete-lined, circular conduit, with a finished diameter of 10 feet. A construction shaft 355 feet deep was sunk at Wynkoop Creek about two miles from the intake chamber at the Neversink Reservoir, and workers tunneled in both directions from this shaft toward the Neversink and Rondout Reservoirs. Working on specially designed and constructed "jumbos" (drill platforms mounted on mine cars), crews drilled, loaded, blasted and mucked out six rounds every 24 hours in each heading for an average daily progress of 50 feet per heading. A superstructure faced with granite was built over the intake chamber, where water sent down the tunnel to the Rondout Reservoir is metered and chlorinated.[24]

A portion of the outlet chamber of the tunnel is utilized to generate electricity. A 1948 agreement between Central Hudson Gas & Electric Corp. and the city allowed use of the tunnel outfall as compensation for the loss of water at the utility's electric generating plants at High Falls and Honk Falls downstream on the Rondout. Central Hudson's Neversink Hydroelectric Plant makes use of the energy difference in water dropping 600 feet in elevation between the Neversink and Rondout Reservoirs. The company received free use of 3.2 billion cubic feet of water a year for 50 years, with the city getting free electricity to operate its control works.[25]

The mutually-beneficial agreement contrasted with a 1931 dispute between the company and the city, which had proposed pumping into the Catskill Aqueduct as much as two million gallons of water a day from the Rondout Creek above the High Falls hydroelectric plant. Central Hudson, and many municipalities, businesses and individuals objected to the plan, according to the *Kingston Freeman* of Nov. 20, 1931. The idea was later dropped.

A major facet of both reservoir projects was the clearing of land and the removal of graves, some of which had lain undisturbed for more than a century. Disinterments from seven cemeteries and burial grounds in the Rondout basin were conducted in 1939 and 1940. Relatives were allotted $40 to hire undertakers to move the bodies and smaller amounts to have headstones or fences moved. A total of 205 people applied for re-burial fees for 1,117 bodies. Another 512 bodies were unclaimed and relocated to a city-owned section of Fairview Cemetery in Stone Ridge, Town of Marbletown, by undertakers who contracted for the job.[26]

The Rondout Reservoir necessitated condemnation of 3,513 acres of land in the basin and marginal areas.[27] Area newspapers reported the first takings in 1936, when about 400 acres were claimed from 55 property owners in the hamlet of Lackawack, Town of Wawarsing, near the site of the Rondout dam. The Neversink project required condemnation of 6,149 acres of land.[28]

Area residents claimed the city took more than was needed by condemning a strip of land 150 to 600 feet deep on the far side of the new highway that was constructed around the Rondout Reservoir. At a mass meeting in Eureka in April 1939, 100 people signed a petition to city Mayor Fiorello LaGuardia protesting the large buffer, claiming that it would require property owners just outside the city land boundaries to build long driveways or access roads from their land to the highway and would restrict the development of roadside businesses. The Towns of Neversink and Wawarsing and Sullivan County legislators took the issue to the Supreme Court, but the city's highway plans were ultimately approved.[29]

Much of the condemned land was productive valley farmland or river frontage prized for its fabulous trout fishing. "The Neversink was a fisherman's paradise," recalled Eureka native Herman Christian in an interview published in the June 1950 *Angler's Club Bulletin*. "In 1900 it was nothing to see 50 trout jumping in a hole. . .you could look them over and take your pick." Christian owned a 176-acre farm bordering the "Big Bend" section of the Neversink River and was a close friend and protégé of famed fly-tier Theodore Gordon, who spent long periods of the year at local hotels and boardinghouses, angling for trout and capturing native insects from which he would pattern realistic flies. Gordon, who was often seen strutting down the road using his bamboo fly rod case as a walking stick, spent the last days of his life just across the river from the village of Neversink, where he died of tuberculosis May 1, 1915, at the home of Anson Knight, a home later taken for the reservoir.

Hundreds of acres owned by wealthy industrialist Edward Ringwood Hewitt were also claimed by the city which his father, Abram Hewitt, had once served as mayor. An avid inventor, Edward Hewitt had developed a one-cylinder automobile

Wetting a line at Leroy's Falls in the Neversink River was inventor and avid flyfisherman Edward R. Hewitt, who lost his favorite trout pools, and much of his extensive land holdings, to the Neversink Reservoir. About 1,500 people in six communities were forced to move from the Rondout and Neversink basins. *Telling on the Trout*, 1926.

and designed a truck engine, establishing the Hewitt Motor Company which was later bought by International Motor Corp., makers of Mack Trucks. A grandson of a founder of Cooper Union, Hewitt was a student of chemistry, maintaining a large laboratory in his home. He was also an ardent angler, fish culturist, photographer and author who wrote six books on fishing. Along with homes in New York City and New Jersey, he owned a Neversink farm, where he raised Brown Swiss cattle and developed a high-protein hay. Hewitt also built a fish hatchery in the Neversink valley. He saw most of his holdings condemned for the Neversink Reservoir. He died in 1957 at the age of 90.[30]

New York City Alderman Thomas Shiels owned a large horse farm and race track called Grand View Farm in Montela, where high spirited trotters and pacers raced before grandstand crowds. His nephew, James Shiels, was proprietor of the elegant Lackawack House, dubbed the Summer Tammany Hall because it hosted the likes of Alfred E. Smith, John Delaney, Congressman William Cleary and other politicians. The area was a popular vacation spot, travelers coming to Liberty, Ellenville or Hurleyville via the Ontario & Western Railroad to stay at places like Vanderlyn's Pines in Neversink or the Maple View Farm in Montela.[31]

Also in Montela, the County Line Farm straddled the Ulster and Sullivan border. Belle Bart owned the place in the 1920s, offering a hotel, casino, boat rentals and dances. Residents and visitors also gathered on the pond there for winter ice skating parties and summer picnics. When the Town of Neversink banned liquor sales, the bar in the hotel was moved down the hall into the Town of Wawarsing, the only establishment in the eight-mile valley where alcohol could be purchased. It was owned in the 1930s by Frank Patruno, who used its unique location to take advantage of the influx of construction workers employed on the two reservoirs.[32]

Most of the 1,500 or so people evicted from the Rondout and Neversink Valleys (1,200 from the former, 340 from the latter), were ordinary folks who'd spent their lives in the area where many of their ancestors had cleared the land to start farms and businesses that were handed down for generations. Bittersweet blacksmith and carpenter Eugene Osterhoudt was a fiddler and square dance caller;[33] Bruce Fuller, a carpenter, electrician and school bus driver, had run the family's grist mill at the confluence of the Rondout and Chestnut Creeks in Eureka until a devastating flood destroyed it and many other valley homes and farms in 1928.[34] Dr. Urban Kemble and his wife, Myrtle, tended to the valley's sick from their home near Montela until the reservoir forced them out. The East End Garage in Neversink was owned by Roy Clark; Charles Freer was a contractor, his wife a paint and wallpaper dealer; John Richards had the general store in Montela; William Evans and his wife kept the Rondout Valley Garage and adjoining store near Lackawack for 32 years until the city claimed the property. The Evanses stayed on, tending to the needs of dam laborers and paying rent to the city, for a year before moving to Woodbourne.[35]

Margaret Dolan was among those whose links to the valley stretched back 150 years. Her great-great-grandfather, Erastus Smith, came to Lackawack from Connecticut in 1827. His son, Samuel, started S. N. Smith & Son General Store in Eureka in 1885. The store, where neighbors could buy union suits and corsets, gum drops and Carter's Little Liver Pills, kerosene, cigars and coffee beans from burlap sacks, was operated by Samuel's grandson George when the city claimed the property. George, who was also Eureka's postmaster, presided over the Cracker Barrel Club, a fraternity of local residents who gravitated to the old box stove in the corner to gossip and play dominoes and eat lunch. The last such meeting of "the club" occurred Feb. 8, 1942, when miller Bruce Fuller, mechanic Grover Hornbeck, chicken farmer George Dierfelter and several others reminisced and said goodbye.[36]

Some of the homes taken by the city were purchased back from the grubbing contractor and were physically moved, a few to "New Nev-

The BWS Watershed Department's annual clambake, complete with marching band, was held near Montela Sept. 6, 1947. NYC DEP.

ersink," the hamlet that sprang up on Route 55 between the Neversink Reservoir and Gra-hamsville. Some of the houses were moved by Eugene Osterhoudt, who himself moved to Fallsburgh when the family's eight-room house, barn and seven acres on the Neversink River were condemned.[37] The old Aden schoolhouse was purchased from contractor S. A. Healy by Otto Lowitz, who moved it to Parksville for use as a storage building. Archie Dean took down several buildings, from barns to bungalows, and used the lumber to build structures on his farm outside Grahamsville and a post office in "New Neversink." The community hall there was built from trees cut from the reservoir basin.[38]

Abandoned buildings, including churches and other public structures, were left to the bulldozers and, along with piles of trees, brush and stumps, were set ablaze in a "final harvest" remembered by Evelyn Hill Huntsberger, who was born in Eureka in 1916. The smoke, she said, hung heavy, "like the haze of Indian summer," and the contours of the now barren valley were "naked and unfamiliar."[39]

Cellars were filled in, privies disinfected, septic tanks and barnyard manure dug up and hauled away. Even the concrete ponds of Edward Hewitt's fish hatchery were broken up and carted off.[40] In an effort to keep its water pure, the city constructed a sewage treatment plant in Grahamsville. Di-Marco & Ciccone were the contractors on the $743,000 job, which began in 1948 and was completed two years later.[41]

And then, at last, The Water came.

Impounding of water in the Rondout Reservoir began May 10, 1951. It was completely filled for the first time Mar. 28, 1955. Storage in the Neversink Reservoir began June 4, 1953. It took just under two years to fill the basin to overflowing.[42]

In 1955, 133 billion gallons of water were sent down the Delaware Aqueduct to New York City. Mingled with the Rondout and Neversink supply was even more water from yet a third source, the huge Pepacton Reservoir. Named by the BWS in 1947 after an Indian word purported to mean "marriage of the waters,"[43] the Pepacton had brought the same scenario of heavy industry and heartache to the East Branch Valley 25 miles to the north.

The Delaware River Basin Compact was signed into law by President John F. Kennedy on Sept. 27, 1961. The President was joined by governors of the basin states and other officials, including New York City Board of Water Supply President Arthur Ford (standing, right), for a formal signing ceremony on Nov. 2. It was the first time in the nation's history the federal government and a group of states joined as equal operating partners in a river basin planning, development and regulatory agency. The Delaware River Basin Commission still manages river activities from its West Trenton, N.J., headquarters. Delaware River Basin Commission.

x

Workers gathered for a group portrait on concrete forms in what is believed to be the diversion tunnel at the Pepacton. Walt Dette photo, Delaware County Historical Association.

18. Pepacton

T HE FIRST PHASE of the Delaware System had barely begun when, in 1937, the State Water & Power Control Commission urged accelerated development of Phase 2, the Pepacton Reservoir, to be created by building a dam at Downsville.

Citing rising pressure being placed on wells supplying Nassau and Suffolk Counties on Long Island, the commission noted, however, that there remained significant groundwater far out on the island. Some had suggested that the city extend its piping system to tap into it. But, conceded the commission in a report issued in March 1937, "It is thoroughly well understood in Suffolk County that the people there will prevent the city from pumping water. They say, with convincing emphasis, 'Why come to Suffolk, which, like Nassau, is rapidly increasing in population, and by over-pumping, spoil our natural supply, when all you have to do is shorten your construction program for the Delaware supply by building without delay the second stage, or Downsville dam?' "[1]

The Board of Water Supply would have liked nothing better than to get started on its largest project to date, for the 147-billion-gallon Pepacton was seen as the solution to its recurring water woes, equal to the combined volumes of the Schoharie and the Ashokan, and 40 percent bigger than the combined storage of 12 Croton System reservoirs.

They had already placed surveyors in the field to plot the course of the 25-mile East Delaware Tunnel, which would carry Pepacton Reservoir water to the Rondout Reservoir. They had pinpointed the location of that tunnel's intake chamber (three miles upstream from the Downsville Dam), and the outlet portal (on the west shore of the Rondout, one mile below Grahamsville.) And they had determined which properties they would need for shaft construction and tunnel easements (a total of 207 acres).[2]

But, despite optimistic forecasts that work would get under way by 1940, and then 1941, and then 1942, construction on the tunnel and the reservoir ultimately took a back seat to World War II. Engineers were called to map-making duty at the former Union Free School in Downsville, purchased in 1943 as BWS headquarters for the project. It was not until late 1947, however, that the growl of bulldozers and the rumble of dynamite were heard in the East Branch Valley.[3]

That's when Walsh Construction Co. and B. Perini & Sons teamed up to submit a successful $13.7 million bid for the construction of a coffer dam and diversion tunnel to redirect the flow of the East Branch of the Delaware River so that the Downsville Dam could be built. These preliminary undertakings took two years, from November 1947 through November 1949, when the same contractors won the job of building the East Delaware Tunnel to the Rondout.[4]

Euclid dump trucks placing fill on the Downsville
Dam, October 1952. Glen Watson.

Sheepsfoot roller compacting newly placed fill.
Glen Watson.

Walsh-Perini's contract called for removal of
199 buildings in the way of the work. These included 31 dwellings and many barns, milk houses
and other farm structures. Some of the homes were
used to house contractors' forces. At first, some 75
laborers arrived to cut brush and run power shovels
to scrape the earth from portal sites. Workers
arrived in greater numbers at the start of 1948.
Downsville's Eagle Hotel was filled to capacity,
and a dude ranch owned by Dr. Charles Markert
and brother-in-law Tom Gunn accommodated another 80 people three miles outside of Downsville.[5]

Wages paid at the start of the unionized project
ranged from $1 an hour for blacksmiths' helpers
and unskilled laborers, to $1.27 for truck drivers,
$1.87 for iron workers, $2.15 for locomotive operators and $2.25 for miners and blasters.[6] These
wage rates attracted scores of job-seeking men fresh
out of the service. "The Main Street of Downsville
is lined every day with autos. The AFL labor union
is enrolling skilled and unskilled laborers day by
day. There are hundreds of inquiries for living
accommodations, most of them unsatisfied," reported the *Downsville Herald*. Residents created
apartments over garages and rented spare bedrooms as the demand pushed up prices in surrounding communities.[7]

The *Walton Reporter* examined a new phenomenon—mobile home living—in a June 25,
1948, article about the new trailer camp established
by Marvin Wynkoop in Downsville. Forty-one
people, including a dozen children, occupied the
park. The wife of mechanic Warren Clark explained they'd opted to buy a trailer in South
Carolina for $3,000 rather than pay rent for a rustic
cabin. "It's the only thing for the family of a
construction worker," she said.

There were so many new families in town that
by June 1948, its enrollment expanding toward
450, the Downsville school district voted to build
an addition on the school, which was originally
designed to handle just 260 children.[8] A second
addition was constructed in 1952, and Downsville's
enrollment eventually reached 600. Margaretville
Central School, at the other end of the valley, also
swelled to just over 600, according to the *Catskill
Mountain News*, Sept. 30, 1955.

Many of the workers were miners, drillers and
career construction men from as far away as Arkan-
sas, Alabama, Oklahoma and Kentucky. One of
those was Earl Barker, who spent 30 years moving
from job to job—Montana, South America, Ha-
waii, Canada and, for four years, Downsville. He
and his family lived in a house in Cat Hollow. He
recalls, "We made friends with local people, but we
mostly took care of our own, and stuck together
on jobs. We had picnics on weekends and parties
on holidays like regular folks, we just never owned
a fancy house or a permanent address."[9]

In the summer of 1948, work on the diversion
tunnel, coffer dam and cut-off wall went forward
around the clock. Estimated materials usage was

impressive: 260,000 barrels of portland cement; two million pounds of steel pilings; 1.9 million pounds of structural steel; 80,000 pounds of steel pipes; 50,000 pounds of cast iron piping; 50,000 feet of timbering; 600,000 cubic yards of earth and rock to be excavated for the cut-off wall.[10]

While the BWS issued condemnation notices to the first two sections of the valley, covering 197 people occupying farms, homes and businesses from Downsville to Pepacton, Walsh-Perini set up offices, a first-aid clinic, cafeteria, machine shop, garage, warehouse, blacksmith shop, powder magazine and other facilities. A sand-and-gravel mine was opened, and a concrete batching plant established.[11]

"Day and night," reported the *Oneonta Daily Star* in the summer of 1948, "the East Branch valley echoes with the roar of diesel powered trucks, earth movers and bulldozers, the chatter of pneumatic drills, the clang of power shovel buckets on rock and the occasional heavy booming of a ton and a half of dynamite going off at once." The article described the "small village" that had sprung up to serve this heavy industry, including a 48-bed bunkhouse, and a cafeteria, open 24 hours a day, that could seat 230 men. "Operated by a concern that specializes in feeding construction personnel, the cafeteria serves excellent food. For $1 a man can get all he can carry out on his back," the *Daily Star* reported.

The diversion works included a temporary dam, 1,800 feet long and 70 feet high, erected across the river bed just below the inlet to a 2,155-foot-long, 40-foot-diameter tunnel. The circular, concrete-lined diversion tunnel was driven in rock along the side of the valley. Inlet and outlet channels at the tunnel portals connected to the existing channel of the river. The entire length of the diversion tunnel was driven from the inlet end, and work was started in late November 1947. A 1,600-foot detour for State Route 30 had to be constructed and five buildings removed before an area could be excavated to launch tunnel driving operations. It was slow going at first, the work hampered by sub-zero weather on 23 separate days and a flood in late March.[12]

Actual tunnel driving commenced May 24, 1948, using the top-heading-and-bench method. This system involved blasting and mucking the top half of the circular tunnel horizontally from its face for the entire length, then dynamiting the bottom half from vertical holes drilled atop the newly-levelled "bench." A specially constructed jumbo accommodated 15 to 18 pneumatic drills. They created 162 blasting holes per round for the heading, which was excavated in 134 advances over 26 weeks. The excavation of the bench took another 72 days, a process delayed when a flood in late December 1948 required the pumping of 10 million gallons of water from the tunnel. *The Delaware Water System News* reported that it took 418,000 pounds of dynamite to remove 140,700 cubic yards of rock and earth for the diversion tunnel.

In November 1948, New York City Council President Vincent Impellitieri ceremoniously threw a switch, setting off a blast that cleared the last rock from the diversion tunnel. City and county officials, contractors and workers stood on a bunting-bedecked dais for the hole-through ceremony, and hundreds of workers took up positions on promontories around the tunnel outlet, ducking as stones flew and smoke and dust blew out the portal. In remarks that presaged the coming drought, BWS President Irving Huie noted that in one hot day that summer, the city had consumed 1.5 billion gallons of water. The need for the Pepacton, and the Rondout and Neversink still under construction to the south, was urgent.[13]

Excavation of the diversion tunnel was completed in January 1949, and concreting was finished by August. In September, when the coffer dam was finished, the river was re-routed and allowed to flow through the tunnel around the site of what would be the permanent dam. State conservation workers retrieved fish from isolated pools in the old river channel and transferred them to the river below the dam.

The inclined tunnel, designed to connect the diversion tunnel with the permanent spillway, was also finished that year. The BWS in its 1949 annual report described the deep excavation as "a mecca for sightseers." Warning signs and barricades

Carrier used to transport explosives into
the East Delaware Tunnel.
Walt Dette photo, Delaware County Historical Association.

couldn't keep people from "going right down to
the edge for a close-up of this deep excavation from
the top of a perilous slope."

In August, Walsh-Perini got to work on the
East Delaware Tunnel. It was driven by workers
blasting toward each other from inlet and outlet
portals, and from the base of two vertical construction shafts. Shaft 1, 605 feet deep, was located in the
Beaverkill Valley at Lew Beach. Shaft 2, 965 feet
deep, was drilled in the Willowemoc Valley. The
distance between the inlet (a half-mile from the
hamlet of Pepacton) and Shaft 1 was 7.3 miles; from
Shaft 1 to Shaft 2 was 9.1 miles; and from Shaft 2
to the outlet (.3 miles southwest of Lowe's Corners) was 8.6 miles. The tunnel's total length was
25 miles.[14]

Shafts were 14 feet in diameter. They were
blasted to the proper elevation and lined with
concrete mixed at the top of the shafts and lowered
in bottom dump buckets. Electric transformer stations were also located at the shafts to provide
power for hoists, air compressors and batteries that
operated locomotives far below. The trains carried
men and equipment from the base of the shaft
through the tunnel to the heading, and hauled rock
and debris back out after each blast.

Headings were drilled from a "jumbo," which
carried six drills mounted on hydraulic booms,

three on the upper deck, three on the lower. "Drill
doctor" benches were located near each heading to
repair drills and sharpen bits. About 20 minutes
after each blast, when the smoke had cleared, men
"scaled" the roof to remove loose or hanging rock,
and a mucking machine was pushed into place by
a locomotive. The machine loaded side-dump cars
with muck, and the cars were pushed back to the
shaft to dump their loads into a hopper that was
hoisted to the surface for removal by truck to spoils
dumps.[15]

Nearly all of the 131,862 feet of tunnel required
roof support. Rather than steel rib and lagging that
had been used in other tunnel projects, roof bolts
were utilized in the East Delaware tunnel. Five-
foot-long steel bolts an inch in diameter were inserted in drill holes in the roof. A six-inch steel
wedge was inserted in the slotted end of the bolt,
and was driven in by a stope drill (similar to an
upside-down jack hammer), expanding the slotted
section of the bolt to anchor it to the rock. The
layers of rock through which the bolt passed were
drawn firmly together by screwing a nut on the
outer end of the bolt. Steel ties, nine feet long and
five inches wide, were secured to the nuts, which
were tightened by compressed-air-operated
wrenches.[16]

Falling rock accounted for many injuries and
at least two fatalities. Richard Morris of Andes and

Spraying gunite on the walls of the East Delaware
Tunnel prior to concreting, December, 1956.
Walt Dette photo, Delaware County Historical Association.

Mucking out the East Delaware Tunnel. Walt Dette photo, Delaware County Historical Association.

Leonard Dauch of Roscoe died in June 1950 when they were crushed by a six-ton rock that fell from the roof as they mucked out the tunnel. It took 12 workers to jack up the rock to free the bodies. Both men were 25 and veterans of World War II. They left their wives and five children.[17]

Each shift would generally drill, load and shoot two rounds, trying for an advance of nine feet per round, remembers Dan Underwood of Roxbury, a chuck tender and miner's helper on the East Delaware Tunnel. Miners would drill a pattern of holes which had been outlined on the rock face in paint by the engineers. Each man was responsible for loading his own hole with explosives, but electricians would then wire the explosives together.

Workers retreated about a quarter mile back down the tunnel while the shift foreman set off the blast with current from a flashlight.[18]

After each blast, the debris would be mucked out, roof bolts and steel implanted, and track and air lines extended. Engineers would determine center line and grade, and mark up the heading. Then the jumbo would be brought forward and drillers would begin again. This went on 24 hours a day.

"Sometimes you'd find a missed hole. If it was your hole, you'd have to wash the powder out. Other guys would stand back, just in case." recalled Underwood. "It was go, go, go. You couldn't hear a thing when the drills were going, you had to use hand signals." The most dangerous part of the job, he said, was the train ride to and from the heading. "It would jump and rattle, we'd duck and hang on. It was always jumping the track. We had guys jump right off the train and start running back toward the portal. A lot of guys couldn't take it. But if you wanted a job, you put up with the conditions."

It was cold, wet, confining and sometimes very dark. "Ain't nothing blacker than a tunnel when the lights go out," said Glenn Watson, who was just 17 years old when he went to work on an East Delaware jumbo for $1.10 an hour. "The Downsville area turned out great drillers," Watson said. "A lot of them were quarry men." Others received on-the-job training, and the admonition that if you hung up a drill (got the bit stuck in the rock) it would cost you a case of beer.[19]

Norman Brazee, a motorman on a locomotive, recalled the day an 11-foot drill got hung up. The crew called for a new one, and he proceeded to deliver it to the heading on the front of the locomotive. As the train bounced along, the drill rolled off the front and stuck in the ground, the back end hitting Brazee in the face, fracturing his cheek bone.[20]

Three tunnel workers injured in 1951, when a blast went off prematurely, sued the powder company, claiming the primers were defective. One man suffered a fractured skull; another lost an eye and two fingers.[21]

In 1953, 34 injuries were recorded in the tunnel. Miraculously, no one was hurt when the hoisting drum of a stiff-leg derrick broke while lifting a 22-ton Caterpillar bulldozer at the Pepacton Intake Chamber. The dozer dropped 80 feet, but the only damage was to the hoisting engine. On December 3 of that year, while lifting a locomotive from the tunnel, the hoist cable at Shaft 1 broke. Fortunately, the cage and locomotive were just a short distance above the bottom landing, and no one was hurt. Men in the tunnel had to get out by way of Shaft 2.[22]

BWS and company officials rode the tunnel rails in March 1953, when the final "hole through" was blasted. A public address system blared "Walking My Baby Back Home" and "God Bless America" before BWS Chief Engineer Karl Kennison

and others descended into the "glory hole" for the explosion, followed by a celebratory luncheon at Antrim Lodge in Roscoe. Work was accomplished under BWS section engineer Frank Duggan at Lew Beach and Albert Krauss at Pepacton. Red Granger supervised the work for the contractor at Shaft 2, Richard Dillon at Shaft 1.[23]

Concreting of the tunnel was finished by November of 1954. Walsh-Perini had built a 400-ton cement elevator in New York Central Railroad yards at Arkville. At 70 feet tall, the storage unit was dubbed "Arkville's first skyscraper." The company expected to use up to eight 80-ton carloads of cement daily on the tunnel, trucking the material from Arkville to mixing plants at the shafts.[24]

The tunnel's outlet works at the Rondout Reservoir were built by Booth & Flinn Co. between May 1952 and February 1955. The job included provisions for an electric generating plant similar to the Central Hudson facility installed at the outlet of the Neversink Tunnel.[25] Orange & Rockland Utilities, Inc. was allowed to use 8.1 million cubic feet of water for free, and would pay for the rest. By 1960, the plant was generating 120,000 megawatt hours per year in electricity, and $417,000 in revenue to the city, according to the BWS annual report for that year.

Carol, Bianchi & Co., Central Construction Co., Munroe-Langstroth, Inc. and G. L. Rugo and Sons combined to submit the lowest of nine bids for construction of the Downsville Dam and related works. The $17.9 million bid was awarded Feb. 3, 1950, and work began Feb. 16. It was to be completed in 54 months, by Aug. 9, 1954.[26]

The contractors took over most buildings and utilities that had been utilized by Walsh-Perini, which had built the dam's cut-off wall, a 2,300-foot concrete barrier across the valley. The wall, extending 110 feet below the surface to bedrock and many more above ground level, formed the heart of the earthen dam.

Bianchi and company added other facilities, including two large "grizzly" plants for grading, separating and processing fill for the dam. These plants, on opposite sides of the valley, produced

Above: Spillway of the Downsville Dam under construction. Author's collection.

Right: No one was hurt in this Jan. 21, 1951, accident on the Downsville Dam. Walt Dette photo, Delaware County Historical Association.

"A" and "B" materials for deposit against the concrete core wall. The first, with a minimum of 12 percent clay content, formed the dense, impervious central portion of the dam. "B" was gravelly material with no clay content, used as a heavy shell atop the "A" material. A specific amount of both types of earth was called for on the dam. Both sides of the dam were to be covered with a rock blanket. The downstream slope would be covered with soil and seeded, the upstream side paved with heavy stone from the crest to 30 feet below the reservoir flow line.[27]

Earth scooped from the valley floor and its hillsides was hauled by bottom-dumping Euclid trucks ("Eucs") to the 550-horsepower grizzlies. There it was dumped into 15-cubic-yard hoppers and fed through screens to conveyor belts capable of handling 30 to 40 tons of material at once. Stones not falling through the screens were stockpiled for later deposit atop the dam. Dirt was loaded into waiting Eucs for transport to the dam, where it was spread in rows and leveled by bulldozers. Sheepsfoot rollers were then dragged over each row several times to tamp down the earth, which was added layer by layer until the required dam height was reached. The processing plants operated 20 hours a day, four days a week.[28]

The earth-laying season was extended in 1951 when a 10-ton fill drier was built on site. Mounted on the reinforced body of a former van, it carried three adjustable burners which were drawn over wet fill to dry it before rolling. Each burner consumed 10 gallons of fuel per hour to generate temperatures of 2200 degrees.[29]

Eighty Eucs were employed on the job: 20 on the top side of the dam, 20 on the bottom and 40 on either side of the valley, remembered Earl Johnson of Margaretville, who operated a Euc on the big dam: "It smelled like diesel fuel all the time. All the vehicles were run wide open, about 25 miles an hour. They wanted progress. If something happened to a vehicle, you took it to the on-site garage where mechanics were on duty all the time. There was the continual roar of machinery, but you got so you shut all that out. There were no people scurrying around. The spotter on the dam was the only person on the ground. It was just machinery."[30]

The 1951 BWS Annual Report figured that about three million cubic yards of fill was placed on the dam that year, but 30 percent of working time was lost to mechanical failure and not enough trucks.

The contractors purchased many of the Eucs new for $25,000 to $28,000 a piece. Tires alone weighed close to half a ton each and cost $1,400. When the earthwork was finished in the spring of 1953, a fortune in equipment was placed on the auction block. Contractors from all over the U.S. came to Pepacton to bid on 86 bottom dump trucks, 16 end dump trucks, 20 bulldozers, cranes, tractors, rollers and both grizzly plants.[31]

Building the overflow weir for the dam was another monumental job. Three-foot blocks of granite were set in mortar along the spillway channel. The 40-foot wall, built by subcontractor Arthur Kappler of Cranston, R.I., was made of granite

shipped by rail from Barre, Vt. to East Branch. It was trucked to the site, measured, cut and washed. Granite coping for the weir was obtained from Massachusetts.[32]

A gatehouse at the north end of the dam was constructed to regulate required water releases to the East Branch below the reservoir. A 200-foot high effluent chamber, as tall as a 21-story building, was built three miles from the dam at the intake to the East Delaware Tunnel to control the amount of water diverted to the Rondout Reservoir. Mammoth motorized valves, electric pumps and other equipment were installed at both locations.

These were boom times in nearby Downsville. The village that two decades earlier had worried it would be drowned by the reservoir was instead awash with new people and their paychecks. BWS engineers bought homes and moved their families up. Workers rented rooms, bought gas, ate out. Local residents found jobs. Bob and Joyce Gladstone Yevich's families were good examples. Bob's parents moved to Downsville from Pennsylvania in 1936 and opened a restaurant named Helen and Jake's. Business was good, and the Yevichs moved their eatery down the street to the Eagle Hotel, owned by Homer and Edna Gladstone. Engineers, surveyors, and later contractors and workers, filled the hotel's 20 rooms, as well as Helen and Jake's dining room, famous for its halupki and paroushki. They served three meals a day, Jake tended bar till

The Eagle Hotel in Downsville was a busy place during the construction of the Pepacton Reservoir. The local landmark was destroyed by fire in 1987. Author's collection.

Left: Steel for the Shavertown Bridge was fabricated in Pottstown, Pa. and shipped by rail to Arkville, then trucked ten miles to the bridge site. This June 4, 1954, photo shows a girder being moved through Main Street, Margaretville. Alton Weiss. *Right:* Building the 1,000-foot-long Shavertown Bridge between 1952 and '54 involved construction of four 100-foot-tall piers. Author's collection.

midnight, and the Gladstones' four daughters waited tables and cleaned rooms. Bob and Joyce also worked for the BWS, Bob as a driller and later a carpenter, Joyce copying deeds and doing clerical work.[33]

During this time, an estimated 1,500 workers were employed on various aspects of the project, including the Shavertown Bridge. In September 1952, the Cayuga Foundation Corp. won the $1.3 million bid to build the piers and abutments for the 1,000-foot-long span. The same company was later awarded the $900,000 job of installing the steel superstructure.[34]

The bridge's roadway would rest upon four concrete piers rising more than 100 feet above the former riverbed. Cement and concrete aggregate from throughout New York, granite facing for the piers from Georgia, and structural steel fabricated at Bethlehem Steel in Pottstown, Penn. were shipped by rail to Arkville and trucked 10 miles to the site.[35] Steel girders weighing 43 tons created quite a stir, as well as traffic problems, as they were transported on double trailers through narrow village streets and winding rural roads. In June 1954 a crane lifting one of these girders at the bridge site

toppled, crumpling the boom and pinning its uninjured operator in the cab.[36]

The Shavertown Bridge was completed in December 1954. Located one mile above the site of the community of Shavertown, the new structure replaced an iron bridge that had crossed the East Branch in the hamlet. That old bridge was being salvaged in November 1954 when it tumbled into the riverbed, where it remains submerged to this day.[37]

The Shavertown Bridge would be the only crossing of the reservoir proper along its 22-mile length.

Back in March 1948, the Savin Co. of East Hartford, Conn. had won the bid to build 10 miles of new highway to replace roads that would be inundated on the western end of the reservoir. The contract included construction of the three-span Downsville Bridge across the East Branch, a project that was started in March 1949 and completed in October.[38] In 1950, the city, seeking to "devote its entire energy to water supply work," opted to request the state Department of Public Works to contract for the remaining 25 miles of substitute highway construction. Seven separate contracts

Arena was one of four communities destroyed by the Pepacton Reservoir. Author's collection.

funded by the city were subsequently let, with all of the work finally accepted by 1957.[39]

The roads—a rebuilt State Route 30 and a city-owned roadway that skirts the south side of the reservoir—encircle a valley where four communities had hugged the East Branch. Proceeding east up the valley from the dam at Downsville were first Pepacton, then Shavertown, Union Grove and Arena. Just east of Arena, the impounded waters narrowed near Dunraven to once again reveal the river in its natural state.

After the first two real estate sections closest to the dam were taken in 1947, six more sections were claimed between September 1950 and April 1954. A total of 13,384 acres—21 square miles—were claimed for the reservoir. Forced to move were 974 people, including 284 children and 46 wards of the state and county. The BWS counted 260 residences, 113 farms, eight churches, eight stores, eight garages, three taverns, three hotels, eight sawmills, two barber shops, two water companies, five schools, four post offices, a Grange hall, a feed store, a fire house and a chiropractor's office. Enumerators even counted livestock—2,336 cows, 6,135 chickens, 103 horses, 99 pigs and 24 sheep and goats.[40]

Also removed were 2,371 graves in 10 cemeteries.[41] The city paid to have bodies disinterred and moved to a cemetery chosen by relatives. Some 600 unclaimed bodies were reinterred on the Ken Sprague farm near Shavertown, a farm the city acquired for that purpose. Sprague, who milked 34 cows on the 168-acre farm, returned from the doctor one afternoon to find a condemnation notice nailed to a shed door. "They gave everyone a number," a neighbor recalled.[42]

Sam Platania was the proprietor of Sam's Place, a Shavertown emporium where you could get a spaghetti dinner, sip a tall ice cream soda or get a haircut, all under one roof. "For years I've been getting up at a certain time in the morning, doing my day's work, visiting with friends, living a pleasant life," Platania told the Catskill Mountain News in September 1950. He anticipated moving in with relatives in New York City, but fretted "You're a nobody there. Some say they're glad to get out, but when the time comes, we all get the shivers."

Separation from their communities was devastating to some. Edmund VanKeuren, who operated a general store in Union Grove from 1928 until 1953, reportedly often told friends he'd prefer to die before the city forced him out. He and wife

Mabel survived the move though, and bought a home in Sidney Center. There he died at the age of 71 in May of 1955. Mabel, 72, followed seven months later.[43]

Some in the valley experienced both gains and losses from the presence of the city in their midst. Ken Sprague's brother Raymond got a job on the reservoir project, as did Arthur Filupeit, whose

Above left: Demolition of the Advent Christian Church in Arena. *Above right:* Moving the James Martin home out of the Pepacton basin Aug. 13, 1954. *Top left:* Agnes Miller handed the last bag of outgoing Union Grove mail to Floyd Tremper. Inez Atkin, postmaster at Shavertown, is at left. *Top right:* Darrell "Mutt" Atkin outside Atkins Store and Post Office, Shavertown. All Alton Weiss.

parents, August and Lena Filupeit, lost their Union Grove farm to the reservoir. James "Bruce" Armstrong, who had taken over his parents' Shavertown store, finally got a chance to make use of the engineering training he'd received at Rensselaer Polytechnic Institute by getting a job with the BWS. He and wife Marian Shaver Armstrong, a fifth-generation descendant of the community's founder, ran the hardware and feed store until they were forced to close it in 1953.[44] That left Atkin's Store and Post Office down the street. They sold meat and hardware and cigars, and Darrell Atkin, a photographer, had his darkroom there. His mother, Inez Atkin, had been the postmaster for 30 years when the last mail left Shavertown Mar. 18, 1954. The auction of the store's contents took place a few weeks later. Two thousand people attended; BWS police directed traffic in the otherwise abandoned town, and a crew from NBC-TV filmed the event.[45]

"It took their heart and soul," recalled Inez's grandson, Gary Atkin. "They could never go home again."[46] Said Marian Armstrong (Scudder), "I remember an awful wave, a terrible sadness. That all of this will be gone, just gone." The home of her parents, Ward and Lela Shaver, had been occupied by the grubbing contractors, Shanahan Construction Company, as they razed vacated homes and barns, burned piles of uprooted trees and removed privies and septic tanks. In the midst of the destruction, trucks rumbled through town transporting vaults and boxes carrying remains from local cemeteries to new resting places.[47]

In August 1954, after the last building in Pepacton (the 13-room home of Herbert Shaver) was put to the torch, nearly all of the hamlet of Arena went on the auction block. The Schutt Construction Company, which had the grubbing contract to clear this part of the reservoir basin, had purchased all buildings as part of the contract with the BWS. It auctioned off 20 dwellings and a similar number of barns and outbuildings. They brought from $15 to $1,500, most selling for from $200 to $400. The buyers either moved them or dismantled them to use the materials in new structures.[48]

Schutt kept three houses that were in particularly good condition, including the Ralph Sanford residence, which they used as their headquarters in Arena. These homes were later moved to an unaffected area of Dunraven where they were placed on new foundations and sold. One, the Katharyn Dickson home, had served for a time as the temporary residence of BWS Division Engineer John Buhrendorf and his wife before the engineer retired in the fall of 1954. Although it escaped the fate of its neighbors, the Dickson house was almost claimed by the East Branch when the tractor hauling it to its new site became mired in gravel as it forded the river. The building was stranded midstream for days before it could be extricated.[49]

Several other buildings were also moved. The Bob and Anne Misner residence, which had housed the Pepacton Post Office, was moved to a new site up Miller Hollow. A small development called Arena Heights included five relocated homes with views of the reservoir above the former community of that name. Ivan and Agnes Miller, who had kept the Union Grove Post Office in their parlor for 18 years until they were forced to leave in 1954, bought it back from the grubbing contractor and used part of it to build their new home in Margaretville. Martin Jobman similarly acquired the barn of George and Letha Hulbert Hoag, whose farm on a fertile stretch along the river in Shavertown was claimed for the reservoir. The Hoags and other neighbors later helped rebuild their barn on the Jobman farm, which escaped condemnation.[50]

Bits and pieces of revered churches----bells, stained glass windows, beautiful woodwork----were also saved by congregations to be displayed in new places of worship. The 150-year-old John Norton home in the Dunraven area was purchased from the grubbing contractor by the Arkville Free Methodist Church, whose members used beams and other parts of the structure to build their new church in Arkville (later used as the Town of Middletown's Justice Court). The door and trim from the beautiful old house were salvaged by a neighbor who intended to give them to Irving Olds, chairman of the board of United States Steel from 1940 to 1952. Mr. Olds, a summer resident of

Huckleberry Brook, had an ancestor who was born in the house.[51]

One area landmark, the Old Stone School in Dunraven, dating back to 1820, was not demolished although it sits within the reservoir buffer zone. It survives to this day as a museum, a meeting hall and a polling place. A covered bridge nearby was razed, however, despite an offer from the contractor that anyone who could cart it away could have it for free. There were no takers, and it became one of four covered bridges in the valley to be removed. The bridge did get a temporary stay of execution, however, when it was pressed into service after a causeway built by the city to replace it and three other spans in the Dunraven area was breached Oct. 16, 1955. A Supreme Court judge had ordered the reluctant city to build a bridge connecting rebuilt Route 30 with the city road on the south side of the reservoir, but instead of a bridge, the city constructed a 25-foot-high earthen causeway pierced by eight sluice pipes. Completed in July of 1955, it was soon battered by three hurricanes----Connie and Diane in August, and Hazel in October. Debris plugged the sluice pipes, forcing the rampaging East Branch over and through the earthwork.[52] The causeway was replaced in 1956 by a 170-foot-long steel bridge.[53]

By that time, one by one, stores, mills and community gathering places throughout the valley had closed their doors. One sunny Sunday morning in 1953, when only three young girls showed up for Rev. Paul Brown's service, the Union Grove Methodist Church rang its bell for the last time.[54] In September, with only four students, the 100-year-old Arena School was permanently dismissed. By the end of 1954, there were just 23 people still living in the reservoir basin.[55]

Many were bitter at the loss of their homes, the businesses they had worked hard to build and the communities where they were comfortable among family and friends. But some saw agriculture declining and viewed the city's condemnation posters as a ticket to a better life. Others simply accepted the situation with pragmatic stoicism. "No man likes to leave his old home, no matter how well paid by the city," said one man interviewed by the NBC film crew at the Atkin auction. "But you can't stand in the way of progress." Instead, they stepped aside; BWS figures indicate that 82 percent of people displaced from the East Branch valley stayed within Delaware County.[56]

On Sept. 15, 1954, impoundment of water in the Pepacton Reservoir began as 30-foot stop logs----30-inch steel bars reinforced by 8x12 western pine timbers----dammed the entrance to the diversion tunnel, halting the flow of the East Branch of the Delaware River. Drought conditions prevailed through October, so the waters rose slowly at first. But six inches of rain in November hastened the process, so that by the end of the year, 51 billion gallons of water covered the western end of the valley.[57] This took the city, and the Margaretville Telephone Company by surprise, submerging the few remaining buildings in the Union Grove area and a half-mile of telephone lines serving families in the Barkaboom valley upstream from the reservoir.[58]

The gates at the inlet chamber were opened Jan. 9, 1955, allowing Pepacton water to flow to the Rondout, and thence to New York City. Regular releases downstream to the East Branch began in July.[59] It took a while longer for the waters to back up to Arena. "Arena is nearly gone," reported the *Catskill Mountain News* on Dec. 9, 1955. "Waters of the Pepacton Reservoir rise each day and in a short time will cover Main Street. The last buildings to go are the former hardware store, the Methodist Church, the fire hall and the school. All are in the process of being torn down, or will be in a few days."

Fed by heavy snows that winter, the reservoir crested the spillway for the first time in April 1956, 19 months and one day after storage began.[60]

In May, a big new billboard appeared on Route 17 near Roscoe, directing tourists to Downsville, 12 miles away in the scenic Delaware Valley, home of the "largest earth dam in the East."[61]

Building reputations, too

The city's reservoir and tunnel projects attracted laborers and professionals from all over the country. Two of those who built substantial reputations during the Pepacton era, and then stayed on to make lasting contributions in the area, were labor leader Clarence "Hank" Mayer and attorney Herman Gottfried.

Mayer was born in Rich Hill, Mo. in 1902, and grew up in Illinois, where he worked in the coal mines, as had his father and grandfather before him. He studied economics and sociology at Illinois Wesleyan University. As a young man, he managed to own a small coal company, but during the Depression of the early 1930s, he became an advocate for the unemployed and later worked on construction jobs. With such jobs in short supply during World War II, he worked for the National War Fund, raising money for international relief, the USO and other aid efforts.

The son of a socialist, Mayer ran unsuccessfully on the Socialist Party ticket for Illinois Senator in 1940. In 1946 he moved his family—wife Ada and sons Scott and Gene—to Vermont to live near and work with Scott and Helen Nearing, who had developed an ardent following for their views on cooperative living and organic subsistence farming. But in 1948, Mayer, in need of a more reliable income, read in *The New York Times* of the big public works project under way near Downsville. And on a 30-below-zero morning he arrived at contractor Walsh-Perrini headquarters and landed a job as a laborer.

He soon became a foreman, and in June his family joined him from Vermont, moving into the Scott and Mary Barnhardt home in Shaver-

Hank Mayer came to the Pepacton project from Vermont as a laborer, and became a union leader. He is shown in this 1949 photo with wife Ada and sons Scott and Gene in front of the "Euc." Ada Mayer.

town that had been claimed by the city. That spring he was tapped to become the business agent for Laborers International Union Local 17.

"I started to make demands on the company," he related in his 1989 autobiography. "There had to be fresh water in the drinking cans, and there had to be better safety conditions." He led a strike protesting contractors' efforts to fire 10 rounds a week while driving the East Delaware Tunnel from Pepacton to the Rondout. And he fought to have an ambulance on site because of the distance to the nearest hospital in Liberty. A serious accident that left several workers injured at the Lew Beach shaft of the tunnel proved his point. "In three days we had ambulances at both shafts and portals. It took an explosion before the company woke up. They didn't move until they were forced to," Mayer wrote.

He continued to work with the union through completion of the Pepacton project and on later construction jobs. In 1952, the Mayers bought the former Ward Shaver farm on Shaver Hill Road in the town of Andes, overlooking the reservoir. There the family operated a small farming operation and hosted many visitors who came to learn about their organic gardening methods. In 1987, after 35 years in Andes, Hank and Ada moved to Vermont, and then to Florida, where in 1993 Hank Mayer died at the age of 91.

As Mayer had fought for the workers, Herman Gottfried fought for property owners being evicted from the reservoir basin. But he started out on the other side.

A Brooklyn native, Gottfried was born in 1910 to German immigrant banker Morris

Gottfried and his wife, Fanny. He earned bachelor's and master's degree in English literature at City College, where he did his thesis on Edgar Allen Poe's theory of the universe. He went on to Brooklyn Law School, then went to work for the city, heading the law department of the comptroller's office during the tenure of Mayor Fiorello LaGuardia.

In 1941 he married court stenographer Margaret "Peggy" O'Neill, daughter of a New York City Board of Water Supply (BWS) engineer. The following year, he joined the U.S. Navy, serving as an officer aboard the *USS Isherwood* and surviving a Japanese kamikaze attack on the vessel. On his return to civilian life, he was named Acting Corporation Counsel in charge of the BWS' Kingston law office. There he supervised a staff of five lawyers, two title examiners and four stenographers preparing the city's land acquisition cases for its upstate reservoirs.

He spent more than three years in that capacity, during which time he argued strenuously before appraisal commissions and Supreme Court justices to persuade them to allow the city to pay as little as possible for the farms, homes and businesses it was taking. Then, in late 1949, Gottfried was urged by colleagues to leave the city's employ and "go west," to Margaretville, to establish his own practice representing the sorts of people whose claims he had been paid by the city to oppose.

"I was called a turncoat. They thought I was probably a spy, with some justification," he recalled in a 1996 interview, noting that his "tobacco road" description of one farmstead at a commission hearing, when he worked for the city, didn't sit well with local residents. "When I was working for the City of New York I had to represent them to the best of my ability, which I

Herman Gottfried, right, congratulates Charles Allen on winning a sizeable property damage award in 1954. Gottfried began his career as an attorney for the city but switched sides in 1950. Alton Weiss.

did, and it worked to the advantage of the city," Gottfried said, admitting to "some regret" that initial Pepacton property damage awards were fairly low. "That haunted me some," he said. "But after we got several awards in 1952 for claimants I represented, they knew I meant business. We hit home runs galore."

Gottfried went on to represent hundreds of people in both the Pepacton and Cannonsville basins, not only those who had lost property to the reservoirs, but merchants who had lost business, workers who had lost jobs and wages, and downstream landowners whose riverside properties had been devalued. An attempt by the city to have him disqualified from representing upstate clients in riparian rights cases because he had "inside information" about the way the city arrived at its appraisals was tossed out by a state Supreme Court justice in January 1957. An effective advocate for his clients, he won substantial awards for them, and in turn profited handsomely while gaining recognition as a specialist in the area of condemnation law.

The Gottfrieds became longtime Margaretville area residents, contributing to the community and its social scene for many years. Among the organizations and institutions they have generously supported are Margaretville Memorial Hospital, Fairview Public Library in Margaretville, the Margaretville Central School Scholarship Fund, Kingston Hospital, and libraries and hospitals in Florida and Cape Cod, where they maintain residences. In 1998, they donated to the Village of Margaretville the office building they built in 1969 to house the Gottfried practice.

Sources: C. H. Mayer's *The Continuing Struggle: Autobiography of a Labor Activist* (1989); interview with Herman Gottfried, August 1996; *Catskill Mountain News*, Sept. 8, 1993, Jan. 6, 1999.

19. Cannonsville

FIVE YEARS before ground was broken starting the Cannonsville phase of the Delaware System, and four years before the U. S. Supreme Court even gave the city the right to do so (Chapter 17), opponents of the project lined up in a losing battle to stop it.

Some 60 municipalities, organizations, businesses and individuals filed as objectors to the project when hearings on the matter were held in Delhi during the spring and summer of 1950. The hearings were conducted by the New York State Water Power and Control Commission, which had to approve the city's plans, already okayed by the New York City Board of Estimate. More than 100 people jammed into the Delhi Village Hall on Mar. 22, 1950, when the hearings opened before five commissioners: Executive Secretary John C. Thompson, who presided; State Conservation Commissioner Perry Duryea; State Public Works Commissioner Bertram Tallam; Edward Ryan, as-

sistant to the State Attorney General and Henry Schiller, senior engineer of the commission.[1]

During nine days of hearings held during March, April, June and July, the commission took 1,200 pages of testimony and viewed 139 exhibits.[2] Board of Water Supply officials and engineers explained their proposal to put up a dam 1,600 feet long and 170 feet high to create a reservoir that would store 95 billion gallons of water. Residents of five communities to be flooded asked that their homes be spared. Delaware County supervisors argued that the county had already sacrificed enough for the Pepacton and other, non-BWS reservoir projects. The Rock Royal Cooperative Creamery claimed that of 153 milk producers using the plant, 50 would be flooded. Predicting that the company, and the local dairy industry, would be ruined, it called the project "inequitable, unconscionable, unjust, and presumptious."[3]

Through much of the hearings, it was the Hudson River, not the Delaware, that was the focus of testimony, as project detractors urged the city to take a serious look at tapping the Hudson River. They brought in Lawrence Beck, a New York City engineer, who proposed building a barrage dam across the Hudson between Poughkeepsie and Chelsea that would raise the river by three feet as far north as Albany. The dam would include locks to permit ship traffic, ladders to allow fish migrations, and a four-lane highway atop to carry the New York State Thruway. The plan would

---

Facing page: Aerial views of Cannonsville before and during demolition (June 25, 1963). The Queens Farms Dairy is in the foreground with the community just across the West Branch of the Delaware River. Cannonsville and four other communities were eliminated to make way for the reservoir that bears the town's name. Bob Gavin photo, Broome County Historical Society.

A BWS surveying party atop Apex Mountain looking south toward Granton in what would become the Cannonsville Reservoir. George Lipp.

have the water pumped from the river, filtered, treated and sent to the city via the Delaware Aqueduct.[4]

The BWS claimed such a project would carry greater maintenance costs and would disrupt countless businesses and utilities along the river, including the New York Central Railroad, which estimated at $200 million the cost of relocating its main line. But for the BWS, the biggest issue was water quality. It found Hudson River water to be "definitely inferior. . .and its use hazardous."[5]

The state Commission rejected the Beck idea and other alternative proposals when, on Nov. 14, 1950, it found the city's Cannonsville plans "justified by public necessity."[6] That approval prompted the city to request the U.S. Supreme Court to amend its 1931 decision and allow it to take additional water from the interstate Delaware River supply. The court obliged in 1954, and the BWS began building the Cannonsville project.

The first contract for the project was awarded in July 1954 to Sprague and Henwood of Scranton, Pa., to do test borings to determine the depth to bedrock at the proposed dam site and along the route of the 44-mile West Delaware Tunnel.[7] The concrete-lined tunnel, with a finished diameter of 11 feet, four inches, would be built from seven shafts ranging from 303 to 780 feet deep. Lengths between shafts ranged from 23,000 to 37,000 feet,

according to the *Delaware Water Supply News* of Nov. 1, 1955.

Five separate contracts for sinking the shafts and drilling the tunnel were awarded beginning in November 1955. Totaling $90 million, they went to three joint ventures.

The intake channel at the Cannonsville Reservoir, plus Shafts 1, 2 and 3 near Readburn, Harvard and Horton, respectively, along with the westerly 19.4 miles of tunnel were built by a consortium of five firms: Johnson, Drake & Piper of New York City; Grafe-Callahan Construction of Los Angeles; Tecon Corp. of Dallas; Winston Brothers of Minneapolis; and Conduit and Foundation of Philadelphia.[8] (The contractors went by the initials D-G-W-T-C, but workers and area residents found it easier to refer to the contractors on this $35 million section of tunnel as "We the People."[9])

The central five miles of the tunnel, including Shaft 4 at Rockland on the Beaverkill creek near the Delaware-Sullivan County line, was built by MacLean-Grove & Company and George M. Brewster & Son for $11.7 million.[10] The remaining 19 miles of tunnel, the outlet channel in the Rondout Reservoir, along with Shafts 5, 6 and 7 at Johnson Hill Road, DeBruce and Halls Mills in Sullivan County, were constructed by D-G-W-T-C under the name West Delaware Tunnel Constructors for $43.8 million.[11]

The 303-foot-deep Shaft 2 was the site of project groundbreaking observances on a bitterly cold Dec. 19, 1955. New York City Mayor Robert Wagner, watched by two busloads of BWS workers and media people, and several city officials in limousines, skipped the speeches and went right to the cab of a crane, where he failed to scoop up a mound of dirt and instead dropped the bucket on the shaft's steel liner. The crowd then departed for the Antrim Lodge in Roscoe where they celebrated the 50th anniversary of the BWS.[12]

The flubbed ground-breaking may have been a portent of things to come for Shaft 2. Six workers were hurt when dynamite that had not fired during a blast in the tunnel heading blew up as holes were being washed out preparatory to renewed drilling. And, about 900 feet into the tunnel from the bottom of the shaft, a vein of water was struck, 300 to 400 gallons per minute gushing into the tunnel, enough to force a two-week shut-down until a 40-foot concrete plug could be poured. Concrete grout was then pumped behind the tunnel perimeter to shut off the flow before tunneling could resume.[13]

In general, though, record progress was made on the West Delaware Tunnel. Overburden ranging from 20 to 40 feet was stripped from the shaft sites with shovels and bulldozers. Once bedrock was reached, jackhammers drilled 60 to 75 holes in the surface rock. The holes were loaded with explosives, blasting about eight feet of rock per round. Drilling, loading and shooting took about one eight-hour shift. It took another eight to 10 hours to hoist debris out of the shaft hole with grapples suspended from the shaft headframe. After the shafts were sunk to required depths (Shaft 6, one-quarter mile from DeBruce, was the deepest at 780 feet), they were "belled out" in wide sections at the bottom, track was laid, and tunnel headings were started in opposite directions. Men riding 36-foot-long, drill-carrying "jumbos" drilled fifty 12-foot-deep holes in the rock face and loaded them with 300 pounds of dynamite to loosen as much as 20 or 25 tons of rock with each shot, extending the tunnel 10 feet per blast. As many as six rounds could be shot in a day, with mucking machines transferring blasted rock to railroad cars and thence to skips at the shaft, where electric hoists raised them to the surface for dumping. Roof bolts and steel liners were placed to prevent rock falls.[14]

Several innovations were employed in tunnel driving. One was the use of a larger "burn" hole at certain of the headings. This center hole, which was not loaded with explosives, was a relief mechanism that allowed the broken rock somewhere to go when the blast occurred. Increasing its diameter from three inches to five or eight inches produced greater headway with each blast. At Shaft 4, a new system of preheating the compressed air used in the pneumatic drills eliminated the "fog" produced during drilling. Compressed air passing through drills undergoes a temperature drop of about 90 degrees in expanding. The dewpoint of the sur-

Above: Concrete being screeded (shaped and smoothed) in the West Delaware Tunnel. Kenneth Kaufman. *Top:* A view toward the east heading at Shaft 2 of the West Delaware Tunnel. Glenn Watson.

rounding air is lowered and the excess moisture is precipitated in the form of vapor, causing fog in the heading. Addition of a heat exchanger kept the exhaust air sufficiently high to prevent such fog from forming. Perhaps it contributed to the accuracy of the tunnel excavation in that section; when the tunnel between Shafts 4 and 5 was "holed through" July 6, 1959, after 4.5 miles of driving by two crews working towards each other, the error in alignment was just half an inch.[15]

Cement for tunnel concreting was shipped by rail to Hancock, while sand and gravel were trucked in from nearby banks. Concrete for the tunnel was mixed at batching plants at certain

Ansco mucker clearing newly blasted rock from the West Delaware Tunnel. Glenn Watson.

shafts, dropped through a steel pipe into a hopper at the bottom, where it was dumped into agitator cars for transport to invert (bottom) and arch forms.

Despite a nationwide steel strike in 1956, which delayed some steel needed for rails and roof support, tunnel-driving went forward at an exceptional pace. By early 1957, 600 men were at work on the tunnel 24 hours a day. In the first seven months of 1957, D-G-W-T-C workers bored 302 feet a day from five headings. Clancy O'Dell of Rockland, project manager for the company, credited good labor-management relations and keen competition between crews on each shift.[16]

At a huge clambake held for 900 D-G-W-T-C officials and workers in East Branch in 1957, the project manager called the tunnel drivers "the Yankees of the construction business," comparing his "team" to the baseball squad that had gained legendary status by winning six out of the eight preceding World Series.[17]

An unusual feature of the tunnel project was the offering of first-aid and safety courses to workers, who took the classes on company time. The classes were instituted following a 1956 explosion of methane gas 880 feet from the intake portal, where earlier in the year a Lake Delaware man had been crushed by a careening muck car. Three men were hurt when a broken electric light bulb ignited a pocket of gas which was allowed to burn for three

days before excavation could resume.[18] The U. S. Bureau of Mines was asked to send instructors to teach workers about gas emergencies, and the enthusiastic response led the contractors to add accident prevention, first aid and mine rescue courses. More than 600 men took the classes, which culminated in a first-aid contest held in Roscoe Central School. Five teams competed, responding to problems posed by Bureau of Mines representatives. The Shaft 1 team won the contest, its prize an all-expense paid trip for the seven team members and their wives to a national first-aid meet in Louisville, Ky.[19]

Not all tunnel casualties involved accidents. Hearing loss was common among workers who chose not to wear earplugs. "Like standing next to a jet engine" was how one man described the sound of six powerful drills biting into solid rock. Air hissing from the pneumatic drills added to the din. Huge compressors at the top of the shaft that ran the drills made the ground shake. And even when the drills weren't running, every sound in the tunnel echoed. Thunder rattling the surface world would ricochet down the shaft and intensify with a subterranean echo.

"Some people had no idea what they were getting into when they took a tunnel job," said Maurice Early, a track-and-top foreman at Shaft 2. "Many of them didn't last a shift. I've seen them get in the muck bucket, go down, and the next bucket up, they're out of there."[20]

Two of the five tunnel contracts were completed in 1959, two years ahead of schedule. With the exception of intake and outlet facilities, the West Delaware Tunnel was finished in 1960. The $2.5 million job of building the intake works at the Cannonsville end of the tunnel went to Johnson, Drake & Piper. Outlet works at the Rondout Reservoir were built by Rosoff Bros. & Foster-Newman Contracting of Brooklyn for $2 million.

Progress on the Cannonsville project was accelerated by another force that was more brain than brawn. An analog computer at New York University was utilized to work out complicated hydraulic problems connected with the design of tunnel control works and water release mechanisms at the dam. "This technique gave a rapid solution to a problem for which only an approximate answer, after prolonged and laborious computations, could be obtained by analytical methods," explained the BWS 1958 Annual Report. Another of these newly introduced computers was also put to the test by the Delaware River Master, who used it to figure out safe yields from the Neversink and Pepacton watersheds. The results, "recorded on special computation sheets," were verified by independent BWS calculation, said the Bureau's 1959 annual report.

The studies, tests and plans conducted by the BWS on every facet of the Cannonsville and other projects were exhaustive. Meticulous drawings for everything from valve and lighting equipment to dam structures and road culverts had to be produced by the Drafting Department. The Proving and Performance Department conducted thousands of tests annually detailing the corrosive qualities of various metals, the chemical composition of cements, the qualities of different paints. And the Reproductions Department spat out many thousands of forms, blueprints, mimeographs and photographs.

The dawn of the Atomic Age added the danger of radioactivity to the concerns faced by the BWS as it developed the Cannonsville project. "Considerable data was available to the Board on A- and H-Bomb explosions, but there was little on discharges from industrial plants employing atomic energy. Furthermore, airborne industrial waste could increase greatly the possible trouble range," explained the BWS in its 1955 booklet produced for the Board's 50th anniversary. Occasional radioactivity testing was conducted on the city's water supply in the early 1950s, and a continuous program was initiated in 1957. Monitoring intensified with the acceleration of atmospheric nuclear testing by Russia, the U. S. and other atomic powers during the height of the Cold War in 1961. Sampling indicated, however, that background radioactivity levels fell well within U. S. Public Health Service guidelines for potable water supplies. The BWS was reassured that their relative remoteness from industrial areas and strategic military targets

provided natural protection for its Catskill and Delaware reservoirs.[21] But just to be on the safe side, the BWS drew up plans to build a tunnel bypassing the Rondout Reservoir as a hedge against sabotage or nuclear contamination. Approved by the Mayor and the city's Board of Estimate, according to the BWS Annual Report of 1965, the project was subsequently abandoned when it failed to receive a budget appropriation.

Work on the Cannonsville Reservoir itself began with the hiring of Queens Structures to build about 1.5 miles of access roads, a 180-foot timber bridge, a 230-foot steel and concrete bridge, a sewer plant, an engineers' office and a soils plant, all in the Town of Deposit.[22] The timber bridge was washed out in a flood in January of 1959, and was rebuilt that summer.

Stream control works, including a 1,280-foot diversion conduit excavated in rock, were built from 1959 to 1962 by the E. J. Albrecht Construction Co. of Chicago at their bid of $2.1 million.[23] The diversion tunnel, 17.5 feet in diameter, was constructed on the south side of the valley to carry the West Branch of the Delaware while the dam was being built. The conduit ended in a stilling pool which discharged into the river. Atop the temporary diversion tunnel was built a permanent release water conduit, a cement-lined steel pipe encased in reinforced concrete. This pipe, 12 feet in diameter, carried water from the reservoir, beneath the dam and back into the river in satisfaction of the Supreme Court's order that the city maintain a steady flow in the Delaware River.[24] The valves fabricated by a Portland, Or., firm for the release works and for the intake and outlet works of the West Delaware Tunnel were designed to withstand pressures up to 400 pounds per square inch. With diameters ranging to 96 inches, these valves were among the largest of their kind, according to the 1961 BWS Annual Report.

In July 1960, Lane Construction Company of Meriden, Conn., was awarded the $11,695,000 contract to build the Cannonsville Dam and associated works. By the end of October, 89 acres of land had been cleared in the immediate vicinity of the dam, two miles east of Stilesville, but actual work on the valley barrier did not begin until the spring of 1961.[25]

The dam was built with a core of impermeable material, not concrete as was used in the city's previous earthen dams. A "key trench" was excavated to bedrock. Joints and crevices in the rock were grouted by drilling hundreds of holes 30 feet deep and pumping grout cement, sand and water into the holes. Compacted clay was layered in the trench and banked with earth. Graded material was placed on the dam in much the same way as on the three preceding Delaware System dams. The Cannonsville Dam required more than 1.5 million cubic yards of rolled impervious material, and 1.1 million cubic yards of semi-pervious material. A small hill left by a retreating glacier eons ago was used as part of the dam, reducing the amount of fill required. A masonry spillway and waste channel were constructed on one end of the dam. Blasted out of rock, some of the material removed for the weir and waste channels was then used for rock embankment and riprap on the dam.[26]

Work on 31 miles of substitute roads to replace those inundated also began in 1960. As was the case at Pepacton, the city paid for the work while the New York State Public Works Department let the bids and coordinated the construction. Nineteen miles of State Route 10 had to be replaced, and eight miles of county highways. Bridges were also built as part of the replacement plan. They included the 420-foot-long Stilesville Bridge, about a mile downstream from the dam; the 1,200-foot-long Cannonsville Bridge that crosses the reservoir a half-mile upstream from the former hamlet of that name; the Trout Creek Bridge that crosses the reservoir midway between Cannonsville and Rock Royal and the 598-foot Apex Bridge, connecting Apex and Cadosia.[27]

The $2 million Cannonsville Bridge was supported by six piers 140 feet high. Built by Walsh Construction Co. of New York, it was begun in September 1961 and was finished two years later.[28] In 1964, that span, and the Apex Bridge built by Lane Construction, was among 20 winners in a nationwide Beautiful Bridges Contest sponsored by the American Institute of Steel.[29]

But it was not a thing of beauty in 1962, when the project claimed the life of one man and a limb of another. William Emans, 36, a Walton father of three, died when he tumbled 101 feet from the top of the bridge on September 19. Two months earlier, Margaretville teenager Joe Duggan, who had graduated from high school only the week before, lost a leg when he slipped beneath the wheels of a dolly supporting the rear of a 144-foot-long, 67-ton steel girder being hauled from Deposit to the bridge site.[30]

The early 1960s was a time of bustling activity, fearsome noise, and strange sights that valley residents could hardly have imagined a few years earlier. A newspaper account on the work of the Yonkers Construction Co. as it built a substitute State Route 10 described long swaths of felled trees and bulldozed clearings along the side of the basin. "At night, the area is dotted with many fires as trees and underbrush are destroyed," related the *Deposit Courier* on Aug. 4, 1960.

The papers also carried dramatic photos of abandoned homes in flames as grubbing contractors cleared all buildings from the floor of the reservoir. The Sidney Center Fire Department made use of a grim opportunity by burning four structures as a training exercise. At least one massive barn, built in Rock Royal of stone and railroad ties, had to be dynamited before it could be removed. The barn, owned by John L. Lewis, was built by his grandfather to withstand fire and flood. It could not resist the power of a city bent on building a reservoir, though. Nor could local churches. "The Lord may have dominion over the heavens and the earth, but he isn't doing too well against the U. S. Supreme Court and the New York City Board of Water Supply," quipped the *Courier* on July 5, 1962, as it reported on the last service of the Rock Royal Methodist Church.

The city claimed a total of 19,910 acres (31.1 square miles) for the Cannonsville Reservoir, which extended about 16 miles up the West Branch to Beerston, and contained a five-mile finger that stretched north up Trout Creek to Rock Royal. Those two communities, along with Cannonsville, Granton and Rock Rift, were eliminated by the

Among the 74 farms claimed for the Cannonsville Reservoir was this one belonging to John and Bernice Lewis on the Trout Creek-Cannonsville Road. Bernice Lewis.

Below left: The former Cannonsville Hotel, later the Community Hall. Edward Reynolds. *Below right:* The Rock Royal Store and Post Office, November 1961. Bernice Lewis.

reservoir. So were 74 farms, two creameries, six stores, three post offices, five churches, four schools, two hotels, three restaurants and a community hall.[31]

Eleven cemeteries and small burial grounds containing 2,150 graves were also unearthed and relocated. Bodies not claimed by relatives were reinterred at the city-owned cemetery near the Pepacton Reservoir.[32] "If you couldn't get a job on the project, you could get a job moving graves," related Hilton Evans. Diggers got paid $12 a grave. "Two guys could dig four graves in a day if they worked hard enough," Mr. Evans said. He tried it, but one day of grave-digging was quite enough. He worked on other elements of the project, and later became editor of the *Deposit Courier*.

Of the three towns that lost land to the project—Deposit, Tompkins and Walton—the Town of Tompkins bore the heaviest loss. One-quarter of the land in the township, representing half of the town's assessed valuation, was acquired by the city, which also claimed the businesses that provided jobs, and the people who lived and worked there. The town's 1950 population of 1,671 had dwindled to 905 by 1970. The town's highway garage was claimed (a new one was built in Trout Creek), and also its supply of gravel, which the city now controlled as well.[33] Of course, the town also gained revenue from taxes paid by the city on the land, but found itself in lengthy assessment battles with the city for years to come.

Cannonsville people first saw the condemnation posters go up on poles and buildings in late fall of 1961. The following year witnessed a mass exodus, as 298 people moved out of the area. "There were people who couldn't wait to get out, people who took it lying down, and people who took what they could get," recalled former Tompkins Town Supervisor Perry Shelton.

Early in 1962, the city attempted to evict 11 property owners immediately so that work could progress on the relocation of State Route 10. About 25 people and attorney Herman Gottfried traveled to a Supreme Court hearing in Binghamton to protest the city's request for immediate possession in the depths of winter. In the courtroom were

Eunice Love, 74, a former teacher; Burnadette Kingsbury, owner of Peg's Tavern; Postmaster Everett Card; former Tompkins Town Supervisor Joseph Judd and Rock Royal Postmaster and store owner Zana Bethel, among others. Two people were in wheelchairs, recalled Mr. Gottfried. Although city attorney Raymond Sweeney argued that people had known about the coming of the reservoir for 10 years and should have appreciated "the penalties of progress," Judge Joseph Molinari said, "No judge will direct people to vacate in 10 or 15 days under such circumstances. I'm not for it, and I don't think that deep in your heart, you are either."[34] The city agreed to allow occupancy of the properties until May.[35]

Cannonsville residents had already said their communal goodbyes at the last Old Home Day celebration, July 4, 1956. Attending were 3,000 people, including four great-granddaughters of Cannonsville founder Benjamin Cannon. The 1790 Cannon homestead, last occupied by Mr. and Mrs. Leland Boyd, was used as a precinct house by the BWS Police during the construction period.[36] The house, with its five fireplaces and a basement door built large enough for a team of oxen to drag in six-foot logs, was among the last houses in Cannonsville to be destroyed in the summer of 1964.[37]

About five miles upstream from Cannonsville was Granton, with a post office, a store, a few houses and, nearby, the 370-acre June Peck farm, with two homes, a pair of dairy barns, a former store and sizeable quarry and timber parcels. Rock Rift, farther up the valley, was remembered by former resident Leonard Rutherford as a hamlet of fewer than 100 people and maybe 20 buildings, most of them company houses dating back to when a wood acid factory was a big employer. Louis Barth had the general store and post office; there was a butcher shop, a bakery, a church, two taverns and the Venetian Inn where Frank and Rachel Fiumera served Italian specialties. The taverns were lively places on a Saturday night, since neighboring Walton was a dry town. Rock Rift had a fair number of talented musicians, and on a summer evening the sound of fiddles and guitars filled the night air.[38]

At the eastern end of the reservoir was the hamlet of Beerston, where another acid factory had consumed great quantities of local hardwoods before it ceased operations in 1924.[39] Up Trout Creek was the Johnny Brook area and Rock Royal, dominated by the cooperative creamery that was owned by the farmers who brought milk there.

Bernice Lewis and her husband, John, who also ran the Rock Royal store and three farms, were among the creamery producer-owners, and she was the bookkeeper at the plant. From her desk one sad day she tearfully watched her home and the boardinghouse owned by her mother-in-law go up in flames as the grubbing contractors, Phillips and Jordan of Robbinsville, N. C., did their work. The Lewises built a new home several miles away. The cooperative rebuilt, too, but it could not recover from the loss of producers, and folded in 1971. The reservoir, Bernice Lewis says, "changed our lives completely."

The lives of Pauline and Sturgis Goodrich were among the many that were altered by the project. They had their Beerston home moved to a new site not far away that was just outside the taking line. Mr. Goodrich sat in a rocking chair on the front porch of the house as L. D. Dexheimer & Son of Guilford transported the building to its new foundation. Recalled Mrs. Goodrich, "They moved the whole house without disturbing anything. Even a quart of water placed on a beam did not spill." [40]

The Cannonsville Covered Bridge, built in 1850 over Trout Creek, was also moved in August 1963. The Sidney Historical Association and the Susquenango Cultural Council planned to use it as an historic site in Unadilla, but a fire believed caused by arsonists consumed the wooden structure the following spring.[41] (The bridge was later repaired and moved to Milford, Pa., where it stands as a historic attraction.)

As vegetation, homes, barns, stores and landmarks were removed from the basin, only filled-in foundations and roadways leading nowhere marked the spots that had been so familiar to generations of valley residents. The trauma of dislocation was felt by animals, too. The Dec. 5, 1963, issue of the *Deposit Courier* carried the poignant story of Missy, a German short-haired pointer owned by the James Moore family. Missy, apparently pining for her old haunts, left her master's new home in Hambletville and was found a week later lying patiently beside the foundation of the Granton home the family had vacated in July 1962.

By the end of 1963, when storage in other city reservoirs had dropped to 29 percent of capacity as a result of a three-year drought, the Cannonsville Dam was 94 percent completed. In September, stop logs had been placed in the diversion conduit and the river directed through the new release water mechanism. In a fortuitous weather turn, a heavy snowfall, quick thaw and then rain in February 1964 made it necessary to siphon water from the nearly-completed reservoir through the new West Delaware Tunnel to allow construction to continue in the basin. This provided a 50-day supply for the city.[42]

The last four residents of the Cannonsville basin vacated in 1964. The dam was completed on Feb. 16, 1965, and the reservoir was placed on line. The first water over the dam's spillway was recorded in May 1967.[43] "The Cannonsville Project has amply justified our faith in it as an excellent source of water supply," said the BWS annual report the following year. "The reservoir refills rapidly after depletion, and permits greater flexibility in operation of all four reservoirs of the Delaware System."

A mere 15 years after the Cannonsville Dam became fully operational, New York State began to explore the potential for expanding the reservoir's capacity by adding stop gates to the spillway. The plan, one of the recommendations in the "Good Faith" agreement made by members of the Delaware River Basin Commission in 1982, would have added 13 billion gallons of storage. The extra water, which would likely have flooded additional acreage at the upper end of the 4,800-acre reservoir, would be controlled by the state and used primarily to maintain conservation releases to the Delaware River. After five years of environmental and other studies, the proposal was deemed to be "not economically feasible."[44]

Instead, the city, in cooperation with the state, decided to pursue installation of a modified valve system that would allow variable releases, improving on the original system which permitted releases of either 45 cubic feet per second, or 325 cubic feet per second, but nothing in between. New valves were installed in 1997 at a cost of $3.4 million.[45]

Today, much of Cannonsville's water, of generally lesser quality than the water in the other Delaware reservoirs, is used to augment the flow of

the Delaware River as mandated in the 1954 U.S. Supreme Court decree.[46] That angers some people, who feel the reservoir didn't need to be built at all. But Bob Weyrauch, one of the thousands of workers who helped build that dam and the other city impoundments in the region, has a different perspective. Says the East Branch man, who worked as a laborer, driller and tunnel bellman on the Pepacton and Cannonsville projects, "There is a feeling of pride. I helped build this. It was a big part of my life. I can look at things along the road that I individually did. And that was a long time ago."[47]

A view of the Cannonsville Dam nearly completed.

Bob Gavin photo, Broome County Historical Society.

When the rains didn't come

The city's protracted efforts at dam-building have, since the very beginning, been plagued—and prompted—by periodic droughts.

Serious water shortages were recorded as early as 1850. In 1864, no water flowed over the Croton Dam for 52 days. In 1870, the outlets to several Putnam and Westchester ponds were cut down to avert a water crisis. Six years later, Boyd's Corners Reservoir ran dry. Droughts in 1910 and 1911 led to creation of a water waste division in the Department of Water Supply, Gas and Electricity. House-to-house inspections and distribution of literature promoting water conservation resulted in a savings of 60 million gallons a day.

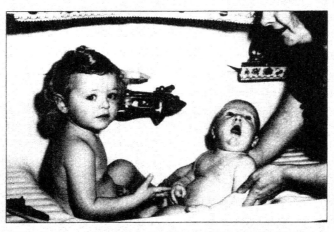

Children were bathed in kitchen sinks to conserve water during the 1949 water shortage in New York City.

As it rushed to finish three Delaware reservoirs, a lengthy dry period coupled with increased consumption in 1949 and '50 pushed the city to unusual lengths to provide water for its residents. The Department of Water Supply, Gas and Electricity enforced water reduction rules. "Thirsty Thursdays" were instituted, when residents were urged to go drinkless and bathless; volunteer civilian "water conservation commanders" went to homes and apartments sniffing out leaks and dripping faucets; car washes were shut down; the Port Authority used waste water to clean tunnels and bridges; the Central Park Zoo even put its elephant and hippopotamus on short water rations. The *Daily Mirror* held a contest to find the best rhyming couplets about saving water, and gave winners free theater tickets to shows like Desi Arnez and his Latin American Review. Residents collected rainwater in rubber life rafts on rooftops and wore armbands urging neighbors to "Save Water." At Tiffany's jewelry shop on Fifth Avenue, gin was used instead of water in a circulating pool in the window. The Brooklyn Dodgers even tried to drill a well in Ebbets Field.

In January 1950, the State Water Power and Control Commission approved a city petition to build an emergency pumping plant at Chelsea on the Hudson River. Tuller Construction Co. and engineer A. J. Dillenbeck won the contract to construct the facility, which included an intake pipe extending 900 feet into the river to draw water into the Delaware Aqueduct.

That spring, the city was desperate enough to engage "rainmaking expert" Dr. Wallace Howell, a Harvard professor, to coax water from the clouds. He assembled a "strike force" that included two police amphibious planes, based at Floyd Bennett Field in Brooklyn, to drop dry ice pellets and silver iodide smoke into clouds above the watershed; two light trucks, carrying silver iodide generators operated by city employees, who would shoot the stuff into low clouds; and a field headquarters near Roscoe, Sullivan County. A meteorologist, radio operator and radar technician manned the headquarters, situated in an abandoned caddie house on an unused golf course near Tenanah Lake. A tower was built atop the caddie house allowing an unobstructed radar sweep that extended 50 miles in three directions from the 2,300-foot elevation, and an advisory committee of six scientists from colleges and universities in the city prepared to compile and review data amassed by the project. But natural rainfall in late March and early April delayed the operation, and some observers claimed it was all a publicity stunt to highlight the need for a dam on the West Branch of the Delaware.

The issue did garner a lot of press. The owners of the Phoenicia Diner placed a birchbark canoe with a mannequin in it on the roof of their establishment with the sign "Let the Rainmakers Come." The Pine Hill and Phoenicia Chambers of Commerce and the Big Indian-Oliverea Board of Trade filed suit to stop the city from rainmaking, calling it "illegal trespass," and the Sullivan County Board of Supervisors passed a resolution urging the city to discontinue its efforts because the threat of rain was scaring off the tourists.

Press accounts indicate that cloud-seeding did occur during that summer, augmented by natural rains. Then, in late November, hunters in the Dry Brook area near Margaretville reported hearing a plane overhead, and being sprinkled with a soft, foreign substance they speculated was silver iodide. A record flood occurred that Saturday night, sending torrents of water through area communities, sailing a 72-ton, 32-foot-tall fuel tank down Route 28 in Arkville, carrying the Pepacton Covered Bridge 1,000 feet downstream, and heavily damaging homes and businesses in Delaware, Ulster and Greene Counties. The city got its water, but it also faced a series of lawsuits from people seeking compensation for losses they said resulted from the rain-making effort. More than 100 claims were filed totalling about $1.5 million, but the suits were later tossed out because it could not be scientifically proven that the downpour had been caused by cloud seeding.

Another extended dry spell in the early 1960s affected much of the Northeast for five years. Perhaps taking its cue from a 1960 report written

by Rand Corporation scientists who concluded that the city could save 150 million gallons a day by eliminating leaks, the city conducted another inspection drive, sending a troupe of 250 leak detectors into apartment houses city-wide. Universal metering was still not in effect, though experts claimed it could save an additional 200 million gallons of water a day.

In 1965, the city issued new rules curbing the use of water-guzzling air conditioners, despite the protests of irritable residents and office workers in high-rise buildings, and the owners of small shops where temperatures sometimes rose to over 100 degrees. The World's Fair, in Flushing Meadows, Queens, operated in air-conditioned comfort, however, because, as an entity set up by the State Legislature, it was not required to abide by city rules.

In July 1965, with the new Cannonsville Reservoir on line, the Delaware River Basin Commission ordered the city to reduce its consumption of Delaware water by 75 million gallons a day. Downstream states had accused the city of hoarding water it was supposed to be sending downstream. George Mekenian, a city engineer whose job was to develop water storage and conservation projections based on hydrology reports and rainfall probabilities, acknowledged that his office's projections prompted the city to suspend its downstream releases.

In 1965 and '66, the emergency pumping station at Chelsea, Dutchess County, was reconstructed for $2.2 million. Built in 1950 but until then never used, the reconfigured plant delivered up to 100 million gallons per day of Hudson River water into the city's supply for 300 days. It was suggested the plant be made part of the city's permanent supply, but consultants engaged by the city to explore additional sources declared that flow restrictions and pumping costs would make that impractical. The 1974 study, by Metcalf and Eddy, instead recommended dam development on the Upper Hudson, the Mohawk and the Black Rivers, proposals that never made the drawing board.

During the 1960s, when, ironically, the city was worried about contamination of its reservoirs from nuclear bomb attacks or industrial accidents, it was also exploring the possibility of teaming up with an atomic power producer to deliver water. The study, conducted in conjunction with seven federal agencies, examined the feasibility of building large-scale atomic energy plants for the dual purpose of desalination of water and generation of electric power. The city also worked with Consolidated Edison on the possibility of utilizing its Indian Point nuclear power plant on the Hudson River for water desalination. The idea required additional technological development and was never brought to fruition.

The Chelsea pumping station was again used in the 1980s, when another drought brought reservoirs to their lowest levels ever. It resulted in a photo opportunity similar to one in January 1964, when Commissioner Armand D'Angelo of the Department of Water Supply, Gas and Electricity led a hardy band of fur-clad engineers and reporters to Monticello in a howling blizzard to measure the snowfall and project how much water the city might have on hand later that year. In a much warmer July of 1985, Mayor Ed Koch also travelled north, this time to Ulster County. There, he stood in the parched bed of the Ashokan Reservoir, beseeching the heavens for rain and announcing both the re-opening of the Chelsea plant and the imposition of strict water conservation measures on eight million New Yorkers.

The Chelsea plant pumped 82 million gallons per day from the river for almost five months in 1985. (For two weeks in May 1989, the plant was also activated to provide 90 million gallons per day.) In July 1985, the city formed an intergovernmental task force to study the water supply needs of the Southeast part of the state. Its subsequent report, unlike the 1974 Metcalf & Eddy study, saw expanded pumping of Hudson River water to be the *only* large source of supplemental supply that could be realistically developed over the next 10 to 15 years. The report urged drawing on the Hudson for 200-300 mil-

lion gallons per day, and suggested renewed study of using Long Island wells to supplement surface supplies in times of drought.

The task force also recommended increased metering and leak detection to make conservation a viable water "source," and that is the path the city chose to follow, adopting a universal metering system in 1986. It began implementing the system in 1988, and by the end of 1997, 456,000 meters had been installed, changing the flat-rate, street-frontage system of billing to one that ascertained actual water usage.

The city also launched a concerted effort to conserve water. By 1997, it had replaced 1.3 million toilets with low-flow models, saving four to five gallons per flush. Daily consumption in New York City dropped from 1,457,000 gallons per day in 1988 to 1,184,000 gallons in 1997. That represents a per capita decrease from 204 to 164 gallons per day. Daily consumption in the four upstate counties that draw on the city's water system also fell during that period, from 125 gallons per capita to 123.

"Based on the results of metering, toilet replacement, leak detection, public information and other conservation programs achieved to date and expected in the future, it is projected that no additional water sources will be necessary for the next 50 years," said the New York City Department of Environmental Protection in 1997.

Sources: Charles Weidner's *Water for A City*; *New York Times*; *New York Herald Tribune*; *New York News*; *New York Mirror*; *New York Journal American*; *New York Sun*; *Hancock Herald*; *Catskill Mountain News*; Albany *Times Union*; *Life Magazine*; BWS Annual Reports for 1950, 1965, 1968; Kingston *Daily Freeman*; Empire State Report (April, 1986); *The Water Hustlers* (Sierra Club, 1971); "Report to the Board of Water Supply on Additional Water Supply for the City of New York," (Metcalf & Eddy, Engineers, New York City, Jan., 1974); "Managing for the Present, Planning for the Future," Mayor's Intergovernmental Task Force on NYC Water Supply Needs (second interim report, Dec. 1987); interview Jan. 28, 1999 with George Mekenian, retired, Bureau of Water Supply, Gas & Electricity; New York City Municipal Water Finance Authority Bond Prospectus, 1997.

Auctions were common as families and businesses dispersed. This one was at the
Norton home in Dunraven, Pepacton Reservoir Basin, in August 1954. Alton Weiss.

20. Assessing the Damage

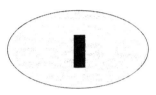

IF there has been one common denominator in the city's multitudinous water projects, it has been the conflict between individual property rights and the needs of the masses.

Wholesale condemnation of private properties to build public-benefit projects brought grief to many, fortune to some, and fresh water to millions of consumers largely unaware of the sacrifices made far away on their behalf.

When the city received state approvals and authorization from its own Board of Estimate and Apportionment to proceed with a reservoir or aqueduct project, it had to file maps with the appropriate county clerks showing the boundaries of its project and the tax parcels it would claim. Upon the filing of the maps, it published, in the *City Record*, in two New York City newspapers and in two newspapers published in each county containing affected properties, notice of application to the Supreme Court for the appointment of three-person Commissions of Appraisal to hear damage claims from property owners. Handbills of the notices were also posted in at least 20 locations in the vicinity of the parcels to be taken.

After the State Supreme Court in the appropriate district granted the petition for the appointment of appraisal commissioners and the oath of each commissioner was filed in the respective

county clerks' offices, the city officially assumed ownership of those properties. However, the city could not take physical possession until property owners were paid one-half the assessed valuation for the year preceding that in which the city acquired title. Often, that sum did not amount to a great deal of money, as assessed valuation was usually much less than actual value.

Once the city had laid claim to an area, it approached property owners with compensation offers. Sometimes, those offers were accepted if the occupants thought them fair, or preferred to avoid a lengthy wrangle. But if the former owners didn't like the offer, they took their case to the commissions, where their attorneys presented evidence and witnesses to bolster claims for more money from the city. The city presented its own witnesses and evidence to try to limit the award.

One or more commissions were named during the life of a project, each handling a numbered real estate section encompassing as many as 50 or 60 parcels. Commissioners---one from the county in which the project was located, one from the city, a third from elsewhere in the state, usually a contiguous county---would hear testimony on each parcel within the section for which they were responsible. After weighing the evidence, they would recommend awards in a report submitted to the Supreme Court. If either the claimant or the city objected to that award, they could ask the court to reject the report and send it back to the commission for

reconsideration. Further objections could be taken
to the Appellate Division. It was years before some
people were paid for their property, but the steam
shovels and bulldozers would not wait, and so
displaced residents often had to borrow money to
acquire new homes and businesses outside the taking lines. When the awards finally came, they came
with interest accruing from the date of the filing of
project maps. Claimants' attorneys' fees and witness fees were also included in awards.

Commissioners not only heard property damage claims from owners of land and buildings
taken. They also heard "riparian rights" cases,
awarding damages to owners of downstream parcels affected by altered water levels. And they
considered claims from people whose businesses
had suffered on account of the project, although
such damages were not compensated when the city
claimed commercial properties within New York
City.

People whose jobs disappeared with their em-
ployers' property were not compensated in the
early Croton takings. Later, however, under terms
of the 1905 act creating the Board of Water Supply,
people were allowed to file claims for wages paid
them for six months prior to the city's taking.
Wage cases were heard in Supreme Court, not
before commissions of appraisal.

Commissioners were sometimes hailed for
their generosity, at other times criticized for their
miserliness. Occasionally, they were vilified for
dining at the public trough. (They were paid $50,
and later $75 per day, plus food, travel and lodging
expenses, to hear damage claims.)

"Most of the people were well satisfied with
the amounts awarded," reported the *Katonah Times*
on Jan. 13, 1899, as awards for 25 properties, including two churches taken for the New Croton
Reservoir, were announced. Two weeks later, the
same paper reported that another group of property owners elsewhere in the Town of Bedford, and
in North Salem, handled by a different commission, were "thoroughly disgusted" with their
awards. "In some instances the money allowed is
but little more than half the original purchase price.
Scarcely a single parcel approaches the market

value. It is simply an outrage on law and equity,"
the paper fulminated.

Those owners, and others whose claims were
awaiting hearings by the same 8th Cornell Commission, held protest meetings at Purdy's Station and
at Golden's Bridge. They petitioned the Supreme
Court not to affirm the awards and to assign pending claims to another commission. Through their
attorney, they argued at a special term of Supreme
Court in Brooklyn that the 8th Commission had
not provided awards comparable to other commissions in Westchester County, and that the commissioners based their judgments on imperfect
information, perhaps because, rather than personally inspect each property, they simply rode past
the premises to view them.[1]

In April 1899, Supreme Court Justice J. F.
Barnard ruled against the property owners, saying
comparisons of awards were difficult, since properties differed so. Soon after, the *Katonah Times*
barely concealed its sarcasm when it reported that
"The Eighth Cornell Commission visited Purdys
and vicinity in a body on Wednesday. As the notice
of their coming was brief, there was no opportunity afforded to give a fitting reception and a public
demonstration by the delighted citizens."[2]

The city also took issue with awards it considered excessive. Westchester County Supreme
Court Justice Arthur Tompkins threw out the
report of one commission in 1907, agreeing with
the city that the three men had used incorrect
methodology to arrive at awards for 11 properties
totalling $95,000.[3]

Without doubt, the task before commissioners
was a difficult one. Presented with conflicting appraisals and property descriptions, they had to
place values on buildings, crops, streams, fisheries,
timber, mineral deposits and more. Parcels ranged
from a fraction of an acre to tracts of several
hundred acres. Henry Clark, for example, counted
478 trees on a half-acre strip of land the city claimed
on the side of Storm King Mountain for the Catskill Aqueduct. He figured those trees were worth
a dollar a piece.[4] David Chadeayne, who owned a
150-acre farm in the Town of Yorktown, farther
south on the aqueduct, claimed his property would

Pythian Hall and the Ira Forbes house in West Shokan, taken for the Ashokan Reservoir in Ulster County.
Town of Olive Archives.

lose $19,640 in value after the city fenced off a strip of it.[5]

Matilda Kurz' property was Parcel 203 in Section 4 of the Kensico Reservoir. Appraisers called by her attorney figured her seven-room house and three-horse carriage barn were worth between $4,600 and $5,150. The city's three witnesses, saying the structures were of "cheap materials," gave appraisals of $3,000 to $3,300. Commissioners William B. Greeley, Henry Gray and H. Hobart Keeler awarded Mrs. Kurz $3,900 in 1907.[6]

In an effort to get every penny they felt their properties were worth, claimants and their attorneys and appraisers itemized absolutely every-

thing, in some cases counting the nails in the walls and the panes of glass in the windows.

Testimony from commission proceedings painted a sometimes heartbreaking picture of what was lost. Parcel #24 in Richmond Park, in the path of Hillview Reservoir, was owned by Eugene Weiblen. His case was heard by the Supreme Court on Oct. 25, 1907: The two-and-a-half story house was situated on a lot 125 feet deep and 150 feet along Ware Avenue, a three-minute walk to the trolley line. The house had 11 rooms, including an oak-paneled reception hall, a 15x22-foot dining room, and a 14x14-foot parlor with a tiled fireplace. There was a wine cellar with a dumbwaiter and gas fixtures and chandeliers throughout the house, which featured both summer and winter kitchens, and a 50-foot-long, glass-enclosed porch along the front. Four bedrooms and a bath comprised the second floor. The top floor consisted of two large rooms topped by a many-windowed "observatory" in a tower with an unobstructed view of Long Island Sound 15 miles to the east. There was a two-stall barn with a coachman's room, a summer house, and beautiful grounds that featured cherry, peach and pear trees, a grape arbor and 100 rose bushes. The property was valued at $18,800 by Mr. Weiblen's witness. The city's appraiser said it was worth $12,757.[7]

Claimants in the Ashokan basin ranged from dressmakers and shopkeepers, to fish sellers and gristmill owners. Emma Cudney wanted $32,000 for her 11-acre ginseng plantation but was awarded $8,700.[8] Gottlieb Mayer's tannery at the confluence of the Esopus and the Butternutkill in Shokan tanned 3,000 to 4,000 pig skins a year on the site of the regionally-famous Hoyt, Fayerweather and Ladew Tannery that years before had made millions for its owners.[9] Cudney's and Mayer's attorney, A. T. Clearwater, also represented heavyweights like Samuel Coykendall, owner of the Ulster & Delaware Railroad. Mr. Coykendall, who had settled with the city for $2.8 million for the relocation of his railroad, objected to the $10,162 award given for his 58-acre bluestone quarry. He took the matter to the Appellate Division. There, attorney Clearwater argued that the property contained more than 33 million cubic feet of marketable bluestone, valued at between 26 and 48 cents per cubic foot. He brought in a plaster of Paris relief map of the parcel, a cross-section model made of 16 glass plates, and more than a ton of bluestone samples. The city, maintaining the tract was a quarry brush lot, prevailed, and the court upheld the award.[10]

That year, 1924, more than 15 years after Ashokan condemnations began, saw $30,290 in awards made, compared to $1,664,279 in dismissals and reductions in awards. Dismissed claims included those amounting to $425,000 filed by merchants in the City of Kingston, who said their businesses were damaged because seven villages had been eliminated for the Ashokan Reservoir, and 1,955 people had relocated. The city pointed to census figures and new building activity to show that 75 percent of former valley residents had moved within 10 miles of the taking line, disproving the merchants' contentions.[11] The E. I. duPont deNemours Powder Company had its claim tried, re-tried and appealed, only to see it reduced by $20,000 because the company had managed to increase production at reduced rates at a new mill in Maine, and so, the court said, had actually benefitted from losing its plant at Winchell's Falls on Esopus Creek.[12]

Ashokan landowner litigation lasted 36 years and resulted in 366 volumes of commission hearing transcripts and Supreme Court proceedings. A total of 954 parcels consisting of 21,138 acres were involved.[13]

Early in the process, it became clear why newspapers sometimes referred to the Ashokan region as "Plumland," alluding to the fruit ready for the picking by lawyers, commissioners and expert witnesses. The Kingston Freeman reported that the city had paid $1,422,000 for Catskill land up to Dec. 31, 1909, but at the same time had paid $1.1 million to engage special counsel and appraisal commissioners, $98,000 for claimaints' attorney fees, $122,000 in interest, $341,000 on advertising, and $205,000 on condemnation engineering expenses.[14] The city, outraged at the fees charged by three attorneys it had engaged as special counsel to argue its cases before commissioners and the courts, charged ex-state Senator John J. Linson, Everett Fowler and Augustus H. VanBuren with fraud and conspiracy in racking up $350,000 in expenses while handling cases from 1907 to 1910. A Supreme Court Justice rejected the city's arguments in 1915.[15]

In its Schoharie Reservoir project, the city faced claims from utilities and others as far north as Cohoes on the Mohawk River, which is fed by the Schoharie Creek. Those firms objected to reductions in the river's flow, although State Conservation Commissioner John D. Monroe said it would amount to less than six percent of the previous flow. "But whatever it is, the Conservation

Commission holds, and will always hold, that the water of this state is primarily and paramountly for drinking and domestic purposes, and it has never yet let a manufacturer or any private interest stand in the way of people's needs for municipal supply, and it never will." Added the commissioner, "Experience in other counties has shown pretty clearly that New York City has richly paid and frequently overpaid, for every bit of damage, direct or indirect, resulting from its work."[16]

Owners of Tri-County Power & Light would likely have disputed that contention. The company, headed by Judge John Grant of Stamford, had a hydroelectric plant on the Schoharie Creek precisely where the BWS wanted to put the Gilboa dam. In July of 1921, the company brought several witnesses before an appraisal commission, including John Harper, identified as a consulting engineer for the hydro-power plant at Niagara Falls. The firm's experts placed the value of its operations at just under a million dollars. The commission awarded it $155,000 in 1922. The city claimed that was excessive and took the matter to Supreme Court, which ordered a re-trial before a new commission. That body, reporting in 1926, further reduced the award to $89,870.[17]

Property damage awards ranged from $10 to more than $12,000. The First Dutch Church got half of what it wanted---$6,200. The Gilboa School District was awarded $1,900, the Gilboa Hose Co. $1,850. A sampling of business damages awarded by Schoharie Commissioners included $6,000 to Joseph Zeh for reduction in the value of his real estate in Fulton and Blenheim downstream; $2,500 to Josiah Mann for disruptions of his Gilboa dental practice; $10,000 to Wallace Stryker for the decrease in his Gilboa dairy business and $3,000 to the Rose Telephone Co. for a decrease in its busi-

The Fuller homestead in Eureka was sacrificed to the Rondout Reservoir. Eugene Fuller.

ness.[18] One claimant, a beekeeper, contended blasting operations on the Shandaken Tunnel jarred his hives, causing the complete loss of a number of colonies and the weakening of others. The city's attorney was forced to study literature on bee culture in order to question eight apiarists who were witnesses in the case.[19]

By 1931, the city had purchased 23,800 acres of land for its Catskill system, including Ashokan, Schoharie, Kensico and Hill View Reservoirs and the Catskill Aqueduct. It had paid out $11.5 million in awards——an average of $486 per acre——and another $7 million, or $296 per acre, for commissioners, attorneys and other expenses.[20]

The city began acquiring property for the Delaware Aqueduct in 1937, when six appraisal commissions were named to evaluate 1,300 parcels being taken in fee and through easements along an 85-mile stretch between the village of Lackawack, site of the Rondout Reservoir dam, and Hillview Reservoir in Yonkers.[21]

In 1938, commissioners began hearing claims of people whose property was condemned in the Rondout Valley. At first, the hearings were held in Kingston, but later they were moved to the Odd Fellows Hall in Grahamsville. There, a steady succession of witnesses provided testimony as spectators warmed themselves by the wood stove. "Claimants liked the shift to Grahamsville," reported the *Ellenville Journal* in a Feb. 8, 1940, article about the activities of the Section 8 Commission. "It was right at home and they could drop in as spectators whenever they had time, as about 30 appeared to have done Friday. Most of them, middle-aged or elderly, appreciated the change because they were not compelled to walk up three flights, as at Kingston." Hearing the claims for Section 8, which covered 65 properties between Lackawack and Grahamsville, including Eureka and Montela, were Chairman Charles Easton, chairman of the Albany County Republican Committee; Rolf Michelsen, a New York attorney; and Howard Beecher, Sullivan County Republican chairman from Monticello.[22]

Examples of awards made in the Rondout Valley included $5,171 to Granville and Glenny

Quick, whose 10 acres on the Ulster-Sullivan County line were confiscated for the Lackawack dam; $27,000 to Sam Lieberman for 38 acres which included a boardinghouse, casino, tennis courts and other facilities on Route 55; and $20,000 for 71 acres owned by William Vandermark near Montela. That land contained valuable timber stands and several small lakes.[23]

The nationwide Depression of the 1930s led to an important case involving Rondout basin property owners Ezra and Marie Empt. The city appealed a commission's award of $19,500, claiming it was excessive. The Empts, however, contended that economic conditions in 1936, the year on which the city based its valuation, were abnormal and did not reflect the real value of the property. They won their case, allowing appraisal commissions to consider testimony as to "normal" (pre-Depression) values in determining awards.[24]

Appraisers, and commissioners, were required to inspect properties prior to the hearings. "We thought they weren't fair in a lot of ways," said Margaret Dolan, whose family lost property in Eureka. "They would come into your home and look at it and say, 'Oh, there's a cracked window in the attic,' or 'There's a door knob off.' "[25]

In the Neversink Reservoir basin, William V. Denman had the same complaint. "The city representatives are careful not to mention what has been put into the property for the past 40 years," the farmer said in a letter to a local newspaper on Mar. 22, 1941. Detailing the money and effort put into improvements to his 203-acre operation, which included a 24-room boardinghouse, a 110-foot-long barn, a large orchard and a productive sap bush, Mr. Denman said city experts "rush(ed) over this property, which practically represents my life work, with prices as though they were going through a five and ten cent store." The commission, he asserted, spent less than two hours on his farm, and "positively refused to view the property until after all stock was sold, farm equipment removed and the house stripped of all furniture, so the entire outfit looked like a deserted homestead instead of a farm home where people were living and doing business." Mr. Denman received an award of $23,960.[26]

Morris Begun, who had operated an inn for 22 years, received an award of $35,500; Frank Vanderlyn, former town supervisor and an appraiser for the city, got $16,200 for his 150-acre farm; and Henie Rubenzahl, owner of a 44-acre resort, was awarded $13,000. Two area churches, the Lows Corners Baptist Church and the Upper Lackawack Methodist Episcopal Church, were awarded $3,365 and $3,950, respectively, less than half of the damages they had claimed, according to the *Ellenville Journal* of May 11, 1939. The smallest award—a mere dollar—went to Mary Smith, for a parcel that was just over a tenth of an acre. Her attorney was allowed five cents for his fee in that case.[27]

Benjamin and Elvira Krum lost their 86-acre farm, and received $5,000 with which they bought another farm near Bradley. Their son, Joe Krum, worked for Edward Hewitt, the wealthy industrialist who owned vast tracts of land and a fish hatchery in the valley. The Hewitts had a house on the river, which was claimed for the reservoir, and another on Blue Hill, which escaped condemnation.[28]

Neversink area resident Will Evans, in an interview in the *New York World Telegram* on Aug. 29, 1938, recalled that his 90-year-old neighbor had a nice farm and testified that while he felt it was worth $7,000, he didn't want to sell it to the city. "Of course, it didn't do no good to talk up like that," commented Evans. "If you don't like the settlement that's made on your property, the city'll reach down through the chimney and take it anyway."

Businesses large and small were affected, too. Some were compensated; others went away empty-handed. Justus Asthalter was 20 years old when he paid $1,600 for two milk routes in the Neversink Valley, carrying 170 cans of milk a day from local farms to a Liberty creamery. When the city bought out the farms, his business disappeared, but, called to the service during World War II, he was not around to file a damage claim. It irritates him to this day. Now 85, Asthalter says, "The city still owes me $1,600."[29]

Neversink damage cases went on through the 1960s. The largest riparian award went to the 8,900-acre Philwood Preserve in southern Sullivan County, where the Neversink River went up and down as a result of fluctuating water releases from the reservoir. After a 13-day hearing in 1957, appraisal commissioners awarded $81,000 in damages.[30]

A landmark riparian rights case involving the city's diversion of the Neversink River went all the way to the U.S. Supreme Court, which, in 1962, ruled that the city must add personal notification to its system of placing property-taking notices in newspapers and posting handbills in affected localities. The case was brought by Madeline Schroeder, who owned a summer home and three acres of land on the Neversink in Orange County 25 miles downstream from the Neversink Reservoir. She contended the reduction in the velocity of the river had hurt boating, swimming and fishing at her property, but she did not file a damage claim within the three-year statute of limitations. In 1960, she took the city to court, contending that since she was in the area only during July and August, she did not see the newspaper notices, or the handbills which had been posted during January 1952. The city, she claimed, had essentially deprived her of the use of her property by failing to notify her directly of her right to file a damage claim.[31] After the Supreme Court, in December of 1962, agreed with Madeline Schroeder, and declared that "notice by publication is not enough with respect to a person whose name and address are known," the BWS was beset by a flurry of claims from people who had not filed during the requisite three years and sought belated recompense.[32]

Following the hearings, it took up to a year for awards to be announced and then for property owners to receive their money from the city, assuming the awards were not contested by either side. Local banks often loaned property owners money in the meantime, and, charging the same interest the city could be expected to pay on the award (six percent), waited until the owners got their checks before calling for payment on the loans.[33]

Idolene and Howard Graham's experience was similar to many. Their Arena farm was claimed for the Pepacton Reservoir in September 1952. Anticipating what was coming, they had hired an attorney in 1950, and in January 1953, appeared before an appraisal commission to state their claim. They offered five years' worth of milk check stubs, receipts and other paperwork as evidence of the value of their property and business. Their appraisers valued the farm at $14,500 (compared to the city's appraisal of $6,500). While waiting for the commission to issue a report of awards, the Grahams paid rent to the city and searched for a new farm throughout New York and Pennsylvania. "We were looking for another place just like the one we had to leave. It took us more than six months to find out there wasn't another place like it. There was something missing in every place we looked at," recounted Graham.[34]

Eventually they settled on a farm in Afton, Chenango County, moving there in June 1953 after buying back from the city some of the equipment in their old barn now owned by the Board of Water Supply. Their property-award check did not arrive until March of 1954. The Grahams also argued claims for lost wages and business related both to the farm and to the sawmill where Howard worked. The business claim was heard in October 1954, and, again, mounds of paperwork were required to prove damages in great detail. "I never knew there were so many different ways to ask the same question," Graham said.[35]

Herman Gottfried, a former city attorney who switched sides in March 1950 to represent upstate claimants, found such property owners to be the best witnesses. "They knew how many cows they had, how many fence posts, how many strands of barbed wire on those posts, when they had to get up in the morning, where they shipped the milk, what the summer kitchen looked like, where the night pasture was. They didn't have to use any fancy words," he recalled in 1996.[36]

Gottfried engaged specialists to dress things up a bit. W. Stanley Munro, local real estate agent and appraiser, used glowing oratory as well as mathematical formulas to describe every element of a piece of property. Even outhouses got special mention, as in the case of one, decorated with expensive wallpaper, characterized by Munro as "early Americana." Fred Hendricks, known as the "Silver Fox" because of his distinguished gray hair, was the owner of a Narrowsburg lumber company who testified about building reconstruction costs. Livingston Manor fly-tier Harry Darby described fishing resources and stream values. Callicoon nurseryman Valleau Curtis appraised trees, shrubbery and other flora that would be lost, and even estimated the amount and value of maple syrup that might be produced from a stand of sugar maples. Architect Jim Burbank drew plans for every room in every building. Walton photographer John R. Clark took pictures of each structure, as well as croplands which, might, for example, show stalks of corn towering over a farmer's head.[37]

The attorney accompanied commissioners on their mandatory visits to his clients' properties. Before one such visit, he had to arrange for the removal of several pet goats from a woman's cellar, which was then fumigated and whitewashed, good as new.

Working behind the scenes for Gottfried were D. T. Williams, a tenacious "genius" who did title searches and tracked down former property heirs to clear land titles; and Edna Scott Gavette, a secretary who helped collect information and laboriously typed forms and records for hundreds of cases in the days before photocopiers, fax machines and computers.

Gottfried's office was first located at the Margaretville Telephone Company (which would later receive the largest damage award in the Pepacton basin----$144,350), then moved to the Masonic Hall's Friendship Room. That room was equipped with a pool table, so, to the accompaniment of "Six ball in the side pocket," the attorney interviewed clients and prepared them for commission hearings.

Paul Eaton Sr., a Walton attorney, also represented numerous clients. He handled the first Pepacton case to come before a commission, ironically against Gottfried, who had not yet switched sides. "I'd never seen one tried before," said Mr. Eaton about his first damage case. "This was kind of a new wrinkle around here. I didn't realize the magnitude of the whole thing. We had nothing to go by." [38]

In spring 1949, Fletcher's Hall at Shavertown was filled to capacity with property owners and attorneys anxious to represent them. Residents thought they'd get a better deal if they organized as the Delaware Valley Chamber of Commerce and actively solicited lawyers. Attorneys who handled Pepacton claims besides Gottfried and Eaton included Alfred Jahr, Edward Bailey of Westchester County, Francis Paternoster of Downsville and J. Taylor Breen of Stamford.[39] Paul Owens and Theodore Lee were among the attorneys representing the city.

During the next several years, numerous legal precedents were set. In 1951, seven Pepacton farmers received the first indirect real estate damage awards. The farmers claimed that although their land was not taken, it was worth less because the reservoir removed farm-related stores and services for which they now had to travel greater distances. The city objected to the $26,972 in awards, but the Supreme Court, and later the Appellate Division, upheld the commission's decision, thereby affirming that a farm is a business.[40]

In another case, attorney Gottfried represented the owner of two contiguous parcels. One was taken for the reservoir, the other was not, but, using the "unity of use" theory, Gottfried convinced the commission that the adjoining parcels were dependent on one another to support the Holstein herd and to make the farm economically viable. Therefore, he argued successfully, both properties must be appraised, and consequential damage awarded for the one not taken.[41]

Gottfried admitted encouraging property owners to spruce up their buildings with fresh paint and make necessary repairs before the commissioners visited, but he defended the practice, claiming it was what anyone should do when trying to sell their property to a prospective buyer for the highest possible price. But New York City attorneys took issue with some cases, claiming that

Sam Platania sold spaghetti and gave haircuts at Sam's Place in Shavertown, an area now under the Pepacton Reservoir. Pepacton Press.

fraudulent evidence was being presented. In 1953, the Supreme Court set aside five awards for business damages after BWS attorneys charged that account books had been manipulated and perjury committed. Citing "hate and prejudice" toward the city in Delaware County, the city also requested that hearings be held in Binghamton, Broome County.[42]

But most Pepacton cases were heard in rooms at BWS headquarters in Downsville, or on the second floor of the Zasloff Building above the Margaretville Post Office. Among the properties described there were August Filupeit's 180-acre farm in Union Grove (awarded $31,500); Arena Postmaster Katharyn Dickson's home and store ($28,250); the house and hardware store of Chamber of Commerce President Ralph Sanford ($41,000); and the farm of Charles and Agnes Allen near Downsville, where gravel found on the property was used to build the dam ($52,000).[43]

The largest individual property award went to Mary Toth, who had operated a farm and a busy boardinghouse one mile from Arena. The 74-year-old widow testified that she had lived there since 1913, welcoming as many as 60 to 70 summer visitors in two 14-room houses. The property included 3,200 feet of frontage on the East Branch of the Delaware, and guests often swam in the river near Hall's covered bridge. The city claimed the property was worth $22,000 in 1954. The commission awarded Mrs. Toth $55,000, an award the Supreme Court upheld.[44]

The first property acquired by the city in the Cannonsville basin was purchased in July 1955. A six-room house on an acre of land just south of Rock Rift was sold by Nelson and Josephine Frazier to the city for $6,500. Richard Burke, secretary of the BWS, which maintained offices in Binghamton and Deposit, said both time and money were saved in directly purchasing property. By the end of October 1955, 20 more parcels were acquired in Rock Rift, Granton and Cannonsville without going through the condemnation process.[45] One satisfied resident was Warren M. Kelly. He sold three parcels totalling 603 acres to the city, which included in the settlement business damages and provisions for a hired farm hand to live in one of the Kelly houses until it had to be razed.[46]

Fred M. Lipp, a former supervisor of the Town of Tompkins, a lumber dealer and a resident of Cannonsville, was the city's local point man, approaching his neighbors and acquaintances to encourage them to sell directly. He also appraised properties for commission hearings, and remained with the city's claims division through the late 1960s, according to his son and daughter.

But while Lipp was successful in convincing some residents to sell direct, there were commission battles aplenty. An award made to Edwin and Amelia Hodam was opposed both by the city and the Hodams' attorney, Herman Gottfried. The $59,700 award was too little, Gottfried said, because the 234-acre farm contained a potential 20-lot subdivision, $15,000 worth of lumber and three stone quarries. The award was too much, the city contended, because the Hodams had only purchased the property in 1946 for $10,000 and had taken in just $100 a year for their quarry stone. Gottfried said the city was using double standards in making generous awards when owners were willing to sell privately, but protesting as too generous the awards that resulted from commission trials. The Hodam award was upheld in 1961 by the Supreme Court.[47]

However, Supreme Court Justice Daniel McAvoy threw out three Cannonsville awards in June 1961, calling them "shocking," "speculative" and "highly problematical." The awards were for three farms: Delview Farm, owned by Theron and Ethel Turner, with house, 45-cow barn and 50 acres of river bottom land ($171,775); Lawrence and Esther Turner's place next door, with a half-mile of river frontage ($123,000); and John and Donald Garrigan's 340-acre farm ($101,600). The judge said the commissioners—Frank Gennett, legal assistant to State Senator Ogden Bush; Anthony Fischetti, a Binghamton attorney; and Edward Blackstone of New York City—had allowed testimony of inflated royalties from quarry stone, sand and gravel, "though nowhere was it shown that a ready market was available within the foreseeable future. . ." The Turner cases were re-tried and the same awards resulted.[48]

Walton attorney Paul Eaton Sr. said he never questioned commissioners about their decisions. "I just argued that the city had come here uninvited, was ruining our lives and our industry. I reminded them about the city's unmetered use of water, and just tried to blacken [the city's] eyes as much as possible."[49] By all accounts, that didn't surprise the city. Paul Blomquist, division engineer of the BWS Bureau of Claims, told *The New York Times* in fall 1963, "No matter what happens, New York City is always on the wrong end of things. We're the intruders. But there are eight million people we've got to take care of. Try selling that idea up here."[50]

City and upstate lawyers became practiced at verbal jousting. Binghamton attorney Bernard Chernin claimed in May 1956 that the city was unduly delaying condemnation claims for Cannonsville valley lands in hopes owners would tire of waiting and settle directly with BWS "hatchetmen." New York City Corporation Counsel Vernon Murphy replied that cases could be hurried along if people were willing to travel to Binghamton, where three claims could be heard at once. In a more conciliatory tone, Murphy offered to make "house calls," to hold hearings in the homes of infirm claimants.[51]

Meanwhile, the hearings continued. The business damage award of $61,000 won by farmer John L. Lewis of Rock Royal was believed to be the biggest ever to a New York State farmer. It was based on testimony that Lewis' three dairy operations, spread out over 1,000 acres, produced a million pounds of milk a year.[52] Lewis was also Rock Rift postmaster. He and his wife, Bernice, owned a store and another home there; his mother owned a 35-room boardinghouse. All were claimed for the Cannonsville Reservoir, and the Lewises were awarded substantial property damages.

Riparian claims brought by owners of land downstream from the dams and on feeder streams also commanded a lot of attention. In August 1958, area newspapers carried lists of awards for 38 properties between Downsville and East Branch. Three months later it was announced that riparian commissioners would be paid $75 per day for their work over the preceding 18 months. Their compensation, ranging from $36,000 to $63,000 each, totaled $270,000, or just over half the $500,000 in awards that had been meted out.[53]

The Tuscarora Club, a private fishing club that owns about seven miles of the Millbrook stream leading to the Pepacton Reservoir near the site of Arena, was among dozens of riparian claimants. Unhappy with an initial award of $7,000, the 40-member club held out for $40,000 granted on appeal. It claimed that not only had the city taken several acres of its land and a quarter-mile of stream, but the presence of the reservoir would allow unwanted fish species like pickerel and perch into the Millbrook to the detriment of the trout the club raised and released in the stream. The club used its award to build a dam of its own, a concrete barricade several hundred yards upstream from the outlet of the Millbrook, equipped with a trout ladder to allow the high-jumping trout to migrate upsteam while keeping other fish out.[54]

For its part, the city produced witnesses at riparian commission hearings who claimed that downstream dam releases were beneficial to fish and plant life. Aquatic biologist John Grim of Rhinebeck testified at a hearing as late as May 1976 that shad had become more abundant in the Delaware River because autumn conservation releases into the West Branch from the Cannonsville Dam had made it possible for the fish to get through the pollution at Philadelphia and Trenton, live to maturity, and re-ascend the stream.[55]

The Lewis boardinghouse in Rock Royal was burned to make way for the Cannonsville Reservoir. Bernice Lewis.

In the mid-1980s, the city, in an attempt to clear the books of more than 800 Delaware business damage and indirect real estate claims that had been filed but never prosecuted, called for anyone with pending claims to come forward. A new Commission of Appraisal was established and met for the first time in October 1986 at Roundup Ranch in Downsville, and later at Kass Inn in Margaretville. The bulk of the cases were dismissed because claimants had died in the intervening 30 years, or could not be located. Many had lost the records to prove their cases. But some engaged attorneys and reinstituted their claims. One of those was Margaretville Memorial Hospital. Its attorney, Richard Harlem, claimed that 301 of its patients had been forced out of the Pepacton Reservoir basin, and quantified the resultant business loss at $101,000. The city's attorney, Robert Travia, contended the hospital was a non-profit corporation and as such was prohibited from engaging in activity for pecuniary gain. He claimed further that the city should not be held accountable for the hospital's reduced potential future profit. Commissioners Ronald Haus of Oneonta, Gary Rosa of Margaretville and Rudolph Barkovich of New York City awarded the hospital $20,598 in 1992, 45 years after the start of the Pepacton project. The last meeting of the final Commission of Appraisal took place in October 1993.[56]

During its long tenure, which began in 1935, the Delaware Commissions of Appraisal settled

6,700 claims totalling $26,806,168.[57] But the money was only partial ointment for wounds that would fester for the next 50 years. Residents, businesses and officials in five counties had grudgingly relinquished their homes, their livelihoods, and what some remember as the most productive lands in the region. They had swallowed the city's presence like a bitter pill that could not be avoided. But they did not forget. And in 1990, when the city imposed new demands on watershed inhabitants, those still-painful memories were employed as an emotional, and very effective, call to action.

Tax disputes

Once the city acquired property to build its reservoirs and aqueducts, it was required to pay taxes on the land. But for years, it was only the unimproved land that was assessed, not the more valuable "improvements," such as dams, gatehouses, shaft structures, valve chambers and pumping stations. In fact, "aqueduct" structures were specifically excluded from taxable property.

Municipalities on both sides of the Hudson challenged the city's exemptions, their first victory coming in 1905 when Westchester County's Board of Supervisors won a court fight to allow local assessors the right to tax reservoir improvements, including the huge New Croton Dam. The case went to the Appellate Division, which ruled that the property, assessed at about $6 million, was taxable. That meant an additional $50,000 in the coffers of the Towns of Cortlandt, Yorktown, Somers, North Salem, Mt. Pleasant and North Castle.

In 1913, the city tried to get the state legislature to adopt a bill exempting it from such taxation, but upstate lawmakers, worried about its impact on their constituents' tax bills, defeated the measure. The city tried again in 1927, but was again rebuffed by legislators.

During the 1920s, a long and bitter battle took place over taxation of the city's newest waterworks, the Schoharie Reservoir. The Town of Gilboa, in 1925, increased the city's assessment from $117,279 on its land holdings (1,024 acres), to $3,742,430 which included the nearly completed Gilboa Dam. In 1926, the assessment on city property in the town was raised again, to $5,085,000, and in 1927, it rose to $5,101,000.

The town sought $55,000 in taxes for 1925, $80,000 for 1926 and $96,000 for 1927. Claiming the increase would mean it would account for five-sixths of the town's tax revenue, and 21 percent of Schoharie County's, the city filed grievances and refused to pay. The county responded by advertising city lands and the Gilboa dam for sale, but a court order prevented the sale while a Supreme Court referee studied the matter.

The referee, appointed in 1925, examined 138 parcels the city had acquired in the Town of Gilboa, and another 88 properties within the town as a basis of comparison. Dozens of court sessions and several field visits were conducted, more than 3,600 pages of testimony recorded, and 60 exhibits introduced.

In 1927, the referee concluded that the dam was subject to taxation, but it had been substantially over-valued during the three years in question, the over-assessment totalling $9.2 million. In 1929, Supreme Court Justice Ellis Staley agreed with the referee, and ruled that the city's structures were indeed taxable.

That opened the floodgates, and the three Ulster County towns housing Ashokan Reservoir appurtances immediately raised the city's assessments: Olive (site of the Ashokan Dam) from $900,000 to $5 million, Hurley from $100,000 to $1,305,000 and Marbletown from $45,000 to $7.5 million. Ulster County billed the

The Schoharie Reservoir Dam figured in a major tax dispute in the 1920s.
Author's collection.

city $189,000 in taxes for 1929, and, when the city refused to pay, offered the Ashokan water system for sale.

Six attempts to auction the property were halted by court-ordered stays, until Supreme Court Justice Staley ruled that the sale could go forward while a referee took testimony on the validity of assessments. In April 1931, County Treasurer Herbert Thomas stood on the courthouse steps in Kingston before a large crowd to take bids on the reservoir property. No buyers came forward, so the treasurer purchased it for the county in the amount of the back taxes.

Assessment battles between the city and upstate towns and counties have been waged ever since. The Town of Colchester in 1955 raised its assessment of city property from $9 million to $22.5 million after completion of the Pepacton Reservoir, whose dam lies within the township. The case was argued before a referee and was finally settled in 1958 when an assessment of $17.5 million was agreed upon. "We made a shake-hand deal that the town would not raise the assessment for the next five years. We haven't

raised it, and the city hasn't challenged it since," said Paul Eaton Sr., former town attorney.

In 1950, Downsville residents voted to dissolve their incorporated village reportedly in part because they felt they would derive greater benefits from taxes paid by the city to the Town of Colchester. The dam was located just outside village limits.

Two lengthy assessment fights took place in the Town of Tompkins, where the city owns 16,000 acres of land categorized as abandoned farmland. The town felt the value should be based on what the city paid to purchase the land and buildings and then to clear the property, according to former Town Supervisor Perry Shelton. State tax law still does not have a category for land that is under water, or watershed lands.

In many upstate towns, the city is the largest single taxpayer, accounting for most of the tax base. In 1997, the City of New York paid a total of $54,999,757 in taxes to municipalities in nine counties. Its buildings, dams, and 84,769 acres of watershed lands were assessed for $333,219,036.

Sources: BWS Annual Reports 1926, 1927, 1928; *Catskill Mountain News* 1928-31; *Katonah Times* July 7, 1905; *Northern Westchester Times*, Jan. 31, 1913; interviews with Paul Eaton Sr. (Jan. 2, 1999) and Perry Shelton (Jan. 16, 1999); NYC Dept. of Environmental Protection Office of Water Supply Lands Assessed Valuations Report FY 1997.

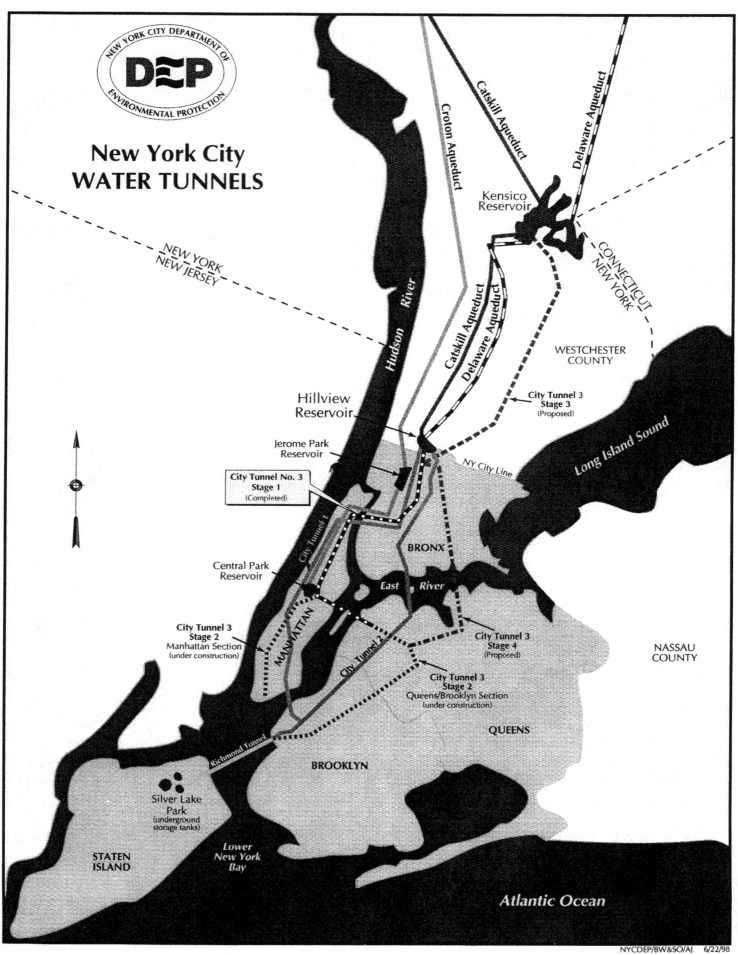

NEW YORK CITY DEPARTMENT OF ENVIRONMENTAL PROTECTION

New York City
WATER TUNNELS

Croton Aqueduct

Catskill Aqueduct

Delaware Aqueduct

Kensico Reservoir

NEW YORK / NEW JERSEY

Hudson River

CONNECTICUT / NEW YORK

Catskill Aqueduct

Delaware Aqueduct

WESTCHESTER COUNTY

Hillview Reservoir

Jerome Park Reservoir

City Tunnel 3 Stage 3 (Proposed)

NY City Line

Long Island Sound

City Tunnel No. 3 Stage 1 (Completed)

City Tunnel 1

BRONX

Central Park Reservoir

East River

City Tunnel 3 Stage 2 Manhattan Section (under construction)

MANHATTAN

City Tunnel 2

City Tunnel 3 Stage 4 (Proposed)

City Tunnel 3 Stage 2 Queens/Brooklyn Section (under construction)

NASSAU COUNTY

QUEENS

Richmond Tunnel

BROOKLYN

Silver Lake Park (underground storage tanks)

STATEN ISLAND

Lower New York Bay

Atlantic Ocean

21. Tunnel Vision

IKE many New Yorkers, Richard DuBois takes the train to work. To catch it, he has to ride in a metal cage down a dark hole in the ground to tracks more than 700 feet beneath the surface. With other mechanics, miners and machinery operators, he hops aboard a small, slow-moving locomotive for the half-hour, four-mile ride far below the streets, subways and sewer pipes of Queens. DuBois' job is at the head of a tunnel where a gigantic rock-chewing machine grinds ancient granite into gravel, adding as much as 75 feet of new, smoothly-bored tunnel behind it every day.

DuBois is an Operating Engineer whose task it is to maintain the multi-million-dollar Tunnel Boring Machine (TBM). He is 28 years old and has been on the job for three years. It is conceivable that he will be ready to retire, his yet-unborn children grown to adulthood, by the time this construction project, which started before *he* was born, is completed.

It is City Tunnel #3, New York's largest, some would say most crucial, public works project to date. The 55-mile tunnel, from 200 to 800 feet underground, will carry water from the balancing reservoir at Hillview in Yonkers to four of the

city's five boroughs. It will improve water pressure, and allow City Tunnels #1 and #2 to be shut down and inspected. Those delivery conduits, completed in 1917 and 1936, respectively, have never been examined because there are no guarantees that once they are shut down and drained, the aging valves that control the flow of water will continue to function properly. If either of the existing city tunnels were to be out of service, even temporarily for inspection, half of the city of eight million people would be out of water, a prospect that could have disastrous social, economic and public health consequences.

But the solution to that potential calamity has been a long time coming. First proposed in 1954, when work on the Cannonsville Reservoir was just getting under way, the tunnel was designed in the early 1960s. Construction didn't start until 1970, however, because the Board of Water Supply was tending to the more immediate water needs of Staten Island (Chapter 11). Litigation with the initial contracting consortium, and the city's acute fiscal problems of the mid-1970s, mothballed the project for nearly three years. It wasn't until 1998 that the first 12.5-mile leg of the tunnel was placed in service. And the entire project is not expected to be finished until 2020, at an estimated cost of $6 billion.

The project is designed in four stages:[1]

- Stage 1 consists of 12.5 miles of concrete-lined tunnel stretching from Hillview Reservoir in

---

Facing page: The route of the third city water tunnel. NYC DEP.

245

Yonkers beneath the Bronx and Manhattan to Astoria, Queens. The tunnel ranges in diameter from 20 to 24 feet. It includes 14 riser shafts from which water is fed to the distribution mains just under the surface, and three underground valve chambers (at Van Cortlandt Park in the Bronx, Roosevelt Island and Central Park in Manhattan). Stage 1 was placed on line in August 1998.

Stage 2 consists of the 10-mile Brooklyn-Queens tunnel, under construction since 1993, and the five-mile Manhattan tunnel, which was expected to be put out to bid in late 1999.

The Brooklyn-Queens section has two distinct legs: The 5.5-mile Brooklyn portion of the tunnel begins in Red Hook (where the Richmond Tunnel currently carries water across the Narrows to Staten Island), and runs beneath Park Slope, Bedford-Stuyvesant and Bushwick to Maspeth, Queens. From Maspeth, the five-mile Queens portion of the tunnel traverses Woodside and Astoria, where it meets the Stage 1 tunnel. The tunnel is 20 feet in diameter in Queens and steps down to 16 feet in Brooklyn. There is an underground valve chamber at 25th Ave. and 72nd St. in Queens.

The Manhattan leg of Stage 2 will be five miles long and 10 feet in diameter. It will start in Central Park at the valve chamber built during Stage 1, and will run south along the west side of Manhattan and then east to the vicinity of South Street Seaport. A total of 16 riser shafts will deliver water from the deep tunnel to street level.

- Stage 3 is a 16-mile tunnel from the Kensico Reservoir in Westchester County to the Van Cortlandt Park valve chamber in The Bronx. This will parallel the Catskill and Delaware Aqueducts, providing additional, and alternative, delivery capacity.
- Stage 4 will be 14 miles long and will provide water to eastern parts of the Bronx and Queens. This final stage will extend southeast through the Bronx from the Van Cortlandt Park valve

chamber, under the East River to Flushing, Queens.

The Board of Water Supply began studying the need for and feasibility of a third city tunnel as early as 1954. By 1962, it had examined population and consumption trends, the number of buildings and their sizes, actual quantities and pressures of water being delivered, geologic formations and potential hydraulic challenges along proposed tunnel routes.[2] Preliminary plans, estimates and recommendations were submitted to the city's Board of Estimate in July 1966, but funds for the preparation of final designs for Stage 1 were not appropriated until 1969. To expedite the process, the BWS engaged consulting engineer Charles T. Main to work with agency engineers on contract drawings and specifications.[3]

On Jan. 12, 1970, three contracts totaling $222 million for the construction of Stage 1, City Tunnel #3 were awarded to a consortium of six companies. The joint venture involved Walsh Construction Co., Dravo Company, S. J. Groves & Sons, Arundel Corp., L. E. Dixon Co. and Ostrander Construction Co.[4]

At first, the project made good progress. A connecting conduit at Hillview Reservoir was built and about 1800 feet of tunnel excavated to the Van Cortlandt Park valve chamber. This complex, designed to be the hub of the entire city delivery system, consists of a series of shafts, tunnels, manifolds and control structures centered in a massive room 250 feet beneath the park. The main chamber is 44 feet high, 44 feet wide and 620 feet long (comparable to two football fields). Two 24-foot manifolds (concrete lined pressure tunnels), 560 and 600 feet long, parallel the north and south sides of the chamber and serve as receiving tanks in routing the flow of water into 17 right-angle laterals. The laterals, concrete- and steel-lined tunnels that are eight feet in diameter, are arranged to direct water from multiple sources to several destinations. A rectangular transfer pit with rails and a car for transport of equipment and materials runs the full length of the chamber[5]

The sinking of shafts to the chamber was begun in April of 1970. Some of the nine vertical shafts built to the chamber complex were constructed using the raised bore method. Rather than excavating them from the surface using standard blast and muck techniques, a hole about a foot in diameter was drilled from bedrock exposed at the surface to the excavated shaft bottom, where a rotary-drilling machine was assembled to penetrate upwards. Debris was removed from below.[6]

Another shaft-sinking technique used along some parts of the tunnel line involved the freezing of wet, unstable ground so excavation could take place. A well-drilling-type rig was brought in to drill a circular pattern of about 50 holes to bedrock. Pipes were placed in the holes and a special plant using ammonia as the refrigerant was set up to circulate chilled salt water through the pipes. Over a period of weeks, the soft ground would freeze in widening cylinders as heat was drawn from the ground and transferred to the brine, which was then recooled and recirculated. With the ground frozen, excavation downward would commence using explosives. Once the shaft was sunk, it was lined with concrete, which sealed off water infiltration, enabling the refrigeration to be discontinued.[7]

Most shaft work at VanCortlandt Park was completed in 1972, when excavation of the chamber itself commenced. Drilling and blasting went on for most of the year, leading to a major dispute between the BWS and the contractor over the structural condition of the chamber. "The rock haunches and walls of the chamber were severely damaged by his (contractor's) methods of blasting, thus removing the portions of the necessary support for the concrete roof arch," explained the 1973 BWS Annual Report. More than 4,500 rock bolts from eight to 14 feet long were installed, along with wire mesh, to provide roof and side wall support and prevent small rock pieces from falling from the arch. Later, under another contract, concrete girders were cast to replace portions of the haunch (the section on either side of the arch).[8]

The contractor suspended work in the valve chamber and associated openings in March 1973, with 90 percent of the excavation complete.[9] Just

Chilled salt water was circulated through pipes to freeze sodden ground so that shafts could be excavated for the construction of City Tunnel #3. Stuart Williams.

6.8 miles of tunnel had been completed by that time.[10]

In addition to the controversy over the chamber blasting, disputes had arisen over change orders and additional compensation sought by the contractors to handle what they contended were unforeseen conditions. The city pointed to excessive use of steel reinforcement in the tunnel; the contractor claimed the city's assessment of rock conditions had been incorrect. The result was the termination of all contracts in July 1975, litigation brought by the joint venture against the city, and related court action brought by the sandhogs union, Local #147. The union, which had 1,200 men at work on the project, sought immediate resumption of work, but they were destined to wait.[11]

The Van Cortlandt Valve Chamber is to be the hub of the city's water delivery system. It was placed into service in 1998 upon activation of the first 13-mile section of City Tunnel #3 from Hillview Reservoir. NYC DEP.

The city's serious financial difficulties of the mid-1970s called a halt to all but maintenance of the excavated portions of tunnel, the hollowed-out valve chamber and hundreds of pieces of construction equipment. There were even calls from some city officials to abandon the project entirely. "I felt like the Dutch boy with his finger in the dike," recalled Martin Hauptman, chief engineer of the BWS at the time.[12] He and others pushed for reinstatement of the work, as they did not want to see the money, effort and lives (16 of them by 1977)[13] thus far expended on the project go for naught.

In 1977, work resumed, and over the next several years a number of individual contracts were let to complete unfinished portions of Stage 1, including tunnel concreting and the valve chambers at Roosevelt Island (122 feet long, 60 feet wide and 70 feet high) and Central Park (70 feet long, 45

feet high and 60 feet high).[14] In 1982, nine years after the Van Cortlandt complex had been left in limbo, a contract was awarded to finish excavation and concrete work there. In 1985, another was let to install 17 massive 35-ton valves, along with meters, and dewatering, lighting and other electrical and mechanical systems.[15] The valves were manufactured in Japan, and city inspectors lived there for more than two years to make sure the equipment was built to exact specifications. Valves for other parts of City Tunnel #3 were built in Austria and South America.[16]

The value of a valve well made was amply demonstrated in the mid-1970s when a water main broke at St. Nicholas Ave. near a shaft from the 60-year-old City Tunnel #1. The gushing water carved a canyon in the street, a canyon that had to be crossed in order to get to the shaft to shut off the water by closing an aging riser valve. A pair of

The 54-mile-long City Tunnel #3 was begun in 1970. It is not expected to be completed until 2020. NYC DEP.
Photos above and opposite by Carl Ambrose.

intrepid emergency workers stretched a ladder across the chasm to reach the valve and shut off the torrent. Had they not been able to do that, officials said they might have had to cut off the supply at Hillview Reservoir, affecting far greater numbers of people. Failure of a tunnel section valve deep down at tunnel level would have the same impact, and that's a prospect city water tunnelers hope to avert by building the third major city conduit.[17]

The tunnel portion of Stage 1 was built in much the same way previous city water tunnels were driven, using platforms called "jumbos" from which men with powerful drills punched holes in the rock face, loaded the holes with dynamite, and then blasted the circular tunnel 14 feet at a time. More than 7,000 such blasts were needed to excavate Stage 1, and two million cubic yards of rock spoil were removed, enough to fill Madison Square Garden five times. Excavation was finished Feb. 11, 1985, when the last two sections of tunnel were joined far beneath 118th St. and Amsterdam Ave. Three-quarters of a million cubic yards of concrete were used to line the 12.5 miles of tunnel.[18]

Some sections of bad ground required additional support. Retired sandhog Stuart Williams recalled the day he "heard the earth groaning and moaning" hours before a 100-foot section of the tunnel collapsed. "There were boulders as big as a room," said Mr. Williams. Workers were at lunch when the cave-in occurred in the tunnel being driven from a shaft at Highbridge Park, not far from the 1848 stone-arched bridge that carried the original Croton Aqueduct across the Harlem River. It took more than three months to fill the crater with concrete and drive the tunnel anew through that concrete plug.[19]

Tunnel driving technique changed with the introduction of the TBM for the construction of Stage 2. The second phase of City Tunnel #3 began in early 1993, when the joint venture of Schiavone-Shea of Secaucus, N.J., won Contract 543B, the excavation and lining of the Brooklyn portion of the Queens-Brooklyn tunnel. Schiavone-Shea, which bid $138.7 million, brought in a refurbished TBM that had already carved subway tunnels in New York City and Montreal, lowered it piece by piece down the working shaft, 23B, in Red Hook, Brooklyn, assembled it below, then set it to work on the tunnel heading.[20] The joint venture of Grow Tunneling, Perini Corp. and Skanska, which had won the $172 million contract for the Queens portion of the tunnel in August, 1995, also purchased a TBM, for $12 million.[21]

Known as "the mole," the TBM chips off sections of bedrock through the continuous rotation of some 50 tungsten carbide cutters mounted on a circular steel head. An operator in an enclosed, computer-equipped cab navigates the huge machine forward along the laser-guided tunnel line. Ground up rock is directed onto a conveyor within the machine, and out the back, where the muck is transferred to a trailing conveyor bolted to the tunnel wall and lengthened as the TBM progresses. The muck is thus transported back to the shaft, where a vertical conveyor carries it to the surface for disposal. (Muck from Tunnel #3 has been used to cover Fresh Kills Landfill on Staten Island, and to line Long Island railroad track beds.) The "mole" requires 13,200 volts to run its 10 motors, which are started two at a time because of the tremendous electricity demand. In addition to two transformers, the 580-ton TBM carries fresh water tanks, pumps and sprayers for wetting the cutter head and keeping the dust down.[22]

Technology for the TBM was perfected during construction of the Chunnel beneath the English Channel. The Brooklyn TBM excavated up to 90 feet per day, averaging 42 feet. In Queens, the TBM managed up to 75 feet in one day.

These machines have several advantages over explosives. The conduit produced by a TBM is very smooth and so requires less concrete lining since there are fewer rock voids to fill. The TBM is safer than explosives, and there is less surface disruption. The muck is much finer, in some cases the size of gravel, making disposal and reuse somewhat easier. The TBM does produce a great deal of dust, however, and that is a health concern for many workers. It's also very noisy for long periods of time.

Another concern is the elimination of jobs. TBMs require one-fourth of the manpower of conventional tunnel excavation procedures. Sandhog Local #147, which had 2,200 members in the early days of Tunnel #3, was down to 650 members in 1999, according to local President Richard Fitzsimmons Sr. But of course TBMs can't run themselves. Such machines require men to operate and maintain them, to clear the base from which they operate, to shore up the roof and sidewalls that surround them. About 150 workers are employed in three daily shifts at Shaft #19B in Maspeth, Queens. One of them is Richard DuBois, whose job it is to crawl through a garbage-can-sized access hole in the body of the TBM to make repairs, or to replace the 400-pound cutters. Excavation is usually done on the evening and night shifts, with maintenance done during the day. Eight to 10 cutters have to be replaced each day, depending on the type of rock being penetrated, DuBois says.

The TBM at work on the Queens tunnel is pointed toward Roosevelt Island, where a "hole-through" into the tunnel dug during Stage I was anticipated by mid-1999. Agents of international firms exploring the possibility of building portions of the enormous Three Gorges hydroelectric project in China have reportedly expressed some interest in buying the Queens TBM, built by Atlas Capco Robbins.[23]

The TBM which in February of 1998 finished its work on the Brooklyn section of the city tunnel was subsequently dismantled, many of its parts sold.[24] "In New York rock, five miles is long enough," remarks Dale Estus, walking boss for Shea-Schiavone. Estus has been working on City Tunnel #3 since 1972. His father, Leonard Estus, worked on the West Delaware Tunnel and then took what he learned around the world, to a huge storm-sewer project in Chicago and a hydroelectric tunnel in New Zealand. The elder Estus was nick-named Haybag, a moniker later assumed by his son, who also inherited his father's affection for the sandhog life.[25]

In early 1999, Dale Estus was supervising the installation of 300 feet of pipe to be used as a liner in two sections of the Brooklyn tunnel, where an area of clay soils made the direct application of concrete inadvisable. The steel pipe was lowered down the 600-foot-deep Shaft 20B at Seigel & White Streets, then transported four miles down the tunnel to be installed. The liner would be concreted to a diameter of 12 feet.

It is stressful work, but Estus acknowledges he makes a very good living at what he does, enough so that the 82-mile commute one way from his home in Middletown doesn't bother him that much. He carpools to the New York job with three other upstate men with family ties to the profes-sion. That is true of many of the sandhogs, who are typically of Irish, Scottish, Caribbean and Eastern European extraction. Many of those now working on City Tunnel #3 had fathers, uncles and grandfa-thers who worked on the Rondout, Neversink, Pepacton and Cannonsville Reservoir and tunnel jobs.

"A lot of people just won't do it, won't go underground, period. But I grew up around it," says David Walker, an operating engineer on the city water tunnel. His father, Joe Walker, was a sandhog, and his grandfather, Alexander Walker, was a blacksmith on the Schoharie Reservoir pro-ject in the 1920s before turning to city tunnel work.[26]

They are a close fraternity, drawn together by a tradition of shared danger and accomplishment. Perhaps that's why Chris Fitzsimmons, 24, took a brief hiatus from his work pumping grout behind

Sandhogs are a tight knit fraternity. Stuart Williams, front, second from right, provided the photograph.

The 24-foot diameter City Tunnel #3 is designed to carry a billion gallons of water per day. NYC DEP.
Photo by Carl Ambrose.

the concrete lining of a section of the Brooklyn tunnel to attend a ceremony marking the initiation of Stage 1 of City Tunnel #3 after several years of testing the complex system.

The brother of sandhog Local #147 Business Agent Richard T. Fitzsimmons, and the son of the union's President, Chris Fitzsimmons said he could not stay away from the event, even though he'd only worked on the project for the past two years. The ceremony was held on a specially constructed platform extending out into the renamed Jackie Kennedy Onassis Reservoir in Central Park, where the fountain that so captivated crowds when Catskill water was introduced to Manhattan back in 1917 was reactivated for the occasion. Mayor Rudolph Giuliani and others proclaimed as "he-

roes" the system's workers, engineers and visionary planners.

Surrounded by politicians and bureaucrats, Chris Fitzsimmons and several fellow sandhogs were not a bit self-conscious in their knee-high, muddy rubber boots, dirty T-shirts and scraped blue hard hats. They were there to pay tribute to the 24 people killed in City Tunnel #3. The names of fellow sandhogs, inspectors, engineers, even a 12-year-old boy who fell into a shaft, were read, accompanied by the tolling of a memorial bell. The memories of some of the men stretched back to 1970, when Charles Gatrell became the project's first victim, falling through a broken board into a shaft. Certainly many remained affected by the more recent death of 33-year-old Anthony Oddo, swept with seven co-workers from two catwalks by a 16-ton winch that pinballed down a shaft just before Thanksgiving in 1993.

Even with the changing nature of the job, there will also be higher-than-average danger associated with working in a subterranean world most of us never see. But Chris Fitzsimmons is not dissuaded by the risks, and chose to return to the tunnel rather than follow up on a college degree in psychology and criminal justice. Says Fitzsimmons, "This is where I want to be."

Taking obvious pride in the new stretch of tunnel were several city engineers, some of whom had spent their entire careers on this project. There was Sam Sigman, who had been Chief of Water Works Construction during the first 20 years of Tunnel #3. (Nearly 60 years earlier, Mr. Sigman had been inspecting fill on the Neversink Dam.) And there was Michael Greenberg, Mr. Sigman's successor, who felt the long wait to see water in the new pipes would be worth it. "It's hard to be complacent," he said. "Everybody feels they're part of something special."

Mr. Greenberg's deputy, George Vaiana echoed that sentiment. An Italian immigrant who came to this country at the age of 18 in 1956, Mr. Vaiana helped plot the big Van Cortlandt valve chamber in the 1960s, and then spent three years surveying the line of the Brooklyn tunnel. "Now they use satellite positioning systems, so that one guy can spend four days doing something it took three people three years to do," says Mr. Vaiana.

During the lengthy prosecution of City Tunnel #3, more than tunnel driving and surveying methodologies had changed. The venerable Board of Water Supply, which had devised, designed and developed most of New York City's enviable water system, faded away in a bureaucratic re-shuffling that left a new agency, the Department of Environmental Protection (DEP), in charge of the system. The BWS, headed by three commissioners, had existed as a separate, semi-autonomous agency until the Koch administration, in 1978, opted to dispense with the commissioners and attach the board to the Department of Water Resources. In 1981, that department's Bureau of Water Supply was merged with the Board of Water Supply.[27]

The move effectively ended the 76-year tenure of the BWS that had for so long represented vision and progress to some, arrogance and indifference to others. Its successor, the DEP, would be forced to come to terms with the legacy of the BWS when, in 1990, it imposed tightened restrictions on the lands and people surrounding its hard-won reservoirs.

More than 80,000 water samples are taken each year from the city's reservoirs
and at points along the distribution system to assure its purity.
Reginald Oberlag, Catskill Center for Conservation and Development.

22. To the Future. . .

ITH the completion of its upstate water collection system, the city settled into an operation and maintenance mode as far as the dams and reservoirs were concerned. To keep the water clean, it relied on rules for land use and activity that were adopted in 1953 and were based on the New York State Sanitary Code. Booklets distributed by the city's Department of Water Supply, Gas and Electricity, which operated the system once the Board of Water Supply finished construction, specified what residents near reservoirs and feeder streams could and could not do: Swimming, wading or washing clothes in water bodies owned by the city were forbidden; barnyard run-off wasn't supposed to reach streams that fed reservoirs; septic tanks and cesspools were relegated to certain distances from streams.

The requirements "aroused considerable consternation among householders. . . One dairyman said he would be unable to retain his livelihood if he had to comply strictly with the regulations at his own expense. . ."[1]

Still, the regulations stood. Over the years, however, faced with a huge watershed and a limited number of inspectors and water supply police, the city's enforcement of the provisions was relatively relaxed. So, in 1990, when the city's Department of Environmental Protection (DEP) issued revised, much tougher, rules of conduct in its watershed,

surprised residents, businesspeople and officials echoed the "consternation" from 40 years earlier.

The city's stricter stance was prompted by new nationwide rules issued by the U. S. Environmental Protection Agency under 1986 Clean Water Act Amendments. The 1989 Surface Water Treatment Rule required all surface drinking water supplies to be filtered, unless municipalities and water suppliers could prove they could otherwise adequately protect their water sources.

Hoping to avoid filtering 1.2 billion gallons of Catskill-Delaware water a day at a plant some estimated could cost as much as $8 billion, the city tightened up its existing regulations and added several new ones. But it did not consult watershed residents, businesspeople or officials, who, through most of 1990, waited and worried about what those new rules would contain, while hearing rumors and reports that land acquisition and the prohibition of development would be at the top of the city's priority list.

Initial rumblings were expressed that spring, as the DEP advised town planning boards and code enforcement officials to withhold building permits for homes and other structures until the agency approved septic system plans for the properties. Real estate brokers and local officials objected, citing the dampening effect that would have on land sales and proclaiming it an infringement on home rule. "Should we roll over and allow New York City to control our economy?" one Dela-

Hard talk and tough choices faced the Coalition of Watershed Towns (CWT) during six years of negotiations with the City of New York about its plans to acquire land and impose strict land use regulations in its 2,000-square-mile watershed. Members of, and alternates to, the executive committee of the CWT at a 1990 meeting included (l. to r.) Robert Homovich, Velma Clark, Ewald Schwartzenegger, Anthony Bucca, Chairman Perry Shelton, Clayton Brooks, James Gorman, Robert Adsit and James Brown. K. O. Wilson.

ware County broker asked. "This would put the future in their hands."[2] "We cannot afford to let New York City buy more of our land and increase its control over the watershed without considering the economic impact these actions will have on our communities. The people of the Catskills will not allow it," opined State Assemblyman Richard Coombe of Grahamsville.[3]

Defiant statements such as those became commonplace---and louder---once the discussion draft of the new regulations was released Sept. 11, 1990. The rules governed activities ranging from parking lot construction and road salt storage to septic system placement and cemetery expansions. It restricted just about everything within unspecified "buffer zones" along watercourses. "This is not an attempt to zone the Croton or Catskill watersheds," explained DEP Commissioner Albert Appleton in unveiling the document at a Kingston press conference. "This is an attempt to preserve water quality." Appleton admitted, though, that he anticipated the debate over the draft rules would get "testy."[4]

Upstate residents did not disappoint him. Two days after the 106-page draft was released, Assemblyman Coombe and State Senator Charles Cook of Delhi exhorted 75 members of the Catskill

Mountain Builders and Contractors Association to fight the proposed regulations. On September 17, the DEP held the first of several informational meetings on the regulations in Delhi, where 250 mostly angry people demanded to see the proof that the water supply was being jeopardized and the science that showed how stricter regulations would improve it.[5]

A citizens' committee, initially launched by Senator Cook to review the proposed state Commission on the Catskills in the 21st Century, concentrated instead on examining the new watershed rules with an eye toward presenting an alternative proposal to the city. Business associations, public agencies, cultural groups and sportsmen's organizations met to discuss potential ramifications of the rules, and to draft their own position papers. The region's farmers, claiming the prohibitions against livestock and farm activities within 100 feet of watercourses would essentially put them out of business, coalesced into an organization that would ultimately bargain for a separate deal with the city, winning major concessions and millions of dollars to support farm improvements.[6]

The State Senate's Local Government Committee held a series of public hearings on the regulations, chaired by Charles Cook. A native of Rock

Royal, the Senator brought to the process his memories of the "slow strangulation" of the Trout Creek valley as the Cannonsville Reservoir was constructed. "In those days, we didn't fight very much. People complained, people cried, but eventually they just packed their belongings and left," Cook recalled, hailing the "popular uprising" that had materialized against the city three decades later. Senator Cook would later introduce unsuccessful legislation to limit the city's authority in the watershed, but he managed to secure considerable public monies to support the fight against the city.

At the hearings, the city defended its intent while suggesting it might revise the details. Commissioner Appleton said because farms and open space were preferable to homesites and associated roads and septic systems, the city might be willing to alter "burdensome" agricultural restrictions. But he said the requirement that municipalities store their road salt and deicing materials in sealed buildings would remain. "Chloride levels in the reservoirs are going up very dramatically," the commissioner said at a Nov. 13, 1990, hearing in Grand Gorge. "If this pace continues, people on low-sodium diets would not be able to drink New York City water."[7]

A few people agreed with the city's need to add more barriers to watershed pollutants, claiming the threat of farmland and mountaintop "urbanization" was real. But most agreed with a Delaware County farmer who said, "For generations, Jersey cows have paid our bills. Is it fair that now they can't drink out of our brook that we pay taxes on?"[8]

During the winter and through the spring of 1991, the watershed regulations were the talk of the towns. The city held scoping sessions to pinpoint issues and options to include in the revision of the rules, which it wanted to see approved and implemented by the end of the year. More than 500 people attended the sessions, at which comments ranged from the succinct "Get off our backs," to dire predictions that the added stress provoked by tougher restrictions would result in more cases of depression and alcoholism among area residents.[9]

In March, recognizing that there was strength in numbers, and that legal arguments and scientific facts would carry more weight with the city than emotional appeals, representatives of towns and villages in five Catskill counties met in the school cafeteria in Margaretville. There, they unanimously approved the creation of the Coalition of Watershed Towns. "The United States had assembled a 'coalition' of nations to battle Iraq in the Persian Gulf War at about this time, so the word 'coalition' had a particularly strong meaning," recalled Kenneth Markert, planning director for Delaware County and one of those who organized the new group.[10]

The CWT was led by a nine-member executive committee: Velma Clark of Delhi, Perry Shelton of Tompkins, Robert Homovich of Colchester, Russell Roefs of Woodstock, Jim Brown of Gilboa, Georgianna Lepke of Neversink, Clayton Brooks of Denning, Anthony Bucca of Hunter and Ronald Wagner of Jewett. The coalition asked member towns (there were eventually 35 of them) to contribute to a legal fund, and then hired the law firm of White, Osterman & Hanna to take on City Hall. Perry Shelton, who had been supervisor of Tompkins since the city's Board of Water Supply had claimed much of the township for the Cannonsville Reservoir 30 years before, was elected the coalition's first chairman.[11]

Thus began four years of difficult relations between the city and upstate towns. More hearings were conducted on the proposed regulations and on the Draft Environmental Impact Statement prepared by the city. One of them, in Walton in September 1993, drew 700 people and elicited six hours of mostly negative comments and testimony. Protesters carried signs reading, "Free the Watershed" and "Remember Arena," a reference to one of the many communities submerged beneath city reservoirs.[12]

The following spring, after a change in city administration led by new Mayor Rudolph Giuliani, DEP Commissioner Albert Appleton was replaced by Marilyn Gelber, a former social worker and city planner, who left a post as executive assistant to the Brooklyn Borough President

Left to right: Robert F. Kennedy, Jr., attorney for Hudson Riverkeeper and a spokesman for environmental interests during the watershed negotiations. Daniel Ruzow, an attorney for Whiteman, Osterman & Hanna which represented the Coalition of Watershed Towns. Albert Appleton, New York City Department of Environmental Protection Commissioner. All K. O. Wilson.

to take the difficult DEP post.[13] Gelber won the respect, even affection, of many upstaters by traveling frequently to the region to talk with local representatives. And there were ancillary efforts to cultivate better upstate-downstate relationships, such as a bus trip in September 1993 that brought representatives from the city mayor's office, the city council and environmental activist groups to visit the source of their water supply and break bread with Catskill residents and leaders.

Meanwhile, the Ad Hoc Task Force on Agriculture and New York City Watershed Regulations came to terms with the DEP on a non-regulatory, voluntary system of curbing farm pollutants. Recommendations prepared by the group in late 1991 led to the formation of the Watershed Agricultural Council, which was allotted $4 million by the city to institute on 10 pilot farms a "Whole Farm Planning" system not only to improve water quality but also to enhance farmers' economic viability. The successful pilot program led to its expansion throughout the watershed and the allocation of an additional $35.2 million from the city.[14] Using "kitchen table diplomacy," WAC representatives convinced fellow farmers of the value of the program, and by 1997, 235 farms, more than 85 percent of those eligible, were participating.[15]

In 1994, the coalition and the city almost agreed on a similar concept for "Whole Community Planning." But late that year, the DEP released the final draft of its proposed Watershed Regulations, which included the federally-mandated acquisition of 80,000 acres of land. (The EPA had required the land purchases in a three-year filtration waiver issued in December 1993.) The city declined to rule out the possibility that it would use condemnation to acquire the land, and the coalition refused to negotiate further without that assurance.[16] The coalition had earlier filed suit against the city and the New York State Dept. of Environmental Conservation (DEC), challenging the environmental review of the watershed regulations, and the land acquisition plan.

In 1995, Governor George Pataki prevailed on the warring factions to come together to hammer out an agreement. Led by Pataki's chief counsel, Michael Finnegan, intense negotiations went on for seven months, involving attorneys and representatives from federal and state agencies, environmental groups, Croton system townships and the coalition. An Agreement in Principle was announced Nov. 2, 1995. It took another 10 months for the complex details of the pact to be developed into the New York City Watershed Memorandum of Agreement (MOA), a three-volume, 1,500-page document that New York City Mayor Rudolph Giuliani called "a model for the future."

Released to the public Sept. 10, 1996, the MOA was seen as a triumph "against what seemed insurmountable odds," according to the governor. The good will evident at that occasion was reflected in the comments of Coalition Chairman Perry Shelton, who called former DEP Commissioner Marilyn Gelber "the sweetheart of the Catskills." (Gelber had been succeeded a month before by Joel Miele, an engineer and former city planning commissioner and building commissioner.) Shelton also then shook hands with environmental attorney Robert Kennedy Jr. Kennedy, prosecuting counsel for Riverkeeper, Inc., had been seen by upstate officials as an adversary seeking to close the Catskills to development, but was now viewed as a partner in the agreement to both protect the natural resources of the region and preserve its communities. Kennedy, who had gained a reputation as a staunch environmental advocate in high-profile cases against Hudson River polluters, later said, "If my whole life's work was to save a chunk of the New York City watershed and nothing more, I would be able to face my children."[17]

Like a proud parent finally able to relax after a long and tortuous labor, a city attorney passed out cigars at the press event where the MOA was at last revealed. But Coalition negotiator Alan Rosa warned that the hard part of actually raising that baby was about to begin.[18]

The MOA was signed with great fanfare Jan. 17, 1997 at the State Capitol in Albany. With 70 municipalities and five environmental organizations as parties. it went into effect in April of that year. The agreement has become internationally recognized as a ground-breaking example of mutually beneficial cooperation between people and agencies sharing a history of conflict and animosity.

The city got what it wanted—a five-year Filtration Avoidance Determination (a waiver) from the EPA, allowing time to prove, through revised regulations and other environmental improvement measures, that an expensive filtration plant is not needed. The city also got a permit from the state to solicit the owners of up to 355,000 acres of vacant watershed land to keep it from being developed.

The federal government got what it wanted—commitment of $1.2 billion from the city for construction of wastewater treatment plants, purchase of sensitive lands, and implementation of water protection programs to assure the health of nine million people who drink New York City's water.

And the upstate communities got what they wanted—most especially a prohibition on the use of condemnation for land acquisition. The West-of-Hudson towns received financial remuneration for costs associated with complying with the new regulations; funds for environmentally sound economic development; and a locally-administered organization—the Catskill Watershed Corporation (CWC)—to develop and run environmental, economic development and education programs in the Catskill-Delaware Watershed.

Most members of the Coalition of Watershed Towns' executive committee became the first directors of the CWC, along with city, state and environmental representatives. Alan Rosa, supervisor of the Town of Middletown, Delaware County, became the first president of the CWC Board of Directors. By the end of its first year, the CWC, based in Margaretville, Delaware County, had a staff of 12 people implementing seven major MOA programs. A study to provide recommended economic development programs for the city-funded $60 million Catskill Fund for the Future was also under way.

East of the Hudson River, the city agreed to pay $68 million to Westchester and Putnam Counties to fund septic repairs, erosion controls, sand and salt storage facilities and other water quality projects identified through a comprehensive watershed planning process.

To seal the deal, the city issued $11 million in "Good Neighbor" payments to towns, villages and counties based on their respective acreages in the watershed. The money could be used for virtually any purpose the municipalities chose, other than tax reduction.

The MOA also provided for a Watershed Protection and Partnership Council made up of the

New York State Governor George Pataki addressed a crowd of officials and media representatives at the formal signing of the New York City Watershed Memorandum of Agreement in January 1997. Pictured behind the governor are, left to right, State Senator Charles Cook, Town of Middletown Supervisor Alan Rosa (partially hidden), Town of Hunter Supervisor Anthony Bucca, Robert F. Kennedy Jr. of Hudson Riverkeeper, New York City Department of Environmental Protection Commissioner Joel Miele, United States Environmental Protection Agency Region 2 Administrator Jeanne Fox, New York City Mayor Rudolph Giuliani, Putnam County Executive Robert Bondi and State Senator Carl Marcellino. NYC DEP.

many parties to the landmark agreement. The council's role is to monitor progress of the MOA, and to provide a forum to resolve disputes that will inevitably arise.[19] The council's first executive director, named in September 1998, is William Harding, former supervisor of the Westchester County Town of Somers and a principal spokesman for the East-of-Hudson towns during the negotiations.

Central to the agreement was the adoption of "Rules and Regulations for the Protection from Contamination, Degradation and Pollution of the New York City Water Supply and Its Sources." The rules went into effect May 1, 1997. They prohibit new septic systems, fuel tanks and imper-

vious surfaces (outside villages) within 100 feet of a watercourse; require stormwater control plans for new construction; and require municipalities to build salt storage sheds. Existing non-complying activities are grandfathered under the new rules.[20]

The DEP reorganized its upstate offices in June 1996 in anticipation of the new protection program, creating the Bureau of Water Supply, Quality and Protection to manage the upstate water supply system as well as the many aspects of the watershed agreement. It has several divisions:[21]

- The Operations and Engineering Division manages the infrastructure (dams, gate houses, reservoirs, sewage treatment plants, and city-owned bridges and roads). An extensive program of rebuilding the city's dams, starting with the oldest ones, in the Croton System, was launched in 1995. By early 1999, the city had also upgraded its eight upstate wastewater treatment plants, and was evaluating the conditions of its tunnels and aqueducts.[22]

- The Division of Drinking Water Quality Control operates the city's laboratories and monitors water quality in reservoirs, streams and city water mains. Crucial to the objective of proving that the city's water quality meets state and federal standards, the division employs 250 bacteriologists, engineers, chemists, hydrologists and limnologists at five laboratories. More than 80,000 water samples are taken from reservoirs and from points along the city's distribution system each year, where a $7 million program to install water quality sampling stations was expected to be completed in 1999.[23]

- The Division of Watershed Planning and Community Affairs oversees the land acquisition program and watershed protection and planning efforts, in concert with upstate communities. By January 1999, the city had acquired just over 5,000 acres of land both east and west of the Hudson River.[24]

- A Watershed Protection Unit inspects septic systems and other potential pollutant sources with a total force of 68 inspectors and supervisors located east and west of the Hudson River.

- The DEP Police provide enforcement capabilities. In February 1999, the DEP had a force of 50 police officers in four precincts.[25]

Former residents of the East Branch Valley reminisce at the
annual Shavertown Old Home Day. Author's collection.

Conclusion: Pride and Sorrow

N the 157 years since the first Croton Reservoir and Aqueduct brought clean water from the wilds of Westchester County to an amazed Manhattan populace, time and changing needs have transformed the New York City water system in ways unimaginable to its founders.

The original 42-mile-long, brick-lined aqueduct, considered such a marvel in its day, is now appreciated more as a hiking trail than a water conduit, although a three-mile stretch of the aqueduct remains in use as a sort of underground "reservoir" for the village of Croton-on-Hudson.

The beautiful arched High Bridge that once carried Croton water over the Harlem River is now an historic, rather than a functional, landmark. The nearby stone tower, that once held water in a tank 150 feet above the ground to maintain water pressure for that district, still looms over its Washington Heights neighborhood, but it was long ago replaced by an electric pumping station.

The Egyptian-styled distributing reservoir at 5th Avenue and 42nd Street (Bryant Park) was removed at the turn of the century, replaced by the New York Public Library. In 1925, the Yorkville receiving reservoir in Central Park was demolished to create the Great Lawn.

But there have been adjuncts to the system, as well. Hydro-electric power plants were installed at Kensico and Ashokan Reservoirs by the New York State Power Authority in the 1980s.

While Croton engineer John B. Jervis and the people of his day would not recognize the city that New York has become, the Big Apple is just as dependent on clean water in 1999 as it was in 1842. "It is taken for granted by just about everyone in the city," acknowledged Mayor Rudolph Giuliani at the initiation ceremony for City Tunnel #3 in 1998. In 1955, another Mayor, Robert Wagner, said much the same thing at the groundbreaking ceremony for the Cannonsville project, adding, "Our water supply has been more responsible for our preeminence as a city than any other natural advantage." Still earlier, in 1922, yet another mayor, George B. McClellan, described the building of the Catskill System as "a fairy tale" and Chief Engineer J. Waldo Smith as the magician: "You have waved your wand and by its magic you have made it possible for six million people to live in this city of ours, where three million were before."

But a fairy tale it most assuredly was not. There was much more hard work than magic involved for countless engineers, surveyors, clerks, contractors and laborers. Their accomplishments, though unheralded today, remain a source of pride for their descendants, people like Josephine Conforti Pofill, who says, "As kids, we would go for rides with my father around the Kensico, and he would say, 'See that wall over there? Your grandfather cut that stone.'"

A sadder inheritance was left to the thousands of families displaced by the reservoir projects. For just as the courses of ancient rivers were shifted by men and machines, so too were the lives of countless men, women and children altered forever. "Unless you have lived through having your home and whole community wiped away, you can't understand the void it leaves in you," explained Evelyn Weaver Norris in 1995 at the rededication of a church bell from the former hamlet of Union Grove. "I can never take my children and grandchildren and show them where I grew up, or where their grandparents and great-grandparents once lived."

Perhaps the best we can do is try to learn, understand, and ultimately appreciate, what it took to build this incredible water system: vision, courage, dedication, public treasure, the sacrifice of land, legacy and lives.

A Chinese proverb reminds us most succinctly----"When you drink the water, remember the spring."

The Old Croton Aqueduct is today used as a recreational trail.

Robert Kornfeld, Jr., AIA

Appendix: The System

COLLECTING

New York City's water comes from 18 reservoirs and three lakes in seven counties to the north and west. The watershed encompasses 1,969 square miles. Two balancing reservoirs and four distributing reservoirs store and release the water to the distribution system. In addition to the surface supply, a pumped groundwater supply serves consumers in Southeast Queens.

Total available capacity of 18 collecting reservoirs and three lakes is 547.5 billion gallons. Total storage capacity of six balancing and distributing facilities is 33.5 billion gallons.

Water finds its way to the Big Apple via underground waterways. Three primary aqueducts convey the water to storage and balancing facilities, while seven tunnels connect the various reservoirs and distributing points. An eighth tunnel—City Tunnel #3—was placed in partial operation during the summer of 1998.

The system is almost entirely gravity-fed; somewhat less than five percent of the supply must be pumped to its destination. The city also operates a system of wells and storage tanks in Southeast Queens which supplies 33 million gallons per day to 500,000 residents.

Some 7,300,000 people in New York City consume 1,184,000,000 gallons of water per day. An estimated one million more in four counties north of the city draw another 123 million gallons of water a day from the principal aqueducts. Fifty-six upstate cities, towns, villages and water districts, along with seven institutions and one airport, rely on this water. That represents 85 percent of the water used in Westchester County, and 7.5 percent of the water used in Putnam, Orange and Ulster Counties.

In addition to its impounded waters, the city maintains a pumping station at Chelsea on the Hudson River to relay water from the river into the Delaware Aqueduct during periods of severe drought. This plant, built in 1950 and reconstructed in 1965, has a pumping capacity of 100 million gallons per day. It has been used during three droughts—in 1965-66, 1985 and 1989.

DISTRIBUTING

New York City is served by a distribution network of 6,181 miles of water mains ranging in diameter from six to 84 inches. More than 88,600 mainline valves are used to regulate flow.

About five percent of the mains—53 miles—were laid prior to 1870. About 3,000 miles of pipe were laid between 1870 and 1930.

The city's water system also includes 15 gatehouses, 15 pump stations and eight maintenance and repair yards. There are 106,851 fire hydrants.

WASTEWATER TREATMENT

The New York City Department of Environmental Protection provides sewer service to virtually the entire city (except for portions of Staten Island, the Queens communities of Breezy Point and Douglaston, and the Brooklyn community of Seagate); as well as to eight upstate communities: Margaretville, Pine Hill, Tannersville, Grand Gorge, Chichester, Grahamsville, Mahopac and Brewster.

Facilities related to sewage handling within the city include 14 treatment plants, 89 wastewater pump stations, nine laboratories, eight sludge dewatering facilities, and three inner-harbor vessels that transport sludge between facilities. Nearly 6,500 miles of sewer pipe, 1,071 miles of which pre-date 1900, carry sanitary and storm wastewater.

The daily sewage flow in New York City is 1.349 billion gallons per day. The upstate flow is 2.7 million gallons per day.

Source: NYC Municipal Water Finance Authority Bond Prospectus, 1997

Collecting Reservoirs (18)

Note: Capacities indicate volume from spillway to minimum operating level, not total volume.

CROTON SYSTEM

Built/acquired 1837-1911

12 reservoirs and 3 controlled lakes drawing from three branches of the Croton River, and its principal tributaries the Titicus, Cross, Kisco and Muscoot Rivers; 375-square-mile watershed.

Provides approximately 10 percent of city demand: up to 250 million gallons per day

New Croton Reservoir
(Terminus for all Croton System reservoirs and lakes)

Location: Westchester County, impounds Croton River, Towns of Cortlandt, Yorktown, New Castle, Bedford, Somers

Constructed: 1892-1905 (replaced Old Croton Reservoir, built 1837-42)

Dimensions: Cornell (New Croton) Dam 2,168 feet long, 174 feet high

Reservoir: 19 miles long (38-mile shoreline), covers 1,962 acres

Capacity: 19 billion gallons

Feeds: Croton Aqueduct (24 miles) to Jerome Park Reservoir; 9 miles to 135th St. Gatehouse

Communities flooded: 4—Katonah, Golden's Bridge, Purdy's Station, Croton Falls

Residents displaced: 2,000

Graves reinterred: 1,500 from 7 cemeteries

Boyd's Corners Reservoir

Location: Putnam County, impounds West Branch of Croton River, Town of Kent

Constructed: 1866-1873; reconstructed 1988-93

Dimensions: Dam 670 feet long, 57 feet high

Reservoir: Covers 300 acres, 5.6-mile shoreline, average depth 25 feet

Capacity: 1.7 billion gallons

Communities flooded: 1—Boyd's Corners

Residents displaced: 11 families

Middle Branch Reservoir

Location: Putnam County, impounds Middle Branch of Croton River, Town of Southeast

Constructed: 1874-1878

Dimensions: Dam 515 feet long, 94 feet high

Reservoir: Covers 404 acres, 6.6-mile shoreline

Capacity: 3.0 billion gallons

East Branch Reservoir
(Connected to Bog Brook Reservoir by 1,778-foot long tunnel)

Location: Putnam County, impounds East Branch of Croton River, Town of Southeast

Constructed: 1888-1893, First in service 1891.

Dimensions: Sodom Dam 500 feet long, 78 feet high. Reservoir covers 521 acres, 11.8-mile shoreline

Capacity: 3.9 billion gallons

Communities flooded: 1—Southeast Center

Land acquired: 1,962 acres (includes land for both East Branch and Bog Brook Reservoirs)

Bog Brook Reservoir
(Connected to East Branch Reservoir by 1,778-foot-long tunnel)

Location: Putnam County, Town of Southeast

Constructed: 1889-1893; first in service 1892

Dimensions: Bog Brook Dam #1: 1,340 feet long, 60 feet high; #2: 1,956 feet long, 24 feet high. Reservoir covers 381 acres, 5.6-mile shoreline

Capacity: 4.4 billion gallons

Land acquired: 1,962 acres (includes land for both East Branch and Bog Brook Reservoirs)

Amawalk Reservoir

Location: Westchester County, impounds Muscoot River, Town of Somers

Constructed: 1889-1897

Dimensions: Dam 1,280 feet long, 80 feet high

Reservoir: 3 miles long, covers 600 acres

Capacity: 6.7 billion gallons

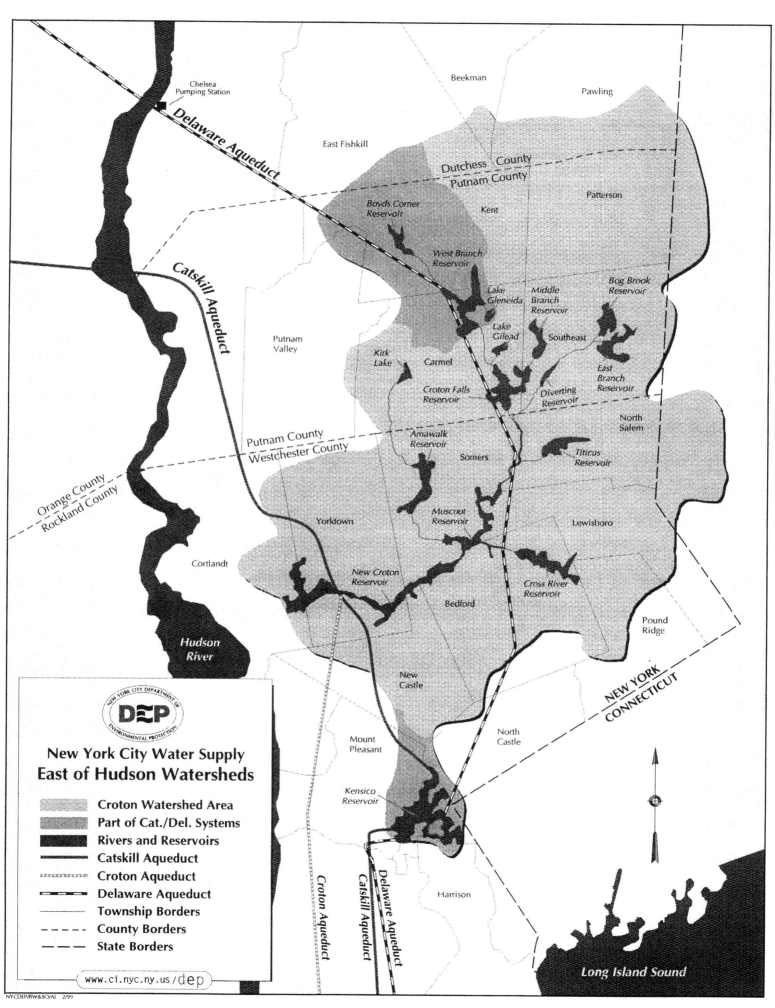

Chelsea
Pumping Station

Delaware Aqueduct

Beekman

Pawling

East Fishkill

Dutchess County
Putnam County

Patterson

Catskill Aqueduct

Boyds Corner
Reservoir

Kent

West Branch
Reservoir

Bog Brook
Reservoir

Lake
Gleneida

Middle
Branch
Reservoir

Putnam
Valley

Lake
Gilead

Southeast

Kirk
Lake

Carmel

East
Branch
Reservoir

Croton Falls
Reservoir

Diverting
Reservoir

Putnam County

North
Salem

Amawalk
Reservoir

Westchester County

Somers

Titicus
Reservoir

Orange County
Rockland County

Yorktown

Muscoot
Reservoir

Lewisboro

Cortlandt

New Croton
Reservoir

Cross River
Reservoir

Bedford

Pound
Ridge

Hudson
River

New
Castle

North
Castle

NEW YORK
CONNECTICUT

Mount
Pleasant

Kensico
Reservoir

Croton Aqueduct

Catskill Aqueduct

Delaware Aqueduct

Harrison

Long Island Sound

New York City Water Supply
East of Hudson Watersheds

NEW YORK CITY DEPARTMENT OF ENVIRONMENTAL PROTECTION

DEP

Croton Watershed Area

Part of Cat./Del. Systems

Rivers and Reservoirs

Catskill Aqueduct

Croton Aqueduct

Delaware Aqueduct

Township Borders

County Borders

State Borders

www.ci.nyc.ny.us/dep

NYCDEP/BW&SO/AJ 2/99

West Branch Reservoir

Location: Putnam County, impounds West
  Branch, Croton River, Towns of Kent, Carmel
Constructed: 1890-96; first in service 1895
Dimensions: Main dam (Carmel Dam), 1800 feet
  long, 65 feet high; auxiliary dam 720 feet long,
  45 feet high
Reservoir: Covers 1.5 square miles, maximum
  depth 43 feet
Capacity: 8 billion gallons
Land acquired: 1,690 acres

Titicus Reservoir

Location: Westchester County, impounds Titicus
  River, Town of North Salem
Constructed: 1890-1896; first in service 1893
Dimensions: Dam 1,519 feet long, 109 feet high
Reservoir Covers 682 acres, 8.6-mile shoreline
Capacity: 7.2 billion gallons
Communities flooded: 1---North Salem
Land acquired: 1,045 acres

Muscoot Reservoir

Location: Westchester County, impounds Croton
  River, Towns of Somers, Bedford
Constructed: 1901-1905
Dimensions: Dam 1,130 feet long, 58 feet high
Reservoir: Covers 931 acres, 28-mile shoreline
Capacity: 4.9 billion gallons
Communities flooded: 3--- Golden's Bridge,
  Purdys, Croton Falls
Residents displaced: 2,000

Cross River Reservoir

Location: Westchester County, impounds Cross
  River, Towns of Bedford, Lewisboro
Constructed: 1905-08
Dimensions: Dam 840 feet long, 170 feet high
Reservoir: 3.2 miles long, covers 899 acres, 13-mile
  shoreline
Capacity: 10.3 billion gallons
Communities flooded: 1---Cross River (including
  Hoyt's Mills)

Croton Falls Main Reservoir
(Connected to Diverting Reservoir
by 3,500-foot paved channel)

Location: Putnam County, impounds West
  Branch, Croton River, Towns of Carmel, South-
  east
Constructed: 1906-1911
Dimensions: Hemlock Dam 1,100 feet long, 173
  feet high
Reservoir: Covers 126 acres, 3.4-mile shoreline
Capacity: 14.2 billion gallons

Croton Falls Diverting Reservoir

Location: Putnam County, impounds East Branch,
  Croton River, Town of Southeast
Constructed: 1906-1911
Dimensions: Dam 1,185 feet long,
Capacity: 900 million gallons

Controlled Lakes
(All acquired 1870 in Town of Carmel,
Putnam County)

Lake Gleneida: 168 acres, 165 million gallons
Lake Gilead: 122 acres, 380 million gallons
Kirk Lake: 101 acres, 565 million gallons

THE CATSKILL SYSTEM

Built 1907-1927
571-square-mile watershed
Provides approximately 40 percent of city demand:
  up to 650 million gallons per day

Ashokan Reservoir

Location: Ulster County; impounds Esopus Creek,
  Towns of Olive, Hurley
Constructed: 1907-1915
Dimensions: Olive Bridge Dam 4,650 feet long, 210
  feet high
Reservoir: 12 miles long (40-mile shoreline), covers
  12.8 square miles, maximum depth 190 feet

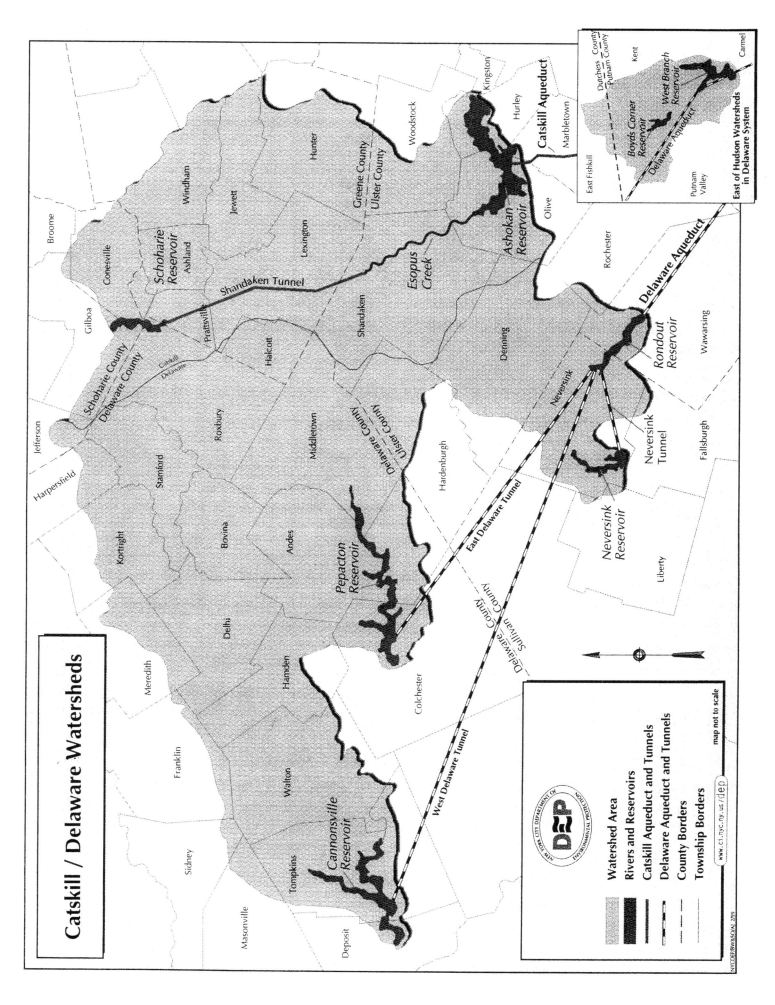

Catskill / Delaware Watersheds

Catskill Aqueduct

Delaware Aqueduct

Schoharie Reservoir

Shandaken Tunnel

Ashokan Reservoir

Esopus Creek

Rondout Reservoir

Pepacton Reservoir

Cannonsville Reservoir

Neversink Reservoir

Neversink Tunnel

East Delaware Tunnel

West Delaware Tunnel

Counties and Townships

Broome, Coneville, Gilboa, Jefferson, Harpersfield, Kortright, Stamford, Meredith, Franklin, Sidney, Masonville, Deposit, Tompkins, Walton, Hamden, Delhi, Bovina, Andes, Roxbury, Middletown, Colchester, Hardenburgh, Denning, Shandaken, Halcott, Ashland, Windham, Jewett, Lexington, Hunter, Woodstock, Kingston, Hurley, Marbletown, Olive, Rochester, Wawarsing, Fallsburgh, Liberty, Neversink, Prattsville

Schoharie County / Delaware County
Catskill / Delaware
Delaware County / Ulster County
Delaware County / Sullivan County

Greene County / Ulster County

East of Hudson Watersheds in Delaware System

Dutchess County
Putnam County
Kent
Carmel
West Branch Reservoir
Boyds Corner Reservoir
Delaware Aqueduct
East Fishkill
Putnam Valley

Legend

Watershed Area
Rivers and Reservoirs
Catskill Aqueduct and Tunnels
Delaware Aqueduct and Tunnels
County Borders
Township Borders

map not to scale

NEW YORK CITY DEPARTMENT OF
DEP
ENVIRONMENTAL PROTECTION

www.ci.nyc.ny.us/dep

NYCDEP/BWS&O/AJ 2/99

Capacity: 123 billion gallons

Feeds: Catskill Aqueduct (75 miles) to Kensico Reservoir

Communities flooded: 8: Shokan, Broadhead's Bridge, Brown's Station, Olive Bridge, West Hurley, Glenford, Olive, Ashton

Residents displaced: 2,000

Land acquired: 15,222 acres

Graves reinterred: 2,637 from 40 cemeteries and burial grounds

Schoharie Reservoir

Location: Schoharie, Delaware, Greene Counties; impounds Schoharie Creek, Towns of Gilboa, Roxbury, Prattsville

Constructed: 1919-1927; first in service 1926

Dimensions: Gilboa Dam 2,000 feet long, 182 feet high

Reservoir: 5.8 miles long (16.5-mile shoreline), covers 1.8 square miles, maximum depth 150 feet

Capacity: 17.6 billion gallons

Feeds: Shandaken Tunnel (18 miles) to Esopus Creek, to Ashokan Reservoir

Communities flooded: 1—Gilboa

Residents displaced: 350

Land acquired: 2,372 acres

Graves reinterred: 1,300 from 7 cemeteries

THE DELAWARE SYSTEM

Built 1937-1965

4 reservoirs; 1,010-square-mile watershed

Provides approximately 50 percent of city demand: up to 890 million gallons per day

Rondout Reservoir

Location: Ulster and Sullivan Counties; impounds Rondout Creek, Towns of Wawarsing, Neversink

Constructed: 1937-1943; 1946-1954. First in service 1951.

Dimensions: Merriman Dam 2,400 feet long, 195 feet high

Reservoir: 7.5 miles long, 19.4-mile shoreline, covers 2,032 acres, maximum depth 175 feet

Capacity: 49.6 billion gallons

Feeds: Delaware Aqueduct (85 miles) to Kensico Reservoir

Communities flooded: 3—Eureka, Montela, Lackawack

Residents displaced: 1,200

Land acquired: 3,513 acres

Graves reinterred: 1,622 from 7 cemeteries

Neversink Reservoir

Location: Sullivan County, impounds Neversink River, Town of Neversink

Constructed: 1941-1943; 1946-1953. First in service 1950

Dimensions: Neversink Dam 2,820 feet long, 195 feet high

Reservoir: 5 miles long, 17-mile shoreline, covers 1,480 acres, maximum depth 175 feet

Capacity: 34.9 billion gallons

Feeds: Neversink Tunnel (6 miles) to Rondout Reservoir

Communities flooded: 1—Neversink, plus settlements of Bittersweet, Aden

Residents displaced: 342

Land acquired: 6,149 acres

Graves reinterred: None

Pepacton Reservoir

Location: Delaware County, impounds East Branch of Delaware River, Towns of Colchester, Andes, Middletown

Constructed: 1947-1954

Dimensions: Downsville Dam 2,450 feet long, 204 feet high

Reservoir 18.5 miles long, 51-mile shoreline, covers 5,178 acres, maximum depth 180 feet

Capacity: 140.2 billion gallons

Feeds: East Delaware Tunnel (25 miles) to Rondout Reservoir

Communities flooded: 4—Arena, Pepacton, Shavertown, Union Grove

Residents displaced: 974

Land acquired: 13,384 acres

Graves reinterred: 2,371 from 10 cemeteries

Cannonsville Reservoir

Location: Delaware County, impounds West
   Branch of Delaware River, Towns of Deposit,
   Tompkins

Constructed: 1955-1967; first in service 1965.

Dimensions: Stilesville Dam 2,800 feet long, 175
   feet high

Reservoir: 16 miles long (51.3-mile shoreline), covers 4,568 acres, maximum depth 140 feet

Capacity: 95.7 billion gallons

Feeds: West Delaware Tunnel (44 miles) to Rondout Reservoir

Communities flooded: 5—Beerston, Cannonsville,
   Granton, Rock Rift, Rock Royal

Residents displaced: 941

Land acquired: 19,902 acres

Graves reinterred: 2,150 from 11 cemeteries

Hillview Reservoir

Receives water from Kensico

Equalizes hourly differences in city consumption

Location: Yonkers, just north of NYC line

Constructed: 1909-1915

Dimensions: No dam (does not impound a waterway)

Reservoir: Dug from a hilltop; surface area 90
   acres, maximum depth 36 feet

Capacity: 900 million gallons

Feeds: City Tunnel #1 to Bronx, Manhattan,
   Brooklyn; City Tunnel #2 to East Bronx,
   Queens, Brooklyn, Staten Island (Silver Lake
   Reservoir); City Tunnel #3 (Phase 1) to parts of
   the Bronx, Manhattan and Queens

Land acquired: 164 acres

Storage/Balancing Reservoirs (2)

Kensico Reservoir

Receives Croton, Catskill, Delaware water

Stores 45-day city supply

Location: Westchester County; impounds Bronx
   River, Towns of Mount Pleasant, North Castle,
   Harrison

Constructed: 1909-1915

Dimensions: Kensico Dam 3,300 feet long, 128 feet
   high

Reservoir: 4 miles long, 35-mile shoreline, covers
   2,081 acres, maximum depth 155 feet

Capacity: 30.6 billion gallons

Feeds: Hillview Reservoir (15 miles south), via Catskill and Delaware Aqueducts

Communities flooded: 3: Kensico, Armonk, part of
   Valhalla

Residents displaced: 500

Land acquired: 4,500 acres

Graves reinterred: None

Distributing Reservoirs (4)

Central Park Reservoir
(originally called Lake Manahatta)

Location: Central Park, Manhattan

Constructed: 1857-1862. Held in reserve for several
   years; taken off line 1993.

Dimensions: Covers 96 acres

Capacity: 1 billion gallons

Serves: Manhattan

Land acquired: 106 acres

Jerome Park Reservoir

Location: North Bronx

Constructed: 1894-1905

Dimensions: Covers 94 acres

Capacity: 800 million gallons

Serves: The Bronx

Land acquired: 300 acres

Silver Lake Reservoir and Tanks

Location: Richmond, Staten Island

Constructed: 1913-1917

Dimensions: Covers 54 acres (1.6-mile shoreline), maximum depth 35 feet

Capacity: 438 million gallons; 100-million-gallon underground storage tanks installed 1965-1970, when open reservoir use was discontinued

Serves: Staten Island

Land acquired: 166 acres

Ridgewood Reservoir

Location: Cypress Hills, Queens

Constructed: 1856-58

Dimensions: Reservoir covers 38 acres

Capacity: 100 million gallons

Serves: Brooklyn

 minimum operating level, not total volume

SOUTHEAST QUEENS SYSTEM
(Pumped groundwater supply)

Location: Jamaica, Queens

Acquired: 1996

Facilities: 69 wells, 12 storage tanks, 700 miles of water mains

Capacity: 33 million gallons per day

Serves: Southeast Queens

Aqueducts and Tunnels

New Croton Aqueduct

Connects New Croton Reservoir (Westchester County) to Jerome Park Reservoir (The Bronx) and 135th Street Gatehouse (Manhattan)

Total length: 33 miles

Transmission capacity: 300 million gallons per day

Type: Brick-lined rock tunnel (24 miles); masonry conduit (9 miles). Diameter 10 to 13 feet.

Constructed: 1885-1893 (first in service 1891); complemented Old Croton Aqueduct (built 1837-1842) until latter was discontinued in 1950s

Cost: $19.6 million; 92 lives

Principal feature: Passes 300 feet beneath high-water mark of the Harlem River.

Catskill Aqueduct

Connects Ashokan Reservoir (Ulster County), to Kensico Reservoir (Westchester) and Hillview Reservoir (Yonkers)

Total length: 92 miles

Transmission capacity: 600-800 million gallons per day

Type: Cut-and-cover (55 miles); grade tunnel (14 miles); pressure tunnel (17 miles); steel siphons (6 miles). Diameter averages 17 feet.

Constructed: 1907-1917. First in service 1915.

Cost: $162 million; 283 lives

Principal feature: Hudson River crossing, between Storm King Mountain on west bank and Breakneck Mountain on east (3,022 feet). Driven through granite 1,114 feet beneath the river bed.

Delaware Aqueduct

Connects Rondout Reservoir (Ulster County), with West Branch Reservoir (Putnam County), Kensico Reservoir (Westchester County) and Hillview Reservoir (Yonkers)

Total length: 84 miles

Transmission capacity: 890-1,400 million gallons per day

Type: Circular, cement-lined pressure tunnel through solid rock; 15-18 feet in diameter

Constructed: 1939-1945; first in service 1943

Cost: $210 million; 58 lives

Principal feature: The Delaware Aqueduct is the longest continuous tunnel in the world. The deepest vertical shaft excavated to build the tunnel was 1,551 feet deep, south of Kerhonksen. The aqueduct passes 600 feet beneath the Hudson River at Chelsea.

Shandaken Tunnel

Connects Schoharie Reservoir (Schoharie County) with Esopus Creek and Ashokan Reservoir (Ulster County)

Length: 18 miles

Transmission capacity: 650 million gallons per day

Type: Concrete-lined pressure tunnel; 11-foot diameter

Constructed: 1917-1924

Neversink Tunnel

Connects Neversink Reservoir (Sullivan County) to Rondout Reservoir (Ulster County)

Length: 6 miles

Transmission capacity: 500 million gallons per day

Type: Concrete-lined pressure tunnel; 10-foot diameter

Constructed: 1949-1954

East Delaware Tunnel

Connects Pepacton Reservoir (Delaware County) to Rondout Reservoir (Ulster County)

Length: 25 miles

Transmission capacity: 700 million gallons per day

Type: Concrete-lined pressure tunnel; 11-foot diameter

Constructed:1949-1955

West Delaware Tunnel

Connects Cannonsville Reservoir (Delaware County) to Rondout Reservoir (Ulster County)

Length: 44 miles

Transmission capacity: 500 million gallons per day

Type: Concrete-lined pressure tunnel; 11 feet in diameter

Constructed: 1955-1964

City Tunnel #1

Connects Hillview Reservoir (Yonkers) with distribution system in The Bronx, Manhattan, Brooklyn, Queens and Staten Island

Length: 18 miles

Transmission capacity: 1 billion gallons per day

Type: Cement-lined pressure tunnel; diameter from 11 to 15 feet, 200-750 feet below surface

Constructed: 1911-1915

City Tunnel #2

Connects Hillview Reservoir with distribution system in The Bronx, Queens and Brooklyn.

Length: 20 miles

Transmission capacity: 1 billion gallons per day

Type: Cement-lined pressure tunnel; diameter 15-17 feet, 200-800 feet below surface

Constructed: 1928-1933

City Tunnel #3

A four-stage project to connect Hillview and Kensico Reservoirs to eastern and southern areas of the city and to allow City Tunnels 1 and 2 to be shut down and inspected.

Planned length: 54 miles

Transmission capacity: 1 billion gallons per day

Type: Concrete-lined pressure tunnel, 24-foot diameter

Constructed: Begun in 1970; Stage 1 (13 miles) in service July 1998. Expected completion date: 2020.

Richmond Tunnel

Connects City Tunnel #2 in Brooklyn to Richmond Conduit and Silver Lake Storage Tanks, Staten Island

Length: 5 miles

Transmission capacity: 350 million gallons per day

Type: Concrete-lined pressure tunnel, 10-foot diameter; carries water 900 feet beneath Upper New York Bay

Constructed: 1962-1970; replaced original and second Narrows pipelines, laid 1913-15 and 1923-25 to service Silver Lake Reservoir

Evening anglers on the Ashokan Reservoir.
Scott Foster photo, NYC DEP.

Chapter Notes

1. The Thirsty Settlement

1. Harry Kessler, and Eugene Rachliss, *Peter Stuyvesant and His New York* (New York: Random House, 1959).
2. William Thomson Bonner, *New York, The World's Metropolis 1623-1923* (New York: R. L. Polk & Co., 1924), p.228.
3. John Duffy, *A History of Public Health in New York City 1625-1866* (New York: Russell Sage Foundation, 1968), p.7.
4. Edward H.Hall, *Water for New York City* (Saugerties, N.Y.: Hope Farm Press, 1993, Excerpted from *The Catskill Aqueduct*, 1917), p.17.
5. Hall, *Water for New York City*, p.17
6. Duffy, *A History of Public Health*, p.30
7. Hall, *Water for New York City*, p.22
8. Charles H. Weidner, *Water for a City, A History of New York City's Problem from the Beginning to the Delaware River System 1897-1966* (New Brunswick, N.J.: Rutgers University Press, 1974), p.16.
9. Hall, *Water for New York City*, p.23
10. "Tea Water Pump," *Valentines Magazine* (1855), taken from *Catskill Water System News* (New York City Board of Water Supply, June 20, 1912), p.100
11. Duffy, *A History of Public Health*, p. 76.
12. Hall, *Water for New York City*, pp. 35-38.
13. Duffy, *A History of Public Health*, p. 75.
14. Ibid., p.76.
15. Bonner, *The World's Metropolis*, p. 219.
16. Duffy, *A History of Public Health*, p. 82.
17. Nathan Silver, *Lost New York* (New York: Schocken Books, 1971), p.4.
18. Weidner, *Water for A City*, pp.15-17.
19. Ibid., p.17.
20. Ibid., p.18.
21. Ibid., pp.20-21.
22. Hall, *Water for New York City*, p.48.
23. Forrest McDonald, *Alexander Hamilton, A Biography* (New York: W. W. Norton & Co. 1979).
24. Harold Syrett and Jean Cooke, eds., *Interview at Weehawken, The Burr-Hamilton Duel as told in the Original Documents* (Middletown, Conn.: Wesleyan University, 1960).
25. Arnold Rogow, *A Fatal Friendship, Alexander Hamilton and Aaron Burr* (New York: Hill & Wang, 1998), p. 187.
26. Hall, *Water for New York City*, p.50.
27. Duffy, *A History of Public Health*, p.392.
28. Weidner, *Water for A City*, p.25.
29. Ibid., p.26.
30. Ibid., p.23.
31. Charles Rosenberg, *The Cholera Years, The United States in 1832, 1849 and 1866* (Chicago: University of Chicago Press, 1962), p. 28.
32. Weidner, *Water for a City*, p. 28.
33. Ibid., p. 30.
34. Ibid., p. 37.

2. Claiming the Croton

1. Daniel Van Pelt, *Leslie's History of the Greater New York* (New York: Arkell Publishing, 1898), p. 300.
2. Martha Lamb, *History of the City of New York* (New York: A. S. Barnes & Co., 1880).
3. Van Pelt, *Leslie's History of the Greater New York*, p. 302
4. Ibid.
5. C. Foster, *An Account of the Conflagration of the Principal Part of the First Ward of the City of New York*, 1835.
6. F. Daniel Larkin, *John B. Jervis: An American Engineering Pioneer* (Ames, Iowa: Iowa State University Press, 1990), p. 83.
7. Neal FitzSimons, ed., *The Reminscences of John B. Jervis, Engineer of the Old Croton* (Syracuse, N.Y.: Syracuse University Press, 1971), p. 12.
8. Larkin, *John B. Jervis: An American Engineering Pioneer*, p. 83.
9. Larry B. Lankton, *The "Practicable" Engineer: John B. Jervis and The Old Croton Aqueduct* (Chicago, Ill: Public Works Historical Society, 1977), p. 8.
10. Ibid., p. 24.
11. David B. Douglass, letter to Stephen Allen, Nov. 24, 1835, from exhibition "The Old Croton Aqueduct: Rural Resources Meet Urban Needs," Museum of the Hudson River at Westchester, 1992.
12. Semi Annual Report of the Water Commissioners, July 1-Dec. 31, 1838, from *Report of the Chief Engineer on the General State of Work on the Croton Aqueduct, 1833-48.*
13. Ibid., p. 59.
14. Washington Irving, letter to unidentified friend, Urban Cultural Park Museum exhibit, Ossining, N.Y.
15. Larkin, *John B. Jervis, An American Engineering Pioneer*, p. 63.
16. FitzSimons, *Reminiscences of John B. Jervis*, p. 124
17. Ibid., p. 122.
18. Lankton, *The "Practicable" Engineer*, p. 24.
19. Fayette Tower, letter to Mrs. D. T. Tower, Waterville, N.Y., Sept. 15, 1837, from exhibition "The Old Croton Aqueduct: Rural Resources Meet Urban Needs," Museum of the Hudson River at Westchester, 1992.
20. Tower, letter to Mrs. D. T. Tower, Waterville, N.Y., Nov. 5, 1837.
21. Charles King, *A Memoir of the Construction, Cost and Capacity of the Croton Aqueduct* (New York, 1843).

22. Jeff Canning and Wally Buxton, *History of the Tarry-towns* (Harrison, N.Y.: Harbor Hill Books, 1975), p. 320.
23. FitzSimons, *Reminscences of John B. Jervis*, p. 125.
24. Report of the Chief Engineer on the General State of the Work on the Croton Aqueduct, Nov. 1833-Dec. 1848, p.242.
25. Ibid., Appendix, p. 4.
26. FitzSimons, *Reminiscences of John B. Jervis*, p. 127.
27. Charles H. Weidner, *Water for a City, A History of New York City's Problem from the Beginning to the Delaware River System 1897-1966* (New Brunswick, N.J.: Rutgers University Press, 1974), p. 42.
28. Larkin, *John B. Jervis, An American Engineering Pioneer*, p. 69.
29. Edward H. Hall, *Water for New York City* (Saugerties, N.Y.: Hope Farm Press, 1993, excerpted from *The Catskill Aqueduct*, 1917), p. 54.
30. Charles King, *Memoir of the Croton Aqueduct*, 1843
31. Ibid.
32. Alvah French, ed., *History of Westchester County, N.Y.*, Vol. 1 (New York & Chicago: Lewis Historical Publishing Co., 1925).
33. *Report of the Chief Engineer*, p. 554.
34. FitzSimons, *Reminiscences of John B. Jervis*, p. 133.
35. Ibid.
36. Larkin, *John B. Jervis, An American Engineering Pioneer*, p. 71.
37. FitzSimons, *Reminscences of John B. Jervis*, p. 138.
38. Weidner, *Water for a City*, p. 45.
39. Hall, *Water for New York City*, p. 61.
40. Ibid., p. 62.
41. Weidner, *Water for a City*, p. 45.
42. Ibid., p. 46.
43. Kenneth Holcomb Dunshee, "George Templeton Strong," *As You Pass By* (New York: Hastings House Publishers, 1952), p. 75.
44. King, *Memoir of the Croton Aqueduct*.
45. Arthur G. Adams, *The Hudson Through the Years* (Westwood, N.J.: Lind Publications, 1983), p. 242.
46. King, *Memoir of the Croton Aqueduct*.
47. Ibid.

3. "Of Life and Stir": The City Grows

1. Charles Dickens, *American Notes*. (New York: St. Martin's Press, 1985), p. 72.
2. Charles H. Weidner, *Water for a City, A History of New York City's Problem from the Beginning to the Delaware River System 1897-1966* (New Brunswick, N.J.:Rutgers University Press, 1974), p. 53.
3. Exhibition text, "The Old Croton Aqueduct: Rural Resources Meet Urban Needs," Museum of the Hudson River at Westchester, 1992.
4. Ibid.
5. Weidner, *Water for a City*, p. 57.
6. Ibid., p. 58.

7. Edward H. Hall, *Water for New York City* (Saugerties, N.Y.: Hope Farm Press, 1993, excerpted from The Catskill Aqueduct, 1917), p. 64.
8. Annual Report of the Croton Aqueduct Department to the Common Council, Jan. 5, 1858
9. Nat Brandt, *The Man Who Tried to Burn New York* (Syracuse, N.Y.: Syracuse University Press, 1986), p. 90.
10. Ibid., p. 71.
11. Ibid., p. 120.
12. Weidner, *Water for a City*, p. 52.
13. *History of Southeastern New York*, 3 vol., (New York: Lewis Historical Publishing Co., 1946), p. 831.
14. William Pelletreau, *History of Putnam County*, (Philadelphia: W.W. Preston, 1886, republished 1975).
15. *Putnam County Courier*, Nov. 24, 1866; July 6, 1867.
16. Pelletreau, *History of Putnam County*, p. 682.
17. Weidner, *Water for a City*, p. 61.
18. Seymour Mandelbaum, *Boss Tweed's New York*, (New York: J. Wiley, 1965), p. 72-86.
19. *Reporter Dispatch*, White Plains, N.Y., Feb. 11, 1979.

4: Lake Effects

1. Charles H. Weidner, *Water for a City, A History of New York City's Problem from the Beginning to the Delaware River System 1897-1966* (New Brunswick, N.J.: Rutgers University Press, 1974), pp. 54, 58.
2. *Brewster Standard*, Sept. 3, 1870.
3. *Putnam County Courier*, Oct. 15, 1870.
4. *Water Rights on the Muscoot River, Supreme Court Proceedings In the Matter of the Application of Allan Campbell, Commissioner of Public Works of the City of New York to take lands and extinguish rights etc. at Lakes Mahopac and Kirk and on the Muscoot River, in Putnam and Westchester Counties, under Chapter 445 of the Laws of 1877*,(New York: Martin Brown), 1882.
5. *Brewster Standard*, Mar. 8, 1873.
6. *Putnam County Courier*, Mar. 23, 1872.
7. *Scribner's Monthly*, June 1877; *Putnam County Courier*, May 18, 1872.
8. H. G. Eastman, *The Water Supply of New York, Suggestions for a Permanent and Economical Settlement of the Question* (Poughkeepsie, N.Y.: Nov. 24, 1876).
9. Weidner, *Water for a City*, p. 54.
10. Ibid., p. 98.
11. Ibid.
12. *Mt. Kisco Recorder*, May 5, 1893.
13. Weidner, *Water for a City*, p. 99.
14. *Putnam County Courier*, May 5, 1893.
15. *Brewster Standard*, Sept. 14, 1894.
16. *Putnam County Republican*, Mar. 3, 1894.
17. *Brewster Standard*, Nov. 3, 1893.
18. *The New York Times*, Dec. 7, 1908.

5: Liquid Links

1. *Putnam County Standard*, June 8, 1877.
2. *Putnam County Standard*, May 4, 1877.

3. Ibid.
4. *Putnam County Standard*, May 5, 1876.
5. *Putnam County Standard*, July 23, 1875.
6. Charles H. Weidner, *Water for a City, A History of New York City's Problem from the Beginning to the Delaware River System, 1897-1966* (New Brunswick, N.J.: Rutgers University Press, 1974), p. 63.
7. Ibid., pp.63-64.
8. Neil S. Martin, "The Lost Village," *North Castle History*, Vol. 10, (Armonk, N.Y.: North Castle Historical Society, 1983), p. 8
9. Alvah French, *History of Westchester County*, Vol. 1 (New York: Lewis Historical Publishing Co., 1925), p. 397.
10. Martin, "The Lost Village," p. 8.
11. Weidner, *Water for a City*, p. 54.
12. Ibid., p. 58.
13. Ibid., p. 65.
14. Ibid., p. 69
15. Ibid, p. 70.
16. Ibid.
17. "Reports on the New Croton Aqueduct, Reservoirs and Dams 1895-1907," (City of New York Aqueduct Commission), p. 81.
18. Weidner, *Water for a City*, p. 81.
19. "Reports on the New Croton Aqueduct," p. 81.
20. "The New Croton Aqueduct," (*Harper's New Monthly Magazine*, Vol. XXXIX, reprinted in *New York, Tales of the Empire State*, Seacaucus, N.J.: Castle Books, 1988), p.45.
21. "Reports on the New Croton Aqueduct," p. 82.
22. Ibid., p. 81.
23. Ibid., p. 81.
24. "The Croton Water System" (Brewster, N.Y: Southeast Museum), undated.
25. *Putnam County Courier*, Carmel, N.Y., Mar. 4, 1892
26. "The Croton Water System"
27. "Reports on the New Croton Aqueduct," p. 85.
28. Ibid., p. 87.
29. Interview of Ella Sweeney by Thomas Purdy for North Salem Historical Society, Nov. 4, 1970.
30. *Brewster Standard*, Nov. 2, 1894.
31. Weidner, *Water for a City*, p. 92; Harza Associates, Investigation of Dams East of the Hudson, 1986.
32. "Reports on the New Croton Aqueduct," p. 86
33. Weidner, *Water for a City*, p. 92.
34. Ibid., p. 89.

6: A New Aqueduct

1. Charles H. Weidner, *Water for a City, A History of New York City's Problem from the Beginning to the Delaware River System 1897-1966* (New Brunswick, N.J.: Rutgers University Press, 1974), p. 71.
2. "A Description of the Water Supply of the City of New York," (Department of Water Supply, Gas and Electricity, 1952).
3. "The New Croton Aqueduct," *Harper's New Monthly Magazine*, Vol. XXXIX (reprinted in *New York, Tales of the Empire State*, Secaucus, N.J: Castle Books, 1988), p. 52-53).
4. "Reports on the New Croton Aqueduct, Reservoirs and Dams, 1895-1907," (City of New York Aqueduct Commission).
5. "Reports on the New Croton Aqueduct and Dams, 1887-1895" (City of New York Aqueduct Commission), pp. 11, 104.
6. "The New Croton Aqueduct," *Harper's New Monthly Magazine*, p. 53.
7. *Brewster Standard*, April 9, 1886.
8. Weidner, *Water for a City*, p. 75.
9. "Reports on the New Croton Aqueduct and Dams, 1887-1895," p. 89-92.
10. Charles Bernard, "The Old Croton Aqueduct," *Century Illustrated Magazine*, Vol. 39, No. 18, pp. 209-210, (reprinted in *The History of the New Croton Dam*, Mary Josephine D'Alvia, 1976), pp.63-64.
11. Weidner, *Water for a City*, p. 77.
12. Undated biographical profile of Angelica Schuyler Church Ossining Historical Society.
13. *King's Handbook of New York* (Boston: Moses King, 1893), p. 199.
14. "Reports on the New Croton Aqueduct, Reservoirs and Dams, 1895-1907."
15. Weidner, *Water for a City*, p. 102.
16. *Scientific American*, July 6, 1901.
17. *New York Herald*, May 23, 1903
18. Various newspaper accounts, 1903, Goldsborough Collection, Croton-on-Hudson Village History Room
19. Weidner, *Water for a City*, p. 104.
20. "Reports on the New Croton Aqueduct, Reservoirs and Dams, 1895-1907."
21. Friends of Jerome Park Web site, January 1999.

7: The New Croton Reservoir

1. Charles H. Weidner, *Water for A City, A History of New York City's Problem from the Beginning to the Delaware River System, 1897-1966* (New Brunswick, N.J.: Rutgers University Press, 1974), p. 84.
2. Reports on the New Croton Aqueduct, Dams and Reservoirs, 1895-1907 (City of New York Aqueduct Commission), p. 91.
3. Weidner, *Water for A City*, pp. 113-114.
4. Reports on the New Croton Aqueduct, 1895-1907, p. 97.
5. Weidner, *Water for A City*, p. 116.
6. Reports on the New Croton Aqueduct, p. 103.
7. Ibid., p. 106
8. Mary Josephine D'Alvia, *The History of the New Croton Dam* (1974), p. 91.
9. Reports on the New Croton Aqueduct, p. 102.
10. D'Alvia, interview by the author, June 4, 1997.
11. D'Alvia, *The History of the New Croton Dam*, p. 121
12. Ibid., p. 105.
13. Ibid., p. 95.
14. *Katonah Times*, July 21, 1905.

15. "Wages Paid During Construction of the New Croton Aqueduct and New Reservoirs," undated, Ossining Historical Society.
16. Various newspaper clippings, April 16-19, 1900.
17. Various newspaper clippings, 1900, 1902, 1903.
18. *New York Tribune*, April 19, 1900.
19. *Katonah Times*, Jan. 18, 1901.

8: Finishing the Croton System— Cross River and Croton Falls

1. Charles H. Weidner, *Water for A City, A History of New York City's Problem from the Beginning to the Delaware River System, 1897-1966* (Brunswick, N.J.: Rutgers University Press, 1974), p. 118.
2. *Katonah Times*, Jan. 25, 1901.
3. *New York Tribune*, Sept. 3, 1907.
4. "Reports on the New Croton Aqueduct, Reservoirs and Dams, 1895-1907," (City of New York Aqueduct Commission), p. 120.
5. Ibid., p. 121.
6. Frances R. Duncombe, *Katonah, The History of a New York Village and its People*, (Katonah, N.Y.: Katonah Village Improvement Society, 1961; republished 1997), p. 218.
7. Weidner, *Water for a City*, p. 119.
8. *History of the Town of Lewisboro* (South Salem, N.Y.: Lewisboro History Book Committee, 1981), p. 226.
9. Fiss, Doerr & Carroll Horse Company brochure (New York City, c. 1902), collection of Katharine Barrett Kelly, Katonah, N.Y.
10. Duncombe, *Katonah, The History of a New York Village*, p. 219.
11. "Reports on the New Croton Aqueduct, Reservoirs and Dams, 1895-1907," p. 121.
12. Weidner, *Water for a City*, p. 121.
13. Ibid., p. 122-123.
14. *Katonah Times*, Aug. 24, 1906.
15. Ibid., Mar. 3, 1907.
16. Ibid., Aug. 24, 1906.
17. Ibid., July 26, 1907.
18. Ibid., August 23, 1907.
19. Ibid., Oct. 23, 1908.
20. Ibid., July 26, 1907.
21. Weidner, *Water for a City*, p. 118.

9: To the Catskills

1. Charles H. Weidner, *Water for A City, A History of New York City's Problem from the Beginning to the Delaware River System, 1897-1966* (New Brunswick, N.J.: Rutgers University Press, 1974), p. 140.
2. Ibid., p. 145.
3. Ibid., p. 147.
4. Ibid., p. 149.
5. Edward H. Hall, *Water for New York City* (Saugerties, N.Y.: Hope Farm Press, 1993, excerpted from *The Catskill Aqueduct*, 1917), p. 79.
6. Weidner, *Water for a City*, p. 152.
7. Ibid., p. 156.
8. Ibid., p. 160.
9. Ibid., p. 162.
10. Ibid., p. 167.
11. Laws of 1905, Chapter 724, Appendix to *First Annual Report of the Board of Water Supply of the City of New York*, Dec. 31, 1906.
12. "1,820,000,000 Gallons Per Day," 50th Anniversary booklet of the Board of Water Supply (New York, 1955), p. 30.
13. *First Annual Report of the Board of Water Supply of the City of New York* (New York, Dec. 31, 1906), p. 24.
14. Weidner, *Water for a City*, p. 18
15. Obituary, J. Waldo Smith, *New York Herald Tribune*, Oct. 16, 1933.
16. "Testimonial to the Chief Engineers, 1905-1965," (Board of Water Supply, City of New York, 1965
17. *First Annual Report of the Board of Water Supply*, p. 70
18. *Kingston Freeman*, Nov. 28, 1905
19. "1,820,000,000 Gallons Per Day," p. 3
20. *First Annual Report of the Board of Water Supply*, p. 20
21. *Ellenville Journal*, Dec. 8, 1905.
22. *First Annual Report of the Board of Water Supply*, Appendix, p. 98-99.
23. Ibid., p. 100.
24. Ibid., p. 208.
25. Ibid., p. 213-215.
26. "Hornets Attack Engineers," unattributed newspaper clipping, Aug. 16, 1906, A. T. Clearwater Collection, Senate House, Kingston, N.Y.
27. *First Annual Report of the Board of Water Supply*, p. 16-19.
28. *Annual Report of the Board of Water Supply*, 1907, Appendix, p. 172.

10: The Catskill Aqueduct

1. Charles Berkey, James Sanborn, "Engineering Geology of the Catskill Water Supply," *Transactions of the American Society of Civil Engineers* (1923, New York), p. 20.
2. Ibid., p. 21.
3. *A Description of the Water Supply System of the City of New York* (New York: Dept. of Water Supply, Gas and Electricity, 1952), p. 35.
4. Edward Hall, *Water for New York City* (Saugerties, N.Y.: Hope Farm Press, 1993, excerpted from *The Catskill Aqueduct*, 1917), p. 113.
5. Lazarus White, *Catskill Water Supply of New York City, History, Location, Sub-surface Investigation and Construction* (New York: John Wiley & Sons, 1913), p. 445.
6. *1907 Board of Water Supply Annual Report*, p. 9-10
7. Charles Berkey et al, "Engineering Geology of the Catskill Water Supply," p. 40.
8. White, *Catskill Water Supply*, p. 270.
9. Ibid., p. 386.
10. Ibid., p. 484.
11. *Cornwall Local*, Feb. 22, 1912; May 5, 1910.
12. *Cornwall Local*, July 27, 1911.
13. *Cornwall Local*, Oct. 20, 1910.

14. *The Catskill Water System News*, Sept. 20, 1911
15. *1910 Board of Water Supply Annual Report*, p. 180
16. Ibid., p. 179
17. *1909 Board of Water Supply Annual Report*, p.200.
18. *Cornwall Local*, Sept. 2, 1909.
19. White, *Catskill Water Supply*, p. 420.
20. Alberta Washburn, interview with the author, Nov. 23, 1997

11: Beneath City Streets

1. *Report of the Board of Water Supply to the Mayor of the City of New York on Completion of the First Stage of the Catskill Water Supply System*, Oct. 12, 1917, p. 6.
2. *Catskill Water Supply, A General Description and Brief History* (Board of Water Supply of the City of New York, January 1913), p. 27.
3. *Catskill Water Supply, A General Description and Brief History* (Board of Water Supply of the City of New York, October 1917), p. 49.
4. Lazarus White, *Catskill Water Supply of New York City, History, Location, Sub-surface Investigation and Construction* (New York: John Wiley & Sons, 1913), p. 591.
5. *Catskill Water Supply, A General Description*, 1917, p. 27.
6. White, *Catskill Water Supply*, p. 588.
7. *Catskill Water Supply, Reports, Letters, Resolutions and Authorizations on the City Tunnel and the Delivery of Catskill Water to the Several Boroughs of the City* (Board of Water Supply of the City of New York, 1912), p. 4.
8. Ibid., p. 7.
9. Ibid., p. 8.
10. *Seventh Annual Report of the Board of Water Supply of the City of New York*, 1912, p. 3.
11. *Eighth Annual Report of the Board of Water Supply of the City of New York*, 1913, p. 250.
12. Edward H.Hall, *Water for New York City* (Saugerties, N.Y.: Hope Farm Press, 1993, excerpted from *The Catskill Aqueduct*, 1917), p. 79.
13. *Catskill Water Supply, A General Description*, 1917, p. 61.

12: Building the Ashokan

1. Board of Water Supply Annual Report, 1907, p. 11.
2. Charles H. Weidner, *Water for A City, A History of New York City's Problem from the Beginning to the Delaware River System 1897-1966* (New Brunswick, N.J.: Rutgers University Press, 1974), p. 19.
3. Bob Steuding, *Last of the Handmade Dams, The Story of the Ashokan Reservoir* (Fleischmanns, N.Y.: Purple Mountain Press, Revised Edition 1989), p. 37.
4. *Board of Water Supply Annual Report, 1907*, p. 85.
5. Ibid., p. 53-54.
6. Weidner, Water for A City, p. 227.
7. Steuding, *Last of the Handmade Dams*, p. 46.
8. Ibid., p. 42.
9. Ibid., p. 43.
10. "Glenford Man Was Waterboy on Ashokan," *Kingston Daily Freeman*, Aug. 5, 1985.

11. "Ashokan Reservoir Stirs Memories," *The New York Times*, Sept. 3, 1985.
12. *Board of Water Supply Annual Report 1909*, p. 153.
13. *Board of Water Supply Annual Report 1936*, Sheets 2, 3.
14. *Annual Report*, 1909, p. 5.
15. *Board of Water Supply Annual Report 1910*, p. 8.
16. *Board of Water Supply Annual Report 1911*, p. 10.
17. *Catskill Mountain News*, Jan. 12, 1912.
18. Vera VanSteenbergh Sickler, *The Town of Olive Through the Years, Part* 1, (1976), p. 77
19. *Catskill Mountain News*, June 13, 1913; also unidentified clipping in diary of Elwyn Davis, 1913.
20. Steuding, *Last of the Handmade Dams*, p. 54
21. Ibid., p. 53.
22. *Annual Report* 1911, p. 99.
23. Ibid., p. 115.
24. *Annual Report* 1912, p. 101-102.
25. *Annual Report* 1907, p. 49.
26. Weidner, *Water for a City*, p. 240.
27. *Kingston Daily Freeman*, Jan. 29, 1910.
28. The Ashokan Reservoir Record Series, Ulster County Clerk's Office, Kingston.
29. Ibid.
30. *Board of Water Supply Annual Report 1922*, p. 11.
31. *Board of Water Supply Annual Report 1913*, p. 23
32. Ibid.
33. Mrs. C. S. Bergner, "Construction Camp Life in Ashokan Reservoir," *York State Tradition*, Summer 1970.
34. *Catskill Mountain News*, March 5, 1915.
35. Weidner, *Water for A City*, p. 262-263.
36. *Cornwall Local*, Oct. 16, 1913, also souvenir program "Celebration of the Beginning of Storage of Catskill Water at Ashokan Dam," Oct. 11, 1913.
37. Edward H. Hall, *Water for New York City* (Saugerties, N.Y.: Hope Farm Press, 1993, excerpted from *The Catskill Aqueduct*, 1917), p. 92.
38. *Board of Water Supply Annual Report 1914*.
39. Hall, *Water for New York City*, p. 95.

13: Kensico and Hill View Reservoirs

1. "Water Supply of New York City" (Republican Club of the City of New York, Apr. 25, 1909).
2. Lazarus White, *The Catskill Water Supply of New York City, History, Location, Sub-surface Investigations and Construction* (New York: John Wiley & Sons, 1913), p. 567.
3. *Board of Water Supply Annual Report, 1910*, p. 171.
4. *Catskill Water Supply, A General Description* (Board of Water Supply, Jan., 1913), p. 13.
5. *Catskill Water Supply, A General Description and Brief History* (Board of Water Supply, Oct. 1917), p. 31.
6. *Northern Westchester Times*, Sept. 15, 1911.
7. *Board of Water Supply Annual Report, 1910*, p. 172-174.
8. *Board of Water Supply Annual Report, 1912*, p. 186.
9. Samuel Taylor, "Large Rock-Crushing Plant for the Construction of Kensico Dam" (*Engineering Record*, Vol. 65, No. 8, Feb. 24, 1912), p. 216.

10. *Board of Water Supply Annual Report, 1912*, p. 190.
11. *Board of Water Supply Annual Report, 1914*, p. 161
12. *Catskill Water Supply, 1917*, p. 31.
13. Ibid., p. 33.
14. "Accidental Blast Kills 8 at Kensico," *New York Times*, Apr. 28, 1915.
15. Michael Paulo, interview with author, Oct. 20, 1998.
16. "Welfare Work at Camp Kensico," Catskill Water System News, July 20, 1913.
17. *Board of Water Supply Annual Report, 1916*, p. 195
18. *Northern Westchester Times*, Jan. 10, 1913; *North Castle Sun*, Dec. 31, 1915 and Nov. 12, 1915.
19. *Catskill Water Supply*, 1917, p. 33.
20. "Great Reservoir to Be Built at Kensico," unattributed, undated clipping, Alvah French Collection, Westchester County Archives.
21. Ibid.
22. *Catskill Water Supply*, 1913, p. 11.
23. "Great Reservoir to be Built at Kensico."
24. Joseph T.Miller, "Historic Kensico and The Hills of North Castle," *North Castle History*, Vol. 2, No. 1, (North Castle Historical Society, Spring 1975), p. 13
25. Del Pietschker, "Kensico, A Special Place," *North Castle History*, Vol. 10 (North Castle Historical Society, 1983), p. 17
26. Neil S. Martin, "The Lost Village, The History of Kensico and Its Inundation," *North Castle History*, Vol. 10 (North Castle Historical Society, 1983), p. 3.
27. "Work on $10,000,000 Dam," *Pine Hill Sentinel*, Sept. 18, 1915.
28 Martin, "The Lost Village. . .", p. 11.
29. "Decided Changes to be Made at Valhalla," *North Castle Sun*, Dec. 22, 1916.
30. White, *Catskill Water Supply*, p. 567.
31. Ibid., p. 568.
32. Ibid., p. 569.
33. *Catskill Water Supply*, 1917, p. 39.
34. Ibid.
35. *Board of Water Supply Annual Report, 1912*, p. 204.
36. Edward H. Hall, *Water for New York City* (Saugerties, N.Y.: Hope Farm Press, 1993, excerpted from *The Catskill Aqueduct*, 1917), p. 120.
37. Charles H. Weidner, *Water for A City, A History of New York City's Problems from the Beginning to the Delaware River System 1897-1966* (New Brunswick, N.J.: Rutgers University Press, 1974), p. 53.
38. *Report of the Board of Water Supply to The Mayor of the City of New York on Completion of the First Stage of the Catskill Water System*, Oct. 12, 1917, p.6-7.
39. "Catskill Aqueduct Formally Accepted," *New York Times*, Oct. 13, 1917.
40. Ibid.

14: Fire and Flood---The Schoharie Project

1. Florence Brandow, interview with author, Apr. 22, 1995.
2. Board of Water Supply Annual Report, 1914, p. 4.
3. *Catskill Mountain News*, Mar. 5, 1915.
4. *Board of Water Supply Annual Report, 1915*, pp. 2, 77.
5. *Pine Hill Sentinel*, Feb. 5, 1916.
6. *Catskill Mountain News,* Feb. 4, 1916.
7. *Board of Water Supply Annual Report, 1916*, pp. 4, 86.
8. *Board of Water Supply Annual Report, 1919*, p. 54.
9. *Board of Water Supply Annual Report, 1917*, p. 52.
10. *Board of Water Supply Annual Report, 1916*, p. 90.
11 *Board of Water Supply Annual Report, 1918*, p. 46-47.
12. Ibid., p. 50.
13. *Board of Water Supply Annual Report, 1919*, pp. 46, 50.
14. R. W. Gausmann, "The Shandaken Tunnel,"(*Transactions of the American Society of Civil Engineers*, Vol. 92, 1928), p. 241.
15. *Board of Water Supply Annual Report, 1920*, p. 50.
16. Edward Scott Swazey, "The Shandaken Tunnel" (New York: Ulen & Co., May, 1923), p. 5.
17. *Board of Water Supply Annual Report, 1920*, p. 48.
18. *Board of Water Supply Annual Report 1921*, p. 46.
19. Swazey, "The Shandaken Tunnel," p. 11-14.
20. Ibid., p. 15.
21. Gausmann, "The Shandaken Tunnel," p. 258.
22. Theodore "Ike" Carmen interview with author, Jan. 10, 1996; also in "Stories from Old Gilboa," (Gilboa-Conesville Central School, 1988-89)
23. Swazey, "The Shandaken Tunnel," p. 17.
24. "Brothers Drop to Their Death," unattributed newspaper article, Nov. 21, 1922.
25. John Ford, interview with author, Jan. 3, 1996; Floyd Kirk, interview with author, December, 1996.
26. Swazey, "The Shandaken Tunnel," p. 24-27.
27. Elwood Hitchcock, correspondence, Apr. 29, 1997.
28. *Board of Water Supply Annual Report, 1919*, p. 56-57.
29. *Board of Water Supply Annual Report, 1920*, p. 69-70
30. Emerson Mead, interviewed in "Stories of Old Gilboa," (Gilboa-Conesville Central School, 1988-89).
31. Charles H. Weidner, *Water for A City, A History of New York City's Problem from the Beginning to the Delaware River System, 1897-1966*, (New Brunswick, N.J.: Rutgers University Press, 1974), p. 279.
32. *Board of Water Supply Annual Report, 1921*, p. 86.
33. Evelyn Haskins, interview with author, Jan. 6, 1996.
34. Harry E. Keator, interview with author, Sept. 8, 1996.
35. *Stamford Mirror-Recorder*, Oct. 21, 1925.
36. "Two Meet Death as Shack Burns at Gilboa," *Catskill Mountain News, Dec. 31, 1926.*
37. *Board of Water Supply Annual Report, 1926*, p. 59.
38. Laurence "Lon" Regular, interview with author, July 16, 1996.
38. *Catskill Mountain News*, May 18, 1928.

15: Fighting for the Delaware

1. *Board of Water Supply Annual Report, 1920*, p. 42; 1921, p. 2.
2. *Board of Water Supply Annual Report, 1921*, p. 42.
3. Ibid., p. 98.
4. *Board of Water Supply Annual Report, 1926*, p. 7
5. *Board of Water Supply Annual Report, 1923*, p. 217
6. "Delaware Basin Gets Water Pact," *The New York Times*, Jan. 29, 1926, p.1

7. *Annual Report 1926*, pp. 103-104.
8. "Ashokan Drained by Leaks Shown by Investigation," *Catskill Mountain News*, Oct. 29, 1926.
9. "Flood Waters Greatly Damage Property Here," *Catskill Mountain News*, Nov. 19, 1926.
10. *Board of Water Supply Annual Report, 1928*, p. 66-76.
11. Ibid., p. 127
12. *Katonah Times*, Feb. 24, 1905.
13. *Catskill Mountain News*, Mar. 9, 1928.
14. *Liberty Register*, Mar. 27, 1924; *Sullivan County Review*, Mar. 9, 1922; *Catskill Mountain News,* July 12, 1912, Oct. 15, 1926.
15. *New York Herald Tribune*, May 26, 1929.
16. "Jersey Objects to Use of Delaware River," *Catskill Mountain News*, May 31, 1929.
17. "New York Begins Work on Delaware Dam," *Catskill Mountain News*, Apr. 10, 1931
18. Charles H. Weidner, *Water for a City, A History of New York City's Problem from the Beginning to the Delaware River System, 1897-1966* (New Brunswick, N.J.: Rutgers University Press, 1974), p. 292-93.
19. Supreme Court of the United States, No. 16, State of New Jersey vs. State of New York and City of New York, decision May 4, 1931.
20. *Catskill Mountain News*, May 1931.
21. *Board of Water Supply Annual Report, 1927*, p. 17
22. Ibid., p. 5-6; pp. 61-62.
23. *Board of Water Supply Annual Report, 1930*, p. 5; pp. 48-54.
24. *Board of Water Supply Annual Report, 1931*, pp. 3, 5-6, 46; Annual Report, 1928, p. 47
25. *Board of Water Supply Annual Report, 1933*, p. 11.
26. "Tunnels," *Guinness Book of World Records*, (New York, Bantam Books, 1995), p. 237.
27. Ibid, p. 14; *Board of Water Supply Annual Report, 1934*, p. 37
28. "Testimonial to the Chief Engineers, 1905-1965," (New York City Board of Water Supply).

16: The Delaware Aqueduct

1. *Board of Water Supply Annual Report, 1932*, p. 3.
2. Charles H. Weidner, *Water for A City, A History of New York City's Problem from the Beginning to the Delaware River System, 1897-1966* (New Brunswick, N.J.: Rutgers University Press, 1974), p. 295.
3. *Board of Water Supply Annual Report, 1933*, pp. 24-26.
4. "Driving 85 Miles of Tunnel," *Engineering News Record*, Aug. 29, 1940, p. 50.
5. *Board of Water Supply Annual Report, 1938* pp. 8-9.
6. *Board of Water Supply Annual Report, 1939*, pp. 52-54.
7. *Newburgh News*, Mar. 24, 1937.
8. *Board of Water Supply Annual Report, 1940-46*, pp. 80.
9. *Annual Report, 1939*, p. 3.
10. *Ellenville Journal*, Mar. 2, 1939.
11. *Engineering News Record*, Aug. 29, 1940, p. 51
12. *Annual Report, 1940-46*, p 101.
13. *Annual Report 1939*, p. 113.
14. *Annual Report 1940-46*, p. 141.

15. Thomas Purdy Jr.,"A Descent into North Salem's Underground River," *Bulletin of North Salem Historical Society*, Vol. 12, No. 1, August, 1985.
16. *Ellenville Journal*, Aug. 22, 1940.
17. *Annual Report, 1940-46*, pp. 73-74.
18. "Waters of Rondout Creek Diverted to City," *The Delaware Water Supply News*, May 1, 1944.
19. *Annual Report, 1940-46*, p. 74.
20. "Digging of Delaware Aqueduct Near End with Toll 58 Lives," (unidentified newspaper clipping, 1941); *Downsville News*, Feb. 23, 1939.
21. *Ellenville Journal*, Aug. 25, 1938.
22. "Silicosis Checked," *Industrial Bulletin* (New York State Dept. of Labor, Jan. 1948), pp. 36-38.
23. *Annual Report, 1940-46*, p. 116-120.
24. Ibid., p. 122.
25. "Last Holing Through on Delaware Aqueduct," *The Delaware Water Supply News*, May 15, 1942.
26. *Annual Report, 1940-46*, p. 184-190.
27. "Tunnel Inspection" *The Delaware Water Supply News, Jan. 1, 1942.*
28. *Annual Report, 1940-46, p. 184-190.*
29. Ibid., p. 238-239.
30. Ibid., p. 245.
31. Jack Burke with Jim Brady, *Tunnel Stiffs Tales* (Minneapolis: American Underground Construction Assoc., 1995), p. 22.
32. Sam Sigman, Dec. 8, 1998, interview with author.
33. *Delaware Water Supply News*, Oct. 18, 1940.

17: Waiting for "The Water"

1. Board of Water Supply Annual Report, 1907, p. 75.
2. Margaret Dolan, interview with author, Grahamsville, N.Y., 1996.
3. *Board of Water Supply Annual Report, 1940-46*, p. 292.
4. *Board of Water Supply Annual Report, 1937*, p. 3.
5. "Caissons for a Cut-off Wall," *Engineering News-Record*, Dec. 5, 1940.
6. *Ellenville Journal*, Mar. 24, 1938.
7. *Annual Report 1940-46*, p. 350.
8. *Annual Report 1940-46*, p. 311-316.
9. *Testimonial to the Chief Engineers, 1905-1965* (NYC Board of Water Supply, 1965), pp. 11, 13.
10. *BWS Annual Report, 1940-46*, p. 296.
11. Charles H. Weidner, *Water for A City, A History of New York City's Problem from the Beginning to the Delaware River System, 1897-1966* (New Brunswick, N.J.: Rutgers University Press, 1974), p. 308.
12. *Annual Report, 1940-46*, p. 352.
13. Weidner, *Water for A City*, p. 312.
14. Horace Sheeley, interview with author, Grahamsville, July 29, 1996.
15. *Annual Report, 1940-46*, pp. 397, 431.
16. *Board of Water Supply Annual Report, 1939*, p. 138.
17. *Annual Report, 1940-46*, p. 405; 1949, p. 115.
18. Sam Sigman, telephone interview with author, Dec. 8, 1998.

19. Ben Musso, interview with author, Grahamsville, NY, July 29, 1996.
20. *Liberty Register*, Nov. 28, 1947.
21. *Annual Report 1940-46*, p. 470.
22. Eugene Fuller, interview with author, Grahamsville, N.Y., April 12, 1996.
23. *Board of Water Supply Annual Report, 1949*, p. 119.
24. W.P. Gillingham, "Driving the Neversink," *Compressed Air Magazine*, May 1950.
25. "The Story of the Neversink Hydroelectric Plant" (Poughkeepsie, N.Y.: Central Hudson Gas & Electric Corp., 1950).
26. *Annual Report, 1940-46*, p. 497.
27. *Annual Report, 1937*, p. 2.
28. *Origin and Achievements of the Board of Water Supply*, City of New York, 1950, p. 34.
29. *Ellenville Journal*, Mar. 2, Apr. 27, May 11, 1939.
30. *Liberty Register*, Dec. 21, 1957.
31. Agnes Kortright, *Old Neversink and Surroundings* (Parksville, N.Y.: 1992).
32. Barbara Wakefield Purcell, ed., *Time and the Valley, Story of the Upper Rondout Valley,*(Town of Neversink Bicentennial Commission, 1978), p. 92.
33. Kortright, *Old Neversink and Surroundings*.
34. Fuller, interview.
35. *Time and the Valley*, p. 86.
36. Dolan, interview.
37. Howard Osterhoudt, telephone interview, Sept. 22, 1996.
38. Archie Dean, interview with author, Grahamsville,NY, Sept. 22, 1996.
39. Evelyn Hill Huntsberger, interview with author, Grahamsville, NY, July 29, 1996; essay "Final Harvest" written August 1981.
40. *Board of Water Supply Annual Report, 1952*, p. 115.
41. *Board of Water Supply Annual Report, 1950*, no page number.
42. *Board of Water Supply Annual Report, 1955*, p. 57.
43. "Pepacton Reservoir," *The Delaware Water Supply News*, Apr. 1, 1947.

18: The Pepacton

1. *Catskill Mountain News*, Mar. 12, 1937.
2. *Board of Water Supply Annual Report, 1937*, p. 57-58; *1938*, p. 60; *1950*, no page number.
3. *Catskill Mountain News*, Dec. 3, 1943; Sept. 20, 1940; Oct. 10, 1941.
4. Contract Data, General Testimony, Pepacton Reservoir Exhibits, Paul F. Cooper, Jr. Archives, Hartwick College, Oneonta, N.Y.
5. *Downsville Herald*, Nov. 27, 1947; Tom Gunn, interview with author,1997, Downsville.
6. *Downsville Herald*, Nov. 27, 1947.
7. *Downsville Herald*, Jan. 8, 1948.
8. *Walton Reporter*, June 4, 1948.
9. Earl Barker letter to author, Sept. 16, 1994, Afton, Okla.
10. *Downsville Herald*, Nov. 27, 1947.
11. Contract Data, Pepacton Reservoir Exhibits; *Board of Water Supply Annual Report, 1949*.

12. "Diversion Tunnel for Downsville Dam," *The Delaware Water System News,*" June 1, 1950
13. *Walton Reporter, Nov. 19, 1948.*
14. *Walton Reporter*, Nov. 4, 1954.
15. Ibid.
16. *Board of Water Supply Annual Report, 1953*, p. 44.
17. *Catskill Mountain News*, June 30, 1950
18. Dan Underwood, interview with author, Jan. 25, 1995, Roxbury, N.Y.
19. Glenn Watson, interview with author, Sept. 20, 1997, Downsville, N.Y.
20. Norman Brazee, letter to author, May 5, 1994.
21. *Catskill Mountain News,* Aug. 24, 1951.
22. *Board of Water Supply Annual Report, 1953*, p. 45.
23. *Walton Reporter*, Mar. 13, 1953
24. *Catskill Mountain News*, Dec. 14, 1951.
25. Contract Data, Pepacton Reservoir Exhibits.
26. *Board of Water Supply Annual Report, 1950*, no page number.
27. Board *of Water Supply Annual Report, 1952*, no page number.
28. *Walton Reporter*, July 6, 1951
29. *Board of Water Supply Annual Report, 1951*, p. 156
30. Earl Johnson, interview with author, Margaretville, NY, Apr. 5, 1995.
31. Unidentified newspaper clipping, scrapbook in collection of Delaware County Historical Assoc., Delhi, N.Y., Apr. 3, 1953.
32. *Board of Water Supply Annual Report 1951,* no pg. no.
33. Bob Yevich and Joyce Gladstone, interview with author, Downsville, N.Y., Aug. 6, 1996.
34. *Board of Water Supply Annual Reports, 1952 and 1953*, no pg. nos.
35. Ibid.
36. *Catskill Mountain News*, June 4, 1954.
37. Alice H. Jacobson, *Beneath Pepacton Waters* (Andes, N.Y.: Pepacton Press, 1988), p. 82.
38. *Board of Water Supply Annual Report, 1949*, p. 65.
39. *Board of Water Supply Annual Report, 1952*; Contract Data, Pepacton Reservoir Exhibits.
40. Summary of Business and Residence Removal, General Testimony, Pepacton Reservoir Exhibits.
41. "Origins and Achievements, Board of Water Supply, City of New York," 1950.
42. Kenneth Sprague, interview with author, Hamden, N.Y., Aug. 5, 1996.
43. *Catskill Mountain News*, Mabel VanKeuren obituary, Dec. 30, 1955.
44. Sprague; Arthur Filupeit (1996, Arkville, N.Y.); Marian Armstrong Scudder(Feb. 2, 1997, Margaretville, N.Y.), interviews with author.
45. Unidentified newspaper clipping, Apr. 18, 1954.
46. Gary Atkin, interview with author, Margaretville, NY, 1997.
47. Scudder, interview.
48. *Catskill Mountain News*, Aug. 20, 1954; Aug. 27, 1954
49. *Catskill Mountain News*, Nov. 4, 1955.
50. Jacobson, p. 20; Ivan Miller, interview with author, Sept. 20, 1995, Margaretville, N.Y.

51. *Catskill Mountain News*, Nov. 11, 1955; USX Corp. communique, Jan. 26, 1999.
52. *Catskill Mountain News*, July 15, Aug. 19, Aug. 26, Oct. 21, 1955; Aug. 17, 1956.
53. *Catskill Mountain News*, Aug. 17, 1956.
54. Evelyn Weaver Norris, remarks at re-dedication service for Union Grove Methodist Church bell, Andes Methodist Church, Sept. 24, 1995.
55. Data Regarding Population, Pepacton Reservoir Exhibits
56. Ibid.
57. *Board of Water Supply Annual Report, 1954*, no page number; *Walton Reporter*, Sept. 1954.
58. *Walton Reporter*, Jan. 14, 1955.
59. *Board of Water Supply Annual Report, 1955*, no page number.
60. *Catskill Mountain News*, April 20, 1956.
61. *Walton Reporter*, May 11, 1956.

19: Cannonsville

1. *Walton Reporter*, Mar. 24, 1950.
2. *Walton Reporter*, Mar. 30, 1950.
3. Roscoe Martin, *Water for New York, A Study in State Administration of Water Resources* (Syracuse, N.Y.: Syracuse University Press, 1960), p. 136.
4. *Delaware Republican-Express*, Delhi, N.Y., Jan. 27, 1950.
5. Martin, p. 138-139.
6. Ibid., p. 143.
7. *Board of Water Supply Annual Report, 1954*, p. 76.
8. Ibid., p. 67.
9. Paul Wadeson, interview with the author, Hancock, N.Y., Apr. 9, 1995.
10. *Board of Water Supply Annual Report, 1956*, p. 77.
11. *Board of Water Supply Annual Report, 1960*, pp. 75, 79.
12. *Deposit Courier*, Dec. 22, 1955.
13. "New York Water Board's West Delaware Tunnel," *Explosives Engineer*, Nov.-Dec. 1957, p. 179.
14. Ibid., p. 179.
15. *Delaware Water Supply News,* Apr. 1, 1959; Apr. 1, 1958; Aug. 1, 1959.
16. "First Holing Through Takes Place Wednesday," unidentified news clipping, August, 1957.
17. "Start Batching Operations for Lining of Tunnel, Nearly 900 Enjoy Engineers Clambake at East Branch," unidentified news clipping.
18. *Board of Water Supply Annual Report, 1956*, p. 78.
19. *Explosives Engineer*, Nov.-Dec. 1957, p. 187.
20. Maurice Early, interview with author, East Branch, N.Y., Apr. 9, 1995.
21. *Board of Water Supply Annual Reports, 1961, 1962.*
22. "Queens Firm Bids Low on New City Job," unidentified news clipping; General Testimony, Cannonsville Reservoir Exhibits, Paul F. Cooper, Jr. Archives, Hartwick College, Oneonta, N.Y.
23. *Delaware Water System News,* (New York City Board of Water Supply), July 1, 1964.
24. *Board of Water Supply Annual Report, 1959*, p. 80.
25. *Delaware Water System News*, April 1, 1965.
26. *Board of Water Supply Annual Report, 1960*, p. 67.
27. *Board of Water Supply Annual Report, 1957*; General Testimony, Cannonsville Reservoir Exhibits.
28. *Board of Water Supply Annual Report, 1961*, p. 98.
29. *Deposit Courier*, Nov. 19, 1964.
30. *Deposit Courier,* July 5, 1962; Sept. 20, 1962.
31. General Testimony, Cannonsville Reservoir Exhibits.
32. *Walton Reporter*, Oct. 31, 1963.
33. Perry Shelton, *Recollections of the Town of Tompkins* (1982); interview with the author, Feb. 16, 1997.
34. *Deposit Courier*, Feb. 8, 1962; Herman Gottfried, telephone interview with the author, Nov. 15, 1997.
35. *Deposit Courier*, Feb. 22, 1962.
36. *Oneonta Daily Star,* undated news clipping.
37. *Delaware Republican Express*, July 1963.
38. Leonard Rutherford, interview with the author, Delhi, NY, 1997; Beatrice Bennett, *Walking Through Time in Rock Rift* (Walton, N.Y.: Walton Historical Society, 1998).
39. Frank Daniel Myers III, *The Wood Chemical Industry in the Delaware Valley* (Middletown, N.Y.: Prior King Press, 1986), no page numbers.
40. Dorothy Kubik, "Water for New York City" (Delhi, N.Y.: *Kaatskill Life Magazine*, Spring, 1992), p. 19.
41. *Oneonta Daily Star*, Aug. 16, 1963; Mar. 15, 1964.
42. *Delaware Water System News*, Apr. 1, 1965.
43. General Testimony, Cannonsville Reservoir Exhibits,
44. *Delaware River Basin Commission Annual Report, 1987*, p. 19.
45. "New Cannonsville Dam Valves Go Into Operation," press release, NYC Department of Environmental Protection, June 3, 1997.
46. Raphael Hurwitz, NYC Dept. of Environmental Protection, telephone interview with author, Feb. 20, 1999.
47. Bob Weyrauch, interview with author, East Branch, N.Y., June 7, 1997.

20: Assessing the Damage

1. *Katonah Times*, February, March, 1899.
2. Ibid., April 21, 1899.
3. Ibid., Nov. 29, 1907.
4. *Cornwall Local,* June 3, 1909.
5. Watershed Condemnation Files, Westchester County Archives, Elmsford, NY.
6. Unattributed Commissioner's Notebook, Westchester County Archives, Elmsford, NY.
7. Watershed Condemnation Files.
8. *The Leader*, July 26, 1909, clipping in A. T. Clearwater Papers, Senate House Museum, Kingston; Bob Steuding, *Last of the Handmade Dams* (Fleischmanns, N.Y.: Purple Mountain Press, 1985), p. 94.
9 Unidentified clipping, Oct. 15, 1909, Clearwater Papers.
10. *Board of Water Supply Annual Report*, 1924, p. 16.
11. Ibid., p. 15.
12. *Board of Water Supply Annual Report*, 1922, p. 12.
13. Ashokan Reservoir Record Series, Guide to the Special Collection, Ulster County Clerk's Office, Kingston, NY.

14. Charles H. Weidner, *Water for A City, A History of New York City's Problem from the Beginning to the Delaware River System, 1897-1966* (New Brunswick, N.J.: Rutgers University Press, 1974), p. 246-47.
15. *The New York Times*, Apr. 18, 1918.
16. *Pine Hill Sentinel*, Nov. 7, 1914.
17. *Catskill Mountain News*, July 1, 1921; *Board of Water Supply Annual Reports* 1922, 1923, 1926.
18. New York City Water Supply Orders Book #2, Schoharie County Clerk's Office, Schoharie, NY.
19. *Board of Water Supply Annual Report*, 1923, p. 12.
20. *Board of Water Supply Annual Report,* 1931, Statement B.
21. *Board of Water Supply Annual Report*, 1939, p. 19.
22. *Ellenville Journal*, Feb. 8, 1940.
23. Ibid., May 9, 1940.
24. *Ellenville Journal*, April 14, 1938.
25. Margaret Dolan, interview with the author, Grahamsville, N.Y., 1996.
26. W. V. Denman, Letter to the Editor, Unidentified newspaper clipping, Mar. 22, 1941.
27. Agnes Kortright, (Parksville, N.Y.: *Old Neversink and Surroundings*, 1992)
28. Joe Krum, telephone interview with author, Jan. 5, 1999.
29. Justus Asthalter, telephone interview with author, Jan. 3, 1999.
30. *Liberty Register*, Mar. 7, 1957.
31. Schroeder vs. City of New York, No. 75, Supreme Court of the United States, Dec. 17, 1962 decision.
32. Board of Water Supply Annual Report, 1962, p. 26.
33. Edna Gavette, interview with author, Margaretville, N.Y., Dec. 5, 1998
34. Idolene Graham, "The City Vs. Me," Deposit, NY: *Courier Magazine*, Oct. 1955), p. 26.
35. Ibid., p. 28.
36. Herman Gottfried, interview with author, Centerville, Mass., August, 1996.
37. Ibid.
38. Paul Eaton Sr., interview with author, Walton, N.Y., Jan. 2, 1999.
39. *Catskill Mountain News*, Jan. 14, 1949; May 20, 1949; Jan. 13, 1950.
40. *Catskill Mountain News*, Oct. 9, 1953; Gottfried, interview.
41. Gottfried, interview.
42. *Catskill Mountain News*, May 11, 1956.
43. *Catskill Mountain News*, Nov. 6, 1953, Dec. 25, 1953; Dec. 17, 1954.
44. Board of Water Supply Transcripts Relating to the Pepacton and Cannonsville Reservoirs, vol. 189, 190, Paul F. Cooper, Jr. Archives, Hartwick College, Oneonta, N.Y.; *Walton Reporter*, Feb. 19, 1954.
45. *Deposit Courier*, July 21, 1955.
46. Unidentified newspaper clipping, "Warren M. Kelly Sells His Farm to New York City," scrapbook, Delaware County Historical Assoc., Delhi, N.Y.
47. *Catskill Mountain News*, Sept. 22, 1961; Herman Gottfried, telephone interview with author, Nov. 15, 1997.
48. *Catskill Mountain News* June 16, 1961; *Deposit Courier* Nov. 10, 1960; Gottfried, interview.

49. Eaton, interview.
50. *Deposit Courier* citing *The New York Times*, Oct. 31, 1963.
51. *Catskill Mountain News*, May 25, 1956; Oct. 19, 1956.
52. *Deposit Courier*, Oct. 17, 1968.
53. *Catskill Mountain News* August 22, 1958; Nov. 14, 1958.
54. Fred Colie, telephone interview with author Jan. 15, 1999; *Tuscarora, A Continuing Story* (Tuscarora Club of Mill Brook, N.Y., 1981), p. 23-24.
55. Board of Water Supply Transcripts Relating to Pepacton and Cannonsville Reservoirs, Vol. 362 (claim of Anna Schuster).
56. Ibid., Consolidated Delaware Sections 14-20A; 30-37.
57. General Testimony Relating to Pepacton and Cannonsville Reservoirs.

21: Tunnel Vision

1. "City Tunnel No. 3," (New York: Department of Environmental Protection), p. 3-4.
2. *Board of Water Supply Annual Report, 1962*, p. 62.
3. *Board of Water Supply Annual Report, 1969*, p. 59-60.
4. *Board of Water Supply Annual Report, 1970*.
5. Malcolm Wane; Victor Feigelman; Samuel Sigman, "The Van Cortlandt Complex," a technical paper, undated.
6. Samuel Sigman, telephone interview with author, Feb. 21, 1999.
7. Michael Greenberg, telephone interview with author, Feb. 22, 1999.
8. Wane et al, "The VanCortlandt Complex."
9. Ibid.
10. *Board of Water Supply Annual Report, 1973*.
11. Paul Delaney, *Sandhogs, A History of the Tunnel Workers of New York*, (New York: Longfield Press, 1983), p. 49.
12. "Environs," (New York: Department of Environmental Protection, Vol. 1, #6, winter 1986).
13. Program, Activation Ceremony and Memorial Service, City Water Tunnel #3, New York City, Aug. 13, 1998.
14. Greenberg, interview.
15. Wane et al, "The Van Cortlandt Complex."
16. Michael Greenberg, interview with author, New York City, Feb. 4, 1998.
17. Ibid.
18. "Fire in the Hole," (New York: Department of Environmental Protection, undated).
19. Stuart Williams, interview with author, Downsville, N.Y., Feb. 28, 1998.
20. Program, Groundbreaking, City Tunnel #3, Stage 2, New York City, June 28, 1993.
21. "State of the Art Tunnel Boring Machine Set to Carve Out Queens Water Tunnel," *U.S. Water News Online*, Dec. 1996.
22. Richard DuBois, telephone interview with author, Feb. 21, 1999.
23. Ibid.
24. Dale Estus, telephone interview with author, Feb. 21, 1999.
25. Ibid.
26. David Walker, telephone interview with author, Sept. 12, 1996.

27. George Mekenian, telephone interview with author, Sept. 12, 1998.

22: To the Future. . .

1. *Catskill Mountain News*, July 11, 1958; *Rules and Regulations for the Protection from Contamination, Degradation and Pollution of the New York City Water Supply and its Sources* (NYC Department of Environmental Protection, May 1, 1997), p. 1.
2. *Catskill Mountain News*, May 3, 1990.
3. Ibid., June 28, 1990.
4. Ibid., Sept. 13, 1990.
5. Ibid., Sept. 20, 1990.
6. Ibid., Oct. 11, 1990; Oct. 4, 1990.
7. Ibid., Nov. 15, 1990.
8. Ibid., Jan. 10, 1991.
9. Ibid., Mar. 14, 1991.
10. Kenneth Markert, communication with author Mar. 1, 1999.
11. *Catskill Mountain News*, Mar. 28, 1991
12. Ibid., Sept. 22, 1993
13. Ibid., Apr. 29, 1994

14. *Whole Farm Planning* (Walton, N.Y.: Watershed Agricultural Council, Jan. 1996).
15. Watershed Agricultural Council records
16. *Summary Guide to the Terms of the Watershed Agreement* (Arkville, N.Y.: Catskill Center for Conservation and Development, October, 1997), pp.3-4.
17. "Somewhere Down the Crazy River," (*Outside Magazine*, Nov. 1997), p. 185.
18. Comments heard by author at Sept. 10, 1996 announcement of watershed agreement, New York City.
19. *New York City Watershed Memorandum of Agreement*, Jan. 21, 1997.
20. *Rules and Regulations*, May 1, 1997.
21. "Watershed Regulations Go Into Effect," New York City Dept. of Environmental Protection press release, May 21, 1997.
22. Bond Prospectus, New York City Municipal Water Finance Authority, Oct. 22, 1998, p. 46.
23. Ibid., p. 50.
24. David Tobias, New York City Dept. of Environmental Protection Land Acquisition and Stewardship office, Shokan, N.Y., communication with author, Jan. 10, 1999.
25. Geoffrey Ryan, New York City Dept. of Environmental Protection Public Affairs office, Corona, N.Y., communication with author, Mar. 1, 1999.

Bibliography

Books

Adams, Arthur. *The Hudson Through the Years.* Westwood, N.J.: Lind Publications, 1983.

Avery, Mrs. A. F. (Ophelia). *Historical Sketch of Katonah, N.Y.* Katonah: Seth Deacon, 1896.

Bennett, Beatrice. *Walking Through Time in Rock Rift.* Walton, N.Y. Walton Historical Society, 1998.

Burkey, Charles P., and James Sanborn. "Engineering Geology of the Catskill Water Supply." Vol. 86. *Transactions of the American Society of Civil Engineers.* New York: American Society of Civil Engineers, 1923.

Bliven, Bruce, Jr., and Naomi Bliven. *New York, The Story of the World's Most Exciting City.* New York: Random House, 1969.

Bonner, William Thompson. *New York, The World's Metropolis, 1623-1923:* New York: R. L. Polk & Co., 1924.

Boyle, Robert H. "New York Down the Drain," *The Water Hustlers.* San Francisco: Sierra Club, 1971.

Brandt, Nat. *The Man Who Tried to Burn New York.* Syracuse: Syracuse University Press, 1986.

Breslin, Jimmy. *Table Money.* New York: Ticknor & Fields, 1986.

Burke, Jack, with Jim Brady. *Tunnel Stiffs Tales.* Minneapolis: American Underground Construction Assoc., 1995

Canning, Jeff, and Wally Buxton. *History of the Tarrytowns, Westchester County, N.Y., from Ancient Times to the Present.* Harrison, N.Y.: Harbor Hill Books, 1975.

Chase, Borden. *Sandhog, The Way of Life of the Tunnel Builders.* Evanston, Ill.: Row, Peterson & Co., 1941.

Cirillo, Joan. *The Westchester Book.* New York: Stein & Day Publishers, 1976.

D'Alvia, Mary Josephine. *The History of the New Croton Dam.* n.p., 1976.

Delaney, Paul E. *Sandhogs, A History of the Tunnel Workers of New York.* New York: The Longfield Press, 1983.

DeNatale, Douglas. *Two Stones for Every Dirt, The Story of Delaware County, N.Y.* Fleischmanns, N.Y.: Purple Mountain Press, 1987.

Diary of Philip Hone 1828-1851. 2 Vol. Ed. Bayard Tuckerman. New York: Dodd & Mead, 1889.

Dickens, Charles. *American Notes.* New York: St. Martin's Press. 1985

Duffy, John. *A History of Public Health in New York City 1625-1866.* New York: Russell Sage Foundation, 1968.

Duncombe, Frances R. *Katonah, The History of a New York Village and Its People.* Katonah: Katonah Village Improvement Society, 1961. Centennial Edition, 1997.

Dunshee, Kenneth Holcomb. *As You Pass By.* New York: Hastings House Publishers, 1952.

Dunwell, Frances F. *The Hudson River Highlands.* New York: Columbia University Press, 1991.

Eastman, H. G. *Water Supply of New York, Suggestions for a Permanent and Economical Settlement of the Question. The Hudson River as an Available and Unfailing Source.* New York. 1876.

Evers, Alf. *The Catskills, From Wilderness to Woodstock.* Woodstock, N.Y.: Overlook Press, 1982.

Finney, Jack. *Time and Again.* New York: Simon & Schuster, 1970.

Foster, C. *An Account of the Conflagration of the Principal Part of the First Ward of the City of New York.* New York. 1835.

Gausmann, R. W. "The Shandaken Tunnel," Vol. 92, *Transactions of the American Society of Civil Engineers.* New York: American Society of Civil Engineers, 1928.

Golden's Bridge, Spanning the Years. Golden's Bridge, N.Y.: Increase Miller PTA, 1976.

Hall, Edward Hagaman. *Water for New York City,* Excerpted from The Catskill Aqueduct, 1917. Saugerties, N.Y.: Hope Farm Press, 1993.

Hewitt, Edward Ringwood. *Telling on the Trout.* New York: Charles Scribner's Sons, 1926.

History of Southeastern New York. 3 vol. New York: Lewis Historical Publishing Co., 1946.

History of the Town of Lewisboro. South Salem, N.Y.: Lewisboro History Book Committee, 1981.

In Celebration of Cornwall, 200 Years. Ed. Martha Schiff. Cornwall, N.Y.: Cornwall Local, 1976.

Horton, Gertrude Fitch. *Old Delaware County, A Memoir.* Fleischmanns, N.Y.: Purple Mountain Press, 1993.

_____. *The Delaware & Northern and the Towns It Served.* Feischmanns, N.Y.: Purple Mountain Press, 1989.

Interview at Weehawken, The Burr-Hamilton Duel as told in the Original Documents. Ed. Harold C. Syrett and Jean Cooke. Middletown, Conn.: Wesleyan University, 1960.

Jacobs, David and Anthony Neville. *Bridges, Canals & Tunnels, The Engineering Conquest of America.* New York: American Heritage Publishing, 1968.

Jacobson, Alice H. *Beneath Pepacton Waters.* Andes, N.Y.: Pepacton Press, 1988.

Jacobson, Alice and Robert. *Echoes Along the Delaware.* Andes, N.Y.: Pepacton Press, 1992.

Kelly, Thomas. *Payback.* New York: Alfred A. Knopf, 1997.

Kelly, Elizabeth Burroughs. *John Burroughs, Naturalist.* New York: Exposition Press, 1959.

Kessler, Henry, and Eugene Rachliss. *Peter Stuyvesant and His New York.* New York: Random House, 1959.

King, Charles. *A Memoir of the Construction, Cost and Capacity of the Croton Aqueduct.* New York: 1843.

King, Moses. *King's Handbook of New York City,* Vol. 1. Boston, 1893. New York: Benjamin Blom, Inc., 1972.

Kortright, Agnes. *Old Neversink and Surroundings.* Parksville, N.Y.: 1992.

Kouwenhoven, John. *The Columbia Historical Portrait of New York*. New York: Doubleday & Co., 1953. Harper & Row, 1972.

Lamb, Martha. *History of the City of New York*, Vol. II. New York: A. S. Barnes & Co., 1880.

Larkin, F. Daniel. *John B. Jervis, An American Engineering Pioneer*. Iowa City: Iowa University Press, 1990.

_____*Pioneer American Railroads: The Mohawk & Hudson & The Saratoga & Schenectady*. Fleischmanns, N.Y.: Purple Mountain Press, 1995.

Law, Anwei Skinsnes. *The Great Flood, Johnstown, Pennsylvania, 1889*. Johnstown: Johnstown Area Heritage Assoc., 1997.

Mandelbaum, Seymour. *Boss Tweed's New York*. New York: J. Wiley, 1965.

Mayer, C. H. *The Continuing Struggle, Autobiography of a Labor Activist*. Northampton, Mass.: Pittenbruach Press, 1989.

Mattice, Beatrice. *They Walked These Hills Before Me, An Early History of the Town of Conesville*. Cornwallville, N.Y.: Hope Farm Press, 1980.

McDonald, Forrest. *Alexander Hamilton, A Biography*. New York: W. W. Norton & Co., 1979.

McFee, Michele. *Limestone Locks and Overgrowth, The Rise and Descent of the Chenango Canal*. Fleischmanns, N.Y.: Purple Mountain Press, 1993.

Miller, James. *Miller's Stranger's Guide for the City of New York*. New York, 1861.

Myers III, Frank Daniel. *The Wood Chemical Industry in the Delaware Valley*. Middletown, N.Y.: Prior King Press, 1986.

"The New Croton Aqueduct, 1889," *New York, Tales of the Empire State*. Comp. Frank Oppel. Secaucus, N.J.: Castle Books, 1988.

Pelletreau, William. *History of Putnam County*. Philadelphia: W. W. Preston, 1886. Reprinted 1975.

Pine III, Joshua. *The Bygone Era, Rafting on the Delaware, 1883*. Ed. Alice H. Jacobson. Andes, N.Y.: Pepacton Press, 1995.

The Reminiscences of John B. Jervis, Engineer of the Old Croton. Ed. Neal FitzSimons. Syracuse, N.Y.: Syracuse University Press. 1971.

Rogow, Arnold. *A Fatal Friendship, Alexander Hamilton and Aaron Burr*. New York: Hill & Wang, 1998.

Rosenberg, Charles E. *The Cholera Years, The U.S. in 1832, 1849, and 1866*. Chicago: University of Chicago Press, 1962.

Shaw, Ronald. *Erie Water West, A History of the Erie Canal, 1792-1854*. Lexington: University Press of Kentucky, 1966.

Silver, Nathan. *Lost New York*. New York: Schocken Books, 1971.

Sketches and Views of the Old and New Villages of Katonah, N.Y. Katonah: Katonah Village Improvement Society, 1900.

Steuding, Bob. *The Last of the Handmade Dams, The Story of the Ashokan Reservoir*. Fleischmanns, N.Y.: Purple Mountain Press, 1985.

Time and the Valley, Story of the Upper Rondout Valley. Neversink, N.Y.: Town of Neversink Bicentennial Commission, 1978.

Township of Neversink, 1798-1998. Neversink, N.Y.,1998.

VanAller Hernick, Linda. *The Gilboa Fossils*. Rensselaerville, N.Y.: Givetian Press, 1996.

Van Pelt, Daniel. *Leslie's History of the Greater New York*, Vol. 1. New York: Arkell Publishing, 1898.

Van Put, Ed. *The Beaverkill*. New York: Lyons & Burford, 1996.

Water Rights on the Muscoot River. Supreme Court Proceedings. New York: Martin Brown, 1882.

Weidner, Charles H. *Water for a City, A History of New York City's Problem from the Beginning to the Delaware River System, 1897-1966*. New Brunswick, N.J.: Rutgers University Press, 1974.

White, Lazarus. *Catskill Water Supply of New York City, History, Location, Sub-surface Investigations and Construction*. New York: John Wiley & Sons, 1913.

The WPA Guide to New York City. New York: Random House, 1939. Reprinted 1982.

Wood, Leslie. *H'olt! T'other Way!* Middletown, N.Y., 1950.

Youmans, George. *Memories of Pepacton*. (n.p.) 1988.

_____*Up and Down the River and Hollows*. (n.p.) 1989.

Articles

Cary, William de la M. "Reminiscences of Old Shokan." *Forest and Stream*. Feb. 14, 1914.

Chiles, James, "'Remember Jimmy, Stay Away from the Bottom of the Shaft!'" *Smithsonian*, July 1994.

"Croton Water." *Scribner's Monthly*. Vol. XIV, no. 2, June 1877, p. 161.

Dane, John Brewster. "Jerome Park Racing Days." *Cosmopolitan*. Vol. 30, 1901. p. 346.

DeNio, Pierre. "Water is Where You Find It." *Courier Magazine*. Oct., 1954.

Heacox, Cecil. "Reservoirs vs. Drought." *The Conservationist*. Feb.-Mar., 1958.

Kubik, Dorothy. "Water for New York City," *Kaatskill Life*, Vol. 5, No. 2; Vol. 6, No. 1; Vol. 6, No. 4; Vol. 7, No. 1. 1990-1992.

"A Mystery of Labor Politics: Who Murdered the Sandhog Leader?" *Life*. Vol. 2, No. 10, Mar. 8, 1937.

Miraldi, Robert. "Draining Upstate." *Empire State Report*. Apr. 1986.

Pauly, Jr., L. J. "The New York Water Board's West Delaware Tunnel." *The Explosives Engineer*. Nov.-Dec. 1957.

Perrin, Noel. "New York Drowns Another Valley." *Harpers*. Aug., 1963.

Swerdlow, Joel. "Under New York." *National Geographic*. Feb., 1997.

Newspapers

(Where public repositories were utilized, they are noted.)

Binghamton Press

Brewster Standard (Brewster, N.Y. Public Library)

Catskill Mountain News (Fairview Public Library, Margaretville, N.Y.)

Delaware Republican, Republican-Express (Cannon Free Library, Delhi, N.Y.)
Deposit Courier (Deposit, N.Y. Free Library)
Downsville News, Herald (Downsville, N.Y. Public Library)
Ellenville Press (Ellenville, N.Y. Public Library)
Katonah Record, Katonah Times, North Westchester Times (Katonah, N.Y. Public Library)
Kingston Daily Freeman
Liberty Register
Livingston Manor Times
Mt. Kisco Recorder
New York Journal, New York Evening Post, New York Tribune, New York Herald, New York Telegram (Croton Village History Room, Croton-on-Hudson, N.Y.)
New York Times (State University of New York at Delhi; New York Public Library)
North Castle Sun (North Castle Library, Armonk, N.Y.)
Oneonta Daily Star
Pine Hill Sentinel (Ulster County Community College, Stone Ridge, N.Y.)
Putnam County Courier (Reed Memorial Library, Carmel, N.Y.)
Putnam County Republican (Southeast Record Center, Brewster, N.Y.)
Roscoe-Rockland Review
Sullivan County Review
Walton Reporter

Special Publications

North Castle History. Vol. 2, No. 1 "Historical Kensico and the Hills of North Castle." Spring, 1975. "Kensico, The Lost Village," "Kensico, A Special Place," and "The Building of the Kensico Dam." Vol. 10, 1983. North Castle Historical Society.
North Salem Historical Society Publications. "Dutch Soldier to Yankee Trader, Early Entrepreneurs in Purdys," Mar. 1980; "Look Ma, They Moved Purdys," 1975; "Heavy Industry for Croton Falls," Winter, 1978; "Views of Croton Falls," Vol. 8, No. 2, Sept. 1981.
"Stories of Old Gilboa." Gilboa-Conesville Central School. 1988-89.

Official Records, Municipal Publications and Technical Reports

"1,820,000,000 Gallons Per Day, 50th Anniversary of the Board of Water Supply." 1955.
Annual Reports of the Board of Water Supply of the City of New York. 1907-1973.
"Catskill Water System News." City of New York Board of Water Supply, June 20, 1911-Dec. 20, 1913
"Catskill Water Supply, A General Description." City of New York Board of Water Supply. Jan., 1913.
"Catskill Water Supply and the Project for an Additional Supply from the Delaware River Watershed and the Rondout Creek." 1936.
Cemetery Reinterments, Pepacton Reservoir. Compiled by Board of Water Supply, City of New York, ed. Russell C. Miller and Robert A. Rowe. 1996.

"City Water Tunnel #3 of New York City's Water Supply System." New York City Dept. of Environmental Protection. (n.d.)
"Delaware Water Supply News." City of New York Board of Water Supply, Aug. 1, 1938-Oct. 1, 1965.
"The Delaware Water Supply for the City of New York." A series of 14 articles reprinted by the Board of Water Supply from *Engineering News.* 1942.
"A Description of the Water Supply System of the City of New York." Dept. of Water Supply, Gas and Electricity. 1952.
"Facts and Regulations for Consumers of Water." Dept. of Water Supply Gas & Electricity, City of New York. Jan. 1, 1911.
Iwan, Gerald. "Drinking Water Quality Concerns of New York City, Past and Present." *Annals of the New York Academy of Sciences,* reprinted from Vol. 501. 1988.
"Managing for the Present, Planning for the Future." Second Interim Report of the Mayor's Intergovernmental Task Force on New York City Water Supply Needs. Dec., 1987.
"Municipal Water Supply System of the City of New York, A General Description." May, 1920.
New York City Municipal Water Finance Authority Prospectus. 1997 and 1998.
New York City Water Commissioners Semi-Annual Report, Jan. 1837-Dec. 1848.
"Origin and Achievements of the Board of Water Supply, City of New York." 1950
Platt, D. H. "Roof Bolting the Delaware Aqueduct." Information Circular #7652. U. S. Dept. of the Interior. Nov. 1952.
Report of the Chief Engineer on the General State of the Work on the Croton Aqueduct, Nov. 1833-Dec. 1848.
Reports on the New Croton Aqueduct Reservoirs and Dams,1883-87; 1887-1895; 1895-1907. City of New York Aqueduct Commission.
"Testimonial to the Chief Engineers, 1905-1965. Board of Water Supply, City of New York.
Wane, Malcolm T. and Victor Feigelman and Samuel Sigman. "The Van Cortlandt Complex." (n.p., n.d.)
"The Water Supply of the City of New York." Dept. of Water Supply, Gas and Electricity. Dec., 1937.

Additional records were reviewed at Hartwick College Archives, Oneonta, N.Y. (Board of Water Supply Transcripts Relating to the Pepacton and Cannonsville Reservoirs); Westchester County Archives, Elmsford, N.Y. (Transcripts and Documents Relating to Croton Aqueduct Commission and Board of Water Supply Projects); Roxbury, N. Y. Library (Gilboa Cemetery Exhumation Records); and at the County Clerk Offices of Sullivan County, Monticello, N.Y.; Schoharie County, Schoharie, N.Y.; Delaware County, Delhi, N.Y.; Ulster County, Kingston, N.Y. (Board of Water Supply Transcripts and Materials Relating to the Neversink, Schoharie, Pepacton, Cannonsville, Ashokan and Rondout Reservoirs, respectively.)

Acknowledgments

The making of this book would not have been possible without the generous contributions of many, many people.

My thanks go out to Wray Rominger of Purple Mountain Press, who first suggested I write an account of the New York City water system's development and then provided support and encouragement when it was most needed.

To my son, Erik Galusha Pickhardt, I offer apologies for the weekends and vacations missed over the past three years when research and writing took priority. I hope one day to reward your love and patience.

Genuine appreciation is extended to more than 100 people interviewed for this book: men and women who worked on the city's water projects, or had family members who did; those who once lived in the reservoir basins; and others with special connections to the work. Space prevents me from naming all who shared with me their memories of accomplishment, community history and personal pain. Please know that I am indeed grateful.

The New York City Department of Environmental Protection, which is now responsible for maintaining and delivering the city's water, provided willing access to vast stores of Board of Water Supply records. Current and former DEP and BWS employees who shared institutional and individual memories and otherwise assisted included Carl Ambrose, Michael Greenberg, Raphael Hurwitz, Joe Landau, Carl Picha, Geoffrey Ryan, Samuel Sigman and Ed Stanton.

The DEP Archives, under the management of Cooper Union, provided numerous photographs. My thanks to Paul Deppe for his help in that regard. Other institutions offering photos and illustrations for reproduction included the Cranberry Lake Preserve in North White Plains, the Cornelia Cotton Gallery in Croton-on-Hudson, the Croton-on-Hudson Historical Society, the Delaware County Historical Association in Delhi, the Delaware River Basin Commission in West Trenton, N.J., Empire State Railway Museum in Phoenicia, the Jervis Public Library in Rome, N.Y., the Town of Olive Archives and the Olive Free Library, the Zadock Pratt Museum in Prattsville, the Ossining Historical Society, the Shandaken Historical Museum in Pine Hill, the Southeast Museum in Brewster, the Staten Island Historical Society in Richmond, and the Trailside Nature Museum in Cross River. Several individuals also contributed photos from their personal collections. I thank each of them. A special note of thanks to Lonnie Gale, Alton Weiss and Elise Hornbeck.

Others deserving mention for their valued assistance include Herman Gottfried and Paul Wadeson. I am beholden to the Roxbury Arts Group for the Decentralization Grant that helped offset some of my research costs. To Joe Michaels and George Mekenian I extend a warm note of thanks for their thorough reviews of the draft manuscript.

More than 60 museums, libraries and official repositories harbor materials related to the building of the New York City water system and the communities affected by it. They are treasure troves of records, diaries, letters, photographs, period newspaper accounts and other documents that were consulted for this book. I thank those responsible for caring for these priceless materials.

Thanks, too, to the historians and authors upon whose research I have drawn when first-person accounts were not available. Each of the city water system's reservoirs deserves its own book and, thankfully, a few have already been written. I regret having to leave out of this work so much that is of specific local interest. But my intent was to bring as much information as possible about the development of this vast system between the covers of one volume, and to show that, indeed, the whole is greater than the sum of its parts. I hope that I have succeeded.

I am honored to dedicate this book to the visionaries whose intellect and skill created the water system that made New York City's development possible, and to those who sacrificed their homes, their health, their very lives for the welfare of millions of distant strangers. May those who provide the water, those who live near its source, and especially those who drink it, be ever mindful of those sacrifices.

Diane Galusha
April 1999

East Branch Dam.
Robert J. Kornfeld, Jr., A.I.A.

INDEX

Acker, Milo, 95
Aden, N.Y., 193, 199
Ad Hoc Task Force on Agriculture and New York City Watershed Regulations, 258
Adsit, Robert, *256*
Advent Christian Church, Arena, N.Y., *211*
African Americans, employed as reservoir and aqueduct workers, 66
  on Ashokan Reservoir, 128, 134, *135*
  on Catskill Aqueduct system, 103, 106-107, 111
  on Cross River Reservoir, 86
  on Shandaken Tunnel, 161
  wages of, 80-81
Albany (boat), 97
Albany, N.Y., 170
Albrecht, E. J., 221
Albright & Friedl, 194
Alkirk Hardrock Tunneler, 123
Allaben, N.Y.
  Board of Water Supply Division office, 163
  Board of Water Supply Police precinct, 137
  during Schoharie Reservoir construction, 157, 160, 161
Allen, Agnes, 239
Allen, Charles, *215*, 239
Allen, Horatio, 24
Allen, Stephen, 21, 22-23
Amawalk Reservoir, Somers, N.Y., *50*, 59
American Condensed Milk Co., 59
American Institute of Steel, Beautiful Bridges Contest, 222
American Jockey Club, 69
American Notes (Dickens), 23-24
American Society of Civil Engineers, 24-25, 54, 67, 146
American Water Works Association, 146
Andes, N.Y., 204-205, 214
Angell, George, 143
Angler's Club Bulletin, 197
"Annabel Lee" (Poe), 27
Ansco mucker, West Delaware Tunnel, *220*
Antrim Lodge, Roscoe, N.Y., 206, 218
Apex, N.Y., 222
Apex Bridge, 222
Apex Mountain, *218*
Apgar, James, 83
Appellate Division, property appraisal awards decisions by, 232, 234, 242
Appleton, Albert, 256, 257-258
Appraisal Commissions, 61, 215, 231-242

appointment of Commissioners for, 231
  criticism of, 39, 232
8th Cornell, 232
property awards claims hearings held by
  Ashokan Reservoir, 132, 234
  Catskill Aqueduct System, 111
  Cannonsville Reservoir, 239-242
  Cross River Reservoir, 83
  Delaware System, 241-242
  fraudulent evidence in, 239
  legal counsel for, 238-239
  Neversink Reservoir, 236-237
  Pepacton Reservoir, 238-239
  Schoharie Reservoir, 234-236
Aqueduct Commission. *See also* Croton Aqueduct Commission
  abolition of, 87
  alleged misfeasance by, 70-71
  approval of Cross River Reservoir project by, 83, 84
  approval of Jerome Park Reservoir project by, 70
  chief engineer of, 63
  New Croton Aqueduct inspection by, 67
  New Croton Reservoir redesign by, 75
  1895-1907 reports of, 73, 79, 84
  president of, 86
Aquifers, as New York City water supply, 47
Archville, N.Y., 25
Ardsley, N.Y., 136
Arena, N.Y., 170
  auction of, 212
  flooding by Pepacton Reservoir, 210, *210, 211*, 213
Arena Heights, 212
Arena School, 213
Arkville, N.Y., 206, 228
Arkville Free Methodist Church, 212
Armonk, N.Y., 150
Armstrong, Charles, 12
Armstrong, James "Bruce," 212
Armstrong, Marian (Scudder), 212
Armstrong, Roger, 172, 189
Army Corps of Engineers, 12, 195
Arnez, Desi, 227
Arson. *See also* Fires
  against New Croton Aqueduct, 67
  against New York City hotels, 38
Arundel Corp., 246
Ashbee, William, 76
Ashokan (boat), 107
Ashokan, meaning of, 139
Ashokan Dam. *See* Olive Bridge Dam
Ashokan Reservoir, 125-139

  aeration system of, 139, *139*

alleged leakage from, 169-170
bid-letting investigation related to, 125
connection with Kensico basin, 148-149
construction of, 149
  "dinky" railroad use in, 130, *131*
  use of mules in, 134-135
  contractors for, 125-126, 132, 134-135
  core borings for, 96-97
  daily water delivery to New York City from, 176
  engineers for, 125, *127*
  as "Esopus Folly," 125
  hydro-electric power plant, 263
  J. Waldo Smith monument, 185
  laborers on, 128, *129*, 130
    African-American, 128, 134, *135*
    criminal behavior of, 136
    injuries and fatalities among, 130-131
    school for children of, *127*, 128
    strike by, 129
    wages, 128-129
  land acquisition for, 126, 128, 129, 130, 132-134, 135
  New York City Mayor Koch's visit to, 229
  during 1926 drought, 169-170
  out-take of, 99
  taxation of, 242-243
  water quality protection of, 151
  during World War II, 137
Ashokan water system, auction of, 242-243
Ashton, N.Y., 128
Associated Contractors, 183
Asthalter, Justus, 237
Astor Hotel, New York City, 30
Astoria, Queens, 246
Atkin, Darrell "Mutt," *211*, 212
Atkin, Gary, 212
Atkin, Inez, *211*, 212
Atkin's Store and Post Office, Shavertown, N.Y., *211, 212*, 213
Atlas Capco Robbins, 250
Atomic-energy plants, for water desalination, 229
AT&T Co., 78
Atwood, NY, 102-103
Austrian immigrants, employed as aqueduct and reservoir workers, 128
"Automatic Respirator & Smoke Protector," 103
Avenire, La, 87
Avery, A. F., 56

Bailey, Edward, 239
Bailey, George F., 47
Baisley's Pond, Brooklyn, N.Y., 46

Baltimore, Maryland, water supply system, 73, 92
Bangston, Martin, 52
Bank of New York, 15
Barclay Building, New York City, 94
Barkaboom Valley, 213
Barker, Earl, 202
Barkovich, Rudolph, 241
Barnard, J.F., 232
Barnhardt, Mary, 214
Barnhardt, Scott, 214
Barrett, Joseph, 76
Barrett, Laban, 39
Barrett Pond, Putnam County, N.Y., 45
Barringer, Claude, 129
Barryville, N.Y., 194
Bart, Belle, 197
Barth, Louis, 224
Basic Creek, Greene County, N.Y., 170
Bavaria (ship), 184
Bear Gutter Tunnel, 143, 150
Bearkill, as dynamite storage site, 158, 160
Beaver Engineering and Contracting Co., 121, 123, 177
Beaverkill (creek), as West Delaware Tunnel site, 218
Beaver Kill, N.Y., 12
Beaver Kill Dikes, 126
Beaverkill Swamp, 96-97
Beaverkill Valley, 194
Beck, Lawrence T., 12, 217-218
Becker, M.J., 54
Bedford, N.Y.
  as Delaware Aqueduct Tunnel site, 180
  as Muscoot Reservoir site, 79, 81
  property condmenations in, 45
  property damage awards, 232
Bedford-Stuyvesant, Brooklyn, 246
Beecher, Howard, 236
Beerston, N.Y., flooding by Cannonsville Reservoir, 222, 271
Begun, Dora, 7
Begun, Morris, 7, 191, 237
Belden & Denison, 51, 52-53
Bell, Herman, 135
Belleayre Mountain, as Crystal Spring Water Company site, 88
Belmont, August, 69
Belmont Stakes, 69
"Bends," 118, 189
Benjamin Odell (ship), 185
Bennett, W. J., 18
Bennett, William, 160
Bergner, C. S., 134
Berkey, Charles, 104, 167
Bernard, Charles, 67-68
Best, S. F., 61

Bethel, Zana, 224
Bethlehem Steel, 209
Bianchi & Co., 206-207
Big Indian, N.Y., 89, 92, 93
Big Indian-Oliverea Board of Trade, 227-228
Bill's Casino, Neversink, N.Y., 7
Billings, Ernest, 165
Binghamton, N.Y., 239, 240
Birch, E. E., 47
Bishop's Falls, N.Y.
  as Ashokan Dam site, 92
  flooding by Ashokan Reservoir, 126, 135
Bittersweet, N.Y., flooding by Neversink Reservoir, 7, 193, 198, 270
Blackburn, Luke, 38
Black Hand Society, 80, 87
Black River, N.Y., as proposed dam site, 12, 228-229
Blackstone, Edward, 240
Blackwell's Island, New York City, 33
Blizzard of 1888, 55
Blomquist, Paul, 240
Blue Hill, Neversink, N.Y., 237
Board of Aqueduct Commissioners, for New Croton Reservoir and Aqueduct, 54-55
Board of Estimate and Apportionment, 46, 83, 217
  approval of City Tunnel #1 by, 114-115
  approval of City Tunnel #2 by, 172
  approval of Delaware System by, 170, 179
  approval of Catskill watershed by, 95
  approval of Schoharie Reservoir by, 157
Board of Fire Underwriters, 94
Board of Public Improvements, 92
Board of Water Commissioners, president of, 30-31
Board of Water Supply
  abolition of, 160, 253
  Administrative Bureau, 94
  Annual Reports
    1906, 96
    1907, 97, 111
    1909, 103, 150
    1910, 106
    1911, 109, 111, 130
    1913, 117
    1916, 152
    1917, 163
    1921, 162-163
    1958, 221
    1961, 221
    1965, 221
    1973, 247
  Ashokan Reservoir bid-letting, investigation of, 125
  Binghamton office, 240
  Bureau of Claims, 240
  employees of
    Civil Service salaries of, 107
    injuries and fatalities among, 108-109
    labor force, 130
    World War II military service by, 182
  Engineering Bureau, 94, 96

expenditures (1911), 130
50th anniversary celebration, 218, 221
  first, 94
  Kensico Reservoir project and, 141, 144
laboratory, Varick St., New York City, 173
laborers' living accommodations regulations of, 106
legal counsel for, 215
legislative basis of, 93-94
Long Island Department, 46
New Sources Division, 194
1926 aqueduct proposal of, 12
Pepacton Aqueduct and, 201, 203, 206, 208, 212
replacement by Department of Environmental Protection, 253
sewage treatment plant proposals, 151-152
Watershed Department, annual clambake, 198
Board of Water Supply Commissioners, names of, inscribed on Kensico Dam, 146
Board of Water Supply Police, 136-138, 149
  horses and equestrian teams, 130, 137, 137, 138
  mascot, 137
  during World War I, 137
  during World War II, 138
Board of Water Supply Police station, 223, 224
Boehmer, Henry, 49
Bogart, John, 67
Bog Brook Reservoir, 55, 86-87
Bog Brook River dams, 56
Boice, John I., 126
Boiceville, N.Y.
  proposed dam at, 89
  relocation for Ashokan Reservoir construction, 128
Boiceville bridge, 130
Bonticou Crag, 103
Bonticou Grade Tunnel, 103
Boonton Dam, New Jersey, 174
Booth & Flinn Co., 206
Borden Condensary, 57, 57
Boston, Massachusetts, water supply, 20
Boutonville Express railway, 84
Bovina Center, N.Y., 170
Bower, C. P., 131
Bowery, New York City, 16, 117
"Bowery" (shanty town), 79
Bowling Green, New York City, 11
Boyd, Ebenezer, 39
Boyd, Leland, 224
Boyd's Corner's Dam, 39, 39, 41, 51
  reconstruction of, 54
Boyd's Corner's Reservoir
  land acquisition for, 39
  during 1876 drought, 227
Bradley Contracting Co., 106
Branch Creek, Putnam County, N.Y., 48
Branchi, Giovanni, 81
Brandow, Florence, 165
Brayton, Albert, 28

Brazee, Norman, 206
Breakneck-Hudson-Modena pressure tunnel system, 104-105
Breakneck Mountain, 104-105, 104, 105
Breakneck Tunnel, rupture of, 107
Breen, J. Taylor, 239
Brewster, George M., 191, 218
Brewster, N.Y.
  Borden Condensary, 57, 57
  "electrozone" sewage-treatment plant, 49
  property relocation in, 48-49, 76
Brewster Gazette, 75
Brewster Standard, 40, 41, 44, 47, 48-49
Briarwood, N.Y., 47
Brick House, Cross River, N.Y., 84
Bridge and Structural Iron Workers Union, 180
Bridges, Lee, 193
British occupation
  of New Amsterdam by, 11
  of New York City by, 14
Broadhead's Bridge, Ulster County, N.Y., 128
Broadway, New York City
  Croton Aqueduct passage across, 25
  1845 fire, 40
  proposed reservoir on, 14
Bronx, N.Y., City Tunnel #1 construction in, 113, 114, 115-117
Bronx Conduit, 53, 142
Bronx River
  concrete batching plant, 173
  proposed dams on, 12, 15
Bronx River Dam. See Kensico Dam
Bronx River Parkway, 146
Bronx Valley, storm sewer, 114
Brooklyn, N.Y.
  City Tunnel #1 construction in, 113, 114, 115, 118, 119, 121
  water delivery system expansion (1923-1925), 176, 177
  water supply system, 46, 83
Brooklyn Dodgers, 227
Brooklyn Hospital, 172
Brooklyn Navy Yard, 19, 191
Brooklyn-Queens tunnel, 246
Brooks, Clayton, 256, 257
Brooks, Mary, 165
Broome Center Road, 162
Brotherhood of Electrical Workers, 180
Brown, James, 256
Brown, Jim, 257
Brown, Paul, 213
Brown, Thomas, 108
Browne, Joseph, 12, 15
Brown's Station, N.Y., 102
  Ashokan Reservoir labor camp, 134, 149
  Board of Water Supply Police precinct, 136
  depot, 125, 128, 130
  robbery of, 138
  flooding by Ashokan Reservoir, 128, 270
  Reservoir Department headquarters, 96

Bryant Park, as City Tunnel #1 location, 117
Bryant Park reservoir, 263
Bryn Mawr siphon, 111
Bryson, T. B., 115
Bucca, Anthony, 256, 257
Buhrendorf, John, 212
Burbank, Jim, 238
Burch, Charles, 171
Bureau of Water Supply, Quality and Protection, 260-261
Burgher, Alonzo, 131
Burgher, Mathias, 131
Burgher Cemetery, Watson Hollow, N.Y., 131
Burke, Richard, 240
Burnaby, Rev. Mr., 13-14
Burr, Aaron, 15-16
Burr, William Hubert, 92, 94, 95, 167, 174
Burr-Freeman-Hering Commission, 92-93, 174
Bush, Ogden, 240
Bushkill bridges, Ulster County, N.Y., 130
Bushwick, Brooklyn, 246
Butler, Benjamin F., 38
Butt's home, Kensico, N.Y., 147
BWS. See Board of Water Supply
Byram Lake, Westchester County, N.Y., 150
Byram River, Westchester County, N.Y., 53, 143

Cableway, use in construction of Sodom Dam, 56
Cadosia, N.Y., 222
"Caisson disease," 118, 189
Caissons
  use in City Tunnel #1 construction, 117-119, 118
  use in Merriman Dam construction, 187, 189
Callahan, W. E., 180
Calvary Cemetery, Queens, 172
Calyo, N., 18
Campbell, Allan, 53, 54-55
Camp Bradley, 106
Camp Columbus, 145
Camp Hillview, 148, 148
Canals
  Chenango Canal, 20, 21, 24
  Delaware & Hudson Canal, 20, 21, 24
  proposals for, 12
Cannon, Benjamin, 224
Cannon homestead, Cannonsville, N.Y., 223, 224
Cannonsville, N.Y., 7-9
  flooding of by Cannonsville Reservoir, 216, 223, 224, 271
  Old Home Day celebration, 224
  as proposed dam site, 12, 168
Cannonsville Dam and Reservoir project, 47, 194, 217-230, 226
  communities flooded by, 216, 223, 224, 271
  completion of, 8-9
  construction of, 219
    problems in, 218-219

West Delaware Tunnel, 218-220, *219, 220*
  contractors for, 218, 220, 221
  design and planning of, 217-218, *218,* 221
    use of computers in, 220-221
  groundbreaking for, 195, 263
  laborers on, 220, 226
    injuries and fatalities among, 218, 220, 222
  land acquisition for, 217, 222-225, *223,* 240
  modified valve system of, 226
  opposition to, 217-218, 224, 226
Card, Everett, 224
Carmel, N.Y.
  Croton Falls Reservoir dam, 86
  Delaware Aqueduct Tunnel, 179-180
  as New York City watershed, 39
Carmen, John, 160
Carmen, Theodore "Ike," 160, 165
Carnegie, Andrew, 54
Carol (construction company), 206
Carpenters and Joiners Union, 180
Cat Hill, N.Y., 102
Cat Hollow, N.Y., 202
Catrell, Charles, 252-253
Catskill Aqueduct, 99-112
  completion of, 176
  construction of, speed of, 180-181
  construction contracts for, 97, 102
  expanded water delivery capacity of, 176-177
  groundbreaking ceremony for, *88,* 97
  laborers on, 103, 106-107, 108-109, 111
    criminal activities of, 137-138
    injuries and fatalities among, 108, *109*
    strikes by, 107
  Northern & Southern Aqueduct Departments for, 102
  Peekskill cut-and-cover section of, *110*
  Silver Jubilee celebration, 111
  terrain transversed by, 99, *100,* 102-103
  tunnels of, *102,* 106, 110
    drilling techniques for, 104-105, *105*
    grade-type, 99, 101, 102, 103
    pressure-type, 99, 101, 103, 106, *108,* 109, *109*
  water conveyance systems of, 99, 101-102, 103
Catskill Creek, 97
  proposed dam on, 170
Catskill-Delaware Supply, Ridgewood Reservoir distribution center for, 47
Catskill Fund for the Future, 259
Catskill Mountain Builders and Contractors Association, 256
Catskill Mountain News, 134, 135, 155, 202, 210
Catskill Plateau, 99
Catskill System, 46, 89-91, 149
  Board of Water Supply and, 78
  cost of, 149
  land acquisition for, 95-96, 149, 236
  legislative basis of, 93
  opposition to, 95

  original distribution system of, 113-114
  preliminary studies and proposals for, 89-97
  Republican criticism of, 141
  watershed, protection of water quality of, 150-153, *150, 151, 153*
Catskill Watershed Corporation, 259
Catskill Water Supply of New York City, History, Location and Sub-surface Investigations and Construction (White), 102, 115-116, 147, 148
Catskill Water System News, 16, 103, 107, 109, 117, 131, 143
Cayuga Bridge, 16
Cayuga Foundation Corp., 209
Cayuga Lake, 16
Cemeteries, grave reinterrments from, 39
  for Ashokan Reservoir, 128, 131, 270
  for Cannonsville Reservoir, 224, 271
  in Croton watershed, 48
  for Kensico Reservoir, 146
  for Neversink Reservoir, 196
  for New Croton Reservoir, 78-79, 266
  for Pepacton Reservoir, 210, 212, 270
  for Rondout Reservoir, 196, 270
  for Schoharie Reservoir, 164
Central Construction Company, 206
Central Hudson Gas & Electric Company, 196, 206
Central Park, New York City, 29, 35
  as City Tunnel #1 location, 116, 117
  as City Tunnel #3 valve chamber location, 246, 248
  Great Lawn, *34,* 263
  Jackie Kennedy Onassis Reservoir, 252
  1917 celebration of Catskill Water System, 149
Central Park Reservoir, *36*
  gatehouse of, 36, *37*
Centre St., New York City, *10*
Century Illustrated Magazine, 67-68
Cesspools, 49
Chadeayne, David, 232-233
Chadwick, Charles N., 94, 97
Chadwick, N.Y., 125
Chaffee, Jerome, 58
Chamberlain, Albert, 87
Chambers of Commerce, 94, 228, 239
Chamber St., New York City, 15
Chapman, James, 77
Chapman family, 77
Chappaqua, N.Y., 110-111
Charles, Meade & Co., 164
Chase Manhattan Bank, 16
Chatham St., New York City, 13
Chelsea, Dutchess County, N.Y., emergency pumping station, 194, 227, 228, 229
Chenango Canal, 20, 21, 24
Chernin, Bernard, 240
Chicago and Rock Island railway, 20
Chicago Post Office, 125
Chichester, N.Y., 151-152
Chlorination facilities
  for Kensico Reservoir, *150,* 152
  for West Branch Reservoir, 183

Cholera, 15, 16-17, 45
Christian, Herman, 197
Christopher St., New York City, 12
Church, Angelica Schuyler, 68
Church, Benjamin Silliman, 37, 63, 68, *68, 73*
Churchill, Jennie Jerome, 69
Churchill, Winston, 69
Cisterns, 16
Citizens Water Supply Company, 47
City Record, 231
City Tunnel #1, 113-121, *114*
  connection with City Tunnel #2, 172
  connection with Long Island City, 177
  construction of
    caisson use in, 117-119, *118*
    construction shafts, 113, 115-119, *116, 118,* 120, *120*
    dynamite use in, 117, 119, 120
  cost of, 114, 115
  engineers, 114
  length of, 162
  planning of, 96, 114-115
  route of, 113, 114, *114-115*
  water main valve shutoff of, 248-249
City Tunnel #2, 172-174, *173, 174,175*
  construction of, speed of, 180-181
  engineers, 189
City Tunnel #3, 245-253
  construction of, 246-253, *247*
    initiation ceremony, 263
    Stage 1, 245-249, 251-252
    Stage 2, 246, 250
    Stage 3, 246
    Stage 4, 246
    tunnel driving techniques, 249-251
  design of, 245
  engineers, 246
  laborers on, 249-252
    injuries and fatalities among, 248, 252-253
  litigation related to, 247
  projected cost of, 245
  projected completion date, 245, 249
Civil War, 35, 38, 39
Clapp, Sidney, 163
Clark, Charles, 95, 163, 172, 189
Clark, Henry, 232-233
Clark, James, 76
Clark, John R., 238
Clark, Mrs. Warren, 202
Clark, Roy, 198
Clark, Velma, *256,* 257
Claverack stream, 169
Clean Water Act Amendments, 255
Clearwater, A. T., 95, 130, 170, 234
Cleary, William, 197
Clifton, Staten Island, 176
Clinton, DeWitt, 16
Clinton, DeWitt, Jr., 17
Clinton, Mass., dam, 83
Clinton Hollow, N.Y., 93
Clinton St., New York City, as City Tunnel #1 site, 113, 117
Clock Barn, Forest View Farm, Cross River, N.Y., *82*
Cloud-seeding attempt, during 1950 drought, 227-228
Clove Conduit, 176

Coalition of Watershed Towns, *256,* 257, 259
Coffin Valve Co., 161
Colchester, N.Y., 243, 257
Cold Brook, proposed dam at, 89
Cold Brook Station, N.Y., 93
Cold Spring, N.Y., 97, 102, 138
Cold War, atmospheric nuclear testing during, 221
Cole, Tillott, 43, 44
Coleman, James S., 73, 81
Coleman, M. S., 59-61
Coler, Bird S., 92
Cole's Mills, 61
Collect, The (pond), 13, 14-15
Collegian (scow), 176
Colles, Christopher, 14
Collier, B. C., 143
Colligan, Rose, 108
Collingwood, John, 67
Colossus (scow), 176
Columbia University, 92
Columbus Day, 149
Commission on the Catskills in the 21st Century, 256
Communities flooded or displaced, by New York City Water System
  Aden, 270
  Arena, 170, 210, *210, 211,* 213, 270
  Armonk, 271
  Ashton, 128, 270
  Beerston, 193, 271
  Bishop's Falls, *126,* 135
  Bittersweet, 7, 198, 270
  Boyd's Corners, 266
  Broadhead's Bridge, 270
  Brown's Station, 128, 270
  Cannonsville, *216, 223,* 224, 271
  Cross River, 8, 76, 268
  Croton Falls, 44, 60, 79, 266, 268
  Dunraven, 212, 213, *230*
  Eureka, *236,* 270
  Gilboa, 155, 164, 165, 270
  Glenford, 270
  Golden's Bridge, 79, 266, 268
  Granton, *218,* 222, 224, 240, 271
  Hoyt's Mills, 84, 86, 268
  Katonah, 76, 266
  Kensico, 52, 271
  Lackawack, 146-147, 270
  Montela, 170, 193, 198, 270
  Neversink, 7, 9, 270
  North Salem, 58, 232, 268
  Olive, 134, 270
  Olive Bridge, 270
  Olive City, 128
  Pepacton, 170, 270
  Purdy's, 57, 60, 268
  Purdy's Station, 76-77, 121, 266
  Rock Rift, 222, 223, 240, 271
  Rock Royal, 222, *223,* 240-241, 271
  Shavertown, 170, 270
  Shokan, 128, 270
  Southeast Center, 48, 56-57, 266
  Union Grove, 210-212, 270
  Vahalla, 146-147, 271
  Wurtsboro, 170-171
Compressed Air, Tunnel and Subway Workers Union, 185

Compressed Air and Foundation Workers' Union, 118
Computers, use in Cannonsville Reservoir project, 220-221
Conduit and Foundation, 218
Conesville, N.Y., 163
Confederate plot, against New York City, 38
Conforte, Saverio, 144-145
Conklin, John, 52
Connecticut, Upper Housatonic watershed, 92
Connolly, "Con," 60
Connolly, P.F., 176, 177
Consolidated Edison, Indian Point nuclear power plant, 229
Constitution Island, 109
Contractors. *See also* names of individual contracting companies
Ashokan Reservoir, 125-126, 132, 134-135, 151
Cannonsville Reservoir, 218
Catskill Aqueduct, 102, 109-110
Chelsea emergency pumping station, 227, 227
City Tunnel #1, 115, 116, 117, 121, 122, 123
City Tunnel #2, 172-173
City Tunnel #3, 246, 247, 250
Cross River Dam, 83-84
Croton Falls Reservoir, 87
Croton Reservoir and Aqueduct system, 23, 59-60, 61, 67, 68, 73, 79
Delaware Aqueduct, 180, 182, 183, 184-185
Downsville Dam, 206-207, 208
Gilboa Dam, 159
Grahamsville sewage treatment plant, 199
Hill View Reservoir, 147
Jerome Park Reservoir, 70-71
Kensico Dam, 141, 142, 145
Kingston sewage system, 152
Muscoot Dam, 81
Muscoot Reservoir, 79
Neversink Dam and Reservoir, 190, 191, 196
Pepacton Reservoir, 201-202
Rondout Reservoir, 187, 188, 189-190
Schoharie Dam, 163
Shavertown Bridge, 209
Yonkers Pressure Tunnel, 106
Contracts
Catskill Water System, 141
City Tunnel #1, 117
Delaware Aqueduct, 180
Neversink Dam, 196
New Croton Aqueduct and Reservoir, 61, 63
Pepacton Reservoir-related highway construction, 209-210
for relocation of cemeteries, 130
Rondout Reservoir, 190
Cook, Charles, 256-257
Coombe, Richard, 256
Cooper Lake, Woodstock, N.Y., 96
Cooper Union, New York City, 145, 197
Cornell, A.P., 73

Cornell Dam, 79
Cornell Steamboat Company, 95
Cornwall Local, 106-107
Cortlandt, N.Y., 102, 242
Cosmopolitan Magazine, 69
County Line Farm, Montela, N.Y., 197
Cowan, John F., 86
Coykendall, Edward, 95
Coykendall, Samuel, 95, 130, 234
Cracker Barrel Club, Lackawack, N.Y., 198
Crafts, N.Y., 59, 60
Craig, Edward, 185
Cranberry Lake, Westchester County, N.Y., 143
Crane, B. D., 48
Craven, Alfred, 35, 59
Craven, H. S., 68
Crimmins, Thomas, 176
Croes, J. J. R., 75
Crosby, Chester, 56
Crosby, W. O., 99
Cross, Pluma, 7
Cross River, Katonah, N.Y., 8, 76
as Cross River Reservoir site, 84, 86
Cross River Dam, 82, 83-84, 125
Cross River Reservoir, 83-84, 85, 86, 94-95
Cross River valley, 81
Croton Aqueduct
New, 63-72
arson attempt on, 67
completion of, 68
construction of, 64-68, 65, 67
defects in, 67-68
design and planning of, 63, 70
dewatering system of, 68
laborers on, 66-67
135th St. gatehouse, 63
tunnels of, 64-68, 65, 67
Old, 17
as Civil Engineering Landmark, 24-25
connection to City Tunnel #1, 113
connection to New Croton Aqueduct, 68
design of, 24-27, 25
engineers for, 17, 20, 21, 73
interest on debt for, 40
location of, 24
maintenance and inspection of, 36-37
as National Historic Landmark, 27
use as recreational trail, 264
station-house keepers for, 36, 37
submerged portion of, 78
watershed for, 38-39
at Yonkers, 22
pressure tunnel of, 114
third, proposal for, 141
Croton Aqueduct Board, 31, 33
Croton Aqueduct Commission, 22, 63
Croton Aqueduct Department, 34-35
replacement by New York City Department of Public Works, 39
Croton Dam, 28
failure of, 27-29
New, 53-55, 84
construction of, 72

demolition and reconstruction of, 54
taxation of, 242
during 1864 drought, 38, 227
Croton Dam keeper, 36
Croton Falls, N.Y., 44, 60, 79
Croton Falls Dam, 84
Croton Falls Reservoir, 86-87
Croton Maid (boat), 30
"Croton Ode," 30
Croton Reservoir, 27-32
Catskill Aqueduct tunnels beneath, 103
completion of, 8-9
New, 53-61, 68, 73-82
communities displaced by, 73, 76-77, 77, 78-79
construction of, 73-81
contractors, 73, 75
design and planning of, 73, 75
engineers for, 73, 75, 78, 94-95
laborers on, 78, 79, 80-81
land acquisition for, 232
superintendent, 79
Old, 17, 27-32
opening of, 30
spillway of, 20
watershed for, 45
Croton River
East Branch, 53, 55-56, 86
Middle Branch, 41
West Branch, 44, 39, 59, 86
Croton System. *See also* Croton Aqueduct; Croton Reservoir
inauguration of, 30-31, 31
land acquisition for, 22-23, 39, 56-57, 59, 61
original, water mains for, 37
protection of water quality of, 151
rebuilding of, 260
Croton Water Department, 51
Crystal Palace, New York City, 40, 40
Crystal Spring Water Company, 88
Cuddebackville, N.Y., 170-171
Cudney, Emma, 234
Curry, N.Y., 170, 191
Curtis, Valleau, 238
Customs House, New York City, 125

Dalton, William, 92
D'Alvia, Mary Josephine, 79
Daly, Michael T., 48
Daly's Raids, 45, 48
Dam Safety Act, 54
Dane, John Brewster, 69
D'Angelo, Armand, 229
Darby, Harry, 238
Dauch, Leonard, 204-205
David R. Page & Company, 56-57
Davis, Carleton, 168
Davis, Charles, 95
Davis, Elwyn, 131
Davis Brook, 147
Dawson, John F., 61
Dean, Archie, 199
Dean's Corners, N.Y., 86-87
Degnon Contracting Co., 157, 158, 160
Delancey St., New York City, as City Tunnel #1 site, 117
Delaney, John, 95, 197

Delaware Aqueduct, 179-185, 217-218. *See also* Delaware System
Board of Water Supply Police precinct for, 138
connection with Catskill Aqueduct, 180
connection with Croton Falls Reservoir, 180
construction of, 178, 180-183
emergency connection with Rondout Reservoir, 190
engineers for, 179, 185
Kensico-Hill View Tunnel section, 180, 183
laborers, 183, 185
injuries and fatalities among, 182
land acquisition for, 179, 236
preliminary surveys for, 171
Rondout-West Branch Tunnel section, 179-180, 183
West Branch-Kensico Tunnel section, 180, 182
as world's largest tunnel, 174
Delaware County
anti-New York City sentiment in, 239
planning director for, 257
proposed Ramapo Water Company's operations in, 89
Delaware & Hudson Canal, 20, 21, 24
Delaware & Northern Railroad, 184
Delaware River, 166
augmentation by Cannonsville Reservoir, 226
East Branch, 168
dam and diversion tunnel on, 201-206
proposed dam on, 170
pollution cleanups of, 194
proposed dam sites on, 12, 170
protection of water quality of, 152
route of, 168
shad population, 241
West Branch, 168, 194
dam on, 228
diversion tunnel for, 221
proposed diversion at Cannonsville, 194
Delaware River Basin Advisory Committee, 195
Delaware River Basin Commission, 195, 199, 228
"Good Faith" agreement of, 225
Delaware River Basin Compact, 199
Delaware River Basin Water Commission, 194
Delaware River Master, 221
Delaware River Treaty Commission, 167-168
Delaware System
communities displaced by, 170-171
master plan for, 194
opposition to, 170
phase 2, 201
proposals for, 167-171
Delaware Valley Chamber of Commerce, 239
Delaware Water System News, The, 182, 183, 185, 189, 203, 218

Delhi, N.Y., 170, 256
    hearings on proposed Cannonsville
    Reservoir, 217-218
Democratic Party, 15, 21, 151
Democratic Register, 75
Denison, H. D., 53
Denman, William V., 236-237
Denning, N.Y., 257
Denniston, Jesse, 107
Deposit, N.Y., 221, 222, 224
Deposit Courier, 222, 224
Devasego Falls, N.Y., 157
Devasego Inn, *164*, 165
Dickens, Charles, 23-24, 33
Dickson, Katharyn, 212, 239
Dierfelter, George, 198
Dillenbeck, A. J., 227, *227*
Dillon, Richard, 206
DiMarco & Ciccone, 199
Dinsmore, Wood & Co., 35
Distributing Reservoir, Murray Hill,
    New York City, 29-30, *29*
Diverting Dam, Dean's Corners,
    N.Y., 86-87
Dixon, L. E., 246
Dobb's Ferry, N.Y., 27, 36
Dolan, Margaret, 187, 198, 236
Double Reservoir I, 55, 56
Douglas, Robert, 81
Douglass, David B., 17, 19, 20, 21, 22-
    23, 25
Dowd, William, 54-55
Downsville, N.Y., 202
    Appraisal Commission hearings in,
    239
    during construction of Downsville
    Dam, 208-209
    Eagle Hotel, 202, 208, *208*
    as New York City Department of En-
    vironmental Protection police pre-
    cinct, 138
    tax income received from Pepacton
    Reservoir dam, 243
Downsville Bridge, 209
Downsville Dam, 201, 206-209, *207*
Downsville Herald, 202
Downsville News, 181, 187, 191
Draft Environmental Impact State-
    ment, 257
Dravo Company, 106, 108, 110, 116,
    180, 182, 246
Droughts, 227-229, *227*
    in Delaware Basin, 195
    1926, 169-170
Duane, James, 70-71
DuBois, Richard, 245, 250
Duggan, Frank, 206
Duggan, Joe, 222
DuMond, Dr., 135
DuMond, Frank L., 134
Duncan, William Butler, 69
Duncombe, Frances R., 76
Dunn, Naughton & Co., 83-84
Dunraven, N.Y., 210, 212, 213, *230*
Dupont Company, 117
DuPont de Nemours Powder Co., 234
Duryea, Perry, 217
Dutch, in New Amsterdam, 11, 13
Dutchess County. *See also* names of in-
    dividual villages and towns

Daly's Raids in, 45
Delaware Aqueduct, 179-180
    Ten Mile River watershed, 92
Dutchess of Connaught, 81
Dutch Reformed Church, West Hur-
    ley, N.Y., 134

Eagle Hotel, Downsville, N.Y., 202,
    208, *208*
Early, Maurice, 220
East Branch, N.Y., 220
East Branch Reservoir, 55-57, *55, 56,*
    86, 169
    land acquisition for, 56-57
    overflow from, 86-87
East Branch Valley, 184, 201
Eastchester Creek, 173
East Delaware Tunnel, 179, 201, 204-
    206, *204, 205,* 208, 214
East Durham, N.Y., 93
East Fishkill, N.Y., 179-180
Eastman, Harvey G., 12, 45
Easton, Charles, 236
East River, 173
    City Tunnel #1 beneath, 117
    gas tunnel beneath, 114
    in Great Fire of 1835, 19
    proposed dam on, 12
East Side Omnibus Corp., 184
Eastview Tunnel, 101, 110
Eastview water filtration plant, 97, 50-
    151, 152, 153, 180
Eaton, Paul Sr., 238-239, 240, 243
Ebbets Field, 227
Eckert, Charles, 131
Edson, Franklin, 54-55
E. J. Albrecht Construction Co., 221
Electrical power, water-generated. *See*
    Hydro-electric plants
Ellenville Journal, 182, 236, 237
Elmendorf family, 130
Elmore & Hamilton Contracting Co.,
    109-110
Elmsford, N.Y., 107
    Board of Water Supply precinct, 136,
    138
Elmsford Tunnel, 110
Emans, William, 222
Emery, David, 108
Emmet, Thomas Eddis, 45
Empire Racetrack, Yonkers, 147
Empt, Ezra, 236
Empt, Marie, 236
Engineering News Record, 181
Engineers. *See also* names of individual
    engineers
    Chelsea emergency pumping station,
    227
    City Tunnel #1, 114
    City Tunnel #2,189
    City Tunnel #3, 246
    Croton Aqueducts, 17, 20, 21, 24, 63,
    65, 66, 68, 70-71, 73
    Delaware Aqueduct, 179, 185
    Hemlock Dam, 87
    Hudson River tunnels, 104
    injuries and fatalities among, 189
    Kensico Dam, 143, 145-146
    Neversink Reservoir, 191, 193

New Croton Reservoir, 73, 75, 78,
    94-95
New York City Aqueduct Depart-
    ment, 172
    Rondout Reservoir, *188*, 189, 191,
    193
    Schoharie reservoir, 163
    Shandaken Tunnel, 160
    water storage and conservation pro-
    jects, 228
English Channel tunnel, 250
Ennist, Harry, 138
Eospermatopteris, 159
Episcobo, Henry, 61
Erie Canal, 20, 21
Esopus Creek, 102-103, 130
    Board of Water Supply-built out-
    houses on, *151*, 152
    connection with Schoharie Creek,
    161-162
    connection with Shandaken Tunnel,
    158
    diversion by Olive Bridge Dam, 130
    oldest gristmill on, 126
    proposed dam on, 95, *95*
    as proposed reservoir site, 93
    watershed of, 92
Esopus Cut-and-Cover, 102
"Esopus Folly," 125
Esopus Valley, 95
    watershed, 120
Estus, Dale, 250, 251
Estus, Leonard "Haybag," 250-251
"Eucs" (Euclid trucks), 190, 207-208,
    214, 250-251
Eureka, N.Y.
    flooding by Rondout Reservoir, 270
    Fuller homestead, *236*
    grist mill, 198
    land acquisition in, 193, 236
    as proposed reservoir site, 93
Evans, Will, 237
Evans, William "Uncle John," 28, 198
Exhibition of the Industry of All Na-
    tions, 40

Fairchild & Co., 35
Fairview Cemetery, Stone Ridge, New
    York, 196
Fairview Public Library, Margaret-
    ville, N.Y., 215
Family Magazine, 16
Farmers Mills, N.Y., 48
Federal Bureau of Factory Inspection,
    129
Federalists, 15
Ferguson, Joseph, 84
Ferrell, Timothy N., 23
Ferris, Jennie, 84
Fifth Ave., New York City
    as Croton Reservoir site, 21
    as Distributing Reservoir site, 29-30
Filtration Avoidance Determination,
    259
Filupeit, Arthur, 211-212
Filupeit, August, 211-212, 239
Filupeit, Lena, 211-212
Finnegan, Michael, 258
Finnish immigrants, employed as reser-
    voir workers, 128

Fire and Water Committee, New
    York City, 17
Fire fighting
    as impetus for New York City water
    system development, 15
    reservoirs as water supply for, 16, 40
Fires
    Benjamin Odell (ship), 185
    during construction of Ashokan Res-
    ervoir, 134-135
    during construction of City Tunnel
    #1, 117
    Gilboa, N.Y., 165
    Great Fire of 1835, *18,* 19, 21, 30-31,
    40
    Imerville, NY, 165
    New York City, *18,* 19, 21, 30-31,
    38, 40
First Dutch Church, Gilboa, N.Y., 235
First National Bank of Kingston, 95
Fischetti, Anthony, 240
Fish, Hamilton Jr., 61
Fish, Virginia, 145-146
Fish's Eddy, N.Y., 194
Fishkill (creek), 12, 93, 169
Fishkill, N.Y., 99, 179-180
Fiss, Doerr & Carroll Horse Com-
    pany, 86
Fitzgerald, John M., 172, 189
Fitzsimmons, Chris, 251-252, 253
Fitzsimmons, Richard T., 252
Fiumera, Frank, 224
Fiumera, Rachel, 224
Flagler Hill, N.Y., 12
Flanagan, William, 79
Flat Brook, N.J., 194
Flatbush Water Works, 47
Fleischmanns, N.Y., 170-171
Flinn, Alfred D., 94, *168*
Floods
    caused by failure of Croton Reser-
    voir Dam, 27-29
    Johnstown, Penn., 54
    1926, 170
    1928, 198
Floyd Bennett Field, 227
Flushing Creek, 173
Forbes, P. S., 69
Ford, Arthur, *199*
Ford, Leonard, 161
Fordham, Bronx, N.Y., 27
Forest View Farm, Cross River, N.Y.,
    82, 86
Fort Amsterdam, 11
Fort Greene Park, Brooklyn, 172, 177
Fort Hamilton, Brooklyn, 176
40th St., New York City, as Distribut-
    ing Reservoir site, 29-30
42nd St., New York City
    as Croton Reservoir site, 21
    as Distributing Reservoir site, 29-30
Fossil ferns, from Riverside Quarry,
    159
Fowler, Everett, 234
Frances, James, 54
Frank, Lincoln, 48-49
Franklinton, N.Y., 93
Frazier, Josephine, 240
Frazier, Nelson, 240

Frazier-Davis Construction Co., 180, 183, 196
Freeman, John, 92, 93, 94, *94*, 95, 141, 167. *See also* Burr-Freeman-Hering Commission
Freer, Charles, 7, 198
Fresh Kills Landfill, Staten Island, 250
Fresh Pond, Staten Island, 121
Fry, George B., 115
Fteley, Alphonse, 54, 55, 59, 65, 68, 73, 75, 78
Fuller, Bruce, 198
Fuller, Gene, 193
Fuller homestead, Eureka, N.Y., *235*

Gardiner, N.Y.
  Board of Water Supply precinct, 136
  Delaware Aqueduct Tunnel, 179-180, 182-183
Gardner, Fred, 84
Garrigan, Donald, 240
Garrigan, John, 240
Garrison, New York, 97, 102, 136
Garrison tunnel, 108-109
Gatun Dam, 146
Gavin, Charles, 107
Gaynor, William, 130, 137-138, 139
Gazzam, Antoinette, 107
Gelber, Marilyn, 257-258, 259
General Electric storage battery cars, 119
Gennett, Frank, 240
George M. Brewster & Son, 218
George W. Jackson Co., 106
German immigrants, employed as reservoir workers, 128
Gilboa, New York, 257
  Board of Water Supply Police precinct, 137
  flooding by Schoharie Reservoir, 155, 164, 165, 270
  as Gilboa Dam site, *156*
  New, 165
  Schoharie project Board of Water Supply division office, 163
  tax income received from Schoharie Reservoir property, 242
Gilboa Dam, 155, *156*, 242
Gilboa Hose Co., 235
Gilboa Hotel, 162
Gilboa School District, 235
Gilboa Telephone Company, 165
Gilkey, Royal, 172
Gillespie, T. A, 103, 104, 176
Gillespie Co., 136
Gilroy, Mayor, 49
Giuliani, Rudolph, 252, 257-258, 263
Gladstone, Edna, 208-209
Gladstone, Homer, 208-209
Gleneida Hotel, 48
Glenford, New York, 270
G. L. Rugo & Sons, 206
Glyndon Company, 110
Godeffroy, New York, 194
Goethals, George Washington, 146
Goldsborough, John B., 79
Golden's Bridge, New York, 79, 232, 266, 268
"Good Neighbor" payments, 25
Gordon, Theodore, 197

Gorman, James, *256*
Gottfried, Fanny, 214-215
Gottfried, Herman, 214-215, 224, 238, 239, 240
Gottfried, Morris, 214-215
Gould's Swamp, Ardsley, N.Y., 63
Gowan, Charles Sewall, 75
Gowanus Canal, 173
Grace, William R., 53-54
Grafe-Callahan Construction, 218
Graham, Howard, 238
Graham, Idolene, 238
Grahamsville, New York, 190-191, 201, 256
  Appraisal Commission hearings in, 236
  Board of Water Supply Police precinct, 138
  during construction of Neversink Reservoir, 193
  sewage treatment plant, 152, 199
Grand Canal, China, 92
Grand Gorge, NY, 257
  Board of Water Supply headquarters, 163
  Board of Water Supply Police precinct, 137
  sewage treatment plant, 152
  during Shandaken Tunnel construction, 158, 160
Grand Hotel, Highmount, N.Y., 95
Grand View Farm, Montela, N.Y., 197
Granger, Red, 206
Grant, Hay Bag, 183
Grant, John, 235
Grant, Ulysses S., 59, 69
Grant, Ulysses S., Jr., 58-59
Granton, NY, *218*, 222, 224, 240, 271
Grant Smith & Co., 115
Gray, Henry, 233
Great Appalachian Valley, 99
Great Fire of 1835, *18*, 19, 21, 30-31, 40
Greeley, William B., 233
Green, George A., 86
Greenberg, Michael, 253
Greenburgh, N.Y., 180
Greene, George S., 35, 39, 73
Greene County, N.Y. *See also* names of individual villages and towns
  proposed Ramapo Water Company's operations in, 89
  as Shandaken Tunnel site, 158
Green family, Olive, N.Y., 130
Grim, John, 241
Grist mills, 126, 198
Groves, S. J., 246
Grow Tunneling, 250
Gulnach, Jerome, 135
Gunn, Tom, 202
Guttridge, Irving, *188*
Guttridge, James, 163, 172

Haggerty, John, 141
Haines Lake, Putnam County, N.Y., 45
Hale, M. M., 107
Hall, A. Oakley, 39
Hall, Edward Hagaman, 149
Hall, F. R., 47

Hall, Mary, 136-137
Hamilton, Alexander, 15-16, 19, 21
Hammer, Red, 183
Hancock, N.Y., 167-168, 194
Hanger, H. B., 108
Hanger, Joseph, 108
Hanover Fire Insurance Co., 94
Hanover Square, New York City, in Great Fire of 1835, 19
Harding, William, 260
Hard Rock Corners, 183
Harlem, Richard, 241
Harlem Railroad, 27, 47-48
Harlem River
  as High Bridge Croton Aqueduct bridge site, 21, 25-27, *26-27*, *32*, *38*, 39, 64, *64*, 263
  as proposed aqueduct bridge site, 17
Harper's New Monthly Magazine, 55-56, 64
Harper's Weekly, 36
Harris, Elmo, 68
Harrison & Burton, 130
Hart, John J., 68
Haskin, Evelyn Young, 164
Hastie, Peter, 24
Hastings-on-Hudson, N.Y., 89
Hatch, Edward Jr., 85
Hauck, William, 87
Hauptman, Martin, 248
Haus, Ronald, 241
Haverstraw, N.Y., 12
Hawthorne, N.Y., 136
Headless Horseman, of Sleepy Hollow, 23
Healey, S. A., *188*, 190, 193, 196, 199
Helen & Jake's restaurant, Downsville, N.Y., 208-209
Hemlock Dam, 86, 87
Hempstead Reservoir, 46
Hendricks, Fred, 238
Hensonville Band, 161-162
Hering, Rudolph, 92. *See also* Burr-Freeman-Hering Commission
Hetch-Hetchy Tunnel, California, 162
Hewitt, Abram, 197
Hewitt, Edward Ringwood, 197, *197*, 199, 237
Hewitt Motor Company, 197
Hibernia, N.Y., 93
Higgins, Frank, 93
High Bridge, Harlem River, 21, 25-27, *26-27*, *32*, *38*, 39, 64, *64*, 263
High Falls, N.Y., 102, 136, 196
Highmount, N.Y., 95
Highway construction. *See also* Route 10; Route 28; Route 30; Route 55; Route 301
  for Ashokan Reservoir, 130, 139
  for Cannonsville Dam project, 222, 224
  for Kensico Reservoir, 147
  for New Croton Aqueduct, 78
  for Pepacton Reservoir, 209-210
Hill, Isaac, 43, 44
Hill, Solomon, 44
Hill, William, 68, 70-71, 75, 78
Hillbourne Farms, Cross River, N.Y., 84
Hilley, Arthur, 170

Hill View Reservoir, 99, 147-149, *148*
  Appraisal Commission claims disputes related to, 233-234
  connection to City Tunnel #2, 167, 172-173
  connection to City Tunnel #3, 245-246
  connection to Shandaken Tunnel, 158
  contract for, 141
  distribution conduits of, 96
  planning of, 97
  recommendation for, 93
Hinman, Florence, 155
Hoag, George, 212
Hoag, Letha Hulbert, 212
Hoagland, Asa, 165
Hoagland, Hazel, 165
Hobby, Harry, 84
Hodam, Amelia, 240
Hodam, Edwin, 240
Hod Carriers Union, 180
Hoerner, Charles, *188*
Holbrook, Cabot & Rollins Corp., 107, 115
Holmes, J. H., 47
Holmes, Oliver Wendell, 171-172
Homovich, Robert, *256*, 257
Hone, Philip, 16-17, 19, 21, 30, 31
Honess, George, 163
Honk Falls, N.Y., 196
Hoosic River, proposed dam on, 12
Hornbeck, Grover, 198
Housatonic Reservoir, proposed, 92, 93
Housatonic River
  as New York City water source, 170
  proposed dam sites on, 12
Howe, Walter, 66
Howell, Wallace, 227-228
Hoyt, Fayerweather & Ladew Tannery, 234
Hoyt, Seth, 86
Hoyt's Mill, 84, 86, 268
Huckleberry Brook, 212-213
Hudler, Henry, 92
Hudson Highlands, 99
Hudson River
  Catskill Aqueduct tunnels beneath, 103
  as Croton Aqueduct and Reservoir water source, 45
  as New York City water source, 45, 93, 194, 217-218, 228
  Pennsylvania Railroad tunnel beneath, 119
  proposed dams on, 12, 217-218, 228-229
  proposed desalination projects on, 229
  proposed linkage with Great Lakes, 14
  water quality of, 218
Hudson River Nightline, 184
Hudson River Railway, 20
Hugh Nawn Contracting Co., 157, 161-162, 165
Huie, Irving, 203
Hungarian immigrants, employed as aqueduct workers, 107
Hunt, Edward, 77

Hunt, John S., 84
Hunt, Wilbur (Mr. and Mrs.), 86
Hunter, NY, 257
Hunter, William, 163
Hunter's Brook, 78, 102
Hunter's Brook Grade Tunnel, 103, 110
Huntsberger, Evelyn Hill, 199
Hurley, N.Y.
    population displaced by Ashokan Reservoir, 134
    tax income received from Ashokan Reservoir, 242-23
Hurricanes, 195, 213
Husted, Willis, 147
Hyde Park, N.Y., 12
Hydrants, 33-34
Hydro-electric power plants, 92, 195, 263

Illustrated American, 45, 47
"Imerville," 165
Immigrant laborers, on New York City Water System, 35, 128. See *also* Laborers, on New York City Water System; specific ethnic and racial groups
Impellitieri, Vincent, 203
Indian Brook, N.Y., 25
Indian Point, nuclear power plant, 229
Insurance rates, 40, 114
International Workers of the World, 129
Interstate Commission on the Delaware River Basin, 194
Irish immigrants, employed as aqueduct and reservoir workers
    cholera among, 16-17
    on Croton Aqueduct, 23-24, 30
    on Hemlock Dam, 87
Irving, Washington, 23
Isa Pond, Yellowstone National Park, 185
Italian Consul General, and Muscoot Dam strike, 81
Italian immigrants, employed as reservoir and aqueduct workers, 106
    Black Hand Society and, 80, 87
    on Catskill Aqueduct system, 106-107
    criminal activity of, 136-137
    on Cross River Dam, 84
    on Croton Falls Reservoir, 87
    on Croton Reservoir and Aqueduct, 59, 66
    injuries and fatalities among, 84
    on Kensico Dam and Reservoir, 142, *144*
    on Muscoot Dam and Reservoir, 79, 80-81
    strikes by, *80*, 81
    wages of, 80-81

Jackie Kennedy Onassis Reservoir, 252
Jackson, George W., 106
Jackson Creek, N.Y., 12, 169
Jahr, Alfred, 239
Jamaica, N.Y., 47
Jamaica Water Supply Company, 47
James Malloy & Co., 87

Jay, John, 84
Jay, William, 83
Jefferson, Thomas, 15
Jenkins, Joshua, 39
Jenkins, Simon, 39
Jerome, Leonard W., 69
Jerome Park, 69, 94-95
Jerome Park Reservoir, 63, 68, 69, 70-71, *71*
    as City Tunnel #1 Shaft 4 site, 116
    controversy regarding, 78
    Gate House, 113
    Keeper's House, *70*
Jervis, John Bloomfield, *20*, 263
    attendance at Croton water system inauguration, 30
    Croton System and, 21, 24, 25, 26, 28, 36, 73
    on failure of Croton Reservoir Dam, 28-29
Jervis, Phebe Bloomfield, 20
Jervis, Timothy, 20
Jervis, William, 24
Jewell's Brook, N.Y., 25
Jewett, N.Y., 257
Jobman, Martin, 212
John J. Hart & Co., 68
John Pierce Co., 125
Johnson, Drake & Piper, 218
Johnson, Earl, 208
Johnson, George, 77
Johnstown Flood, 54
Jones, Alice, *146*
Jones, Valentine, 14
J. P. Shirley, 180
Judd, Joseph, 224
"Jumbos," 181, 249

Kalm, Peter, 11, 13
Kappler, Arthur, 208
Kass Inn, Margaretville, N.Y., 241
Katonah, N.Y., 181
    effect of Muscoot Reservoir on, 79
    relocation of, 76, 266
    typhoid cases in, 85
Katonah, The History of a Village and Its People (Duncombe), 76
Katonah Times, 76, 77, 78, 80, 81, 84, 85, 86, 87, 89, 232
Keator, Harry, 164-165
Keeler, H. Hobart, 233
Keeler, Richard C., 146
Kellogg, H. W., 76
Kellogg family, Katonah, N.Y., *8*
Kelly, Isaac, 51
Kelly, Warren M., 240
Kemble, Myrtle, 198
Kemble, Urban, 198
Kemp, J. F., 99
Kennedy, John F., 195, *199*
Kennedy, Robert Jr., 259
Kennison, Karl, 206
Kensico, N.Y.
    Board of Water Supply precinct, 136
    flooding by Kensico Reservoir, *52*
    "New," 146-147
    second flooding of, 146-147
Kensico Dam, *140*
    construction of, 142-147, *142*
    contractors for, 141, *142*

laborers on, 144-145, 147
    allegedly entombed within the dam, 145
    injuries and fatalities among, 145
    labor camp for, *142*, 143
    new, 53
    during World War I, 149
Kensico-Hill View Tunnel, 180
Kensico Reservoir, 101, 181-182
    aeration system, 183
    chlorination system, *150*, 152
    communities displaced by, 146-147
    connection with City Tunnel #3, 246
    connection with Shandaken Tunnel, 158
    connection with West Branch Reservoir, 180
    construction of, 141-147
        quarry and stone yard, 143, *144*
    contract for, 141
    filling of, 148-149
    hydro-electric power plant, 263
    influent chamber, 183
    land acquisition for, 146-147, 233
    old, *52*, 53
        diversion of Wampus River into, 150
        drainage of, 142
    planning of, 97
Kensico Station, 53
Kent, N.Y., 39, 179-180
Kerbaugh, H.S., 141, *142*, 143, 149
Kerhonkson, N.Y., 138
Kew Gardens, N.Y., 47
Keystone State Construction Co., 147
Killeen, Jack, *188*
Kinderhook, N.Y., 169
King, Rice & Ganey, 152
Kingsbridge, N.Y., 53
Kingsbury, Burnadette, 224
Kings County, N.Y., 47. See *also* Brooklyn, N.Y.
Kingston, N.Y.
    Board of Trade, 95
    Chamber of Commerce, 95
    merchants' protest of Appraisal Commission decision, 234
    opposition to Catskill Water System development, 95
    sewer system reconstruction in, 152
    water sources for, 96
Kingston Daily Freeman, 92, 132, 135, 196, 234
Kingston Hospital, 215
Kingston Weekly Leader, 89
Kirk, Floyd, 161
Kirk Lake, Putnam County, 43, 44, 45
Kissing Bridge, New York City, 13-14
Kline, Ardolph, 139
Knapp, Abram, 84
Knight, Anson, 197
Koch, Ed, 229, 253
Kortright, Albert, 193
Kortright, Milton, 193
Kortright, Sherman, 193
Krauss, Albert, 206
Krum, Benjamin, 237
Krum, Elvira, 237
Krum, Joe, 237
Kurz, Matilda, 233

Labor camps
    Ashokan Reservoir, 128, 129, 149
    Croton Falls Reservoir, 87
    Kensico Dam, *142*, 143, 145
        racial and ethnic segregation of, 106, 128
    Shandaken Tunnel, 158
    typhoid in, 158
Laborers, on New York City Water System
    Ashokan Reservoir, *127*, 128-129, 130-131, 134, *135*, 136
    Cannonsville Dam and Reservoir, 218, 220, 222, 226
    Catskill Aqueduct, 103, 106-107, 108-109, *109*, 117, 118, 119
    City Tunnel #3, 248, 249-252
    criminal activity of, 60, 107, 111, 136-138
    Cross River Dam and Reservoir, 84, 86
    Croton Aqueduct, 60-61, 66-67
    Croton Falls Reservoir, 78, 79, 80-81
    Croton System, 51, 52
    Delaware Aqueduct, 180, 183, 185
    first-aid training for, 220
    hearing loss among, 220
    Hill View Reservoir, 148
    injuries and fatalities among, 66, 80, 84, 108, *109*, 130-131, 165, 193, 204-205, 206, 218, 220, 222, 248, 252-253
    Kensico Dam, *124*, 143, 147
    living accommodations for, 106, *106*. See *also* Work camps
    Muscoot Reservoir, 79, 80-81
    Neversink Reservoir, 193
    Pepacton Resrvoir, 202, 203, 204-206, 211-212, 214, *214*
    Schoharie Reservoir, 165
    Shandaken Tunnel, 160, 161
    strikes by, 23, *80*, 81, 107, 129, 196, 214
    wages of, 51, 52, 66, 128-129, 180, 202, 206
Laborers and Hod Carriers Union, 193, 196
Laborers International Union Local Seventeen, 214
Labor unions, 180
Lackawack, N.Y., 93, 193, 270
Lackawack Dam. See Merriman Dam
Lackawack House, 197
LaGuardia, Fiorello, 138, 180, 181, 191, 196
Lake Gilead, Putnam County, 43, 45
Lake Gleneida, Carmel, Putnam County, 43, 44-45, 47, 61
Lake Hill, Putnam County, proposed dam at, 89
Lake Kensico, Westchester County, 53
Lake Mahopac, Putnam County, 44, 48, 49
Lake Manahatta, New York City, *34*, 35, 39
Lake Minnewaska, Ulster County, 180
Lakes, in Putnam County watershed, 43-45, 47-48, 49
Lake View Hotel, Kensico, N.Y., 53

Land acquisition, for New York City Water System
  for Ashokan Reservoir, 126, 128, 129, 130, 132-134, 135
  for Cannonsville Dam and Reservoir, 217, 222-225, 223, 240
  for Catskill project, 95-96, 149, 236
  compensation for, inadequacy of, 87
  condemnation use for, 9, 22, 39, 45, 59, 86
    prohibition of, 259
  for Cross River Reservoir, 83, 86
  for Croton Reservoir and Aqueduct System, 22-23, 39, 56-57, 59, 61
  by Croton Water Department, in Putnam County, 43-45, 47-49
  for Croton watershed, 45, 47, 48
  for Delaware Aqueduct, 179, 236
  Department of Environmental Protection's involvement in, 261
  in Dutchess County, legislative opposition to, 93
  for Hudson River tunnels, 104, 105
  for Kensico Reservoir, 146-147, 233
  for Lake Manahatta, 35
  legislative basis for (McClellan Act), 93-94, 95, 96
  McClellan Act, 96
  for Neversink Reservoir, 191, 193, 196, 197-198
  for New Croton Reservoir, 73
  opposition to, 196-197
  for Pepacton Reservoir, 210, 212, 215
  process of, 231-232
  in Putnam County watershed, 43-45, 47-49
  for Rondout Reservoir, 187, 196-197
  for Schoharie Reservoir, 163-164, 164, 165
  taxation issue, 242-243
  for Wampus River water quality preservation, 150
Land use regulations, of Department of Environmental Protection, 255-260
Lane, George W., 54-55
Lane Construction Company, 221, 222
Lane's Saloon, Kensico, N.Y., 147
Larkintown, 79
Latting Observatory, New York City, 40
Lavelle, Michael J., 180
L'Avenire, 87
Law, George, 26-27
Lawrence, J. L., 31
Lawrence, William, 7
Laws of 1905, Chapters 724 and 724, 93-94, 95
Laws of 1906, Chapter 314, 96
Laws of 1923, Chapter 630, 152
Lederle, Ernst, 85, 95
L. E. Dixon Co., 246
Lee, Gideon, 61
Lee, Theodore, 239
Lepke, Georgianna, 257
Leroy's Falls, N.Y., 197
Leslie's History of the Greater New York, 17
Lew Beach, N.Y., 170, 206, 214
Lewis, Bernice, 223, 241

Lewis, John L., 222, 223, 240-241
Lewis, Leland, 165
Lewis boardinghouse, Rock Royal, N.Y., 241, 241
Lewisboro, N.Y., 180
Lexington, N.Y., 89
Liberty, N.Y., 7, 214
Liberty Register, 191
Lieberman, Sam, 236
Lincoln, Abraham, 97
Lincoln, Mass., water system, 94
Linson, John J., 234
Lipp, Fred M., 240
Little Delaware River, 170
Little Delaware Valley, 194
Little Falls, N.J., 94
"Little Italy," 79
Livingston Manor, N.Y., 170, 238
Livingston Manor Times, 171
Lloyd, N.Y., 89
Lobdell, Darius, 59
Local #147, 247
Locher (construction company), 115
Lockwood, David, 48
Lockwood, Louis, 185
Lockwood, Samuel, 159
Long Island
  Coastal Plain, 99
  groundwater sources, 170
  wells on, 93, 229
  as New York City water source, 46, 95, 229
  water supply of, 47
Long Island Department, of Board of Water Supply, 96, 97
Long Island Railroad, 250
Long Island Sound, proposed dam on, 12
Love, Eunice, 224
Low, A. A., 184
Low, Seth, 70, 92, 184
Lowitz, Otto, 199
Lows Corners Baptist Church, property damage award to, 237
Lupfer & Remick, 163

Maben, Winfield, 164, 165
Mabie, Henry, 61
MacArthur Brothers Co., 125-126
MacArthur Brothers & Winston, 149
MacDonald, George, 167-168
Mackey, Mary, 52
Mack Trucks, 197
MacLean-Grove & Company, 218
Macomb, Robert, 12
Madison Square, New York City, City Tunnel #1 construction in, 117
Main, Charles T., 246
Malaria, 79, 109
Malcolm Pirnie, 194
Malloy, James, 87
Mamakating Valley, 170-171
Mamaroneck, N.Y., 73, 75
Manhattan Company, 10, 15, 16
Manhattan tunnel, of City Tunnel #3, 246
Mann, Isaac, 14
Manor Kill, N.Y., 157, 163

Manufacturers' Association of Brooklyn, 94
Maple View Farm, Montela, N.Y., 197
Marbletown, N.Y.
  population displaced by Ashokan Reservoir, 134
  tax income received from Ashokan reservoir, 242-243
Marchand, Jules Henri, 159
Marcy, William, 17
Margaretville, N.Y., 208, 212
  Appraisal Commission hearings, 239
  Catskill Watershed Corporation, 259
  cloud-seeding experiment near, 228
  during construction of Shavertown Bridge, 209
  as proposed dam site, 168
  sewage treatment plant, 152
Margaretville Central School, 202
  Scholarship Fund, 215
Margaretville Memorial Hospital, 215, 241
Margaretville Telephone Company, 213, 238
Markert, Charles, 202
Markert, Kenneth, 257
Marlboro, N.Y., 89, 99, 179-180
Marsh, Luther, 35, 38
Martin, James, 211, 212
Martin, Robert, 38, 73
Martineau, John, 25
Mase, Lottie, 165
Mase, Starr, 165
Mason, Arnold, 26-27
Mason & Hanger, 106-107, 108, 110, 115, 189-190
Maspeth, Queens, 246
Massachusetts, Upper Housatonic watershed, 92
Massachusetts Institute of Technology, 92, 94
Mathews, D. N., 135
Mattice, V. D., 164
Mayer, Ada, 214, 214
Mayer, Clarence "Hank," 214, 214
Mayer, Gene, 214, 214
Mayer, Gottlieb, 234
Mayer, Scott, 214, 214
McArthur Bros. Company, 83-84
McAvoy, Daniel, 240
McClellan, George, 97
McClellan, George B., 93, 95, 97, 139, 149, 263
McClellan Act, 93-94, 95, 96
McCulloch, Back, McManus & Hepborne, 29
McDonald, John B., 70
McGoldrick, Joseph, 181
"McGovern's Tunnel," 172
McGrath, Joseph, 60-61, 134
McGregory, John, 23
McKay, Douglas, 136
McKeel, N.Y., 102
McKeel's Store, Purdy's Station, 77
McLean, Genevieve, 129-130
McNally, Thomas, 97, 102
McQuaid, John, 59
Meade, Emerson, 163
Mealy, William, 35
Mekenian, George, 228

Meland, Alvin, 163
Mellon, Andrew, 54
Merchant's Association, 70
Merchants Exchange, destruction in Great Fire of 1835, 19, 21
Merchants Society of N.Y., 12
Merchant St., New York City, in Great Fire of 1835, 19
Merrick, Slim "Six Fingers," 183
Merrill Reservoir, N.J., 195
Merriman, Thaddeus, 95, 163, 168, 172, 189
Merriman Dam, 187, 189, 188, 190, 189-191
  Board of Water Supply Police protection for, 138
  land acquisition for, 236
Merritt, James S., 80, 87
Merritt & Chapman Derrick and Wrecking Company, 121, 122
Merritt-Chapman & Scott Corp., 176
"Merryweather" (house), 58-59
Metcalf & Eddy, 228-229
Methodist Church, Cross River, N.Y., 84
Methodist Church, Gilboa, N.Y., 165
Methodist Church, Kensico, N.Y., 147
Methodist Church, Purdy's Station, N.Y., 76-77
Mexico City, water supply, 92
Michelson, Rolf, 236
Middle Branch Reservoir, 51-53, 50
Middletown, N.Y., 89
Miele, Joel, 259
Millard Construction Co., 147
Millbrook stream, 241
Miller, Agnes, 211, 212
Miller, J. G., 44
Miller Hollow, N.Y., 212
Mill River. See also Pocantico River
  Croton Aqueduct station house on, 36
Mill River Valley, 25
Mill Town, N.Y., 48
Minerva Publishing Co., 87
Mink Hollow Stream, 96
Misner, Anne, 212
Misner, Bob, 212
Misner family, Neversink, N.Y., 7
Mitchel, Purroy, 120
Mitchell, "Jughead," 183
Modena, N.Y., 138
Mohawk & Hudson Railway, 20
Mohawk River, 160, 228-229
Mohonk, N.Y., 136
Molinari, Joseph, 224
"Monell's Fill," 101
Monroe, John D., 234-235
Montela, N.Y., 170, 193, 198, 236
Montezuma Swamp, 16
Moodna Creek valley, 103
Moodna Pressure Tunnel, 107, 108, 114-115
Morgan, Ellen, 48
Morrisania, annexation to New York City, 53
Morrisania Creek, 12
Morley, James, 38-39
Morningside Park, as City Tunnel #1 shaft location, 113

Morris, George Pope, 30
Morris, Richard, 204-205
Morris, Robert, 30
Morris, Robert E., 66
Morrison-Knudsen Co., 123
Mosholu Ave., Bronx, 63
Mosholu Golf Course, Van Cortlandt Park, 152
Mount Kisco, N.Y., 48, 49, 85
Mount Pleasant, N.Y., 25, 92
  Kensico-Hill View Reservoir, 180
  Kensico-Hill View Tunnel, 180
  tax income received from New Croton Dam, 242
  water filtration plant, 150-151, 152, 153
Mount Prospect, N.Y., 46, 176
Mucking machines, 110, 119, 154, 160, 181, 220
Mud Pond, Putnam County, 45
Munro, W. Stanley, 238
Munroe-Langstroth, Inc., 206
Munyers, Henry, 36
Murphy, Vernon, 240
Murray, William, 134
Murray Hill Reservoir, 21, 29-30, 29
Muscoot Creek, 48
Muscoot Dam, 79
Muscoot Mountain, 79
Muscoot Reservoir, 76, 79-81, 94-95
Muscoot River, 50, 59
Musso, Ben, 191, 193, 193

Napanoch, N.Y., 93
Napanoch Prison, 138
Nassau County, water supply, 201
Nassau Water Company, 46
National Guard, 80, 81, 137, 149
National Industrial Recovery Act, 173-174
Native-Americans, employed as reservoir workers, 161
Nawn, Hugh, 157, 161-162, 165
NBC-TV, 212, 213
Nearing, Helen, 214
Nearing, Scott, 214
Neversink, N.Y., 7
  acquisition for Neversink Reservoir, 193
  Board of Water Supply Police precinct, 138
  displacement by Delaware System, 170
  "New," 198-199
  New York City Department of Environmental Protection police precinct, 138
  opposition to Rondout Reservoir, 196-197
Neversink Dam, 186, 189, 192, 193, 193, 193
Neversink Hydroelectric Plant, 196
Neversink Inn, 7, 191
Neversink Reservoir, 191, 193
  completion of, 195
  filling of, 199
  historical marker for, 7
  laborers on, 193, 196
  land acquisition for, 191, 193, 196, 197-198

Neversink River
  riparian rights on, 237
  trout fishing on, 197, 197
  water quality of, 185
Neversink River bridge, 191
Neversink Tunnel, 179, 188, 192, 192, 193, 196
  electricity generating plant, 206
  outlet portal, 193
New Amsterdam, 11, 13
Newburgh, N.Y., 181, 183
Newburgh Iron and Steel Workers Local 417, 193, 196
Newell property, Garrison, N.Y., 97
New Gilboa Cemetery, 164
New Hamburg, N.Y., 99
New Hurley, N.Y., 136
New Jersey, opposition to Delaware System development by, 171-172
Newman, E. B., 76
New Netherlands, 11
New Netherlands Bank, New York City, 120
New Paltz, N.Y., 89, 136
Newsboys' Home, New York City, 184
Newton, Isaac, 53, 73
Newtown Creek, 177
New York (ship), 33
New York Central & Hudson River Railroad Company, 73, 75, 78, 143
New York Central Railroad, 86, 110, 206, 218
New York City
  consolidation of, 83
  daily water consumption, 53
    during 1890s, 73
    during 1940s, 203
    1988-1997, 229
  early water sources for, 11, 12, 13-18
    during 17th century, 11, 13
    during 18th century, 12, 13-15
    during 19th century, 10, 12, 15
  mayors
    Allen, Stephen, 21
    Gaynor, William, 105
    Grace, William R., 53-54
    Guiliani, Rudolph, 252, 257-258, 263
    Hall, A. Oakley, 39
    Hone, Philip, 16-17, 19, 21, 30, 31
    Kline, Ardolph, 139
    Koch, Ed, 229, 253
    LaGuardia, Fiorello, 138, 180, 181, 191, 196
    Low, Seth, 70, 92, 184
    McClellan, George B., 93
    Mitchel, Purroy, 120, 149
    names of, inscribed on Kensico Dam, 146
    Wagner, Robert, 218
    Wickham, William, 45
  population, 33, 53
New York City and Northern Railroad, 64
New York City Aqueduct Department Divisions of, 115
  establishment of, 172
New York City Board of Estimate. See Board of Estimate and Apportionment

New York City Board of Public Improvements, 89
New York City Board of Water Supply. See Board of Water Supply
New York City Department of Environmental Protection, 229, 253, 260-261
  commissioners, 256, 257-258, 259
  Watershed Regulations of, 255-260
New York City Department of Public Works, 39, 53
  Commissioners, 44, 45, 54-55
  construction of Amawalk Reservoir by, 59
New York City Department of Water Resources, 253
New York City Department of Water Supply, Gas, & Electricity, 87, 227
  commissioner, 229
  Esopus watershed surveys by, 92
  sanitary regulations of, 255
New York City Health Department, 85
New York City Tunnels, 244
New York City Watershed Memorandum of Agreement, 9, 153, 258-260, 260
New York City Water System. See also specific aqueducts and reservoirs
  Confederate conspiracy against, 38
  East-of-Hudson, 170
  proposals for, 12
  radioactivity monitoring of, 221
  tax assessment value of, 243
  taxes paid by, 242-243
  water quality of, 150-153
  Westchester County's access to, 93
New York Fertilizer Company, 49, 49
New York Harbor Narrows
  as City Tunnel #1 site, 96, 113, 114-115
  as Siphon #2 site, 176
New York & Harlem Railway, 58
New York Herald, 79, 85
New York Herald Tribune, 170
New York Merchants Association Pollution Committee, 85
New York Milk & Cream Company, 48
New York & New England Railroad, 57
New York Polyclinic, 85
New York Public Library, 29-30, 263
New York Sacred Music Society, 30
New York State Board of Health, 45
New York State Conservation Commission, 155, 160, 234-235
New York State Constitution, 93
New York State Department of Environmental Conservation, 258
New York Department of Health, 151
New York State Department of Labor, 183
New York State Department of Public Works, 209-210, 222
New York State Legislature. See also New York State Senate
  Act for construction of New Croton Reservoir and Aqueduct, 54

authorization of Ramapo Water Company by, 89
defeat of sanitation bills by, 151
New York State Museum, 159
New York State Police, 137
New York State Power Authority, 263
New York State Sanitary Code, 255
New York State Senate
  Local Government Committee, 256-257
  resolution for New Croton Rreservoir and Aqueduct, 53-54
New York State Thruway, 12
New York State Water and Power Control Commission, 152, 170, 201, 217, 218
New York State Water Supply Commission, 46, 95, 96, 115
  wage claims cases before, 232
New York Times, 35, 69, 83, 84, 107, 163, 214, 240
New York Times Magazine, 184
New York Tribune, 84, 86
New York University, 21, 220-221
New York World, 125
New York World Telegram, 237
Nicaragua Canal, 174
Nicetown, Penn., 105
Nicholls, Richard, 11
Nile River, Assouan dam on, 81
Norris, Evelyn Weaver, 264
North American Civic League for Immigrants, 145
North Castle, N.Y., 180, 242
North Castle Sun, 148-149
Northern Aqueduct Department, 96, 97
North Salem, N.Y., 58
  Delaware Aqueduct Tunnel in, 180
  property damage awards in, 232
  tax income received from New Croton Dam, 242
North Salem Board of Health, 59
Norton home, Dunraven, N.Y., 230
Nostrand, Peter Elbert, 89
Nuclear contamination, of New York City's water supply, radioactivity monitoring for, 221

Oak Hill, N.Y., 93
Ocker, Edward Sr., 136-137
Oddo, Anthony, 253
Ogbin, Frances, 159
O'Grady, P. W., 107
Old Croton Trailway State Park, 27
Olds, Irving, 212-213
Old Stone School, Dunraven, N.Y., 213
Olive, N.Y.
  New York State Energy Protection Police precinct, 138
  population displaced by Ashokan Reservoir, 134, 270
  Ramapo Water Company's proposed operations in, 89
  tax income received from Ashokan reservoir, 242-243
Olive Bridge, N.Y., 270
  as Board of Water Supply precinct, 136

as prospective dam site, 93, 95, 99
Olive Bridge Dam, 125-126, *126*, *127*, 130, 144, 149
Olive City, N.Y., 89, 128
Olive Hall, Brewster, N.Y., 40
O'Dell, Clancy, 220
Olmstead, B. S., 76
Olmstead, G. S., 76
Onassis, Jacqueline Kennedy, 252
135th St. Gatehouse, of New Croton Aqueduct, 63, *65*
Oneida County, N.Y., 24
O'Neill, Alice, 79
O'Neill, Mrs, Jack, 79
O'Neill, Nora, 79
Oneonta Daily Star, 203
Ontario & Western Railroad, 197
"On the Move" (Rowe), 77
Operating Engineers Union, 180
Orange and Rockland Utility, Inc., 206
Osborne Drilling Co., 172
Oscawana and Cornell Railroad, 73-74, 75
Osterhoudt, Eugene, 198, 199
Ostrander Construction Co., 246
Oullen, A.C., 84
Outhouses, 151, 238
Owens, Paul, 239
Ozone Park, N.Y., 47

Page, David R., 56-57
Paino, Angelo, 176
Paladino, Angelo, 61
Palmer, Van, 165
Palmer Block, Carmel, N.Y., 48
Panama Canal, 92, 146
Pantzer, Kurt F., 194
Paolo, Jack, 145
Parent, Henry, 77
Parker, Platt, 39
Park Slope, Brooklyn, 176, 246
Parksville, N.Y., 199
Passaic River, New Jersey, 12
"Passing of Old Gilboa, The" (Mattice), 164
Pataki, George, 258, *260*
Patchin sand pit, 163
Paternoster, Francis, 239
Paterson, New Jersey, 12
Patrick McGovern, Inc., 172
Patruno, Frank, 197
Patterson, N.Y., 39, 48
Peach Lake, Putnam County, 45
Peak Grade Tunnel, 102
Pearl St., New York City, proposed reservoir on, 14
Peck, June, 224
Peconic Valley, N.Y., 46
Peekskill, N.Y., 102, 136
Peg's Tavern, Cannonsville, N.Y., 224
Pennsylvania Railroad, 114
Pennsylvania Railroad tunnel, 119
Pepacton, N.Y., displacement by Delaware System, 170, 270
Pepacton Covered Bridge, 228
Pepacton Dam, 201, *202*, 243
Pepacton Intake Chamber, 206
Pepacton Post Office, 212
Pepacton Reservoir, 7-8, 12, 199, 201-216

completion of, 195
connection with Rondout Reservoir, 201
East Delaware Tunnel of, 179
laborers on, *200*, 226
land acquisition for, Appraisal Commission claims hearings for, 238-239
population displaced by, 213
taxation of, 243
Perini Corp., 123, 187, 250. *See also* Walsh-Perini
Persons, Henry, 95
Peters, Curtis, 130
Pfister's General Store, Kensico, N.Y., 147
Phelps, Francis B., 12, 17
Philadelphia, Penn., water supply, 194
Philwood Preserve, Sullivan County, 237
Phipps, Henry Clay, 54
Phoenicia, N.Y., 170
proposed dam at, 89
proposed sewage treatment plant in, 151-152
Phoenicia Diner, 228
Pietschker, Del, 147
Pietschker, Pearl, *146*
Pine Hill, N.Y.
Crystal Spring Water Company of, 88
proposed sewage treatment plant in, 151-152
rainmaking experiment near, 228
Pine Hill Sentinel, 108, 139, 152
"Pioneer" (locomotive), 51
Pittsburgh Contracting Co., 107, 110, 115, 116
Platania, Sam, 210, *239*
Platner Farm, Prattsville, N.Y., 155
Plattkill, N.Y., 179-180
Pleasantville, N.Y.
Board of Water Supply precinct, 136
sediment-removing coagulation plant, 152, *153*
Pleasantville Constructors, 183
"Plumland," 234
Pneumatic Engineering Co. of New York, 68
Pocantico River, 23, 63
Poe, Edgar Allen, 27
Pofill, Josephine Conforte, 144-145, 263
Poisoning plot, against New York City water supply, 38
Polish immigrants, as reservoir workers, 128
Pollution. *See also* Water quality protection
of watersheds, Department of Environmental Protection regulations for, 255-260
of wells, 11, 13
Porter, Eugene, 85
Port Jervis, N.Y., 168, 171
Potter's Field, Putnam County Farm, 48
Poughkeepsie, N.Y., 97
Poughkeepsie Evening Star, 135
Prattsville, N.Y.

Board of Water Supply Division office, 163
Board of Water Supply Police precinct, 137
proposed Ramapo Water Company operations in, 89
as proposed Schoharie Creek dam site, 155, 157
Preston Hollow, N.Y., 93
Proper, Churchill, 161
Proper, Edward, 161
Proper, Keith, 161
Prospect Park, Brooklyn, N.Y., 46
Pulitzer, Joseph, 125
Purdy, Isaac, 76
Purdy, John F., 69
Purdy, Thomas, 76
Purdy, Thomas L., 59
Purdy, Thomas L. Jr., 181
Purdy's Bridge, N.Y., 79
Purdy's, N.Y., 57, 60, 368
Purdy's Station, N.Y., 76-77, 232, 266
Putnam County. *See also* names of individual villages and towns
Croton Water Department's land acquisition in, 43-45, 47-49
Delaware Aqueduct, 179-180
New York City water quality project funds for, 259
population decline in, 57
reservoir sites in, 38-39, 31
watershed lakes in, 43-45, 47-48, 49
Putnam County Courier, 39, 41, 43-44, 56, 59, 60-61, 67
Putnam County Republican, 48, 61
Putnam County Standard, 45, 51, 52
Putnam Valley, Delaware Aqueduct Tunnel in, 179-180

Quaker Bridge, N.Y., 73
Queens, N.Y.
City Tunnel #1 in, 119
Jamaica Water Supply Company in, 47
wells in, 47, 83
Queens Farms Dairy, *216*
Queens Structures, 221
Quick, Glenny, 236
Quick, Granville, 236
Quinby, Howard, 149

Radioactivity monitoring, of New York City's water supply, 138, 221
Rainmaking attempt, during 1950 drought, 227-228
Raisch's Casino Hotel, Staten Island, 121
Ramapo River, 89
watershed of, 92
Ramapo Water Company, 89, 92
Randall's Island, New York City, 33
Raven, Catherine, 53
Raven, John, 53
Ravens Farm & Hotel, Kensico, N.Y., 147
Ray Shea's Corner Bar and Grill, 183
Reade St., New York City, 10
Real Estate Board of New York City, 160
Red Hook, Brooklyn, 246, 250

Red Mills, N.Y., 48
Redwood, R. Norman, 184-185
Regular, Ettie Mercer, 165
Regular, Hatward, 165
Reiner, Rudolph, 167-168
Rensselaer County, 169
Rensselaer Polytechnic Institute, 212
Renwick, James, 24
Report of the Commission on Additional Water Supply for the City of New York, 93
Reports on the New Croton Aqueduct, Reservoirs and Dams, 1895-1907, 73, 79, 84
Republican Club of the City of New York, 141
Republican party, 15
Reservoir Department, 96
Reservoir M., 57
Reservoirs. *See also* specific reservoirs communities flooded by. See Communities flooded or displaced, by New York City Water System
covers for, 152
Department of Environmental Protection regulations for, 255-602
proposals for, 12, 15
Revolutionary War, 14
Reynold's Hill Tunnel, 103
Reynold's Hotel, Purdy's Station, New York, 77
Reynolds, Hiram, 84
Reynolds, William S., 84
Rhinebeck, N.Y., 241
Rice & Ganey, 161, 163, 176
Richards, John, 198
Richmond Conduit, 121, 122
Richmond Hill, N.Y., 47
Richmond Tunnel, 246
Ridgewood Reservoir, Brooklyn, N.Y., 46, 47
Ridgewood System, 46, 47
Ridgway, Robert, 102, *168*
Riekert family, 79
Riley, Ed, 147
Rinehart & Dennis Co., 145
Riots, by Croton Aqueduct laborers, 23
Riparian rights claims, 44, 93, 215, 232, 237, 241
Rivenberg, Della, 165
Riverkeeper, Inc., 259
Riverside Quarry, 159, *159*, 162
Roach, Edward, 39
Roberts, Samuel, 26-27
Robertson, William Henry, 76
Rochdale, N.Y., 93
Delaware Aqueduct Tunnel in, 179-180
Rock Mill, 43
Rock Rift, N.Y., 222, 224, 240, 271
Rock Royal, N.Y., 222, *223*, 240-241, 256-257, 271
Rock Royal Cooperative Creamery, 217
Rock Royal Methodist Church, 222
Rock Royal Store & Post Office, *223*, 224
Rodgers, James, 141

Rodgers, John, 141
Roefs, Russell, 257
Roeliff Jansen Kill, 93, 169
Rome, N.Y., 20
Rondout Creek, *169*
  emergency diversion of, 181-182
  as proposed reservoir site, 93
  sewage treatment plant on, 152
Rondout Pressure Tunnel, *98, 110,*
  103, 114-115
Rondout Reservoir, 12, 171
  Board of Water Supply Police pre-
    cinct, 138
  completion of, 195
  connection with Hill View Reservoir,
    179
  connection with Neversink Reser-
    voir, 191
  connection with Neversink River, 7
  connection with Pepacton Reservoir,
    208
  East Delaware Tunnel outlet at, 206
  filling of, 199
  land acquisition for, 193, 197-198
  proposed bypass tunnel for, 221
  West Delaware Tunnel outlets at,
    218, 220
Rondout River, water quality of, 185
Rondout Valley, land acquisition in,
  appraisal claims hearings for, 236
Roosevelt, Theodore, 81, 85, 125, 136
Roosevelt Island, 246, 248
Rosa, Alan, 259
Rosa, Gary, 241
Roscoe, N.Y., 170, 204-205, 206, 213
  Antrim Lodge, 206, 218
  rainmaking experiment near, 227-228
Roscoe Central School, 220
Rosendale, N.Y., 89, 193
Rose Telephone Co., 235-236
Rosoff, Samuel Rufus, 183, 184-185
Rosoff Bros. & Foster-Newman Con-
  tracting, 220
Rotella, Angelo, 81
Rotello, Anita Douglas, 81
Roundup Ranch, Downsville, N.Y.,
  241
Route 10, 222, 223
Route 28, 228
Route 30, 163, 44, 193, 55, 193, 210,
  213
Route 55, 7, 198-199, 236
Route 301, 61
Rowe, John, 77
Roxbury, N.Y., 152, 205
Rubenzahl, Henie, 237
Rubenzahl Brothers' chicken hatch-
  ery, Neversink, N.Y., 191
Rucci, Lena Pettinato, 79
"Rules and Regulations for the Protec-
  tion from Contamination, Degra-
  dation and Pollution of the New
  York City Water Supply," 260
Ruscoe, George, W., 84
Russian immigrants, as reservoir work-
  ers, 107, 128, *158*
Rutherford, Leonard, 224
Ryan, Edward, 217
Ryan, John, 71
Ryan-Parker Company, 83

Rye Lake, 143
Rye Outlet Bridge, *142*, 143
Rye Pond, 12, 53, 142

S. A. Healy Co., 188, 190, 193, 196,
  199
St. Catherine's, Ontario, 53
St. Elmo Brook, 101
St. Francis de Sales Church, Phoenicia,
  134
St. Michael's Chapel, 79, 81
St. Nicholas Ave., as site of City Tun-
  nel #1 fire, 117
St. Nicholas Hotel, New York City
  fire damage to, 38
  water use by, 35
"St. Patrick's Cathedral," Phoenicia,
  N.Y., 134
Salem Center, N.Y., 58
Sam's Place, Shavertown, N.Y., 210,
  239
Sanborn, Gilbert, 136
Sandhog Local 147, 250
"Sand hogs," 118
Sanford, Ralph, 212, 239
San Francisco, Calif., 92, 162
Sanitation facilities. *See also* Out-
    houses; Sewage treatment plants;
    Sewer systems; Waste water treat-
    ment plants; Water filtration plants
  for Schoharie Reservoir, 163
Sanitation regulations. *See* Water qual-
    ity protection
Savin Co., 209
Sawmill River, 63, 66
Schiavone-Shea, 250
Schiller, Henry, 217
Schoharie Creek
  connection with Esopus Creek, 161-
    162
  hydroelectric power plant, 235
  as New York City water source, 92
  proposed dam for, 12
  surveys of, 97
Schoharie Dam, 162-163, *162, 243*
Schoharie Reservoir, 155-165, 176
  Board of Water Supply Police pre-
    cinct in, 137
  engineers, 189
  laborers on, injuries and fatalities
    among, 165
  land acquisition for, 163-165
  taxation of, 242
Schoharie water supply, 149
Schroeder, Madeline, 237
Schunnemunk Co., 163
Schutt Construction Company, 212
Schuylkill River, 194
Schwartzenegger, Ewald, *256*
Scientific American, 89
Scribner's Monthly, 36, 37
Sebal, Fred, 165
Secor, Benjamin, 61
Seibert, A., 85
Seventh Ave., New York City
  as site of Croton Reservoir, 21
  as site of Yorkville Reservoir, 29
79th St., New York City, as site of
    Yorkville Reservoir, 29
Sewage treatment plants, 199

in Brewster, 49
in Catskill watershed, 151-152
for Delaware System, 170
in Port Jervis, 171
Seward, William, 30
Sewer systems, 16, 85
Seymour, Bradford, 12
Shad, in Delaware River, 241
Shaft 25, Croton Aqueduct, *62*
Shanahan Construction Company, 212
Shandaken, N.Y., 89, 93
Shandaken Tunnel, 157-158, 160
  completion of, 161-162, *161,* 176
  damage claim related to, 236
  during 1926 flood, 165
  engineers for, 189
  gatekeeper for, 161
  police protection for, 137
  Shaft Five, *154*
Shandaken Tunnel Corp., 160
Sharp's Sanitorium, Cross River,
  N.Y., 84
Shaver, Herbert, 212
Shaver, Lela, 212
Shaver, Ward, 212, 214
Shavertown, N.Y., 170, 209, *209,* 210,
  214
  Atkin's Store and Post Ofice, *211,*
    212, 213
Shavertown Old Home Day, *262*
Shaw, Charles A., 94
Shawangunk Mountains
  Catskill Aqueduct tunnel construc-
    tion in, *102*
  Delaware Aqueduct shafts and tun-
    nels construction in, 180, 184-185
Shea, Ray, 183
Sheeley, Earl D., 190-191
Sheeley, Horace, 190-191, 193
Shelton, Perry, 224, 243, *256,* 257, 259
Sheppard, Thomas S., 160
Shiels, James, 197
Shiels, Thomas, 197
Shinhopple, N.Y., 164
Shirley, J. P., 18
Shokan, N.Y.
  Board of Water Supply precinct, 136,
    138
  relocation for Ashokan Reservoir
    construction, 128, 270
Shrady, George, 137
Sidney Center Fire Department, 222
Siemon, George, 135
Sigman, Sam, 185, 191, 253
Silicosis, 182
Silver Lake, Staten Island, 158, 176
Silver Lake Hotel, 121
Silver Lake Park, 121
Silver Lake Reservoir, 96, 113, 121,
  122, 123, 176
Simmons, J. Edward, *88,* 94, 97
Sing Sing (Ossining), N.Y.
  Croton Aqueduct in, 24-25, *25*
  Croton Aqueduct station house in, 36
  fire in, 40
Sing-Sing Kill, Ossining, 21
Sing Sing Prison, 34, 136
Sing Sing Republican, 73, 75
Sixth Ave.
  as site of Croton Reservoir, 21

as site of Yorkville Reservoir, 29
S. J. Groves & Sons, 246
Skanska (construction company), 250
Sleepy Hollow, Tarrytown, N.Y., 23
Sleicher, John A., 95
Smalley's Hotel, Carmel, N.Y., 44-45
Smith, Alfred E., 167-168, 197
Smith, C. Elmore, 87
Smith, Edwin, 75
Smith, Erastus, 198
Smith, George, 198
Smith, Hauser & Locher, 115
Smith, J. Waldo, 78, 94, *94,* 95, 125,
  127, 145, 163, 167, *168,* 169, 170,
  189, 263
  death of, 174
  monument to, 185
  retirement of, 172
Smith, Joseph, 43
Smith, Mary, 237
Smith, Merritt Haviland, 102, 145, *168*
Smith, Robert, 28
Smith, Samuel, 198
Smith Dutchess County Act of 1904,
  93
Snare, Frederick, 176
Socialist Party, 214
Sodom Dam, 55-56
Somers, N.Y., 59, 60
  Amawalk Reservoir, *50,* 59
  Delaware Aqueduct Tunnel in, 180,
    181
  as Muscoot Reservoir site, 79
  tax income received from New Cro-
    ton Dam, 242
Southeast, N.Y., 39, 51, 86, 266
Southeast Center, N.Y., 48, 56-57
Southeast Queens System, 47
Southern Aqueduct Department, 96,
  97
South Fork Dam, Johnstown, Penn.,
  collapse of, 54
South Fork Fishing & Hunting Club,
  54
South St., New York City, as City
  Tunnel #1 de-watering site, 113
South Street Seaport, New York City,
  246
Spear, Walter, 46, 95, 115, *168,* 179,
  189
  as Thaddeus Merriman's successor,
    174
Spencer, James C., 54-55
Sprague, Ken, 210, 211
Sprague, Raymond, 211-212
Sprague & Henwood, 218
Sprout Creek, N.Y., 12, 169
Spruceton, N.Y., 161
SS Thaddeus Merriman (ship), 189
Staley, Ellis, 242, 243
State Conservation Commission, 46
Staten Island, 113
  City Tunnel #1 connection with,
    113, 121, 122, *122,* 123
  City Tunnel #2 connection with, 123
  pipe and conduit system of, 176-177
  water delivery system expansion in,
    176, 177
  water sources for, 121, 123
Stearns, Frederic, 94, *94,* 95

Sterling, George, 95-96
Stevens, Samuel, 30-31
Stevens Mountain Quarry, 162, 163
Stewart-Kerbaugh-Shanley Co., 102
Stilesville, N.Y., 221-222
Stilesville Bridge, 222
Stilesville Dam, 271
Stillwater, N.Y., 14
Stone & Webster, Inc., 160
Stony Kill, 169
Stone Ridge, N.Y., Fairview Ceme-
     tery, 196
Storm King Mountain, 99, 104-105,
     104, 232
*Stranger's Guide for the City of New
     York* (Miller), 27
Strauss, Charles, 151-152
Strikes
  against Samuel Rosoff, 185
  by Ashokan Reservoir workers, 129
  by Croton Aqueduct workers, 23
  by Italian workers, *80*, 81
  by Neversink Reservoir workers, 196
  by Pepacton Reservoir workers, 214
Strong, George Templeton, 30, 40
Stryker, Wallace, 235
Stuyesvant, Peter, 11
Subway system, New York City, 70,
     97, 119, 184
Sudbury, Mass., water system, 73
Suffolk County, N.Y., 46, 201
Sullivan, John L., 12
Sullivan, Rider & Dougherty, 55
Sullivan County. *See also* specific vil-
     lages and towns
  proposed Delaware River dam in, 168
  West Delaware Tunnel shafts in, 218
Sullivan County Board of Supervisors,
     227-228
Sullivan County Legislature, opposi-
     tion to Rondout Reservoir, 196-197
Sullivan County Review, 168
Summitville, 194
Sunnyside, Tarrytown, 23
Supreme Court decisions, 58, 83, 84,
     171-172, 187, 194-195, 196, 213,
     215, 217, 218, 221, 222, 224, 232,
     235, 240, 242
Surface Water Treatment Rule, 255
Susquehanna River, proposed dam
     sites on, 12
Swedish immigrants, as reservoir
     workers, 128, *158*
Sweeney, Raymond, 224
Sweet, Elnathen, 75
Swenson, Ophelia, *146*
Symons, Thomas, 125

Taghkanic, 169
Tallam, Bertram, 217
Tammany Hall, "Summer," 197
Tammany Society, 39, 31. *See also*
     Tweed, William Marcy "Boss"
Tannersville, N.Y., 152
Tappan, N.Y., 89
Taxation, of land acquired for reser-
     voirs and aqueducts, 242-243
Teamsters Union, 180
"Teawater men," 13
Tea Water Pump, New York City, 14

Tea Water Spring, 13
Tecon Corp., 218
Temperance Hall, West Hurley, N.Y.,
     134
Tenanah Lake, 227-228
TenEyck, William, 71
Ten Mile River, 92, 93
Terrorism, as threat to New York
     City water system, 138
Teton River Dam, Idaho, collapse of,
     54
Thomas, Herbert, 243
Thomas McNally Company, 97, 102
Thomasville, N.Y., 47
Thompson, Hubert, 53, 54-55
Thompson, Jefferson DeMont, 167-168
Thompson, John C., 217
Three Gorges hydroelectric project,
     China, 250
Tibbits Brook, N.Y., 36, 63
Tiffany and Company, 97, 227
Tilford, William, 49
Tilly Foster Mine, flooding of, 57
Tilly Foster Reservoir, 51
Titicus Dam, 58, 59-60
Titicus Reservoir, 57-59, 76
Tocks Island, proposed dam on, 195
Toilets, low-flow, 229
Tombs prison, New York City, 13
Tompkins, Arthur, 232
Tompkins, N.Y., 224, 240, 257
  tax assessment dispute by, 243
Tompkinsville, Staten Island, 121, 123
Tonetta Brook, N.Y., 47, 48
Tongore, N.Y., 95
Toth, Mary 239
Tower, F.B., 28
Tower, Fayette, 24
Towners, N.Y., 47-48
Townsend, Frank, 47, 48
Traband, Harold, 145-146
Tracey, Edward H., 24, 43, 44-45
Trailer camp, Downsville, 202
Traver Hollow Bridge, 130, 131, 134
  discovery of bomb planted at, 138
Travers, William R., 69
Travia, Robert, 241
Tremper, Floyd, *211*
Tri-County Power & Light, 235
Triest Construction Co., 187, 189
Tri-State Rock, 170
Trout Creek Bridge, 222
Trout Creek valley, 256-257
Tuller Construction Co., 227
Tunnel Boring Machine, 245, 250-251
Turner, Esther, 240
Turner, Ethel, 240
Turner, Lawrence, 240
Turner, Theron, 240
Tuscarora Club, 241
Tweed, William Marcy "Boss," 39, 41,
     43
Twiname, John, 58
Typhoid, 15, 49, 85, 135

"Ulalume" (Poe), 27
Ulen Contracting Corp, 154, 160, 161,
     162
Ulster County. *See also* names of spe-
     cific villages and towns

Delaware Aqueduct in, 179-180, 182-
     183
  proposed Ramapo Water Company's
     operations in, 89, 92
  tax income received from Ashokan
     Reservoir, 242-244
Ulster County Clerk, 89
Ulster & Delaware Railroad, 95, 125-
     126, *128*, 151
  owner of, 95, 234
  relocation of, 128, *128*, 130, 184
  Shandaken Tunnel, 158
Underwood, Dan, 205
Union Grove, N.Y., 239
  destruction by Pepacton Reservoir,
     210-212, *211*, 213, 270
Union Grove Methodist Church, 213
Union Grove Post Office, *211*, 212
Union Square, New York City, as
     City Tunnel #1 site, 117
United States Bureau of Mines, 183,
     220
United States Environmental Protec-
     tion Agency, 152, 255, 258
United States Maritime Commission,
     189
United States Military Academy, West
     Point, 17, 21
United States Public Health Service,
     221
United States Steel, 212
University of Missouri School of
     Mines, 68
Upper Lackawack Methodist Episco-
     pal Church, 237
Upper Housatonic watershed, 92
Utah Construction Co., 185
Vaiana, George, 253
Vail's Gate, N.Y., 107
Valhalla, N.Y., 142, 143, 145, 146-147,
     150, 271
  as Board of Water Supply precinct,
     136
Van Buren, Augustus H., 234
VanCortlandt, Augustus, 14
VanCortlandt, Frederick, 14
VanCortlandt, Pierre, 22
Van Cortlandt Park, as City Tunnel
     #3 valve chamber site, 246, 247,
     248, *252*, 253
Van der Donck, Adriaen, 11
Vanderlyn, Frank D., 7, 237
Vanderlyn's Pines, Neversink, N.Y.,
     197
Vandermark, William, 236
Van Dyke, Lawrence, 161
Van Dyke, Nelson, 161
Van Etten's ice house, West Shokan,
     N.Y., 135
VanKeuren, Edmund, 210-211
VanKeuren, Mabel, 210-211
VanSteenbergh, Vera Sickler, 130
VanTassel, Will, 84
Venetian Inn, Rock Rift, N.Y., 224
Vermilyea, Ashbel G., 87
Vernooy Creek, 183
Voris, Edith Martin, 77
Voris, Nathaniel, 77
Vorndran, C., 48

Waccabuc Lake, 45
Wachusett Dam, Massachusetts, 81
Wagner, Robert, 218, 263
Wagner, Ronald, 257
Waldo, Rhinelander, 136
Walker, Alexander, 251
Walker, David, 251
Walker, Fred E., 137
Walker, Jimmy, 170
Walker, Joe, 251
Wallabout Canal, 172
Wallkill, N.Y., 136
Wallkill Pressure Tunnel, 103, 109,
     114-115
Wallkill River, 12
  watershed of, 92
Wallkill River valley, 103
Wallkill Valley Railroad, 183
Wallpack Bend, N.Y., 194
Wall St., New York City, 15
  1845 fire on, 40
Walsh, Patrick, 134
Walsh Construction Co., 201, 202,
     222, 246
Walsh-Perini, 203, 206, 214
Walters, Frederick, 83-84
Walton, N.Y., 224
Walton Reporter, 202
Wampus River, 150
Wappinger, N.Y., Delaware Aqueduct
     Tunnel in, 179-180, 181
Wappinger Creek, 12, 93, 169
Ward, Edmund, 147
Ward's Island, New York City, 33
Waring steam drill, 52
War of 1812, 14
Washburn, Abbie, 110-111
Washburn, Alberta, 110-111, 137
Washburn, Oscar, 110-111
Washburn, Shaler, & Washburn, 57
Washington, George, 15
Wastewater treatment plants, 9, 153,
     260-261
Water bonds, 93
Water closets, 33, 34, 44
Water conservation programs, 195,
     227, 228, 229
Water desalination, atomic-energy
     plants for, 229
Water filtration plants, 71, 85, 92, 94,
     150-153
Water for a City (Weidner), 75
Water meters, 34-35, 92, 93, 141, 195,
     229
Water quality, of New York City
     water supply, 150-153
Water quality protection
  for Ashokan Reservoir, 151
  by Bureau of Water Supply, Quality
     and Protection, 260-261
  for Catskill watershed, 151-152
Water rates, 33, 34
Watershed(s)
  Catskill, 89
  of Croton Aqueduct and Reservoir
     system, 38-39, 41
  pollution of, 71, 85
  Esopus, 46
  radioactivity monitoring of, 138, 221
  security for, 138

wastewater treatment plants within, 9
Watershed Agricultural Council, 258
Watershed Protection and Partnership Council, 259-260
Watershed Regulations, 255-260
Water Supply of the City of New York, 1658-1895 (Wegmann), 58
Waterville, N.Y., 24
Watson, Albert, 107
Watson, Glen, 206
Waverly House, New York City, 40
Wawarsing, N.Y., 187, 189
  Delaware Aqueduct Tunnel in, 179-180
  opposition to Rondout Reservoir in, 196-197
Webster Act, 45
Webster Ave. sewer, 114
W.E. Callahan, 180
Weehawken, N.J., 15
Wegmann, Edward, 75
Weiblen, Eugene, 233-234
Weidner, Charles, 75
Wells
  in Ebbetts Field, 227
  as Nassau and Suffolk Counties' water source, 201
  in New York City
    at Bowling Green, 11
    contamination of, 15
    of Fort Amsterdam, 11
    of Manhattan Company, *10*
    pollution of, 11, 13
    private, 16
    public, 15, 16
  in Queens, 83
  for Ridgewood System, 46, 47
Wells, J., 23
West Branch-Kensico Tunnel, 180, 182, 183
West Branch Reservoir, 59-61, *60*, 181-182
  connection with Kensico Rerservoir, 180
  dams, 59

influent and effluent chambers, 183
Rondout-West Branch Tunnel connection of, 179
Westbrookville, N.Y., 170-171
Westchester County. *See also* individual villages and towns
  access to New York City water supply by, 93
  Croton Aqueduct land purchases in, 22-23
  Daly's Raids in, 45
  New York City water quality project funds for, 259
  opposition to Cross River Reservoir in, 83
  partial annexation to New York City, 53
  Piedmont region of, 99
Westchester County Board of Supervisors, 151, 242
Westchester County Clerk, 89
Westchester Creek, 70
West Conesville, N.Y., 164
West Delaware Tunnel, 218-220, *219, 220*
West Delaware Tunnel Constructors, 218
West Farms, N.Y., 53
West Hurley, N.Y., 99
  relocation for Ashokan Reservoir construction, 128
  relocation of buildings from, 134
West Kill, N.Y., 137
Weston, William, 15
West Shokan, N.Y.
  Pythian Hall, 135, *233*
  relocation for Ashokan Reservoir construction, 128
Weyrauch, Bob, 226
Whimpenny's rag carpet mill, 147
White, Canvas, 25
White, Lazarus, 101, 103, 104-105, 110
  The Catskill Water Supply, 102, 147, 115-116, 148
White Plains, N.Y., 102, 107

Whiteman, Osterman & Hanna, 257
  Southern Aqueduct Department headquarters, 97
White Plains Daily Argus, 145
White Pond, 45
White St., New York City, proposed reservoir on, 14
Whitlockville, N.Y., 76
Whitman, Clarence, 76
Whole Farm Planning system, 258
Wickham, William, 45
Williams, D. T., 238
Williams, Stuart, 249, *251*
Williamsbridge, New York City, 15
Williamsbridge Reservoir, 53, 142, 150
Williamsburg Conduit, 177
Williams & Gerstle, 79
Willow, N.Y., 93
Willowemoc Creek, 12
Willowemoc River, 170
Willowemoc Valley, 204
Winchells Corners, N.Y., 129
Winchells Falls, N.Y., 234
Windolph, John, 71
Winifred, Goldring, 159
Winne, A. D., 135
Winne, Davis, 92
Winson, Frank, *168*
Winston, James, 86
Winston, James O., 130
Winston Bros., 218
Winston & Co., 83, 87, 125-126, 130, 134
Wittenberg, N.Y., 93
Wolf, Alfred E., 49
Wong, Eddie, 183
Woodhaven Water Company, 47
Woodman's farm, Kensico, N.Y., 147
Woodside, Queens, 246
Woodstock, N.Y., 96, 257
  Ramapo Water Company's proposed operations in, 89
Workmen's Compensation Law, 182
World's Fairs
  1940, 138

1964, 228
Worthen, F.E., 54
Worth Monument Park, 117
WPA Guide to New York, 27
Wright, Benjamin, 20
Wurtsboro, N.Y., 170-171
Wyckoff, Imer, 165
Wyckoff's General Store, Kensico, N.Y., 147
Wynkoop, Marvin, 202
Wynkoop Creek, 196

Yankees, 220
Yellow fever, 1798 epidemic, 15
Yellowstone National Park, 185
Yevich, Bob, 208, 209
Yevich, Joyce, 208, 209
Yonkers, N.Y.
  Board of Water Supply precinct, 136
  Catskill Aqueduct pressure tunnels, 103
  Croton Aqueduct at, *22*
  Croton Aqueduct land acquisition in, 23
  Croton Aqueduct station house, 36
  Hill View Reservoir of. *See* Hill View Reservoir
  Kensico-Hill View Tunnel, 180
Yonkers Construction Co., 222
Yonkers Pressure Tunnel, 106
  laborers hospital for, *109*
Yonkers Raceway, 147
Yorktown, N.Y., 138, 232-233, 242
Yorktown Heights, N.Y., 136, 151
Yorkville Reservoir, New York City, 29-30, *34*, 35, 263
Yosemite National Park, 162
Young, Emma, 164
Young, Evelyn, 164
Young, Henry, 164
Young, Sarah, 164
Young & Scott, 24

Zeh, Josiah, 235
Zena, N.Y., 134

DIANE GALUSHA is a former journalist with a passion for history. She was the editor of the Catskill Mountain News in Margaretville from 1989 to 1996. Since 1998, she has served as communications director and education coordinator with the Catskill Watershed Corporation, which has its headquarters in the former newspaper plant. The author of several books of local and regional history, Diane is the founding president of the Historical Society of the Town of Middletown, Delaware County.